MW00784992

The Churches and Democracy in Brazil

The Churches and Democracy in Brazil

Towards a Public Theology Focused on Citizenship

Rudolf von Sinner

with a foreword by
Vítor Westhelle

WIPF & STOCK · Eugene, Oregon

THE CHURCHES AND DEMOCRACY IN BRAZIL
Towards a Public Theology Focused on Citizenship

Wipf & Stock
An Imprint of Wipf and Stock Publishers
199 W. 8th Ave., Suite 3
Eugene, OR 97401

www.wipfandstock.com

ISBN 13: 978-1-60899-385-7

Manufactured in the U.S.A.

for my beloved daughter Taís Alessandra (b. 2002)
who has the privilege of growing up in a democratic and flourishing Brazil

Contents

Foreword

by Vítor Westhelle

Conto o que fui e vi, no levantar do dia. Auroras.

João Guimarães Rosa, *Grande Sertão: Veredas*

PRESENTING A PANORAMIC SCENARIO of a theological landscape, be it a country or a continent, is an arduous undertaking. Its implications are far reaching and complex. Portraying the Brazilian situation even when focusing mostly, but not only, on its religious and theological landscape is such a task, daring and daunting. The reader will be introduced to the milieu of theology and church life in Brazil, one of the major players that four decades ago launched liberation theology. Now times and tides are upon Latin America and Brazil in particular that are significantly different from the yore to which the pages that follow are a travel guide. Rudolf von Sinner is aware of the dangers and challenges in this undertaking. His musing of the old adage, "after spending a short time in Brazil, you write a book, after a longer period, you write an article, and after a very long period you stop writing because you're so confused,"[1] is a telling observation that is true for Brazil as it is for Latin America in general. US historian and Latin Americanist, Richard Morse, concurs with this as he compares the works of Tocqueville, Weber, and Huizinga—who were able to grasp the North American ethos with precision and clarity that made their studies classics—with those "that could hardly be regarded as of a lesser caliber, as a Humboldt or a Saint-Hilaire, who could only offer fortuitous glimpses of the Ibero-American condition, even if they stayed longer."[2] Von Sinner has been in Brazil for a long time, and yet, contrary to the adage, he does advance a comprehensive reading of the Brazilian situation in general and of three of the representative Christian religious organizations: the Roman Catholic Church, a mainstream Protestant church (Lutheran) and a Pentecostal church (Assemblies of God). The reading is persuasive and the constructive proposal for a public theology grows naturally out of what he observes in his case studies of the different ecclesial formations in the interface between faith and the *res publica*, the public thing or affairs. As a Brazilian living in the diaspora, I am enthralled to see a Swiss theologian present a view of my own country, its challenges and promises, with constructive alacrity and hope. The words of the Brazilian writer, João Guimarães Rosa, in the epigraph, could not be more apt to describe this book: "I tell what I was and saw, at the awake of the day. Dawns."

Public theology, the operational concept the author is developing, is not common currency in Brazilian theological and ecclesial circles as noted by the author. This is probably the single most important insight in the pages that follow, namely, to detect and describe a theological practice that

1. Below, IIB, p. 128.

2. Richard Morse, *O Espelho de Próspero: Cultura e Ideias nas Américas* (São Paulo: Companhia das Letras, 1988), 157-58.

is encompassing enough to address the interface between the life of faith in different communities and the public domain. Implicit is a suspicion that liberation theology's significant contribution to Latin American and, in particular, to Brazilian theology has not been able to be owned in the same way by different faith communities or sectors of a single church to account for the nature of their intervention in the public sphere. The novel concept of public theology for those latitudes promises an inclusivity and a contiguity at the same time; inclusive of the heritage of liberation theology and contiguous to cover a broader spectrum while being ideologically more neutral and in a tone more realistic and pragmatic. The commitment of public theology clearly expresses the concern for the common good articulating in the public arena a voice that addresses the core values and practices of faith communities.

Liberation theology when initially launched as a theological program in the late 1960s and early 1970s became the emissary for voicing these concerns when many countries in Latin America, notably Brazil, were under military dictatorship and civil society was severely repressed. Regular channels for public intervention and manifestation were impaired, political parties illegalized or coopted, and public meetings prohibited or censored. At the time it was church communities, religious gatherings, that inherited the extra burden of taking upon themselves the tasks commonly assigned to regular organs of civil society. Church Base Communities were the most celebrated expression of this intense concentration of tasks that added to the religious sphere proper (worship, bible study, prayer, etc.) also economic issues affecting the community, the need for political articulation, and the basic task of community organizing. Liberation talk thus became the language of expression and communication to get out into a more open and freer society.

By the mid-1980s, however, most of the Latin American continent was experiencing a slow process of political liberalization, or, as it was then called in Brazil, "opening" (*abertura*). Democratic processes were beginning to be restored or created, new constitutions drafted, and general elections being held. And Brazil, occupying about half of the territory of South America, was at the center of these events and of this chronology. The church as well as Chuch Base communities slowly started to retrench to their more traditional religious practices as civil society was progressively undertaking, through their own regular channels, political and economic agendas.

Towards the end of the 1980s, the radical rearrangement of global geopolitics that had dominated world politics and allegiances for the previous seventy years collapses and with it also fell the concrete expectation that an alternative to the western hegemonic capitalist model was viable. Nothing was more symbolic for the ensuing change in atmosphere than the downfall of the Berlin wall in 1989 and the erosion of its ideological buttress. Some form of Marxism, Leninism, Trotskyism, or Maoism was believed to sustain the viability of another social order, even as it was already a commonplace that the eastern European models were debased and corrupt. Remnants of such expectations were confined, to a certain degree, in Cuba, an island in the vicinity of the USA, the most powerful capitalist country in the world, though it has to be acknowledged that probably more than Cuba itself, what was magnetizing was the iconic figure of Ché Guevara, an Argentinian that became one of the leaders of the 1959 Cuban revolution. However, the proclivity of many a liberation theologian toward some form of Marxist analysis of society was no secret. "Instruction on Certain Aspects of the 'Theology of Liberation,'" issued by the Vatican's Congregation for the Doctrine of the Faith, already in 1984, only hardened this perception. The same opinion found echo in the voice of several theologians in Europe, North America, and in Latin America itself. As a North American theologian phrased it: "Liberation theology is the Trojan Horse of a communist plot." With the drastic changes in the geopolitical scenario, a sense of theoretical disorientation was inevitable and a new or renewed paradigm and public voice had to be fashioned. Some concepts and idiosyncratic expressions indebted to the Marxist tradition, once taken *prima facie*, had to undergo a radical reassessment as to their analytical usefulness and political effectiveness.

There is a telling anecdote from the 1990s which throws some light into the critical phase affecting liberation theology to the extent it was indeed committed to some form of Marxist analysis. The story suggests the perplexity that ensued from the aftermath of the fall of the Berlin Wall and the dissolution of the Soviet Union. The graffiti on the walls of the University of Bogotá, Colombia speaks volumes in conveying the Zeitgeist: "Cuando teniamos casi todas las respuestas, se nos cambiaran las preguntas" ("When we had almost all the answers, the questions were changed."). Von Sinner's text is a rigorous and sustained attempt to detect, locate, and articulate the "new questions" pointing to pathways that lead to answers that are less self-assured of their certainties, ideologically more flexible in their assertions, and above all pragmatically relevant to address the common good of the *res publica*.

By the 1990s in Brazil the churches were progressively unencumbered from the direct task of undertaking activities of political and economic nature (except for the traditional diaconal services) to become a voice of national conscience in addressing public issues and concerns on the basis of their social teachings and within the proviso of its constitutional mechanisms. For theology the biblical paradigm shifts. It was no longer the Exodus narrative that was most helpful for the new moment. The Exodus motif had served liberation theology richly as a template to organize a discourse under political oppression and the repression of civil society. With the process of political liberalization and democratization what comes to the fore are other texts, such as Paul's famous public address at the Areopagus in Athens. Exemplarily, this is one of boldly making a public case for the Christian story in the public square, announcing that in the God of Jesus Christ they already had their being and attained their freedom unawares (Acts 17:28). Paul's speech might not have been as effective as he had hoped, but definitely set the tone for a public theology. It was not an attempt to offer an alternative and exclusive option in the religious market, but to give voice to what the Athenians already acknowledged, yet could not name it: the "unknown god."

Paulo Freire, one of the seminal figures at the inception of liberation theology offered his own version of the law-gospel dialectics in saying that the task of the theologian is to denounce and announce. The denunciatory tone, the *j'accuse* posture typical of early liberation theology's discourse, and demanded by the circumstances, slowly gravitated to the other pole or, better, found a balance in the Freirean dialectics: the freedom of boldly speaking (*parrhesia*) and humbly announcing the gospel. This seems to be the critical verve of von Sinner's careful argumentation and lengthy documentation. The concluding reflection of this book, on "boldness and humility," significantly lifts up the Greek concept of *parrhesia*. It is significant because the choice of the Greek notion for "bold speech" stands in notable contrast to the notion of "prophecy," one of the most endeared words in liberation theology. Michel Foucault in his final lectures at the Collège de France in 1983-1984 offered a typology of different rhetorical forms of truth-speaking. He discerns the discourses of the sage, the technician, the prophet, and the parrhesiast. The distinction that he elaborates between the prophet and the parrhesiast is important in this context. While the prophet makes all-encompassing (and in this being similar to the sage) denouncements of the state of affairs, the parrhesiast is the one that risks it all, even life itself, for a *particular* (in this being similar to the technician) statement of a truth for the sake of truth itself, relinquishing all negotiation and strategic calculations. By emphasizing this distinction Foucault created a divide, which von Sinner implicitly adopts, between the prophetic orientation of liberation theology's discourse and the commitment to *parrhesia* that he sees in the practice of a public theology. He does not consider one in exclusion of the other, but rather regards *parrhesia* as a form of truth speaking that comes about when the work of prophesying has produced its fruits.

The notion of *parrhesia* further implies another central concept of the book: citizenship. *Parrhesia* can only be exercised by the one who has responsibility to the public affairs and that is the condition for being a citizen. On this point von Sinner makes a robust theological claim supported by the early Luther's distinction of régimes (*Regimente*), on which he was followed by other reformers (Melanchthon, Bucer, Calvin among them). The theological point is that the responsible participation in the secular sphere is as much a divine calling as serving the church as a priest or a bishop. This is what is implied in Paul's use of the words, "In him we live and move and have our being" (Acts 17:28), quoting an early Greek source. A citizen is one who is accountable for the common good and speaks responsibly on public affairs in a secular sphere entitled by faith alone and guided by the scriptures to do so. Citizenship, in this sense, does not cancel the private sphere, but does proscribe secrecy when the common good of the *res publica* is at stake. And that is done for God's sake and for the sake of the world.

This text is a discourse hinging on hope, addressing challenges, offering vision, and sketching a program for theology in a country as Brazil, and so many others in the third world, so often marked with cynicism when it comes to the public domain of things. Indeed he gives an account of what he has been and saw, at the break of a day. Dawns!

Preface

I remember, when I first came to Brazil in 1996, the saying went that "Brazil is the country of the future," quoting Stefan Zweig's famous book title and adding: "and always will be." The future was seen with distrust, as something distant and unreachable. Fourteen years later, the mood has changed. It seems that people now believe the future has arrived, and that Brazil has a proper place in its own right and within the world community. The time it took me to write this book from its tentative beginnings in 2003 to its completion at the end of 2010, coincided with the long awaited and much praised presidency of Luiz Inácio Lula da Silva, the first worker in Brazil's history ever to receive the presidential sash. It also coincided with the presidency of Walter Altmann in the church I serve, the *Evangelical Church of the Lutheran Confession in Brazil* (IECLB). Altmann was an outspoken Protestant Liberation Theologian who later also became the Moderator of the *World Council of Churches'* Central Committee. So many things have changed, even in the eight years of my professorship at the *Lutheran School of Theology* (Escola Superior de Teologia, EST) at São Leopoldo, and many of them for the better. This is a rapidly emerging country, and it has been most fascinating and, indeed, a privilege to live and work here during all these years, and to have time to read and reflect on this changing reality.

This book could not have been written and prepared for publication without the interaction and help of many persons. I cannot name all of them here, but I hope that all will feel well represented in the names I shall mention as a sign of gratitude. First of all, my thanks go to Professor Wolfgang Lienemann, who generously agreed to accompany this study and has most competently and vigorously done so. He also received it for evaluation as my Habilitation Thesis, and wrote the first, extensive evaluation report. It was submitted to and accepted by the University of Bern in 2009, which bestowed on me the title of *Privatdozent* in early 2010. Together with his wife, Professor Christine Lienemann-Perrin, my former dissertation guide, he has promoted investigations into *The Churches and the Public Sphere in Societies in Transformation*, which has been a source of inspiration and thorough discussion in the early stages of the present study. It is in this context also that I met and interacted with Professors Paulo Krischke and Sérgio Costa. The former introduced me to many important authors and discussion groups in Brazil. The latter interacted with me on many occasions, giving very valuable input, and also kindly and generously produced the third evaluation report in the Habilitation process. The second report was written by Professor Heinrich Bedford-Strohm, an expert in Public Theology and a teacher of mine since the days of undergraduate study at Heidelberg University in the early 1990s. My heartfelt thanks to all of them and to the other colleagues in the Lienemann research group, which have given very important feedback to my texts.

During the first years of the research, the EST under its then-principal Professor Lothar Carlos Hoch provided an excellent environment for this work. Although it required much teaching and supervising, thus restricting time for research, I have grown immensely through my contacts with colleagues and students. The research group on *Theological Ethics and Society* (now *Public Theology in a Latin American Perspective*) that I created in 2003 has become a very important place for thorough discussion of students', colleagues', and my own project. I especially thank Professors Roberto Zwetsch and Valério Schaper, as well as Drs. André Musskopf and Antonio Carlos Teles da Silva, who formed the first nucleus. The *Swiss National Foundation for Research* granted me a fellowship for research abroad and generously maintained it (2003-2006) even as I was called to the chair of Systematic Theology, Ecumenism and Inter-religious Dialogue at EST. Research assistants were also made available to me for work on documents, and my deep thanks go to them: Rodrigo Gonçalves Majewski, Hênio de Almeida, Daiana Ernest and Guilherme Brinker. The IECLB archive service as well as the CNBB headquarters have been very helpful in finding and copying relevant documents. Professor Hermann Brandt [in memoriam] and Rev. Sílvio Schneider read the chapter on the IECLB and gave important and precise feedback.

Real and thorough writing became only possible away from teaching and administration, during a sabbatical leave at the *Center of Theological Inquiry* in Princeton, New Jersey. I would like to thank all my colleagues during our seven months there, especially the director, Professor William Storrar, who brought me on track for Public Theology and into the *Global Network of Public Theology*, created at Princeton in 2007. Special thanks go to colleagues Professors Graham Maddox, Piet Naudé, Herman Paul, and Scott Sunquist who read part of the text and shared their insights and criticism with me. Professors João Biehl, Paul Sigmund, and Robert Wuthnow at Princeton University also gave me precious time and insights during that period and beyond, as did Professors Alfred Stepan and Ralph Della Cava and Dr. Miguel Carter at Columbia University. Professor Della Cava, Professor Heike Walz (then in Buenos Aires), Dr. Katrin Kusmierz, and Professor David Plüss (at the time both in Basel, now in Bern), whose friendship I cherish, read parts of the text and gave very valuable comments. A very relevant and innovative South-South exchange also started at Princeton, in 2007, and has since grown considerably, notably with *Stellenbosch University*, where colleagues Professor Nico Koopman and Dr. Clint Le Bruyns are most involved. Professor Ronaldo Cavalcante, a Brazilian Presbyterian, has become a very competent and important partner in the emerging Public Theology project in Brazil, and so have many students who have taken up research on the matter, namely Eneida Jacobsen, Felipe Gustavo Koch Buttelli, and Rodrigo Gonçalves Majewski.

As I was looking for a place to publish the book, Professor Vítor Westhelle, formerly and now again at EST and for many years in Chicago, guided me to *Wipf & Stock*, and has been very helpful and supporting. He has kindly agreed to write the foreword. His assistant, Dr. Mary (Joy) Philip, has given invaluable support in reformatting the text for submission to the publisher, and has done indexing. Additional help was found with Mr. Kevin A. Byrnes, who provided a thorough format and language revision. I thank the publisher for accepting and competently seeing the text through to publication in the person of the Assistant Managing Editor, Christian Amondson. Finally, Christian Kamleiter, a German exchange student to EST, and Steffen Goetze, my research assistant in Göttingen, have given support in checking references. The Lichtenberg-Kolleg at the Georg-August-University in Göttingen, an institute of advanced study supported by the Deutsche Forschungsgemeinschaft (DFG), which hosted me as a fellow in the year 2011, provided an excellent environment for the final revision of the book, for which I have received valuable advice from my colleagues Professors Charles Zika and Shalini Randeria, as well as from the director, Professor Dagmar Coester-Waltjen. My deep gratitude goes to all of them.

As with all long-haul academic works, the family knows best what it means to bear with the affliction of one who is trying to finish a book. I thank my wife, Helena Santos von Sinner, for her love and often tested patience, and for bringing me back from letters to life now and again. I dedicate the book to our daughter, Taís Alessandra Santos von Sinner (b. 2002), who was born prematurely and thus did not have an easy start into life, but has endured and become such a strong and lovely personality, and who now has the privilege of growing up in a democratic and flourishing Brazil.

Abbreviations

	Portuguese	*English*
ABI	Associação Brasileira de Imprensa	Brazilian Press Association
ABONG	Associação Brasileira das Organizações Não Governamentais	Brazilian Association of Non-Governmental Organizations
AD	Assembléias de Deus	Assemblies of God
AEVB	Associação Evangélica Brasileira	Brazilian Evangelical Association
ALCA	Área de Livre Comércio das Américas	Free Trade Area of the Americas (FTAA)
ALN	Aliança Libertadora Nacional	National Liberating Alliance
AP	Ação Popular	Popular Action
ARENA	Aliança Renovadora Nacional	National Renewal Alliance
BC		Before Christ (or Common Era)
BI	Boletim Informativo (IECLB)	Information Bulletin
CA	Confissão de Augsburgo	Augsburg Confession
CAPA	Centro de Apoio ao Pequeno Agricultor	Center of Support for the Small Farmer
CAPES	Coordenação de Aperfeiçoamento de Pessoal de Nível Superior	Coordination of Continuous Formation of Graduate Personnel
CCB	Congregação Cristã do Brasil	Christian Congregation of Brazil
CEB	Confederação Evangélica do Brasil	Evangelical Confederation of Brazil
CEBs	Comunidades Eclesiais de Base	Church Base Communities
CECA	Centro Ecumênico de Evangelização, Capacitação e Assessoria	Ecumenical Center for Evangelization, Capacitating and Consultancy
CEDI	Centro Ecumênico de Documentação e Informação	Ecumenical Center for Documentation and Information
CELAM	Conselho Episcopal Latinoamericano	Latin American Episcopal Council
CERIS	Centro de Estatística Religiosa e Investigação Social	Center for Religious Statistics and Social Research
CESE	Coordenadoria Ecumênica de Serviço	Ecumenical Coordination of Service
CGADB	Convenção Geral das Assembléias de Deus	General Convention of the Assemblies of God
CIMI	Conselho Indigenista Missionário	Missionary Council for Indigenous Peoples
CLAI	Conselho Latinoamericano de Igrejas	Latin American Council of Churches

	Portuguese	*English*
CLT	Consolidação das Leis do Trabalho	Consolidation of Labor Laws
CM	Comunicado Mensal (CNBB)	Monthly Bulletin
CMI	Conselho Mundial de Igrejas	see WCC
CNBB	Conferência Nacional dos Bispos do Brasil	Brazilian National Bishops' Conference
CNPB	Conselho de Pastores do Brasil	Brazilian National Pastor's Council
COMIN	Conselho de Missão entre Índios (IECLB)	Council of Mission among *Índios*
CONAMAD	Convenção Nacional de Ministros da Assembléia de Deus da Madureira	Madureira National Assemblies of God Ministers' Convention
CONIC	Conselho Nacional de Igrejas Cristãs	National Council of Churches [Brazil]
CONTAG	Confederação Nacional de Trabalhadores Agriculturais	Nacional Confederation of Agricultural Workers
CPAD	Casa Publicadora das Assembléias de Deus	Assemblies of God Publishing House
CPT	Comissão Pastoral da Terra	Pastoral Land Commission
CST		Catholic Social Teaching
EATWOT		Ecumenical Association of Third World Theologians
ECA	Estatuto da Criança e do Adolescente	Statute of the Child and the Adolescent
ENEM	Exame Nacional do Ensino Médio	National High School Examination
EST	Escola Superior de Teologia (IECLB)	Lutheran School of Theology at São Leopoldo
FGTS	Fundo Nacional de Garantia por Tempo de Serviço	Guarantee Fund for Time of Service
FLD	Fundação Luterana de Diaconia	Lutheran Foundation for Diakonia
FONAPER	Forum Nacional Permanente de Ensino Religioso	Permanent National Forum for Religious Education
FTAA	see ALCA	
FTL	Fraternidade Teológica Latino-americana	Latin American Theological Fraternity
FUNAI	Fundação Nacional do Índio	National Foundation of the *Índio*
GEELPA	Grupo de Empreendedores Evangélico-Luteranos de Porto Alegre	Group of Evangelical-Lutheran Business Persons of Porto Alegre
IBGE	Instituto Brasileiro de Geografia e Estatística	Brazilian Institute for Geography and Statistics
IBRADES	Instituto Brasileiro de Desenvolvimento	Brazilian Institute of Development
ICAR	Igreja Católica Apostólica Romana	Roman Catholic [Apostolic] Church
IELB	Igreja Evangélica Luterana do Brasil	Evangelical Lutheran Church of Brazil
IELCB	Igreja Evangélica de Confissão Luterana no Brasil	Evangelical Church of the Lutheran Confession in Brazil

	Portuguese	*English*
IMF	[Fundo Monetário Internacional, FMI]	International Monetary Fund
IPB	Igreja Presbiteriana do Brasil	Presbyterian Church of Brazil
IPT	Instituto Pré-Teológico (IECLB)	Pre-Theological Institute
ISAL	Igreja e Sociedade na América Latina	Church and Society in Latin America
ISER	Instituto de Estudos da Religião	Institute for the Study of Religion
IURD	Igreja Universal do Reino de Deus	Universal Church of the Kingdom of God
JAC	Juventude Agrária Católica	Rural Catholic Youth
JEC	Juventude Estudantil Católica	Student Catholic Youth
JIC	Juventude Independente Católica	Independent Catholic Youth
JOC	Juventude Operária Católica	Workers' Catholic Youth
JOREV	Jornal Evangélico (IECLB)	Evangelical Journal
JUC	Juventude Universitária Católica	University Catholic Youth
LDB	Lei de Diretrizes e Bases da Educação	Law of Guidelines and Bases of Education
LGBT		Lesbian, Gay, Bisexual or Transgendered
LW		Luther's Works
LWF	[Federação Luterana Mundial, FLM]	Lutheran World Federation
MASTER	Movimento dos Agricultores Sem Terra	Movement of the Landless Farmers
MDB	Movimento Democrático Brasileiro	Brazilian Democratic Movement
ME	Movimento Encontrão	Encounter Movement (IECLB)
MEB	Movimento de Educação de Base	Base Education Movement
MEP	Movimento Evangélico Progressista	Movement of Progressive Evangelicals
MEUC	Missão Evangélica União Cristã	Evangelical Mission Christian Union (IECLB)
MLST	Movimento da Libertação dos Sem-Terra	Movement of the Landless´Liberation
MST	Movimento dos Trabalhadores Rurais Sem Terra	Movement of Landless Workers
MTST	Movimento de Trabalhadores Sem-Teto	Movement of Homeless Workers
NGO	[Organização não-governamental, ONG]	Non-Governmental Organization
OAB	Ordem dos Advogados do Brasil	Brazilian Bar Association
PAMI	Plano de Ação Missionária (IECLB)	Plan for Mission
par.		Parallel references (in the Bible)
PCJP		Pontifical Council for Justice and Peace
PDS	Partido Democrático Social	Social Democratic Party

	Portuguese	*English*
PMDB	Partido do Movimento Democrático Brasileiro	Party of the Brazilian Democratic Movement
PNRA	Plano Nacional de Reforma Agrária	National Plan for Land Reform
PPL	Pastoral Popular Luterana	Popular Lutheran Pastoral Action
PSDB	Partido da Social Democracia Brasileira	Party of Brazilian Social Democracy
P-Sol	Partido Socialismo e Liberdade	Party for Socialism and Freedom
PT	Partido dos Trabalhadores	Workers' Party
RCC	Renovação Carismática Católica	Catholic Charismatic Renewal
SOTER	Sociedade de Teologia e Ciências da Religião	Brazilian Society for Theology and Religious Studies
SPI	Serviço de Proteção aos Índios	Service of Protection to the Indians
STM	Supremo Tribunal Militar	Supreme Military Court
SUDENE	Superintendência de Desenvolvimento do Nordeste	Northeast Development Agency
TFP	Sociedade Brasileira de Defesa da Tradição, Família e Propriedade	Brazilian Society for Defending Tradition, Family and Property
UDR	União Democrática Ruralista	Ruralist Democratic Union
USP	Universidade de São Paulo	University of São Paulo
WCC	see CMI	World Council of Churches

Introduction

Since the 1970s, Brazil has become well known for its progressive Roman Catholic Church, outspoken Theology of Liberation, fervent Church Base Communities, and social movements with church support. Outstanding prophets like archbishops Dom Hélder Câmara and Dom Paulo Evaristo Arns, as well as theologians like Leonardo Boff have become known worldwide for their charisma, poetic and prophetic writing and speech, courage, and power of mobilization. Under the military regime, such persons and communities became *nuclei* of resistance as they maintained a certain degree of freedom, while other forms of organization suffered prohibition and repression. Now that the military regime has been overcome by democracy, freedom of organization and opposition restored, and the "citizen" constitution promulgated (1988), what has become of the highly praised "progressive church" in Brazil? Has it gone back to "business as usual"? And what about the ever growing Pentecostal churches? Are they alien to political engagement, or utterly conservative? What, after all, has happened to the public role of Brazilian churches since the transition to democracy has been completed (1985/1989)?

The task of the present study is to give an answer to these questions. To pursue such a task is, in my view, justified from the beginning in that it will provide evidence and interpretations on the recent trajectory of one of the most visibly emerging countries in the world and its churches. Brazil is part of the so-called "BRIC" countries—Brazil, Russia, India, and China, in an expression coined by financial analyst Jim O'Neill from the Goldman Sachs Bank in 2001.[1] The country itself is investing highly in partnerships with India and South Africa, on political, social, economic, technological, and scientific matters, among others. In 2003, the IBAS/IBSA Forum was founded based on the *Brasilia Declaration,* as "a trilateral, developmental initiative between India, Brazil and South Africa to promote South-South cooperation and exchange."[2] Brazil is still the country with the world's largest Catholic population. But it now also hosts the world's largest Pentecostal population, with a booming increase over the last thirty years. And even if less visible today, Liberation Theology is still very active and productive.[3] In particular, Leonardo Boff continues to receive enormous

1. See http://www.itamaraty.gov.br/temas/mecanismos-inter-regionais/agrupamento-bric (accessed on 12/12/2010). Internet references, if not referring to a full article, are given only in the footnotes.

2. http://www.ibsa-trilateral.org (documents) (accessed on 12/12/2010).

3. This is visible, for instance, in the annual congresses of the Brazilian Society for Theology and Religious Studies (SOTER) and the World Forums on Theology and Liberation, held in 2005 (Porto Alegre), 2007 (Nairobi), 2009 (Belém), and 2011 (Dakar), see Susin, *O mar se abriu, Sarça ardente, Terra prometida, Teologia para outro mundo possível*; Althaus-Reid, Petrella and Susin, *Another Possible World*; Getui, Susin and Churu, *Spirituality for Another Possible World*; Santos and Susin, *Nosso planeta, nossa vida;* SOTER, *Gênero e teologia, Deus e vida, Sustentabilidade da vida e espiritualidade*; Freitas, *Teologia e sociedade, Religião e transformação no Brasil*; also Sanchez, *Cristianismo na América Latina e no Caribe*, just to mention the collective works.

publicity both inside Brazil and worldwide. For his themes and resonance—today mainly on account of ecology—, he is to be considered a truly public theologian.[4]

This would seem to be enough reason to undertake such a study, given that no extensive, ecumenical, and theologically interested project has been undertaken on the public role of the churches in Brazil after transition, as is done here. However, such a role is relevant also in a comparative perspective. The so-called "third wave" of democratization[5] ended military regimes in Portugal, Spain, and Greece, but also in a number of East Asian and Latin American countries, including Brazil,[6] and finally in Eastern Europe. In many instances, organized religions, not least Christian churches, have contributed significantly to such transitions from an authoritarian to a democratic system. This fact, however, has received little attention from researchers in general, even though there has been substantial research on the Roman Catholic Church in Brazil under the military regime. Thomas Bruneau and Scott Mainwaring have to be named here in the first place.[7] Alfred Stepan, an expert on military rule and its overcoming, has prominently stated that "by the mid-1970s the Brazilian Church had become the most theologically progressive and institutionally innovative Catholic Church in the world".[8]

From 2002–06, a group of researchers, most of them from theology, but also from political science, law, and ethnology, has examined the role and contribution of religions, namely Christian churches, in the public sphere before, during, and after transitions to democracy. This examination has included both theoretical reflections and six case studies, on South Africa, Mozambique, Brazil, South Korea, the Philippines, and Indonesia.[9] These discussions and their findings have served as a constant resource for this study. My contribution to that project became, in a way, the basic script for the present book.[10] My interest in the subject has come from long acquaintance: As I was writing my doctoral dissertation on a Trinitarian, contextual, and catholic theology in dialogue with Leonardo Boff and Raimon Panikkar and their respective Brazilian and Indian contexts, I was able to spend six months in each country for research. During my first stay in Brazil (1996), it struck me how the State tends to be thought of as "them" by many people I spoke to, while their own activity,

4. On Boff see my earlier works "Ecumenical Hermeneutics for a Plural Christianity"; *Reden vom Dreieinigen Gott in Brasilien und Indien*; "Leonardo Boff—a Protestant Catholic"; *Leonardo Boff und die protestantische Theologie*, and the collective work in the Brazilian Intellectuals series, Guimarães, *Leituras críticas sobre Leonardo Boff*.

5. Huntington, *The third wave*.

6. Hagopian and Mainwaring, *The Third Wave of Democratization*; Sinner, "Der Beitrag der Kirchen zum demokratischen Übergang in Brasilien."

7. Bruneau, *The political Transformation of the Brazilian Catholic Church*, *The Church in Brazil*; Mainwaring, *The Catholic Church and Politics in Brazil*. The churches' role has, of course, been of different degrees in different cases, and has been both transition-enhancing and transition-hindering; see for instance McDonough, Shin and Moisés, "Democratization and Participation." An important study on the public role of religion has been undertaken by Casanova, *Public Religions in the Modern World*. More recently, not least propelled by the September 11 attacks on the World Trade Center in 2001, political theologies and public religions have received notable attention by a number of experts in a book edited by Vries and Sullivan, *Political Theologies*. Norris and Inglehart, *Sacred and Secular*, based on empirical studies, evaluating and differentiating the highly challenged classical theory of secularization from Durkheim and Weber to Berger, state that while some, mainly "advanced industrial societies," have become more secular during the last fifty years, the world as a whole has become more religious, not least due to the higher fertility rate of those holding religious values (ibid., 235). Berger, *The Desecularization of the World*, and others have rediscovered the importance of religion for public life. Juergensmeyer, *Religion in Global Civil Society*, and others have studied the role of religion in global civil society. However, on the whole, there is still little recognition of the contribution of churches and religions to processes of transformation, see Lienemann-Perrin and Lienemann, *Kirche und Öffentlichkeit*, 14.

8. Stepan, *Democratizing Brazil*, XII.

9. Lienemann-Perrin and Lienemann, *Kirche und Öffentlichkeit*.

10. Sinner, "Der Beitrag der Kirchen zum demokratischen Übergang in Brasilien."

in their perception, had certainly nothing to do with politics. People did not seem to feel part of the State.[11] There seemed to be a widespread distrust of politicians, but also towards the police and other governmental agencies. At the same time, the famous Brazilian *jeitinho* (a smart way of doing things, something like cunningness), while it serves as an important and creative mode of "social navigation" (Roberto DaMatta), seems to run contrary to the reliability of the rule of law even on a popular level.[12] It is, for instance, very common to be asked in taxis or restaurants what amount the waiter should write on the receipt to be presented to one's company or university for reimbursement. It is, thus, considered normal by many that you cheat on your firm in order to get more for yourself. While such things are not uncommon even in long established democracies, I would contend that the extent of their acceptance in Brazil is remarkable.[13]

This impression was confirmed as I came to live in the city of Salvador in Northeastern Brazil (2001–02), where I worked in an ecumenical Non-Governamental Organization and lived in a modest *bairro* (city district) on the periphery of this metropolitan region of three million people. There, the Roman Catholic parish with very active Base Community work at the time had fostered political participation through a critical evaluation of candidates and a conscientious vote. In 1996, political articulation was high. Especially the young people in the parish brought forward their own candidate and finally succeeded in getting him elected into the state legislative assembly in 1998 —he was reelected in 2002, but not in 2006.[14] A good number of those who supported him became, however, more and more disillusioned as they saw how he sent his children to a private school and lived in a security-protected apartment block in a more sophisticated *bairro*, something the others thought to be impossible for themselves. He was apparently using his now higher salary also for his own sake, even though he accounted for it and also donated a considerable amount to his Worker's Party (PT).[15] Later, it seemed that he was employing *laranjas* ("oranges") in his office, i.e. persons appointed as staff in order to receive money from the State, but who had to return most or all of their salary to the deputy. Thus, he could use State money destined for his collaborators for other purposes—not necessarily for himself, but rather for his party. Some might consider this legitimate, and it is indeed a common practice among many politicians, but it is certainly illegal, and the PT with its ethically sound message was not supposed to fall into such practices. Nothing was ever proven, despite the installation of a parliamentary investigation commission, and the charges were dismissed; but some of the supposed or real "oranges" spoke out to their friends in the parish and contributed to the disillusionment. The once so strong and hopeful support in the parish had gone:

11. "State" will be used with capital "S" when referring to it generically, conceptually or as a specific nation-state as a whole, namely Brazil, with its governing and administrative bodies; "state" will be used for particular states like Rio Grande do Sul.

12. Cf. DaMatta, *Carnivals, Rogues and Heroes*, *A Casa & A Rua*, *O que faz o Brasil, brasil?*; Hess and DaMatta, *The Brazilian Puzzle*; Sinner, "Menschenrechte in Brasilien." According to a recent empirical study, Brazilians themselves are deeply divided and ambiguous over the *jeitinho*, see Almeida, *A cabeça do Brasileiro*, 43–71.

13. In terms of corruption, commenting on the scandals affecting the PT government from 2005 onwards, a columnist in Porto Alegre's main daily newspaper, *Zero Hora*, claimed that while there was corruption in the whole world, only in Brazil it would be considered so normal. While this is certainly an exaggeration, Brazil does not have to be a unique case in having a serious problem in this field to call for a much more rigorous morality in politics – but, as I would contend, also among the population.

14. However, Yulo Oiticica (PT) was able to step in as substitute for another deputy and had become an effective state deputy again by the end of 2007; see http://www.al.ba.gov.br/ deputadolegislatura.cfm?varCodigo=16 (accessed on 2/11/2009).

15. Specific documentation on this and what follows is in my possession or has been shown to me personally.

People became as distrustful as anybody else who could not be motivated to collaborate in political mobilization in the first place.

What seemed, initially, to be at least a partial realization of God's kingdom, now appeared as just one more proof of the dirty business of politics, and that popular mobilization could, after all, not make any lasting difference in politics. At the same time, new priests with little interest in social justice and transformation took care of the parish and returned to a more traditional way of being the church. The parish I mentioned earlier is a case in point: although "religiously" stronger than ever, with frequent masses, processions, and other activities of this kind, social justice and ecumenism, while not completely absent, are relegated to minor importance. I have been able to observe this in regular visits over the past 13 years. Traditional Catholic values and practices are stronger again, to the detriment of political discussions. On the other hand, the sense of impotence that I perceived, mixed with a strong distrust of "them" in politics, has been confirmed by surveys that rated interpersonal trust particularly low in Brazil and politicians among the most distrusted actors in society.[16] The churches, in turn, rank constantly high—which gives them an excellent potential for building trust, indispensable in any democracy.[17]

It had been Liberation Theology that brought me to Brazil in the first place, this contextual and political theology *par excellence* that has defended the churches' task of helping the voiceless to get their voices heard and to transform society in order to eradicate the appalling poverty. Strangely, although Liberation Theology is still alive and outspoken, it has spent little time reflecting on such factors and engaging in a reconstruction of the State in Brazil after the return to democracy in 1985. Had the changing context not brought about changes in contextual theology? As I shall show, it has, but the utopia of a system change—overcoming neo-liberal world capitalism by replacing it with some kind of socialism—seems to continue to prevail over effective changes. Mediation, negotiation, and the building of new and possibly unusual partnerships are still regarded with a lot of distrust.[18] It is my conviction, however, that in order to make efficient changes that effectively improve the lives of the poor and, indeed, the excluded, such partnerships are needed. To be sure, the founding element of Liberation Theology, the preferential option for the poor, still holds true in a world—and in a Brazil—where despite considerable improvements in a number of areas, poverty and, indeed, social and economic exclusion continues on a wide scale.[19] But I fear that the tendency towards maintaining a dualist view (rich and poor, foreign and national, "them" and "us," powerful and powerless, etc.), or else "escaping" to rather vague notions of "paradigm changes" and "spirituality", both visible in the yearly Congresses of the Brazilian Society for Theology and Religious Studies (SOTER) and the World Forum on Theology and Liberation,[20] might be obstructing rather than helping a necessary "new social contract."[21] As I shall show, there is also a general lack of interest in questions of law and little confidence that a stable legal system and an effective rule of law could indeed be a keystone to the deepening of democracy in Brazil. However, there are signs—although still relatively timid—to include *cidadania* (citizenship) into a liberative theology.[22] Citizenship

16. See Latinobarómetro 2003, 2005; IBOPE, *Confiança nas instituições.*

17. Sinner, "Trust and convivência."

18. See, for instance, the analyses in Maclean, *Opting for Democracy?*; Petrella, *The Future of Liberation Theology.*

19. See, in a strong plea out of broad experience and intellectual reflection, Farmer, *Pathologies of Power*, explicitly referring to Liberation Theology, its method of "see-judge-act" and its option for the poor (ibid., 139–59 and passim).

20. Cf. above, note 3.

21. Streck, *Educação para um novo contrato social.*

22. Assmann, "Teologia da Solidariedade"; Castro, *Por uma fé cidadã*; Pauly, *Cidadania e pastoral urbana.*

starts as "the right to have rights" (Hannah Arendt) and comprehends the concrete rights and duties as foreseen by law. In a wider sense, it includes the real possibility of effective access to those rights and consciousness of one's duties, as well as the extension of citizen participation in the social and political life of the country. In both its narrower and wider senses, often with a utopian character, citizenship has become the key term qualifying Brazilian democracy since transition.[23] This is visible in both Brazilian and foreign studies on politics and law.[24] Thus, a stronger reception of the term in theology could be expected than has effectively happened. Similar moves can be seen in South Korea, where a "theology of the citizen" is claimed as a timely continuation of liberative *Minjung* theology.[25] But, again, it has not (yet?) become a widely accepted concept. After considerable attention given to the *shimin* (citizen, citizenship) in Korea during the preparation of the new constitution in 1986/87, it lost momentum shortly thereafter, either because of disinterest in a further discussion of democratization, or because it was thought to be too "bourgeois."[26]

What role, then, does religion play in society; what influence do, or should churches have (or not have) on politics? Of course, *political theology* is not a new subject. The term was coined by the *Stoa* and described by Marcus Terrentius Varro (116–27 BC), as recorded, with criticism, by Augustine in *De Civitate Dei* VI,5ff.[27] There, within a "tripartite" theology, poets would tell stories about the gods and the cosmos in the *theologia mythike* (in Latin *fabularis*), philosophers would ponder on the nature of things in the *theologia physike* (*naturalis*), and priests were to sustain and legitimate the State through public cult, which was "political theology" (*theologia politike* or *civilis*). Augustine scolded and ridiculed Varro namely for the first and the last of these as being men's work for the theater and the city. For him, not only are such gods not worthy of being worshipped for the "earthly goods" (VI,12), but indeed most unfit to provide eternal life.

The relationship between Church and State, religion and politics has been a constant subject in Western theology, located by Augustine's well-known work in the tension between the *civitas Dei* and the *civitas terrena* or *diaboli*, and reworked by Luther in what was developed much later into a doctrine of the two kingdoms or regiments.[28] Concrete relations changed over time. Following John Witte, Jr., there are four main phases to be described: (1) Since Constantine, when the Roman Empire gradually adopted Christianity as its official religion, there has been *symphonia* (or caesaropapism)[29] between political and spiritual power, with the pendulum swinging towards the predominance of the first. (2) In the West, the pendulum swung to the other side with the

23. The long transition process started in 1974 with General-President Ernesto Geisel and is taken to have ended with the handover to a civilian government in 1985 or the first popular presidential election in the new republic, held in 1989.

24. For studies on politics and law, see Carvalho, *Cidadania no Brasil*; Benvenides, *A cidadania ativa*; DaMatta, *Brasileiro: cidadão?*; Herkenhoff, *Direito e Cidadania*; Pinsky and Pinsky, *História da Cidadania*; Pinsky, "Os profetas sociais e o Deus da cidadania." For education, see Buffa et alii, *Educação e cidadania: quem educa o cidadão?*; Pauly, *Ética, educação e cidadania*; Streck, *Educação para um novo contrato social*. For sociology, see Demo's *Cidadania menor*, *Cidadania tutelada*, *Cidadania pequena* and Costa's *As cores de Ercília*. For anthropology, see Caldeira, *City of Walls*; Biehl's *Vita* and *Will to Live*; Holston, *Insurgent Citizenship*.

25. Min, "From the Theology of Minjoong to the Theology of the Citizen" and "Towards a Theology of Citizenship"; cf. Lienemann-Perrin, "Neue sozialethische Konzeptionen Öffentlicher Theologie."

26. Lienemann-Perrin and Chung, "Vom leidenden Volk zur Staatsbürgerschaft. Koreanische Kirchen zwischen Minjung und Shimin," 327f.

27. ". . .die segenbringenden Stadtgottheiten! Sind sie nicht noch lächerlicher als die Narrenpossen der Theater?" Augustinus, *Vom Gottestaat*, 305 (De Civ. Dei VI,9).

28. Duchrow, *Christenheit und Weltverantwortung*.

29. Witte, *God's Joust, God's Justice*, 11.

Gregorian Reform beginning in 1075, when the Roman Catholic Church was established "as an autonomous legal and political corporation."[30] (3) The Reformation of the 16th century shifted power, law and property largely to the State in yet another swing of the pendulum. (4) Finally, the enlightenment brought (in the West) the definitive secularization of politics and law, promoted by prominent Christians like Hugo Grotius, for whom natural law can exist *etsi Deus non daretur.*[31]

At the beginning of the 20th Century, Carl Schmitt[32] understood political theology as religious concepts secularized into State concepts, namely God's omnipotence translated into the State's sovereignty.[33] His personal friend Erik Peterson differed from him in rejecting analogies between a God and politics on the grounds of the nature of God as Trinity, proclaiming the end of any political theology—at the time a subtle, but clear critique of the Nazi State and its pseudo-religious undergirdings.[34] The so called *New Political Theology* of Johann Baptist Metz, Jürgen Moltmann, and Dorothee Sölle claimed a more active role for the churches, not in legitimizing the *status quo*, but in questioning not the State as such, but specific political decisions.[35] A similar, but stronger and more general critique of a repressive State and an oppressive national and world economy was formulated by Liberation Theology in the same period, the late sixties and the seventies of the twentieth century. Clodovis Boff[36] described its method as a theology of the political. In the same period, Martin E. Marty[37] brought up the concept of *Public Theology* in referring to Reinhold Niebuhr's interpretation of U.S.-American political and religious culture. Max L. Stackhouse's works have connected public theology with (global) civil society. Theologians in the anglo-saxon world from Niebuhr to Duncan Forrester,[38] but also Liberation Theology inspired the creation of the *Global Network of Public Theology* in May 2007, in Princeton, New Jersey, USA, and its *International Journal of Public Theology.* For the purpose of the present study, South Africa—whose *Beyers Naudé Center for Public Theology* at Stellenbosch University is one of the main founding members of the Global Network—is especially interesting in comparison to Brazil because of certain contextual similarities and, not least, because of the need to formulate theology anew in a situation where mere resistance has given way to a more constructive (while still critical) approach. Public Theology is very rarely used as a term in Brazil or Latin America, but its content matches in many respects what Liberation

30. Ibid., 12.

31. For sources on Christian political thought from Irenaeus to Grotius (100–1625), see O'Donovan and Lockwood O'Donovan, *From Irenaeus to Grotius.*

32. Schmitt, *Politische Theologie.*

33. "Alle prägnanten Begriffe der modernen Staatslehre sind säkularisierte theologische Begriffe" (Schmitt, *Politische Theologie*, 43). Schmitt has regained prominence in recent discussions on politics, also in Brazil, where four of his books have been published over the last years by Del Rey law editors in São Paulo, including his *Political Theology.* A recent prominent critique of his doctrine of sovereignty and the connected concept of the state of exception is to be found in Giorgio Agamben's works *Homo Sacer* and *State of Exception*, which have also been translated into Brazilian Portuguese.

34. Both Jürgen Moltmann (*The Trinity and the Kingdom of God*) and Leonardo Boff (*Trinity and Society*) have referred to Peterson's thesis of the end of all political theology through the doctrine of the Trinity as developed by the Cappadocian fathers. But while Peterson defended that no political analogy of God was possible after the discovery of the Trinity, they affirmed the contrary and developed social analogies of the Trinity; on this see my reflections in Sinner, *Reden vom Dreieinigen Gott in Brasilien und Indien*, 108–12.

35. Political Theology has come unto us as what I call an aggregating concept for different kinds of relating theology and politics, broadly defined in the Blackwell Companion to Political Theology as "the analysis and criticism of political arrangements (including cultural-psychological, social and economic aspects) from the perspective of differing interpretations of God's ways with the world" (Scott and Cavanaugh, *The Blackwell Companion to Political Theology*, 1).

36. Boff, *Theology and Praxis.*

37. Marty, "Reinhold Niebuhr."

38. See Storrar and Morton, *Public Theology.*

Theology and its followers, but also other theologies in that context have been seeking to think and do, much *avant la lettre*. There is, today, a growing interest in this concept in Brazil, created not least by the somewhat coincidential, but eventually very fruitful membership of the Lutheran School of Theology at São Leopoldo (EST) in the Global Network.[39]

Indeed it is my hypothesis that public theology is an appropriate aggregating concept for a liberative theology in Brazil which aims at achieving social justice and transformation through fostering citizenship. The focus on citizenship is necessary, because public theology is, in itself, not sufficiently defined for concrete action. It unites a number of ethical principles under the horizon of the public dimension of theology and, indeed, the churches. The specific way in which this public dimension becomes visible in Brazil is an object of this study; but I believe that its findings are relevant also for other contexts.[40]

Why do the *churches* have such a great potential to foster citizenship, notably in Brazil? There are a number of factors which will be developed during this study. *First*, theologically speaking, churches have a longstanding tradition of distinguishing between this world and the world to come, the sinful state of the actual world and its overcoming through Christ who will bring about God's Kingdom. While this can lead to a dangerous dichotomy separating loyalties to political authorities and to God, an eschatological reserve can (and, indeed, must) maintain a healthy tension between what is now and what is to be, what is and what should be. Even for many of those who are not believers, but concerned about the well-being of society, there is, in Habermas' words, "something" that the churches (and indeed, religions) keep alive that is able to show "societal pathologies," as well as the "failure of individual life plans."[41] The church tries to bring a foretaste of the world to come into today's world. The churches' mission to proclaim the Gospel, worship God, serve the poor and witness to God's saving grace is propelling it into public space—it cannot keep this good news for itself. Christianity is by definition public.[42] While it has a local, contextual presence, it is

39. An Indian colleague, J. Jayakiran Sebastian, had mediated an invitation by William F. Storrar to join a book project on Trinity, Church and Civil Society, combined with the invitation for an international congress at Edinburgh University (A World for All? Ethics for a Global Civil Society), in September, 2005, where the first meeting of those interested in creating the Global Network was held and to which I was invited spontaneously. In 2007, while I was a resident member of the Center of Public Theology in Princeton, which hosted the first global meeting of the Network, EST joined it as a full and founding member, and was elected on its Executive to represent South America. These points of encounter have helped to give shape to this study's argument, from which in turn insights have been shared with colleagues from the Network, and a major article was published in its journal (Sinner, "Brazil: From Liberation Theology to a Theology of Citizenship as Public Theology"). The first issue of the *International Journal of Public Theology* in 2012 will be wholly dedicated to the emerging Public Theology in Brazil.

40. I am aware of the fact that, in Europe, the discussion on citizenship tends to focus on nationality, on the difference between those who are by citizenship nationals of a specific country, or members of a specific agreement (like the Schengen agreement), and those who are not. In Brazil, however, the main problem is to be found in the lack of effective citizenship for its residents, namely its nationals. The U.S. discussion on citizenship tends to focus on both aspects, rights for immigrants and rights for citizens on the whole, given the historical inequalities vis-à-vis the black and hispanic population.

41. Habermas, "On the Relations Between the Secular Liberal State and Religion," 257.

42. Lienemann, "Kirche und Öffentlichkeit in Transformationsgesellschaften"; Wolfgang Huber, since his seminal study *Kirche und Öffentlichkeit*, has insisted in this public character of the church. Ironically, according to a survey carried out by Huber's then doctoral student Wolfgang Vögele (*Zivilreligion in der Bundesrepublik Deutschland*, 421, n. 158), the term "öffentliche Theologie" disappeared in German writings until 1992, with the only reference he could find—without further explanation—being located in the German translation of the Boff brothers' work *Introducing Liberation Theology*. Boff and Boff (*Introducing Liberation Theology*, 85–87) speak of a "public" and "prophetic" theology, pointing to Liberation Theology's presence in the media and among both left- and right-wing politicians. Since the 1990s, however, a series of important studies related to public theology have been published notably by Huber's students in the series Öffentliche Theologie, like Vögele (*Zivilreligion in der Bundesrepublik Deutschland*; *Menschenwürde zwisch-*

at the same time worldwide, ecumenical, and catholic.[43] This also creates a tension—ideally fruitful—between the church and a particular State. From this angle, churches are prone to participating in public debate and contributing towards the improvement of society, through a critical and constructive attitudes, selective cooperation with the State and civil society, and public statements on issues of public interest.

A *second*, sociological factor is that the churches, in the case of Brazil especially the Roman Catholic and the Pentecostal churches, reach in some way or another the greatest part of society. Although all might not actively participate in church life, 92.7 percent of the population affirm that they belong to some religion, and 89 percent indicate that they belong to a Christian church (see below, IIB1). The churches' capillarity is very high.[44] In many instances, churches are the only institutions reaching very poor populations, working with prisoners, bringing people off alcoholism or drug addiction, and catering for the socially abandoned. Of course, these works are not free from ambiguities, and might not necessarily foster political participation or the transformation of structural illnesses in society. They might indeed help rather to cope with than to change the situation.[45] But is this not a necessary first step? Is it not, after all, more efficient than political rhetoric that puts off most of the population?

Thirdly, churches themselves provide a space for education and the development of skills, including leadership skills, and can function as "schools for democracy."[46] There is some empirical evidence for this, as important leaders of civil society and political institutions have come from Church Base Communities and even from the—usually conservative—Pentecostal churches.[47]

---

en Recht und Theologie) and Bedford-Strohm (*Vorrang für die Armen*; *Gemeinschaft aus kommunikativer Freiheit*). See also Huber, "Öffentlichkeit und Kirche," who insists that "Die Herausbildung von Öffentlichkeit im neuzeitlichen Sinn [. . .] die Einsicht [verstärkt], dass die Verkündigung der K. [Kirche] den Charakter öffentlicher Kommunikation hat. Sie veranlasst zu der Einsicht, dass kirchliches Handeln nicht auf den innerkirchlichen Bereich beschränkt sein kann. [. . .] in diesem Horizont [sc. der Botschaft von der Rechtfertigung des Sünders und der Orientierung an Glaube, Hoffnung und Liebe im Horizont der Gottesherrschaft] aber erweisen sich das Eintreten für die Wahrheit, der Einsatz für die bessere Gerechtigkeit und die Kultur der Barmherzigkeit als wichtige Leitlinien ihres öffentlichen Handelns" (ibid., 1170).

43. See Sinner, *Reden vom Dreieinigen Gott in Brasilien und Indien*, 34–53.

44. This is a typical expression in Brazil (*capilaridade*) to express that the churches are present even in the most remote and downtrodden places, like the hair-thin veins (capillaries) of the body that oxygenize even the most remote parts of the body with their blood.

45. Mariz, *Coping with Poverty*.

46. In their differentiated table, such function is called by Mathwig and Lienemann, *Kirchen als zivilgesellschaftliche Akteure in aktuellen politischen Transformationsprozessen*, 119, the "Sozialisierungsfunktion"; Huber in 'Öffentlichkeit und Kirche,' 1173 calls it the "Bildungsaufgabe," and the churches' contribution toward the development of a "Kultur des Helfens." This contribution is often discussed in terms of the churches' role in the production of social capital (Putnam, *Making Democracy Work*, *Bowling Alone*, *Gesellschaft und Gemeinsinn*; Wuthnow, *The United States*). According to Putnam (*Bowling Alone*, 66), "faith communities in which people worship together are arguably the single most important repository of social capital in America." This is largely confirmed by the comparative empirical data interpreted by Norris and Inglehart (*Sacred and Secular*, 180–95), but they stress that it is difficult to establish causalities here, and that membership in a religious organization seems to be more significant for civic participation than church attendance, although the latter enhances membership in religious and also some non-religious organizations. It is, for them, not clear whether secularization has in fact weakened social capital and civic engagement.

47. The São Leopoldo mayor, elected in 2004 and very honorably reelected in 2008, Ary José Vanazzi (PT), is one of them; he has made his way through the CEBs movement from a poor farming family to a pastoral agent and missionary among indigenous peoples, and then as a politician. Assemblies of God member Benedita da Silva from Rio de Janeiro has been a senator, vice-governor, governor and federal government minister. Marina Silva, originally from the "progressive" Catholic Church, later converted to Pentecostalism in the Assemblies of God, served as the federal government minister for the environment until 2008, when she resigned and returned to her seat in the senate. In the 2010 presidential election, she gained a remarkable 20% support at the ballot competing for the Green Party.

While the "Protestant,"[48] in fact predominantly Pentecostal, contribution to the consolidation of democracy or to economic and social transformation is certainly ambiguous and not immediately evident, my contention is that they do have an important positive contribution in the long run, as I shall argue, although there is not sufficient empirical evidence that this is necessarily so.[49]

The present study pursues, then, an interaction between theological reflection and the history and sociology of democratic transition in Brazil. It takes stock of the literature available from foreign "Brazilianists", Brazilian researchers living and teaching abroad and Brazilian researchers in their homeland, predominantly those working in the fields of political science, sociology, and anthropology. These contributions are connected to the wider debate on "transitology," i.e., system transformation.[50] However, most of these do not give much attention to the role of religion, and therefore, in line with the above mentioned research project,[51] special attention is given to religion here, notably the Christian churches.[52] The restriction on Christian churches is due to the numerically very small percentage of (declared) non-Christians in Brazil.

Although the importance of the *Roman Catholic Church* for opposing military rule and working as a catalyst for civil society during authoritarianism is widely recognized, its continuing contribution has not received the same attention. *Pentecostal churches*, on the other hand, have become a focus in sociological research,[53] but there is still little theological reflection on their contribution, and their place in civil society is subject to controversies.[54] The *historical churches*, among them the Evangelical Church of the Lutheran Confession in Brasil, have received very little attention in this regard, despite their reasonable size, age, and influence, which gives a strong argument for including the named church here.

48. Terminology is often vague. In Brazil, non-Catholic Christians are usually called *evangélicos* (literally "evangelicals"), which tends to refer primarily to Pentecostals. "Protestants" is more often used in foreign literature; in Brazil, it normally refers to the historical Protestant churches which have come to Brazil through immigration or foreign mission in the 19th century, and is used even for those who explicitly oppose such denominator for themselves, as Baptists and Anglicans.

49. Gaskyll, "Rethinking Protestantism," 86, reviewing the then available literature, concludes: "While the empirical literature is still small it gives us no particular reason to believe that Protestants intrinsically [!] constitute a cultural or organizational opposition to patterns and structures of traditional, authoritarian political and social domination in the democratic era." That might be true, but does not exclude elements, often without or even against the official discourse, which in practice contribute toward citizenship.

50. Merkel, "Theorien der Transformation," *Systemwechsel 5;* O'Donnell, "Democracia delegativa?", "On the State, Democratization and Some Conceptual Problems," "Polyarchies and the (Un)Rule of Law in Latin America"; O'Donnell and Schmitter, *Transitions from Authoritarian Rule*; Linz and Stepan, *Problems of Democratic Transition and Consolidation*; B. Lienemann, "Deskriptive und normative Grundlagen der politologischen Transformationsforschung"; "Vergleichende Betrachtungen zu den Transformationsprozessen."

51. Lienemann-Perrin and Lienemann, *Kirche und Öffentlichkeit.*

52. Herbert, *Religion and Civil Society*, 68 and passim speaks of a "neglect of religion in mainstream studies of democratization." This is also true for non-theological academics in Brazil. By 1989, as political scientist, sociologist, and Anglican layman Burity noted, "religion and politics" had not yet become a field of interest (*Os protestantes e a revolução brasileira*, 7; cf. "Religião, política e cultura", 91 n. 8). He himself has contributed greatly to the inclusion of religion as a variable in academic analyses (see among others Burity, *Radical Religion*, *Redes, parcerias e participação*).

53. Martin, *Tongues of Fire* and *Pentecostalism*; Freston, *Evangélicos na Política Brasileira*, *Evangelicals and Politics*, *Evangelical Christianity and Democracy*; Stoll, *Is Latin America Turning Protestant?*

54. Interestingly, even the Pentecostals' own reflections draw heavily on other, namely sociological research (Paul Freston, Ricardo Mariano) to understand their own political role, cf. the entry "política" in the Dictionary of the Pentecostal Movement (Araujo, *Dicionário do Movimento Pentecostal*, 703–12), which indicates that this is still an incipient issue for Pentecostal self-reflection.

This study is and has to be interdisciplinary. It makes use of (1) *anthropological* studies as well as my own experience since 1996, and makes occasional use of stories in order to check what is argued against the reality in a deep experience, even if limited in scope, to give people, namely "the poor," a concrete face.[55] This deep perception of the life of some few persons is verified against (2) *sociological* studies that help to expand such perceptions and measure their relevance within broader movements in society. (3) *Political* and, to a minor degree, *legal* studies help to understand better the functioning of political institutions and possibilities (and hindrances) of political participation. (4) *Historical* studies help to situate the present within short- and long-term developments and understand it in its roots, without wanting to fix it there. Finally, (5) *theology* is at stake to identify and interpret the churches' positions as well as the contemporary challenges, and to ultimately propose elements for a public theology focused on citizenship. While literature is used from the United States, Western Europe, and South Africa, the main focus is on Brazilian authors and literature, thus making them available for the reader who is proficient in English. The reason why, as a non-native speaker, I opted for writing this text in English is so that it might serve as a bridge between the quadrangle of countries or regions involved, even if that means that my Brazilian colleagues, many of whom are not fluent in English, will have more trouble in reading. Still, some parts of this study have, in their previous and adapted versions, already been published in Portuguese as articles, chapters, and presentations recorded in proceedings. More will certainly follow. In any case, the Brazilians' voice is to be well heard throughout the text, which is what I owe the many authors, discussion partners, and fellow citizens (in the wide sense) whose experience and expertise has informed me. I hope that what I am giving back here will be meaningful to them.

The *first part* of this study is dedicated to Citizenship and Democracy in Post-Transition Brazil. The task of this part is to introduce the reader to Brazilian democracy and citizenship, both descriptively and conceptually, and to consider the treatment of these key issues and concepts in its most expressive theology, Liberation Theology. The first section (A) is about transition itself, its advances and setbacks. The second section (B) deals with the concept and reality of civil society in Brazil, followed by a section on the new key concept for Brazilian democracy that has emerged from there, citizenship (C). Finally, the possible emergence of a theology of citizenship from Liberation Theology is explored, and the question asked what a public theology might mean in the Brazilian context and how it might be connected to the existing theological discourse (D).

The *second part* contains case studies on the contribution of the churches towards citizenship. First, methodological considerations are made as preliminaries (A), followed by a panoramic overview of churches and religions in Brazil, their ever-growing diversity and legal status, and the appearance of religion in public space without the presence of institutional representation (B). Thereafter, through the necessarily selective analysis of official documents, newspapers or bulletins, websites and books, as well as existing empirical research, the three churches named above, the Roman Catholic Church (C), the Evangelical Church of the Lutheran Confession in Brazil (D), and the Assemblies of God (E) are presented in an analogous way: Preceded by a historical survey, documentation is analyzed as to the discourse that emerges from it and, as far as possible, verified empirically, and followed by theological elements that relate to democracy and citizenship, church and State, church and society, and the connection between political and ecclesial citizenship.

55. This happens, with the necessary but not excessive theoretical grounding, in a fascinating way in Biehl, *Vita*, where the story, self- and outsider-interpretation of one single woman in the context of a "zone of social abandonment" becomes emblematic for the reality of many persons in Brazil.

The *third part* sketches out the author's own proposal for a public theology focused on citizenship. The first section (A) is on citizenship, describing theologically what it means to *be* a citizen in the first place, to *live* as a citizen on the basis of trust, to *endure* as a citizen within the ambiguity of existence, and to *serve* God as a citizen in liberty under two regiments. This section draws on traditional theology, namely within the Lutheran tradition, where I am situated and which I came to find especially helpful, though it is little known in today's Brazilian context. This tradition is interpreted in the light of the challenges and possibilities identified in the first and second parts. The second section (B) is on public theology, a new, but in my view promising term for the Brazilian context within an ecumenical, i.e., interconfessional, intercultural, and international perspective. Public theology, with an emphasis on academic theology, is differentiated from public religion. As the common weal is set as the necessary goal for the action of the churches in the public sphere, boldness and humility alike are needed for a meaningful contribution, faithful to the Gospel and in cooperation with others who ". . .seek the welfare of the city," even when it is seen as being located in exile (Jer 29:7).

PART I

CITIZENSHIP AND DEMOCRACY IN POST-TRANSITION BRAZIL

Democratic transition in Brazil is generally taken to have occurred between 1974, when President General Ernesto Geisel took power and initiated a "slow, gradual and secure" process of political decompression, and 1989, when the first direct presidential elections were held, thus completely restoring, at the least, an electoral democracy. Another important year was 1985, when power was handed over to a civilian president; this became a milestone in Brazil's history of transition. It marks the beginning of the period the present study is examining more closely.

Democratic consolidation was considered achieved when Luis Inácio Lula da Silva assumed office in 2003, after a remarkably smooth government transition.[1] In a moving ceremony, for the first time in over 40 years, a democratically and directly elected president, the distinguished sociologist Fernando Henrique Cardoso, handed over the presidential sash to another democratically and directly elected president.[2] Lula had been elected by nearly 53 million voters (61 percent) on October 27, 2002.[3] A charismatic metal worker from a humble, North-Eastern background, who became a powerful trade-union and, later, Worker's Party (PT) leader, Lula had been the hope of all those longing for change in the country, over three consecutive election campaigns (1989, 1994, 1998), until he eventually made it in his fourth run. He won over common people and entrepreneurs alike with his program of marrying strict economic responsibility[4] to an extensive fight against hunger.[5] However, as we shall see, while the economy prospered, social transformation

1. Codato, *Political Transition and Democratic Consolidation*, IX.

2. The last one had been president Juscelino Kubitschek (1956–60), handing over to Jânio Quadros (1961). Quadros resigned still in 1961, and vice president João Goulart took over. Goulart was deposed by the military in 1964. The first civilian president after military rule, Tancredo Neves, was elected by an electoral college, and died without taking office. Vice president José Sarney assumed the presidency. In 1989, Fernando Collor de Mello was elected president by the people, but again had to leave office without completing his term due to his impeachment in 1992. Vice president Itamar Franco handed over the sash to Fernando Henrique Cardoso for his first mandate. Only at the end of Cardoso´s second mandate (the possibility of reelection was a novelty, introduced only in 1997 by the Constitutional Amendment number 16, of June 4), on January 1, 2003, 43 years after Kubitschek and Quadros, the passing of office ceremony came back to normality.

3. Almanaque Abril, *Brasil 2003*, 44.

4. This implied continued fighting against inflation, maintenance of a high primary budget surplus and loyal and even anticipated payment of debts (interest and capital).

5. The *Fome Zero* ("no hunger") program has become the flagship of this policy, executed, among others, by the well known liberation theologian Frei Betto who was promoted to the post of presidential adviser; however, the program has been facing numerous criticisms (for being inefficient and insufficient, as well as assistentialist rather than transforming) and Frei Betto resigned "for personal reasons" at the end of 2004. For an extensive critique and well documented

continued to be slow. A huge scheme of Government bribery involving deputies, which came to the fore in 2005, was a major blow to democracy.[6] The democratic institutions withstood the blow, and the remarkable transparency of the investigation—with hearings broadcast live on TV—as well as the fact that some representatives lost their seats, showed that all was not simply doomed to end up in "pizza."[7] On the other hand, Lula was convincingly reelected in 2006 for a second (and last possible) term—partly because of his undeniable achievements in the economic area, partly because of a weak and divided opposition. Lula won not least because, unlike his government ministers and PT politicians, he was regarded by many as somehow above corruption—although it is barely imaginable to the observer that he really didn't know anything and was simply "betrayed" by his staff. In any case, Lula succeeded in communicating that impression and showed that he was still representing people's hopes of social ascent: if a humble mechanic from the poor and backward Northeast who had not even finished school could become president, then anything seemed possible. There is, of course, a dose of populism in this direct relationship between the president and the people, and indeed when he underwent the strongest pressures, Lula sought reassurance through direct contact with them.

In terms of democratic institutions and, partly, of their agents, I think it is still fair to consider Brazil a consolidated democracy. There is a fair degree of institutional stability and little chance of a breakdown. However, in terms of participation of the people and the effective availability of their rights and performance of their duties, there are considerable deficiencies, and "civil" democracy or "civil citizenship"[8] cannot be considered consolidated.

The word *cidadania* (citizenship), which has emerged (especially since the 1980s) as a central term in the process of democratization, will accompany my reflections throughout this study, both in general terms and in theological use. The abundant literature using the concept rarely spends much time on a sharp definition; rather, it denotes a conceptual field for political participation and social inclusion, assuming the role of a utopian and open concept. *Cidadania* is, in the first place, the "right to have rights" in a situation of "social apartheid" where exclusion prevails.[9] Thus, a major challenge to effective citizenship is for all people to realize that they indeed *do* have rights, that they *are* citizens. This may sound obvious, but it is not in a society with millions of people struggling for mere survival, living with less than two ore even one US-Dollars a day to spend, in appalling contrast to the income and wealth of a small number of very rich people. It is not obvious in a country where there are people whose first photograph ever is taken on the day of their death,

---

description of his activities during office see Betto, *A mosca azul*, *Calendário do poder*.

6. The Federal Republic of Brazil (*República Federativa do Brasil*) is composed of 26 states and the federal district, with a total of 5,563 municipalities. It has two legislative chambers: the Chamber of Deputies (513), composed by different numbers (between eight and 70) of deputies per state according to its population, and the Senate (81 members), with three senators per state. The federal executive is led by the president who is head of state and government, the state executive by a governor, and the municipality by a mayor, all of them elected by direct popular vote, each together with one vice-president, vice-governor, or vice-mayor.

7. This is a common expression in Brazil, used to denote the dilution of investigations that go on for a long time and end up with no palpable result. It is used constantly in cartoons and paper headlines, as well as in everyday gossip: The idea is that everything ends up in a nice meal with a tasty pizza (which everybody likes), and then one forgets about problems and conflicts. As all are being nice to each other (especially parliamentary colleagues, police corporations and the like), they are expected to prefer a good meal to a thorny investigation.

8. O'Donnell, "Polyarchies and the (Un)Rule of Law."

9. Dagnino, Os movimentos sociais, 108,105. It was Hannah Arendt who saw in this the most fundamental right for human dignity: to be the subject of rights; 'Es gibt nur ein einziges Menschenrecht,' in *Die Wandlung* 4 (1949), 745–70, quoted in Huber, "Menschenrechte/Menschenwürde," 598. For an extensive exploration of the concept of citizenship, see below, IC.

where many newborns are not registered and thus do not exist legally, where people suffer total social abandonment, and where the police are known to be corrupt, incompetent, and violent. It is also not obvious in a country with a traditionally strong patriarchal and clientelistic social and political organization, where it is not the law that defines or even protects relationships.

This being the case, the concept of citizenship must be broader than just indicating the rights—and duties—foreseen by law. It must include the possibility of real access to rights and the consciousness of one's duties, a positive attitude over against the constitutional State as such, as well as a constant molding and extension of the citizens' participation in the social and political life of their country. It is a way of overcoming the distinction between "them" and "us," making people feel they are part of the story. If others are not doing their part, especially those in public office, citizens have the right to denounce that and to press for improvement. Aspects of a citizen's effective participation are, then, becoming central, as is the political culture by which such participation is encouraged or hindered. It is not least in this area, I contend, that churches can make a difference.

In this first part of my study, I shall describe and examine the story of transition in Brazil, with a short presentation of the preceding situation in which the "March/April Revolution,"[10] or rather the coup d'état occurred, and the consequent advances and setbacks in democracy and citizenship (A). I then focus on the role of civil society, which in the present setup was arguably born during the phase of transition, and locate the churches within it (without yet exploring their contribution in depth) (B). The next chapter is dedicated to the concept of citizenship as it is currently being used and interpreted in Brazil, with some references to the wider debate (C). Finally, I shall look at the continuation of Liberation Theology and their hesitant entry into issues of citizenship (D).

10. As the important events occurred on March 31 and April 1, it is called either "March" or "April" Revolution.

A. The Story of Transition in Brazil—Advances and Setbacks in Democracy

THIS FIRST CHAPTER IS dedicated to a description and evaluation of transition to democracy in Brazil, using available national (i.e. Brazilian) and international literature, mainly from political scientists and historians. First, I shall tell the story of what happened as Brazil came under military rule in 1964, as well as the main episodes of its development, followed by a more detailed account of the transition period (1974–85) and the phase of consolidation (since 1985) (1). I then present evaluations of Brazil as an (un)consolidated democracy, using a set of criteria and recent information to assess these evaluations (2). The third chapter explores "disjunctions" in citizenship, i.e., the deficiencies, defects, restrictions, or whatever else might be called the shortcomings in Brazilian citizenship that are in contrast to the important advances that have occurred over the last two decades (3).

1. TRANSITION TO DEMOCRACY

Minha dor é perceber que apesar de termos feito tudo, tudo que fizemos
ainda somos os mesmos e vivemos como nossos pais.
Belchior[11]

In order to understand how the present situation came about, and to familiarize the reader whose knowledge of Brazilian history is restricted, it is necessary to recount the story of previous democratic and authoritarian phases, especially the developments from the watershed of the 1930 "lieutenants" revolution to the 1964 March/April revolution and the fiercest phase of the military regime under president Médici, which shows how decisive a power the military had become (a). A second section tells the story of transition to democracy, until 1985/89 (b), and the third explores the process of consolidation that followed (c). These accounts are based on the available, already classical literature both of Brazilians and (mainly U.S.) Brazilianists, with special weight given to the groundbreaking work of Thomas Skidmore.[12] The voice of the churches is not yet the focus of

11. "It hurts to perceive that, despite all we did, we are still the same and we live like our parents." This song, written by Antônio Carlos Gomes Belchior Fonetenelle Fernandes (*1946), in 1976, and later masterly performed by Elis Regina Carvalho Costa (1945–82), arguably the most popular Brazilian singer at the time, became the song of a revolutionary generation which, because of the military government, felt their dreams were frustrated and that, after all, they were not able to go beyond their parents.

12. Skidmore (*Politics in Brazil*, *Politics of Military Rule*, "Brazil's Slow Road to Democratization") is the most recognized authority here and has so far given the most comprehensive historical account of Brazilian democracy between 1930 and 1985; focusing on political history, Schneider, *Order and Progress*, looking back on 30 years of research in

this subchapter, but will be heard here and there to indicate how churches reacted to events like the 1964 revolution.

a) The Authoritarian Turn and the Military Regime 1964–1973

Initially, it is necessary to recall the pre-history of the 1964 "revolution" or coup d'état and the reasons for the turn to authoritarianism.[13] Independent Brazil had first become a constitutional monarchy under an emperor, descended from the Portuguese royal family. Under this constitutional monarchy, which lasted from 1822 to 1889, the emperor was to function as "moderating power" (*poder moderador*) in the State, between (and indeed above) the two chambers, the Chamber of Deputies and the Senate.[14] A limited democracy was established by the foundation of the Republic following a military coup on November 15, 1889. The straightforwardly secular Constitution of 1891—the first of only two not to invoke the name of God in Brazil's independent history—established a limited franchise qualified by property and education, and limited to men.[15] A year earlier, the decree No. 119-A had disestablished religion, introduced freedom of worship, recognized churches as corporations that could acquire goods in their name, and formally abolished the *padroado*, that papal concession by which the political ruler was responsible also for church matters.[16] This was the so-called "Old" or "First Republic." It was ended in 1930 by a military coup with the support of a "revolutionary" coalition. This coalition was made up by liberal constitutionalists and semi-authoritarian nationalists, among them junior military, called the "lieutenants" (*tenentes)*. It was further supported by senior military, coffee growers, and dissident members of the political elite. The provisional president, Getúlio Dornelles Vargas (1883–54), who was indirectly elected in 1934, managed to function as a kind of new "moderating power"—both arbitrating and securing his own power—between these competing factions.[17] Parties were few and weak, while more radical groups surfaced on the left and right, both the Communists under Luís Carlos Prestes (1898–90) and the

---

and on Brazil, also gives a comprehensive account from colonial times to Fernando Collor de Mello. Both use vast documentary and bibliographical material, as well as personal interviews from and in Brazil. Among the Brazilians, Iglesias's *Trajetória Política do Brasil* covers, in a more panoramic view, the political trajectory from 1500 to 1964, and Fausto's *História do Brasil* is the reference for a general historical account of Brazil. A previous and shorter version of what is being said here has been published in Sinner, "Der Beitrag der Kirchen," 271–78.

13. For this section, I am drawing mainly on Skidmore, *Politics in Brazil*, 253–302.

14. Herkenhoff, *Direito e Cidadania*, 67–73; Bonavides and Andrade, *História constitucional do Brasil*, 87–105. According to the 98th Article of the Constitution, "the Moderating Power is the key to all the political organization and is delegated privatively to the Emperor, as Supreme Head of the Nation and its representative, so that he may, incessantly, watch over the maintenance of independence, balance and harmony among the other political powers." Ibid., 91.

15. Herkenhoff, *Direito e Cidadania*, 78 states that the Republican Constitution "excluded from the [electoral] listing mendicants, illiterates, soldiers [not officers] and religious subject to votes of obedience" [cf. article 70 of the Constitution of the Republic of the United States of Brazil, of February 24, 1891], but "abolished the requirement of income through raw goods, commerce, industry or arts, as a criterion for the exercise of political rights." On the invocation of God in the Brazilian constitutions, see the booklet by the deputy attorney-general of the Republic Nóbrega, *Deus e constituição*. The other one not to invoke God was the 1937 Constitution in the *Estado Novo*.

16. Decree nr. 119-A, of January 7, 1890. Like all legislative texts since Independence, this decree can be found on the Federal Senate's homepage (http://www.senado.gov.br), under the category "legislação." It is from there that I cite, unless otherwise stated, throughout this study. On the Portuguese patronage see Boxer, *The Portuguese Seaborne Empire*, 228–48. The *padroado* "can be loosely defined as a combination of rights, privileges and duties granted by the Papacy to the Crown of Portugal as patron of the Roman Catholic missions and ecclesiastical establishments in vast regions of Africa, of Asia, and in Brazil" (ibid., 228–9). In effect, this meant that the Portuguese king and his representatives had (or at least acted as if they had) dominion over virtually any decision concerning the church in their lands overseas.

17. Standard works on Vargas are the 16 volumes of Hélio Silva, published by the Civilização Brasileira in the 1960s and 1970s, and the political biography by the same author, *Vargas*, as well as Fausto, *Getúlio Vargas*.

fascist *integralistas* led by Plínio Salgado (1895–75). "In 1937 an exhausted Brazil ended her political experimentation and began eight years of authoritarian rule under the *Estado Nôvo*" (1937–45), as Skidmore[18] sums up this period. Through a coup in November 1937, Vargas assumed rule as a dictator and imposed a new Constitution, which still foresaw a legislative power—but elections were never held.

Vargas, a highly centralizing nationalist-populist leader, sought out those who could strengthen his support among the people.[19] Thus, the Roman Catholic Church under Cardinal Sebastião Leme was able to re-establish its leading role and influence over the State. As was the case with Rome at the time, democracy was not a predilection of the Catholic Church in Brazil, which preferred a strong centralist government. It conceived of itself as the national church, while it considered other churches as foreign intruders. To be Brazilian was to be Catholic, and the Church exerted significant efforts in this period to reach its (mostly nominal) members and fortify its structures, schools, and social works.[20] While the regime became increasingly authoritarian, with restricted civil and political rights, the Vargas period saw important advances in social matters, especially in labor legislation. The 1934 Constitution reflected "to a remarkable degree the ideals both of political liberalism and of socio-economic reformism."[21] It was also a time of important economic changes, with home industrialization beginning to replace the traditional importation of processed goods, while exporting primary products, mainly agricultural crops.

With the end of World War II, authoritarian government lost its legitimacy, even more so as Brazil had entered the war on the side of the allies, fighting for democracy. Protests arose in various camps. Elections were announced, but Vargas vacillated over how they would take place. Once again, it was the military, not the politicians, who were responsible for the change in government, deposing Vargas on October 29, 1945.

The *Estado Nôvo* was followed by a phase of democratic restoration under former War minister General Eurico Gaspar Dutra (in office 1946-1951) , as elections were held on December 2, 1945, during the interim presidency of chief justice José Linhares. Dutra could count on ample support from the traditional and emerging elites who had already supported Vargas, and from urban workers organized in paternalistically organized unions. His party, the Social Democratic Party (*Partido Social Democrático,* PSD) which despite its name gathered the traditional political elites, won 42 percent of seats in the Chamber of Deputies, and the urban worker's Brazilian Labor Party (*Partido Trabalhista Brasileiro,* PTB), 10 percent. While Dutra represented a politics of *tranqüilidade* (in this context, "normalcy,"[22] although it included the banning of the Communist party on the grounds that it was seen as "anti-democratic" (i.e. against party pluralism and fundamental human rights, as foreseen in the 1946 Constitution, art. 141, § 13)), Vargas skillfully prepared for a new bid, now in a democratic election. In 1950, he was voted back to the presidency (1951–54) with support from

18. Skidmore, *Politics in Brazil,* 8.

19. Skidmore, *Politics in Brazil,* 67 comments that "the populist politician would have been unthinkable before 1930, since his success presupposes a relatively free vote. He is a personalistic leader whose political organization centers upon his own ambitions and career." Skidmore notes that the electorate grew considerably in that period, and elections were organized more freely and correctly than in the Old Republic, where they were highly manipulated. In the 1934 Constitution, women were included in the electorate, and the voting age was reduced from 21 to 18 years (Constitution of the Republic the United States of Brazil, of July 16, 1934, Art. 108).

20. On the relationship of church and State and the constitutional implications, see below, IIB, and specifically on the Roman Catholic Church, IIC1.

21. Skidmore, *Politics in Brazil,* 19; see especially Art. 121 of the 1934 Constitution. Cf. also Herkenhoff, *Direito e Cidadania,* 83–89; Bonavides and Andrade, *História constitucional do,* 317–27.

22. Skidmore, *Politics in Brazil,* 65.

mixed sources, including, in some states, his most important opponent, the National Democratic Union (*União Democrática Nacional,* UDN), and mainly another populist, São Paulo governor Adhemar de Barros (1901–69, in office 1947–51 and 1963–66).[23]

While urbanization and industrialization continued, Vargas followed a developmentalist and nationalist line ("the oil is ours"),[24] which worked for some time. However, in the midst of an economic crisis, rising opposition to Vargas, and the implication of his entourage in an attempt to kill one of the opposition's main leaders, Carlos Lacerda (1914–77), it was once more the military that decided on the head of State's destiny. Met with an ultimatum, Vargas shot himself on August 24, 1954, as he had announced he would do should he be deposed. Vice President João Café Filho (1899–1970), a Presbyterian and thus the first Protestant president of Brazil, completed the term of office.

The next elected president, Juscelino Kubitschek (1902–76, in office 1956–60), commonly known as "J.K.," launched an ambitious development program under his famous dictum "fifty years in five," made visible symbolically through the construction of the new capital, Brasília. His successor, Jânio Quadros (1917–92, in office January to August, 1961), promised to wipe the political scene with his "broom" (the symbol of his electoral campaign), claiming to bring morality, correctness, and efficiency into the administration, which evidently aroused people's hopes. However, he had no luck in presidential politics and resigned unexpectedly after only seven months in office. According to the Constitution, the vice-president would succeed him. But João Goulart (1918–76, in office 1961–64) had been minister of labor under Getúlio Vargas and was seen as a leftist and, thus, mistrusted by the elites. The Armed Forces nearly took power, but met strong resistance from the South which guaranteed that Goulart could take office.[25] The price was the introduction of a parliamentary system of government, allowing stronger control of the executive by Congress. Tancredo Neves (1910–85), who in the later transition process would be elected the first civilian president, was made prime minister, but resigned after just one year in office. In 1963, a referendum was held and the former system of presidentialism was restored. In this period, anti-communism was a common position among many, not least in church circles. At the same time, extreme poverty and the lack of viable politics, especially in rural areas, ushered laborers into the hands of communist organizations like the Rural Leagues (*ligas camponesas*). Various types of revolutionary projects seemed to throw the country into chaos.[26] "Impatience on the far left, disillusionment among the moderate left, alarm in the center, conspiracy on the right— it added up to a volatile political cauldron," in Skidmore's assessment.[27] Goulart tried to attend to both the exigencies of a policy of austerity as imposed by the creditors, and to the demands of his electoral basis, the working class. Once he seemed to be on a successful course with the former, he then courted the

23. Ibid., 78 comments that "one could hardly have found greater proof of the non-doctrinal character of parties in the economically backward states!," in this case, the Northeastern state of Pernambuco. Barros' unofficial campaign slogan, till today popular as a designation for efficient, albeit corrupt politicians, was "he steals but gets things done" (*rouba, mas faz*), see ibid., 68.

24. In 2006, President Lula could proudly quote Vargas to announce Brazil's full self-supply in petrol, see below, IA3a.

25. The outstanding leader of the resistance was Goulart's brother-in-law Leonel Brizola (1922–2004), then governor of the state of Rio Grande do Sul, together with the 3rd Army based in Porto Alegre. Brizola would remain one of the important— however scintillating and populist— figures of Brazilian politics until his death, which aroused an impressive, nationwide wave of sympathy and mourning.

26. On revolution in the discourse of the Brazilian left see Burity, *Os protestantes e a revolução brasileira*, 56–86; Sodré *Introdução à Revolução Brasileira*.

27. Skidmore, *Politics in Brazil*, 294.

latter, seeking popular support for changing the Constitution to give him more powers to carry out reforms that Congress might block. Many of his advisors, including the renowned anthropologist Darcy Ribeiro (1922–97), had long urged him to turn to the people and combat those they considered Brazil's exploiters. In a political rally on March 13, 1964, held in Rio de Janeiro with a crowd of 150,000 strong, Goulart spoke out in a radical, leftist way, arousing fears among the elite that "he had rejected the rules of the democratic game."[28] One of the key issues was his promise of an agrarian reform by appropriating public lands.[29]

After considerable hesitation by some of the generals, the military eventually came forward and took power in the "revolution" of March 31 and April 1, 1964, in which General Humberto de Alencar Castelo Branco (1900–67, in office 1964–67), the Army Chief of Staff and one of the leaders of the coup d'état, was elected president by Congress.[30] Congress itself remained in session and the 1946 Constitution was upheld, but the military commanders considered themselves empowered to rule by "institutional acts" legitimized by the "victorious revolution" itself and immediately sought to strengthen the power of the executive. Although he and his followers, the *castelistas* (like future president Geisel, who would later initiate the transition), are generally regarded as more moderate, different from the "hardliners" Costa e Silva (1967–69) and Médici (1969–74), it was Castelo Branco who expanded executive power and abolished the existing political parties in the Institutional Act number 2, of October 27, 1965.[31]

At the time, many were relieved that order was being re-established and that the "communist threat" was effectively being contested. The National Roman Catholic Bishops' Conference (CNBB) welcomed the coup:

> As we give thanks to God who attended to the prayers of millions of Brazilians and freed us from the communist danger, we thank the military who rose, facing great risks to their lives, in the name of the supreme interests of the nation, and we are thankful for those who ran to free her from the imminent abyss.[32]

The bishops, however, expected an early return to the democratic order and called for a struggle against the root causes of the rise of communism, i.e. social injustices and materialism.

On the Protestant side, the São Paul Synod of the Brazilian Presbyterian Church (IPB) also hailed the "revolution":

28. Ibid.

29. Sader and Silverstein, *Without Fear of Being Happy*, 56; on the whole episode see Skidmore, *Politics in Brazil*, 284–93, and the whole chapter on the breakdown of democracy, 253–302; on João Goulart Ferreira and Benjamin, "Goulart, João," 1504–21, especially 1517–20.

30. The Institutional Act number 1, of April 9, 1964, and its preceding address to the nation considered the event a revolution, as it represented "the interest and the will of the nation." It also considered that "the constitutional processes did not work to depose the Government which deliberately headed towards bolshevizing the country"; text reproduced in Bonavides and Andrade, *História constitucional do Brasil*, 771.

31. The extended power of the executive included dismissal of legislative representatives on all levels, depriving them or any other citizen (this was stated more clearly than in the earlier Institutional Act) of their political rights for up to 10 years, including their freedom of movement, and the possible submission of citizens to military justice. The president could now declare or extend the State of Siege for up to 180 days, without having to be voted upon by Congress, and could decree a Congress recession. The 18th article bluntly states, without any justification: "The actual political parties are abolished and their respective registers cancelled," and then refers to the regulations which would allow a two-party-system to come into being. The text is to be found online: www.acervoditadura.rs.gov.br/legislacao_3.htm (accessed on 1/24/2007).

32. Official declaration of 2/6/1964, in Matos, *Nossa história*, 171.

> All true Christians rejoice in the results of the glorious March-April [military] revolution: the purge of communists and sympathizers from the government of our beloved Brazil . . . God acted at the right moment, using the courage and patriotism of the armed and civilian forces.[33]

Other churches issued similar statements. The editor of the Baptist Journal *(Jornal Batista)* interpreted the coup as a victory of democracy over communism:

> as we were living in a heavy climate of provocations, threats, agitations, which took from us the minimum of calm necessary to be able to work and progress. Necessary, inclusively, for the preaching of the Gospel. Now things have changed. It was time.[34]

More ambiguous, i.e. subtly critical, was a telegram to the new president, Castelo Branco, for his inauguration, sent by the Evangelical Confederation of Brazil (*Confederação Evangélica do Brasil*—CEB). The CEB

> greets Your Excellency [. . .] formulating wishes to God [for] continuous divine support to the Government of Your Excellency, illuminating [the] way [toward] the Christian-democratic reconstruction of our Fatherland, guaranteeing human rights, promoting social justice and [the] wellbeing [of the] people, defending national sovereignty, Christianizing [the] development [of the] Brazilian society, leading the Fatherland [to] high destinies [in the] concert [of] free nations, [this is the] sense in which Your Excellency shall have constant moral support and loyal cooperation [from] *evangélico* Christians.[35]

The Armed Forces themselves had diverging opinions on the duration of their regime. In any case, they never fully institutionalized it, not even in the Constitution of January 24, 1967. The most extraordinary powers continued to be given to itself by the executive in Institutional Acts, which modified the Constitution, but upheld it as a whole. The climax of such powers was reached by decreeing, on December 13, 1968, the Institutional Act Nº 5 (AI-5), which maintained and expanded all earlier rights for the executive— freed from juridical appreciation— and now also suspended the *habeas corpus* rule "in the case of political crimes, against national security, the economic or social order and people's economy."[36] More clearly than the earlier institutional acts, its preamble stated that the "Revolution" intended

> to give to the country a regime which, attending to the exigencies of a juridical and political system, assured an authentic democratic order, based on freedom, respect of the dignity of the human person, the combating of subversion and ideologies contrary to the tradition of our people, the struggle against corruption [. . .][37]

While much of this sounds nothing but cynical— even as the authors presumably did not think so—the act indeed gave more power to the executive to combat corruption and imposed serious restrictions on personal enrichment in public service. The regime had morally fairly high standards, although of course not against its political enemies, and it was far from living up to them

33. *Brasil Presbiteriano*, May 1964, p. 7, in Cavalcanti, "Political Cooperation and Religious Repression," 100.

34. José Reis Pereira, in *Jornal Batista* of April 12, 1964, cited in Reily, *História Documental do Protestantismo no Brasil*, 315. While it states the total incompatibility of "communism" – which is said to have infiltrated also some of the church's youth – and Christianity, the text does note that "many things" in the social realm are to be conquered, namely land reform, and ends by stating: "Justice, liberty, truth, honesty, purity, these beautiful ideals are only achieved when Jesus dominates the hearts. Let us live and struggle so that Jesus Christ may reign in our fatherland" (ibid., 317).

35. Printed without any comment in the *Órgão Oficial* of the IECLB number 9 of May 1964, p. 6 [Historical Archive of the IECLB in São Leopoldo]. The omissions are due to the typical abbreviated style of a telegram.

36. Text reproduced in Bonavides and Andrade, *História constitucional do Brasil*, 791, art. 10.

37. Ibid.

comprehensively. Even so, the fight against corruption and the imposition of surveillance in the name of security was perceived by many as a blessing. For those, however, who were considered a threat to "national security," media censure, political repression, imprisonment, torture, and killings became common. The torturers continued their cruel work even after the several small guerrilla groups had been defeated.[38]

It is a Brazilian peculiarity that a certain democratic routine was maintained. Although there were only two parties allowed, the ruling National Renewal Alliance (*Aliança Renovadora Nacional - ARENA*) and the opposition Brazilian Democratic Movement (*Movimento Democrático Brasileiro*—MDB), there were elections with a degree of real competition and not an institutionalized single "revolutionary" party as in Mexico. Congress was suspended from time to time, but never dissolved; elections for president, although not competitive, followed the compulsory rotation after each term —there never was one single dictator. In Chile, Uruguay, and Argentina, normal political processes were disrupted. "In Brazil, in contrast, political society functioned within military-set limits."[39] This is why Juan Linz has called it an "authoritarian situation" rather than an "authoritarian regime."[40] It never consolidated, as it lacked a sufficient ideological basis and a clear idea of (and if!) Brazil was going to be an authoritarian State.[41] There was a constant ambiguity between the tendency to perpetuate the authoritarian regime and the reiterated perspective of a return to democracy. Differently from the Vargas period, there was neither a thorough reorganization of State and society, nor a charismatic and populist leader to have it implemented.[42] And despite its fervent anti-communism and hailing of national security, Brazil was the least repressive of the so called bureaucratic-authoritarian regimes, with a death toll considerably lower than in its neighboring countries. According to the *Brasil: Nunca Mais!* ("Brazil: never again!") report published in 1985, 333 persons were killed between 1964 and 1981, a per capita toll 100 times lower than in Argentina.

The regime's "legitimacy," or rather, endurance, was greatly helped by the so-called "economic miracle." President General Emílio Garrastazú Médici (1905–85, in office 1969–74) governed the country during those years with strong repression of political opposition. Nevertheless, he was very popular, as salaries rose, economic growth reached nearly 12 percent in 1972, and employment opportunities were abundant.[43] Even the Secretary of the Treasury of the United States looked with envy on the Brazilian performance and affirmed it should serve as a model for the U.S.[44] As this came to an abrupt end with the 1973 oil crisis, more moderate commanders came to power and commenced a slow and controlled transition process in 1974, to which I now turn.

38. See *Brasil: Nunca Mais*; Skidmore, *The Politics of Military Rule*; Weschler, *A miracle, a universe*.

39. Hagopian, *Traditional Politics and Regime Change*, 259.

40. Linz, "The Future of an Authoritarian Situation," 235 and passim. Linz presented his thesis at a 1971 conference at Yale and was proven right by subsequent history, as Skidmore, "Brazil's Slow Road to Democratization," 6 affirms.

41. According to Alfred Stepan, the military were, however, fairly confident of their legitimacy and capacity to govern, as the ruling doctrine of the *Escola Superior de Guerra*, in which the vast majority of the "revolutionary" generals had been formed, had insisted on a necessary combination of development and security; Stepan, *The Military in Politics*, 172–87.

42. See Skidmore, "Politics and Economic Policy Making," 37–46.

43. According to a poll carried out in 1971, 82 percent of the population approved of Médici's government, see Gaspari, *A ditadura derrotada*, 25f. Baer, *The Brazilian Economy*, 75 gives an average 11.3 percent of growth for the period 1968–74.

44. Gaspari, *A ditadura derrotada*, 26.

b) Transition to Democracy 1974–1985 (1989)

In 1974, the newly elected General Ernesto Geisel (1908–96, in office 1974–79), descendant of a German Lutheran immigrant family from Rio Grande do Sul, initiated a process of, as he said, "slow, gradual and secure liberalization," sometimes also called "decompression."[45] This, however, did not mean that repression was immediately reduced. Geisel and his crew, among them notably the versatile General Golbery do Couto e Silva (1911–87), had to fight on a double front. On the one hand, he needed to secure maximum authority in the presidency against the military command in order to deter the hardliners, while showing full control over the "subversives." On the other hand, he wanted full control of the decompression process, which was not really meant to become a fully participatory democracy, but a more legitimate and less repressive system. While the military were to gradually leave politics, the main authority should remain in the executive.[46] Thus, ironically, presidential authoritarianism increased under Geisel as the process of transition commenced. However, once the process was under way, it did not remain as controlled as Geisel wanted it to be. The growing space the political opposition and civil society found for action was used to influence the outcome of transition.

The Roman Catholic Church became one of the main sources of opposition (see below, IIC1), together with the increasingly audible voice of the Brazilian Bar Association (*Ordem dos Advogados do Brasil*—OAB). The people expressed their will by exercising their right to vote and in November 1974 gave a landslide victory to the opposition which had focused its campaign on social justice, civil liberties and resistance against denationalization, i.e. foreign influence on Brazilian economy. Although the power of civilian politicians was limited, it is significant that the government lost its two-thirds majority in Congress, which was necessary for constitutional changes. At the same time, the elections were a clear sign of what people wanted, and indicated that this was not in line with the government's plans. Dissatisfaction with military rule rose as the economy worsened—high inflation, economic recession, rising unemployment, and a growing external debt left people with ever less money to spend.

Incidents like the alleged "suicide" in custody of Jewish journalist Vladimir Herzog (1975), whereby the army publicly defied the president's policy of "decompression," showed how much

45. The expression of a "slow, gradual and secure liberalization" [*distensão lenta, gradual e segura*] is from a programmatic speech delivered on August 29, 1974, Coutinho and Benjamin, "Geisel, Ernesto," 1453. For information on Geisel's biography and personality, see Gaspari, *A ditadura derrotada*, 25ff.; on his biography and political activities Coutinho and Benjamin, "Geisel, Ernesto." Like many descendants of immigrants, he could not get rid of his hated nickname *Alemão* ("German"), although he tried hard to evade this mark. On transition as a whole, see Skidmore, *The Politics of Military Rule in Brazil*, 160ff.; "Brazil's Slow Road to Democratization"; Schneider, *Order and Progress*, 267ff.; Kinzo, "Transitions."

46. Skidmore, *The Politics of Military Rule*, 163–71. One of the voices heard in the reflecting process on the best form of decompression, beginning still under Médici from 1972 onwards, was Harvard political scientist Samuel P. Huntington (1927–2008), who recommended a controlled process favoring institutionalization, quoting as successful examples Mexico and Turkey; cf. ibid, 165, based on manuscripts and personal information from Huntington. The contact with Huntington was mediated by Catholic layman and political scientist Candido Mendes de Almeida, co-moderator of the "bipartite commission," whose brother Dom Luciano Mendes de Almeida (1930–2006) would be president of the CNBB (cf. below, IIC1c). The main respondent to Huntington was Brazilian political scientist and Stanford PhD Wanderley Guilherme dos Santos, publishing his position in *Estratégias de descompressão política* (Brasília: Instituto de Pesquisas, Estudos e Assessorias do Congresso, 1973, in Skidmore, *The Politics of Military Rule*, 363, note 11). While he concurred with the need for a controlled process, he insisted more than Huntington on the reintroduction of classical liberal rights. It is interesting to note that Golbery again called on Huntington in 1974 for intensive talks, focusing on his (Golbery's) part on "'intermediary bodies' such as the Church, the press, universities, and labor" (ibid., 167).

would still have to be done to return to democracy.[47] The above mentioned AI-5, that was hoped to simply "fade away from lack of use,"[48] gained new momentum in fierce raids against (supposed or real) communists or former guerrillas, as well as in stripping awkward legislators of their mandates. When an opposition congressman and leading critic of the regime, Protestant lawyer Lysaneas Maciel (1926–99),[49] came out in defense of two deputies who were close to losing their mandates, his name was immediately added to the list of those to be discharged. There were also some eruptions of "rightist terrorism"[50] against the press and the Roman Catholic Church—even a bishop was harassed—to destabilize the process of decompression. At the same time, the opposition made ground in municipal elections in 1976, winning majorities in the municipal councils of the most important cities.

With his power base considerably weakened, Geisel had to resort to rule by decree, making it necessary to close Congress, which he did on April 1, 1977. He then announced constitutional changes known as the "April package," designed to strengthen ARENA's position for the next elections.[51] Public reaction was strong, forcing the president to reconvene Congress only two weeks later. Throughout the year, the regime had to face ever growing protests from the opposition, university students and intellectuals, and although the "April package" was successful in preventing a MDB majority in Congress in the 1978 elections, the tendency to vote for the opposition was evident. At the end of the year, the AI-5 was finally abolished, diminishing considerably the president's power, bringing back *habeas corpus* for political prisoners and lifting prior censorship from the mass media. The National Security Law was revised, though still allowing for detaining political prisoners without communication and, thus, keeping possibilities for torture open. Banishment was lifted for 120 political exiles. Metal workers, led by Luís Inácio Lula da Silva, launched waves of strikes involving up to three million workers in the São Paulo area, with strong support from civil society, not least from the Roman Catholic Archdiocese under Cardinal Arns.

Geisel's successor, João Baptista Figueredo (1918–99, in office 1979–85), continued the process of *abertura.* Congress approved an amnesty bill in August 1979, which freed over 700 political prisoners and brought many exiles back to Brazil, among them Communist Party leaders. It also restored political rights to those who had lost them. However, torturers were also understood to be covered by the amnesty law, which included "perpetrators of both 'political crimes' and 'connected crimes,'" under which torturers were understood to be covered.[52] Also contrary to the general mood

47. On the reaction of exponents of the Jewish community and ecumenical partners, who ostensively celebrated an ecumenical funeral service, see below, IIB1, IIC2.

48. Skidmore, "Brazil's Slow Road to Democratization," 13.

49. According to Freston, *Evangélicos na Política Brasileira*, 108, Maciel was stripped of his office because he denounced torturers. He came back into parliament in 1982 and remained one of the most progressive Protestant politicians, following the principle that "the vital problems of the Brazilian people are the vital problems of the Gospel" (ibid.). While Skidmore in *The Politics of Military Rule,* 166, says he was a "Methodist preacher," Freston holds that Maciel belonged to a secession of the Presbyterian Church of Brazil (IPB), the Christian Church of the Reformed Confession (*Igreja Cristã de Confissão Reformada*).

50. Skidmore, *The Politics of Military Rule in Brazil,* 190.

51. The "April package" extended the following president's mandate to six years, maintained the indirect election of governors, shortened the mandate of mayors and city councilors to be elected in 1980 to two years (for the new election to coincide with Congress election in 1982), decreed the indirect election of one third of the senators (the so-called "bionic senators", *senadores 'biônicos'*), increased the number of seats of minor states (where ARENA was stronger), reduced the majority necessary for passing constitutional amendments to simple majority, and extended the already existing restrictions for political propaganda on radio and TV ("Lei Falcão," bearing the name of Geisel's Minister of Justice) to the general elections; Coutinho and Benjamin, "Geisel, Ernesto," 1456.

52. Skidmore, *The Politics of Military Rule,* 219.

of liberalization was the rather tough law introduced in August 1980 to regulate the entry and residence of foreigners in Brazil, which was to hit a good number of foreign Roman Catholic priests.[53]

Following the principle of *divide et impera,* new parties were allowed to be formed, in the hope that this might split the opposition and ensure the government's hold on power. Among others, the Workers's Party (*Partido dos Trabalhadores,* PT) was founded.[54] The Social Democratic Party (*Partido Democrático Social,* PDS) succeeded the ARENA, while a considerable part of the former MDB entered the new PMDB (*Partido do Movimento Democrático Brasileiro,* Party of the Brazilian Democratic Movement), apart from other, minor parties.

Elections held (belatedly) in 1982 brought back direct elections for state governors for the first time since 1965. The opposition won a remarkable 10 out of 22 governorships. On the national level, it received 59 percent of the votes, but failed to gain a majority in Congress or the electoral college that would vote on the next president, due to the restrictive modalities of the election fixed by the Government in 1981, known as the "November package."

Huge rallies demanded direct presidential elections in 1984 (the famous *Diretas Já!* campaign). On April 16, 1.7 million took to the streets in what became the largest public demonstration the city of São Paulo had ever seen. But the opposition was not strong enough to see the necessary amendment approved by Congress. However, their candidate for the presidency, Tancredo Neves, made it by a large margin in the electoral college, gaining support from dissenters of the ruling party PDS, and was to become the first civilian president since 1964. The New Republic (*Nova República)* was born. As Tancredo fell seriously ill on the eve of his inauguration, the conservative vice-president José Sarney (PDS, later PMDB) took over and would remain in office due to Tancredo's subsequent death. "Brazil's transition to democracy had taken yet another unexpected turn."[55]

It is debatable whether the transition process ends here or only with the first direct presidential elections in 1989. In any case, the phase of consolidation began with the end of the military regime. Thus, I shall speak about these years in the following section.

c) The Process of Consolidation

Under Sarney, a president who lacked legitimacy and was associated with the former military regime, the process of transformation took an important step forward, but democracy remained fragile, having to face a growing economic and social crisis. From 1986 to 1994, Brazil saw four different currencies being introduced and went through six stabilization plans, all of which—except the last one, the *Plano Real*—failed to bring lasting economic stability and, especially, to contain inflation.[56] The 1980s are generally called "the lost decade," resulting in instances of reduced *per capita* income and a continuously high foreign debt.[57] Approval for democracy was considerably

53. The imprisonment of two French priests in the Araguaia region, formerly an area of guerilla activity and disputed between landlords, settlers and indigenous peoples, generated movements of solidarity and gave birth to an ecumenical movement in the state of Pará, still existing today with some of the original leadership, including Lutheran pastor of German origin, Rosa Marga Rothe; see the thesis of Silva, "As origens do movimento ecumênico na Amazônia paraense."

54. On the history and importance of that fact see Sader and Silverstein, *Without Fear of Being Happy*; Keck, *The Workers' Party and Democratization in Brazil*; Branford and Kucinski, *Lula and the Workers' Party in Brazil*, 13–53.

55. Skidmore, "Brazil's Slow Road to Democratization," 31.

56. Cf. Baer, *The Brazilian Economy,* 145–219, according to whom the previous plans failed for not including strong fiscal adjustment and for financing government deficits through the Central Bank, thus pushing up inflation. For him, the main unresolved question was for the government to decide "which group would bear the burden of financing government programs and/or fiscal stabilization" (ibid., 199). This problem still looms large, as we shall see (below, IA3a).

57. See the contributions on the Brazilian economy in Briesemeister, *Brasilien heute*, 265ff., all written before the

lower in Brazil than in other countries undergoing transition (both Latin American and European, namely Spain, Portugal, and Greece), presumably a consequence of the modest concrete effect democratization was able to make in the lives of the people, namely the workers and unemployed. In 1988, 21 percent affirmed that "under certain circumstances, a dictatorship is better than a democratic regime" (Argentina: 13 percent), and 26 percent agreed that "it doesn't matter whether the government is a dictatorship or a democracy" (Argentina: 10 percent).[58] Among the elites 64 percent saw a "high likelihood that Brazilian democracy would achieve consolidation during the 1990s," but 48 percent did not rule out military intervention, and maintained elitist tendencies, according to surveys quoted by Weyland.[59]

Still, this phase brought significant advances, in particular the promulgation of the 1988 Constitution which came to be called the "citizen" Constitution due to its impressive list of "individual and collective rights and duties" contained in the 77 paragraphs of the 5th article (Brasil 1996). With its decentralized structure, popular participation and ample negotiations, the Constituent Assembly "was the most democratic experience in Brazilian constitutional history" (see also below, IB).[60]

However, the new was to coexist with the old, including the continuing influence of landowners and the military, which had to be left untouched after the return to democracy—a kind of "Truth and Reconciliation Commission" was installed only very belatedly (in 1995), different from South Africa and other Latin American countries like Argentina and Chile.[61] The Constitution itself was the fruit "of a mosaic of contradictory interests of a heterogeneous and unequally organized society."[62]

The definitive end of the transition process was marked by the direct election of a new president in 1989, where the little known Fernando Collor de Mello (b. 1949) won with a small majority over the PT candidate Lula in the second round. The influence of the media and the vote of Pentecostal churches, who were worried about a possible "communist" and anti-religious government under Lula,[63] probably made a considerable difference. Collor seemed to embody a new, fresh politics as he was young, good-looking, and sporting. However, he was exposed as corrupt and ousted after remarkable public rallies called for his impeachment, in 1992.[64] Vice-president Itamar

Plano Real. Wöhlke, "'Land der Zukunft'?," 374, diagnosed even a "chronic crisis" and foresaw its endurance. Already the year 1994 with the *Plano Real*, but certainly the year 2003 with Lula´s economic success indicate that Brazil is well back on track, even though the social disparities (and these seem indeed to be chronic) improve at a much slower pace than the economy as a whole.

58. Moisés, *Os brasileiros e a democracia*, 161 (the reference in the bibliography is from 1994); see also Linz and Stepan, *Problems of Democratic Transition and Consolidation*, 171–78.

59. Weyland, "The Growing Sustainability," 112.

60. Kinzo, "Transitions," 31.

61. There were also no *madres de la plaza* as in Argentina and Chile to press for the truth about the killed and disappeared (on the Argentinian movement see Walz, "Madres appear on the public Plaza de Mayo in Argentina"), although there were movements of women for amnesty for political prisoners (Moraes, "Cidadania no feminino," 510). According to Pereira ("An Ugly Democracy?," 222–28), the legal façade maintained throughout the military regime in Brazil weakened public pressure as there was much more of a conceived normalcy than in the named countries. The commission mentioned above is the Special Commission on the Political Killed and Disappeared (*Comissão Especial dos Mortos e Desaparecidos Políticos*), installed under President Cardoso, to come to terms with cases brought before the commission, issuing death certificates, trying to locate the remains and compensate victims' families once proven the State's responsibility. See also Guider, "Reinventing Life and Hope"; Maclean, *Reconciliation, Nations and Churches.*

62. Kinzo, "Transitions," 32.

63. Mariano and Pierucci, "O envolvimento dos pentecostais na eleição de Collor."

64. In 2006, he was elected senator for Alagoas and has registered the project for a constitutional amendment to install parlamentarianism instead of presidentialism; http://www1.folha.uol.com.br/folha/brasil/ult96u91332.shtml

Franco (b. 1930) succeeded him, but was unable to mark a new phase; this would be the role of his finance minister Fernando Henrique Cardoso (b. 1931) who forged the *Plano Real* in 1994, bringing inflation down and opening new opportunities for the economy. He was elected president at the end of the same year, not only defeating Lula but gaining an overall majority (54.27 percent) in the first round.[65]

Cardoso's tenure can be considered strong in terms of consolidating political democracy, i.e. ensuring the stability of democratic procedures. For this, the fact that he succeeded in introducing an amendment to the Constitution in 1997, allowing for the President's (single) re-election, and to be indeed re-elected even in the first round in 1998, probably was an asset. On the other hand, there was still no comprehensive political reform, the electoral system (proportional-representative with an open party list) continued to favor individual politicians rather than parties, and the parties themselves remained weak, with high intra-party competition and low voter loyalty.[66] Furthermore, there was little progress in social terms, and Cardoso's policy of privatization of flourishing state companies (like the *Companhia do Vale do Rio Doce*, a mining company) was questioned by many.[67] Cardoso had been a sociologist of the left in the 50s and 60s and became known for his defense of dependency theory against the then prominent developmentalism.[68] He was exiled and later elected senator for the state of São Paulo for the PMDB. In 1988, he founded, together with others, the center-left Party of Brazilian Social Democracy (*Partido da Social Democracia Brasileira*—PSDB).[69]

A first national plebiscite since the new Constitution, held in 1993, had confirmed the presidential system of government.[70] A good number of researchers consider presidentialism to be a hindrance for the development of democracy.[71] It is certainly a matter of discussion whether this must or merely can create problems that parliamentarianism would not have.[72] Governance has

(accessed on 10/1/2008).

65. Data from http://www.tse.gov.br. (accessed on 10/1/2008).

66. Cf. Power, "Political Institutions in Democratic Brazil"; Mainwaring, *Rethinking Party Systems*. The book edited by Lamounier and Figueredo (*A era FHC*) makes a generally favorable evaluation of Cardoso's tenure. While it does not include a chapter on democracy, it features various aspects of economic, political, and social changes. For Cardoso's own vision, see his political memoirs in Cardoso, *A arte da política*.

67. This is mentioned, among others, by Weyland, "The Brazilian State in the New Democracy,"53, who, on his part, takes a positive look on the privatizations.

68. Cardoso and Faletto, *Dependência e desenvolvimento na América Latina*.

69. In the 2006 elections, the PSDB constituted the fourth largest party in the House of Representatives (57 of 513) and elected five senators, totaling thirteen (the 81 strong senate undergoes election in a one third/two thirds model, the mandate being eight years). They also conquered six governorships, including São Paulo, Minas Gerais and Rio Grande do Sul. In every presidential election since 1994, a PSDB candidate has run against a PT candidate,,winning twice and losing twice. See http://www.psdb.org.br; http://www.camara.gov.br and http://www.senado.gov.br (accessed on 1/27/2008).

70. Hagopian, "Politics in Brazil," 557 states that "despite the fact that parliamentarism was favored by a wide margin by every segment of civil elite – including intellectuals, association leaders, high public administrators, and union leaders (. . .) the proposal did not arouse any enthusiasm among the general electorate." The decision was by a two-thirds vote, although only 55 percent of the electorate cast valid votes.

71. See Linz and Stepan, *Problems of Democratic Transition*, 169; Mainwaring, "Multipartism, robust federalism, and presidentialism"; Zaverucha, *FHC, forças armadas e polícia*.

72. Juan Linz' thesis that presidentialism is intrinsically less conducive to stable democracy than parliamentary government is discussed critically by Mainwaring and Shugart, "Juan Linz, Presidentialism, and Democracy"; they insist that even if there is truth in this statement, both systems depend on the specific constitutional and institutional setup, arguing that "providing the president with limited legislative power, encouraging the formation of parties that are reasonably disciplined in the legislature, and preventing extreme fragmentation of the party system enhance the viability of presidentialism" (ibid., 166). Linz' position is to be found in "Presidential or Parliamentary Democracy:

been a problem since transition, especially for presidents Sarney, Collor, and Franco, and has compelled negotiation, opening doors for patronage, clientelism, and all kinds of exchanges of favors—a phenomenon Brazilians commonly call *fisiologismo*. Mainwaring quotes Guillermo O'Donnell's observation that "Brazilian presidents oscillate between omnipotence and impotence."[73] More specifically, presidents have suffered from a "combination of undisciplined parties, party system fragmentation, and federalism,"[74] which results in an exaggerated dispersion of power and constant negotiation with Congress—and its changing power constellations—to establish support to implement policies.

This would not be different for the following government.[75] As mentioned above, Luis Inácio Lula da Silva (b. 1945) was elected in his forth run in October 2002, and became the first president who was neither an academic nor a military. Born in the Northeastern state of Pernambuco, where he was taught to read and write (he never completed school, not even on the primary level[76]), Lula's family migrated to São Paulo state in 1952 and to the state capital in 1956, where they lived with eight children in one room at the back of a bar. As many of his fellows and still many children today, he started working at 12 in a dyeing mill and gained some extra money as a shoeshine boy, among other services.[77] He later became a metal worker and, in 1975, president of the metal worker's trade union of São Bernardo do Campo in São Paulo's industrial belt, later leading the above mentioned strikes in 1978. He was one of the founders of the PT, for which he stood for governor of São Paulo in the 1982 elections. He was not elected then, but became federal representative in the Constituent Assembly in 1986. Since 1992, he has been a council member of the Citizenship Institute (*Instituto Cidadania*) which formulated "proposals of national public policy as well as [promoting] campaigns to mobilize civil society on the way to the conquest of the rights of citizenship for all the Brazilian people."[78]

At the beginning of Lula's political career, the PT was too small and too isolated to be a successful party. Also, electoral support from the progressive church, namely the CEBs, was less than

---

Does It Make a Difference," in Juan J. Linz and Arturo Valenzuela, eds., *The Crisis of Presidential Democracy: The Latin American Evidence* (Baltimore: Johns Hopkins University Press, 1994). The notorious weakness of the party system is certainly one of the main obstacles to a functioning parliamentarism.

73. Mainwaring, "Multipartism, robust federalism, and presidentialism," 107.

74. Ibid.

75. The so-called *mensalão* (monthly stipend, in an ironic tone), supposedly the PT government's way of buying the support of representatives of other parties through monthly payments—its existence has been largely confirmed by the report of the Parliamentary Investigation Committee (*CPI dos Correios*), presented to the public in April 2006 in Brasilia—is a sad sign for the use of improper means to facilitate political projects.—Confirming the problem, it is one of the historical ironies that the PT, while in the opposition, had been one of the strongest opponents of the president's ruling by provisional decree (*medida provisária*), but once in government, Lula even in the beginning issued more such decrees than his predecessor. On a critical evaluation from people highly sympathetic to the PT on principle see Chauí, *Leituras da crise*.

76. The Brazilian school system foresees eight (since 2006: nine, cf. Law nr. 11.274 of February 6, 2006) years of primary education (*ensino fundamental*) and three years of secondary school (*ensino médio*). Access to universities (*ensino superior*) is through entry exams (*vestibular*) and, increasingly, through an examination system linked to secondary education to facilitate university access (*Exame Nacional do Ensino Médio*, ENEM). The main regulating document is the Law of Guidelines and Bases of Education (*Lei de Diretrizes e Bases da Educação* - LDB), nr. 9.394 of December 20, 1996.

77. Since the Constitutional Amendment nr. 20 (1998), work has been forbidden for children below 16 years of age (1988 Constitution: 14 years), unless as apprentice, where the minimum is 14 years; Brasil, *Constituição da República Federativa do Brasil*, 25, Art. 7–XXIII. The main regulating document for Youth is the Statute of the Child and the Adolescent (*Estatuto da Criança e do Adolescente* - ECA), nr. 8.069 of December 20, 1990.

78. Cited from President Lula´s website, http://www.presidencia.gov.br/presidente/biografia/ (accessed on 10/1/2008).

anticipated. Then, as he ran for president, it is interesting to note that most Pentecostal and Neo-Pentecostal churches (see below, IIB) had fiercely opposed him in the first campaigns, but a good number of them now joined with him in 2002, including the Neo-Pentecostal Universal Church of the Kingdom of God (*Igreja Universal do Reino de Deus*—IURD), who had earlier called him a "demon."[79] At a breakfast that sealed the accord that an expressive part of *evangélico* leaders would be joining the Lula campaign in the second round, a document signed by all stated:

> We support Lula for president because we recognize that various proposals of his government program identify with the prophetic calling of the Church of Jesus Christ, like the defense of social inclusion, of the oppressed, of the ethics of relationships, of the distribution of income and the proclamation and seeking of justice and fraternity between people.[80]

Lula, for his part, said to the group that

> never, in the history of the Evangelical Church [singular!] in this country, the believers have been called to the responsibility to participate in the building of the nation as we will do it from now on." He also said that "one of the advantages of counting on the partnership of the churches in assistance to the poor is the certainty that the money will reach its destiny, without interference of corruption.[81]

In 2004 and beyond, the country enjoyed considerable economic growth with continued low inflation and a strengthened currency, being applauded by economists inside and outside of Brazil.[82]

While forming new alliances, Lula has had to face strong criticisms, not least from within his own party, for maintaining an austere economic policy and doing far too little for the long overdue redistribution of wealth and income. Having fought for more ethics in politics during its campaigns, the PT government was itself drawn into a series of corruption affairs in 2005.[83] Even so, not least due to its economic achievements and to the lack of strong opponents, Lula was clearly reelected on October 30, 2006, by over 58 million voters (61 percent) for another four year term until 2010.[84]

79. See Freston, *Evangelicals and Politics*, 55ff., according to whom the IURD's strongly anti-left position began to wane in late 1995, and some exponents even adopted a leftist language, like saying that "globalization is the domination of the underdeveloped countries" (Bishop Rodrigues, in *Folha Universal* of 17/10/1999) or speaking of a "Satanic trinity in capitalism," comprising the market, capitalism and the IMF (Bishop Alfredo Paulo, in *Folha Universal* of 25/04/1999), ibid., 56.

80. *Revista Eclésia* 11/2002, 41. There had been "evangelical" support for Lula in earlier elections, but it was on a much smaller scale and restricted to numerically insignificant groups like the Evangelical Progressive Movement (*Movimento Evangélico Progressista* - MEP). The Assemblies of God joined with Lula's adversary in 2002, José Serra.

81. Ibid.

82. Among others, U.S. Secretary of the Treasury John Snow "hailed Brazil's 2004 gross domestic product (GDP) growth of 5.2 percent—the country's highest growth rate in 10 years," http://usinfo.state.gov/wh/Archive/2005/Mar/28-165770.html (accessed on 10/1/2008).

83. At the end of March, 2006, even the highly respected and supposedly unbeatable finance minister, Antonio Palocci, had to resign due to an alleged case of corruption referring to his mandate as mayor of Ribeirão Preto in the state of São Paulo, before he became a federal government minister.

84. Data according to http://www.justicaeleitoral.gov.br (accessed on 10/1/2008).

2. A CONSOLIDATED DEMOCRACY?

In contemporary Brazil, democracy really is 'the only game in town'.

Kurt Weyland[85]

Can Brazil be considered a consolidated democracy? Anyone reading the newspaper would expect the answer to be mixed, and so it is. There has been, however, considerable progress, and it is probably safe to say that a breakdown of democracy as a system is more unlikely than ever in Brazil's history. At the beginning of the 1990s, it was clear that Brazil's democracy was not consolidated, both for institutional and for social reasons.[86] Guillermo O'Donnell counted Brazil among the "delegative democracies"[87] because of a concentration of power in the executive, namely the president, combined with a lack of accountability and a malfunctioning of horizontal checks and balances. This is reinforced by Weffort,[88] pointing to the "general predominance of [. . .] personalistic leaderships, plebiscitary elections, clientelistic vote, and so on, over parliamentarian relations, party relations, et cetera." Despite representatively organized institutions, behavior is, then, "predominantly delegative." President Collor was certainly an emblem of such a kind of democracy, as were Fujimori in Peru and Menem in Argentina. By the end of the nineties, Brazil was still counted among, in Philippe Schmitter's words, "the excluded middle" of post-authoritarian regimes, which neither suffered a breakdown, nor could be considered consolidated.[89]

At the dawn of the third millennium, however, a Brazilian collective work on transition and consolidation stated that, since Lula assumed office as president in 2003, "there is a consensus among scholars today that the latter event marks what can be considered the consolidation of current Brazilian democracy."[90] This judgment is not wrong, but needs to be qualified. To be sure, the quoted book was completed by the end of 2003, so authors didn't know yet about the very serious corruption scandals that were to come in 2005. A survey carried out in 2000 saw 46 percent respond that "Brazilian democracy is consolidated because elections are held regularly," while 36 percent disagreed, showing a split population on this issue.[91]

Of course, all depends on the criteria to be applied.[92] These can lead to a much more skeptical evaluation, judging that Brazil—like South Africa and Mozambique—is an "exclusive" and "illib-

85. Weyland, "The Growing Sustainability of Brazil's Low-Quality Democracy,"120.

86. See Weffort, "Brasil: condenado a modernização," 22, who mentions low party institutionalization, stalemates between the presidency and Congress, and military presence, being the first two more accentuated than in the 1945–64 period, and the third less important than in that period. On the social level, Weffort considers the situation clearly worse, and for a democracy to consolidate, minimal social equality is required.

87. O'Donnell, "Democracia delegativa?"; Power, "Political Institutions in Democratic Brazil," 23; Lienemann, "Deskriptive und normative Grundlagen," 155f.

88. Weffort, "Brasil: condenado a modernização," 26.

89. Kingstone and Power, *Democratic Brazil*, 4.

90. Codato, *Political Transition and Democratic Consolidation*, IX.

91. Weyland, "The Growing Sustainability," 115.

92. In his response to Weffort's paper given in 1992, Guillermo O'Donnell stated that "we do not yet know clearly when, after a transition from totalitarian rule, a new democracy becomes consolidated," in Weffort, "New Democracies, which Democracies?,"41. As an example of the aporias in the debate, he cites India, a relatively old democracy and usually taken as consolidated, but this can be questioned on the grounds of its weak social basis and its character of a "delegative democracy" with strong leaders—from Nehru via Indira Gandhi to (after O'Donnell's writing) Atal Bihari Vajpayee and now Manmohan Singh, of course with different political (and religious!) positions. In the same debate, Arturo Valenzuela highlighted the importance of the protection of minorities and certain values in a democracy, ibid.,

eral" democracy, i.e. with (socially) restricted political participation and precarious guarantees of civil rights, and thus has only partially reached consolidation,[93] representing still a "low intensity citizenship."[94] But even those who still call Brazilian's citizenship a "small citizenship" (cidadania pequena), like Demo,[95] agree that significant democratic advances have occurred. At the same time, it is a fact that these advances have not reached all sectors of the population, which seems to result in a rather pragmatic relationship to democracy. The affirmation "Democracy is preferable to any other form of government" showed the lowest rate of consensus among Brazilians, where only 37 percent (Latin America: 56 percent) adhered to it without reservations.[96] After the period of political turmoil and constant economic reform plans was over by 1992 and 1994, respectively, one would certainly expect a much higher consensus on democracy. But nothing indicates a "mass commitment to democracy," as even under Cardoso's fairly well succeeded tenure, support for democracy declined from 50 percent in 1996 to 39 percent in 2000 and 27 percent in 2002, being the lowest score of all countries in the corresponding *Latinobarómetro* surveys.[97]

Apparently, dissatisfaction still looms large, and idealizing memories might wish back enforced "law" and order and the economic miracle of the seventies.[98] Even a priest-activist admitted, in 1996, that "frankly, I prefer military rule to what we have now. The military was largely predictable. Now one does not know when or why violence will strike."[99] Others see arbitrary state violence as a serious problem which makes Brazil's democracy look "ugly."[100]

Let us now look more closely at criteria that could be considered for the consolidation of democracy in Brazil. Applying Robert Dahl's criteria for a polyarchy, Brazil can rightly be counted as a democracy.[101] O'Donnell insists that Dahl's is a necessary, but insufficient definition of democ-

55. I would add that it is precisely there that the country and today still various states in India are acting in a most problematic and anti-democratic way through anti-conversion laws, mostly on the basis of the Hindutva-Ideology.

93. Lienemann, "Vergleichende Betrachtungen," 410f.

94. O'Donnell, "On the State, Democratization and Some Conceptual Problems," 1361.

95. Demo, *Cidadania pequena*.

96. See Latinobarómetro, *Informe Latinobarómetro* 2005, 52. *Latinobarómetro* is an NGO based in Santiago de Chile, which between 1995 and 2007 has been carrying out 12 surveys in originally 8, now 18 countries on their opinion regarding democracy, citizenship, welfare and related issues, interviewing a total of 216.998 respondents. Its databases are available at http://www.latinobarometro.org and have recently also been made available for research to universities in the U.K. Its work is supported by the Organization of American States (OAS) and international development agencies. The latest report (2007) is based on 20.212 interviews, including 1.204 in Brasil, carried out by the main Brazilian opinion poll institute IBOPE, http://www.ibope.com.br. The data in the 2007 report, which does not specify the numbers per country, indicates an even lower total for Latin America: Only 54 percent affirm that democracy is always the preferable form of government; Latinobarómetro, *Informe Latinobarómetro 2007*, 77.

97. Weyland, "The Growing Sustainability," 114.

98. This is confirmed by the considerably low rate of positive reactions to the affirmation that the respondent would, "under no circumstances, support a military regime": 56 percent in Brazil, in front of Paraguay (31 percent), Honduras and Peru (both 48 percent), as well as Ecuador (51 percent), but lower than the Latin American average (62 percent). The highest response rate opposing a military regime was found in Costa Rica (94 percent), followed by Panama (77 percent); see Latinobarómetro, *Informe Latinobarómetro 2005*, 47.

99. Quoted in Cleary, "The Brazilian Church and Church-State Relations." The internet version of this article is available only in a html-format and does not indicate the page as in a .pdf file. In any case, the quote is at note 4 of the text.

100. Pereira, "An Ugly Democracy?" 235.

101. Dahl's attributes are (*Democracy and its Critics*, 221): (1) elected officials; (2) free and fair elections; (3) inclusive suffrage; (4) right to run for office; (5) freedom of expression; (6) alternative information; and (7) associational autonomy. O'Donnell ("Polyarchies and the (Un)Rule of Law") adds: (8) elected officials (and some appointed persons, such as high court judges) should not be arbitrarily terminated before the end of their constitutionally mandated terms;

racy as it views democracy as a political regime in the first place and does not consider the role of the citizens as legal persons with autonomy and responsibility. For him, political citizenship and civil citizenship have to go together. He argues that it is mainly the civil part which is deficient. O'Donnell, then, draws an interesting conclusion that runs contrary to the leftist critique of "liberal" democracy (see below, IB and ID):

> Even if in the origins of polyarchy liberalism sometimes (often, throughout the history of Latin America) acted as a break to democratic impulses, in the contemporary circumstances of this and other regions of the world the more promising democratizing impulses should come from demands for the extension of civil citizenship.[102]

Thus, the issue is, precisely, "to undertake liberal struggles for the effectiveness of formal, universalistic civil rights for everyone."[103] This, of course, is not to underestimate in any way the fact that social disparities are also a strong hindrance to citizenship.[104]

According to the *Freedomhouse* surveys, which rate civil and political rights, Brazil has improved its mark since the return to democracy, rising from a double 5 in 1972 to a double 2 in 1985. However, it deteriorated between 1993 and 2001 (partly free: 3 or 2 in political and 4 in civil rights, respectively), due mainly to violence, corruption, the ineffectiveness of the judiciary and the police resulting in "public distrust," creating a "climate of lawlessness."[105] These same factors hold Brazil still behind the ideal double 1 rating. In 2005, the country could at least rise to a double 2 after some years of a 3 in civil rights; this rise was justified with the "continued governmental steps to enhance racial equality."[106] In 2006, Brazil maintained the double 2 rating, but with a downward trend arrow[107] because of "increased political corruption, including the involvement of the governing party in many of the country's most serious corruption scandals."[108] These scandals indeed show a very serious setback in terms of political ethics and public trust (or distrust). Lula had come close to

(9) elected officials should not be subject to severe constraints, vetoes, or exclusion from certain policy domains by other, nonelected actors, especially the armed forces; and (10) there should be an uncontested territory that clearly defines the voting population.

102. O'Donnell, "Polyarchies and the (Un)Rule of Law," 78.

103. Ibid.

104. In his analysis of the state of democracy after the election of Collor which he made attending to a request of a Jesuit priest, Lamounier (*Depois da transição*), referred to two main criteria for a consolidated democracy: The strength of the representative system and the "disconcentration" of income, privileges, power related to property and social status, which he saw in analogy to the *liberté* and *égalité* of the French revolution. A third aspect, political culture (in analogy to *fraternité*) is also mentioned, but none of the three is related to civil rights.

105. Country Information Brazil 2006, available at http://www.freedomhouse.org/template.cfm?page=22&year=2006&country=6928 (accessed on 12/14/2010). Rating is from 1 (free) to 7 (not free). "A Free country is one where there is broad scope for open political competition, a climate of respect for civil liberties, significant independent civic life, and independent media," Puddington, "Freedom in Retreat," 3, emphasis omitted. For a comparative table 1972–2005, see http://www.freedomhouse.org/uploads/fiw /FIWAllScores.xls (accessed on 12/14/2010).

106. Country Information Brazil 2006, available at http://www.freedomhouse.org/template.cfm?page=22&year=2006&country=6928 (accessed on 14/12/2010).

107. Puddington, "Freedom in the World," 7; http://www.freedomhouse.org. (accessed on 1/17/2007). In the following report, Freedom in the World 2008:6, http://www.freedomhouse.org/uploads/fiw08launch/FIW08Tables.pdf (accessed on 12/14/2010), the downward arrow disappeared. For the 2007 period, Puddington, "Freedom in Retreat," 10 affirms that, despite the frequent headlines about Venezuelan President Hugo Chavez, the "significant story was the durability of the [Latin American] region's democratic institutions in the face of multiple problems. [. . .] Latin America today is largely governed by parties of the center-left or center-right that have demonstrated a commitment to the electoral process, freedom of expression, and a broad range of civil liberties." Brazil is not mentioned specifically in this summary of the 2008 report, which indicates stability.

108. Ibid., 16.

facing an impeachment process when the scandal took on ever greater dimensions. However, the opposition seemed to fear the possible instability that would follow such a process, and not least did not want to see the vice-president in office, much less the then Congress president, Severino Cavalcanti, constitutionally second in line for substituting the president.[109]

A quite different rating was developed by the *Global Integrity Country Assessment,* which will be explored in more detail below (IA3b). The overall score is 73 out of 100, considered "moderate," where "elections" come out as "strong," while "administration and civil service," as well as "civil society, public information and media" score "weak."

The cited data indicate that Brazilian democracy, while apparently stable and consolidated at least in terms of electoral procedures, as well as improving in many respects over the last years, is still far from being satisfactory, especially in terms of effective civil rights. There is still "low intensity citizenship" (Guillermo O'Donnell), albeit growing, and there are "disjunctions" in citizenship, as Holston and Caldeira[110] called them. From this perspective, I shall present three main subjects that appear to be the most urgent challenges: economic inequalities, faults in the rule of law, and conflicting cultures.

3. "DISJUNCTIONS" IN CITIZENSHIP

O Brasil vai bem, mas o povo vai mal.

Ernesto Geisel[111]

A society of the wretched is not a society of citizens, nor can it be.

José de Souza Martins[112]

Brazilian Citizenship is typical [. . .] in the resilience of its regime of legalized privileges and legitimated inequalities.

James Holston[113]

In the previous section, I followed O'Donnell and others in their conclusion that the question about the consolidation of Brazilian democracy is to be answered in a mixed way: While political institutions and procedures are fairly consolidated (especially the elections), there is a great deficit

109. Calvacanti's election was a tragic outcome of party negotiations. Blunt in his will to power, insensitive to the climate in the house and the population, and eventually proven corrupt and ousted, the office suffered a severe loss of credibility during his occupation.

110. Holston and Caldeira, "Democracy, Law, and Violence".

111. "The country is well, but the people are badly off," quoted by Dressel in *Brasilien*,190.

112. Martins, "Changes in the Relationship between Society and the State," 80. In order to avoid quoting this out of context, it has to be said that Martins is not only referring to those – indeed existing – persons who are so poor that they are also "below the threshold of active participation in the destinies of society," but also to the abstract image constructed of them by middle class social movements, some of them supported by the churches. He sees there an "interpretative reductionism" which does not take into account that "in today's world there is a broad diversity of poverties, well beyond the mere lack of what is essential for a person's physical survival" (ibid.).

113. Holston, *Insurgent Citizenship*, 4.

in "liberal," civil rights and, thus, citizenship beyond political rights. Holston and Caldeira have called this, appropriately in my view, "disjunctions" in citizenship, which means that

> although their [sc. emerging democracies'] political institutions democratize with considerable success, the civil component of citizenship remains impaired as citizens suffer systematic violations of their rights. In such uncivil democracies, violence, injustice, and impunity are norms. As a result, the institutions of law and justice lose legitimacy, the principle of legality is obstructed, and the realization of democratic citizenship remains limited.[114]

The main factors these authors refer to are lawlessness and violence, i.e. a serious defect in the rule of law and, especially, law enforcement. I consider this one of the most important factors that hinders effective citizenship for a very large group of citizens (b). At the same time, these factors are imbedded in problems of economic inequalities, the "hard facts" (a), and are also linked to cultural dimensions that make it difficult for citizenship to work, the "soft facts," as it were, as they are much more difficult to measure (c). These latter are especially important as it comes to a possible contribution of the churches to social and cultural change.

a) Economic Inequalities

Is Brazil a poor country or a rich country? This is, of course, a simplistic question. But the answers to it say something about the perception people have about their own country. I hear quite frequently, for instance among pastor colleagues who graduated in the 1970s and 1980s, that Brazil is a "poor" and "dependent" country, pointing to poverty and external debt. But they are at the same time being conscious that Brazil is "rich," for instance in natural resources, and of course has a small, but rich or even very rich elite. Both statements are somewhat true, but the latter more than the former, as economically the country is currently stronger than ever, with its Gross Domestic Product (GDP) having passed 1 trillion U.S.-Dollars in 2006, according to data from the World Bank.[115] Brazil is ranked 10th among global economies by GDP, just after Spain and before Russia. Brazil's currency since 1994, the Real, is strong and has gained constantly against the dollar since 2002, from over 3.50 Reais to one U.S.-Dollar (December 2002) to around 1.80 Reais in early 2008; inflation is constantly low and the "Risk" index went down to as low as 187 points (January 2007), while at the end of Cardoso's term it stood at 2,436 points (September 2002).[116] External debt, which held the whole continent in its grips since the late 1960s, and was a common feature of discourses on social justice by NGOs and churches with reference to the

114. Holston and Caldeira, "Democracy, Law, and Violence," 263.

115. See the Brazil Data Profile available at http://www.worldbank.org (accessed on 1/13/2008).

116. The "Brazil risk," more precisely the ranking of Brazil in the "Emerging Markets Bond Index Plus" (EMBI+) is an instrument developed by the U.S. Bank J.B. Morgan Chase. It indicates the assessed risk degree a country's bonds bear in relation to U.S. Treasury titles, i.e., how sure an investor can be of getting his money back, as well as the due interest. If trust is low and the index is high, the country's bonds are expected to pay more in interest than its U.S. counterparts to make up for the investor's risk – an index of 100 points would be equivalent to a 1% surcharge to be paid on the bonds. Cf. http://g1.globo.com/Noticias/Economia/0,,AA1431760-5599,00.html of 1/23/2007 (accessed on 1/2/2008); http://www.portalbrasil.net/indices_dolar.htm#consulta for the Dollar exchange rates in December 2002 (accessed on 1/2/2008); http://g1.globo.com/Noticias/ Economia_Negocios/0,,MUL19707-9356,00.html for the 2002 Risk Brazil points. – The crux of updated information is that it tends to get outdated very easily. The worldwide financial crisis which started at the end of 2008 has, of course, had its effect on Brazil as well, for instance bringing the Dollar exchange rate back to around 2.30 Reais per Dollar. The consequences are still to be seen, but according to the newspapers, they seem to be far less devastating on Brazil than they are on, for instance, the United States.

debt cancellation of the Sabbath Year (cf. Lev 25), is well below half of all debt in Brazil, and debt service has been diminishing considerably.[117]

Even if numbers have to be taken with caution because they so highly depend on the way data are obtained and interpreted, it seems safe to conclude that Brazil is not a poor country, nor simply dependent on countries in the Global North, although, of course, there are dependencies as in all countries in today's globalized world. Thus, while the euphoric developmentalist thriving of the 1950s and 60s was fiercely criticised both for not taking into account international dependency relationships and questioning the Western model as the one to be achieved by the "delayed" and "underdeveloped" countries, factual development towards better life for many people has shown considerable improvements, as I shall show below. And if Brazil is "dependent" within international trade relations, it is not only dominated, but also dominates, as clearly shown by the conflict around the Brazilian gas extraction from Bolivia in 2006, and around the bi-national hydroelectric Itaipu plant with Paraguay in 2008. In fact, there are today a good number of respectable multinationals based in the country, like the Gerdau metal industry, the Odebrecht construction company (which built the Miami Airport in the U.S.), the IBOPE opinion poll institute, and Embraer, which exports airplanes into the whole world.[118] In 2006, a bit more than 50 years after Getúlio Vargas' famous dictum "the petrol is ours," on securing nationalized extraction of petroleum and heading towards auto-sufficiency in the country, president Lula could proudly announce that Brazil is now producing 100 percent of what it consumes by the state-owned Petrobrás, itself a powerful multinational company.[119] And Ethanol produced from sugar cane as biological car fuel is becoming an internationally noted export product.[120] The trade balance has been positive for much of Cardoso's and throughout Lula's government, exportation exceeding importation by nearly 45 billion U.S.-Dollars in 2005.[121]

We could perhaps say that Brazil is an amazingly rich country with appalling poverty.[122] It is infamously known to be one of the most unequal countries in terms of distribution of income and wealth, and indeed Latin America is the most unequal continent. Although Brazil has grown over the past 40 years to become one of the leading economies of the world, this has not been felt by

117. According to the already quoted World Bank data, total debt service in percentage of exports, services, and income has been reduced by more than half from 93.7 percent (2000) to 44.8 percent (2005). Between 2003 and 2006, the net total debt has been reduced from 57.2 to 51.2 percent of the Gross Democratic Product, according to data from the Brazilian Geographical and Statistical Institute (IBGE *Brasil em números*, 299). On February 21, 2008, the Brazilian government even proudly announced that, for the first time, its international reserves surpassed foreign debt, standing at 188.5 billion and 184 billion U.S.-Dollars, respectively. Thus, theoretically, Brazil could liquidate all its foreign debt and still have 4.5 billion U.S.-Dollars in reserves, which was all the country held in 1983 (with a debt of 93.75 billion then). This good news is also bringing Brazilian issues close to trustworthy for investment rather than speculative (BB+ grade, one below the necessary BBB-); see *Zero Hora* of February 22, 2008, 4–5.

118. Gerdau's director-president until 2007, Jorge Gerdau Johannpeter, a Lutheran, was invited by Lula to join his ministry in the second mandate, but declined. – The Brazilian Institute for Public Opinion and Statistics (IBOPE) is present in 16 countries of the Americas, including the United States, http://www.ibope.com.br (accessed on 4/4/2007).

119. http://www.estadao.com.br/ultimas/nacional/noticias/2006/abr/21/120.htm (accessed on 1/2/2007).

120. Cf. UNDP. *Human Development Report 2007–2008.*

121. IBGE, *Brasil em números*, 310.

122. This formula came out, among others, as a consensus from a Master's course I taught, in January 2008, for professionals with 35 high school teachers, church ministers, lawyers and other liberal professionals, from the states of Bahia, Distrito Federal, Goiás, Rio Grande do Sul and Santa Catarina. There, we discussed the initial, simplistic question on whether Brazil was a rich or a poor country, looking for arguments on both sides. As was to be expected, the issue became quite emotional – after all, feelings of pride and shame mix into the arguments. But it proved a good start towards getting a clearer picture of the issues at stake.

everyone in a satisfactory way. At last, after decades of constantly high ratings in the Gini index, a standard economic measure of income inequality, a considerable, if still small improvement was noted in 2007. Brazil gained five places from the sixth among the most unequal countries in 2002 to eleventh in 2007, due to a growth of inequality in Bolivia and Colombia, but also an improvement from an index of 59 in 2004 to 57 three years later.[123] As the UNDP reports of 2006 and 2007 indicate, this was attributed mainly to the *Bolsa Família* welfare program, which extends to 7 million families. The reports of 2005–7 say that while in 2001 the richest 20 percent had a share of 63.2 percent and the poorest fifth 2.4 percent of national income, in 2004 this was slightly better: 61.1 percent against 2.8 percent.

Indeed, while improvements have been made, 25 percent of Brazil's population are still counted to have no "guarantee of access to food in quantity, quality and regularity considered sufficient."[124] 13.9 million citizens suffer from hunger, and 72 million (out of a population of some 181 million, i.e. nearly 40 percent) are victims of some type of food insecurity. As would be expected, this is especially true in the North and Northeastern regions, traditionally the poorest.[125] Black or "mulatto" people are much more likely to suffer mal- and sub-nutrition than whites. Even among those who receive some kind of government subsidy, many households are subject to hunger (14.9 percent) or at least food insecurity (66 percent).

In terms of the UN Human Development Index, which is based on life expectancy, education (literacy rate and enrolment ratio) and GDP per capita, Brazil improved steadily from 1975 to 2005, from an index of 0.647 to 0.800, ranking high at 70 in 2007 and being located, for the first time in its history, among the countries with "high human development," even if it occupied the last position in this category. Comparing Brazil with its neighboring countries, it is behind Argentina (38), Chile (40) and Uruguay (46), but ahead of Venezuela (74), Colombia (75), Peru (87), Paraguay (95), and Bolivia (117).[126] In the Human Poverty Index for developing countries, Brazil comes in at 23, well behind Uruguay (2), Chile (3), Argentina (4), Colombia (14), Paraguay (20) and Venezuela (21), which indicates it has a particularly serious problem in this area. According to the table, 21.2 percent of the population live with less than 2 US-Dollars per day, and 7.5 percent with less than 1 US-Dollar, among other relevant indicators .[127]

According to the Brazilian Institute of Geography and Statistics,[128]which undertakes regularly general censuses and specific surveys, the fertility and child mortality rates have changed at an astounding pace within 30 years, approaching European figures, while Europe is said to have taken some 100 years for a similar development.[129] Between the 1930s and 2000, life expectancy rose from 43 to nearly 72 years, with an especially strong rise after 1960. Between this same year and 2000, the fertility rate dropped from six children per woman to 2.39, and infant mortality was reduced around 75% in the same period, with a projected decline of 15 percent in the five years

123. *Zero Hora* of November 28, 2007:36, based on UNDP data, UNDP, *Human Development Report 2006*, 336 and http://www.pnud.org.br/noticias/impressao.php?id01=2390 (accessed on 12/14/2010), and UNDP, *Human Development Report 2007*, 282. *Human Development Report 2006*, 272, quoting national sources, even speaks of an improvement from 56 in 2001 to 54 in 2004. The Gini index measures from 0 (perfect equality) to 100 (perfect inequality).

124. *Zero Hora* of May 18, 2006:36, based on IBGE data.

125. The percentage of those "who have suffered from hunger in the 90 days preceding the survey" is highest in the Northern state of Maranhão (18 percent) and lowest in the Southern state of Santa Catarina (2 percent).

126. UNDP, *Human Development Report 2007*, 234ff.

127. Ibid., 238.

128. IBGE, *Brasil em Números*.

129. IBGE, 62.

between 2000 and 2005. This also means that an upcoming challenge for the State is to cater for its elderly people, even more so as ever smaller families find it increasingly difficult to take care of them. Together with so-called "mad" people (*loucos*), the elderly are under a particular threat to suffer what João Biehl so accurately described as "social abandonment."[130] Brazil is often quoted as a model in health policy, especially in terms of distributing anti-retroviral therapies free of charge for bearers of HIV/AIDS, which indeed reduced considerably the illness' impact.[131]

As to consumers, there has been a considerable shift in consuming classes. Over the last five years, and especially since mid-2006, around 20 million Brazilians over 16 years of age have migrated from the D and E classes (lower middle class and low class) to the C class (middle middle class). Thus, the last two classes diminished from 46 percent of the population to 26 percent, while the C class increased from 32 percent to 49 percent, that is, about half of the 125 million person electorate. The A and B (upper and upper middle) classes remained virtually stable, increasing by a mere 3 percent to 23 percent of the population.[132] This is a significant change, and mixes well with news of high internal consumption as well as high spending on travels abroad (due to the low exchange rate against the dollar).[133]

A serious problem for consumers, however, is the high tax load levied by the states on consumer goods and services; in Rio Grande do Sul state, no less than 43 percent of the phone bill, to give just one example, goes to the state, with tax (theoretically 30 percent) being included in the value to be taxed, resulting in a *de facto* higher percentage. The fact that the (federal) income tax works with only three tiers[134] puts an especially heavy tax load on the (upper) middle class, i.e. those who earn enough to have to pay the highest rate but not enough to have a generous leftover. The generally weak public education system incites the middle class to invest in private schools for their children, which might give them access to the (generally very good) state and federal universities, where tuition is free. Those who cannot afford to pay for private primary and secondary education are unlikely to pass the public universities' entry exam and *numerus clausus* and will have to work all day to study at night at some private university, which is expensive. Consumer credit is extensively available at high and sometimes growing interest rates, and many lose control of their payment commitments, which might sum up to a considerable portion of their income over months or even years (to buy a car, for instance, or a house). The entrenched bureaucracy dampens private initiative for building up one's own, even small business. According to data from the World

130. Biehl, *Vita. Life in a Zone of Social Abandonment.*

131. Biehl, "Pharmaceutical Governance," tells this story in a precise and concise way and highlights it as an interesting case of cooperation between social movements, NGOs, the State and agencies like the World Bank, correcting many prejudices against either of these institutions.

132. *Folha de São Paulo* of December 16, 2007, section "dinheiro." The classification is made according to the Brazilian Association of Research Companies (ABEP) and works with a point system based on the ownership of consumer goods (like color TV and car) and monthly employed domestic workers, as well as the degree of education of the "head" of the household; see the 2003 Economic Classification Criteria at http://www.abep.org. While the Association itself cautions on restrictions as to the degree of information such system is able to furnish, it is most commonly used in consumer surveys.

133. In 2007, according to data from the Brazilian Central Bank, Brazilian tourists spent 8.2 billion US-Dollars abroad, a growth of 42 percent in comparison with 2006. In the same year, foreign tourists spent 4.9 billion US-Dollars in Brazil; http://g1.globo.com/Noticias/ Economia_Negocios/0,,MUL277101-9356,00.html (accessed on 10/1/2008).

134. Up to a monthly income of R$ 1,257.12, there is tax exemption; those who earn up to R$ 2.512.08 pay 15 percent, and those above 27.5 percent of income tax. Capital as such is not taxed, but must be declared, and gains on capital are subject to taxation. Taxes on land property (according to the area where one lives) are levied by the municipality.

Bank, it takes an average 152 days (as of 2005) to get started, against 32 days in Argentina.[135] It is true that it is much easier legally to start a church in Brazil than to open a shop.

What has been said applies mainly to those who live in the cities, which is over 80 percent of the population. In rural areas, land is extremely concentrated and slave-like work persists, including the exploration of child labor, while land reform, although advocated since decades, is notoriously slow and ineffective. Land conflicts claim victims, often lives, while both the landless (e.g. in the National Confederation of Agricultural Workers—*Confederação Nacional de Trabalhadores Agriculturais,* CONTAG, founded in 1963, and more recently the Movement of Landless Workers—*Movimento dos Trabalhadores Rurais Sem Terra,* MST, founded in 1984) and the landowners (e.g. in the Ruralist Democratic Union—*União Democrática Ruralista,* UDR, founded in 1985), mobilize.

Thus, we can say that life in Brazil has improved in many aspects, the middle class has grown and the number of poor diminished, although the problem of poverty is far from being resolved, and inequality continues to be very high, certainly too high. However, in general, economic and social indicators are positive and show an improving trend.

b) The Law and its (Non-)Rule

As shown above, the rule of law and its (non-)functioning is at the heart of the disjunctions in Brazilian citizenship. This refers, on the one hand, to civil rights and liberties, pointing to deficiencies in the "liberal" part of democracy. On the European continent, civil rights were among the first to be conquered, as rights of protection against undue state action. The State should only act upon its citizens in cases foreseen by law, mainly to levy taxes and punish crime, thus ensuring that the rights of all were being respected. Among these, the rights to life, freedom, and property had received a special emphasis, as formulated notably by John Locke in his *Second Treatise of Government* (1690), the classical manifest of political liberalism. Such protection was, at the time and under any modern authoritarian system, an important front against an absolutist State which arrogated to itself whatever rights it found fit over its citizens.[136]

However, under politically democratic circumstances, another aspect comes to the fore that is just as important as protecting citizens from the State. Identifying "the civil" as the main component of citizenship concerning liberty and justice, Holston and Caldeira can say that it not only differentiates society from the political system, but also "integrates the two by utilizing state power against the relations of inequality and domination within society itself."[137] For civil society to function, it needs the State's regulating power and monopoly of coercion. It does so by the rule of law which regulates and restricts society and the State in their actions. If this is not working well, then both the State and society cannot work properly. Unfortunately, it is easy to show that this is precisely the case in Brazil. Thus, Brazilians "experience the delegitimation of many institutions of law, resulting in the privatization of justice, escalation of both violent crime and police abuse, criminalization of the poor, and massive support for illegal and/or authoritarian measures of control."[138] Anthony Pereira stated that, while "lethal violence" was relatively low under the military, "under democracy, Brazil's state violence increased to become the highest in the region."[139] A movie released in 2007,

135. See the country profiles at http://www.worldbank.org (accessed on 1/17/2007).

136. See Huber, 'Menschenrechte/Menschenwürde'; Karnal, "Estados Unidos, liberdade e cidadania"; Odalia, "Revolução francesa."

137. Holston and Caldeira, "Democracy, Law, and Violence," 264.

138. Ibid., 265.

139. Pereira, "An Ugly Democracy?", 217.

"Elite Squad" (*Tropa de Elite*), based on facts,[140] showed that while the well-equipped and "thoroughly" trained elite police was loyal to its principles and, thus, not corrupt in the sense of being buyable, it would not hesitate to torture or kill whenever found necessary to fight Rio's traffickers.[141]

Let me now give a few examples to illustrate the issue of violence in Brazil.

A case in point was the disarmament referendum. A new law on firearms had been adopted by Congress and sanctioned by the president in 2004, imposing more severe restrictions on the possession and use of firearms, as well as nationalizing the registration of firearms, whereby everyone owning an arm was forced to (re-)register it.[142] This process was accompanied by a nationwide campaign carried out by the police forces in cooperation with sectors of civil society, including the churches, encouraging people to hand in their arms rather than hiding them or going through the expensive process of re-registering them. On October 23, 2005, a referendum asked the voters to decide whether the sale of firearms should be banned completely, which was turned down by a clear 64 percent majority. This result was probably also the consequence of not too few policemen supporting armed citizens in their arguing that disarming the population would expose the population even more to crime. They thus admitted that the police were unable to control the situation. At the same time, the fact that the weapons used by criminals often come from their raids in private households, and citizens who choose to defend themselves with their own arms frequently pay with their lives, which was also defended by a good number of policemen, was not sufficient as a counterargument.

In fact, the police too often are part of the problem rather than the solution. The "executions" of street children in Candelária (Rio de Janeiro) in 1993 and the invasion of Rio's Vigário Geral *favela,* where 21 residents were killed[143] to name but some of the most renowned cases, were committed by policemen off duty as the victims were sleeping. Most had no criminal record. As the Carandirú House of Detention in São Paulo underwent a mutiny, military police stormed it and killed 111 inmates in 1992. In one of the photographs published just after the massacre, an inmate holds up the Human Right's Declaration booklet published by the Ecumenical Coordination of Service (*Coordenadoria Ecumênica de Serviço*—CESE), indeed a strong message.[144]

Another important aspect are the regional differences. The vast lands in the Amazon region, for example, have their own laws *de facto*, and the State is absent or inefficient in many instances. When the U.S.-American missionary Sister Dorothy Stang (b. 1931) was murdered in 2005 in the state of Pará, her death followed a very common logic in that region.[145] She knew her murderers and knew that they had come to execute a landlord's order to kill her, which they did despite her appeals with Bible readings that she said were her "weapon." She had been opposing landlords and their gunmen for "too long." The case only gained so much notoriety because she was a Catholic

140. Soares, *Elite da Tropa.*

141. Another book on the subject was published in 2003 by Brazilian journalist Caco Barcellos. Among others, he analyzed 3.846 deaths by arms from the Military Police (the Brazilian security police force) which occurred in São Paulo between 1970 and 1992, and found that 65 percent of the victims were innocent (Barcellos, *Rota 66*, 327).

142. Law number 10`826 of December 22, 2003.

143. Holston and Caldeira, "Democracy, Law and Violence," 266.

144. *Revista Visão,* 1992, front cover cf. CESE, *Declaração universal dos direitos humanos,* 1. The said publication contains all the articles of the Universal Declaration of Human Rights of 1948, together with biblical quotations and excerpts of documents of CESE's member churches. It was published for the first time shortly after CESE's foundation, in 1973; since then, more than two million copies have been distributed.

145. According to the *Folha de São Paulo online,* 40 percent of the 1,237 deaths of landworkers between 1985 and 2001 were committed in this state; see http://www1.folha.uol.com.br/folha/cotidiano/ult95u105580.shtml, where Stang's assassination was noticed on December 2, 2005 at 17:22 hs.

nun and a foreigner. Federal Police, at present the most reliable and efficient police force, rushed in to investigate and indeed caught the culprits (whom everybody knew). Given that their own local stations had no computers, they had to use the Bank of Brazil's computer facilities, to quote but one fact of the State's weak position in those lands.

But even in the megacities, there are zones free of the State's influence. Many slum hills are occupied by drugdealers. They are not necessarily liked, but fare much better in the dweller's opinion than the police, who are either straightforwardly violent or try to make money by threatening everyone. The traffickers, in turn, sponsor cultural institutions and maintain "law" and order in the slum. The kids who join them know they probably won't live long and cannot leave their zone because of gang rivalries, but they gain respect through their firearms, are recognized as members of a group and, not least, earn much more money than they would earn in any job they might be eligible for—if they could find one at all.[146] Throughout 2006 and continuing in 2007, São Paulo and Rio de Janeiro were places of an outright war between criminal factions and the police. Criminal organizations like the "First Command of the Capital" (*Primeiro Comando da Capital*—PCC) in São Paulo were able to steer from and within prisons multiple mutinies and attacks on police installations and even directed killings of individual policemen and prison guards, on or off duty.[147]

There can, thus, be no doubt that the Rule of Law is one of the major challenges to democracy and citizenship in Brazil, especially law enforcement and its main actor, the police, who—except for the cited elite forces—are extremely vulnerable, badly paid, poorly equipped, and not well trained for the specific challenges they have to face. The strict corporation rules in the militarily organized security police (*Polícia Militar*) make changes extremely difficult.[148] One indicator of the ill functioning of the police is that in shootouts with criminals (real or supposed), often called "marginals" (*marginais*), many fewer policemen are injured or die than criminals, and far more of the latter die than get injured, which indicates that the police are quick to issue lethal shots.[149] The prison system suffers from constant overloading and is far from being able to rehabilitate people for "normal" life, while powerful criminals can lead their organizations even while in custody, usually by bribing the prison staff. The saying went that one of the most powerful traffickers, Luiz Fernando da Costa, *vulgo* Fernandinho Beira-Mar, would make a better justice minister, as he disposed of more funds than the actual office bearer.

There are few days when middle and upper class people do not mention "security" as an issue—there is a constant "talk of crime."[150] One result of widespread crime and fear is that cities become "Cities of Walls" with closed condominiums and private security.

146. Although this situation is not new, a documentary video shown in the famous Sunday evening programme *Fantástico* of the main TV network, the *Rede Globo*, stirred up public opinion. Well known rapper MV Bill, himself a slum dweller, accompanied 17 adolescents from various cities in Brazil. When he finished the film, only one of them was still alive; see Bill and Athayde, *Falcão*.

147. See, for instance, "Maior ataque do PCC faz 32 mortos em SP," in *Folha de São Paulo* of May 14, 2006, http://www1.folha.uol.com.br/fsp/cotidian/ff1405200601.htm (accessed on 10/24/2006)

148. A female police major in Belo Horizonte gained a great deal of confidence in direct contact with the people, creating various social projects. As she took off her weapons, anti-bullet jacket and other gear in public in order to show that police were just as human as anyone, the corporation considered this a severe violation of their code of honor and took her off the project; Lima, *A major da PM que tirou a farda*.

149. See Caldeira, *City of Walls*, 138–210 with ample data.

150. "The everyday narratives, commentaries, conversations, and jokes that have crime and fear as their subject counteract fear, and the experiences of being a victim of crime, and simultaneously make fear circulate and proliferate." Caldeira, *City of Walls*, 2.

> Even under democratic rule, the police in Brazil frequently act outside the boundaries of the law, abusing, torturing, and executing suspects, and the justice system is considered ineffective by the population. As a result, an increasing number of residents of São Paulo are opting for types of private security and even private justice (through either vigilantism or extralegal police actions) that are mostly unregulated and often explicitly illegal. Frequently these privatized services infringe on, and even violate, the rights of citizens. Yet these violations are tolerated by a population that often considers some citizenship rights unimportant and even reprehensible, as evidenced in the attack on human rights. [. . .]. This widespread violation of citizenship rights indicates the limits of democratic consolidation and of the rule of law in Brazil. The universe of crime not only reveals a widespread disrespect for rights and lives but also directly delegitimates citizenship. This disrespect for individual rights and justice represents the main challenge to the expansion of Brazilian democracy beyond the political system, where it has been consolidated in recent decades.[151]

It is indeed not rare that citizens take justice into their own hands and practice lynching—fear and resulting counter-aggression seem to be so strong that it ultimately does not matter whether the person killed was really the culprit. "Justice" had been done by a type of substituting sacrifice.[152] More than half of Brazil's population is also in favor of the death penalty.[153] Violence has superseded unemployment as the main problem of the country, as seen by its population.[154]

The sense of insecurity is cited by many who wished the military regime back, when order had been enforced more efficiently—even at the price of torture and death. "In the context of crime, fear, and the failure of the institutions of law, people consider discussions about the legitimacy of the military occupation in Rio or of the prison assault in São Paulo and the threat they pose to the consolidation of democratic rule largely irrelevant."[155] It is a fact that violence has grown considerably in Brazil, and that life does not seem to count much: From 1994 to 2004, murder numbers rose by 48.4 percent, and 64.2 percent among young people (age 15–24), which puts Brazil into rank four worldwide in general and three among the youth. Nearly 40 percent of deaths in this age group were because of murder (2004). More and more, crime is also reaching the to date complacent

151. Caldeira, *City of Walls*, 3. Already in 1994, according to Brazilian sources quoted by Pereira, "An Ugly Democracy?," 230, there were more private security guards than military police, while the latter, some 400,000 strong, outnumbered the Armed Forces.

152. According to the survey carried out by economist and public affairs researcher Carlos Alberto Almeida among a representative sample of 2,363 persons between July and October 2002, 28 percent of the population believe that lynchings are "always correct" or "mostly correct" in cases of "suspects [!] of very violent crimes." 39 percent think it is "always correct" (26 percent) or "mostly correct" (13 percent) that somebody convicted for rape is raped by his fellow prisoners. To beat prisoners in order for them to confess a crime is considered always or mostly correct by 36 percent of the sample. Asked more generally, however, whether it was correct "to do justice with one's own hands," only 13 percent said that this was mostly or always correct, while 85 percent affirmed this was "always wrong"; Almeida, *A cabeça do Brasileiro*, 135. The main difference to the result was made by the degree of education, as in all issues dealt with in this study. As one of the few issues, the difference made by religion was analyzed here; people who are religious (i.e. frequent church services and pray regularly) "are considerably more recalcitrant [refratários] in relation to any type of illegal punishment than the less religious"; ibid., 145. The author explains this by both a "more institutional world view" (reluctance to breaking the law) and, maybe more important, Christian "humanism" that rejects the law of talion and preaches the golden rule.

153. 55 percent according to a *Datafolha* poll carried out in March 2007, *Folha de São Paulo* of 8 April, 2007, section Brasil. This is a new peak, equal only to numbers in 1993, when Brazilian was in political and especially economic turmoil. Such polls have been carried out by *Datafolha* since 1991.

154. 31 percent affirmed this according to the *Datafolha* poll; *Latinobarómetro* 2007:21 cites "delincuencia" (delinquency) as named by 17 percent in Brazil as the country's most important problem; 13 percent quoted unemployment. The Latin American average is 17 percent for delinquency and 18 percent for unemployment.

155. Holston and Caldeira, "Democracy, Law, and Violence," 267.

backlands, no longer being restricted to the cities and their peripheries; and the most violent cities in relation to the population are no longer Rio and São Paulo, but Recife and Vitória, and more recently also Porto Alegre.[156]

Interestingly, the Rule of Law has been rated "strong" in the Global Integrity's 2006 Country Report.[157] This essentially refers to the independence of the judiciary and the enforcement of judicial decisions. However, when it comes to accessibility of the judiciary for citizens, scores are considerably lower, and the category of "law enforcement," which covers the police, is rated "weak."

All these factors combine to create or foster a generalized climate of mistrust, which is an extremely serious problem for any democracy. This will be the main aspect of the following section.

c) Conflict and Ambiguity: "Persons" and "Individuals"

The constantly appalling poverty in large parts of the population is due to economic factors, the failures of the State to comply with its own regulations and, in some respects, with international standards. Apart from these, there are problems of political culture that tend to undermine change. If citizenship is to be available to all, it is not enough that "they" in the state do something, or that "they" in the multinationals, the World Trade Organization, the International Monetary Fund, the Worldbank, the G8, the Bush administration, or whoever powerful might be "outside there," do something. It has to be sustained by a population conscious of their rights and duties and actively involved, at least on the micro-level, in attaining citizenship.

One of the cultural problems is the generalized lack of trust.[158] According to the regular inquiries of *Latinobarómetro*, "most Latin American publics are [. . .] skeptical—if not actively cynical—about key institutions of democracy, and Latin Americans manifest some of the lowest levels of interpersonal trust observed anywhere in the world."[159] Asked whether one could generally "trust the majority of persons," in 2002 only 4 percent of Brazilians answered "yes," against a 17 percent average on the continent and a maximum of 36 percent in Uruguay.[160] Five years later, this was only slightly better: 6 percent in Brazil against (again) 17 percent in Latin America, with a new maximum of 31 percent, now in Guatemala.[161]

156. *Zero Hora* of November 17, 2006, p. 4; of October 20, 2007, p. 4. After a peak in 2003 (51,043 murder cases), numbers have dropped to 44,600 in 2006, down 12.5 percent, according to data from the Health Ministry cited by the paper. This is, possibly, a consequence of the disarmament campaign, as most murders are carried out with firearms, and unauthorized bearers of arms can now be imprisoned without bail. The campaign of giving up arms to the police against payment rendered 426,000 firearms between July 2004 and October 2005. In Rio Grande do Sul state, where violence with firearms is still on the rise, rejection against the 2004 arms referendum was highest. Porto Alegre reached a peak of 29.86 homicides per 100,000 inhabitants in 2007, well above São Paulo, which in 2000 figured a rate of 51.33 and is now down to 18.36; *Zero Hora* of January 6, 2008, version online: http://zerohora.clicrbs.com.br/zerohora.

157. See http://www.globalintegrity.org/reports/2006/BRAZIL/ (accessed on 1/17/2007). The score follows a set of categories which can be viewed online in detail, and receive comments by peers, which makes it a transparent and reasonably reliable source of evaluation. Comments are helpful in contextualizing the necessary generalizing criteria.

158. See Sinner, "Trust and Convivência."

159. Lagos, "Between Stability and Crises," 137.

160. Latinobarómetro, *Informe Latinobarómetro 2003*, 26.

161. This is a standardized question, which in its full version reads: "Generally speaking, would you say that most people can be trusted or that you can't be too careful in dealing with people?" Besides the Latinobarómetro survey of 2007 (p. 93), it is used in national (as in the U.S., Wuthnow, "Der Wandel des Sozialkapitals in den USA," 672–75) and the World Value Surveys (Norris and Inglehart, *Sacred and Secular*, 191). The question offers, obviously, a very simple dichotomy, and says nothing about how people understand "trust." Wuthnow, "Der Wandel des Sozialkapitals in den USA," 675, also mentions that when respondents were given the possibility to answer both parts of the question, many affirmed either one (62 percent for trust and 71 percent for caution), apparently not understanding them as contradic-

This does not mean that there is no trust at all, but that one does not trust strangers. However, to construct a democratic State, it is necessary that trust can be presupposed among citizens in general and not only among family, friends, and neighbors.[162] If I cannot—or believe I cannot—trust my fellow citizens, why should I possibly behave as a "good citizen," complying with the law and asking others to do the same? Am I not, then, exposing myself to ridicule, as I presumably would be too naïve to understand "how things are" or work, and that they just don't work the way the law foresees it? To cite an example, in a case known to me personally:

On buying a house in big city, in a modest periphery neighborhood, one of the local brokers promised the new owners he would do the paperwork for them. He asked them for a considerable, but for a foreigner still very reasonable amount of money, "to speed things up," as "you know how things work here." But then they insisted the registering should be done following the letter of the law, including noting in the register the amount that was effectively paid and the house in its real dimensions. Both have a direct bearing on the estate property tax, so many indicate a lower amount or a smaller house. As the broker obviously had no idea of how to do things according to the law, he was unable to "speed things up" through his contacts and bribery, but rather took much longer and, in fact, eventually proved unable to accomplish the process. To be just, however, it has to be said that he was not helped by frequent strikes of the judiciary and changing rules, tariffs, and deadlines, keeping track of which would require a degree of professional formation and infrastructure that he did not have at his disposal.

Foreigners and Brazilians alike would say these buyers should not have trusted the broker, but at least a good number of neighbors would also say they should not have tried to trust the law and comply with all regulations. Their real error, then, was not to do things through persons rather than laws, but to have chosen the wrong person to do it. But how to find "the right person," especially on being a foreigner?

Brazilian anthropologist Roberto DaMatta, analyzing day-to-day language and action, argues that part of the problem lies in the duality between "person" and "individual."[163] While the former is incorporated in some sort of a hierarchical network of relationships, the latter is equal before the abstract law, but isolated. "For my friends, anything; for my enemies, the law," as the saying goes.[164] While being a "person" can be crucial for one's survival, and indeed guarantees access to services that would not be available without a well-positioned "godfather," a democratic, constitutional State presupposes "individuals" with equal rights and duties. Brazilian society is, according to DaMatta, a mixture of "persons" and "individuals." It works both on the basis of rights and duties before the law and with the *jeitinho*, this famous indirect way of those who are cunning enough to get help

---

tory. Nevertheless, the question still serves as an indicator for the presence or lack of trust, especially as numbers are so significantly different between countries – very low in Brazil, diminishing in the US. (from 54 percent in 1964 to 34 percent in 1994, ibid., 674), and even higher in Scandinavia (from 57 percent in 1981 to 67 percent in 1997, Rothstein, "Schweden," 166).

162. See Offe, "How can we trust our fellow citizens?"

163. See DaMatta, *Carnivals, Rogues and Heroes;* Id., *A casa & a Rua*; Hess and DaMatta, *The Brazilian Puzzle.*

164. O'Donnell, "Polyarchies and the (Un)Rule of Law," 53 uses this saying, attributed to Getúlio Vargas, as an introducing quote for his article: "Aos meus amigos, tudo; aos meus inimigos, a lei." DaMatta conducted a survey together with graduate students. Asked as to "'how would you classify a person who obeys the laws in Brazil?', [the answer] was invariably negative" (DaMatta, "The Quest for Citizenship in a Relational Universe," 317). Holston, *Insurgent Citizenship*, 4 rightly remembers the negative connotation of citizen in the 1980s: "[. . .] generally, they used 'citizen' to refer to the insignificant existence of someone in the world, usually in an unfortunate or devalued circumstance. People said 'that guy is a *cidadão qualquer*', to mean 'a nobody'." Holston calls this "differentiated citizenship," as rather than for all, this is only for the others, those who "deserve the law" (ibid., 5).

where they would otherwise get stuck. One changes from the insignificant status of anybody to somebody who belongs to the "family" of an important person through the famous question "do you know who you're talking to?"[165] thereby claiming a privileged treatment.[166] Based on DaMatta, Carlos Alberta Almeida[167] has tested this attitude recently in a survey, and found that Brazilians generally accept that many (and they themselves) use the *jeitinho,* while they differ almost evenly over whether this is right or wrong, and there are differences in evaluating whether something is to be considered *jeitinho*, a favor, or corruption. He also showed the persistence of a considerable amount of hierarchical thinking, with difference according to region, age, gender, employment, and, predominantly, the degree of formal education.

Thus, the public and the private, the "street" and the "house," the "individual" and the "person" are overlapping realms that coexist and make structural changes difficult. The struggle around defining and keeping the frontier between the public and the private has been studied in extensive works earlier and shown as an important feature of Brazilian society; even if one does not want to necessarily agree with the width of the argument and the theoretical explanations (and certainly not with a "culturalist" attitude that would suggest that changes are impossible), there are striking historical indicators for what Raymundo Faoro had called "patrimonialism" of the powerful,[168] including those running the State, and, earlier, Sérgio Buarque de Holanda had described as the ambiguous behavior of the "cordial man."[169] Once one focuses on the actual behavior of people and not on written rules—be they legal, religious, moral, or otherwise—there appears to be significant creativity among Brazilians to make out what is most useful for them, rather than sticking to just one or, indeed, to any particular doctrine.[170]

In any case, there seems to be the lack of a vision of the whole rather than for securing group interests. According to Reginaldo Prandi, the poor live in a "pre-ethical" position, following the principle of "save himself [or herself] who can," getting hold of whatever possible to survive, while the rich live in a "post-ethical" position, "saving" items of public space conceived as "no man's land," thereby both invading the public with private interests.[171] That public space would include a value of equality and the responsibility also for the other's well-being, does not find an anchor in either of these positions.

165. DaMatta, *Carnivals, Rogues and Heroes*, 137–97.

166. As I could observe, however, this way of claiming privileged treatment seems to suffer increasing restrictions, for instance when it comes to queues in banks and public services, where clerks keep quite clearly to the order established by the "first come, first serve" of an electronically processed number you take as you come in. Certainly, regional, sectorial and urban/rural differences apply here. Against an "a-historic" reading of reality which Vidal ("Die Sprache des Respekts", 138f.) applies as a critique against DaMatta, one has to state a development in different speeds, a "non-coincidence" (*Ungleichzeitigkeit*) of relationships as they are changing through democratic achievements on different levels.

167. Almeida, *A cabeça do Brasileiro.*

168. Faoro: *Os donos do poder.*

169. Holanda, *As raízes do Brasil*; see Chauí, "Raízes teológicas do populismo no Brasil"; id., *Brasil.*

170. Recent doctoral studies in the religious (Adilson Schultz) and sexual, notably gay, lesbian, bisexual and transgendered (GLBT) realm (André Musskopf) confirm this, as does other scholarly work in this field. In many fields of research, there has been a strong emphasis on real, daily life (*o cotidiano*) rather than on doctrine and ideology in, say, the last ten years. The fact that there are certain highly doctrinally conscious groups – like certain historical Protestants, many Pentecostals and the military, does not undo the general sense of ambiguity through which people culturally navigate. It points, however, to the fact that there is no absence of doctrines, rather a plurality of these, which is prone to give rise to all kinds of syncretism, but also of antagonisms and contradictions.

171. Prandi, "Perto da magia, longe da política," 84f.

It is important to stress that such cultural factors are, at the same time, to be seen as a strength and as a problem. While the *jeitinho* is a form of intelligence and creativity necessary to survive in difficult circumstances, a way of "social navigation" as DaMatta says, it makes it difficult to adapt to a system of law where procedures are to be followed rigorously. Also the categories of "person" vs. "individual," where Brazil is being located between the United States (wholly individual) and India (wholly personal, given the caste system), are not to be understood as playing one against the other and suggesting to follow one or the other comparative models; rather should their mixture be improved in order to be compatible with a contemporary democracy. If seen in this way, Brazilian society would mark a point on a scale whose aspects are to be found also in other societies.[172] Thus, one should neither glorify the *jeitinho* nor dismiss it as simply backward.

Another case in point is "respect." According to Dominique Vidal, who developed empirical studies in Rio de Janeiro and used Avishai Margalits "decent society" as a theoretical reference, stressed that the lack of respect (*falta de respeito*) is often cited by poor people as even worse than economic shortage. The "exaggerated focus" of social sciences on economic inequalities is blinding, Vidal contends, against the "relevant dimensions of democratic citizenship." He says that "for the Brazilian urban poor it is considerably more important to feel to belong to humanity than to diminish social inequalities."[173] It is certainly difficult to weigh one against the other, but I would agree that there is an utterly important element here that tends to be overlooked by social scientists and theologians alike—although it is precisely here that churches can make an important difference. What is alarming, however, is that the claim to respect—which presupposes a fundamental equality among human beings who, then, are entitled to a respectful treatment regardless of social difference, color, gender, religion, or other categories—is, from the perspective of many, able to be forfeited by non-compliance with certain moral rules, as Vidal's informants clearly stated. These rules are not identical with positive law, but somehow situated in a kind of natural law, which prevails over any law code. Thus, they exempt "criminals" from such rights, and lay them bare to "justice" to whomsoever takes the lead in executing it.

It seems plain, then, that democracy is something that has to be learned—not only as to how to fill out a ballot, which might have caused serious problems in the first post-military general elections as the mostly young electorate had never voted before,[174] and which is still not dominated by everyone, but has certainly improved much since then. In fact, elections are one of the most reliable elements in Brazilian democracy, and since 2002 carried out entirely by electronic ballot, which gives very fast results.[175] However, how should candidates be chosen? And, once chosen, how should they be "accompanied," i.e. held accountable? What should happen in between electoral

172. Precisely because of its apparent claim to Brazilian uniqueness, as well as its pressupposition of Brazilian "un-authenticity" (as a continuation of lusitan culture), DaMatta's theory has been fiercely critized by Souza, *A modernização seletiva*, 183–204. According to Souza, DaMatta would, in his theory which relies heavily on the people's "common sense," follow too uncritically the formers' (wrong) notion of cultural determinism, according to which Brazil would be unable to change. I doubt that this criticism is really valid for DaMatta, anyway for his more recent writings (Hess and DaMatta, *The Brazilian Puzzle*, 281: "We are not dealing merely with contradiction, cynicism, or out-of-place ideas but with a social logic that interrelates the system and exploits the ambiguities of its intermediate ranges. [. . .] I interpret the Brazilian system as *substantively functional* and exhibiting original sequences of *social compensation*.")

173. Vidal, "Die Sprache des Respekts," 133.

174. See Schneider, *Order and Progress*, 365f.

175. It is no wonder, then, that "elections" is the only category rated "strong" in the Global Integrity Report (http://www.globalintegrity.org), with, however, a weak subcategory in terms of campaign financing, which many see as an incentive to take money from questionable sources and leave it undeclared (all campaign donations have to be declared publicly by law).

campaigns? And, more importantly, how could democracy be extended to the grassroots level, to be felt as making a real difference to people's lives, not only during electoral periods when politicians tend to sponsor sports areas, road improvements, and the like?

Evidently, civil society and, within it, the churches play an important role here.[176] This will be treated extensively in part II of the present study. Here, I want to give just one very important example of an ecumenical NGO, founded in 1973, the "Centre for Evangelization, Capacitating and Consultancy" (*Centro Ecumênico de Evangelização, Capacitação e Assessoria*—CECA).[177]

CECA has been training, for the last ten years, so-called "popular attorneys" *(promotoras legais populares)*, whose task it is to mediate between the population and the State, namely the police and the judiciary, but also the health system.[178] Thus, one story I was told is that a child, while being examined by the public health service doctor, vomited and splashed it on the doctor's apron. The latter then told the mother to take her daughter away. By coincidence, one of the popular attorneys had followed the scene and reminded the doctor of her lawful duty to examine the child. The doctor then asked: "Who are you?" in a way to suggest that this "Ms. Nobody" had no right to question the person in charge, who held a degree, was State employed, and entitled to the status of a doctor. Lawyers and physicians are commonly called *doutor*—although they generally do not hold a doctoral degree—and spoken to in the formal way, while they address clients and patients the informal way, indicating a clear hierarchical asymmetry. But the popular attorney, well aware of her own and the patient's rights and thus confident, just cited the law, and the doctor gave in to such confidence and examined the child.

Such cases are not uncommon. Biehl confirms this for AIDS patients under the otherwise exemplary policy of free anti-retroviral treatment: "Specialized health care is provided only to those who dare to identify themselves as AIDS patients in an early stage of infection at a public institution, and who autonomously search (they literally have to fight for their place in the overcrowded services, for continuous treatment)—those whom I call patient citizens."[179]

Much depends, then, upon the self-confidence people can show towards those who are assumed to be higher up in the hierarchy, and upon knowledge of the law and how to handle it. It is sad to note that "citizen" is used, in everyday language, in a derogatory way: *Cidadão* is somebody unknown, weak, with no (relevant) relationships, abandoned, as it were, to an ineffective law. Rather, people who take their reassurance in law's rights and duties, should be proudly called, and call themselves, citizens.

Following this sketch of challenges and the situation of a disjunctural democracy and citizenship, I shall now turn to the role of civil society during and after transition.

176. See Krischke, *The Learning of Democracy.*

177. See Stoffel, *Ecumenismo de justiça: reflexão e prática.*

178. See Parlow, *Fruto maduro não volto a verde.*

179. Biehl, "Pharmaceutical Governance," 231.

B. The Role of Civil Society in Brazilian Democracy

In a word, we need to build civil society
because we want freedom.

Francisco Weffort[1]

Give us this day democracy, the kingdom
and our daily utopia.

Joanildo Burity[2]

IT IS WIDELY KNOWN and accepted that Brazilian civil society has had an important influence on the transition and consolidation of democracy, and continues to do so, albeit in different ways and with different concepts. In his evaluation of democracy at the end of Cardoso's mandate, Mauricio Font states that

> the density of politically active civil society and the increased levels of citizen participation provide reasons for optimism. The enhanced third sector [i.e. NGOs] is itself an important dimension of societal democratization, while the more complex civil society makes relentless demands for political incorporation into a democratic polity.[3]

Font points specifically to the growth of labor unions, but a recent survey counted a huge diversity of 276,000 foundations and non-profit associations, employing no less than 1.5 million people in 2002.[4]

After repression relaxed, an ever more diversified civil society emerged, initially under the umbrella of the Roman Catholic Church, namely its Church Base Communities (*Comunidades Eclesiais de Base*—CEBs), but more and more independent of it as decompression and opening progressed. Along this way, both concepts, "projects," forms of organization and institutionalization, concrete actions and, not least, the relationship to the State changed considerably. Thus, the terms used in this debate denote conceptual fields rather than clearly defined concepts, both due to historical changes and their increasingly diverse constituency.

1. Weffort, "Why Democracy?," 349. This is the final sentence in Weffort's emphasis on the need of civil society as a bulwark against what he calls a "monstrous State in front of us."

2. Burity, *Radical Religion and the constitution of new political actors in Brazil*, 162. This is the title of Burity's doctoral thesis' final chapter, which adds "religion and permanent transition."

3. Font, *Transforming Brazil*, 165.

4. ABONG, *Ações das ONGs no Brasil*, 4.

In what follows, I shall first explore the concept of civil society, historically and systematically (1.), followed by a more specific reflection on religion and civil society, and namely the churches in it (2.). Following these conceptual clarifications, I shall take a historical and contextual perspective, given that civil society in Brazil developed as space was opened for it, both by the State's initiative and, increasingly, by its own conquests. I then go on to treat the more recent development under a conceptual aspect. Thus, a third section seeks to describe civil society before and during the military regime (3.), followed by its "(re-)birth" during the process of transition (4.) and the description of the major shifts in concept, organization and activity during the 1990s and beyond, from "civil society" to "citizenship" as key concepts in civil society (5.). Throughout the chapter, religious and non-religious elements and organizations will be present, as they indeed are intertwined in many aspects.

1. THE CONCEPT OF CIVIL SOCIETY

Much has been written on civil society and its origins,[5] as well as the specific role the churches play in it.[6] The concept begins its history with the political body as *societas civilis* or κοινωνὶα πολιτική, in Aristotle, when State and society were not distinguished. It was, however, seen as separate from the sphere of the house and the family. In the natural law and contractual theories of the 17th and 18th centuries, it implied a "civilized" society protected by some recognized authority, as opposed to a barbarian, natural state of affairs, and was synonymous with political society.[7] The term also acquired, in the enlightenment discourse, a utopian meaning of peaceful and tolerant living together by mature citizens.[8] Later, it came to be clearly distinguished from political society, i.e. the State, and was identified as an intermediary between the State and the market,[9] the private and the public, the family and the State in Hegel's *bürgerliche Gesellschaft*, already with a critical stance over against the rising dominance of the economy as he seeks to favor the corporations.[10] Marx radicalized a bourgeois concept of civil society with a capitalist economy at its heart, to the detriment of the citizen, and made it a polemical concept. Different from the English "civil society", which has not suffered such polemics, the *bürgerliche Gesellschaft* became suspect and had, in its 20th century

5. E.g. Bobbio, "Sociedade Civil"; Cohen and Arato, *Civil Society and Political Theory*; Costa, *As cores de Ercília*, 37–63; Kocka, "Civil Society in Historical Perspective"; Gohn, *O protagonismo da sociedade civil*.

6. E.g. Bedford-Strohm, *Gemeinschaft aus kommunikativer Freiheit*; Lienemann, "Öffentlichkeit und bürgerliche Gesellschaft"; Mathwig and Lienemann, "Kirchen als zivilgesellschaftliche Akteure"; more widely on Religion and Civil Society see Herbert, *Religion and Civil Society*, esp. 61–94.

7. Locke, *Second Treatise of Government*, 47 (§87) affirmed: "Those who are united into one body, and have a common established law and judicature to appeal to, with authority to decide controversies between them, and punish offenders, are in civil society one with another: but those who have no such common appeal, I mean on earth, are still in the state of nature. . . ." Kant also distinguished between a natural state („Naturzustand") "in welchem jeder seinem eigenen Kopfe folgt" and a civil state ("bürgerlicher Zustand"), where humans unite with others in submitting to a public legal external coercion; Kant, "Die Metaphysik der Sitten," 430 (Rechtslehre, § 44); cf. Bobbio, "Sociedade Civil", 1206f.

8. Kocka, "Zivilgesellschaft als historisches Problem und Versprechen," 16.

9. Ferguson, *Essay on the History of Civil Society*.

10. Hegel, *Grundlinien der Philosophie des Rechts*, 339 (§182, Zusatz): "Die bürgerliche Gesellschaft ist die Differenz, welche zwischen die Familie und den Staat tritt, wenn auch die Ausbildung derselben später als die des Staates erfolgt; denn als die Differenz setzt sie den Staat voraus, den sie als Selbständiges vor sich haben muss, um zu bestehen"; cf. Lienemann, "Öffentlichkeit und bürgerliche Gesellschaft, " 73. The *bürgerliche Gesellschaft* has been criticized as being biased toward the *bourgeois* as economic citizen rather than the *citoyen* as political citizen. Conversely, the latter is seen to be implied in a "civil society" or "citizen society" (*Bürgergesellschaft*), precisely the concepts that are being retrieved internationally since the 1980s; see Kocka, "Zivilgesellschaft als historisches Problem und Versprechen"; cf. Mathwig and Lienemann, "Kirchen als zivilgesellschaftliche Akteure," 93; also Soosten, "Civil Society," 140–44.

renaissance, to give way to *Zivilgesellschaft*.[11] Tocqueville stressed the importance of voluntary associations—not least congregational Christianity—in their contribution to social cohesion and democracy in the United States of America.[12] Communitarians like Michael Walzer and Charles Taylor[13] added the importance of social cohesion through associations, among them religions, neighborhood associations and the like. Systematizing the diverse influences in recent debate on the importance of civil society, Croissant et al. extract five essential "democratic functions of civil society" from a variety of traditions, namely its protecting function (from the liberal tradition), its mediating function (from Montesquieu), its socializing function (from Toqueville), its community function (from communitarianism), and its communicative function (from Habermas).[14]

The Tocquevillian and communitarian accent is taken up by Brazilian thinkers to stress the importance of associations in which people organize themselves to "defend their rights," among them a "minimum of social equality" needed for real citizenship.[15] Another important aspect is the stress on subjectivity and an ethical stance in civil society, following Gramsci's concept. Different from Marx, Gramsci—highly influential in Brazil and Latin America—saw civil society not as part of the structure and, thus, the relations of production, but of the superstructure.[16] Civil society, then, is not seen "merely as a posthumous justification of a power whose historical formation is dependent on material conditions, not merely as rationalizations of a power which already exists, but as forces capable of shaping and creating a new history and contributing to the formation of a new power which will progressively emerge."[17] The State (i.e. political society) would, ultimately, be reabsorbed into civil society. Gramsci, according to Bobbio, was especially interested in hegemony as cultural rather than political leadership (without dismissing the latter), thus even more stressing the importance of civil society and its possibilities for transformation against dominion by

11. Kocka, "Zivilgesellschaft als historisches Problem und Versprechen,"17.

12. On South America, Tocqueville (*Democracy in America*, 388f.) affirms that perspectives are positive due to European and Christian values: "Today civil war and despotism desolate these vast regions. The movement of the population halts, and the few men who inhabit them, absorbed in the care of defending themselves, hardly feel the need to improve their lot. But it cannot be so forever [. . .] South America is Christian like us; it has our laws, our usages; it contains all the seeds of civilization that have been developed within the European nations and their offshoots; besides, South America has our example: why should it remain ever barbaric? Here it is evidently only a question of time: a period more or less distant will doubtless come in which South Americans will form flourishing and enlightened nations." And also: "One cannot doubt that Americans of the north of America are called upon to provide one day for the needs of the South Americans." He sees the same advanced state of civilization and consequent responsibility in North as against South America as for the English in relation to the Italians, Spanish, and Portuguese.

13. Costa, *As cores de Ercília*, 45ff. distinguishes between an "emphatic current" of civil society with Keane, Cohen and Arato, Walzer, Taylor, Habermas and the new Frankfurtians Rödel, Frankenberg and Dubiel, and a "moderate" version with Edward Shils and Ralf Dahrendorf. While the former is highly normative in seeking a "radically democratic project," the latter is mainly empirical and descriptive, even if prone to contribute to the growth of liberal democracy by fostering civic virtues (ibid., 49).

14. Croissant et alii, "Zivilgesellschaft und Transformation," 11ff.; I use the list as provided by Mathwig and Lienemann, "Kirchen als zivilgesellschaftliche Akteure, " 99.

15. Weffort, "Brasil: condenado a modernização."

16. Bobbio, "Sociedade Civil,"1208f. highlights that Marx understood civil society as "independent individuals that proclaim themselves free and equal before the state" (ibid., 1208), and that thus it was to be understood as "bourgeois society," composed by egoistic human beings benefited by what is called human rights. For him, "the anatomy of civil society is to be sought in political economy" (*Critique of Political Economy*, quoted ibid., 1209). For Marx, civil society was the state of war of all against all which Hobbes had, precisely, seen as the natural state to be overcome by civil society and its social contract.

17. Bobbio, "Gramsci and the Concept of Civil Society," 88.

the State and being determined by structural factors.[18] In *Past and Present*, Gramsci defined civil society as "the political and cultural hegemony which a social group exercises over the whole of society, as the ethical content [sic!] of the State," with reference to Hegel.[19] Civil society constituted an autonomous space in the system, and by the conquest of hegemony would arrive at the conquest of power. All these aspects form a prominent conceptual framework for Brazilian civil society, as I shall show. It has influenced at least progressive religious political thinking from the early 1960s, with a "Gramscian boom" after 1975, identifying precisely civil society (rather than the private sphere, as in the Protestant realm, or direct intervention with State authorities, as in the case of the Roman Catholic Church) as the *locus* for the churches' contribution.[20] The debate on the "content" of democracy rather than its mere "form" has accompanied Brazilian society well into the 1990s, including the theologians (cf. below, ID), with references being "post-marxists" like Argentinian Ernesto Laclau and Frenchwoman Chantal Mouffe.[21]

In addition to these, the ideas of Hannah Arendt are being invoked, projecting civil society as an effective means against totalitarianism.[22] Habermas' works on the public sphere and its discourse[23] are yet another important point of reference, not least because of his strong distinction between civil society and the economy, which the widely anti-liberal discourse in Brazil has been very happy to adopt.

18. "Breaking with the tradition which translated the old antithesis 'state of nature—civil state' into the antithesis 'civil society—state', Gramsci translates another great historical antithesis, between the Church (broadly speaking, the modern Church is the party) and the state, into the antithesis 'civil society—political society'" (Bobbio, "Gramsci and the Concept of Civil Society," 95). Even in its terminology, such reflection could be read, in the Brazilian context, to be open to a positive contribution of the churches. Further on Gramsci and religion in the *Prison Notebooks* see Löwy, *A guerra dos deuses*, 26ff., where the utopian force of religion is recognized and can be a "necessary form of will of the popular masses," as long as it is an innocent religion of the people and not the "jesuitic Christianity" which is "pure narcotic for the popular masses" (ibid., 27, with quotes). Living in Catholic Italy, Gramsci idealized the Protestant Reformation (of Luther and Calvin, not only Müntzer), while Germans like Karl Kautsky called the latter "a thing of barbarians" and hailed the Italian Renaissance, criticized in turn by Gramsci as aristocratic and reactionary (ibid., 29).

19. This is seen in Bobbio, "Gramsci and the Concept of Civil Society," 84.

20. On Gramsci and revolution in progressive Protestantism in the early 1960s, see Burity, *Os protestantes*, *Radical Religion*. He affirms that "from that moment [sc. the 70s], he [sc. Gramsci] became a *lingua franca* of the *basista* discourse of building a hegemonic project 'from below', 'in the grassroots', which went against the grain of the whole tradition of Leninist politics represented by the left, and elite bargaining represented by the Brazilian mainstream political culture. This created some internal displacements in the Marxist front, where 'Gramsci' was vigorously set against 'Lenin' and 'stalinism', and hegemony was associated with a cunning version of 'dual power', supposed to prepare a confrontation of liberal democracy with popular, grassroots democracy" (Burity, *Radical Religion*, 146). On Gramsci's reception in Brazil in general see Secco, *Gramsci no Brasil*, who mentions that theology also "incorporated Gramsci": "Theorists like Gutierrez, Hinkelammert, Frei Betto, Leonardo Boff, Hugo Assmann, Pablo Richard created a true space for mutual understanding of Christians and Marxists. And the emergence of the PT expanded this space" (ibid., 54) Some authors started to write on Gramsci and religion and to translate foreign works on the matter. The interaction between Christianity and Marxism from the latter's point of view is positively described in Löwy, *A guerra dos deuses* , which includes a chapter on Protestantism, 176–202.

21. Laclau and Mouffe, *Hegemony and Socalist Strategy*; Mouffe, *Dimensions of Radical Democracy*; cf. Burity, *Radical Religion*, "Religião, política e cultura." Burity, an Anglican layman and political scientist from Recife, developed his doctoral thesis on *Radical Religion and the Constitution of New Political Actors in Brazil: The Experience of the 1980s* under Laclau's supervision at the University of Essex.

22. Many of her works have been translated into Portuguese, among them *The Origins of Totalitarianism*, *The Human Condition*, *On Revolution*, *On Violence*, among others, and the Minister of Exterior Relations (in Brazil called Chancellor) under the Cardoso government, Celso Lafer, is a renowned specialist on Hannah Arendt; cf. Lafer, *Hannah Arendt*. For a list of translated works and secondary sources published in Brazil see ibid., 195–97.

23. Habermas, *Strukturwandel der Öffentlichkeit*, *Faktizität und Geltung*.

Historically, there has been a revival of the concept of civil society in the 1970s, both in Eastern Europe, as a form of resistance against the restrictions of freedom and citizens' organization and participation under real existing socialism, and in Latin America as a resistance against authoritarian regimes.[24] The concept also re-emerged in Western Europe within, for instance, the *deuxième gauche* in France, in solidarity with Eastern European civil society, but also protesting against the welfare State's tutelage in the West.[25] In Brazil, at the time, certainly due to constant threats, the restrictions of public space and communication, and a sense of urgency under political repression, the concept was more "political-strategic" than "analytical-theoretical."[26] Until the 1980s, the concept was very "diffuse" and included anything "from base organizations to the progressive church, via the then so-called 'new unionism' [. . .], 'progressive' business sectors [. . .], to the 'democratic' parties and politicians."[27] According to Costa, this unlikely alliance broke apart as democratization progressed in the early 1980s. In the 1990s, a significant number of civil associations and social movements sought to mark quite clearly the frontier between civil society and the State, no longer presupposing that the latter would incorporate the former's aspirations. On the other hand, a number of organizations sought to assimilate into public agencies or business organizations.

Both internationally and in Brazil, the debate on the meaning of civil society continues. Not only are there diverse definitions, dimensions, and contexts, but the way the concept is used varies widely. It ranges from endowing it with messianic hopes, connected to the dawn of the "popular," "the people" organizing themselves and deciding as subjects on their fate, as envisioned by Paulo Freire's Pedagogy of the Oppressed, to the more concrete, but very modest notion of the "third sector." The latter essentially includes Non-Governmental Organizations (NGOs), more or less representative of a diversity of social movements and sectors of society, that are called "third sector" because they are different both from the State (all public) and the economy (all private), inasmuch as they constitute private organizations with public goals.[28] This double boundary between the State and society, quite in line with Habermas, Cohen, and Arato, but in different degrees contested by Kocka and Stackhouse, among others, is certainly questionable, as both State and economy are necessary for the existence and survival of a civil society, and it might be wise not to define civil society too narrowly, given that market economy and civil society can and should benefit each other, and have historically done so.[29]

On the other hand, not all NGOs want to belong to a third sector, which they see as co-opted by the State, abandoning the utopian horizon of social transformation; much less do the social

24. Ironically, even moderate military associated themselves to the concept, together with their allied middle- and upper-class sectors of Brazilian society, which "by the mid-1970s [. . .] began referring to themselves as 'civil society' and to their ongoing effort to acquire minimal civil liberties as 'opening up spaces'" (Della Cava, "The People's Church," 148).

25. Cohen and Arato, *Civil Society and Political Theory*, 29–82; Costa, *As cores de Ercília*, 42ff.

26. Costa, *As cores de Ercília*, 55.

27. Ibid., 57. In the same period, democracy came to be seen by the left as a "universal" and not merely instrumental value through precisely a Gramscian rather than Marxist understanding of civil society: Coutinho, *A democracia como valor universal*; cf. Burity, *Radical Religion*, 15 and the whole chapter, 6–33.

28. Fernandes, *Privado porém público*, Doimo, *A vez e a voz do popular.*

29. Kocka, " Zivilgesellschaft, " 22s. insists on this and affirms: "Fehlt die für funktionierende Marktwirtschaften typische Dezentralisation von Entscheidungen und Macht, hat die Zivilgesellschaft schlechte Chancen," but also: "Die Entstehung und der Erfolg von Marktwirtschaften werden durch zivilgesellschaftliche Strukturen zumindest erleichtert, wenn nicht gar erst ermöglicht. Denn zu dieser gehören sozialer Zusammenhalt, Vertrauen und ‚soziales Kapital', die die Marktwirtschaft stützen, von dieser allein aber nicht hervorgebracht werden können. " See also Stackhouse, "Civil Society, Public Theology and the Ethical Shape of Polity in a Global Era."

movements want to belong to this category.[30] In short, the conflict is between professionalism, cooperation with the State, and efficiency on the one hand, and utopia, transformation of the State and society, and popular participation on the other, and any imaginable intermediate position between these two extremes. Furthermore, the growing internationalization of many organizations is a relevant factor, not least for the churches, many of which are part of an international network or institution. While this is helpful and has made possible many actions that would otherwise not have been realized, it can lead, at the same time, to an inadequate imposition of foreign models on different national contexts.[31]

In any case, civil society is more than a descriptive category. It has a normative, ethical dimension to the extent that not all non-State and non-profit organizations are counted as belonging to it.[32] Many authors claim the importance of a utopian element, inasmuch it seeks to transform not only a specific element or group in society, but society as a whole.[33] Therefore, the terminology, especially in the 1980s and 1990s, often indicates civil society as a goal rather than a fact, something to be "constructed," "developed," "reinforced," and the like.[34] According to the Association of Brazilian NGOs, their focus is on private initiative founding institutions in the public interest "for the development and defense of rights, for the promotion of the environment and for rural development."[35] Under this definition, NGOs are separated from churches, hospitals, private schools and universities, cultural and sports clubs, and professional organizations. A restriction is thus made both in empirical ways (the NGO as a specific type of organization) and normative ways (advocacy for rights, the environment, and the land).

Without questioning the right of a broader and more descriptive concept, I shall adopt here a quite narrow and normative concept of civil society as an ideal type. Civil society is, then, a diverse

30. Gohn, *O protagonismo da sociedade civil.*

31. This is the leading subject in Costa's habilitation thesis, *Vom Nordatlantik zum "Black Atlantic,"* where he criticizes the application of anti-racism models from the U.S. on the Brazilian contexts. In Brazil, however, the history, concrete life, practice and concept of being black and "blackness" (*negritude*), as well as the concepts and practices of racism and anti-racism, are not equal to the U.S. and thus make specific, contextual approaches necessary. See also my review in Sinner, "Sérgio Costa."

32. Mathwig and Lienemann, "Kirchen als zivilgesellschaftliche Akteure," 103–7 exclude the military, the State, the parties, the economy, associations (at least some like sports clubs), confederations ("Verbände") as interest groups, the family and the churches. Although especially three of the latter four (without the family) have much in common with civil society and present features of it, they cannot be as such subsumed under civil society. Kocka, ("Zivilgesellschaft," 25f.) questions too clear a distinction of civil society from the family, as the definitions of "public" and "private" are in constant flux, and, as we have seen (cf. IA3c), especially problematic in Brazil where family structures tend to be influential in the public sphere and even the political system. Berger in "Religion and Global Civil Society" distinguishes between a structural aspect (civil society *in between* the private sphere, the State and the economy), and a civil aspect (institutions that mitigate conflict and foster social peace)—the first excludes General Motors from civil society, the other the Mafia, to cite Berger's examples. Indeed, the normative (Berger: civil) element is to distinguish between destructive (for example, skinhead groups, the Ku-Klux-Klan) and constructive movements and organizations of civil society (peace and environment groups, for example), and among them those who benefit not only their own members (like sport clubs), but reach out to larger parts or, intentionally, the whole of society or even the world (environment, trade and foreign debt issues etc.).

33. Cf., descriptively, Burity, *Radical Religion*, 160, who states that "both 'progressive' religion and social movements speak the impossible language of democracy to convey the longings for solidarity, difference, extended citizenship (beyond mere political liberties), peace, and a new world order, among other metaphors (or would they be referents?) of democracy. [. . .] They wish to be part (in both sense of taking part, and of being affected by) of the invention they voice for." Such democracy was to be built "from scratch" out of authoritarianism, and to be different from "neo-liberalism and conservatism."

34. Fernandes, "Sociedade civil e ecumenismo," 56.

35. ABONG, *Ações das ONGs no Brasil*, 4.

conglomerate of non-governmental and non-profit organizations and movements of voluntary, private initiative engaged in fostering citizenship in the public sphere to promote the common good for the whole of society. Apart from specific claims and actions, such organizations and movements provide a space for learning how to actively participate as a citizen in matters of society, fostering personal and interpersonal trust and civic virtues. The primary field of civil society's action is the national (or sub-national) setting, as it is there that concrete goals can be achieved through mediation between sectors of the population and government, whether administration, legislative, or judiciary. Civil society, however, is embedded in transnational networks, from which it receives criticism and support, morally, personally, technically, and financially, and into which it infuses its own contribution.[36] This is especially so for religious organizations, especially the Christian churches, and among them prominently the Roman Catholic Church, which seeks global coherence and obedience. But I would say that there is, as yet, no global civil society, properly speaking, because it lacks both a constituted power and a concrete populational constituency between which it could mediate.[37]

2. RELIGIONS AND CIVIL SOCIETY

Many have stated, and rightly so, that religions tend to be left out of transformation studies, although in many places, and certainly in Brazil, they have made an indispensable contribution to the formation of civil society. Even where this is recognized, the fact seems to leave the discussions of sociologists and political scientists untouched.[38] Researchers and thinkers about civil society like Jürgen Kocka, Wolfgang Merkel, and their colleagues tend to highlight, historically, dissident churches like the Quakers, but are very skeptical of the great religions and churches, namely the Roman Catholic Church.[39] My hypothesis is that such minimal attention to religions and, especially, Christian churches has to do with the German situation of the public law status of both the Roman Catholic and Protestant churches and their history of political influence and dominance, where they do not seem to foster emancipated citizen participation. This seems especially true where churches do not maintain internal democratic relationships and thus seem to be unfit for a democratic society with a strong civil society. Another factor is certainly the still widespread presupposition that modernization and, with it, secularization will eventually turn religion obsolete,

36. Danièle Hérvieu-Leger speaks, in this context, of an "ecumenism of human rights" that permeates what is seen as a global civil society, quoted by Berger, "Religion and Global Civil Society," 14.

37. Keane in *Global Civil Society?* identifies global civil society as an ideal type, given the problems of the availability and interpretation of empirical data, with five main features: (1) it is non-governmental, (2) a dynamic of social processes ("society"), (3) marked by civility (respect, politeness, non-violence), (4) contains both traces of pluralism and strong conflict potential, not least because of its economic (sic!) features (it is not a "global community," as Keane insists against the communitarians), and (5) it is global, not in the sense "of a 'vast empire of human society, as it is spread over the whole earth' (Wordsworth)—global civil society is neither a new form of empire nor encompassing of the whole earth—but it certainly is a special form of *unbounded* society marked by constant feedback among its many components" (ibid., 17); it is a "vast, dynamic biosphere" (ibid., 18), "a vast, interconnected and multi-layered non-governmental space that comprises many hundreds of thousands of self-directing institutions and ways of life that generate global effects" (ibid., 20). It is strange that religions, although occasionally mentioned, are not treated as an issue in themselves, although they certainly have been responsible for globalizing trends from early on and many of them provide more or less strong and unified transnational networks. On this see Stackhouse, "Reflections on How and Why We Go Public" and "Civil Society, Public Theology."

38. See, for instance, Crane, "Civil society and theology"; Bedford-Strohm, *Gemeinschaft aus kommunikativer Freiheit*; Herbert, *Religion and Civil Society*; Mathwig and Lienemann, "Kirchen als zivilgesellschaftliche Akteure"; Stackhouse, "Civil Society, Public Theology."

39. Cf. Mathwig and Lienemann, "Kirchen als zivilgesellschaftliche Akteure", 102.

at least in its public role and influence.[40] Apart from the fact that such interpretations are certainly one-sided (even a church undemocratic in faith matters can foster participation in democratic movements) or have to be modified (due to the shortcomings of a teleological modernization and secularization theory)[41] they are certainly not appropriate for a religiously highly plural situation like Brazil, where churches are "religious societies" of civil law and religious groups abound (cf. below, IIB).[42] There is, however, a renewed and growing interest in religion in its public role,[43] and some have even stated, with Brazil among its examples, that "the third wave of democratization was predominantly a Catholic wave"—which means, to be sure, the fact that many of the third wave countries were predominantly Catholic at the time, rather than being the consequence of this church being "intrinsically" or "essentially" democratic.[44] Although Catholic sectors were active in resistance against authoritarian regimes in other countries, it was mainly in Brazil that the hierarchy gave such strong support, so that Stepan could conclude that "by the mid-1970s the Brazilian Church had become the most theologically progressive and institutionally innovative Catholic Church in the world. With the initial support of the Vatican, it also became in Brazil the most legitimate, most nation-wide, and most useful organizational resource for the opposition forces of civil society."[45] Alongside the Catholic Church, ecumenical organizations were among the most outspoken against repression and for social transformation. Their independent legal status as NGO's and their external founding gave them a great deal of independence, creating, as Doimo called it, a "secular ecumenism."[46]

Charles Taylor[47] identifies a number of historically important aspects of the Western concept of society: the early Middle Ages already had a notion that political authority was only one organ among others, and that society was not solely defined through its political organization like in the Greek and Roman States and empires. This was helped by the idea of the Church as an autonomous society, which created a "bifocal" Western Christianity, subject to "two swords," even if they served

40. Burity, "Religião, política e cultura."

41. Casanova, *Public Religions,* 11–39; Herbert, *Religion and Civil Society*, 29–59.

42. This was the impression I got from discussions with Jürgen Kocka and colleagues during a seminar at the São Paulo Goethe Institute in March, 2008. I am grateful for the interactions we had there, and for the kindness to send me manuscripts which are of difficult access here in Brazil.

43. Casanova, *Public Religions;* Vries and Sullivan, *Political Theologies,*

44. Casanova, "Civil society and religion," 1041, who also refers to Huntington, *The Third Wave*. The usual absence of religion in terms of "political-cultural features of Brazilian society" is noted by Moisés in *Os brasileiros e a democracia,* 243, but he states (against Huntington) that the variable does not have any significant effect on "satisfaction with real existing democracy." This is discussed by Burity in "Religião e cultura cívica," who, based on qualitative research, says that, rather than to expect a statistically significant variation in the motivations of individuals, a "conjunctural" emphasis can "catch oscillations of political culture of the religious sectors, which project them as relevant partners [*interlocutores*] in public discussion." He also stresses that religious influence on political behavior is not one-sided or strictly causal, but emerges in interaction with non-church activities and shows considerable variation. Thus, it remains an important element for a wider democratic culture.

45. Stepan, *Democratizing Brazil*, XII, Birle, "Zivilgesellschaft in Südamerika," 246, confirms that "in keinem anderen Land spielte die Kirche und insbesondere der Wandel innerhalb der katholischen Kirche eine ähnlich wichtige Rolle für das Verhältnis zwischen Zivilgesellschaft und Staat wie in Brasilien." See also Mainwaring, *The Catholic Church*; Hagopian, "Politics in Brazil," 530f.

46. Cf. Burity, *Radical Religion* and Doimo, *A vez e a voz do popular* where in the glossary of abbreviations out of 112 nothing less than 50 are partially or wholly church organizations and movements. A case in point is the Boff case, whose documentation was edited by the National Movement of Human Rights which Boff himself helped to create (cf. Sinner, *Reden vom Dreieinigen Gott*, 67ff.), and the case was looked at through this category, not distinguishing between Church and world here. On p. 32 Doimo talks of "secular ecumenism."

47. Taylor, "Die Beschwörung der Civil Society."

the same God. A third important aspect, according to Taylor, is the idea of subjective rights, present even in feudal relationships, as they not only obliged the vassal, but also the landlord. The existence of relatively independent and autonomous cities and the fact that the monarch had to constantly negotiate with an unstable bunch of estates further reinforced a view of political structure as being within society as a whole rather than identical to it. These five elements were further modified, but already laid the ground for what was to become civil society.[48]

According to José Casanova, the Catholic Church with its hierarchical structure (and wherever it was in the majority) was able to constitute an "autonomous public space" vis-à-vis the State. As such, when using this power against an authoritarian State—Casanova quotes Poland as an example, but Brazil would also be in place— it can help the constitution of a civil society. But this does not make the church as such an institution of civil society, nor is the presence of a "powerful autonomous church an indication of the existence of civil society."[49] The Church can, however, become an institution of civil society when it ceases "being a church in the Weberian sense of the term: when it gives up its monopolistic claims and recognizes religious freedom and freedom of conscience as universal and inviolable human rights,"[50] which is, in Brazil, at least partially the case, as we shall see, and which has become possible worldwide through the aggiornamento of the Vatican II.

Within society, churches can provide social capital for society, and collaborate both critically and constructively with other actors in civil society and with the political authorities. They have access to the people like nobody else and, in many places and not least in transformation societies, rank among the institutions with the highest credibility. Churches also provided organizational skills, both nationally and transnationally, for the articulation of social movements and the struggle for human rights, against racial discrimination, slavery and the like. There is, however, no reason for any kind of triumphalism, given that many of the situations now condemned as sin, such as slavery and apartheid, long received theological and ecclesial support. Any contribution churches can make in civil society should be given with conviction, indeed with boldness, but also with humility (see below, IIIB4). Mathwig and Lienemann[51] distinguish a variety of roles of churches as actors in civil society, structurally, normatively, and functionally. I here presuppose that churches are, structurally, mediators and in this sense part of civil society. In this study, I shall work mainly on the normative level, as to how churches understand themselves, and comment on issues of citizenship in society, which is, within the limits of a bibliographical study, checked against empirical

48. In "Die Beschwörung der Civil Society" Taylor further works with two strands of the concept of civil society: the one coming from Locke (the government as trusteeship installed by society through a contract, which can be undone and the government deposed, later radicalized by Thomas Paine; this implied also an autonomous economic sphere, criticized by Hegel and his followers, especially Marx), and the other from Montesquieu (monarchy has to be tamed by laws, where free society is identified by a particular political constitution; a line followed by Hegel and Tocqueville, where the *bürgerliche Gesellschaft* is a separate, but not autonomous sphere), fostering the idea of a self-regulated public sphere and a constitutional structure of a society defined by its political organizations, respectively. Both are important. Stackhouse in "Civil Society, Public Theology" takes a similar double strand as constitutive, with Locke and Hegel, who disagreed on "whether civil society can construct and legitimately deconstruct and reconstruct the political society or whether the political order must comprehend and control the institutions of civil society" (ibid., 2). But they agreed on three important points, according to Stackhouse: (1) They share a two-agent theory of society, i.e., institutions independent of the State and a power that can use coercive force legitimately; (2) commerce, markets and corporate enterprises are part of civil society; (3) "they presumed that religion would have a role in forming persons and associations in civil society" (ibid., 3).

49. Casanova, "Civil society and religion," 1044.

50. Ibid., 1046.

51. Mathwig and Lienemann, "Kirchen als zivilgesellschaftliche Akteure," 117–19.

data and studies, i.e. the functional, descriptive level. Returning to my definition of civil society introduced above (IB1), we can say that churches are non-governmental and (normally) non-profit organizations of a voluntary nature, with membership based on private decision, but transcending it in that it creates an identifiable community with a public mission and impact.[52] In part II, I will examine the extent to which churches in Brazil foster citizenship and seek to promote the common good for the whole of society and what virtues they proclaim. Furthermore, I will consider the extent to which churches provide a space for learning to participate in democracy as an active citizen; and then the extent to which, if it is at all measurable, churches contribute to interpersonal trust. My hypothesis is that they indeed have an important record in these matters, although not free of ambiguities, as we shall see.

3. CIVIL SOCIETY IN BRAZIL BEFORE TRANSITION

In the period before the military took power, Brazilian civil society was generally restricted to a limited number of organizations with elitist character or steered by the Government, like the trade unions. However, the fifties and sixties were a time of social and cultural effervescence. The great educator Paulo Freire (1921–97) started his work for popular literacy during this period. He interacted intensely with the churches and worked for ten years with the World Council of Churches in Geneva (1970–80).[53] "Conscientization" became a key word in this period, as Freire's Pedagogy of the Oppressed sought to assist the oppressed in freeing themselves by resisting both the external oppressor and the internalized structure of oppression, becoming the "subject" of their liberation. "Popular education" (*educação popular*) became another key term, which meant that intellectuals should become "organic" (Gramsci), working with and among "the people," understood as economically poor, socially despised, and culturally different, thus overcoming the strata imposed by class and education in the traditional sense. Popular education, then, should help people discover their dignity and worth and empower them to make decisions of their own, rather than just repeat phrases and information in what Freire called "bank-like education" (*educação bancária*), in which knowledge is deposited like money in a bank account.[54]

While the diversity of organizations and movements is, today, seen as a sign of democracy's strength, at the time many considered such effervescence to be highly dangerous for democracy (as then understood). Samuel Huntington, who often served as an adviser to Brazil and other Latin American governments, has become notorious for such a position, claiming that modernization would lead to aspirations by the lower layers of society, which in turn would lead to anomic political mobilization, thus presenting a serious threat to government.[55] As many "projects" had a more

52. In his review of the post Berlin Wall discussion on civil society, Joachim von Soosten in "Civil Society" insists on the church as part of the public space and an element of civil society with its specific contribution: ". . .die sozialen Erfahrungsräume, die der christliche Glaube eröffnet, bilden ein Element im Netzwerk einer lebendigen Zivilgesellschaft, zu der die *Kirche als Interpretationsgemeinschaft* in der ihr eigenen Weise beizutragen in der Lage ist" (ibid., 155). Thus, the empirical aspect of the churches' location in society is clearly—and rightly so, cf. IIIA ad IIIB below—transcended to state its normativity from the interpretation of its founding document, Scripture, in relation to the specific context within a hermeneutical community.

53. Andreola and Ribeiro, *Andarilho da esperança*.

54. As this criticism was taken up by student movements in many countries, including Brazil, in the late 60s, Pink Floyd's *The Wall* (1979/82) is an excellent visualization of this type of education. Not surprisingly, as we speak about popular education in the graduate course on *Panorama of Latin American Theology*, students invariably refer to that film. On the *basista* aspect, fostering popular participation and mobilization, on which church groups and leaders insisted more than the tendentially elitist militants of the left, see Burity, *Radical Religion*, chapters 4 and 5.

55. Huntington, *Political Order in Changing Societies*; cf. Rodrigues, "Autonomous Participation and Political

or less clearly revolutionary connotation, they seemed to call for the 1964 coup, itself somewhat strangely called a "revolution" that promised to establish order and prevent a real turnover from happening, usually subsumed under the heading "bolshevist" or "communist" (see above, IA1).

During the fiercest period of repression (1968–73), the establishment of an active and organized civil society was practically impossible. The very limited attempts through guerrilla warfare to topple the Government had been crushed, important leaders had been tortured and killed or exiled, political parties were reduced to two with little power, trade unions were under fierce control, and the media were under heavy censorship. In the seventies, "the only institution able to assert itself against the military government was the [Roman Catholic] Church."[56] Furthermore, as it suffered considerable aggressions even once *abertura* was in course, "the hardliners had helped propel the Church into becoming a powerful and aggressive voice of civil society."[57] Thus, the Roman Catholic Church, and, on a much smaller scale, the ecumenical organizations founded by Protestants, which co-operated with the Roman Catholic Church, served as a protective umbrella for opposition to the State.

Among Protestant circles, the "Evangelical Confederation of Brazil" (*Confederação Evangélica do Brasil*, founded in 1932), especially its Sector for Social Responsibility, played an important role in forging a critical societal awareness. The latter organized four major conferences from 1955 onwards, among them the "Northeast Conference" in Recife on "Christ and the Brazilian Revolutionary Process" (1962), which became a landmark.[58] Its keynote speaker was the North American Presbyterian missionary Richard Shaull (1919–2002), a seminal figure for a whole generation of theologians and church activists.[59] He was also one of the main speakers at the World Council of Churches' "Church and Society" Conference in Geneva (1966). At the "Northeast Conference," political and social conscience was confirmed through exposure to the particularly poor and non-democratic northeastern region, where the so called *coronéis* (colonels), usually rich landowners, were in power. Initially, the progressive forces seemed to prevail. However, when the 1964 coup came, the Confederation quickly lost its space and influence, the sector on public responsibility was dismantled, and "Brazilian Protestantism [was] submerged in the legitimizing limbo of the military regime."[60] With support from the international ecumenical movement and in collaboration with representatives from other countries, those involved in the former Sector could continue their work in the movement "Church and Society in Latin America" (*Igreja e Sociedade na América Latina*—ISAL), which had been founded in the aftermath of an ecumenical consultation

Institutions."

56. Skidmore, "Brazil's Slow Road to Democratization," 35.

57. Skidmore, *The Politics of Military Rule*, 184. Even bishops were not spared: In 1976, the bishop of Nova Iguaçu, Dom Adriano Hypolito, known for his support for the grassroots neighborhood organizations in his diocese, had been kidnapped, stripped of his clothes, and abandoned on the road, while his car was blown up in front of the CNBB headquarters.

58. Burity's *Os protestantes* provides an extensive analysis of the discourse of revolution among Brazilian intellectuals and the same discourse among progressives in the Protestant churches which led to the said conference. He identifies similarities in the view of history, expecting the imminence of a new social order, which, however, turned out to be a failure—for the Protestant progressives even earlier than for the utopian left, as Protestantism closed itself up in orthodoxy and a supportive stance toward the regime. In his already mentioned doctoral thesis, *Radical Religion*, he takes up the existing strands of "radical religion" and what became of it in the 1990s.

59. The issue of citizenship was already discussed then. Shaull read, with small groups, Karl Barth's "Christengemeinde und Bürgermeinde" and J. Bennet's book on "The Christian as Citizen," see Dejung, *Die Ökumenische Bewegung*, 300, note 30.

60. Burity, *Os protestantes*, 124.

on "Church and Society" in Huampani (Lima, Peru) in 1961.[61] Being ecumenical became synonymous with being associated with the struggle for social justice. In the early seventies, a number of seminal ecumenical organisms were founded, among them the Ecumenical Coordination of Service (*Coordenadoria Ecumênica de Serviço*, CESE, 1973) and the Institute for the Study of Religion (*Instituto de Estudos da Religião*, ISER, 1970/1973).[62] Within the evangelical (in the Anglo-Saxon sense) spectrum, a theologically conservative but socially progressive, transconfessional movement was founded in 1970 in Cochabamba, Bolívia, in a certain sense as an alternative to ISAL. It gave important inputs on the struggle for social justice as intrinsic to mission into the Lausanne Evangelization Movement.[63]

However, most churches were concerned, in the first place, with their survival, trying to keep their flock together and to be recognized as good Brazilian citizens and not as foreign intruders. Given their foreign origin as immigrant or mission churches (see below, IIB, IID1), neither ecumenism nor the struggle for justice were well regarded, and it was left to individuals to carry on the churches' prophetic message.[64] While the progressive wings of some churches, mainly Presbyterian, Methodist, Lutheran (IECLB), and some Pentecostals, were indeed active and influential, it seems safe to assume that the majority of the faithful remained traditional and reserved in terms of political and social engagement. With a variety of revolutionary projects and political utopias competing with each other and a lack of clear political direction, insecurity and fear of chaos (associated, for many, with communism) was widespread and fostered a sense of longing for a strong hand. Thus, as mentioned above (IA1), many church leaders welcomed the military's "revolution" and the establishment of an orderly situation controlled by the government.

61. ISAL united Church and Society commissions from seven church federations: Argentina, Brazil, Chile, Cuba, Mexico, Puerto Rico, Uruguay, and later also from Bolivia, and there were "fraternal relations" with another six (Plou, *Caminhos de unidade*, 126–33). According to Bastian, *Geschichte des Protestantismus*, 236f., ISAL's protagonists were "essentially young white intellectuals of Protestant origin from the corridor São Paulo—Montevideo—Buenos Aires." On the ecumenical reception of the debate in Latin America, as protagonized by ISAL and, namely, Richard Shaull and Miguez Bonino, see Dejung, *Die Ökumenische Bewegung*, 296–321. The Latin Americans especially criticized a liberal, reformist view of development and advocated a more revolutionary stance, without, however, falling into an uncritical appraisal of communism. Quite to the contrary, Shaull was outspokenly critical of it. Theologically central was the notion of God's presence and intervention in history, namely in the realization of social justice and the recognition of human dignity in a new society. At the same time, ISAL was very critical of the Latin American Protestant churches, who were considered ill prepared for the renewal of society. Rather, they were seen as part of the problem and as isolated from reality, for which US-American missionary praxis was blamed. On the continuation of the ecumenical debate, see Zaugg-Ott, *Entwicklung oder Befreiung?* and Stierle, *Chancen einer ökumenischen Wirtschaftsethik*, the latter more specifically on an ethics of economy.

62. The ISER was founded in 1970 as the Institute of Theological Studies (*Instituto de Estudos Teológicos*—ISET), "formed exclusively by Catholic and Protestant radicals who were facing trouble in their churches" (Burity, *Radical Religion*, 89, n. 31). It renamed itself in 1973 and developed more and more into a diversified research institute.

63. See Longuini, *O novo rosto da missão* esp. 171f.; Zabatiero, "Um movimento teológico." The central concept that developed within this movement was "holistic mission" (missão integral), with C. René Padilla among its most prominent defendants; on this see now the doctoral thesis of Zwetsch, *Missão como com-paixão*.

64. President Lula da Silva, however, thanked the churches for this engagement, as he addressed the 9th Assembly of the World Council of Churches in Porto Alegre on February 17, 2006: "As we fought, decades ago, for democracy in our country, we found not only moral and spiritual incentives in the World Council of Churches, but also active solidarity and effective support to, confidently, pursue those struggles." He namely thanked the WCC for having hosted Brazilian educator Paulo Freire, then prosecuted by the military regime, from 1970 to 1980, as he was able to work in the WCC; Silva, "Discurso do presidente da República," 2.

4. THE DEVELOPMENT OF CIVIL SOCIETY DURING TRANSITION

From 1974 onwards, alongside the Roman Catholic Church, the Brazilian Bar Association (*Ordem dos Advogados do Brasil*, OAB) also gained momentum. Like the Church, it could count on a well-organized nationwide structure and its own, efficient network of communication, not having to rely on the highly censured mass media. The press, although limited in reach, could less easily be controlled and some publications were fairly critical of the government. The Brazilian Press Association (*Associação Brasileira de Imprensa*, ABI) became another organ of opposition. Political weeklies appeared that survived despite heavy censorship and high costs of production, showing that there were some niches left for the opposition. Artists and intellectuals developed means of indirect criticism through cartoons, poetry, and music, for which the military bureaucrats lacked any sense. By relaxing censorship, President Geisel "was helping to reawaken civil society, but was unprepared to hear what society's voice would say."[65]

At the grassroots, new groups appeared and grew like the already mentioned CEBs, neighborhood associations, and anti-racist movements, often with women in the leadership. Catholic influence was strong in many of these groups, but more Pentecostals collaborated than is generally assumed.[66] The concrete influence of these groups is difficult to measure, due to the frailty, heterogeneity, and limited representivity of social movements.[67] As for the Roman Catholic Church, Bruneau and Hewitt,[68] based on surveys carried out in 1982 and 1984, concluded that, despite the church's undeniable transformation in terms of social commitment, even progressive archdioceses and episcopal regions had not succeeded in persuading practicing Catholics to adopt more progressive postures. The church has, they say, "largely been unable to cultivate a mass following of committed progressives, even among its closest adherents," while their real success has been in dealing with "elite institutions, civil and military, including the media," and anticipated that it would turn, increasingly, to "issues involving education, morality, and the family."[69] As we shall see, they were largely correct in this prognosis (IIC).

Still, it is without doubt that church and non-church groups and movements had a significant impact, since the government was forced to be concerned about them.[70] Their common struggle was initially facilitated by the common enemy, i.e., the perceived coalition between the military regime and the economic elite, both landlords and managers, as well as international capital in terms of debts and multinational companies active, for instance, in the exploration of the Amazon rainforest. As this common enemy multiplied its face and became, especially in the case of the State, more cooperative, civil society became aware that it lacked a common "project" and was unclear as

65. Skidmore, *The Politics of Military Rule*, 188. In the left's terminology, this is what turned the regime's "project" of liberalization into a "process" of democratization, which went much further; Burity, *Radical Religion*, 22. The emerging "social movements of the period [sc. from the late 1970s onwards] came next to be a synonym for democracy itself" (ibid., 30).

66. Ireland, *Kingdoms Come*; Burdick, *Looking for God in Brazil.*

67. For a critical analysis of the neighborhood associations, based on a 1981/82 survey, see Boschi, "Social Movements and the New Political Order." For him, in Brazilian literature on the topic, such associations are usually treated with an ideological bias and overvalued in their concrete impact, but may still, in the long run, "operate and diffuse the ethos of a new political culture, especially in view of their emphasis on the values of participation and internal democracy" (ibid., 190). Such associations had existed since the 1950s, but similarly to the CEBs, become politicized under the military regime, and expanded particularly after 1979.

68. Bruneau and Hewitt, "Patterns of Church Influence."

69. Ibid., 60.

70. Mainwaring, "Grassroots Popular Movements."

to how to react to the changing context.[71] One of the consequences of the changing context was the creation of NGOs in order to help social movements to better organize and articulate their claims. Professionally trained and often university graduates, NGO agents assisted people with little formal education and organizational experience to get funding and support from other groups, politicians, and other influential people, as well as addressing their claims to the right person or body in an effective way. They also provided a legal structure and corporate bank account needed for receiving funds. In those years, financial and moral support from outside agencies was readily available and came with very modest obligations, which guaranteed both the viability and the autonomy of those organizations and the movements they assisted.

The strikes that began in the São Paulo area in 1978, which succeeded in pressuring managers and politicians alike, were additional important and indeed more visible manifestations of civil society. Mass rallies were at their height with the *Diretas Já* campaign for direct presidential elections in 1984. Both showed a growing influence of civil society on politics. Thus, the process of transition in Brazil, while initiated and dominated by the government, became more and more a "dialectic between regime concession and societal conquest."[72] Associations of all kinds became important places for the learning of democracy as they tried to pressure the government to fulfill its promise of returning to democracy, apart from specific rights issues.[73] The CEBs can be considered an important birthplace and school for the activists who would later found their own organizations.[74] The foundation of the Worker's Party (PT) in 1979 was an important conquest in itself, as it was arguably the first party not founded by highly educated and well-related elites (although many intellectuals, church and not, contributed to it), but by the workers themselves, with generally poor formal education and little insertion into the realm of political and economic power—and among whom Lula had emerged as one of their most important leaders. Frei Betto called for a redefinition of the popular pastoral work's role in civil society, as with the process of abertura "the popular movement can emancipate themselves, doing without their links with the pastoral. . . ."[75]

Changes in terms of mobilization and organization were accompanied by a further diversification of their subjects and thematic foci (women's, blacks', environmental, landless, and, more recently, also hip-hop and gay movements). A survey carried out in 1988 counted 1,010 NGOs, listed as "organizations at the service of the popular movement" (422), organizations of women (185) and ecological organizations (403) .[76] Between 1996 and 2002, such organizations nearly

71. See Burity, *Radical Religion*; Doimo, *A vez e a voz do popular*; Martins, "Changes in the Relationship between Society and the State"; Gohn, *O protagonismo da sociedade civil.*

72. Stepan, *Democratizing Brazil*, XI

73. See Krischke, *The Learning of Democracy.*

74. McDonough, Shin and Moisés in "Democratization and Participation" come to a noteworthy conclusion in their comparative perspective on Spain, Brazil and South Korea: ". . . it is religiosity that most dramatically conditions levels of political participation among the postauthoritarian regimes. Its net impact is strongly positive in Brazil and Korea, and just as negative in Spain." Avritzer, "Modelos de sociedade civil," 288 highlights that "the church contributes to the development of a process of reflexivity [i.e., in which the relationship between the individual and the political system is being debated] in the relationships between the population and political power, a process which has to be located at the root of a number of urban movements and the tendency of creating civil associations, which come to the fore in Brazil at the end of the seventies." While the Roman Catholic Church's contribution is generally acknowledged and well researched, the specific role of the Protestant churches has not yet found sufficient consideration, cf. Burity, *Radical Religion*, 85 and passim. There are, however, the pioneering works of Freston titled "Breve História," "Evangelicals and Politics," and *Evangelical Christianity and Democracy.*

75. In Burity, *Radical Religion*, 115.

76. Landim, *Sem fins lucrativos.*

tripled, from 2,800 to 8,600 in a similarly narrow definition,[77] which suggests that they had already more than doubled between 1988 and 1996. Although there are serious statistical shortcomings[78] to discerning with precision the number of associations and NGOs throughout the last four decades, their number has beyond doubt increased, both in general terms of non-profit institutions and, specifically, those that favor development and the defense of rights. It is plain that the social movements did not disappear after the end of State repression, but have indeed grown and changed.[79] Gradually, an external differentiation between economic agents and political society, along with an internal heterogenization in terms of their degree of professionalism and specialization and the degree of cooperation with the State, has taken place.

In her study of the development of social movements between 1975 and 1990, covering the transition period from its beginnings to the direct presidential elections, Doimo[80] speaks of a "crisis of social movements," due to a host of contextual elements that changed during the years she researched. Among those elements she mentions the retreat and inward-looking tendency of the Roman Catholic Church, including internal debate on the role of CEBs that gradually lost their mobilizing force, and the decision by ecumenical and secular NGOs to favor direct political action instead of mere consultancy to movements.

Doimo identifies an "erosion of an ethical-political camp through the gradual disaggregation of its local movementalist networks and the successive disarticulation of its cognitive and symbolic universe," i.e. the dissolution of social movements—taken to be ethically superior because of their assumed high degree of participation—in favor of more hierarchical and bureaucratic NGOs. On the other hand, for Doimo there has been "a stimulus for active-propositional efforts, especially in terms of the aeration of the political-administrative apparatuses, the conquest of new institutional dispositions towards direct or semi-direct participation and the struggle for the amplification of social rights." Thus, discourse moved from "base democracy" to "democracy as universal value," from "popular movement" to "organized social movements" and from "struggle against the state" to "society's participation in decision-making" through state-civil society partnerships, accompanying the dislocation from movements to organizations.[81]

Thus, the utopian radicalism of change that envisioned some kind of revolutionary turnover of the State and/or the system of capitalism, gave way to a more collaborative style, seeking at least selective collaboration with the state, while being more or less cautious about a possible cooptation by the latter.

> What is known is that the revolutionary dream of the great transformation of society is losing territory to the reorganization of the system of interest representation, in view of the greater opening of possibilities of social integration, toward the amplification of the rights of citizenship.[82]

This tendency is confirmed well beyond the period of transition (see below, IB5).

It is significant that religious pluralism also expanded considerably from the later 1970s onwards, creating a similar heterogenization both in theological and institutional terms, in what

77. ABONG, *Ações das ONGs no Brasil*, 4.

78. Landim, "Associativismo e organizações voluntárias."

79. Hochstetler, "Democratizing Pressures from Below?"

80. Doimo, *A vez e a voz do popular*, 201f.

81. Ibid., 222.

82. Ibid., 218.

Campos[83] calls a "pulverization" of the religious field. While these churches disagree on many issues, they agree on the importance of religious freedom, i.e., equal footing in legal and political terms with the Roman Catholic Church (cf. below, IIB). Pentecostals traditionally shunned politics, affirming that "the believer does not muddle with politics" (*crente não se mete em política*). But they later constituted a considerable group in the Constituent Assembly, nearly doubling the number of seats held previously, in what came to be called the *bancada evangélica* ("evangelical bench"; cf. below, IIE1c).

As indicated, theoretical debate about civil society—in its empirical vs. normative aspects and their respective theoretical frameworks—continues broadly, and the adaptation of agents of civil society to the development of democracy, for instance through professionalism, is underway, though not free of ambivalence.[84] The latter becomes evident, for instance, considering the fierce debate on the methods of the landless worker's movement (MST): Are land occupations legitimate means to force land reform or, rather, illegal and undemocratic forms of violence? This became particularly evident through the invasion and devastation of a tree school in Barra do Riberio in Rio Grande do Sul on March 8, 2006, by some 2,000 women of the international movement La Via Campesina, in a protest against eucalyptus monocultures maintained by the Aracruz cellulose industry, a highly polemicized event.[85] The conceptual and organizational changes in Brazilian civil society, as well as these questions shall be the focus of the next section.

5. AFTER TRANSITION: THE EMERGENCE OF CITIZENSHIP AS THE NEW KEY CONCEPT

Nada será como antes.

Regina Novaes[86]

In her concise exploration of civil society's protagonism, *O protagonismo da sociedade civil: movimentos sociais,* Maria da Glória Gohn expressed a certain perplexity and frustration at the considerable changes civil society has undergone since it became an important social actor in the later 1970s. While she values the efficiency and the professionalism of many NGOs today, she also articulates the disappointment at their apparent pragmatism, which seems to have given up any major "project." Thus, she concludes that

> something more is needed to oppose the model which is being implemented in the country; it is required that the NGOs' actions have links [. . .] with all the organized groups that have constructed the hard and difficult transition from the military regime to democracy, with all those who fought for social rights in the country.[87]

Somewhat on the other side of the spectrum, José de Souza Martins, an expert on the politics of land and former defender—now biting critic—of the landless workers' movement, writing towards the end of president Cardoso's second mandate, affirms that the State had been more agile than civil

83. Campos, *Teatro, Templo e Mercado.*

84. Cf. Costa, "Atores da sociedade civil e participação política"; Birle, "Zivilgesellschaft in Südamerika."

85. http://www1.folha.uol.com.br/folha/brasil/ult96u76373.shtml (accessed on 2/19/2009)

86. Social scientist Novaes, a collaborator of the Institute for the Study of Religion (*Instituto de Estudos da Religião—*ISER) drew this conclusion in 1989 following an in-depth evaluation of the *pastoral popular* which she developed on the request of its leaders; apud Doimo, *A vez e a voz do popular,* 202 and 239.

87. Gohn, *O protagonismo da sociedade civil,* 106

society in adapting to the new historical circumstances; in regard to social movements, however, he says that "their ideological references correspond neither to the historical circumstances nor to the possibilities of transformative intervention that are opened within it."[88] Moreover, "social movements often became aggressive, authoritarian and intolerant organizations, with their own bureaucracies, hindering the emergence of new and authentic social movements."[89] In his view, this leads to a situation of anomy, to "[outdated] practices worthy of the time of the dictatorship, namely, destabilizing the government, precipitating institutional crises, and questioning its legitimacy," linked with a "notorious messianism"[90] and a strong dichotomy between good and evil.

These two positions, the frustration with "pragmatism" on the one hand and the criticism of "ideologies" on the other, can serve as markers of an increasingly controversial debate within civil society as to what it is, what it should seek, and how it should act. This has been the case especially since the 1990s: not only was transition complete, but real socialism fell with the Berlin wall, the Sandinista government fell in Nicaragua, and Lula lost the 1989 elections.[91] The "project" many in civil society had fought for, which for most was some kind of socialism, and in which it was supported by some sectors of the churches and church-related organizations, was profoundly questioned.

Fourteen years later, when a much more moderate Lula and PT won the elections, it seemed that what had been civil society in the role of opposition had now become the government. Although many organizations and movements hastened to affirm that, even with "their" president in place, they would continue to watch the government critically and, if necessary, resume their actions to press the government on their issues, there was a kind of truce at the beginning. Expectations on all sides were high, but it was civil society that became most critical of the government it had helped to bring to power. Conversely, praise came from where it was least expected (and, by some, most hated): entrepreneurs, bankers, the U.S., and even the International Monetary Fund and World Economic Forum. These had no problem in turning their pre-election alarms into applause for the president, once in office. Then U.S.-president George W. Bush quickly dropped the idea that Lula would be part of an "axis of evil" together with Venezuela and Cuba. Civil society, however, seemed stunned. Pressure soon resumed, and the debate on what kind of cooperation with the government should be promoted was as hot as ever. An extreme event showed that the line between legitimate civil demonstrations and anti-democratic violence was thin.

A group of 700 members of the the Movement of the Landless' Liberation (*Movimento da Libertação dos Sem Terra*—MLST), a radical breakout from the MST, invaded the Chamber of Deputies on June 6, 2006, in order to bring forward their claims in a drawing room adjacent to the Chamber's plenary. Official and MLST sources do not agree on what triggered the following act, whether it was premeditated or a consequence of the resistance with which their entry was met by security, but in any case members of MLST carried out an unexpected and unacceptable raid of destruction, all well documented on videotape. Ironically, the Chamber's president at the time was Aldo Rebelo, of Brazil's Communist Party (PCdoB), who refused to see them and provided security

88. Martins, "Changes in the Relationship between Society and the State," 73.

89. Ibid., 79.

90. Ibid., 84.

91. On the international importance and impact of the 1989 events as a "turning point in the history of Christianity" see now Koschorke, *Falling Walls*, which includes five texts on Latin America, namely Brazil and Liberation Theology.

measures to detain the invaders. The event came as a shock both to social movements and society at large, and damaged the former's image considerably.[92]

Not surprisingly, there is a continuous debate as to whether Lula and the dominating faction in the PT are still to be considered as the legitimate political representatives of civil society, or whether another political project had to be put in place. The far left of the party indeed founded a new party, the "Party for Socialism and Freedom" (Partido Socialismo e Liberdade, P-Sol), whose prominent leader Heloisa Helena, a former senator from Alagoas, ran for the presidency in 2006 and collected a respectable 6.9 percent of valid votes (over 6.5 million voters), as she came in third after Lula (48.6 percent) and Geraldo Alckmin (PSDB, 41.6 percent) in the first round.[93] Still, it was clear that society as a whole and even large parts of civil society preferred the moderate and economy-friendly, but government-capable PT to the radical left, which had no chance of winning. One of the continuous aporias in civil society and parties related to it is, then, either to maintain a radical posture and remaining in opposition, or head for the government by compromise and negotiation. The former might be more faithful to a "project" and avoid being coopted by the forces in power, but is bound to have very limited effect, while the latter can certainly be very effective, but might drown in political business and lose sight of any proper "project." It becomes evident in this conflict that civil society, as defined above, would lose its non-State, representative, and intermediate character if it were to simply serve as a prolonged arm of "its" government. It would be equally disastrous if the president saw himself as civil society's (or at least some of its sectors') mouthpiece and forgot that he was elected to be the president of a constitutional State—who should hear civil society, but not be steered by it.

One of the crucial questions is precisely the degree of cooperation with the State. Undeniably, opportunities for such intervention are much wider today than they were twenty years ago. A good number of Councils have been created to oversee the implementation of specific policies and their respective legislation (e.g. children and youth, social assistance, food security), with a strong participation of civil society. A good number of NGOs receive money today from the government (federal, state, or municipal) on mandates to implement government policies, and institutions of civil society are sought for assistance with programs like "No Hunger" (Fome Zero), as they enjoy a high degree of trust among the people and reach many of them more easily than the State. According to law number 9,790, of March 23, 1999, NGOs can qualify as "Organizations of Civil Society of Public Interest,"[94] provided they are non-profit organizations and pursue activities in the area of social assistance, culture, (free) education, (free) healthcare, food security, protection of the environment, voluntary engagement, combating poverty, experimentation in alternative systems of production and commerce, rights (including their expansion in the construction of new rights), studies and research into the development of alternative technologies or on the other areas indicated above, and "the promotion of ethics, peace, citizenship, human rights, democracy and other universal values" (Art. 3, XI). Religious organizations are explicitly excluded from qualifying as an OSCIP (Art. 2, III). This does, however, not apply to church-founded NGOs. In any case, it shows how churches at the same time are and are not counted among civil society: legally, they can participate in civil society through specific, legally autonomous organizations, namely in the field

92. One of the first notices is to be found in http://www1.folha.uol.com.br/fsp/brasil/ fc0706200602.htm (accessed on 4/17/2008); many more followed.

93. Data according to http://www.tse.gov.br (accessed on 2/14/2007)

94. Organizações da Sociedade Civil de Interesse Público, OSCIPs. cf. Paes, *Fundações, Associações e Entidades de Interesse Social*, 590–637.

of social assistance and education, which many churches have indeed founded; but not as churches with their—more narrowly—religious activities of worship, evangelization, and the like.

Money from outside is also coming in, including from State or transnational sources (like the European Union). According to Brazilian sources cited by Hochstetler,[95] in the mid-1990s, nearly 5,500 Brazilian NGOs received USD 400 million annually from international agencies, and were controlling USD 1.2 billion (1996) from Brazilian government ministries and international banks. While this is positive in principle, it lays bare the lack of a tradition and practice of national fundraising to access private sources and makes NGOs nearly totally dependent on government and international sources. This, of course, raises questions about the degree to which these flows of money influence (and indeed alter) the programmatic work of those organizations. To handle such enormous amounts and the projects they fund, professional application, planning, monitoring, and reporting is needed. They are usually centered on concrete, regionalized, time-restricted projects, making it virtually impossible to obtain support for long-term processes of social movements with a low degree of organization and professionalism. Thus, important spaces of open-ended formation, dialogue and experiment are being lost, and finding and keeping specialized personnel at modest salaries is not an easy task.

An interesting example of a rather unusual cooperation was the enhancement of "patient citizenship" through "pharmaceutical governance," providing antiretroviral treatment to AIDS patients free of cost. Anthropologist João Biehl underlines that this became possible "through an inventive combination of activist forces and the interests of a reforming state, transnational organizations, and the pharmaceutical industry—all in a context of deeply entrenched inequality."[96]

On the conceptual level, the key concept has shifted from "democracy" to "extending citizenship,"[97] from "civil society" to "citizenship,"[98] from "autonomy" to "citizenship"[99] and from "opposition to the military" to "citizenship" as a "master frame."[100] As is to be expected, this new term is again a field rather than a clear-cut concept, and how it is to be understood differs as much as the diversity in civil society goes. It is usually connected to the language of "exclusion" and "inclusion," in which ("full") citizenship is expected to expand inclusion gradually to all citizens. Such inclusion is, however, not easy, not even among the movements and organizations of civil society themselves:

> Nearly all use the language, but some are more included than others. On the other hand, social movements find those limits to their commonality precisely because they are trying to stretch across social divides that are not often bridged in Brazil except through more hierarchical relations. [. . .] In the 'social apartheid' that characterizes Brazil, the efforts social movements make to share and extend citizenship do make them, perhaps, incubators of new social and political relations.[101]

Terminology tells much: Gohn[102] distinguishes between NGOs of the third sector—viewed very critically—and "citizen" NGOs—which fare better—and finally "militants properly speaking"

95. Hochstetler, "Democratizing Pressures from Below?" 179.
96. Biehl, "Pharmaceutical Governance," 207.
97. Hagopian, "Politics in Brazil," 538.
98. Costa, *As cores de Ercília.*
99. Gohn, *O protagonismo da sociedade civil.*
100. Hochstetler, "Democratizing Pressures from Below?"
101. Hochstetler, "Democratizing Pressures from Below?" 169.
102. Gohn, *O protagonismo da sociedade civil,* 83.

(*militantes*), i.e., persons engaged in social movements who strive towards a greater transformation. Today, however, all do use the terminology of citizenship in one way or another. I shall try to explore its meaning and function in the following chapter (IC). But it is necessary to add that this does not mean that the concept of civil society has totally lost its use and meaning. Costa[103] affirms it as continuously important as a "specific field of social relations characterized rather by solidarity than by competition." The two concepts are not synonymous, although they are related as civil society, with its organizations and movements that mediate between the established public authorities and the population or specific sectors of it, strives to foster citizenship. Rather than substituting the concept altogether, we could say that the utopian, visionary element has moved from "civil society" to "citizenship." Civil society is recognized to exist; citizenship is seen to be at least partially absent and still to be conquered.

103. Costa, *As cores de Ercília*, 61.

C. The Concept of Citizenship in the Brazilian Context

A Constituição empenha-se em tornar o homem cidadão. Entretanto, só é cidadão quem recebe salário adequado e justo. Só é cidadão quem pode ler e escrever, tem casa, acesso a hospitais, médicos e lazer.

Ulysses Guimarães[1]

Sobald der öffentliche Dienst aufhört, die Hauptsorge der Bürger zu sein und sie lieber mit ihrer Geldbörse als mit ihrer Person dienen, steht der Staat bereits vor seinem Ruin.

Jean-Jacques Rousseau[2]

As stated in the previous chapter, citizenship (*cidadania*) has become the new key concept for democracy in Brazil. In this perspective, all are considered—and are expected to consider themselves—citizens, can (and should) effectively claim and work on expanding their *rights*, enjoy the freedom given by them and perform their *duties* with responsibility, although it has to be said that the latter aspect has been less central than the former. Civil society has, increasingly since the time of "decompression" and "opening," taken on the role of articulating and claiming citizenship on behalf of those who are considered to be deprived of "full" citizenship. Both are, thus, complementary concepts and include the really existing citizens, organizing themselves to give shape to their (and others') citizenship. Civil society, as Fernandes put it, is the "top of an iceberg which sustains itself above the beliefs and deep practices encountered among Latin Americans."[3] He uses the expression to indicate that it is in danger of becoming an abstract idea, but at the same time it is used to signal the most visible space for working and reworking the concept and molding it into concrete claims and actions. It provides, thus, a prominent mediating space between the citizens and the State, different from the economy and, to some extent, from the wider field of voluntary, non-profit and non-state organizations (above, IB1).[4] Citizenship is a legal status and, moreover, a "socio-political identity."[5] It includes not only rights and duties, but also civic virtues, an attitude

1. "The Constitution strives to make Man [sic] a citizen. However, only he who receives an adequate and just salary is a citizen. Only he who knows how to read and write, has a house, access to hospitals, doctors and leisure is a citizen," in Weffort, "Brasil: condenado a modernização," 188. Guimarães (1916–1992), an eminent politician, was president of the Constituent Assembly from 1987 to 1988 and had an important hand in the drafting process of what he called the "citizen constitution," as which it has been known ever since.

2. Rousseau, "Vom Gesellschaftsvertrag," 157 (III/15); cf. Benevides, "Cidadania e democracia," 6.

3. Fernandes, *Privado porém público*, 106.

4. Cf. Vieira, *Os argonautas da cidadania*, 36f.

5. Heater, *A Brief History of Citizenship*, 1.

on the part of the citizen towards his status and the relationship to others and to the State implied in it.[6] Civil society is, to some degree, the institutionalized expression of citizens' struggle to give shape and effectiveness to citizenship, and its presence is a sign of democratic, active, participatory citizenship far beyond voting, which it seeks in turn to encourage.

As indicated, "citizenship" denotes a conceptual field rather than a clear-cut concept, due to the ever increasing plurality of subjects, issues, goals, and policies. The concept has been historically forged in the West, having as its initial references Athens and Rome[7] and passing through the 18th century revolutions in the United States and France. From there, the liberal notion of citizenship has had its bearing on the Imperial Constitution of independent Brazil, and its further constitutional history.[8] Another matter is how it came to be applied and how it has worked (or not) within Brazil, given its specific multicultural and socially disparate context. Immigrants were called into the country not least to safeguard the white, dominant population against a possible uprising of the slaves brought over from Africa, then already in the majority.[9] But some of them were brought to replace the slaves, and there were restrictions in their citizenship, especially if they were Protestant (see below, IID1). Indigenous peoples had been gaining a proper status throughout the 20th century, culminating in the 1988 Constitution when they emerged from State tutelage into equal citizenship with a particular right to difference. Racism against black people has finally led to affirmative action in the early 21st century. These three examples show from the outset that it is impossible to restrict citizenship to an issue of passport and Brazilian nationality.

The issue of nationality is a difficult one in Brazil. What is it that characterizes the nation? Cultural studies like those promoted by the Indian Homi Bhabha have shown that nations are a construct, promoted both by national discourses reinforcing the common origin and essentials that tie the "compatriots" together and the constant reinterpretation of national symbols.[10] For a long time in Brazil it had been clear that speaking Portuguese and being Catholic were all that

6. This has been precisely the focus of a renewed debate on citizenship in the West since the 1990s (cf. Kymlicka and Norman, *Citizenship in Diverse Societies*, 1ff.). Rather than analyzing institutions, this new debate is looking to the people's engagement, stating the importance of civic virtues and citizen's attitudes, which forms a modern democracy's "social capital" (Putnam, *Making Democracy Work*; *Bowling Alone*; *Democracies in Flux*). In the emerging theories of citizenship, citizen's duties (like tax-paying and military service) have also become prominent (Janoski, *Citizenship and Civil Society*). Another important strand of recent Western theories of citizenship has been on minority rights, which emerged in the same period but surprisingly independent. The volume edited by Kymlicka and Norman, *Citizenship in Diverse Societies*, seeks to connect them.

7. Pinsky and Pinsky, *História da Cidadania*; Heater, *A Brief History of Citizenship*.

8. According to Bonavides (*Curso de direito constitucional*, 361ff.), there are three constitutional periods to be distinguished in Brazil: The first, in the 19th century Empire, was influenced by the French and English constitutional models, including individual rights and a constitutional, parliamentary monarchy; the second, in the Republic, was informed by the U.S. model with its presidentialism and constitution, and the third, from the 1934 constitution onwards, shows traces of the Weimar constitution and later the *Grundgesetz* (with its long catalogue of fundamental rights), namely including dimensions of social welfare. See also Mendes, Coelho and Branco, *Curso de direito constituticional*, 151ff.

9. The history of slavery in Brazil, abolished formally only in 1888, and the mixing of black, indigenous and white people all along is, by the way, another chapter to be seen in its specific development, strikingly different from the U.S., starting with the absence of any policy of racial segregation. No law has since used race or ethnicity as a criterion for discrimination. Still, there are blatant social asymmetries, and there is racial discrimination based on the phenotype in people's perception, as recently shown once more by Almeida, *A cabeça do Brasileiro*, 215–34. On the issue of racism and the reacting anti-racism movements in Brazil see Costa, *Vom Nordatlantik zum "Black Atlantic."* For Costa, the so-called *pardos* (literally "grey," "dark," meaning "brownness") and other phenotypes resulting of the mixture of Europeans, Africans and Indigenous, are to be seen as an identity in its own right, to be distinguished also empirically and statistically, and not simply to be seen as a "false" identity (which supposedly should be either "white" or "black," *tertium non datur*).

10. See Homi Bhabha, ed., *Nation and Narration* (London: Routledge); cf. Costa, *As cores de Ercília*, 115.

was necessary to be Brazilian. According to Carvalho,[11] until 1930 there were "no people politically organized nor a consolidated national sentiment." Despite some national identity having been forged, for the first time, in the war against Paraguay (1865–1870), patriotic feeling was in the provinces, and a number of revolts during the 19th century were a reaction against central government, against the republic, even against vaccination campaigns in a defense of local and regional life, culture, and religion.[12]

The "myth of racial democracy," propagated based on the seminal study of Gilberto Freyre, *The Masters and the Slaves*, first published in 1933, presented Brazil as inherently syncretistic, mixing, in a process of *mestiçagem.*[13] This was a considerable advance in terms of earlier biological determinism,[14] in what Darcy Ribeiro called "the most important work of Brazilian culture," even if indicating that the book is pervaded by Freyre's "nostalgic vision of lord of the sugar-cane farm [*senhor do engenho*] and of slave" which he sentimentally expresses throughout the book.[15] It now seemed possible to construct one nation from so many diverse influences, namely the European (Portuguese), Indigenous, and African. One could also recall the 1920s with their so-called anthropophagic movement in the arts, which stressed mixture and syncretism, "swallowing" elements from all sides, and the fact that it was in this time that the syncretistic *Umbanda* came into being, considered by some the Brazilian religion *par excellence.*[16] However, the 19th (and 20th) century immigrants do not have a place in such a unifying vision. Getúlio Vargas, who translated this new notion of nation into politics, made efforts to press on the brazilianization (*abrasileiramento*) of the immigrants, namely the Germans and their descendants, of course directly confronting their own tendencies of linking up to Nazism.[17] Consequently, the use of the German language was forbidden in schools and, generally, in the public. Since, a smoother assimilation has occurred, while at the same time a new ethnic consciousness has taken root, visible for instance in the belated (1984) introduction of an *Oktoberfest* in Blumenau and subsequently in other towns of German immigration. This is true even if there are, of course, strong economic interests in such an event prone to—and in fact effective in—attracting tourists from other Brazilian regions. Brazil is today more consciously multi-cultural and multi-ethnic, namely, in terms of indigenous and African Brazilian rights.[18] It is today clearer that despite a general consciousness to be Brazilian, there are social, racial, ethnic, and cultural differences and asymmetries among Brazilian citizens. An appropriate

11. Carvalho, *Cidadania no Brasil*, 83.

12. While Rio de Janeiro tried to introduce sanitary measures, houses were destroyed and the population expelled, beggars and dogs prohibited on the streets, and it was forbidden to spit on the street or on cars. Vaccination against pox was made compulsory. It was applied into the upper arm, but news spread that doctors would apply the injection into the hip or the buttocks, which mobilized the men who did not want to have their wives' and daughters' intimate parts being touched by strangers. The following uprising shows that people did have a sense of their rights having to be protected, and that the State had to observe limits in infringing on their privacy; Carvalho, *Cidadania no Brasil*, 73–75.

13. Stephan Zweig (*Brasilien*) is among those who "bought" this new image and wrote, quite enthusiastically about this "Land der Zukunft": "Während in unserer alten Welt mehr als je der Irrwitz vorherrscht, Menschen 'rassisch rein' aufzüchten zu wollen wie Rennpferde oder Hunde, beruht die brasilianische Nation seit Jahrhunderten einzig auf dem Prinzip der freien und ungehemmten Durchmischung, der völligen Gleichstellung von Schwarz und Weiss und Braun und Gelb" (ibid., 13).

14. Cf. Costa, *Vom Nordatlantik zum "Black Atlantic,"* 177-222.

15. In Freyre, *Casa grande e senzala*, 11, 25.

16. Cf. below, IIB1.

17. Cf. below, IID1.

18. Cf. Costa, *As cores de Ercília*, 115–129; *Vom Nordatlantik zum "Black Atlantic,"* 145–176.

equilibrium between equality and difference is evidently necessary and becoming a central issue for the debate on citizenship, in Brazil as, today, globally.

What does citizenship mean beyond the formal attribution by law to those duly registered? Although mentioning the origins and some definitions of the term, I shall not try to impose a clear concept on a diffuse field, nor present a unified theory of citizenship, but rather explore dimensions that, based on my perception of the contemporary Brazilian context and pertinent literature, seem useful for the debate at the interfaces of State, civil society, and the churches. While it can be most clearly defined in legal terms, citizenship cannot be reduced to its legal and especially constitutional dimensions. Still, I consider these latter aspects fundamental to the concept, without which citizenship is prone to become a balloon that flies up high, leaving reality far below. In my perception, this is not always being taken into account sufficiently by civil society and, even less so, by its supposedly most obvious partner, the Theology of Liberation (see below, ID).

Initially, I shall describe the origins and development of the concept as seen, primarily, in Brazilian contemporary literature on the issue, relating citizenship to the concepts of democracy and public space (1.). Then, I shall explore theories of citizenship in Brazil (2.), followed by an analysis of citizenship in its constitutional implications (3.).

1. CITIZENSHIP, DEMOCRACY AND PUBLIC SPACE

As practiced throughout this study, in what follows I shall privilege Brazilian sources, while maintaining contact with the wider debate that they in fact widely reflect. The literature on both ends is enormous, and while I cannot and do not claim to be exhaustive, I still hope to catch the main issues and positions as far as they are relevant for this study. In the case of citizenship, when it comes to conceptualization, it is significant that even recent Brazilian works[19] largely rely on secondary sources, Brazilian or foreign.[20] While recognizing the Western, namely modern origin of the term, it is seen to be useful for the Brazilian context, although with necessary adaptations especially in regard to culture or multiculturalism.[21] Given that even in the West the concept is not univocal, a "unitary theory of citizenship is inappropriate."[22] Furthermore, here and there new and specific issues have come up through the black and women's movements, pacifist and ecological concerns and, more recently, in the struggle for rights of sexual orientation. As the concrete reality reshapes the concept, many authors seem to prefer developing it "alongside" their text, exploring its theoretical and empirical dimensions, rather than defining it as a concept in a specific paragraph or chapter.[23]

19. Vieira, *Os argonautas da cidadania*; Gohn, *O protagonismo da sociedade civil*.

20. Janoski, *Citizenship and Civil Society*; Pinsky and Pinsky, *História da Cidadania*.

21. Avritzer and Domingues, *Teoria social e modernidade no Brasil*; Avritzer, *Democracy and the Public Space*.

22. Turner, *Citizenship and Social Theory*, 11. Citing examples beyond it (like Argentina and South Africa), but focusing on Europe and the U.S., Heater, *A Brief History of Citizenship*, 140–43 names four basic dilemmas of citizenship: (1) The balance between duties and rights; (2) compatibility between civil/political and social citizenship; (3) the "most beneficial mix of participation in and abstinence from public affairs" (ibid., 142); and (4) the paradox of a heightened interest in citizenship and its apparent conceptual disintegration. He further mentions the increased consciousness of multiple identities and of globalization. How to relate multiple identities, belongings, loyalties? As indicated, this is a question crucial also to the Brazil context.

23. Cf. for instance Castro, *Por uma fé cidadã*; Pinsky and Pinsky, *História da Cidadania*, start with T.H. Marshall's definition (see below, IC1a), but want to show its diverse and changing definitions and dimensions precisely through a historical approach. Herkenhoff, *Direito e Cidadania*, and, as a resource for the 1988 Constituent Assembly and the discussion around it, Quirino and Montes, *Constituiçoes brasileiras e cidadania*, have been written for a wider public and therefore avoid lengthy conceptual explorations; they give a working definition and then elucidate it through the

In what follows, I shall explore the concept of citizenship in its relationship to two key concepts to which is related, i.e. the political system it belongs to: democracy (a) and the *locus* where debate on its implications, practices, and ways of expansion are most visible, apart from the legal democratic institutions: public space (b).

a) Citizenship and Democracy

The most comprehensive Brazilian resource on the origin and the development of the concept of citizenship is the "History of Citizenship" (*História da cidadania*), edited by historians Jaime and Carla Pinsky.[24] It starts off with the coming to the fore of "ethical monotheism" in national Israel, as claimed by the prophets, via the different forms and phases of city-states in Greece and the rise of the Roman Empire, the first Christian communities and the city-states in Italy that gave rise to the renaissance, which are all taken as the "pre-history of citizenship" or as citizenship *avant la lettre*. The "foundations of citizenship" are then seen in the English Revolution in the 17th century, and the American and French revolutions in the 18th century. The part on "the development of citizenship" explores the contribution of socialism, social rights, women's rights, national self-determination, minority rights, Amnesty International, and ecological concerns, before going on to analyze aspects of "citizenship in [contemporary] Brazil," as experienced by indigenous, black people, workers, women, and voters, the environment and the new possibilities for the exercise of citizenship in the third sector. It thus provides a panoramic view of the concept of citizenship, both as it developed from Antiquity to this day, and in Brazilian reality.[25] While it states that there is a tendency towards constant expansion of citizenship and especially its rights, it should not be seen as a "unique, deterministic and necessary sequence"[26] that would be universally valid. There are variations in time and space.

As in other authors, also in Pinsky and Pinsky it is clear that citizenship developed as a Western concept, with roots in the Mediterranean and its elaboration and expansion in modernity. There is no major introductory discussion of methodological questions as to the possibilities and limits of connecting historical to contemporary citizenship, which is perhaps wisely left to the individual authors to comment upon. In any case, it is clear that the addressees of the book are contemporary readers who are to realize that "the advances of citizenship, if they have to do with the country's richness and indeed the distribution of riches, also depend on the struggle and claims, the concrete action of individuals." Thus, the book "wants to participate in the discussion about public and private policies which can affect each one of us, in their quality as engaged citizens."[27] It is precisely this search for the historical foundations of today's Brazilian citizenship that makes the book interesting

---

successive Brazilian Constitutions. Zeron, "A cidadania em Florença e Salamanca," 97, points out that in the standard work *Dictionary of Politics*, edited by Norberto Bobbio, Nicola Matteucci and Gianfranco Pasquino, there is no specific entry for citizenship, and according to Janoski (*Citizenship and Civil Society*, 8), this is true for another six major social science surveys or dictionaries.

24. Most of its authors, mainly historians but also experts of other areas like anthropology, law, sociology, and theology, teach at the renowned University of São Paulo (*Universidade de São Paulo*—USP) or have degrees from there. The USP was founded in 1934 and figures today among the 100 most eminent universities in the world and is considered the first ranking in Brazil; cf. http://www.usp.br (accessed on 2/26/2007). The editors stress that such a comprehensive work was not only missing in Brazil, but even worldwide: Pinsky and Pinsky, *História da Cidadania*, 12. A year later, Heater, *A Brief History of Citizenship* offered at least a "brief" history of citizenship, stating that this was an innovation.

25. The reality was further described in a follow-up volume called "Practices of Citizenship," Pinsky, *Práticas da cidadania*.

26. Pinsky and Pinsky, *História da Cidadania*, 10.

27. Pinsky and Pinsky, *História da Cidadania*, 13.

for the purpose of this study. I shall thus try to show the main aspects and turning points in the development of citizenship as presented, with occasional comments, reflections, and references to further literature.

The story told along the book is one of an ever-expanding participation of all sectors of society in molding their own destiny. In a rather short and less substantiated article than most others in the book, Pinsky highlights "ethical monotheism" and the prophetic critique against the monarchy and its compulsory temple cult. Amos and Isaiah broke, he says, "with ritualism and with the small national god"; they "give up the god of the temple, of any temple, and create the god of citizenship."[28] As to Antiquity's city-states, Guarinello takes as a lesson—and in contrast to the somewhat amorphous citizenship in the Roman Empire—that "there is only effective citizenship in the midst of a concrete community, which can be defined in different manners, but which is always a privileged space for collective action and for the construction of projects for the future."[29] In the Roman context, among other aspects, Funari emphasizes that ". . .there was a public opinion which accepted women, freedmen and poor as supposed authors of public discourse," which can be established not least by the fact that they were criticized by Cicero as "simple and obscure men" [*humiles et obscuri homines*, Cicero, Diu. 1,40,88].[30] Identifying an astonishingly strong coincidence between Roman and modern citizenship, as life was *de facto* less controlled by aristocracy than generally assumed and magistrates had to seek popular support, Funari concludes that "the *forum* can be considered the major symbol of a political system with strong participation of citizenship," stressing also Roman Law as written and thus public law, handed down to us through the *Codex Iustinianus*. Still, formal citizenship was restricted, and thus to be a *civis* or not altered one's treatment considerably. A well known example of this is Paul's insistence on his Roman citizenship as described in the Book of Acts.[31]

We can say, then, that in the Mediterranean city-states, particularly far-reaching in Athens, and then in Rome, some forms of public opinion and participation in decision-making are visible, although they remain restricted in a society stratified on hereditary and property grounds, where status was all and could be changed only within limits and invariably dependent on decisions by the rulers, even if public pressure could make a difference (like in the plebeians' march out of Rome in 494 BC). Social critique had been present in Israel, as especially clear in the prophets, who could criticize the rulers by referring to God's word in a way that was not possible for its great and powerful neighbor, Egypt.[32] A case in point is also Christianity, which through its practice of hospitality, diaconia, and inclusiveness especially for the lower strata of society, "won," according to Hoornaert "not by the preaching of its apostles or bishops, nor by the fearless testimony of his martyrs, nor by the sanctity of its heroes, nor by the virtues or the miracles of its saints [. . .] but by a persistent and courageous activity at the basis of the social and political edifice of society."[33] At least within the communities *status* could be renounced and the commandment of love provided a degree of equality among the first congregations and remained preserved in Scripture.[34] Important not only for Europe, but for Iberian America in the time of the *conquista*, Francisco de Vitória (ca.

28. Pinsky, "Os profetas sociais e o Deus da cidadania," 27.
29. Guarinello, "Cidades-estado na Antigüidade Clássica," 46.
30. Ibid., 69.
31. Acts 22-28; cf. Funari, "A cidadania entre os romanos," 65f.
32. Cf. Assmann, *Herrschaft und Heil*.
33. Hoornaert, "As comunidades cristãs dos primeiros séculos," 94.
34. Cf. Theissen, *Die Religion der ersten Christen*.

1480–1546) condemned power based on secular and religious rulers alike by referring to natural law as equal to all the peoples, already providing a ground for individual rights, as it is prior to social and political organization.[35]

There is a wide consensus that the most important turning-points are the cited revolutions of the 17th and 18th centuries, when those who were considered *subjects* of a ruler came to claim to be *citizens* who are not at the bottom, but at the basis of the State, which is now defined from, by, and for its citizens, and not vice versa. The Protestant Reformation, which is not given a specific chapter in the Pinskys' book but mentioned at various points,[36] had already established a direct relationship between God and the believer, thus fostering the individual's religious and social responsibility and providing a basis for criticizing human authority with the Bible as reference. It presupposed that the believing reader had the authority to correctly understand it, which meant effectively breaking the magisterium's monopoly.

Further important turning points were, as the book highlights, not so much the Puritan Revolution as the Glorious Revolution of 1688, which sealed the end of absolutist monarchy and produced the *Bill of Rights* the following year. The State is no longer an "organic" given, as in Aristotle's conception, but a human construction, and instead of Hobbes' insistence on absolute power to protect human beings from each other, State power indeed has to be limited and civil rights established against it, based on Locke's arguments. The "age of rights"[37] began, which Locke understood as the preservation of "property," more precisely life, liberty, and goods.[38] In North America, the *Virginia Bill of Rights* and the *Declaration of Independence* (both in 1776) as well as the Constitution of 1787 and the ten amendments of 1791 constituted the body of principles valid till this day and model to many other States, including Brazil. According to the Declaration of Independence "all men [sic] are created equal" and were "endowed by their Creator with certain unalienable Rights," namely "Life, Liberty and the pursuit of Happiness." Governments are instituted "to secure these rights" and derive "their just powers from the consent of the governed."[39]

While acknowledging this, Karnal rightly insists that the direct line from the Pilgrim Fathers to Independence and today's U.S. democracy is a powerful construction, as it leaves out both the dark sides of history and important earlier attempts at installing a "charismatic and democratic power" against constituted authorities, namely governor Sir William Berkeley, as was the case of Nathaniel Bacon in Virginia, in 1676. Bacon's arguments resemble in many aspects the Declaration of Independence 100 years later, and indeed insisted in including poor whites in the political system, while, however, despising indigenous communities.[40] Still, Karnal sees Puritanism and a specific reading of colonial history as bases for the freedom tradition, together with Locke's *Second Treatise of Government* and Thomas Paine's widespread pamphlet on *Common Sense* (January 1776). But the story did not stop there, and the expansion of the franchise, the diffusion of media, the amplification of public education and, not least, the flourishing of "popular Protestant groups, with more emotive appeals and worship services considered 'very noisy' by the conservative elite"[41]—in a reference that resounds well with present-day religious diversity in Brazil—were to follow. Karnal

35. Zeron, "A cidadania em Florença e Salamanca", 106–110.

36. E.g., Karnal, "Estados Unidos, liberdade e cidadania,"140.

37. Bobbio, *A era dos direitos*.

38. Mondaini, " O respeito aos direitos dos indivíduos."

39. Text as reproduced in http://www.ushistory.org/declaration/document (accessed on 2/27/2007).

40. Karnal, "Estados Unidos, liberdade e cidadania," 137f.

41. Ibid., 147.

also highlights the equilibrium noted by Tocqueville between individualism and life in society, which somehow could be solved, as shown by the fact that "in nearly 230 years of independent life, the USA never suffered a *coup d'état* or a social convulsion of such an order that it implied a change in the political structure itself."[42] The paradox of citizenship Karnal identifies, then, is the contradiction between the domestic expansion of rights and the "self-confirmatory" democracy in the U.S. that made a "fusion between the signified and the signifier," universalizing it at the expense of other forms of democracy outside, where he calls it "excluding for many."[43]

In his short text on the French Revolution of 1789, Odalia is keen to remember the importance of science and reason, where empirical induction became the partner of deductive reason. The industrial revolution made it possible "to dream of a new type of society, in which misery, poverty, illiteracy and illness could be reduced and the project of a happy society could be thought and imagined not as an utopia, but as a reality to be constructed."[44] If indeed all are born equal, as natural law has it, "it is necessary to concretize and make public this possibility."[45] The French revolution did proclaim and concretize it through the three key terms of "liberty, equality and fraternity," translated into rights in the "Universal Declaration of the Rights of Man [sic] and the Citizen," namely "freedom, property, security and resistance against oppression."[46] Apart from the rights of freedom of movement, opinion, religion and the binding of all penalty to the prior existence of a law, and the institution of a "public force" with the separation of powers, installed for the benefit of all, levying a common contribution for its expenses and properly accounting for it, the 17th article emphasizes the right to property as an "inviolable and sacred right." As Odalia emphasizes, the law is a norm to be followed by all and must not be disobeyed, a "quite considerable [*ponderável*] restriction."[47]

Of course, the kind of citizenship conquered by these revolutions was, in the first place, a bourgeois revolution, with liberal rights and a restriction of the State's influence over people's lives, but with property as an important element, and anyway far from being all inclusive, as the poor, black people, strangers, and women continued to be deprived of political participation.[48] The social aspects and worker's concerns are highlighted by Leandro Konder in his article on socialism, some of whose main claims can be summed up in the 1891 Erfurt program, which called for "universal franchise; direct elections on national, state and municipal levels; popular participation in the decisions of foreign policy; democratization of the judicial apparatus (election of judges); free and compulsory basic education for all; freedom of expression and organization; abolition of the death penalty; a tax on the riches' income; laws of workers' protection; free medical assistance for the population, including expenses with births and funerals; and the revocation of all legal dispositions

42. Ibid., 150.

43. Ibid., 153.

44. Odalia, "Revolução francesa," 160.

45. Ibid., 162.

46. *Déclaration des droits de l'Homme et du citoyen* of August 26, 1789, 2nd article, see http://www.assemblee-nationale.fr/histoire/dudh/1789.asp (accessed on 10/19/2011).

47. Odalia, "Revolução francesa," 167.

48. See Olympe de Gouges' (Pseudonym of Marie Gouze, 1748–1793) "Declaration of the Rights of Woman and the [female] Citizen" (*Déclaration des Droits de la Femme et de la Citoyenne*). This text was intended to be adopted in complementation of the Declaration of the Rights of Man and the Citizen, but did not achieve this goal. Its 10th article stated that "woman has the right to mount the scaffold; she should equally have the right to mount the tribune." While the latter was not implemented, de Gouges herself suffered the fate of the former as she was put to death by the guillotine in 1793 after strongly criticizing the Jacobin reign of terror. De Gouges had also written theatre plays in favor of the abolition of slavery; cf. Heater, *A Brief History of Citizenship*, 123f.

which result in discrimination against women."[49] Paul Singer reviews the coming to the fore of social rights in his text on "Citizenship for All."[50] Such rights, according to Singer, are directed towards the workers, both those with a salary (as employees or autonomous workers) and those unemployed. He recalls the rise of the workers' movements along with the industrial revolution, and the gradual recognition of their rights in the revolutions and their following constitutions. The French Constitution of 1793 stated in its 21st article that "the public aids are a sacred debt. Society owes subsistence to the unfortunate, be it by providing them with work, be it by guaranteeing the means of existence for those who do are not in a condition to work."[51] The main advances of social rights, however, came into place in the first half of the 20th century, not least following the social pressures of the two wars and the Great Depression between them. The founding of the International Labor Organization by the Versailles Treaty, in 1919, was a major step forward in this line. Singer highlights its 1944 Philadelphia Declaration, which affirmed: "Believing that experience has fully demonstrated the truth of the statement in the Constitution of the International Labour Organization that lasting peace can be established only if it is based on social justice, the Conference affirms that—(a) all human beings, irrespective of race, creed or sex, have the right to pursue both their material well-being and their spiritual development in conditions of freedom and dignity, of economic security and equal opportunity."[52] Singer takes this as perhaps the first international document that understands social rights as human rights on the same level with liberal rights. As we shall see (below, IC2), Brazil also introduced social rights in this period, even during the dictatorship of the *Estado Novo* (1937–45), and clearly in the post-transition 1988 constitution. For Singer, however, the welfare state envisioned by the constitution "is, today, nothing more than a stillborn in Brazil,"[53] given the adoption of neoliberal policies with president Collor and his followers. In any case, the initiative of the struggle for social rights that used to be the State's is now in the hands of "civil society itself which becomes the protagonist of the solution of the problems social rights wanted to prevent."[54] Further articles focus on women (Carla Bassanezi Pinsky and Joana Maria Pedro), political citizenship (Osvaldo Coggiola), minorities (Peter Demant), freedom of expression (Rodolfo Konder), and the environment (Wagner Costa Ribeiro). As these themes are taken up again in discussing specifically Brazilian citizenship, I shall not deal with them here.

Following this presentation of the history of citizenship, as perceived by the contributors to Pinsky and Pinsky,[55] it is plain that it is a history with advances and setbacks, but overall of important conquests upon which the following generations could build. What now of the specifically Brazilian situation? The fourth part of the book is dedicated to citizenship in Brazil, focusing on indigenous peoples, *quilombos*, workers, women, democracy (voting), environmental citizenship, and the third sector.

As M. Gomes shows in his chapter, indigenous rights were discussed throughout the centuries through prophets like Bartolomé de Las Casas (1474–1566), the Jesuits (with many ambiguities),

49. Konder, "Idéias que romperam fronteiras,"186.

50. Singer, "A cidadania para todos."

51. In ibid., 217.

52. *Declaration Concerning the Aims and Purpose of the International Labour Organization*, available at http://www.itcilo.it/english/actrav/telearn/global/ilo/law/phila.htm (accessed on 5/6/2007).

53. Singer, "A cidadania para todos," 252.

54. Ibid., 260.

55. Pinsky and Pinsky, *História da Cidadania*.

the pope's affirmation of their humanity, and extensive and controversial legal debates.[56] But it was in the Republic that their rights came to be recognized more thoroughly, not least through the insistence of positivist (following Comte) politicians. One of them was marshal Cândido Mariano da Silva Rondon (1865–1958) who headed the Service of Protection to the Indians (*Serviço de Proteção aos Índios*—SPI), founded in 1910, until his death. In 1967, the military regime extinguished the SPI and created the National Foundation of the *Índio* (*Fundação Nacional do Índio*—FUNAI). The 1988 Constitution sealed the new policy of recognition of their specific rights (e.g. to their own, original land) and overcame the acculturation policy adopted initially. While still counted as legally incapable (like women) in the Civil Code of 1916, the indigenous' assumedly inferior status has been revised since the 1934 Constitution. Nearly destroyed through imported illnesses, killings, and slavery since the arrival of the colonizers (the original indigenous population is estimated at around 5 million), indigenous peoples are now growing again at a pace of up to 6 percent per year and number over 400,000 in 218 peoples with 160 languages.

Of the 10 million (or more) Africans brought as slaves to the Americas between the 16th and 19th centuries, Brazil has received 40 percent.[57] Alongside indigenous slaves, they worked on the huge sugar cane plantations (*engenhos*) in the Brazilian Northeast. Fugitives created so-called *quilombos*, which in Bantu languages means "camp," but possibly also refers to the Kimbundu word for a ritual of initiation for warriors, including those from conquered regions. As Africans were invariably separated on arrival in Brazil in order to destroy their family, linguistic, and ethnic networks and to hinder their collaboration, the *quilombos* had to construct a community of Africans from various origins, as well as their descendants, which possibly included such a ritual.[58] They were economically quite successful, and one of them, the *Quilombo dos Palmares* in Pernambuco, resisted for over a hundred years, from 1585 to 1695. Till today, descendants of *quilombos* exist and make evident the ethnic component of the claims to land. One could add that they recall by their very existence that the economic, social, and cultural (and religious) inequalities and asymmetries were by no means ended through the law that formally abolished slavery in 1888.

The chapter written by Moraes on women shows a historical situation similar to other places: women were confined to the private space, the house, and subordinate to their fathers or husbands, without an independent legal personality.[59] In 1827, they were admitted into formal education, and in 1879 into higher education. In the eyes of society, women were divided into "pure" mothers and "dirty" prostitutes—*tertium non datur*. During the last fifty years, however, women have conquered many new rights, and especially a status compatible in many respects with men's: They are legally independent and have equal rights and responsibility with the family. Still, different from the majority of men, they continue to bear the double responsibility of being (co-)providers for the family and taking care of the children. According to a research carried out by the Perseu Abramo Foundation (linked to the PT), some 43 percent of women affirmed having suffered some kind of violence from men.[60] Women's suffrage was achieved in 1932, and both authoritarian regimes (of Vargas' and the military, respectively) saw women grouping together to press for amnesty. In view of the International Year of Woman, in 1975, they circulated and assembled signatures for a

56. Gomes, "Sonhando com a terra, construindo a cidadania."

57. Ibid., 448.

58. Ibid., 449.

59. Moraes, "Cidadania no feminino."

60. The punishment of sexual harassment became a law in 2001 (number 10,224). Possibilities for the State to interfere with domestic violence have been widened considerably through law number 11,340, of August 7, 2006.

Manifest of Brazilian Women for Amnesty, which stated that "We, Brazilian women [. . .] take up our responsibility as citizens in national politics. [. . .] the Nation [can] only fulfill its goal of peace if ample and general amnesty will be granted to all those who have been affected by the acts of exception."[61] There were, of course, also conservative movements, mainly defending religion and the family.

Other chapters deal with voting, an important conquest which had to overcome, among others, a deep (and at times fully justified) distrust among voters[62]; social rights (Tânia Regina de Luca), environmental democracy (Maurício Waldmann) and the third sector (Rubens Naves). These issues are being dealt with in other contexts of this study (IC2, IB) and thus are not presented here.

There are, if I see correctly, three main developments that are at the heart of today's democracy and citizenship, without presupposing that all of the necessary conditions are satisfactorily met today. Still, with all of its setbacks and problems, the world has certainly never been so widely democratic and inclusive of citizenship as today.

(1) The basis for public organization and government is turned upside down to attribute *sovereignty to the people* rather than the rulers, who are balanced by a representative legislative and an overseeing judicial power, and in all held accountable for their actions. A ruler's subjects have become citizens, and the State has become, to some extent, dependent on society (i.e., the totality of citizens), in a system that distinguishes between the two. Democracy has become the standard political system, and is seen as the most appropriate way of living together: what concerns all should be decided by all, even if guided by constitutions and laws that set boundaries to simple majority rule. More countries today practice a democratic form of government (even accounting for differences, such as direct versus representative, or parliamentary versus presidential) than autocratic-democratic or autocratic forms.[63]

(2) A number of characteristics are attributed to all human beings without distinction, and where there is distinction, it has to be justified by reasonable argument.[64] *Human rights*, based on the intrinsic dignity of all human beings, have become a normative concept for a set of constitutive principles and executive rules incorporated into national constitutions, based on the fundamental equality of all human beings, with only a limited number of privileges reserved to national citizens.[65] Protection of life, liberty, and property, for instance, are guaranteed to all. These rights and

61. Moraes, "Cidadania no feminino," 510.

62. One of the curiosities was the candidateship of "Cacareco," a rhino in São Paulo Zoo, which received nearly 100,000 votes in the 1959 elections for the municipal chamber. Cacareco had been launched by a journalist which said he felt "disappointed by the actions of the public men" (Canêdo, "Aprendendo a votar," 517).

63. In 2005, *Freedom House* counted 87 of a total of 191 countries as democratic (double 1 rating in civil and political rights, cf. above, IA2), 56 in the middle range and 48 at the bottom (not at all free, rank 7 in both categories); in Schmidt, "Demokratie (J)," 329.

64. The universality of such natural law in a "metaphorical, notional universal moral community" forms the κοσμοπολίτης with his double loyalty both to his particular "city" and to the "world city," as described by the Stoa (Heater, *A Brief History of Citizenship*, 38f.) and resurging today, of course passing through Kant's "perpetual peace." The relation between the two loyalties is, till today, an unresolved matter. Religious loyalty over against political loyalty has been at stake in Christianity since Jesus' famous dictum: "Give to the emperor the things that are the emperor's, and to God the things that are God's" (Mark 12.17 par.), passing through the *clausula Petri* in Acts 5.29, Augustin's *civitates* and Luther's *two kingdoms or regiments*, to name the most prominent. See on this part II and especially IIIA5.

65. In Western Europe today, the tendency is to at the same time expand such rights to people in a larger territory (the European Union), applying them to all nationals belonging to EU states, while restricting them for those coming from outside. Travelling and even migrating through Europe has become easier for those with European passports (and some on good bilateral terms with them, like the Swiss), it has become much more difficult for those who hold other nationalities. Brazilians are quite regularly being refused entry into the EU through Madrid Airport, even if their

principles, as we know them, have admittedly originated in a Western, modern setting, but interaction with the New World contributed early to their formulation, as the status of "Indians" had to be clarified, and as slavery became a matter of heated debate. Today, a globalized society has yet to come to terms with cultural differences and, thus, the universality and particularity of such rights and principles. The creation of new generations of rights, beginning with social and then cultural and even environmental rights, is a consequence of this ongoing debate.

(3) The *number of those entitled* to contribute to the political organization and management has been ever expanding to include the poor, women, black and indigenous people, illiterates, and other formerly excluded groups. This development implied changes in anthropological presuppositions, as the hitherto excluded were now held capable of understanding and contributing to the democratic processes. The principle of universal education has been an important factor here—a citizen has to be prepared to know, understand, reflect, and act on his rights and duties. Another necessary precondition is at least a minimum of economic conditions to meet the necessities in food, health, and clothing and, thus, to have time to accompany the democratic process. This constant expansion has brought in a new aspect, which is not entirely new, but has come to the fore through globalization and its accompanying processes of fragmentation, and has been accentuated through migratory movements: how to do justice both to the principle of equality and to the right to difference and multiculturalism, on a global as on State level.

All these aspects are relevant for democracy and for citizenship, and in retelling the history of citizenship, the history of democracy was retold. It is, therefore, time to distinguish and relate these two complementary concepts. *Democracy* is a system of government based on the power exercised (κράττειν) by the people (δῆμος). There is a long tradition of distrust in the people—beyond a circle restricted by criteria like birth and status, gender, education, profession, and wealth—as to their capacity and willingness to contribute in a positive way to their government, which would make them prone to manipulation, a notion prominent since Plato in a large part of democratic theories,[66] which made "democracy" nothing like univocally positive. This stands in striking contrast to the 20th century, especially the post-war period and even more so after the "third wave" of democratization, when democracy came to be widely recognized as the best and, indeed, only legitimate government. As Schmidt formulates,[67]

> to the great majority of philosophers, state scientists and politicians [principally up to the 20th century, but still existing in a good number of countries], democracy has been, for a long time, a particularly bad form of state, not rarely as a fickle 'mobocracy', at best as an order which could only be realized in the framework of smaller communities and—if at all—would only be acceptable if strongly mixed and, thus, tempered by elements of other state forms, namely monarchy, aristocracy and oligarchy.

Different from the embryonic democracy in Athens, where women, slaves, and foreigners were not considered part of the δῆμος and were, therefore, not entitled to vote in the Assembly or exercise any office, today "the people" would include all adult male and female nationals ("full citizens"), who are entitled to vote, hold office, pay taxes, and possibly do military or an equivalent service in return. While restricted in their political rights and duties, and usually exempt from

travel purpose is clearly transitory (such as participating in an academic congress). Even worse, immigration laws and deportation rules get ever more tight. All this leaves the impression that human, supposedly universal rights are, after all, not so universal.

66. Cf. Schmidt, "Demokratie (J)."

67. Ibid., 25.

military service, resident foreigners enjoy all other rights and are subject to all other duties, and might under specific circumstances become full citizens through naturalization.[68]

Abraham Lincoln's famous dictum in his 1863 Gettysburg address, stating that democracy is "government of the people, by the people and for the people"[69] still holds true as a starting point: The State, i.e., the political system with government and administration within a specific territory, serves a politically (not ethnically) defined society, its governors being elected by its members (*of* the people), the elected themselves being members of society (*by* the people) and their goal being to foster and maintain the well-being of all (*for* the people). Apart from participation, again as wide as possible, a commonly agreed constitution with a system of law depending on it is fundamental to democracy. A normative notion of the common good, although in principle changeable through the ages, cannot be taken for granted as emerging naturally from participation as such, as historical examples of disastrous politics carried out with popular support have clearly shown. *Vox populi vox dei* is a highly suspicious principle, and yet the population as a whole has to remain the origin and testing field for a democracy worth its name. Mechanisms are, thus, needed to ensure the smooth functioning of the rules of the game, as well as both enable and limit the process of defining and redefining these rules.

Inasmuch as the subjects of democracy, in a politically defined society, are the *citizens* (*cives*) of a State with their rights and duties over against the *societas civilis* or *civitas* (in Greek κοινωνὶα πολιτική or πόλις / πολιτέια), democracy and citizenship are direct corollaries.[70] It is, of course, possible to be the member of a political system that is not democratic, but for instance a monarchy, and thus be a citizen in a non- or only partially democratic system. A merely descriptive concept of citizenship would be able to fit here. But as the modern notion of citizenship began to define government in a normative way from "below," i.e., the citizens, it had sooner or later to arrive at some form of participative politics and, thus, democracy. In the debate that is in focus in the present study, it is in fact the debate on citizenship that informs the discourse on democracy as a political system, analyzing its principles and reality and seeking to deepen its constituency, ensure its efficiency, and foster the participation of as many persons as possible: citizenship is "the concrete expression of the exercise of democracy."[71] It is, so to speak, the "subjective side" of democracy, not as a psychological category, but to indicate that democracy refers to human beings who are, together with others, subjects of their collective organization. Democracy, thus, becomes evident not as an abstract system, but as a way of socio-political being, concrete in citizens who are part of it as they share rights and duties of a society constituted as State under laws and contribute to its wellbeing. The debate on citizenship is, thus, much more popularly accessible than the apparently abstract and theoretical discussion of democracy. This brings us to the *locus* of such discourse, which is best expressed through a notion of "public sphere" or "public space," whose prominent, but not exclusive actors are organizations of civil society (see above, IB3).

68. In Brazil, resident foreigners can apply relatively soon for naturalization. However, in a country that favors the *ius solis* over the *ius sanguinis*, while there must not be distinction between born and naturalized Brazilians in the law (Art. 12 §2 of the Constitution, Brasil, *Constituição da República Federativa do Brasil*), some offices are restricted to born Brazilians: President and vice-president of the Republic, president of the chamber of deputies, president of the senate, minister of the supreme federal court, diplomat and officer of the armed forces (Art. 12 §3).

69. In Schmidt, "Demokratie (J)," 22.

70. Etymologically and also historically, the citizen is the (free) inhabitant of a city, which from medieval times brought specific privileges with it (Turner, "Outline of a Theory of Citizenship," 203).

71. Pinsky and Pinsky, *História da Cidadania*, 10.

b) Citizenship and Public Space

The molding of democracy and citizenship as different from, but related to the work done by elected representative bodies and heads of state, brings us to another correlate concept: "Public space" or "public sphere." Like the German term *Öffentlichkeit*, the public (*publicus*) has a long tradition for instance in Roman Law, where it designated the law applicable to all as different from the relationships of citizens among themselves (*ius privatus*).[72] It is also etymologically linked to the people (*populus*) and indicates the *space of the public as different from the private*. The distinction between the public and the private, the πόλις and the οἶκος, has been common since Aristotle's *Politics*. In Brazil, Da Matta reflects this in his distinction between the "street" and the "house."[73] In any case, in Greek antiquity as well as in Brazilian contemporary society, these are not totally separable spheres, but interact in many ways, and the borders are fluid. It has been an achievement that the State can and does interfere in cases of domestic violence, turning such violence in the "private" space public, while still preserving "intimacy" not subject to rules made for and by the general public. It is, on the other hand, important that families debate and participate in politics and exercise their citizenship, while they should never act in public as if this were their home—a principle that, of course, applies primarily to politicians and other persons holding public office.

Public is also *opposed to "secret,"* which both points to legitimate rights to secrecy (i.e., of personal data, telephone conversations, letters, religious confessions, and medical consultations) and the right to publicity when it comes to acts that have a consequence for all and/or that constitute crime. As Kant stated in his *Perpetual Peace*: "All actions related to the right of others, whose maxim is incompatible with publicity, are illegitimate."[74] Publicity serves the interest of the public, which uses reason to verify whatever is at stake. Thus, for Kant, peace is possible only in a republic, where at least in principle all can be referred to the will of the (free) people. This will is not empirically grounded, but is an "idea of reason." Publicity is, thus, a "transcendental formal principle of constitutional legality [Rechtsstaatlichkeit] and politics," as the categorical imperative is for morality. The decisive feature is, according to Lienemann[75], "the unhindered, free use of reason, directed towards public knowledge of truth."

While this insistence on reason and its normativity was certainly a historical advance, it is problematic in its universalizing assumptions in view of cultural differences, and it also does not make clear—except for the principle of representation and, thus, republican institutions—where the *locus* of an effective participation of people in the molding of their own destiny would be. In not being empirical, but normative, Kant's rational principle seems safeguarded against a misled popular will, but in this supports the longstanding distrust of people's participation in politics.[76] While stressing that "public opinion" as such has to be differentiated from Kant's principle of publicity, Lienemann holds it necessary to verify the real public discourse: "The principles of legality

72. For the explications on "public" I am indebted to Lienemann, "Öffentlichkeit und bürgerliche Gesellschaft in der europäischen Tradition," especially 52–62.

73. Da Matta, *Carnivals, Rogues and Heroes*, *A Casa & A Rua*.

74. "Alle auf das Recht anderer Menschen bezogene Handlungen, deren Maxime sich nicht mit der Publizität verträgt, sind unrecht," Kant, "Zum Ewigen Frieden," 245. On this see also Huber, *Kirche und Öffentlichkeit*, 13–15.

75. Lienemann, "Öffentlichkeit und bürgerliche Gesellschaft," 66.

76. Furthermore, Kant himself held a racially differentiated view of human beings: "In den heißen Ländern reift der Mensch in allen Stücken früher, erreicht aber nicht die Vollkommenheit der temperierten Zonen. Die Menschheit ist in ihrer größten Vollkommenheit in der Race der Weißen. Die gelben Indianer haben schon ein geringes Talent. Die Neger sind weit tiefer und am tiefsten steht ein Theil der amerikanischen Völkerschaften." This was written in his *Physische Geographie*, published in 1802; in Costa, *Vom Nordatlantik zum "Black Atlantic,"* 42.

and (representative) democracy have to constantly complement each other and need a social basis for their realization."[77] Still, it seems that Lienemann maintains a certain uneasiness about public opinion and would, I presume, have reason (which?) prevail in cases of doubt.

It was Habermas[78] who most prominently elaborated on the coming into being of a changed public sphere through new forms of communication in bourgeois society, which he showed from its development in England, France, and Germany in the late 18th and early 19th century. It was in their associations that "the political norms of equality of a forthcoming society could be trained."[79] The separation between State and society in the autonomy of a *bürgerliche Gesellschaft*, as described by Hegel and Marx, was followed by a turn in trend in the later 19th century, where a "societization of the State" and a "statization of society" occurred. Over against the real intermingling of the two systems, Habermas highlighted a normative conception of the "self-organization of society, which suspends the separation of State and economic society in a radical democracy."[80] Thirty years after his seminal work first appeared, Habermas has, however, become doubtful of "holistic concepts of society" and recognized, not least in view of the fall of State socialism, "that a modern, market steered economic system cannot be at will redirected from money to administrative power and democratic formation of will without putting in danger its efficiency."[81] Also the popular basis of the public sphere has to be extended, both by paying more attention to the structural exclusion of women and to include the issues of "political culture." The straight line from a "culturally reasoning to a culturally consuming public" was, Habermas says, too pessimistic and too "short" a conclusion.[82]

Habermas' notion of the public sphere is of great interest for our study, and in fact has been widely received by Brazilian authors on the issue, as we shall see, who expand and modify it. The main problem in Habermas' view, as far as this study's interest goes, is that morality had to be inserted into the democratic process of the formation of opinion and morality as such, under the presupposition of (secular) rationality, which of course greatly relativizes the contribution of churches and other "producers" of morality. Habermas has always recognized that churches and religions played a role in supplying citizens with moral attitudes, but this was somehow peripheral to the "real" democratic process, which is to be held free of moral presuppositions outside its own procedural morality. More recently, however, Habermas has come to recognize a more important role of religion, to the point that

> the ideological neutrality of state authority, which guarantees the same ethical freedoms for every citizen, is incompatible with the political generalization of a secularistic worldview. Secularized citizens, insofar as they act in their role as citizens of a state, may neither deny out of hand the potential for truth in religious conceptions of the world, nor dispute the right of believing fellow citizens to make contributions to public discussions that are phrased in religious language.[83]

As has become evident in the telling of the story (IA1), there was only a very limited public sphere during the military regime in Brazil. Most intermediary institutions were more or less

77. Lienemann, "Öffentlichkeit und bürgerliche Gesellschaft in der europäischen Tradition," 69.

78. Habermas, *Strukturwandel der Öffentlichkeit.*

79. Ibid., 14.

80. Ibid., 23.

81. Ibid., 27.

82. Ibid., 30

83. Habermas, "On the Relations Between the Secular Liberal State and Religion," 260.

controlled, with only the family and the church maintaining some kind of autonomy and commitment to moral values.[84] What should be public, then, was debated in private or indirectly through art. But neither did the revolutionary concepts from the left, as elaborated in the 1950s and 60s, think of a public sphere properly speaking, as they tended to homogenize "the people" on the one hand, "the State" as an instrument for the change of system on the other. As decompression and opening proceeded, however, space was made by the government and conquered by civil society, in a dynamic that saw initiative shifting increasingly towards civil society and its allies in politics.

Brazilian political scientist Leonardo Avritzer, in his seminal book on *Democracy and the Public Space,* insists on the importance of a public space or sphere as a fundamental element of democracy, which he sees as particularly accurate for the Latin American context.[85] This concept, according to Avritzer, overcomes two conceptual models in effect after World War II that both fail either to understand or to build democracy in Latin America: democratic elitism and transition theory. As he develops his concept in interaction with mainline democratic theory on the one hand, the Brazilian context on the other in a very recent attempt at a democratic theory for Latin America, it is worthwhile to have a closer look at his argument.

First, he analyzes *democratic elitism* in the theories of Schumpeter and Downs. The former, in his *Capitalism, Socialism, and Democracy* (1942) defined democracy essentially as "a political method, that is to say, a certain type of institutional arrangement for arriving at political—legislative and administrative—decisions and hence incapable of being an end in itself."[86] He thus overcame the problem of a not necessarily democratic majority and the issue of rational governability, problems laid bare by World War II and especially the success of Nazism in Germany, presupposing that the whole people and not only their representation are to be understood as sovereign. The people are, then, essentially "the arbiter of competing elites."[87] But are people indeed incapable of an ethical consensus in view of the common good, if they pursue their own interests, and is the citizen so irrational he needs to be represented politically by an elite? And how does he rationally choose, if he is so irrational, between competing elites, Avritzer asks?

The latter, Downs, in his *An Economic Theory of Democracy,* attributes to individuals the now decidedly rational choice not only of the elites who should represent them, but also of a hierarchy of political proposals. However, he defines interests as economic and individuals as egoistic. The elitist conception of democracy, then, "bypasses the idea of a public consensus prior to the distribution of material goods."[88] Specifically in terms of the "second reverse wave of democratization,"

84. Cf. Avritzer, *Democracy and the Public Space,* 81.

85. Avritzer is professor of political science at the Federal University of Minas Gerais in Brazil. He holds a doctorate from the New School of Social Research in New York and has been twice a fellow at the Massachusetts Institute of Technology.—On models of public space and its use in Brazil, see one of Avritzer's partners in dialogue, Sérgio Costa, *As cores de Ercília,* 15–36. Costa distinguishes two main models: the market and mass communication model and the discursive model which recognizes civil society, informal networks and other instances to be constitutive of public space, with reference to Habermas. As to Brazil, one prominent way of thinking about public space is to name it "non-State public sphere" (a term often used by Tarso Genro, now minister of justice, but also, I add, by Wanderley "Educação, cultura e democracia," 71, in relation to the Catholic schools which he understands as non-State, but public), criticized by Costa and others as being too strongly fixed on the State and thus risking to be instrumentalized by it. He concludes that "public space has to be represented as an arena which [. . .] mediates the processes of articulation of normative consensuses and reflective reconstruction of values and moral dispositions which orient social life [*convivência*]" (ibid., 35).

86. As quoted by Avritzer, *Democracy and the Public Space,* 17.

87. Ibid.

88. Ibid., 23.

a concept Avritzer derives from Huntington,[89] of which Latin American failures of democracy in its breakdown between 1964 (Brazil) and 1973 (Chile) are a part, the author insists that elitist democratic theory was unable to point out factors of inter-elite competition, and did not relativize moments of mass-society theory that declared mass participation as such to be anti-democratic; it did, furthermore, not take into account institutional questions, nor link up conflict over material goods with the issue of a normative consensus on democracy.

Avritzer then analyzes *democratic transition theory*, which took into account ambiguities as to democracy among the elites and the process character of democratization, as well as the importance of mass mobilization/participation and the role of political institutions, although with categories imported from Western constitutionalism. Finally, they also drew increasing attention to the importance of culture, but did not "bind cultural traditions to democratic design," that is, "to understand how a cultural transformation of an instrumental tradition in relation to democracy needs to be supplemented by institutions capable of strengthening innovation."[90] It was, however, still too much centered on society's participation in electoral competition, as if this would exhaust it. Theories of democratic consolidation stepped in to point to a necessary change in culture, so as to adapt to "the only game in town."[91] The question of society's participation is reduced to adherence to "the parameters of democratic procedure"[92] and to "public opinion's trust of political institutions."[93] Avritzer then recalls O'Donnell's notion of "delegative democracy," where there is a gap between democratic institutions and their norms and actual practices that stem from "various sorts of non-universalistic relationships ranging from hierarchical particularistic exchanges, patronage, nepotism, and favors to actions that, under the formal rules of the institutional package of polyarchy, would be considered corrupt."[94] While such democracies can endure, they are not consolidated, and so the teleological aspect of many consolidation theories is broken. Latin American democracies, which introduced democratic norms and institutions but could not change patterns like paternalism and clientelism would lead to "a durable semi-democratic relation between state and society, an outcome not predicted by transition theories."[95] But Avritzer claims that O'Donnell does not move beyond the elites' culture into what he is proposing, i.e., a conception of the public space that approaches "both deeper cultural continuities and renewal."[96] Following Cohen and Arato,[97] the author distinguishes between a "societal logic" of movements and associations, and "state logic" that aims at the institutionalization of the delegation of power. He then arrives at his own proposal, which he calls "participatory publics."

In developing this concept, Avritzer takes up Habermas' concept of a discursive public sphere as a widening of democratic participation beyond administrative bureaucracy and a mere voting population. The public sphere comes in as an important level of public discourse, different from the State and from the economy, where there are not only private interests driven mainly by economic

89. Huntington, *The Third Wave*.

90. Avritzer, *Democracy and the Public Space*, 31.

91. Ibid., 32, quoting Linz and Stepan, *Problems of Democratic Transition and Consolidation*.

92. Linz and Stepan, *Problems of Democratic Transition and Consolidation*, 5.

93. Avritzer, *Democracy and the Public Space*, 33.

94. O'Donnell, Guillermo, "Illusions about consolidation", in *Journal of Democracy* 7/2 (1996), 34-51, here 40, quoted by Avritzer, *Democracy and the Public Space*, 33.

95. Avritzer, *Democracy and the Public Space*, 34.

96. Ibid.

97. Cohen and Arato, *Civil Society and Political Theory*.

factors, but where people organize themselves in movements with the possibility of generalizing interests at the public level. However, Habermas restricts the role of the public sphere in democratic systems in that "it is not to produce decisions or deliberations but through a symbolic form of communication he calls influence to demand that the consensus which emerges at the level of public opinion be reflected in administrative decisions."[98] The public sphere is not seen as a "forum for practicing democracy" in its own right, but geared towards law-making that is, still, done by power-holders helped by "experts."

Avritzer's own proposal aims at going beyond Habermas in that the public sphere is not only a discursive space that communicates with the political system through influence, but it has a proper *deliberative* dimension through providing public fora, which monitor the administrative implementation of policies. He also locates political parties in this sphere, while associations can interfere directly with the political system through the courts. By strengthening this intermediate level, Avritzer believes he avoids both a blurring of the difference between democratic participation and administrative rationality and leaving out an institutional dimension proper to the public sphere. What he calls "participatory publics" is based on four elements: (1) Face-to-face deliberation, free expression and association to address specific issues; (2) the introduction of alternative practices by social movements and voluntary associations; (3) a challenge to the exclusivity of "experts" being heard by decision-makers and the importance of monitoring of their decisions as implemented by the political administration; and (4) the binding of deliberation by participatory publics to the search of institutional formats which do justice to the issues raised at the public level.[99] Thus, such publics do not confuse their role with that of the competent administration, but give them a higher competence in interacting with it and suggesting even the latter's institutional adaptation, rather than just pressing for issues which are then dealt with at the discretion of governmental agencies with the help of "experts."

I believe this proposal to be helpful in that it takes public participation seriously and aims at expanding it to include both as many people as possible and provide them with a real chance of change at the administrative level, without presupposing a homogenous notion of social movements or "the people"—something that was common both to elitist thinkers distrustful of the masses and those using Marxist revolutionary thinking, for which these publics were merely instrumental—nor underestimating the (permanent) role of the State administration and its specific competence. There are indeed interesting new forms of intermediate deliberative fora, like the already mentioned councils on specific policies (children and youth, food security, social assistance and the like), and the experiences of "participatory budgeting," an idea that came out of the neighborhood associations and is drawing on their experiences in deliberative assemblies.

Participatory budgeting was first introduced by the PT city government of Porto Alegre (1989), and then in Belo Horizonte (1993), as well as in a good number of other municipalities, usually administered by the PT. My city, São Leopoldo, introduced it in 2005, when a PT mayor assumed office.[100] In this system, a part of the public budget, not previously bound to education, health services, and government administration, is invested in projects in a range of previously established areas (like pavement, sewage, housing, education, health and social assistance, transportation, sports, leisure, culture, and the like), on the basis of popular deliberation and representa-

98. Avritzer, *Democracy and the Public Space*, 49.

99. Cf. ibid., 52f.

100. The following description is based on Avritzer (*Democracy and the Public Space*) and my own experience in the popular budgeting process in São Leopoldo in 2006.

tion. Assemblies set up in the city districts, where all inhabitants (including resident foreigners) are invited to make proposals, lobby for them, and have them approved by the assembly, as well as to be elected as delegates to the monitoring council. At first people are informed about previous decisions and their implementation, learn about the rules of the process, which are simple but strict, and then can present and lobby for their specific projects, which are ranked in their priority by secret ballot. The assemblies also elect delegates to the monitoring council according to the number of people present, usually one delegate for ten persons (the ratio is decreasing as the number of assembly participants increases). The council mediates between the assemblies and the city government and monitors the implementation of the prioritized projects. The prioritization of projects is based on three elements: "previous access to a public good [e.g., pavement], population of the region, and popular deliberation in intermediary assemblies."[101] Thus, two criteria other than deliberation in popular assemblies are introduced, not leaving the decision exclusively to the dynamics of such an assembly and forcing it to recognize aspects of justice beyond their possibly self-oriented interest.

This system seems to me a promising process of popular participation in governance, in which the government, civil society, and the population at large cooperate. The process becomes a learning place for democracy and can, thus, help to overcome popular distrust in politics and the idea that politics is "them" rather than "us." Of course, there are regional differences, well articulated pressure groups, and shy first-time participants in the same assembly, which potentially benefits the well-spoken and good networkers. However, as this is known to all, all can prepare accordingly, which in itself is a training place for discursive, participatory democracy. Overall participation is still modest, but numbers have increased fairly constantly.[102] For Avritzer, participation varies due to "previous traditions of association and the perceived effectiveness of the process."[103] In any case, the system has shown considerable success in including people to a much higher degree than voting every two years for federal and state or municipal elections, respectively, and serves as an important place to experience democracy at work, making possible unusual alliances as projects like new lines in public transportation, leisure areas, space for cultural events for young people, or "incubators" to facilitate mounting small businesses cut across party divides.

Avritzer's proposal, grounded both in empirical examples and theoretical reasoning, including eminent international and national authors, institutional and cultural factors, is helpful in giving shape to the "public space" where the churches' intervention is particularly interesting. It is a pity that Avritzer does not venture more into questions of religion and the churches' contribution, and in his focus on social movements and public budgeting, important examples as such, does not take into account informal ways of networking and resolving of problems, as healers and spiritual counsellors, and in some way or another religions and notably Pentecostal churches do provide assistance in this line. According to Fernandes,[104] who extensively takes into account the contribution of churches and non-organized religious phenomena, "the traditional forms of mutual help continue alive and acting, and are to be counted among the principal sources of help in moments of affliction."[105]

101. Avritzer, *Democracy and the Public Space*, 154.

102. Numbers rose from 976 (1990) to 12,518 participants (1998) in Porto Alegre, and from 15,216 (1993/94) to 21,175 in Belo Horizonte (1999/2000), although the latter suffered a decrease after the peak (31,795) in 1996/97, which Avritzer (*Democracy and the Public Space*, 152f.) explains with doubts about the continuation of the process, as linked to the (non-) continuation of the PT in government.

103. Avritzer, *Democracy and the Public Space*, 154.

104. Fernandes, *Privado porém público*.

105. Ibid., 109.

Two concrete examples can illustrate what Fernandes is saying: In the first one, the [Pentecostal] Church of the Four-Square Gospel in Porto Alegre has a temple close to one of the main parks in the city, and calls it "spiritual first aid"—"*pronto-socorro espiritual*," where spiritual counseling and healing through prayer are to be expected. Similar types of attendance under a variety of expressions are to be found all over the country.

The second example is of an innovative partnership between doctors, the municipal government and "women prayer healers" (*rezadeiras*) in the town of Maranguape (90,000 inhabitants) in a semi-arid region of the Northeastern state of Ceará. Social assistants found out that infant mortality was very high due to dehydration. While this can be resolved by a very simple, homemade infusion of filtered water, salt, and sugar, mothers used not to see the doctors or nurses, but the prayer healers, who prayed for the child but did not suggest any medical treatment. The prayer healers represent an old tradition of spiritually gifted women (and some men), who discovered their gift and learnt a syncretistic type of prayer and treatment by plants (often roots) from others. Although mostly Catholic, there are, today, such prayer healers in most, if not all denominations, including Pentecostal and Lutheran. The program called "Infusion, Roots and Prayers" (*Soro, Raízes e Rezas*) registered the 188 prayer healers active in the town and had the doctors send patients to them and vice-versa, to ensure double treatment, medical and spiritual, with the result that infant mortality was reduced from 36 (1998) to 13 in 1,000 live births (2003), far below the national average of 27. The health post even set up a space for attendance by one of the prayer healers within its premises. Only through this partnership of modern and traditional means of healing, and thus taking traditional wisdom seriously, was it possible to save lives.[106]

Fernandes dedicates a whole chapter to what he calls, as different from organized social movements and NGOs, "other dynamics, below the waterline." He concludes that "either civil society finds means to dialogue with the moral authorities that dwell at the margins, or it will continue to impose itself like an external and distant force, always in debt with the problems that present themselves there."[107] It is furthermore interesting that social movements themselves do use religious symbols like blood and the cross, which they have learnt from the church, but use them without any explicit reference to a church or the presence of a priest or pastor, in what possibly might amount to a kind of "civil society religion."[108]

Avritzer does indeed pay attention to cultural aspects and refers to the concept of "hybridization," namely in Nestor Canclini's works,[109] much referred to in today's academic works in Brazil and elsewhere. Argentinian anthropologist Canclini tries to overcome empirically the normative and evolutionist opposition of modernization and tradition, where instead of the former overcoming the latter the two mix in an, in Avritzer's words, "association among economic modernity [with its economic interests], political power, and cultural tradition that allow for the continuity of eminently traditional activities on a modern basis."[110] Since the beginning of colonization, there have been syncretistic mixings in culture and religion, "created by Spanish and Portuguese matrices mixing with indigenous representation."[111] While recognizing the empirical value of Canclini's

106. See the report: Cotes, Paloma, Um santo remédio, in *Revista Época* 298 (2004) of 01/29/2004, available at http://revistaepoca.globo.com/Revista/Epoca/0,,EDG62468-6014-298,00.html (accessed on 3/5/2007)

107. Fernandes, *Privado porém público*, 126.

108. Cf. below IIB3; Sinner, "Brazil."

109. Canclini, *Hybrid cultures.*

110. Avritzer, *Democracy and the Public Space*, 65f.

111. Canclini, *Hybrid cultures*, 241f

thesis, Avritzer claims it is not clear as to whether, in terms of a theory of democratization, "hybridization is a vice or a virtue," except for the production of "cultural goods," where, as Canclini says, "consumption becomes a fundamental area for establishing and communicating differences."[112] Avritzer rightly criticizes that making hybridization a normative concept on the political level "has strong anti-democratic consequences"[113] as it is unable to foster equality. He notes that, despite their cultural hybridism, Latin American countries did refer to liberal tradition for their constitutions as they became independent, not proposing an alternative model, while at the same time beginning to value a supposedly homogenous—and non-democratic—"popular culture" in the building of nations, rather than trying to overcome it as happened in the West. Thus, there was no clear differentiation between the private and the public, as emphasized by Roberto Da Matta, among others (see above, IA3c), nor was there a "tradition of plural and democratic associations," among them the Catholic "third orders," associations of lay believers with a specific commitment, which were racially homogenous and religiously intolerant.[114]

The concept of hybridity and hybridization is used widely today. It helps to see the often unexpected mixing of influences and that the "result" of hybrid cultures (and religions) is unpredictable and difficult to categorize. Thus, the observer is free to see reality in its contradictions, flowing together of strands and *sui generis* results, and an artificial homogenization and, with it, potential domination and hierarchization can be avoided. There are numerous singular, new "plants," recalling the origin of the term in biology. But hybrid plants by definition cannot reproduce themselves, they are sterile. How could, then, democracy and citizenship possibly be fostered, where similarities and equality are, even with the recognition of difference, central? Would it not stop at an aestheticism of a huge variety of "plants," to the awe of some and the horror of others?[115]

In sum, Avritzer's proposal provides a good ground for defining the *locus* of the discourse on citizenship, a public space where churches and organized religions in general can contribute directly and indirectly. I shall now turn to theories of citizenship commonly used in Brazilian pertinent literature.

2. THEORIES OF CITIZENSHIP

Não vejo a cidadania apenas como um conceito jurídico e político.
Vejo a cidadania como uma dimensão do 'ser pessoa'.

João Baptista Herkenhoff[116]

There is currently no full-fledged theory of citizenship available from a Brazilian's pen, although elements of it are to be found in the abundant literature on the matter, generally focused on rights,

112. Avritzer, *Democracy and the Public Space*, 67; Canclini, *Hybrid cultures*, 16.

113. Avritzer, *Democracy and the Public Space*, 67

114. Ibid., 73.

115. See also the critique of Costa, *Vom Nordatlantik zum "Black Atlantic*," 106 n. 9, who calls Canclinis definition of hybridity "schwammig" and stresses that Canclini himself, different from post-colonial authors like Homi Bhabha, does not attribute a political connotation to the concept: "Waren Hybridisierungsprozesse in der Region entweder mit der Legitimierung despotischer Herrschaften oder mit emanzipatorischen Versuchen verbunden, so meint Hybridität heute lediglich eine allegorische und unorganisierte Mischung und ist viel mehr ein Ausdruck des Ästhetischen als des Politischen." On the whole see ibid. 103–109.

116. "I don't see citizenship only as a legal and political concept. I see citizenship as a dimension of 'being a person,'" Herkenhoff, *Direito e Cidadania*,17f.

their applications and expansion, and to a much lesser degree on its correspondent obligations.[117] Janoski,[118] followed by Vieira,[119] defines citizenship as "passive and active membership of individuals in a nation-state with certain universalistic rights and obligations at a specified level of equality." Most Brazilian authors refer to British sociologist Thomas H. Marshall's (1893–1981)[120] three categories of rights, civil, political, and social, conquered in this order in the 18th, 19th, and 20th centuries, respectively, with Great Britain as his reference.[121] Brazilian political scientist and historian José Murilo de Carvalho[122] argues that the order of conquest was inverted in Brazil.[123] Although civil rights, inspired by the French Constitution of 1791 and the Declaration of the Rights of Man and Citizen, had already been included in the Brazilian Imperial Constitution of 1824, Carvalho makes a reservation: "But if these rights still today are dead letter for a great portion of the population, what to say about Brazil in the 19th century, when there was still slavery and nearly all the population called free lived under the strict control of landlords?"[124]

117. A search with the title word "citizenship" (*cidadania)* on the website of Brazil's biggest online bookshop, *Livraria Cultura,* which offers nearly 2.6 million titles, resulted in 303 matches; "theory of citizenship" (*teoria da cidadania*) gave one match: José Alfredo de Oliveira Baracho, *Teoria geral da cidadania: a plenitude da cidadania e as garantias constitucionais* (São Paulo: Saraiva, 1995). The booklet, of 68 pages, is no longer in print. See http://www.livcultura.com.br (accessed on 2/24/2009). The fact that citizenship is often talked or written about, but rarely defined with precision, both in Brazil and beyond, is noted by Domingues, "Cidadania, direitos e modernidade,"213; Corrêa, *A construção da cidadania,* 216.

118. Janoski, *Citizenship and Civil Society,* 9.

119. Vieira, *Os argonautas da cidadania,* 34.

120. The most extensive text is the 1949 [Alfred] Marshall lectures delivered in Cambridge (UK), to be found in the collection of essays Marshall, *Class, Citizenship, and Social Development,* 71-134. The Brazilian translation of 1967 (*Cidadania, classe social e status*) is, unfortunately for the whole discussion, no longer available in print. Beyond the three types of rights, Marshall also argued that the equality of citizenship was "not inconsistent with the inequalities which distinguish the various economic levels in the society," as quoted by Heater, *A Brief History of Citizenship* 113.—Other frequent references are to Reinhard Bendix (*Nation-building and Citizenship*), and Norberto Bobbio (*A era dos direitos*).

121. Carvalho, "Interesses contra a cidadania," *Cidadania no Brasil*; Herkenhoff, *Direito e Cidadania*; Vieira, *Os argonautas da cidadania*; Gohn, *O protagonismo da sociedade civil*; Corrêa, *A construção da cidadania*, among others. Also British and American authors Turner ("Outline of a Theory of Citizenship"; "Contemporary Problems in the Theory of Citizenship") and Janoski (*Citizenship and Civil Society*) follow Marshall's path, although criticizing—among others for providing a historical description rather than an explicative theory—and expanding his approach in terms of the importance of conflict, especially as carried by social movements and including religious elements, or, as Janoski (*Citizenship and Civil Society,* 4f.) put it as to the changing context, in view of the decline of the welfare state, the breakdown of real existing socialism in Eastern Europe and the increasing citizenship issues related to international migration, as well as the need to balance rights and obligations.

122. Carvalho "Interesses contra a cidadania,"; *Cidadania no Brasil*; also O'Donnell, "Polyarchies and the (Un)Rule of Law in Latin America."

123. It becomes clear through Carvalho's historical study that notions and portions of the other categories of rights were present earlier, but there were serious setbacks. Independence was not the conquest of popular revolts or great liberators like Simón Bolívar, as was the case in other Latin American countries. It was a negotiation between the national elite, the Portuguese crown and England, mediated through Prince Pedro, who later became Emperor. The people had little participation in this. Slavery was not mentioned in the Constitution, but remained in place. However, it is interesting to note that suffrage was extended, in the Empire, even to the illiterate (more than 85 percent of the population at the time!). All free men over 25 (or 21 for some) with a minimum salary of 100 mil-réis (which was a modest rate) could and had to vote. Although elections were indirect and in fact a market of buying and selling (not without rationality in this, however), the electorate at the time came up to 13 percent of the population, much higher than in many European States at the time. In 1881, direct voting was established, but the minimum salary required to qualify as voter was elevated to 200 mil-réis (still modest), the vote of illiterates prohibited and in general no longer compulsory. Under these conditions, 80 percent of the male population was excluded from voting (Carvalho, *Cidadania no Brasil,* 29ff.).

124. Carvalho "Interesses contra a cidadania," 97.

Still following Carvalho, first came the social rights, which were introduced under Getúlio Vargas' dictatorship in the *Estado Novo* (1937–45). These included the creation of a Ministry of Labor, Industry and Commerce, and especially the enormous collection of labor legislation with numerous protections and a pension system, which was finalized in 1943 as the "Consolidation of Labor Laws" (*Consolidação das Leis do Trabalho*—CLT), still in effect today. This allowed Vargas to create for himself an image of a benevolent "father of the nation," while civil and political rights were highly restricted, the media were censured and disliked intellectuals and politicians were harassed.[125] Under the military regime (1964–85), further advances such as the creation of a unified pension system were introduced, now extended also to rural workers, domestic employees, and autonomous workers, and the Guarantee Fund for Time of Service (FGTS) was created to function as an unemployment insurance. Political rights were, again, highly restricted, but democratic structures and the vote remained in place, although as little more than a façade. It is remarkable that in this period the number of voters rose from 12.5 million in 1960 (18 percent of the population) to 65.6 million (1986), representing 47 percent of the population, and I add that it nearly doubled to roughly 126 million in 2006 (about 67 percent of the population).[126] As transition progressed, political participation became a possibility for the people. While significant advances were made in social and political rights, it is civil rights that remain "deficient in terms of their being known, their extension and guarantees,"[127] which is confirmed by the Freedom House Rating (see above, IA3b), and also sustained by Guillermo O'Donnell for Latin America, namely Brazil and Argentina.[128]

An important tendency is to attribute the conquest of citizenship historically less to the *citoyen* than to the *bourgeois*, and seeing rights primarily as liberal rights serving the bourgeoisie. Marx and Gramsci are, of course, patrons of such discourse (see also above, IB1). Namely in the beginning of the New Republic, opposition against repression and inequality made thinkers suspicious of liberal discourse, and socialist utopia (pre-1989) and the hope for revolution were still strong,[129] which had its bearing on theology (see below, ID). This utopian tendency is reinforced by the perception that citizenship in Brazil was, originally, not "conquered" from below, but "given" from above, i.e., the State run by the elites, in a *cidadania regulada*[130] or *cidadania tutelada*.[131] What is meant becomes clear through recalling Vargas' promotion of social rights: this was not the conquest of the people, but the populist act of a ruler to incorporate the subaltern classes into a bourgeois order, as interpreted by Wanderley Guilherme dos Santos and others.[132] The basic contradiction is, of course, the one between freedom and social justice, which has prompted liberals like John Rawls to intro-

125. Cf. Fausto, *História do Brasil*, 364–389.

126. I have calculated the percentage from "population clock" estimate on http://www.ibge.gov.br, which stood at 188.3 million on March 1, 2007; the total number of entitled voters for the 2nd ballot on October 30, 2006 is to be found on http://www.justicaeleitoral.gov.br/2turno/br1.html (accessed on 03/01/2007).

127. Carvalho, *Cidadania no Brasil*, 210.

128. O'Donnell, "Polyarchies and the (Un)Rule of Law in Latin America."

129. Cf. Buffa, Arroyo and Nosella, *Educação e cidadania: quem educa o cidadão?*

130. Corrêa, *A construção da cidadania*, 215.

131. Sociologist Pedro Demo has been criticizing restrictions on citizenship, which he still calls "small" (Demo, *Cidadania pequena*). Earlier, he contrasted "patronising [tutelada] citizenship" as the one based on patriarchy, and "assisted citizenship," which he still considers paternalistic as the State appears as the nurturing father, with "emancipated citizenship" (Demo, *Cidadania menor*), based in his evaluation on empirical data from the UN Human Development Report and from the domestic sample survey carried out by the national IBGE institute. Writing at the beginning of the nineties, he concludes that Brazilian society is not only materially poor, but "politically poor."

132. Wanderley Guilherme dos Santos, *Cidadania e justiça: a política social na ordem brasileira* (Rio de Janeiro: Campus, 1979), in Corrêa, *A construção da cidadania* , 216.

duce a double principle of justice as fairness, trying to correct the fact that there is no real equality of opportunity for all.[133] But it is plain that social rights have never attained the same fundamental, universal validity as have civil rights and political rights, precisely because the principle of equality in this field is a matter of continuous debate, and and has fuelled the debate between capitalists and socialists. Corrêa introduces into his definition of citizenship the economic and social aspects: "Citizenship is [. . .] the democratic realization of a society, shared by all the individuals to the point that all have their access to the public space and conditions of a dignified survival guaranteed, having as its basic value the fullness of life."[134] It is plain that such a definition surpasses the issue of rights (and duties) as foreseen by law, but introduces a utopian, even eschatological dimension when speaking of the "fullness of life" (cf. John 10.10, often cited in Christian social movements and NGOs). "Access to public space" seems to include both the political and juridical system and the discursive space, while a "dignified survival" indicates having the basic needs met appropriately. He clearly wants to go beyond the insufficiencies of Marxism and its reception in Latin America, where even a movement called "critique of law" was formed in the 1970s.[135] While maintaining the utopia of "another possible world," to take up the World Social Forum's slogan, Corrêa seeks to affirm the law and the State as indispensable, even if insufficient for citizenship: "the State as idealized representation of public space takes on the form of law."[136] Three important affirmations are implied here: (1) The State is an "idealized" representation, i.e., its central values as formulated in the constitution are valid even if far from being put into action. Thus, the common opposition of "abstract" and "concrete" human rights is overcome by the "idea" of human rights, which remains as symbolic orientation and, thus, a constant reference for the struggle for their concrete enactment. (2) The State is a "representation," i.e., the already mentioned inversion happens: the public is prior to the State. The latter is, however, indispensable, and becomes a truly representative agent, not reduced to a simple mechanism to defend the bourgeoisie. (3) The "law" is indispensable, not least to serve as a reference to facilitate the struggle of those still excluded from its benefits. This does not mean merely a "passive" status, but rather an "active" contribution of the citizen as a truly political and not merely legal subject.[137] Corrêa shows how it is possible, while somehow remaining within the Marxist flock, to adapt to the new democratic situation and value the law as an instrument to materialize the utopia of human dignity.

One could say that if traditionally the elites distrusted the ability of the masses to govern themselves, it is the masses—as represented by civil society with a Marxist-Gramscian philosophy—who distrust "liberal" or "formal" citizenship as an instrument benefiting only the elites. Corrêa signals a way to continue in that line, opening up to a more constructive and collaborative "active" citizenship, without abandoning a hermeneutics of suspicion. One does not have to share his philosophical position in order to agree with his conclusion, but as such philosophy is widespread among Brazilian intellectuals and leaders of civil society, it is important to acknowledge that they are willing to enter the discourse rather than leave it aside in a generalized critique.

133. Rawls, *A Theory of Justice*; for an analysis of Rawls' proposal in view of the option for the poor, so prominent in Liberation Theology (cf. below, ID1a), see Bedford-Strohm, *Vorrang für die Armen*, 150–203.

134. Corrêa, *A construção da cidadania*, 217.

135. Ibid., 207.

136. Ibid., 223.

137. One can also recall that in a country where many still find it hard to get from the State and its organs what is due to them—as well as contributing what is due to the citizen—an "active" citizenship starts with the simple registration of one's child to become a legal citizen. Of course it does not stop there, but beginning here is crucial as not even such activity is common for a good number of Brazilians.

The frequent use of "conquest," "participation," "emancipation," and "active citizenship" in Brazilian literature indicates the hope and, indeed, expectation of those active in civil society to construct a new society with inverted roles—a society from "below,"[138] with more emphasis given to the social than to the individual, even some form of socialist republic.[139] The theologians of liberation, strongly articulated with leaders of civil society, blew into the same horn, as I shall show below (ID). Both for the former and the latter, a certain overstatement of the potential of the people (as well as a rather abstract notion of them, without sufficiently specifying differences) and their movements was underlying.[140] This strong hope was frustrated (but not extinguished) by a number of events in 1989, not only the fall of the Berlin Wall, but the non-election of Lula to the presidency and the non-continuity of the Sandinista government in Nicaragua. Thus, new forms of participation within a more modest horizon (the "construction" of citizenship in a "process") had to be elaborated. The participatory budgeting is part of this new vision, relatively modest quantitatively, but still important in indicating a concrete increase in popular, democratic participation. The means of popular vote (referendum, plebiscite, and popular initiative), foreseen in the 1988 Constitution and propagated in a major study by Benevides[141] as elements of an "active citizenship," were only used twice: On the form of government (1993) and on the prohibition of the commercialization of firearms and ammunition (2005). This is deplorable, because it would be another important advance of popular participation in politics. But it also shows the problem of what kind of issue should be submitted to the people's vote. The death penalty has not been put to the vote, because it is taken as being against the logic of fundamental rights.[142] But according to opinion polls, it would find a clear majority in favor.[143]

Another trend, identified globally by Janoski and taken up by Vieira, includes an emphasis on *civic culture* and specifically *virtue*, in line with Tocqueville and Durkheim and again among communitarians like Bellah, Etzioni, and Walzer.[144] This tendency is less strong in Brazil and Latin America, although there are signs of it in speaking of "responsibility," "duty," "behavior."[145] This is why the "learning" of democracy[146] and education[147] are so central. It is also no surprise that this aspect is of particular interest to theologians, namely those who think society in terms of a large community, like Boff, who emphasizes "virtues for another possible world,"[148] these being hospital-

138. E.g. Demo, *Cidadania pequena, Política social, educação e cidadania*: 43ff.; Jelin "Construir a Cidadania."

139. Citizenship, for sociologist Pedro Demo, is "a historical process of popular conquest, by which society acquires, progressively, conditions of becoming a conscious and organized historical subject, with a capacity to conceive and make effective [=emancipation] a project of one's own. The contrary signifies the condition of a mass of manipulation, periphery, marginalization" (Demo, *Cidadania menor*, 17).

140. E.g. Dagnino, *Anos 90*,"Sociedade Civil"; cf. Hochstetler, "Democratizing Pressures from Below?"

141. Benevides, *A cidadania ativa*, "Cidadania e democracia."

142. Cf. below, IC3.

143. Cf. above, IA3b.

144. Cf. Janoski, *Citizenship and Civil Society*, 7.

145. See, for instance, Jelin "Construir a Cidadania," who speaks (from Argentina, but in a similar situation to that of Brazil) of the need to reconstruct and transform the institutions of the State and civil society, but also emphasizes that "people have to adopt adequate and coherent behaviors and beliefs in relation to the notion of democracy, learning how to act in a renewed institutional system" (ibid., 55).

146. Cf. Jelin, "Construir a Cidadania,"; Benevides,"Cidadania e democracia"; Krischke, *The Learning of Democracy in Latin America.*

147. Cf. Buffa et al., *Educação e cidadania*; Pauly, *Ética, educação e cidadania*; Streck, *Educação para um novo contrato social.*

148. Boff, *Virtudes para um outro mundo possível.*

ity, conviviality (*convivência*) and sharing of the table (*comensalidade*; see below, ID). The churches are, or at least can be—and in Brazil historically certainly have been, namely through the Church Base Communities—schools of democracy, where ways of linking up motivation, analysis, and action in a participatory discussion are tested.

Civil society, as already mentioned, is an important correlate of citizenship and has in Brazil and elsewhere without doubt played a considerable role in the expansion and enhanced efficiency of rights, although not rarely downplaying (or leaving out on) duties. In this context, it is important to stress that the State is not something barely instrumental and transitory, but an indispensable institution to keep law and order with a monopoly of coercion; indeed, civil society with its mediating, claiming, educating, and project executing role would be meaningless without the State. History seems to have shown that the important experiences of small scale "popular" organizations like Church Base and other communities and movements cannot make up for the whole of society and guide its path with its long-term processes of reflection and decision-making—which is, however, not to say that its experiences could not be valued, as happens in the experiences of public budgeting. In fact, such movements can only exist inasmuch as the State provides and guarantees space for them, which even the military regime did to some extent, if only because it could not directly supervise all these localized experiences. As rightly stated by Vieira: "civil society cannot constitute the *locus* of the rights of citizenship, as it does not cover the State sphere which assures official protection through legal sanctions."[149] The dimensions of State and the law it establishes and guarantees, with equal and universal validity, are, thus, indispensable (even if insufficient) dimensions of citizenship.

At the same time, civic culture, i.e., the significance attributed to being a citizen and the attitudes of pride, rejection, or disbelief held by citizens toward their citizenship, has a direct influence on the degree to which citizenship can be effective and participative, not least because those in power and working in the administration are also citizens, and their shortcomings reflect all citizens' potential or real shortcomings. The churches, to some degree part of civil society and certainly mediating institutions, can have influence on laws, inasmuch as their members and representatives directly negotiate with the state on these, and on civic culture, inasmuch as they train, inform, and legitimate it among their members.

I fully agree with the Brazilian authors that citizenship cannot be reduced to rights and duties in a national State. For one, the law as written needs grounding in something that is prior to it, to which the people at least broadly agree and feel committed to. Morality and normativity come in here, as do human rights, which by definition go beyond national boundaries. Secondly, the law is useless unless it is effectively available for the people, which includes both how it is handled by the instituted authorities and perceived by the citizens. Third, citizenship is molded by discourse and practice in the public sphere, where civil society as the organized part based on "private initiative engaged in fostering citizenship in the public sphere to promote the common good for the whole of society" (my definition above, IB1) has a specific task. Here also, the question is to be asked if this civil society is to be seen in a national or global perspective.

Initially, the answer will be "both, of course," recalling the crucial role Brazil has played in bringing about and sustaining one of the most visible forums of a globally interacting and networking civil society, the World Social Forum. There certainly are conceptions of a global citizenship (since Antiquity, as we have seen), and it is true that national boundaries have become

149. Vieira, *Os argonautas da cidadania*, 37.

flexible to some extent.[150] A globalized economy as well as ever faster means of communication seem to make nonsense of national boundaries. But fragmentation, ethnic issues, migration with subsequent reactions of xenophobia, and closing of borders have also created new boundaries and reinforced old ones. In any case, it is the national setup that puts into practice concrete rights and claims duties. The national State and its laws are a concrete correlate to civil society, which is not the case globally, although there are regional and certain global conglomerates that assume a certain degree of supra-national power (the European Union, or the United Nations with its political, judiciary, and military institutions and regulations). There is no World State, and it is questionable whether it would be desirable to exist, as some would be more powerful than others in running it, and it might undermine rather than foster a world democracy. A kind of federation, based on international law, as advocated already by Kant in his *On Perpetual Peace* might be, *mutatis mutandis*, more appropriate.

Be this as it may, it is legitimate to focus on a national constitution to analyze what it says about citizenship, because it is in reference to this citizenship that people can struggle for the improvement of their lives and effective participation. And if I agree, as indicated, that citizenship is much more than rights and duties, to become effective for people's lives it is prominently about rights and duties. I thus go on to look into citizenship and constitution in Brazil.

3. CITIZENSHIP AND CONSTITUTION

Tão frágil como o papel e, quase sempre,
com seus direitos assegurados apenas no papel.
Assim se resume a cidadania no Brasil. . .

Gilberto Dimenstein[151]

It has become clear that citizenship is not exclusively, but also and prominently about having rights and duties. Such rights and duties are meaningless if they are not formulated by a set of public rules, enforced by an efficient administration, overseen by an impartial judiciary and known, adopted and supported by the citizens themselves, which includes their questioning and alteration if laws themselves are against citizenship, for instance when they give unjustified privileges.[152] Thus, while citizenship can by no means be reduced to a legal definition, it is there that it is made most explicit. Citizenship, in its narrow legal sense, refers to the rights and duties of the born and naturalized inhabitants of a certain State, as foreseen and guaranteed by its constitution and laws. In what follows, I will give at least an indication of what is at stake in Brazil today. I shall concentrate on the 1988 constitution, but at least mention that far-reaching laws with ample protection for the citizen in general or specific groups of citizens have come into effect: The *Statute of the Child and the Adolescent* (ECA, Law nr. 8,069 of July 10, 1990), the *Code of Defense of the Consumer* (Law nr. 8,078 of September 11, 1990), the *Law of Directions and Bases for National Education* (LDB, Law nr. 9,394 of September 20, 1996); the *Statute of the Elderly* (Law nr. 10,741 of October 1, 2003).

As shown above (IA2), political citizenship in Brazil can by now be considered consolidated in terms of its basic processes like elections, the existence of a constitution with a long list of

150. Cf. Vieira, *Os argonautas da cidadania*; Keane, *Global Civil Society?*

151. "As fragile as paper and, nearly always, with your rights guaranteed only on paper. That's how citizenship can be summarized in Brazil. . ." Dimenstein, *O cidadão de papel*, 4.

152. Cf. Holston, *Insurgent Citizenship*.

fundamental rights and an elaborate body of laws drawing on it, and a fairly impartial judiciary. The constitution is an especially important indicator of the existence of citizenship as it contains the principles that guide the State in its laws and policies. The constitution is a fundamental element of the State's self-definition after the transition to democracy,[153] which happened in Brazil when a constituent assembly was elected less than a year after the civilian government took power.[154] It was, probably, unfortunate that the assembly was to sit through a mandate as congress beyond the promulgation of the Constitution, and thus lost part of the independence and creativity that an exclusively constituent assembly might have had.[155] Still, in Herkenhoff's evaluation,[156] the text that came out of the process was much more than could have been expected, not least due to the 122 "popular amendments," supported by a total of over 12 million signatures that were submitted by a variety of movements and institutions—mostly, but not exclusively social movements and related NGOs, including churches—and had to be taken into account by the constituent assembly.[157] The issues were, among others: the rights of as well as the respect for and care of senior citizens, children, youth, persons with disabilities, women, workers, consumers, indigenous people, black people, "oppressed minorities," prisoners, and the environment, as well as the "ample exercise of citizenship," popular action, *habeas corpus* and *habeas data,* free public schools and universities, and the freedom of expression of thought.[158] As Herkenhoff states, these themes all point to a "culture of citizenship and human rights."[159] Apart from the popular amendments, there were other kinds of demonstrations, artistic events, public debates, participation in public audiences, proposals submitted to the preparatory committee of the constitution and the like. Having examined carefully all the material, formal and informal proposals and manifestations, Herkenhoff concludes that "popular participation was decisive for the directions the constitution was to take"[160] and that, thus, a "much better constitution than the one to be expected of the constituent congress"[161] came into being.[162] Of course, nobody explicitly advocated a return to military rule or promoted racism, torture, censorship, or women's discrimination; however, the military was still active in the background, as were the ancient elites of landlords, entrepreneurs, and "colonelist" *(coronelista)* politicians (not rarely in a combination of such attributions), and, last but not least, the sitting president, José Sarney, whose extensive power was still based on the authoritarian 1969 constitution. All of these had their influence on the political process, including the constitution.[163]

153. Cf. Gremmelspacher, "Kirchen als Nicht-regierungsorganisationen."

154. A comprehensive analysis of the constituent process, through documents and interviews with leading figures, is to be found in the dissertation of Swiss political scientist Markus Eugster, *Der brasilianische Verfassungsgebungsprozess.*

155. Herkenhoff, *Direito e Cidadania,* 129ff.

156. João Baptista Herkenhoff, a Roman Catholic, is a judge and professor at the Federal University of Espírito Santo and has accompanied closely the constituent process in 1987–88.

157. Michiles et alii, *Cidadão Constituinte*; CNBB, *Participação popular e cidadania.*

158. Herkenhoff, *Direito e Cidadania,* 135f., referring to Assembléia Nacional Constituinte—Comissão de Sistematização, *Emendas Populares,* vols. 1-2 (Brasília: Centro Gráfico do Senado Federal, 1987).

159. Herkenhoff, *Direito e Cidadania,* 137.

160. Ibid., 139.

161. Ibid., 140.

162. Consequently, he deplores that the future constitutional amendments were done without popular consultation (Herkenhoff, *Direito e Cidadania,* 141), with the two exceptions already mentioned (IA1).—Also Eugster, *Der brasilianische Verfassungsgebungsprozess von 1987/88,* 305 concludes that "not only in the Brazilian context, but also in an international comparison, it becomes evident that the present constituent process is unique and could virtually become a model," precisely for its ample inclusion of citizens and their elected representatives.

163. Eugster, *Der brasilianische Verfassungsgebungsprozess von 1987/88*; Zaverucha, *FHC, forças armadas e polícia.*

The 1988 constitution is the country's eighth after those of 1824 (Empire), 1891 (Old Republic), 1934 (following the 1930's "lieutenant's" revolution), 1937 (during the dictatorial *Estado Novo*), 1946 (following the return to democracy), 1967, and 1969 (both under the military regime), the latter being replaced by the new constitution, in the first constitutional process that did not follow the rupture of a political institution (independence, republic, the installation and deposition of authoritarian regimes), as it followed a relatively smooth process of transition. The new constitution was promulgated on October 5, 1988, by decision of the constituent assembly, without a popular referendum.

It contains 245 articles in its main text and 70 articles in the transitory dispositions. The preamble states:

> We, the representatives of the Brazilian people, united in the national constituent assembly to institute a democratic state, destined to secure the exercise of social and individual rights, freedom, security, well-being, development, equality and justice as supreme values of a fraternal and pluralist society free of prejudices, founded on social harmony and committed, in the internal and international order, to the pacific solution of controversies, we promulgate, under God's protection, the following CONSTITUTION OF THE FEDERATIVE REPUBLIC OF BRAZIL."[164]

The constitution is organized under nine headings: (1) Fundamental principles; (2) fundamental rights and guarantees; (3) organization of the State; (4) organization of the powers; (5) defense of the State and the democratic institutions; (6) taxation and budget; (7) economic and financial order; (8) social order; (9) general constitutional dispositions. For the interest of the present study, the first two headings are the most relevant, as are the (few) dispositions in relation to religion(s).

The first heading names five fundamental principles: Sovereignty, citizenship, the dignity of the human person, the social values of work and free initiative, and political pluralism, and states that "all power emanates from the people" (Art. 1). The second article defines the legislative, executive, and judicial powers as "independent and harmonious among each other," while the third article states as the four fundamental goals of the Republic to "construct a free, just and solidary society"; "guarantee the national development"; "eradicate poverty and marginalization and reduce the social and regional inequalities," and to "promote the good of all, without prejudice of origin, race, sex, color, age or whatever other forms of discrimination," thus implicitly naming poverty, marginalization, inequality, and discrimination as the most pressing challenges of the country. The fourth article names the principles of international relations, which should be based on, among others, the "prevalence of human rights," "self-determination of peoples," "non-intervention," "defense of peace," "rejection of terrorism and racism," and the "concession of political asylum," and explicitly names engagement in the "economic, social and cultural integration of the peoples of Latin America," in view of "the formation of a Latin American community of nations."

The following heading intends to name the "fundamental rights and guarantees" implied in citizenship, whose "defining norms [. . .] have immediate applicability" (Art. 5, § 1). Its most cited part are the 77 numbers of the Fifth Article's initial paragraph, which extensively affirm the "individual and collective rights and duties."[165] The ingress reads as follows: "All are equal before the law,

164. Brasil, *Constituição da República Federativa do Brasil*, xvii. As to the invocation of God, the 1988 constitution upholds the tradition of most Brazilian constitutions; only the 1891 and 1937 texts did not include it. In the interpretation of the (Roman Catholic) lawyer and judge Francisco Adalberto Nóbrega (*Deus e constituição*), the invocation of God is "ecumenical, as our society is pluralist and non-confessional" (ibid., 73).

165. "Duties" are explicitly mentioned only in the chapter heading and come up in the text only indirectly (like in

without distinction of any nature, guaranteeing to Brazilians and foreigners resident in the country the inviolability of the right to life, freedom, equality, security and property." I shall mention some of the articles that most strengthen people's rights and participation, and clearly seeking to leave authoritarianism behind. Those related to religion will be named below (IIB2).

Unarmed and peaceful meetings—i.e., including demonstrations—in public places do not need authorization, they only need to give notice to the competent authority in order to avoid interfering with another meeting (xvi). Also the foundations of associations and, as determined by law, cooperatives do not need authorization and may not suffer State intervention (xviii), which also applies to religious organizations.

The right to property is guaranteed; however it is to "attend to its social function" (xxiii), which has, of course, bearings on the issue of land reform, and indeed a landowner can be disappropriated "because of public necessity or utility, or for social interest," being entitled to a "just and previous monetary compensation" (xxiv).

"Exceptional judgment or courts" are forbidden by number xxxvii. Racism is considered a crime without bail nor limit of time (xlii), as are "the practice of torture, the illegal traffic of narcotics and similar drugs, terrorism and those crimes defined as heinous" (xliii) and the "action of armed groups, civil or military, against the constitutional order and the democratic State" (xliv). The death penalty is forbidden "unless in cases of declared war" (xlvii, a), as are life sentences, forced labor, banishment, and "cruel" punishments (xlvii, e). Nobody must be held incommunicable, but any imprisonment has to be communicated immediately "to the competent judge and the prisoner's family or to the person he indicates" (lxii), and those who imprison or interrogate him have to identify themselves (lxiv). Many of the legal services are to be offered free of charge for those who cannot pay, and especially are to be free "for the recognizedly poor," as specified by law, the registers of birth and death (lxxvi)—which, in practice, are being offered free of charge to all citizens today.

Among the *social rights* are counted "education, health, work, leisure, security, social security, maternity and infancy protection, and assistance to the defenseless [*desamparados*]" (Art. 6). The rights secured for workers, urban and rural, are protection against arbitrary dismissal, unemployment insurance, Guarantee Fund for Time of Service (FGTS), minimum wage as fixed by law, nationally unified, which is to be "capable of attending to his [or her] and his [or her] family's basic vital needs with habitation, food, education, health, leisure, clothing, hygiene, transportation and social security" (Art. 7, iv), guarantee of salary, 13th salary, maternity and paternity leave, and the prohibition of difference in salary based on gender, age, color or marital status, among other items.

Further highlights are the introduction of the voluntary vote for 16-18 year olds, giving them the opportunity to grow into their exercise of citizenship (Art. 14 § 1), and the possibilities of the exercise of "popular sovereignty" not only by the vote, but by "plebiscite," "referendum," and "popular initiative" (Art. 14), i.e., a popular vote on the (in)convenience of a legal or constitutional innovation to be elaborated by congress (plebiscite), a vote on an already passed constitutional amendment or law (referendum), and the popular proposal of a new law to be elaborated by congress (initiative), respectively.[166]

The 1988 constitution is an extensive constitution, having received contributions from many—often contradictory—forces. While the *constituent process* is to be hailed as exemplary, the same is not true for the *text*, which was unable to solve some of the most enduring problems of the

---

the "social function" of property). The index also shows no entry under "duty" (*dever*).

166. Herkenhoff, *Direito e Cidadania*, 177f.

Brazilian political system, like the separation of powers and potential deadlocks when differences remain. The necessary reforms of the political process, the judiciary, the pension system and land reform were not sufficiently backed up by it and still remain unresolved. Also, while some articles ended up as a compromise, other, somewhat contradictory articles were just juxtaposed to attend to the pressure of the lobbies involved, resulting in a "chaotic [*unübersichtlich*] patchwork,"[167] difficult to understand even for experts.

As the assembly opted for a comprehensive rather than a summarizing constitution, it considerably restricted the legislator in his flexibility to live up to the constitutional principles in a contextually sound manner. Naturally, in view of the constant violations of human rights during the military regime, those abuses had to be prevented from repeating, and everything had to be done to secure citizenship in its civil, political and social dimensions. The price for this, however, is that it is from the outset extremely difficult to translate such far reaching principles into positive law, and even more so to enforce it. For instance, the admirably strong protection of workers is, in many cases, ineffective because of informal work contracts, and the latter at least partly a consequence of small and middle businesses being unable to cope with the amount of paperwork and social contributions prescribed by law. It will take a long time till such principles and laws can be really enforced without crushing smaller elements of the economy. Another common problem is the old fashioned style and ineffectiveness of the judiciary, and the fact that a lawyer is always needed, which makes it hardly attractive.[168] The work justice is probably the most effective one, with workers having a good chance of winning their cause. In any case, such far reaching rights and guarantees are virtually impossible to meet effectively, although that fact does not make them wrong.

In 1992, law professor José Murilo de Carvalho stated in his address within a series of lectures on "The Brazilian: a citizen?" (*Brasileiro: cidadão?*)[169]: "I confess to you that in my 52 years of age, and in my knowledge of the history of the 19th century and the First Republic, I never experienced a similar climate of disenchantment and frustration, of lack of loyalty with the political system and with the country itself."[170] According to a survey he cited, 40 percent of Brazilians at the time affirmed to feel ashamed of being Brazilians. Although much has changed in the years since the aftermath of the disastrous experience with president Collor's impeachment and the failing economic plans, a more or less subtle shame about their country's "being behind" industrialized and "civilized" nations still looms large.

This is reminiscent of what was said earlier on the "disjunctions" of democracy and citizenship, especially of the importance of political and civic culture (IA3c), i.e., a lack of ownership of the country and its political institutions and procedures, as well as the public sphere as the space were citizenship is most directly practiced and, indeed, enhanced. In some cases, citizens are not conscious of their rights. In others, they are conscious of their own rights, but seem to ignore the other's.

Carvalho counts that a TV documentary in Rio, produced at the beginning of the New Republic (after 1985), told the following story: "A young citizen played soccer in the middle of a pavement of a busy street in southern Rio de Janeiro. The reporter asked him if he did not consider his exercise dangerous, as the ball could hit some baby carriage and hurt the child, or hit the eyes of a person. The answer came quickly and with conviction: 'I pay taxes and do whatever I want, and where I want.'"[171]

167. Eugster, *Der brasilianische Verfassungsgebungsprozess von 1987/88*, 322.

168. Nalini, "Justiça e cidadania."

169. DaMatta et alii, *Brasileiro: cidadão?*.

170. Carvalho, "Interesses contra a cidadania," 100.

171. Ibid., 101.

In Carvalho's reading, this is the reverse of the complete lack of a notion of rights present in other cases. It is, he says, the famous "Gerson's law" (*Lei de Gerson*): to make profit for oneself wherever possible. Gerson, a soccer star in the 1970 national team, had propagated this principle in a cigarette advertisement in 1976, "it's time to take advantage of everything" (*é hora de levantar vantagem em tudo*). In his case, this principle referred to the soccer player taking a sportive advantage of every situation by talent, while since it has become synonymous of corruption and opportunism.

Another case in point which can be mentioned here is traffic, where those who run too fast or in a zigzag style often return horn or hand signals with ugly fingers or words.[172] In popular city districts, it is common to have the whole district listen to the most potent P.A. installed in the back of their cars—whether the inhabitants wanted it or not. When asked to turn it down even just a little, the equipment's owner often continues without bothering or might even curse you.

In any case, these ways of egoistic behavior might be, at least as far as they occur among the poor population, an aggressive way of self-assertion in a context where all common reasons for respectability fail—education, profession, economic status, powerful family, good connections, and the like. Where people are not respected, they enforce respect by sheer force—be it the potency of the car and its driver's (supposed or real) ability, or the power of a firearm, for example—or emotional power, as in the case of those girls who have children at a very young age and, although very risky on various levels, can thus earn respect, affection, and also protection from people around them.

This statement, which enlarges the implications of citizenship, is building a bridge to the next section, where I shall explore the implications of the effective exercise and enhancement of citizenship.

Citizenship is, I repeat, not restricted to a legal status and its rights and duties, much less to the actually guaranteed ones. However, it passes through these to become effective, and partnerships are needed between the state, economy, the population, and the organizations that seek to represent them, civil society. As public space, where the named realms overlap, becomes a real space for debate, manifestation, claim, and exercise of citizenship, involving people and bridging the gap between "them" (the politicians, patrons etc.) and "us," democracy is fostered and citizenship becomes effective.

What these debates leave for the upcoming chapters is, in my view, a double question: (1) In what way have the churches helped to work on the legislation and to turn it effective, as well as to extend citizenship to become more participatory? (2) To what extent have churches sought to and been able to motivate their members to claim and exercise their citizenship, and assisted them in training for it? First, however, I shall look into theology to see what difference the debate on citizenship has made to it.

172. Despite a fairly severe Traffic Law, number 9,503, of September 23, 1997, and the recent abolition of tolerance in the amount of alcohol drivers may have in their veins while driving (law number 11,705, of June 19, 2008), insufficient police action with the related sense of impunity leads to dangerous streets. On the last weekend of summer holidays in 2009, Federal Road Police fined 2,598 drivers in only ten hours of radar control for excessive speed, i.e. over four in a minute, which sheds some light on the reality.

D. Liberation Theology and Citizenship

An der Befreiungstheologie führt kein Weg vorbei.
Clodovis Boff[1]

HAVING DESCRIBED THE ROLE of the churches before, during, and after the process of transition, this chapter shall look at the theology which, in the first place, claimed and subsequently fostered such an active role, especially that of the Roman Catholic Church. It is true that this theology, which has become known worldwide as "Theology of Liberation" or "Liberation Theology," has never been the theology of the majority, nor has it been defended by all those who opposed the military regime. It has also been questioned to what extent this theology had always and unanimously supported democracy.[2] The background to this question is the diagnosis of a strong critique among liberation theologians toward a "liberal"—understood as bourgeois, individualistic, and capitalist—notion of democracy and the expectation of a real socialist alternative, thoroughly disappointed by 1989 at the latest. However, this position has given way to a more pragmatic attitude and the claim of a *participatory*, as opposed to a merely liberal or procedural democracy. Citizenship, which as has been shown is a key term in Brazilian democracy, appears as a plausible and useful focus for theological reflection on democracy in Brazil today, capable of retrieving the important insights of Liberation Theology, while re-contextualizing it.

Liberation Theology has laid the groundwork for a way of thinking that argues for and makes plausible the foundational importance of the contextual aspect of theology, especially in view of its economical, political, and social dimensions.[3] It is a theology stemming from an interaction with a specific context, while not being restricted to that context; it has links with worldwide Christian theology, interacts with worldwide Christian bodies (confessional or ecumenical), the academy and national and international civil society. Hence, it has gained recognition and visibility far beyond national or continental borders. It is, therefore, plausible to focus on this theological line, present as it is in literature and public perception, having become virtually hegemonic in Brazil and Latin America, and question it in terms of new and further developments within it. As Clodovis Boff defended in a brief and clear statement: "There is no way past the Theology of Liberation"[4]—not

1. "There is no way past the Theology of Liberation." Boff, "Die Theologie der Befreiung," 216.

2. Maclean, *Opting for Democracy?*

3. I have shown this in detail in relation to Leonardo Boff's theology, Sinner, *Reden vom Dreieinigen Gott in Brasilien und Indien*, 77–98. A first version of this chapter (ID) has been published in my article, "Brazil: From Liberation Theology to a Theology of Citizenship as Public Theology."

4. See also Boff, "Die Theologie der Befreiung," 222, where he explicitly speaks of a "hegemonic theology, which showed the Church the way on its pastoral trajectory, morally and intellectually"; he also calls it an "epochal," a "historically necessary" and not only "conjunctural" theology; he even states that "every theologian must adopt a liberation

in terms of its content, much less in terms of its historical impact. In a first step, I shall describe and discuss the most important foundations of Latin American Liberation Theology, focusing on Brazilian authors, and its recent developments (1). Then, I shall present formulations and argue for what I consider to be one of the most promising and necessary thematic focal points today: A theology of citizenship (2). Finally, I shall attempt to link up the outline of this theology to the worldwide debate on public theology, which, so far, has received little attention in Brazil and Latin America (3).

1. LIBERATION THEOLOGY: RECENT DEVELOPMENTS

Before we do theology, we have to do liberation.

Clodovis Boff[5]

In this first section, I shall present the foundations of Liberation Theology, both in terms of its historical origins and of its main concepts and method (a). Recent developments in Liberation Theology as to its subjects and themes follow (b), and I finally discuss the lack of a "historical project" in contemporary Liberation Theology (c).

a) Foundations of Liberation Theology

Without doubt, the forerunners of what came to be known as (Latin American) Liberation Theology, Presbyterians Richard Shaull and Rubem Alves,[6] and the Liberation Theology, which was formulated mainly by Roman Catholic theologians in the late 1960s and in the 1970s, most prominently by Peruvian Gustavo Gutiérrez,[7] have provided an important theoretical foundation for social and political action. This theological movement has brought, internationally, "theology in[to] movement,"[8] providing the grounds for a real awareness of the contextual character of theology[9] and bringing to the fore the "theology from the edge,"[10] in contact with similar movements on various continents, which originated in the same period. They are collectively defined as "Third World

theology" (Boff, "Epistemology and Method of the Theology of Liberation," 59f.; 61). While these statements are rather bold, Maduro, "Once Again Liberating Theology?" 20 positions it again (or still?) in the fight against the dominant theologies, affirming that "Liberation Theologies are subaltern."

5. Boff, "Epistemology and Method of the Theology of Liberation," 73.

6. Shaull's relevant contributions on Liberation Theology are *Encounter with Revolution* and "Die revolutionäre Herausforderung an Kirche und Theologie." Alves' 1968 Princeton dissertation is arguably the first book on a Theology of Liberation, which indeed was its original title (then changed for the published book to "A Theology of Human Hope"): "Towards a Theology of Liberation: An Exploration of the Encounter Between the Languages of Humanistic Messianism and Messianic Humanism." It was translated into Portuguese only in 1987, with an explicatory preface that counts the story of the book's coming into being. On Shaull, Burity, *Os protestantes e a revolução brasileira*, 101ff.; César, "Church and Society"; Faria, *Fé e compromisso*; Shaull, *Surpreendido pela graça*. A "Theology of Revolution" and, more generally, a revolutionary mood had been in effervescence since the 1950s (cf. above, IA1, IB1, IB4; below, IIC1, IID1), with an influence on and help by the Ecumenical Movement.

7. Gutiérrez, "Notes for a Theology of Liberation," *A Theology of Liberation*.

8. Segundo, *Liberation of Theology*.

9. I have dealt with the polarity of contextuality and catholicity in Sinner, *Reden vom Dreieinigen Gott in Brasilien und Indien*, 34–53, using it as the perspective for the whole book, and citing pertinent literature. I just mention here Schreiter, *Constructing Local Theologies*; newer publications include Brinkman and Keulen, *Christian Identity in Cross-Cultural Perspective*; Sanneh, *Whose Religion is Christianity?*; Bevans and Schroeder, *Constants in Context*.

10. Boff, *Faith on the edge*.

Theologies," visible in the foundation of the *Ecumenical Association of Third World Theologians* (EATWOT) in 1976, which has been providing an important platform for the decolonialization of theology.[11] "Third World," in this context, was a protest term against the dominance of the so-called First (the industrialized West) and Second (the socialist East) worlds, quite in line with the movement of non-aligned countries. Also in the so-called First World, black and feminist theologies emerged as theologies of liberation from oppression based on race, ethnicity, and gender. Thus, there are "theologies of liberation" in the plural. When I use the singular, and with capital letters, I am referring to Liberation Theology as developed in Latin America, which, despite its diversity, can be clearly identified historically, personally, and bibliographically. It sought to present itself, not as homogenous, but as united by a common struggle, and so it seems legitimate to use this singular.[12]

Liberation Theology's backbone is, without doubt, the (preferential) option for the poor, as officially adopted by the second and third continental assemblies of the Latin American Episcopal Council (CELAM) in Medellín (1968) and Puebla (1979) and maintained ever since.[13] As Gustavo Gutiérrez recalls,[14] it is a "preferential" option because of the "universality of God's love that excludes no one." The same universal love of God commits Christians to "give people a name and a face," especially those to whom it is denied; precisely, the poor."[15] "Option," on the other hand, does not mean that it is optional in the sense of not being necessary, but the "free commitment of a decision," a "matter of a deep, ongoing solidarity, a voluntary daily involvement with the world of the poor."[16] Jesuit Jon Sobrino and Methodist José Miguez Bonino insist, in this context, on the importance of Liberation Theology as "intellectus amoris."[17] Sobrino even said that Liberation Theology is, "first and foremost, an *intellectus amoris*, an intelligence of the realization of historical

11. Miguez Bonino, "Latin America"; Parratt, *An Introduction to Third World Theologies.*

12. Various attempts have been made to provide a comprehensive view of theology and its answers to contemporary challenges through the perspective of liberation. The series "Theology and Liberation," started in 1980 with a project of 55 volumes to be translated into seven languages, stopped in its Portuguese edition at 28 volumes, all of which have not been translated. Sixteen titles have been translated into German, none of which is currently available on the market (cf. Sinner, *Reden vom Dreieinigen Gott in Brasilien und Indien*, 77, n. 3). A more condensed reference work is the *Mysterium Liberationis* by Ellacuría and Sobrino , translated from the Spanish original [1990], while omitting 14 titles as listed on page iv. Marty, "Befreiungstheologie I. Kirchengeschichtlich 2. Nordamerika,"1209 affirms that, differently from Catholic Latin America, "the plurality of denominations and traditions has forestalled a coherent appearance here [i.e. in the U.S.]." – Petrella (*The Future of Liberation Theology* and *Beyond Liberation Theology*) today advocates a new unity in liberation theologies.

13. Cf. Gutiérrez, "Option for the Poor," "Renewing the Option for the Poor"; the preferential option was already present at Medellín, although not in these precise words; it states "preference to the poorest and neediest," (as quoted by Gutiérrez, "Option for the Poor," 239). It was present explicitly at Puebla, where a whole chapter of the final document was headed "the preferential option for the poor." Pope John Paul II, in his encyclical *Sollicitudo Rei Socialis* (n. 42) formulates it as "the *preferential option or love* of the poor" (in ibid., p. 240, original italics), and the Santo Domingo Episcopal assembly in 1992 adopted the language of "advancement" [promoción], a certainly much less radical formula. The latest CELAM assembly, held in May 2007 in Aparecida (São Paulo state), Brazil, takes up the formula of "promotion of human dignity," under which it reiterates the "preferential option for the poor and excluded" and explicitly expresses the will "to ratify and strengthen [*potencializar*] the preferential option for the poor made at earlier Conferences" (CELAM, *Documento de Aparecida*. nr. 396).

14. Gutiérrez, "Renewing the Option for the Poor," 74f.

15. The same thought is reflected by Pope John Paul II in his Apostolic Exhoration *Ecclesia in America*, nr. 67, as quoted by CELAM in *Documento de Aparecida*, nr. 392: "Jesus Christ is the human face of God and the divine face of humankind."

16. Gutiérrez, "Option for the Poor," 240.

17. Sobrino, "Teología en un mundo sufriente"; Miguez Bonino, "Love and Social Tansformation in Liberation Theology"; cf. Mueller, "Um balanço da Teologia da Libertação como intellectus amoris."

love for the poor of this love and of love that makes us open [*afins*] to the reality of the revealed God," and that this is "the major theoretical novelty of Liberation Theology."[18]

The poor are both the main focus of Liberation Theology and its intended subject—its practical and epistemological locus whence theology is to be developed—hence the importance of "popular education" (*educação popular*) in the line of Paulo Freire and the Church Base Communities (*Comunidades Eclesiais de Base*—CEBs), where this could become concrete. Theologians were to share people's lives and work among them as "organic intellectuals" (to use Gramsci's phrase) or, to use the common Portuguese expression found in Brazil, *assessores*, which translates into something like "consultants" or "advisors."[19] They underwent a real conversion to the people, as clearly visible in Leonardo Boff's self-description on returning from his doctorate in Munich (Germany) to the Brazilian reality in 1970.[20] Many sought to combine academic work with parish or base community contacts in poor areas, trying to provide a space where people's suffering was taken seriously and turned into positive action.[21] As Clodovis Boff puts it: "Before we do theology, we have to do liberation," which is, then "pre-theological," and theology is always the "second act" following proper action.[22] This implies what is called an "epistemological rupture," as praxis is given epistemological priority over theory, herein following Marxism, but also Maurice Blondel's "*l'action*" and the Second Vatican Council's call to pastoral commitment in reading the *signs of the times* (*Gaudium et Spes* 44).[23] "Theology is a critical reflection on Christian praxis in the light of the Word," Gutiérrez affirms.[24] Although not dismissing it entirely, it takes issue with traditional, deductive theology, namely as identified with scholasticism.[25]

Liberation Theology is a theology that started, and continues to start, from the indignation at the appalling poverty to which millions of people in Latin America and beyond are subjected, in

18. Jon Sobrino, Teología en un mundo sufriente: la Teologia de la Liberación como *intellectus amoris*, in *Revista Latinoamericana de Teologia* 15 (1988), 243–66, at 259 and 261, quoted in Mueller, "Um balanço da Teologia da Libertação como intellectus amoris," 42.

19. Comblin (*Called For Freedom*, 201) affirms, at the end of his treatise on freedom, while often being critical of Liberation Theology, that "the best thing about what the church in Latin America has done during the past thirty years has been that it has set itself up in the midst of the poor, sharing directly in their everyday life, in the midst of great struggles to be able to live more humanly despite everything. [. . .] Christians (whether conscious or unconscious) who decide to share in this grace [i.e. of God which enables to overcome the limits of normal human possibilities] have entered into the struggle for liberation."—For progressive Protestants and ecumenical organizations at the time see Burity, *Os protestantes e a revolução brasileira*, who deals extensively with Gramsci.

20. Boff, *Teologia à escuta do povo*, "Um balanço de corpo e alma"; Sinner, *Reden vom Dreieinigen Gott in Brasilien und Indien*, 61–76.

21. On the theme of suffering in Latin American Liberation Theology, see Weber, *Ijob in Lateinamerika*; also Stålsett's (*The crucified and the Crucified*) study on the Liberation Christology of Jon Sobrino, linking the crucified people to the Crucified God, and most recently Westhelle, *The Scandalous God*, albeit not exclusively dedicated to Liberation Theology, but having it as one of the sustaining pillars.

22. Boff, "Epistemology and Method of the Theology of Liberation," 73.

23. Libânio and Murad, *Introdução à Teologia*,184f. formulate that Liberation Theology is a theology *of* praxis, *for* praxis, *in* praxis, and *through* praxis: Praxis provides material for theological reflection, it is intended to "illuminate the intra-ecclesial or socio-political practice," being "given back to the practice of the faithful or citizen," the theologian has to be related to the practice he reflects, being committed to the cause of the liberation of the poor, and led to an *orthopraxis*, preserving faith in this practice. Westhelle, "Befreiungstheologie II. Systematisch," 1213 recalls the Aristotelian distinction between praxis and poiesis, which translates into action (Tun) and work (Arbeit). The latter is, then, understood as society's production necessary to satisfy the human needs, while the former is taken to be "performative action which is defined through interaction and aims at the transformation of social *relations*" (original italics). See also the comprehensive study by Schäfer, *Praxis—Theologie—Religion*.

24. Gutiérrez, *A Theology of Liberation*, 11.

25. Gutiérrez, *A Theology of Liberation*, 3ff; Boff, *Theology and Praxis*, *Teoria do método teológico*, 185f.

sharp contrast with the enormous wealth a tiny minority have. The issue was "how to be Christians in a world of destitution."[26] As the poverty of many was seen as the consequence of the wealth of the few, this situation was duly called a situation of oppression from which liberation was needed. An important theoretical undergirding became, at the time, dependency theory, which sought to move beyond the then predominant developmentalism. The latter theory suggested that the developing countries will reach, in due time, the level of the developed countries, and the whole focus was on modernizing "backward" countries, while the former theory stated the impossibility of development because of structural dependency in a world divided between center and periphery.[27] Economic and social oppression was further aggravated by political oppression through military regimes. Resistance against such oppression and utopias envisioning a liberated world facilitated a dialogue between Christians and other thinkers and movements, including Marxists, while it divided Christians among those who supported, consciously or not, the *status quo*, and those who struggled for its transformation.

Possibly the most evident influence of Liberation Theology has been its elaboration of Cardinal Cardijn's methodological tripod of "See – Judge – Act," or, in more technical language, "socio-analytical," "hermeneutical," and "practical mediation."[28] The important shift was from philosophy as the traditional dialogue partner for theology to taking seriously the contribution of sociological and economic investigations. This was meant to help in exploring the context *before* interpreting it in the light of a biblically oriented theology—although being rooted in reality while doing religious and/or social work—in order to contribute finally towards the transformation of social reality, and thus being inductive rather than deductive, moving away from the predominant Thomistic-scholastic model in Roman Catholic Theology. For many theologians of liberation a specific reading of Marx became important.[29] There are many parallels between European political theology and North American black theology that emerged in those same years.[30] Also the French *Nouvelle Théologie* was influential, as found in the works of Yves Congar, among others.[31] The articulators of Liberation Theology had been trained abroad, mainly in Europe, where especially the Catholic University of Louvain in Belgium had become a center for theologians from the Third World,

26. Boff and Boff, *Introducing Liberation Theology*, 1.

27. Frank, *Capitalism and Underdevelopment in Latin America*; Cardoso and Faletto, *Dependência e desenvolvimento na América Latina*; Dussel, "Theology of Liberation and Marxism."

28. Boff, *Theology and Praxis*; "Epistemology and Method of the Theology of Liberation." As Petrella (*The Future of Liberation Theology*, 29) rightly observes, the social sciences are only allowed in the analysis of reality, but not in the "practical mediation," where concrete solutions could be developed; cf. for the same critique already Sung, *Teologia e economia*. —The CNBB (Eleições 2006, 22–24) added the fourth element 'review', as it suggested the model for a critical preparation and accompaniment of the elections. 'Celebration' is also commonly added as an element.

29. Dussel ("Theology of Liberation and Marxism," 87) affirms: "First it was Jacques Maritain, then Emmanuel Mounier, and afterward Lebret [. . .], whom we followed. [. . .] But then came Marx, by way of the Cuban revolution (1959), and we began to read, simultaneously, the young Marx and works like those of Che Guevara, Antonio Gramsci, and Lukács. That is, we read a 'humanistic' Marx—as he was called at the time, clearly neither dogmatic, nor economistic, nor naively materialist." Kern (*Theologie im Horizont des Marxismus*) emphasizes that Marxism was received primarily through dependency theory and through Gramsci with his "cultural hegemony" and "organic intellectual," and some other authors like Marcuse (especially in Alves, *A Theology of Human Hope*) and Althusser (in Boff, *Theology and Praxis*), while the Frankfurt School was influential in ideology criticism, not least via the European political theology of Metz and Moltmann. Marx itself was read mainly in view of his "theses on Feuerbach," where the notion of praxis comes to the fore.

30. Cf. Blaser, *La theólogie au XXe siècle*, 219ff.; Batstone et al., *Liberation Theologies, Postmodernity, and the Americas*; Gibellini, *A teologia no século XX* , 347ff.

31. E.g. Boff, *Theology and Praxis*, xxviii; Gutiérrez, *A Theology of Liberation*, 3; Libânio and Murad, *Introdução à Teologia*, 145–7.

counting on the seminal contribution of François Houtart.[32] They knew the theological tendencies there and the thrust given to new developments by the Second Vatican Council (1962–65). Yet it was Latin American Liberation Theology that most decisively installed the notion of liberation and undersigned it, so to speak, with its martyrs' blood, among them such famous ones as Archbishop Oscar A. Romero of San Salvador, assassinated at the altar in 1980, and Jon Sobrino's six fellow Jesuits and two women, murdered in that same city nine years later.[33] But there are many more, unknown laypersons and clergy who died for their resisting the powers and defending the poor.

Liberation became the central hermeneutical category, and a considerable amount of ink was spent in a *relecture* of traditional concepts through the lens of liberation. Both the production of "small literature" for the use in communities and of academic books for use in seminaries has been remarkably comprehensive. Apart from systematic theology, biblical studies became especially important and a decisive vehicle in including laypersons into the debate, for many of whom (Catholics in particular) the Bible had been virtually unknown. Liberation theologians declined to separate secular history from the history of salvation, as the latter was located at the very heart of the former: "there is only one history—a 'Christo-finalized' history," states Gutiérrez.[34] Thus,

> building the temporal city is [. . .] to become part of a saving process which embraces the whole of humanity and all human history." ". . .the historical, political liberating event *is* the growth of the Kingdom and *is* a salvific event; but it is not *the* coming of the Kingdom, not *all* of salvation. It is the historical realization of the Kingdom and, therefore, it also proclaims its fullness.[35]

Many of Liberation Theology's authors have suffered repression from the State and/or the church as they criticized all kinds of repressive and hierarchical structures. The Vatican issued two "Notifications" on the Theology of Liberation.[36] Leonardo Boff is certainly a case in point, since, while he narrowly escaped direct State repression, the Vatican treated him harshly, which resulted, eventually, in his resignation from the Franciscan order and priesthood.[37] Others, like Gustavo Gutiérrez, Clodovis Boff and, most recently (March 2007), Jon Sobrino, came under the Vatican's scrutiny and suffered measures against their theology and its divulgation.[38] Indicating how difficult matters of sexuality and reproductive rights are in the Catholic Church, Augustinian nun Ivone Gebara was silenced by her order (1994–96) because she dared to advocate a de-criminalization of

32. Houtart, a sociologist of religion, founded the *Centre Tricontinental* in 1976, facilitating the interaction and study of scholars from Africa, Asia, Latin America and Europe. It is a "center of research, publication and documentation on the development of North-South relations"; see http://www.cetri.be (accessed on 10/19/2011).

33. Sobrino himself was absent at the moment, surviving the slaughter; his Christology of the Crucified linked to the crucified people took its decisive impulse from that event. Moltmann, *God for a Secular Society*, 197 counts that his "The Crucified God," fallen from a shelf, was found in the blood of one of the dead, and is now preserved in a showcase as a symbol of martyrdom; he paid homage to this on a "pilgrimage" in 1994.

34. Gutiérrez, *A Theology of Liberation*, 86; cf. Ellacuria, "The Historicity of Christian Salvation."

35. Gutiérrez, *A Theology of Liberation*, 91, 104.

36. *Libertatis Nuntius* (1984) and *Libertatis conscientiae* (1987); see Congregation for the Doctrine of Faith, *Libertatis Nuntius. Liberatis Conscientiae.*

37. Cf. Sinner, *Reden vom Dreieinigen Gott in Brasilien und Indien*, 67–70.

38. The "Notification on the works of Father Jon Sobrino, SJ: *Jesuscristo libertador, Lectura histórico-teológica de Jesús de Nazaret* and *La fe en Jesucristo. Ensayo desde las víctimas*," of 26 November 2006 and an "Explanatory Note" only became public in March 2007; see Congregation for the Doctrine of Faith, *Notification on the works of Father Jon Sobrino S.J., Explanatory Note on the Notification on the Works of Father Jon Sobrino, S.J.* As perceived in Brazil and Latin America (I have a good number of e-mails on this in my possession), the Notification is against Liberation Theology as such, and does not take seriously material poverty in citing Pope Benedict XVI's 2006 Lenten Message, where he affirms that "the first poverty among people is not to know Christ" (in *Explanatory Note*, 2).

abortion based on her experiences with women in Northeastern Brazil, many of whom die due to clandestine abortions. Her position was explicitly based on Liberation Theology and its option for the poor.[39]

It was also Leonardo Boff[40] who most effectively propagated a new *ecclesiogenesis* from the "popular church." However, it was not only the Vatican which sobered high expectations, inasmuch as he did not strongly support the upcoming of a "new way of being the Church" (*um novo jeito de ser Igreja*), much less the more radical "new being of the whole Church" (*um novo jeito de toda Igreja ser*).[41] Even the CEBs were not able to fulfill the high ecclesiological and political expectations invested in them. It is true that their number is still high and estimated at up to 100,000.[42] Their national "inter-ecclesial" meetings also continue to be vibrant and with large numbers of participants; in fact, the latest national meeting of CEBs, its 11th edition, was held in Ipatinga in the State of Minas Gerais, in July 2005, and brought together some 4,000 delegates, including fifty Roman Catholic and two Anglican bishops.[43] However, they no longer have the same appeal they had in the 1970s and 1980s, and there has been a considerable shift from CEBs to social movements, Afro-Brazilian religions, and Pentecostal churches.[44] Thus, in a certain way, both the base and the once strongly committed church leadership eroded as the democratic transition proceeded and political repression faded.

b) Developments in Liberation Theology: New Subjects, New Themes

It has been stated repeatedly, and on principle rightly so, that the events at the end of 1989 caused a great perplexity among liberation theologians in many respects and made changes inevitable. The utopian vision of an imminent new social order was thoroughly frustrated. Lula was, by a narrow margin, not elected to the presidency in Brazil, the socialist alternative broke down with the Berlin Wall, and Nicaragua did not hold to the Sandinista path. Expectations had been very high, given, in the eyes of many, the considerable achievements of civil society, CEBs, and liberation theologians.

39. Burdick, "Das Erbe der Befreiung," 30f

40. Boff, *Ecclesiogenesis*.

41. Boff, "CEBs: Que significa 'novo modo de toda a Igreja ser'?"

42. See, for instance, Boff, "The Contribution of Brazilian Ecclesiology to the Universal Church," 80. Sociologist Pedro Ribeiro counted in 1996, based on a survey carried out by the *Center for Religious Statistics and Social Research* (CERIS) in Rio de Janeiro in 1994, 70,000 such groups, defined by the following wide criteria: The celebration of dominical worship services without the presence of a priest, communal self-administration and the existence of Bible reading groups; cf. Sinner, *Reden vom Dreieinigen Gott in Brasilien und Indien*, 87.

43. Anthropologist John Burdick (*Legacies of Liberation*) cites these events as some of the continuing signs of the progressive church, in an attempt to counterbalance, as it seems, his earlier more critical view (*Looking for God in Brazil*). Maclean remains more critical, considering the CEBs' effective impact on democratization "exaggerated" (*Opting for Democracy?* 176). Another anthropologist, Nancy Scheper-Hughes (*Death Withouth Weeping*) offers a sobering description of the development and importance, but also frailty of both the neighborhood association and the base communities organized in the Alto do Cruzeiro district in Bom Jesus da Mata (both fictitious names) in rural Pernambuco she first knew as a community worker in 1964–66 and then as an anthropologist in the 1980s; see esp. the last chapter (505ff., "De Profundis"). Another sobering account is Robin Nagle's (*Claiming the Virgin*) study on a CEB stronghold in Recife whose priest, Reginaldo Veloso, was dismissed by the new conservative archbishop in 1990, and the parish was "taken back" rather quickly by Charismatic Catholics, showing the (im-)balance of tendencies within Roman Catholic parishes and the weight of the (non-)existence of sacerdotal and episcopal support. On the same subject see Burity, "Religião e cultura cívica" with a qualitative, empirical study on the contribution of churches toward democracy and citizenship.

44. Ireland, *Kingdoms Come*, "Pentecostalism, Conversions, and Politics in Brazil"; Burdick, *Looking for God in Brazil*.

While it might have been possible to swallow a mere delay, any concrete alternative now seemed to have lost its plausibility altogether. Only a good number of years later, liberation theologians could speak more calmly and self-critically about that moment.[45]

However, it would be wrong to either consider Liberation Theology dead after 1989 or to affirm that changes came about only because of the named events, although they certainly served as a catalyst, fostering the adaptation of Liberation Theology to a changed context. For one, the appalling poverty has transformed its face to some extent, and some changes have come about (cf. above, IA3b), but it is still there. Globalization and notably neo-liberal politics have given to many Latin Americans the impression of, to use the expression coined by Franz Hinkelammert, being "below a sky without stars" (*bajo un cielo sin estrellas*, in Spanish), without solidarity, without space for humanity to be realized.[46]

Secondly, the 1980s had in fact already seen considerable shifts in terms of subjects and themes.[47] Subjects, because "the poor" or, more widely, "the oppressed" came to be seen and described more and more clearly as concrete persons with a face rather than as a supposedly homogenous category. Already in the 1970s, Leonardo Boff wrote about Mary and the "maternal face of God," striving to take seriously women's experiences and their divine source in the Trinity.[48] But it was mainly in the following decade that women began to claim openly their specific role and to cry out for liberation.[49] A theology from the experience of African Brazilians also came to the fore, as it did in the case of indigenous peoples. Thus, the poor and oppressed became more specifically identified; among them persons who were not all materially poor, but still oppressed. As Gutiérrez tentatively defined it: "the poor are the non-persons, the 'insignificant ones', the ones that don't count either for the rest of society, and, far too frequently, for the Christian churches."[50] It has become customary to speak also about the triple oppression that poor, black women are enduring.

Other new subjects are still struggling to be recognized even among liberation theologians, namely, lesbian, gay, bisexual, or transgendered (LGBT) persons. Gay theology and queer theory are having great difficulties in taking root in Latin America, unlike North America and Europe where LGBT has gained considerable, although certainly not unanimous, recognition.[51] Persons

45. An example for this would be Assmann, "Por uma teologia humanamente saudável".

46. Cf. Tamez, *Bajo un cielo sin Estrellas*, 13. Biblical key references, notably from the Old Testament, appear to accompany the different phases of Liberation Theology: Central was, of course, the Exodus narrative (liberation from Egyptian bondage), but under a situation of "captivity" (L. Boff) in the worst years of repression, the Babylonian Exile became an important reference, and under new circumstances, Tamez ("When the Horizons Close Upon Themselves") makes a reading of Qohélet to formulate hope in the midst of absurdity.

47. An excellent overview on *desdobramentos* (follow-ups), i.e., the continuing development of the same argument, like the shift from "the poor" to "the excluded," and *deslocamentos* (dislocation of focus), i.e., theology being developed from new subjects and around new themes, is to be found in Carlos G. Bock's (*Teologia em mosáico*) doctoral dissertation, unfortunately unpublished and available only in Portuguese. The translated title reads as follows; *Theology in a Mosaic: the New Latin American Theological Scenario in the 1990s.*

48. Boff, *The Maternal Face of God*; cf. Sinner, *Reden vom Dreieinigen Gott in Brasilien und Indien*, 154.

49. For recent overviews see SOTER, *Gênero e teologia*; Ströher, Deifelt and Musskopf, *À flor da pele*.

50. Gutiérrez, "Renewing the Option for the Poor," 72.

51. See the provocative challenge posed by Maduro, "Once Again Liberating Theology?"; also Althaus-Reid, *Indecent Theology*; *Liberation Theology and Sexuality*. Musskopf ("Até onde estamos disposto(as) a ir?"; "Who is not afraid of Gay Theology") has recently finished the first major study based on queer theory and gay theology from a Brazilian perspective: "*Via(da)gens teológicas: itinerários para uma teologia queer no Brasil.*" PhD diss., Escola Superior de Teologia, 2008. Online: http://tede.est.edu.br/tede/tde_busca/arquivo.php?codArquivo=96 (accessed on 10/19/2011). Marcella Althaus-Reid, an Argentinian, passed away on February 20, 2009. She was professor of contextual theology at Edinburgh University. Only one of her books, *Indecent Theology*, has been translated into Spanish, and this in Spain, not

with disabilities are being recognized by churches and their diaconal sectors, and they are beginning to formulate a specific theology from their experience.

Besides these new subjects—which in fact are not new, but are coming to the fore in an explicit self-affirmation and are recognized and supported increasingly in this venture—new themes have emerged also. Again, Leonardo Boff is a pioneer when he insists on the dignity not only of human beings, namely the poor, but of the earth.[52] The economy, although constantly an issue in Liberation Theology, is analyzed more thoroughly, as neo-liberal market capitalism becomes a kind of religion in its own right, denounced as idolatrous from a Christian point of view.[53] However, there is a lack of concrete alternatives for effective change.[54] This is also true for concrete politics, and especially law, which have not become a theme of interest among liberation theologians. This is somewhat surprising, given that Liberation Theology is a political theology *par excellence*. However, in a number of publications, the law is seen as merely oppressive, confused with what is perceived as pharisaic legalism, and rejected as if it were still serving only the interests of the powerful.[55] There is, as Ivan Petrella states,[56] a lack of a "historical project"; precisely what used to define most clearly Liberation Theology. I'll come back to these shortcomings below (ID1c).

The *1st World Forum on Theology and Liberation*, held January 21–25, 2005, in Porto Alegre with about 200 participants, showed very clearly that Liberation Theology and, indeed, liberation theologies in the plural are alive. It also showed that they are, today, as diverse as the challenges to which they are exposed.[57] This can also be seen looking at the publications of the (Brazilian) Society for Theology and Religious Studies (*Sociedade de Teologia e Ciências da Religião*, SOTER), which had been founded in 1985 from among Liberation Theologians as an independent civil association—where bishops could not interfere—and understood as ecumenically open.[58] Some of the yearly congresses and following publications are balances of (Liberation) theology in Brazil and Latin America,[59] but all can be understood as indicators of the burning issues.[60] Apart from

in Argentina, which shows how difficult it is to launch issues of sexuality in a heterodox way in Latin America.

52. Boff, *Ecology and Liberation*; *Cry of the Poor, Cry of the Earth*.

53. Hinkelammert, *The Ideological Weapons of Death*; Assmann and Hinkelammert, *A idolatria do Mercado*; Sung, *Teologia e economia*.

54. Brandt, "Befreiungstheologie nach der Wende" (esp. 969) is critical in relation to 'effectiveness', as it tends to instrumentalize theology and secularize the analysis of reality, and cites Vitor Westhelle and Rubem Alves as testimonies of this criticism. However, he insists on "the prophetic" as the continuous task of Liberation Theology and its enduring heritage. I don't see this as precluding what I am arguing here: That the churches and theology are, and should be, contributing to effective changes in people's lives, which is not to say that they are to be restricted to this or would need to undergo a secularization to this end.

55 Tamez, *Contra toda condena*. More positive is Miguez Bonino ("From Justice to Law and Back"), who calls for an adequate combination of "justice, law and power."

56. Petrella, *The Future of Liberation Theology*.

57. Number 5/2004 of the international theological review *Concilium* was dedicated to the theme of "A Different World is Possible." Presentations have been published in Susin, *Teologia para outro mundo possível* (English edition: Althaus-Reid, Petrella and Susin, *Another Possible World*). A second edition was held in Nairobi, Kenya, January 20–25, 2007, with the texts published by Getui, Susin and Churu, *Spirituality for Another Possible World* (in English). The third Forum, focusing on "Earth and Water" was held in Belém, in the Amazon region, from January 21–25, 2009, see Santos and Susin, *Nosso planeta, nossa vida*. The fourth Forum happened in Dakar, Senegal, from February 5-11, 2011, see http://www.wftl.org.

58. They, thus, effectively applied a doctrine of the two regiments, escaping into the secular regiment to be free of any ecclesial influence—but precisely to do theology in a free, academic space; see below, IIIA5, IIIB2b.

59. Susin, *O mar se abriu*; *Sarça ardente*.

60. Anjos, "Teologia e ciências da religião no Brasil."

continuously relevant issues of necessary social transformation and the persistent exclusion of the poor,[61] challenges of (post-)modernity, the development of technology and science, the place of theology in the university, and questions of gender have been dealt with.[62] Academic theology is located more and more clearly at the interface of church and science, not least due to the fact that theology has been recognized by the Brazilian Ministry of Education as a duly academic subject matter in 1999 (cf. below, IIIB2b). This will certainly bring a certain distancing from the churches, a greater diversification and a more strongly academic character to theology, whose long term consequences are not yet to be seen. In any case, theology is well underway towards achieving its citizenship in juridical terms and also in terms of state support for research projects.[63]

c) The Lack of a "Project" in Liberation Theology

A lack of innovative reflection in Liberation Theology is to be stated not only in the evasion of its personal basis, i.e., the apparently higher attractivity of Pentecostal and Neopentecostal churches and Charismatic Movements within the historic churches, like the Catholic Charismatic Renewal (cf. below, IIB1), but also in a vacuum created within its own foundations: There is no actual "project" Liberation Theology would be fighting for, as Petrella notes.[64] In Miguez Bonino's definition,

> 'historical project' is [. . .] a midway term between an utopia, a vision which makes no attempt to connect itself historically to the present, and a program, a technically developed model for the organization of society. [. . .] It is in this general sense that we speak of a Latin American socialist project of liberation.[65]

For Hugo Assmann, faith "implies a consciousness of the fact that the real act of faith, as a concrete bodily realization of a praxis placed within the historical process, always includes an option related to historical projects."[66] And Gustavo Gutiérrez, as cited by Petrella[67] affirms that "the mediation of the historical project of the creation of a new man," while not identical to the God's Kingdom, "assures that liberation from sin and communion with God in solidarity with all men—manifested in political liberation and enriched by its contributions—does not fall into idealism and evasion."

61. Susin, *Terra prometida*; Freitas, *Religião e transformação no Brasil.*

62. The themes of the congresses, apart from those who explicitly take stock of (Liberation) theology in Brazil and seek to develop it further, or deal with issues of social transformation have been, over the last ten years: Theology and New Paradigms (1996); Religious Experience: Risk or Adventure? (1998); Mysterium creationis: An Interdisciplinary Look at the Universe (1999); Gender/Feminist Theology: Challenges and Perspectives for Theology (2002); Corporeity and Theology (2004); Relevance and Functions of Theology in Society (2005); God and Life: Challenges, Alternatives and Future of Latin America and the Caribbean (2007); Sustainability of Life and Spirituality (2008); Religion, Science and Technology (2009); Religions and World Peace (2010); Religion and Education for Citizenship (2011)

63. Cf. Anjos, "Teologia e ciências da religião no Brasil," 481. The author mentions that "strangely, theology is to be found among the subject matters with the highest number of scientific publications in Brazil," although it is, at the same time, underrepresented in the Ministry of Education's departments and generally subsumed under the area of "Philosophy," ibid., 485.

64. Petrella, *The Future of Liberation Theology.*

65. Miguez Bonino, *Doing Theology in a Revolutionary Situation*, 38f.

66. Quoted by Petrella, *The Future of Liberation Theology*, 14, translated from Assmann, *Teología desde la praxis de la liberación*, 168. As Petrella rightly observes, the English edition of Assmann's book (*Theology for a Nomad Church*) omits the whole second part of the original, precisely where the more concrete chapters are to be found, including an entire chapter on "Church and historical project" (*Teología desde la praxis de la liberación*, 157–170).

67. Petrella, *The Future of Liberation Theology*, 16.

In his sharp analysis, Ivan Petrella identifies three not mutually exclusive, but still distinct ways of reacting to the fall of socialism and the consequent lack of a real alternative: First, reasserting core ideas, namely the preferential option for the poor; secondly, reformulating basic categories to highlight humanity, everyday life, and civil society; thirdly, denouncing capitalism as idolatry.[68]

The *first* position is to reassert core ideas, namely the preferential option for the poor, the Reign of God, and liberation, while disassociating them from a concrete historical project as was socialism. As genuinely theological concepts, not tied to any particular historical project, then, these would not really be affected by the 1989 events. The *second* is to reformulate basic categories, seeking a middle way between the earlier revolutionary worldview and the contemporarily dominant neo-liberal market-based model. "Humanity" serves as a basic category against the reigning individualism, and "everyday life" replaces the notion of the poor as "revolutionary subjects." According to Pedro Trigo, quoted here as the main example of such a reformist position: "We insist that the historical strength of the poor is not exercised in politics as a privileged realm but in the sphere of everyday life recreating, healing and strengthening the social fabric."[69] Another element is the emphasis on the importance of civil society, which, as we have seen, links up well with the reaction of other formerly revolutionary movements (cf. above, IB). In sum, this position takes on board the first position's theological core, but goes beyond it in its "rejection of a unified revolutionary subject of history, the refusal to accept the dichotomy of reform and revolution, and an espousal of popular culture and civil society as the privileged arenas for liberation."[70] While acknowledging the importance of this position, Petrella is correct in criticizing the idealization of civil society as a supposedly bottom-up venture and a "downplaying [of] the importance of state power" (cf. above, IC2). I would add in this category those who venture into pluralism and inter-religious dialogue, which they, however, invariably do without taking into account *Christian* pluralism and ecumenism.[71] The *third* tendency is critiquing the market as idolatry, spearheaded by Franz Hinkelammert[72] at the Ecumenical Department of Investigations (DEI) in Costa Rica. As even Michael Camdessus, former head of the International Monetary Fund (IMF), could use Liberation Theology's terminology to explain the IMF's mandate to Christian businessmen,[73] cooptation seems to be easy and capable of turning this originally critical theology into an asset for the IMF and its customary policy of austerity through cuts in social spending. Against this idolatrous god who asks for sacrifices, Hinkelammert invokes the biblical witness as to the God of life who opposes sacrifice. As Petrella underlines, the critique of idolatry goes both against capitalism and real existing socialism as people forced under a logic of profitability, imposed by the State.[74] While there

68. Ibid. Ivan Petrella is of Argentinian origin, holds a PhD in Religious Studies and Law from Harvard University and is currently Associate Professor of Religious Studies at the University of Miami. Together with Marcella Althaus-Reid and others he has been working on the formulation of a "next generation" Liberation Theology, cf. Petrella, *Latin American Liberation Theology*.

69. Trigo, Pedro, "El futuro de la Teologia de la liberación", in Comblin, José et al. (eds.), *Cambio Social y Pensamiento Cristiano en América Latina* (Madrid: Trotta, 1993), 297–317, here 314, in Petrella, *The Future of Liberation Theology*, 6.

70. Petrella, *The Future of Liberation Theology*, 6.

71. Tomita et al., *Pluralismo e libertação*.

72. Hinkelammert, *The Ideological Weapons of Death*; "Liberation Theology in the Economic Social Context of Latin America."

73. Petrella, *The Future of Liberation Theology*, 8.

74. Unger, *What should Legal Analysis Become?; Democracy Realized: The Progressive Alternative.*

is, thus, a necessary unmasking of economy's idolatries, this position does not provide a viable alternative option and, furthermore, relies on a unitary, restricted reading of what capitalism is.[75]

By not presenting a new project and, indeed, abandoning the notion of historical project altogether, Liberation Theology is, according to Petrella, giving away what once was most central to it; that is, a concrete mediation of liberation in view of the reign of God for social transformation in order to overcome poverty. Petrella's own proposal is not to provide a new historical project, but to pave the way for it. He follows Roberto Mangabeira Unger's reflections within critical legal thought.[76] He thus suggests that Liberation Theology "must" [sic!] follow these three steps: "theorizing society as frozen politics, recognizing the variety of capitalisms, and incorporating critical legal thought's process of mapping and criticism."[77] "Frozen politics" refers to the political and economic institutions as "the result of contained political and ideological strife"; that is, presupposing that society is heterogeneous and institutions are not simply a given. Thus, it is "institutional imagination" that has to prevail in its specific context, which leads to a "step-by-step process" rather than an "empty imaginative leap between a monolithic capitalism to an equally monolithic socialism or abstractly defined participatory democracy."[78]

Indeed, Liberation Theology should deal with concrete problems of society in order to contribute to their solution. Apart from pointing to shortcomings of an incomplete democracy and an excluding neo-liberal market economy, and the danger of idolatry in this economy's religious features, Liberation Theology should, in interdisciplinary cooperation not least with political scientists and specialists of law, look for possibilities of alternatives in society, while at the same time continuing to strive for reform within the church. As Maclean's earlier study on *Opting for Democracy?* aptly showed, liberation theologians were slow in adapting to the changing context and lagging behind the political left in terms of finding more pragmatic approaches and building new alliances, which led to their isolation in the 1980s.[79] Nearly a decade later, Petrella is right in pointing to continuous shortcomings in Liberation Theology's adaptation to the new political situation, especially following the 1989 events. There is an as yet unmet need for constructive

75. Sigmund, *Liberation Theology at the Crossroads.*

76. Unger, *What Should Legal Analysis Become?* Unger, a Brazilian-U.S. double citizen, born in Rio de Janeiro in 1947, has been Professor of Philosophy of Law at Harvard University since 1971 and has published both in the United States and in Brazil. He is a founder of the Brazilian Republican Party (PRB; http://www.prb.org.br), of which he is a vice-president. It is noteworthy that the Vice-President of the Republic, José Alencar, is a prominent member of this party, founded to escape the bad image created by the 2005 *mensalão* corruption scandal (see above, IA1) in relation to his former party, the Liberal Party (*Partido Liberal* – PL). Both had and have strong links to the IURD, with Bishop and Senator Marcello Crivella among its leaders. In April 2007, despite his fierce criticism of the first mandate, Unger received and accepted President Lula's invitation to become a minister in his second government, in a special secretariat for long-term actions. Later, the ministry was called "Extraordinary Ministry for Strategic Issues," and Unger started to travel from state to state to analyze possible actions with transforming potential. In an interview, the (liberal) main newspaper in Porto Alegre asked him whether he felt he was being taken seriously, showing the scepticism many hold against this somewhat enigmatic job of a philosopher-politician; *Zero Hora* of February 13, 2008, 12. One result has been a bold development project for the Amazon region which, however, clashed directly with environment minister Marina Silva's plans of environmental protection in the region and led to her resignation on May 13, 2008. A bit over a year later, in June, 2009, Unger also resigned and returned to Harvard. Silva, a member of the Assemblies of God, ran for the presidency in 2010 for the Green Party and won a remarkable 20% of the vote.

77. Petrella, *The Future of Liberation Theology*, 111.

78. Ibid., 107.

79. South African theologian's Iain Maclean's study, completed as a doctoral dissertation in 1996 at Harvard Divinity School and published in 1999, gives a competent overview on Liberation Theology's positions towards democracy until the mid-1990s. I have been able to draw on a good number of its bibliography for that period, which is to be thankfully acknowledged here.

proposals. At the same time, to speak of a "historical project," as Petrella does, seems to me to reinforce an either/or alternative, a change of the system as such.[80] Such either/or alternatives, however, are precisely what Petrella wants to avoid, since he emphasizes a "step-by-step process" and "mapping and criticism." His concrete positive examples are to reshape property rights through associational networks and to include the population in political decisions through major popular mobilization before elections (something that seems rather on the decline in contemporary Brazil, but also in many other countries, including Europe and the U.S.) and through more referenda and plebiscites. Especially the latter is certainly an interesting proposal, and has been brought forward also by Brazilian authors, shortly after the 1988 Constitution was promulgated.[81] Also the others are noteworthy, but imply a number of factors—social, political, educational—that are not to be drawn up in a comprehensive and concrete "historical project." I thus think that Leonardo Boff's rather generic discussion of democracy[82] is right from a theological standpoint, which however should not prevent him or others from discussing concrete institutional frameworks that might correspond better to a theological ideal.[83] Christian contributions should be brought into the discourse in politics, civil society, the academy, media and, of course, the churches themselves to see what contribution they could make, from there entering into dialogue on concrete political issues. Social sciences should come in, as Petrella is right in reminding us, not only in the analysis of the situation, but also in the practical section. This means that theology and politics, as well as theology and the social sciences, are to be correlated in a creative tension; not being identical, or mutually exclusive, or simply complementary. What is lacking, then, is not only a more concrete spelling out of how a liberating theology could contribute to concrete politics, law, and the public sphere, but also fresh look at how, under the present circumstances, theology and politics are to be related.

One promising way of recontextualizing Liberation Theology, in the light of what has been said on the importance of citizenship in Brazil, are moves toward a "theology of citizenship," which I shall present and discuss in the following section.

2. TOWARDS A THEOLOGY OF CITIZENSHIP

As I have shown above (IC), citizenship has become the key term for democracy in Brazil, although there are considerable differences as to what this precisely means. There has been some repercussion of this in Liberation Theology. Thus, José Comblin states that "the greatest flaw in Latin American nations is the lack of citizenship,"[84] adding that political participation is restricted to a tiny minority. As an important move forward, he mentions Herberto "Betinho" de Souza's

80. This is reinforced in his latest book, where he re-advocates the centrality of class analysis as being at the heart of Liberation Theology ("liberation theology cannot be a liberation theology unless issues of class are at the forefront," Petrella, *Beyond Liberation Theology*, 3). He also signals that one might be more of a liberation theologian outside theology than inside it, asking "could the future of liberation call for the dissolution of liberation theology as an identifiable field of production?" (ibid., 150). The concrete example he refers to is the U.S. physician Paul Farmer who provides health care to poor communities in Haiti and elsewhere, and "rethinks medical anthropology from the perspective of liberation theology" (ibid., 149; Farmer, *Pathologies of Power*). Theology seems to disappear here as a discipline worth to be developed, as does faith inasmuch as it is not entirely put into a practice of martyrdom (an aspect also present in Brandt, "Befreiungstheologie nach der Wende", but there with a strong theological and faith connotation). It is no wonder, then, that only Gutiérrez' earlier works are cited and not those of the 1980s in which he focuses on spirituality and faith, including its gratuity (on this shift in Gutiérrez see Weber, *Ijob in Lateinamerika*, 171–219).

81. Benevides, *A cidadania ativa*; cf. above, IC2.

82. Cf. Petrella, *The Future of Liberation Theology*, 110.

83. Boff, *Trinity and Society*; cf. Sinner, *Reden vom Dreieinigen Gott in Brasilien und Indien*, 117–42.

84. Comblin, *Called For Freedom*, 122.

"Citizenship's Action against Hunger, Misery and for Life" (*Ação da Cidadania contra a Fome, a Miséria e pela Vida)*,[85] and insists on the importance of the people of a nation pursuing their common good, stating: "The nation becomes strong and united when its citizens are able to understand and assume together the common tasks entailed in shared life, striving to get along with one another and thereby establishing the 'national project.'"[86] Where society is split between the elites and the "popular masses," however, nation-building becomes utterly difficult.

Like Comblin, other authors spoke about citizenship through concentrating on the city, both for the conceptual intertwining of city and citizenship, and for the massive rural exodus that occurred in the last fifty years.[87] More than others, Comblin underlines the possibilities of freedom found by the people there, even if under poor conditions, stating: "The new content of liberation consists of learning to be a citizen, a member of the city." The rural poor, according to Comblin, opted for the city and preferred "to live in a shantytown [. . .] than on a plantation [. . .]. Despite everything, they have more freedom."[88] He is, therefore, critical of models of liberation and community that still reflect rural models of life and, not least, a community centered on a powerful priest rather than made up of autonomous lay people. Rather than a theology of liberation in the previous molds, a theology of freedom is needed. He cites a number of challenges to be met, among them citizenship, but does not develop a specific proposal.

Protestant authors also follow in locating citizenship primarily in the city. For the IECLB, this is especially important, as their traditional model was the immigrant or his descendant living as a small farmer. As urbanization has not left the IECLB untouched, "urban pastoral action" (*pastoral urbana*) has become urgent. From his experience as a Lutheran pastor in the metropolitan area of Porto Alegre and his membership in the PT, which at the time started to build up its program of popular budgeting (cf. above, IC1b), Evaldo Luis Pauly reflected on "Citizenship and Urban Pastoral Action".[89] In a rather unusual combination of references, he writes about the "house" as a hermeneutical key to the city, while analyzing the latter's heavy habitation deficits; uses psychoanalysis to explain the subjectivity of citizens; highlights the 1988 constitution and its importance for the churches and the city; examines urban technology and how it could be used fruitfully by the churches; and presents, finally, urban pastoral action from a theological and ecclesial point of view. I shall come back to some of his theological insights as I present the IECLB case study (IID). In any case, Pauly adopts a deeply pastoral attitude[90] in trying to retrieve people's citizenship in a

85. Betinho (1935–1997), a Roman Catholic sociologist and longstanding political militant who was among the exiled during the military regime, was a voice respected and heard by Liberation Theology and civil society alike. In 1993, he founded Citzenship's Action, cf. http://www.acaodacidadania.org.br. He died of AIDS contracted by blood transfusion in the mid-1980s, which made him one of the most important militants for those infected by the HIV-virus. In the same line as Comblin, highlighting Betinho's emphasis both of solidarity values and the concrete conquest of citizenship, see Assmann, "Teologia da Solidariedade e da Cidadania," 33. In a small booklet on "Christians: how to do politics," it was Betinho who most clearly advocated an unequivocal affirmation of democracy, given that, historically, basing political action on faith has easily led to authoritarian regimes. As the society sought for in Brazil is to be for those with faith and those without faith, it is necessary to affirm democracy above faith's contribution to it (Souza, "Os cristãos e a democracia").

86. Comblin, *Called For Freedom*, 123.

87. Comblin, *Called For Freedom*; Libânio and Murad, *Introdução à Teologia*; Antoniazzi and Caliman, *A presença da Igreja na cidade*.

88. Comblin, *Called For Freedom*, 91.

89. Pauly, *Cidadania e pastoral urbana*.

90. Among others, he points to the importance of listening and pastoral care, Pauly, *Cidadania e pastoral urbana*, 69–73. This branch of theological training had to defend itself from being considered too individualistic and not liberating enough, but has in the meantime flourished most, at least at the Lutheran School of Theology in São Leopoldo

democracy, reviewing what the new constitution has to offer and, not least, showing what society expects from the Church: "There is a lot of literature on what the churches expected of the constituent assembly, but there is no theological reflection to date about what Brazilian society, after 1988, expected of the Church."[91] This call for citizenship is also radically applied to the church itself, as "of this half citizenship [i.e., what many are, *de facto*, living in], urban pastoral work heads toward the ecclesial, political, social and cultural construction of double citizenship,"[92] that is, citizenship in society as well as in the Church through the fostering of the laity, their autonomy and responsibility and, not least, their wishes [*desejos*], which Liberation Theology has often forgotten to take seriously. As he retells stories from the parish in which he served as a minister, Pauly makes plain that striving for political changes often times did not come through the correct discourse, but through encouraging lay people to make their own decisions.

Pauly recounts that, as a pastor, he tried to introduce a "materialist" reading of the Gospel of Mark in a Bible reading group.[93] He points to the fact that, usually, "the poor hear the Bible and speak of the Bible in a moralist and imposing way."[94] He was, thus, disappointed that the group wanted to go to a pietistic evangelistic meeting, despite the class discourse the pastor had introduced. He agreed, however, to join them and, after that, the persons in the group became more honest; they told the pastor that they thought if they did something against his will, he would no longer come to see them. The group then passed from a materialist to a moralist and directive reading of Mark, seemingly contrary to the liberation message and its class discourse. The pastor let them do it and continued to visit them. Shortly after that, they started to organize a group, together with the neighborhood association, pressing for access to school. Without liberationist discourse, they did what liberationists were striving for. Pauly concludes: "Their discourse was moralist only in my ear. For them, it was liberating."[95]

One of the most challenging essays of Liberation Theology in the 1990s was an article by Roman Catholic theologian and professor of education Hugo Assmann, where he claimed the continuation of liberation theology as a "theology of citizenship and solidarity."[96] His criticism of classical Liberation Theology included the lack of a perception of who the poor—or, more realistically, the excluded and the discarded—in fact are, having held an idealized view of them as

(EST), with specialization courses invariably booked out, and now also including a professional Master's course. Beyond this, themes like subjectivity, corporeity and resilience are in the air, seeking to combine personal identity and strength with citizenship; cf. Hoch, "Aconselhamento pastoral e libertação"; "Healing as a Task of Pastoral Care among the Poor"; Hoch and Rocca, *Sofrimento, resiliência e fé*. See also the pastoral emphasis in Knebelkamp, "Believing without belonging?" explicitly centered around citizenship (*cidadania*). Ari Knebelkamp is a Brazilian IECLB pastor who spent some years in an exchange program in northern Germany.

91. Pauly, *Cidadania e pastoral urbana*, 16.

92. Ibid., 173.

93. Ibid., 59f.

94. Ibid., 59.

95. Ibid., 60.

96. Assmann, "Teologia da Solidariedade e da Cidadania." Assmann (1933–2007), a Brazilian Catholic lay theologian, philosopher and sociologist, taught in São Leopoldo and Porto Alegre, as well as in Münster (Germany), Chile and Costa Rica, where he founded, in 1977, the Ecumenical Department of Investigations (DEI) in San José (http://www.dei-cr.org). He also collaborated with ISAL (cf. above, IB3) from 1970–74. Since 1981, he has been Professor of Education at the Methodist University of Piracicaba in the state of São Paulo, and has published widely read books on matters related to this field. His ecumenical experiences made him critical of Liberation Theology's "catholicocentrism" and "catholicalist distortion" (*distorção catolicona*, Assmann, "Teologia da Solidariedade e da Cidadania," 28). Assmann's article has received attention by many as marking a new tendency in Liberation Theology, see for instance Brandt, "Befreiungstheologie nach der Wende," 970f.

subjects of their own liberation while not perceiving their genuine desires and aspirations. Thus, he counts among the pendent challenges "a theology of the right to dream, to pleasure [*prazer*], to fraternal tenderness [*fraternura*], to creative life [*creativiver*], to happiness," summed up in the notion of embodiment [*corporeidade*].[97] At the same time, as the poor have become dispensable for the dominant neo-liberal market capitalism, they only come into sight for those "converted to solidarity."[98] Thus, Assmann has consistently worked on the necessity of educating for solidarity.[99] He further insists that it is necessary to "join values of solidarity with effective rights of citizenship."[100] Presupposing the lasting presence of a market economy, there is need for the compensation of the logic of exclusion's effects, combining market and social measures by democratically installed institutions. Assmann does not elaborate further on this, but he criticizes the exaggerated emphasis given by Christians – and, one should add, many liberation theologians insisting on the notion of community—

> to the communitarian relationships, as if they were a sufficient – although indispensable – basis to make solidarity effective in large, complex and accentuatedly urbanized societies. [. . .] there's a dangerous non-observance of the use of law as the weapon of the weakest [. . .], especially a fallacious anti-institutional stance.[101]

Theology, then, is obliged to think about the social aspect of conversion, which goes beyond individual conversion, although the latter is a precondition of solidarity, which, in turn, is to become a "social value culturally available in the social environment one lives in."[102] While Assmann situates his argument more in the economic sphere, I would add that the new situation of political participation, rather than a new economic situation, makes a new kind of theology possible and necessary, precisely as a theology focused on citizenship.

A few years later, Assmann's self-critical balance at the SOTER annual congress took up many of these aspects again, even in its title, looking for a "humanely healthy theology." Assmann asks whether theology, namely Liberation Theology, has been a "healthy phenomenon." Has it helped "many people to 'be in tune' with their own life and to irradiate social sensitivity? Has it been, effectively, a source of solidary energy?"[103] Without giving a straight-forward answer, Assmann affirms that the "negativism" often present in "progressive" ideas is "humanely harmful." And he explains why he feels more at ease now in education than in theology, stating: "Against the backdrop of the emergence of a learning society, with market economy and changing ways of employability, there is no doubt that to educate is to struggle against exclusion. In this context, to educate means to save life."[104]

Methodist theologian Clovis Pinto de Castro dedicated a major study to the theme of citizenship, in which he claimed a *pastoral da cidadania* (pastoral action for citizenship) as "public

97. Assmann, "Teologia da Solidariedade e da Cidadania," 30f. *Fraternura* and *creativiver* are neologisms created by Leonardo Boff and Hugo Assmann, respectively. The issue of embodiment becomes more and more common in both theology, especially as developed from a perspective of gender, and education, see Assmann, *Paradigmas educacionais e corporeidade*; SOTER, *Gênero e teologia*; Deifelt, "The Body in Pain"; Walz, *Nicht mehr männlich und nicht mehr weiblich?*

98. Assmann, "Teologia da Solidariedade e da Cidadania," 31.

99. Assmann and Sung, *Competência e sensibilidade solidária.*

100. Assmann, "Teologia da Solidariedade e da Cidadania," 33.

101. Ibid.

102. Ibid., 34.

103. Assmann, "Por uma teologia humanamente saudável," 124.

104. Ibid., 130.

dimension of the church."[105] His central concept is that of an "active and emancipated citizenship," which he develops based on Hannah Arendt's *vita activa*, Marilena Chauí's[106] reflections on Brazil's foundational myth—which fostered paternalism and messianism, contrary to a democratic and participatory notion of citizenship—and Pedro Demo's[107] critique of a paternalizing (*cidadania tutelada,* as in a liberal state) or social assistance based citizenship (*cidadania assistida,* as in a welfare state), in favor of an emancipated citizenship (*cidadania emancipada*), in which the effective participation of the people is being central to democracy (cf. above, IC2). Castro also refers to the "new political theology" of Johann Baptist Metz and Jürgen Moltmann. Theologically, he grounds the *pastoral da cidadania* on God as the one who loves justice and right, on the commandment to love one's neighbor, good works and justice according to the witness of the New Testament; on the concept of *shalom* ("peace") as comprehensive well-being, and finally on the notion of God's Kingdom. From there, he deduces the church's mandate to live not (only) its private, but its public dimension (*pastoral*), oriented towards human beings in their daily, real life, and not only towards the church's members. Faith conscious of citizenship (*fé cidadã*) is oriented by the three dimensions of faith as confession (knowing God), as trust (loving God) and as action (serving God), of which none must be absent, all being of equal value. Although the *pastoral da cidadania* emphasizes the aspect of action, the other two are present concomitantly. This *pastoral* has to be, furthermore, a "*meta-pastoral*," i.e., a dimension of all forms of pastoral action. Its non-renounceable aspects are the dimensions of action, the formation of subjects of *cidadania* (*sujeito cidadão*), participation of Christians in democratic administration of cities, and finally the missionary paradigm of *shalom.* In this way, Castro takes a position somewhere in between Liberation Theology (of which he takes up a good number of aspects) and a "postmodern mystical religion," in which the action dimension is underestimated or misunderstood in an individualistic manner. He thus avoids separating faith and action, while not fusing them either. While Castro does not offer any specific insights as to what concretely such a pastoral of citizenship might imply, he lays out a theological basis for it. This is especially noteworthy in a church where strong charismatic sectors tend to overstate faith to the detriment of (transforming) action, and which gained a majority in the 2006 Methodist Church's General Council, which decided to withdraw from all ecumenical institutions where the Roman Catholic Church is present. As ecumenical and social engagement have been very closely related in Brazil and Latin America historically, and, in fact, received many insights from Methodist theologians, they appear as synonymous in the perception by supporters and adversaries alike.

Citizenship, then, has made its way into theology, namely those who follow the basic insights of Liberation Theology; economic exclusion has made it urgent and political change has made it possible. It is urgent to engage more concretely and decisively in issues of citizenship, both theologically and practically, inside and outside the churches; I see this as an adequate recontextualization of Liberation Theology's insights. It is somewhat surprising that this aspect has not gained its own "citizenship" in Brazilian theology, despite the cited attempts to implant it right there. A reason for this might be, apart from the general lack of concrete proposals in Liberation Theology as identified above, that theologians who take the challenge seriously tend to pursue citizenship in other fields, like education and anthropology, or through engaging in NGOs rather than in the churches. The latter are contributing to this situation by being apparently more concerned about their own survival than about a new type of theology, linked with "Liberation Theology" or "ecumenism," both

105. Castro, *Por uma fé cidadã.*

106. Chauí, "Raízes teológicas do populismo no Brasil."

107. Demo, *Cidadania tutelada e cidadania assistida.*

of which have a negative connotation for many clergy and lay people. Sadly, this means that both theology and the churches are being deprived of important challenging voices.

It is noteworthy that a similar insistence—but similarly isolated—can be identified in Asian, namely South Korean theology as developed by Anselm K. Min,[108] who insists that citizens themselves have to be the focus of attention, "agents" rather than "agendas," overcoming "tribal" tendencies in Asian traditional culture and a simplistic blame of poverty and corruption on outside forces alike. Min urges a recontextualization in *Minjung*-theology, understanding that its logical continuity in a changed context would be the "theology of the citizen," which is essentially a theology of solidarity with others which overcomes "tribal," i.e., closed, group-centered solidarity. As with Latin America, however, theology in Korea or Asia on the whole has not taken this up as a central point to date.[109]

In part II, I shall present case studies on three major Brazilian churches representative of different church traditions, before presenting elements of a public theology focused on citizenship in part III. Before going on to this, however, I would like to make a connection to the international debate on public theology. With all setbacks, I believe it is fair to say that democracy in Brazil has advanced to a degree where new forms of popular participation, as well as an insertion of churches into civil society's quest for an effective citizenship and accountability in government's instances, have become possible. Thus, a wider term than "liberation" is needed. Public theology seems to me to be useful to this end, but is too unspecific. Therefore, I would opt for a public theology focused on citizenship. In the following section, I shall explore in what way the debate on public theology might be useful, and how the international and contextual dimensions can be linked.

3. A PUBLIC THEOLOGY FOR BRAZIL?

"Public Theology" is not a term commonly used in Brazil.[110] There is only one place I know of which has made it one of its programs: The "Humanitas" Institute at the Jesuit University in São Leopoldo (UNISINOS). Founded in 2001, the Institute organizes yearly symposia, publishes books and articles under the heading of *Teologia Pública*, with a very wide range of topics, mainly in the systematic field (inter-religious dialogue, ecology, ethics, theology at the university, method in theology etc.). According to the programme's website

> the Public Theology Program aims at resituating theological discourse in the academic environment and promote the active participation of theology in the debates which develop in the public sphere of contemporary society. In this perspective, it proposes a theological reflection which, in dialogue with the sciences, seeks to contribute to the elucidation of the principal questions of our time and in the search for responses for the same.[111]

Somewhat ironically, this program is located at a university that originates from a seminary founded at the outset of the 20th century by German Jesuit missionaries, but does not host a theo-

108. Min, "From the Theology of Minjoong to the Theology of the Citizen"; "Towards a Theology of Citizenship as the Central Challenge in Asia."

109. On this, see Lienemann-Perrin and Chung, "Vom leidenden Volk zur Staatsbürgerschaft," 327–30; Lienemann-Perrin, "Neue sozialethische Konzeptionen Öffentlicher Theologie," 439–41.

110. I shall say more on the origin and possible implications of the concept below (IIIB).

111. http://www.unisinos.br/ihu/index.php?option=com_programas&Itemid=25&task=categorias&id=5 (accessed on 3/20/2007). According to the program's coordinator, Cleusa Andreatta, the main references are David Tracy (his *Analogical Imagination* of 1981 has been translated and published by the Institute in 2006), and Jürgen Moltmann (cf. note above).

logical faculty.[112] It is, then, the Humanitas Institute that guarantees more explicitly the presence of religion and theology in the environment of a confessional university.

In 2004, the institute organized an international symposium "Theology at the University in the 21st century," with David Tracy, Michael Amaladoss, Andres Torres Queiruga, and John Milbank among its speakers, and paying homage to the centenary of Karl Rahner's birthday.[113] This underlines the two main aspects of public theology as understood by the institute: a theology in dialogue with contemporary society and, more specifically, with the scientific community.[114] It is important to remember that theology and religious studies have been recognized only as recently as 1999 by the Brazilian Ministry of Education as bachelor's level subjects, which is expanding its visibility. However, theology is virtually exclusively left to non-State, confessional institutions of higher education, including seminaries and universities like the Pontifical Catholic Universities (PUCs) in various parts of the country (cf. below, IIIB4).

As stated before, public theology is not a common term currently in Brazil and Latin America.[115] One important reason for this is certainly its origin in the English speaking part of the world,[116] with which Brazilian and Latin American theology especially has not interacted much; partly due to language restrictions and partly due to resentment towards the United States' support of some of the military regimes and, in general, its anticommunist tendencies. It is important to remember, however, that the appeal made to the Roman Catholic Church in the U.S. to send missionaries to Latin America did not have the expected effect, and although up to 50% of the clergy were foreigners, most have come from Europe, mainly from Latin countries, but also from Germany and Poland.[117] Thus, one cannot speak of a U.S.-American clerical dominance. In any case, while some of the foreign missionaries attended primarily to the immigrant communities, and others might have brought with them a conservative theology, not too few foreign missionaries have been in the forefront of what became Liberation Theology—including Belgian José Comblin, Dutch Carlos Mesters, Spanish Pedro Casaldáliga, and U.S.-American Tomás Balduino, to name just those who are very well known.

112. The UNISINOS was created in 1969, a hundred years after Jesuit education first came to São Leopoldo. The Jesuit's seminary moved to Belo Horizonte in the state of Minas Gerais, in 1982, where it runs the Jesuit Faculty of Philosophy and Theology (FAJE), http://www.faculdadejesuita.edu.br (accessed on 3/20/2007).

113. Neutzling, *A teologia na universidade contemporânea.*

114. Neutzling, *Teologia pública.*

115. Recently, however, the Editora Sinodal in São Leopoldo has started a series on *Teologia Pública*, whose first volume has been published (Cavalcante and von Sinner, *Teologia pública em debate*), and the *International Journal of Public Theology* is dedicating its whole issue 6/1 (2012) to "Public Theology in Brazil", where the certain notoriety the concept is acquiring in Brazil can be measured.

116. This differs notably from post-transition theology in South Africa, where interaction with North American theologians like David Tracy, Max Stackhouse, Reinhold Niebuhr and others has led to its interaction with a "broader ecumenical public theology" (Gruchy, "From Political to Public Theologies," 45) and to the foundation of the *Beyers Naudé Center for Public Theology* in Stellenbosch in 2002, see Kusmierz and Cochrane, "Öffentliche Kirche und öffentliche Theologie," 217; http://academic.sun.ac.za/tsv/Centres/beyers_naude_sentrum/bnc.htm (accessed on 10/19/2011).

117. In 1946, a third of Brazil's Roman Catholic clergy were foreigners, in the 1970s this ratio came up to 50%, see Della Cava, "Catholicism and Society in Twentieth-Century Brazil," 21. U.S.-American missionaries were mobilized among those coming back from Asia or Africa, where decolonization had resulted in their expulsion. They came to counter "U.S.-financed Protestant proselytism" and "Soviet-inspired labor union agitation" (ibid., 23). However, the plan to dispatch some 20,000 North American missionaries to Latin America in a decade, articulated by Maryknoll missionary John Considine on Pope John XXIII's request, failed, and the number of missionaries going to Latin America was much more modest—about 1,700 by 1966.

Another reason points to the same argument that used to be brought forward against liberalism and liberal democracy: the concept sounds too bourgeois, not radical, or not specific enough.[118] However, as with democracy, I believe that public theology could become a useful term for theology in Brazil as it intends: *first*, to address issues of contemporary society; *second*, to confirm its place at the university and, *third*, to be communicable to the scientific, the religious, and the political community (namely, civil society, but also the economy). By qualifying it more specifically as a theology focused on citizenship, the main actual challenges can be addressed, while holding the concept open to other and new challenges in society. Citizenship might, at some point in time, become less of a burning issue; which would be the case when most or, ideally, all citizens can understand themselves and act effectively as such. Public issues, however, will always be there to be addressed by the churches and theology. In a new context where a "critical-constructive" approach[119] has become plausible, rather than a (merely) conflictive view, it seems promising that, as formulated in South Africa, "Public theology [as compared with liberation, political, black, feminist, African and other particularistic theologies] has more of a dialogical, cooperative and constructive approach,"[120] without, however, being naively too positive about democracy and the neo-liberal capitalist market economy.[121]

Breitenberg, in his overview about public theology, arrives at the following definition:

> Expressed in terms of the Christian tradition, public theology intends to provide theologically informed interpretations of and guidance for individuals, faith communities, and the institutions and interactions of civil society, in ways that are understandable, assessable, and possibly convincing to those inside the church and those outside as well.[122]

This is a useful initial definition. However, as we look at the Brazilian context, we have to be clear that while religions, namely Christian faith communities, abound in an ever more diversified religious field—often characterized as a religious market— thoroughly academic reflection on it is a relatively young phenomenon. In general, only 13.9 percent (2008) of the population between age 18 and 24 are enrolled in higher education in Brazil,[123] and, as mentioned, theology has made its way only recently into a recognized field of higher education. It is true that at least public and non-confessional universities in Brazil have a tradition of strong reservations towards religion and theology, and thus a more qualified communication with them is needed (cf. below, IIIB4). But the greater challenge, in my view, is to ensure communication between faith communities, namely churches, among themselves and between them and society. Religious competition and the strongly exclusivist character of Pentecostal and most historic Protestant churches on the one hand, and the still hegemonic behavior and self-consciousness of the Roman Catholic Church on the other makes such communication enormously difficult.

One interesting result of the recognition of theology by the Ministry of Education is that many ministers holding a seminary degree are now looking for booster courses to obtain a recognized diploma.[124] It might be, thus, that academic formation can provide a more thorough mediation

118. Cf. Maclean, *Opting for Democracy?*

119. Altmann, *Lutero e libertação*; cf. Sinner, "Healing Relationships in Society."

120. Koopman, "Some Comments on Public Theology Today," 7.

121. As in Brazil, similar criticism against too harmonious and potentially "Western" theology is to be found in South Africa, cf. Kusmierz and Cochrane, "Öffentliche Kirche und öffentliche Theologie," 220.

122. Breitenberg, *To Tell the Truth,* 86.

123. As quoted by Amaral, "Projeções para o financiamento da expansão das IFES", 10.

124. I'm not sure about the motivations that lie behind this amazing demand for what is called "integralization," by

between the churches' clergy and wider society than church-run seminaries tend towards; while advanced courses, undertaken by Pentecostal theologians, could lead to an increased awareness of the churches' role and task in the public sphere. By insisting on rational, communicable, and pluralist reflection, such formation forces students to engage with colleagues from other traditions and with different positions, breaking the ghetto-like homogeneity they tend to experience in their own churches. There is, of course, no guarantee of making a lasting difference, but it is a promising space for testing alternative visions on the churches, their task, and activity in the public sphere. These issues will be taken up below, in IIIB. For now, I turn to the case studies, exploring the contributions of the Roman Catholic, Lutheran, and Assemblies of God churches toward citizenship in Brazil.

which former seminary alumni have to do 20 percent of the full bachelor's course to get their State recognized degree, which is usually done by extension and block courses. In any case, it does give ministers more job options. As State recognized Bachelors of Theology, apart from having a formal degree as such, they can apply for post-graduate studies also in other fields and do, say, a Master's Degree in Education without having to do another undergraduate degree.

PART II

THE CONTRIBUTION OF THE CHURCHES TOWARD CITIZENSHIP

The first part of this study was dedicated to setting the stage for a contextually and conceptionally situated analysis of the churches' contribution toward citizenship. It is this latter task I now turn to in the present second part. Methodological preliminaries (A) will describe how exactly this analysis is to be done, what material is to be used and how it is to be interpreted, just as what is to be expected from this analysis and what are its limitations. The second chapter describes the religious situation in Brazil, situating historically and sociologically the three churches analysed here and justifying the choice made for them rather than for others (B). The following chapters are dedicated to these three churches: the Roman Catholic Church (C), the Evangelical Church of the Lutheran Confession in Brazil (D) and the Assemblies of God (E), respectively. Concluding remarks summarize and compare the three case studies (F).

A. Methodological Preliminaries

As we have seen, there is little doubt that the churches in Brazil have been and are making important contributions to democracy and citizenship, being present in the public space and interacting with other organizations of civil society. Notably the Roman Catholic Church (henceforth ICAR)[1] has become widely recognized for its providing a sort of incubator for the emerging civil society in the late 1960s and the 1970s. The contribution of the historical Protestant churches, among them the Evangelical Church of the Lutheran Confession in Brazil (henceforth IECLB)[2] is less visible. They have often been criticized for their quietism or even outright support of the military regime. Pentecostal churches, the fastest growing segment of churches in Brazil and, indeed Latin America, have increasingly become an object of study, mainly from sociologists, more recently with a focus on these churches' political role as they have come to name and support specific candidates for political offices. The Assemblies of God (henceforth AD)[3] have even made it into ministerial ranks under the Lula government.

I have already indicated that the churches are to be understood as part of civil society, at least inasmuch as they contribute to debate and action in public space (IB2). This was done on the background of the history of transition and civil society's crucial role in it. I have argued that the church, namely the ICAR, served as an apt ally for civil society, as did ecumenical organizations composed of some of the historical Protestant churches, including the IECLB and the Anglican and Methodist churches. Other historical Protestant churches and Pentecostals remained largely absent from the debate or were supportive of the authoritarian system. The ICAR, its organs and communities were able to maintain a considerable degree of autonomy during the military regime, which has made it an incubator for the emerging civil society. Feeling repression in its own ranks, it became outspoken on human rights. In its midst, innovative and even revolutionary movements, although dismantled at the height of the authoritarian regime, had left their seed to grow, a strong awareness of the need for social transformation. The Church Base Communities provided an excellent local basis for such action, mainly in the countryside and on the periphery of the cities. The "discovery" of the Bible in a rather direct way, with straight parallels being made between people's lives in biblical and contemporary times, with special emphasis on the liberating experience of the Exodus, sustained these groups in their daily struggles. Many leaders of civil society and politicians of the Workers' Party have come from these communities. Finally, the church's role was strengthened through a theological reflection that has become recognized worldwide for its insistence on

1. The acronym stands for the official Portuguese name: *Igreja Católica Apostólica Romana* and has become customary in Brazil. The English abbreviation RCC could be misleading, as it is used in Brazil for the Catholic Charismatic Renewal, *Renovação Carismática Católica*.

2. *Igreja Evangélica de Confissão Luterana no Brasil*.

3. *Assembléias de Deus*. For a justification of the plural see below, IIE.

the contextuality of theology, the importance of a more precise perception of reality with the help of social sciences, the epistemological priority of praxis and, of course, the "(preferential) option for the poor" (cf. ID1). Both the church and theology were helped by international solidarity and, not least, by the innovative thrust of the Second Vatican Council. These remarkable features faded, however, during and after transition, with a more introspective and traditionalist church, more obedient to a more conservative Rome under Pope John Paul II, and Liberation Theology having great difficulties in reformulating its precepts in a new context.

The following case studies will show that a closer look demonstrates a more differentiated scenario. This is especially true for the role of Pentecostal churches, whose self-imposed political absence—*crente não se mete em política*, "the believer does not mingle with politics"—underwent considerable changes with the constituent process. They are now electing and supporting candidates for political offices. More subtly, they are making indirect contributions through empowerment, giving believers a sense of dignity and respect. The IECLB, numerically the smallest of our case studies and still largely considered the "German church," has been active in the Pastoral Land Commission (CPT) and a partner in the struggle for indigenous rights, and is today leading in academic theology as well as social work, with a recognized position in councils on social policies.

The timeframe for the case studies is from 1985 to 2006, i.e., from the return to a civilian government to the end of the first mandate of President Lula. As to the *terminus a quo*, of course the churches' actions and positions cannot be properly understood unless they are situated in more long-term developments. Thus, a brief historical account will show the arrival of each respective church in Brazil and its development up to the end of the military regime, with a special focus on its political contribution. In the same way, earlier events and statements are quoted whenever necessary in order to understand a contemporary event or statement. As to the *terminus ad quem*, the original project was to go up to the end of the second mandate of President Cardoso (2002), an indeed documental research has been based on this timeframe. However, with the (by many, including many theologians and church activists) long expected election of Lula to the presidency and the subsequent policy changes, advances and setbacks, I could not have left out this period entirely. In order to be able to set a date and not enter into a never-ending spin of including new data, the end of Lula's first mandate on December 31, 2006, has become the final reference point.

The material analyzed is exclusively documentary, although personal interactions, for instance during courses taught to persons who have been striving for social transformation in church and civil society during and after the military regime, and interviews with church leaders have informed this study and are referred to occasionally. I am trying to identify the main thrust in regard to the churches' self-defined role in public space. In order to verify how this discourse is received and put into practice, I contrast it with empirical studies, as they are available. However, I admit that there is a kind of "normative surplus" in my approach, i.e., I do value theological positions from the churches and their theologians, even if they are not necessarily adopted by believers or movements they belong to. While I strongly believe that the priesthood of all believers is needed to live out the mission of the church, and that it collectively guarantees the apostolicity of the church, there is a specific role for theology in securing, by argument, the correctness of the churches' position. Its criteria are not only the *consensus fidelium*, but Scripture and its tradition as text, and—in this case—Brazil as context.[4] This implies that theology has to be informed and corrected by empirical

4. Drawing on Faith and Order work on hermeneutics (WCC), Liberation Theology and a Theology of Religions, I have described this as the hermeneutical circle between catholicity and contexuality (Sinner, *Reden vom Dreieinigen Gott in Brasilien und Indien*).

research, but it is not determined by it. It is also the reason why I believe it to be appropriate to take statements from the churches' leadership as a means to measure its position, although they might not be shared by all or even a majority of church members.

In the first place, *primary sources* were consulted. The idea was to include material from the church leadership (like pastoral letters, official documents, websites) as well as widely available bulletins and journals. This did not prove equally viable in all cases, both for the material itself, which did not always render the information sought for, and for restrictions of time and personnel. Especially in the case of the AD issues of citizenship are, if present, usually only implicit in its official newspaper, and this proved to be astonishingly difficult to get hold of (the few complete archives are not, at this time, open to the public). Thus, other sources had to be used, like training course material for pastors and Sunday school subsidies.

Secondly, *published studies* on the churches, mainly from sociologists, church-related or not, but also from political scientists, historians, and anthropologists, Brazilian and foreign, were used in order to assess the churches' role from an outsider's view. Wherever available, studies grounded on empirical material were especially sought, as well as comparative studies with continental or worldwide amplitude.

Thirdly, *theological* publications from prominent theologians were reviewed as to their arguments in relation to the mission of the church in the public sphere. In the case of the AD, I had to work mainly with few, but important books on the matter. Although they often use translated books from U.S. authors, there are works in ethics by Brazilian writers belonging to the AD, and these were analyzed. In the other churches, books and articles of individual authors or collections of contributions that speak out on the public role of the church and its theological foundation were taken into account.

In terms of analysis, a mainly empirical perspective from outside—even if from church-related institutions and researchers—and a mainly normative perspective from the inside are constantly being balanced. While the former helps to assess the effective contribution of the churches in the public sphere, the latter serves to evaluate the theological foundations and arguments for their specific action. For both perspectives, local, national, and international sources are important as the churches interact very directly with the Vatican, the World Council of Churches, the Lutheran World Federation, the German (and increasingly North American and Norwegian) churches, and the Assemblies of God and Pentecostal theology in the United States, respectively. Many of these, in turn, interact with globalized movements of civil society and international agencies with government representation, notably the United Nations.

Four aspects appear to be particularly important: 1. The churches' own practice; 2. their pedagogical role; 3. their action in public space and 4. their theological reflection. I shall explain these four dimensions briefly, with the hypotheses that are implied in them. From the outset, it is important to acknowledge that all aspects are not treated equally in all the case studies; both for reasons of emphasis given to a particular aspect in the respective church, and for the (non-)availability of material and its limitations.

1. *The churches' own practice*: The way persons are recognized within the churches' practice, in worship, catechesis, retreats, Bible reading groups, social programs, and the like will reflect on their ways of feeling and behaving like citizens conscious of their rights and duties. Such practice covers activities developed by the churches and can include church members or the larger population beyond membership. Most, if not all activities will count on baptized and non-baptized, contributing or non-contributing members, even more so as most churches

do not have a reliable registration system. Special attention, though, will be given to outreach programs, where the churches deliberately make a contribution to the wider population's well-being, grounded in their faith but directed to all, regardless of their religious affiliation or lack thereof.

2. *The churches' pedagogical role*: It is acknowledged that the churches reach more people than any other organization in Brazil. Many of their activities include some sort of education, be this directly—through sermons, lectures, catechesis, retreats—or indirectly, through developing people's practical, organizational, and leadership skills. Explicitly or implicitly, issues of citizenship can be part of such educational processes. Another point in case are the churches' own schools, many of which belong to the best private schools in the country, and there are also confessional universities with very good standards (see below, IIIB2b). It would be the matter of a specific research as to how they deal with their confessionality in view of a usually middle and upper middle class public of all kinds of denominations and religions, or none.

3. *The churches' action in the public sphere*: The churches, through their leadership, congregations, media, or specialized organizations and ministries, collaborate with civil society and with the government on all levels (municipal, state, and federal) and make their contributions through seeking solutions, offering concrete support, and partaking in the debate on the course social action is to take, as well as by offering a religious legitimation to such activity. Given the increasing competition between the churches, however, they are not only part of the solution, but also of the problem, in terms of corporatist tendencies and enmities that reflect on their action and, of course, on the public perception of their contribution.

4. *Theological reflection*: Although not always explicit, theological reflections undergird the churches action both *ad intra* and *ad extra*. The Theology of Liberation has made a special, but not exclusive contribution here (cf. above, ID). Official church documents usually carry with them a theological foundation of their argument, even if it is stated rather than developed, or implicit rather than explicit. At the same time, they relate to issues from the wider debate on democracy, citizenship, politics, public space, poverty, and the like, which therefore provided the thematic focus for the selection of primary sources.

There can be no doubt that the churches do have a public role to play. This is so empirically, because of their numerical weight, their influence on the lives of many people as well as the political system, their innumerous educational and social institutions and projects, and the great amount of trust they still hold among the population. But this is also so theologically and, thus, normatively, since its mission following Jesus is public from the outset, there are many insights to be identified toward fostering citizenship. This will be further elaborated in part III. At this point, rather than developing a specific theological grounding for the churches' task in public space at the outset, I shall see what theological arguments emerge in the official, journalistic, and theological literature, and dialogue with them as I highlight a number of theological aspects from the analyzed traditions that I find particularly challenging and helpful in the present situation.

After a description and discussion of the religious panorama in Brazil and its implications for the present study (IIB), the following case studies all follow the same pattern: In a first section, the respective church or collective of churches is situated in its historical development since it arrived or emerged in Brazil (1.). This section includes sociological "readings," i.e., the interpretation of data on the composition and positions of the churches' membership, with due attention to the internal diversity of each church. The second section analyzes the discourse and practice of the church in relationship to issues related to citizenship as defined above (IC) (2.). Discourse, as explained earlier, refers to official documents, official or semi-official journals, websites, theological reflections, and other available material of this kind. Practice looks at concrete action developed on a specific issue. Finally, the third section seeks to present the theological elements explicit or implicit in the church's discourse and practice in terms of the foundations of democracy and citizenship, the relationship between church and State, between church and society, and between political and ecclesial citizenship (3.).

B. Churches and Religions in Brazil

Bem no meio dos funerais de Deus e do réquiem à religião,
uma chuva de novos deuses começou a cair
e um novo aroma religioso encheu
os nossos espaços e o nosso tempo.

Rubem Alves[1]

É o caso de dizer mais uma vez . . . "bye bye," Brasil tradicional!

Antônio Flávio Pierucci[2]

The saying goes that after spending a short time in Brazil, you write a book, after a longer period, you write an article, and after a very long period you stop writing because you're so confused. There is some truth in terms of such feelings, and indeed the highly irruptive realm of religions, in the vast majority varieties of Christianity, is an enigma, fascinating and alarming at the same time. Fascinating, because nothing seems impossible, and if it is in fact God's Spirit that moves the ever-growing Pentecostal churches and charismatic movements within the historical churches—who are we to control the Spirit, who "blows where it chooses" (John 3.8)? Another saying goes that in Brazil, everything becomes religion. A clear proof of this is that even Auguste Comte's positivism, designed to overcome theology and metaphysics by science, became the Church of the Positivist Apostolate (*Igreja do Apostolado Positivista*) in Brazil, with two temples (in Rio de Janeiro and Porto Alegre) still active and the legacy of its humanist, scientific religion even on Brazil's national flag: "Order and Progress."

All depends, of course, on what is to be understood by "religion," and such definitions are as diverse as is the "religious field" (*campo religioso*), in the expression commonly used in Brazilian sociological literature, following Bourdieu.[3] As to the emerging discipline of religious studies in

1. Alves, *O enigma da religião*, 167."Right in the midst of God's funerals and the requiem on religion, a rain of new gods has begun to fall and a new religious aroma has filled our spaces and our time."

2. Pierucci, "Bye bye, Brasil," 24. "It's the case of saying, again . . . bye bye, traditional Brazil!"

3. Bourdieu, *Economia das trocas simbólicas*, 27-98. According to Brazilian Catholic sociologist Pedro Ribeiro de Oliveira, Bourdieu, building upon Marx, Durkheim, and Weber, considered that "religion performs the symbolic function of conferring to the social order a transcendent and unquestionable character," reinforcing "a given hierarchical order between groups, classes or ethnic groups" (Oliveira, "A teoria do trabalho religioso em Pierre Bourdieu," 180f.). But beyond them, trying to overcome the dichotomy between idealistic and materialistic understandings of religion, he speaks of "religious labor" in terms of religious practices of specific groups, among which some develop specialized agents and distinguish them from the laity. Thus, the "religious field" is constituted by "the whole of relations which religious agents maintain among them and in attending to the demand of the 'laity,'" while the agents are sustained in their

Brazil, they do not hesitate to speak of an "essence of religion" or a "religious *a priori*," in an evident contrast in relation to tendencies elsewhere, namely in Germany, where the phenomenology of religion is generally held in very low esteem.[4] If the former, the sociologists, seek to transmit distance to their object of study in their texts, the latter, most of them theologians by training, strive for combining scientific objectivity with religious subjectivity. Theological thinking, for this matter, has to be constantly informed and challenged by empirical studies to see what motives and factors are leading people to change or abandon their church affiliation. This is why both sociological and religious studies research are indispensable for theology. Doctrine tends to be marginalized by both, as their priority is to understand lived religion by concrete subjects. Furthermore, reasons for religious practice, syncretism, and mobility are identified predominantly as unrelated to doctrinal issues.[5] Theology, however, cannot dispense thorough reflection of doctrine, and the fact that all do not believe or follow what a religious institution proclaims states the need to rethink doctrine in its relation to context, but not to leave it out. Doctrine, even if implicit or not public (e.g. in the case of African Brazilian religions) is an essential part of a religion's, and certainly of a church's, identity and profile.

In order to situate the three churches that will be presented as case studies in the following chapters (IIC, D, E) in the wider religious field, I shall present a panorama of religions in Brazil at this beginning of the 21st century (1), followed by an analysis of the legal status of religions (2), and a brief description of the presence of religious symbols in the public realm as detached from organized religion, more specifically the churches (3).

---

maintenance by the working laity, which presupposes the existence of a considerable economic surplus (ibid., 184). This obviously reflects the application of a market model with monopolistic tendencies on the "religious field"; it is precisely the religious agents that fight any kind of "religious production of self-consumption" and seek to gain and hold complete control over the "religious goods," resulting in a double tension between religious agents and the "laity" and among different agents and types of agents—like Weber, he distinguishes priests, prophets and magi, who represent, sociologically speaking, a church, a sect and a freelance religious activity (ibid., 185ff.). As Oliveira ("A teoria do trabalho religioso em Pierre Bourdieu," 193) rightly criticizes, the types and terms used by Bourdieu clearly reflect its European origin with its specific religious constellation, which has limitations in its application to a Brazilian, religiously dynamic and ever more pluralistic "religious field." I think that he is so appealing in Brazil because he shows how specific types of religion resist dominant ones, as many intellectuals feel is happening in Brazil over against Roman Catholic and European or U.S.-American hegemony. Religious diversity is, then, a sign of anti-hegemony and liberation of the "laity" or "religious consumer," without, however, questioning the highly economicized language and conception of religion, which might precisely not take seriously enough the religious subject. It does also not solve the problem of whether there are—or should be—any criteria for judging what can be duly called a religion and what that should imply in terms of protection and privilege by the State (cf. below, IIB2). On the theological reception of Bourdieu see IIIB5; on reflections on praxis, theology, and religion following Bourdieu by a German theologian who has worked for eight years (1995-2003) in Central America, see Schäfer, *Praxis – Theologie – Religion*.

4. For a comparative analysis of recent publications in Brazil and Germany see Brandt, "As ciências da religião numa perspectiva intercultural."

5. Montero, "Religião, pluralismo e esfera pública no Brasil"; Fernandes, *Mudança de religião no Brasil*; Fernandes and Pitta, "Mapeando as rotas do trânsito religioso no Brasil."

PART II: THE CONTRIBUTION OF THE CHURCHES TOWARD CITIZENSHIP

1. THE RELIGIOUS PANORAMA IN THE 21ST CENTURY: DEVELOPMENTS AND TENDENCIES

Sou católica, como todo o mundo

Candomblé priestess[6]

Pode-se pertencer ao candomblé e à irmandade do Senhor do Bonfim,
filiar-se à ordem terceira franciscana e ao movimento carismático,
ser católica, estudar teologia com os luteranos e consultar-se com um guru espírita ou budista.
Eis-nos diante da complexidade do fenômeno religioso atual e da nossa incapacidade de abordagens fechadas.

Ivone Gebara[7]

The religious field in Brazil is vast, ever-growing, and diversifying, and thus a fascinating ground for researchers, mainly from the social sciences. Not rarely, their interest ventures into issues of public presence and politics. In Brazil, researchers in the sociology department of the University of São Paulo (USP), the Superior Institute of the Study of Religion (ISER), and the Center for Religious Statistics and Social Investigation (CERIS), linked to the CNBB, are the main, but not only references here. There are also researchers from other centers at State universities,[8] some with strong links to a church or church movement, even being religious ministers.[9] But international researchers have also been attracted to the new developments, mainly from North America.[10] They come from anthropology, sociology, or theology, stunned at the wide, diverse, and ever irruptive religious field in its interactions with other social fields. Regular congresses are held with religion as their main topic. Theories of modernity, late modernity, or post-modernity serve as references, generally starting from Max Weber with his theory of secularization and disenchantment of the world. At the same time, given the strong presence of religion in daily life, such theory is insufficient to understand the Brazilian religious field: neither is Brazil really disenchanted, nor has religion simply become a private matter.[11] But there is a certain distraditionalization, as Pierucci

6. "I am Catholic, as everybody." Quotation given in Souza, "As várias faces da Igreja Católica," 77, without citing the name of "a famous Bahian *babalorixá*" —indicating she was a woman, but actually using the expression for a male priest (a priestess would be *ialorixá*). He probably refers to Mãe Menininha (1894–1986), one of the most famous Candomblé priestesses, leader of a traditional *terreiro* (African Brazilian sanctuary).

7. "One can belong to Candomblé and the Catholic brotherhood of the Senhor do Bonfim [Our Lord of the Good End], join the Franciscan Third Order and the Charismatic Movement, be Catholic, study theology with the Lutherans and seek counsel with a Spiritist or Buddhist Guru. Here we are before the complexity of the contemporary religious phenomenon and our incapacity to [generate] closed concepts." Gebara, *Teologia ecofeminista*, 100. I would like to thank my former doctoral student André Musskopf for drawing my attention to this quotation.

8. Birman, *Religião e espaço público*; Giumbelli, *O fim da religião*, "Religião, Estado, modernidade."

9. Freston, *Evangélicos na Política Brasileira*, "Breve História do Pentecostalismo Brasileiro," *Evangelicals and Politics*; *Religião e Política, sim*; *Evangelical Christianity and Democracy in Latin America*; Campos, "Historischer Protestantismus und Pfingstbewegung in Brasilien," *Teatro, Templo e Mercado*.

10. Stoll, *Is Latin America Turning Protestant?*; Martin, *Tongues of Fire*; Burdick, *Looking for God in Brazil*; Ireland, *Kingdoms Come*, "Pentecostalism, Conversions, and Politics in Brazil"; Corten, *Pentecostalism in Brazil*; Chesnut, *Born Again in Brazil*; *Competitive Spirits*.

11. Giumbelli, *O fim da religião* presents the debate between Lísias Negrão, an expert on Umbanda, and Pierucci: While for the former the effervescence of religion(s) defies Weber's secularization model, the latter holds that it is being confirmed, saying that the world would only be "re-enchanted" if religion came to reassume its role of a "totalizing

remarks, as the most traditional religions, the Roman Catholic Church, the Lutheran church(es), and the Umbanda[12], have all lost considerable numbers of members.[13]

Well into the 20th century, it was common to affirm—*pace* the few Protestant and liberal voices—that to be Brazilian is to be Catholic, and other churches were branded as foreign and, thus, non-Brazilian. While it is true that the so called historical Protestant churches (Anglicans, Lutherans, Congregationalists, Presbyterians, Methodists, Baptists) have come to Brazil by immigration, mainly from Europe, or mission, mainly through missionaries from the United States, their members have long been Brazilians, albeit not all of Portuguese descent.[14] They certainly had to fight for being recognized as citizens and for their full right to religious liberty (see below, IID). At the same time, for a variety of reasons, immigration communities themselves kept apart from whom they called "Brazilians" (i.e., those who spoke Portuguese), and maintained their language, culture, and way of living. This was, it has to be said, true also for Catholic immigrants, which did not necessarily integrate more easily than their Protestant counterparts, and would not accept a priest if he were not also an immigrant.[15]

The fastest growing and diversifying sector, however, are the Pentecostal Churches. It has become customary to distinguish, historically and theologically, three "waves" or types of Pentecostals.[16] The *first* Pentecostal churches were introduced by European missionaries who had passed through Pentecostal experiences in the United States. In 1910, Italian Luigi Francescon started the Christian Congregation of Brazil (*Congregação Cristã do Brasil*—CCB) among the Italian community in São Paulo, while the Swedes Gunnar Vingren and Daniel Berg arrived in 1911 in the Northern city of Belém (Pará state) and commenced what became the Assemblies of God (*Assembléias de Deus*—AD). From there, they migrated along with many Northerners and Northeasterners to the big cities in the Southeast. These first Pentecostal churches, which featured

---

cultural matrix." For Pierucci, as for his colleague Reginaldo Prandi, the diversity of the "religious market" would in itself confirm the existence of "religious liberty," and thus complaints about its infringement were unfounded. Giumbelli contests this thesis by critically analyzing the accusations against the IURD made against its economic success, saying it was not really a religious, but an economic enterprise. cf. Montes, "As figuras do sagrado"; Montero, "Religião, pluralismo e esfera pública no Brasil."

12. Umbanda is a Brazilian bred syncretistic religion which originated in the 1920s in Rio de Janeiro and was, in the 1960s, taken to be the Brazilian religion *par excellence:* syncretistic, inclusive and national (cf. above, IC), with elements from African Brazilian and indigenous religions, spiritism, and popular Catholicism.

13. Pierucci, "Bye bye, Brasil."

14. It has to be noted that Anglicans and Baptists reject being called "Protestants." This is the case for Anglicans because they consider themselves to stem from the catholic church in Britain, albeit separated from the pope, and see themselves as an inclusive middle way between Catholicism and Protestantism (cf. http://www.ieab.org.br, accessed on 3/5/2009). As to the Baptists, they could never count on state support, thus not being part of the 1529 Speyer "protestation" which gave origin to the "Protestants." Furthermore, Baptists or "Anabaptists," which see themselves as having existed throughout the centuries even before the Reformation, were persecuted by Lutherans and Reformed alike in the 16th century (cf. http://www.solascriptura-tt.org/EclesiologiaEBatistas/BatistasNaoSaoProtestantes-Lyons.html, accessed on 3/5/2009).

Still, as the term "historical Protestants" is commonly being used for all churches which have their roots in the 16th century Reformation, I will also use it here in this inclusive sense, *cum grano salis.*

15. Leonardo (civil name: Genézio Darci) Boff, a third generation Italian immigrant who learnt to speak Portuguese only at the age of twelve, tells about this in his interview with Horst Goldstein, see Sinner, *Reden vom Dreieinigen Gott,* 62, n. 2: "Brasilianer waren für uns Hinterwäldler, die Mischlinge, die von entlaufenen Sklaven und von Indianern abstammten, die es da und dort bei uns gab, oder waren Weiße mit wohlklingenden portugiesischen Namen. . . So oder so, 'Brasilianer' klang für uns ein wenig abschätzig, war für uns gleichbedeutend mit faul und ohne Kultur."

16. Freston, "Breve História do Pentecostalismo Brasileiro"; Campos, "Historischer Protestantismus und Pfingstbewegung in Brasilien"; Mariano, *Neopentecostais*, "Expansão pentecostal no Brasil."

elements like speaking in tongues, prophecy, and the discernment of spirits, are till this day among the largest and have consolidated over nearly a century, with considerable (AD) or virtually no changes (CCB). This is why they are duly called "classical" Pentecostalism.

The *second wave* counted, in part, on foreign missionaries, as was the case of the Church of the Four-Square Gospel (*Igreja do Evangelho Quadrangular*), who came from the United States and organized a local church in 1953.[17] But Brazilians also were pioneers in that period: Manoel de Mello founded the Pentecostal Church Brazil for Christ (*Igreja Pentecostal O Brasil para Cristo,* 1955), which for some time was a member of the World Council of Churches, and Davi de Miranda founded the Pentecostal Church God is Love (*Igreja Pentecostal Deus é Amor,* 1962). The center of this second wave of Pentecostalism was São Paulo, and its main feature the emphasis on healing as a gift of the Spirit, as well as the incipient use of mass media (radio and then TV) for evangelization.[18]

The *third wave* marks a yet stronger difference, which is why it is called Neo-Pentecostalism[19] or even Post-Pentecostalism.[20] Its main representative is the Universal Church of God's Kingdom (*Igreja Universal do Reino de Deus*—IURD), founded in Rio de Janeiro in 1977 by three pastors coming from other churches, among them Edir Macedo[21] who is leading the church till this day in a strongly verticalized line of command. Other churches in this category are the Evangelical Community Heal Our Earth (*Comunidade Evangélica Sara Nossa Terra,* 1976), home to a good number of people from show business, the International Church of Grace (*Igreja Internacional da Graça,* 1980), and Rebirth in Christ (*Renascer em Cristo,* 1986). While classic Pentecostal gifts of the Spirit, like prophecy and speaking in tongues, vanished together with the moral rigor of most Pentecostal churches, cure, exorcism, and prosperity became the main features in a world populated by evil spirits that are to be fought in a spiritual battle (*batalha espiritual*). I shall come back to this type of church below. First, however, let us see the astounding numeric development of this whole segment, commonly called *evangélicos.* This originally meant the historical Protestants, but is in today's use virtually synonymous to Pentecostals. In distinction from the U.S.-American and British use of "evangelical," where it usually denotes a specific kind of belief, piety, and missionary practice (in the German neologism, *evangelikal* as different from *evangelisch*), I shall use the Portuguese *evangélico* when generically talking about historical Protestants and Pentecostals.

The following table shows a clear trend in religious affiliation: While the Roman Catholic Church is losing ground, *evangélicos,* namely Pentecostals are growing at an astounding pace. However, another group, while still small, is also growing: those "without religion" (*sem religião*), i.e., those who do not belong to any religious community, but might still believe. I'll come back to this below.

17. These and other churches, namely the (not Pentecostal) Seventh-Day Adventists, Mormons, Jehova's Witnesses and the like are being subsumed under a supposed U.S.-American conspiracy to combat communism and progressive Catholicism in Brazil, according to Lima, *Os demônios descem do norte*, with his suggestive title: "The Demons Come Down from the North". The hypothesis of American supported "sects" that alienated people through their otherworldliness has been quite common, but, even if there is a grain of truth in it, largely proven wrong.

18. See Fonseca, *Evangélicos e mídia no Brasil.*

19. Mariano, *Neopentecostais.*

20. Siepierski, "Pós-pentecostalismo e política no Brasil."

21. See Tavolaro, *O bispo: a história revelada de Edir Macedo.*

Religious affiliation in percent of the population

Religion/Church	*1980*	*1991*	*2000*
Roman Catholic	89.0	83.0	73.6
Pentecostals	3.2	5.6	10.4
Without religion	1.6	4.7	7.3
Hist. Protestants	3.4	3.0	5.0
Spiritists	0.7	1.1	1.4
African Brazilian	0.6	0.4	0.3
Other	1.2	1.8	1.6
No reply	0.3	0.3	0.2

IBGE, Censo demográfico 2000[22]

A more long-term comparison confirms the trend, namely for Catholics, evangelicals and those "without religion":

Development 1940-2000 (in percent of the population)

	1940	1950	1960	1970	1980	1991	2000
R.Cath.	95.2	93.7	93.1	91.1	89.2	83.3	73.8
Evang.	2.6	3.4	4.0	5.2	6.6	9.0	15.4
No rel.	0.2	0.5	0.5	0.8	1.6	4.8	7.3

IBGE, Censos demográficos[23]

This amounted, in 2000, to over 26 million persons declaring themselves to be *evangélicos*. This might sound like a small group when compared to 125 million declared Catholics. But it is most remarkable in percentage and, especially, its growth rate. While in earlier decades the average annual growth was at around 5 percent, between 1991 and 2000 it came up to 7.9 percent.[24] Interestingly enough, in the Southern region, where Protestant immigration had been strong throughout the 19th and at the beginning of the 20th centuries, the smallest growth rate was registered.

Two thirds of the *evangélicos* are Pentecostals and Neo-Pentecostals, and among them the Assemblies of God (AD), the Christian Congregation of Brazil (CCB), and the Universal Church of the Kingdom of God (IURD) unite 74 percent of this category, around 13 million believers.[25]

22. IBGE 2000; Follmann, "O Mundo das Religiões e Religiosidades." The Pew Forum's survey, albeit restricted to urban environments and adults ages 18 and older, found an even greater diversification: 21 percent for all "Protestants" (i.e., evangélicos) as over against a mere 57 percent of Catholics, and 13 percent of other religions. "Renewalists" (i.e. members of Pentecostal churches and charismatic believers in historical churches, cf. below, IIE – introduction) make up 49 percent among the urban population as a whole, 57 percent of Catholics and 78 percent of Protestants, according to the same survey (The Pew Forum on Religion and Public Life, *Spirit and Power*, 73).

23. Pierucci, "Bye bye, Brasil," 20. The difference in percentage between the two tables (Roman Catholics in 2000: 73.6 percent and 73.8 percent, respectively, is according to the sources quoted and probably due to rounding differences. In any case, the general tendency holds true with either number.

24. Mariano, (*Neopentecostais*, 134, note 5), a sociologist and expert on Pentecostalism and Neo-Pentecostalism, trained at the USP and now professor at the Pontifical Catholic University of Rio Grande do Sul in Porto Alegre (PUC-RS), says that the high growth rates even among historical Protestants can at least partly be explained by flaws in the 1991 census, which understated their effective numbers at the time.

25. One could also add the strong charismatic movements within the historical churches, both Catholic and Protestant.

While the AD and especially the IURD are very visible publicly, through their active religious propaganda, the use of mass media and political articulation, the CCB stands there somewhat oddly, as it does not make any use of such media nor undertake evangelization campaigns, and still continues as one of the largest churches.[26] But churches multiply at an astounding pace. A survey carried out in the Rio de Janeiro metropolitan area in the early 1990s found that six new churches were being founded every single week.[27] Some are just the size of a garage, with maybe fifty members, others have expanded to hundreds or thousands of adherents. The names are getting more and more "creative": Evangelical Church of the Abomination of Awry Life, Church Explosion of Faith, Evangelical Pentecostal Church of the Last Embarkation to Christ, Automotive Church of the Holy Fire, Evangelical Association Faithful even Below Water, Baptist Church Blast of Blessings, Evangelical Crusade of Pastor Waldevino Coelho the Supreme, Church of the Seven Trumpets of the Apocalypse, I. A. W. B. Church (I Also Want the Blessing), Evangelical Pentecostal Church Spit of Christ, and the like.[28]

There are regional differences to be mentioned. Evangelical churches as a whole are strongest in the Central-Eastern and Northern regions (19.1 percent and 18.3 percent, respectively), and weakest in the Northeast (10.4 percent), where the Roman Catholic Church is strongest (80.1 percent). Rondônia is the state with the largest "evangelical" population (27.8 percent), followed by Espírito Santo (27.5 percent), Roraima (23.7 percent) and Rio de Janeiro (21.1 percent), states in which the number of those not confessing any religion are also very high: Rio de Janeiro comes first (15.5 percent), followed by Rondônia (12.5 percent) and, in fifth, Espírito Santo (9.7 percent) which is, as we shall see (IID), also one of the states with the strongest Lutheran presence. Roman Catholics are strongest in the Northeastern states of Piauí (91.4 percent), Ceará (84.9 percent) and Paraíba (84.3 percent).[29]

More close readings of the 2000 census show that historical Protestants tend to be well-educated and have a reasonable, middle class salary, as well as a higher proportion of white members, all above Brazilian average.[30] Pentecostals are among the poorest and least educated, work as domestics in others' houses and have a higher number of black people and *pardos* (*mestiços*). They are also generally younger than historical Protestants.[31] Both groups are composed above average by women and an urban population. Statistics confirm, thus, what has been said above (ID): The poor opted for the Pentecostals.

These data indicate a dramatic change in religious affiliation over the last twenty years. Over 15 million Catholics left their church and joined another church or religion, mostly a Pentecostal church (58.9 percent).[32] However, fluctuation is, by percentage, much higher among Pentecostals,

26. Mariano, *Neopentecostais*, 122.

27. Fernandes, "Governo das almas,"166; Fernandes et al., *Novo nascimento*.

28. The original names are: *Igreja Evangélica Abominação à Vida Torta, Igreja Explosão da Fé, Igreja Evangélica Pentecostal a Última Embarcação para Cristo, Igreja Automotiva do Fogo Sagrado, Associação Evangélica Fiel Até Debaixo D'água, Igreja Batista Incêndio de Bênçãos, Cruzada Evangélica do Pastor Waldevino Coelho, Sumidade, Igreja das Sete Trombetas do Apocalipse, Igreja E.T.Q.B. (Eu Também Quero a Bênção), Igreja Evangélica Pentecostal Cuspe de Cristo;* "Igrejas para todos os gostos," in *Eclésia*: a revista evangélica do Brasil 8/91 (2003), 44-49.

29. For more data and detailed local surveys in the Porto Alegre metropolitan area see Follmann, "O Mundo das Religiões e Religiosidades".

30. A considerable number of indigenous, above average, is also to be noted, see Jacob et al., *Atlas da filiação religiosa e indicadores sociais no Brasil*, 77; historical Protestants are here classified as "evangelicals of mission."

31 Ibid., 49.

32. Fernandes and Pitta, "Mapeando as rotas do trânsito religioso no Brasil." The survey used 2,870 questionnaires from 23 state capitals and 27 municipalities. The percentage of Catholics in the surveyed area was found to be below

where 84.6 percent said they had changed their church affiliation at least once (there are cases of five or even more such changes). Although 68 percent of the informants have not changed their church affiliation since they were born, it is estimated that 23 percent have done so once or even more often during their lifetime. According to the survey, these are mainly university trained persons between 46–55, often divorced, women and men alike.[33] Another research showed that "one of the primary motivations for joining specific religious groups is the search for protection and welcome [*amparo*] because of the sentiment of loneliness after conjugal separation."[34] A significant number of 30.9 percent affirmed that they joined their present church "because you feel well in it,"[35] indicating the importance of subjective emotions far beyond doctrinal contents, although these are not necessarily unimportant. At the same time, it was confirmed what all other surveys indicate, namely that "adherence to Pentecostalism is strongly related to social vulnerability."[36] Another interesting finding is that those "without religion" (*sem religião*), or rather, those without belonging to an organized religion, whose number has doubled in the 1990s like the Pentecostals, are not simply secularized or even atheistic. 41.4 percent indicate that they consider themselves "without religion" because they "have a proper religiosity without church affiliation," which corresponds to the situation in most Western, namely European countries.[37]

The IURD has attracted great interest by social scientists because of its strong public presence, its efficiency in filling huge theaters or supermarkets turned into churches and keeping people as a kind of clients in loyalty with its "program."[38] This great interest and the fact that the church is today present in most countries of the world both call for a brief excurse on it and a justification why it is not being taken into account more broadly in this study.

Despite the IURDs insistence (and efficiency) on the payment not only of tithes, but of more than it—based on the salary one would like to earn rather than on the one people in fact are getting paid—the IURD is frequented by mostly poor people. Their contributions are "sacrifices," signs of faith, which in turn allow believers not only to pray to God for something, but to have the *right* to *ask from* Him the immediate fulfillment of His promises. The implications of such sacrifice and its importance for subjectivity in a globalized, capitalist world, as well as its narcissist effects have been studied by Esperandio.[39] The church's message of "Stop Suffering!" (*Pare de Sofrer*!) and "Jesus Christ is Lord" (*Jesus Cristo é o Senhor*) is sustained by few biblical references, but by many symbols—including the Bible as a book—charged with magic power to heal, to exorcise and to bring prosperity. While the IURD's discourse is straightforwardly anti-Catholic and against the African Brazilian

the IBGE (2000) census at 67.2 percent (73.9 percent IBGE), while the percentage of Pentecostals was higher, at 13.9 percent (10.6 percent), confirming the trend of the 1990s.

33. Fernandes, *Mudança de religião no Brasil*; Fernandes and Pitta, "Mapeando as rotas do trânsito religioso no Brasil."

34. Fernandes and Pitta, "Mapeando as rotas do trânsito religioso no Brasil," 10. The mentioned research, called "New Ways of Believing" (*Novas formas de crer*), carried out in 2004, evaluated qualitative interviews with 435 persons, from the Assemblies of God, the Roman Catholic Charismatic Renewal, the CEBs and from among those without religious belonging (cf. http://www.ceris.org.br/pesquisas/_read.asp? codDoc=117, accessed on 4/9/2007). According to the first author, Sílvia Fernandes, the publication of this research was abandoned due to financial and structural constraints (information by e-mail of 4/10/2007).

35. Fernandes and Pitta, "Mapeando as rotas do trânsito religioso no Brasil," 28.

36. Ibid., 15.

37. Ibid., 18.

38. Campos, "Historischer Protestantismus und Pfingstbewegung in Brasilien"; Mariano, *Neopentecostais*, "Expansão pentecostal no Brasil"; Oro et al., *Igreja Universal do Reino de Deus*.

39. Esperandio, "Narcisismo e sacrifício."

religions—of whose divinities people are to be freed in "liberation" sessions—it is in fact highly syncretistic and, as scholars argue, precisely for this reason attractive to many. The Pentecostals' asceticism is largely absent, except for the prohibition of the consumption of alcohol, tobacco, drugs, pre-marital sex, and homosexual relationships.[40] By adapting to the general lifestyle—not requiring specific clothing, for instance—, by their presence in the center of the cities—you walk into a IURD temple as if you walked into a shopping center—, their workers' (including full-time pastors') continuous availability, mediatic presence, and immediatist verifiable response—rather than waiting for Christ to return and believing in things unseen and unproven—, the IURD seems to be an apt response to contemporary people's wishes, and effective in its marketing.[41] If Liberation Theology once formulated that "faith [is] in search of efficiency" (Míguez Bonino),[42] the IURD has found it and measures it by attendance and income. Theological training is not only unimportant, but has been clearly rejected by the church's founder and leader, Bishop Edir Macedo, who said that faith and church had to be liberated from a theology that was, rather than speaking about God and experiencing God, simply "the study of the studies on God."[43] According to him, "all forms and branches of Theology are futile."[44]

The IURD has also become a matter of controversy in many respects. Macedo came under lawsuits for unduly extracting money and practicing charlatanism. He comments on this in the interviews with Douglas Tavolaro.[45] The boldness of Bishop Sérgio von Helde in kicking a replica of the national patron saint, *Nossa Senhora da Conceição Aparecida,* on the very holiday dedicated to her (October 12, 1995) aroused strong protest among Catholics and (mainly historical) Protestants alike, and Macedo was forced to remove von Helde from office.[46] The main Brazilian TV network, *Rede Globo*, is always interested in enhancing negative attitudes against what is becoming its main rival, *Rede Record,* bought by the IURD for 45 million U.S.-Dollars in 1989. Politicians linked to the IURD, which amounted to a considerable 22 representatives in the 2002 elections, have come under scrutiny for involvement in corruption schemes, and one of its federal deputies, Bishop Carlos Rodrigues, resigned in the course of investigation. On the other hand, the IURD even elected a senator, Bishop Marcelo Crivella, who in 2006 had a respectful turnout in the elections for governor of the state of Rio de Janeiro, although he lost.

In spite of this high public visibility and the ever growing amount of literature by and on the IURD, I have opted not to include it as a case in this study. One reason is theological: It is nearly impossible to situate the IURD theologically, as it is both highly syncretistic in practice and highly exclusive in discourse, while using very few biblical references. If Christianity is rightly considered a religion of the Word rather than of the book, the IURD is indeed practicing a religion of the book. If it is strong and outstanding in numbers and public presence, it is at the same time isolated from the rest of even the Pentecostal flock (and in any case of the historical Protestants), and in terms of citizenship inserts persons into the economic rather than into the political system or civil society.[47] While such economic inclusion is far from being illegitimate,

40. Mariano, *Neopentecostais.*

41. Campos, *Teatro, Templo e Mercado.*

42. *Fe en busca de eficacia;* Bonino, *Doing Theology in a Revolutionary Situation.*

43. Macedo, *A libertação da teologia*, 15.

44. Ibid., 17.

45. Tavolaro, *O bispo.*

46. Giumbelli, "O 'chute na santa'"; Almeida, "Dez Anos do 'Chute na Santa.'"

47. It does, however, a remarkably good job in assisting the government with the *Fome Zero* program, as Frei Betto—

it goes together with a highly questionable practice of asking for money from those who barely have any, and a theology of demand and immediatism that has no grounds in a biblically grounded theology as developed throughout the centuries. The absence of theological reflection and, indeed, of a coherent doctrine is only aggravating the problem. Thus, the IURD's contribution to a theological reflection on citizenship is very limited. Saying this does not imply a judgment *ex ante* on whether the IURD is or not to be considered a Christian church. There are, however, serious doubts from a theological point of view, which would make a more thorough analysis and discussion necessary than can be offered here. The second reason for not including the IURD as a case, more objective and certainly easier to argue, is that the AD are still the largest, the second oldest, and a prominent member of the first wave of Pentecostalism, with more than three times the IURD's size according to the 2000 census.

Apart from this strong, but ever more diversified Christian fold, there are other religions. Numerically the strongest are the Spiritists (2.3 million), which go back to the teachings of Allan Kardec, pseudonym for Frenchman Denisard Léon Hyppolite Rivail (1804-1869), thus also called *kardecismo*, following his doctrine as formulated in the "Book of Spirits." They believe in a Westernized notion of reincarnation and hold spiritual sessions, in which spirits of deceased persons are invoked through mediums. Many Spiritists consider themselves Catholics, whereby the cited number might be too small. While they often defend their belief as a "philosophy" rather than a religion, they do understand themselves as the synthesis and harmony of all religions. According to the study by Jacob et al.,[48] they form the best educated and best remunerated religious group.

Another considerable category are the "neo-Christians" like Jehova's Witnesses (1.1 million) and the Mormons (some 200,000).

Further religions include African Brazilian religions like Candomblé (118,000) and the (syncretistic, Brazilian bred) Umbanda (397,000).[49] African religions have survived under the umbrella of the Roman Catholic Church. They could camouflage their feasts as they celebrated them on the days of Catholic saints and paralleled their divinities to those saints. They were not generally organized in churches, rather in independent "houses" under the leadership of a (mostly) female or male priest. As their knowledge is not published in books, but passed on orally via initiation and successive stages of teaching, and involves periods of closure, rituals with blood (cuts in the head scalp for initiation), and animal sacrifices, they tended to be classified as "sorcery" or "magic" rather than "religion."[50] They had to organize themselves in order to claim their due share of religious liberty, which is still in process (cf. also below, IIB2). While they are becoming more visible as

then still an adviser to President Lula on the program—affirmed in a conference I attended in July 2003. On the specific place of the IURD see anthropologist Emerson Giumbelli's extensive study (*O fim da religião*, 423): "The persistence of a 'church' without legitimation or 'religious' normatization is reflected both in the paradoxical terminologies of the intellectuals about Brazilian Protestantism and in the condemnation without any power of imposition, so often observed in the coverage of the IURD's activities by the media's organs." This is similar to the "sects" in France, although the latter are subject to government policies, while legal action against the IURD, in the absence of such policies, has always been on very weak grounds ("fraud," "charlatanism") and no case was won. Furthermore, the term commonly attributed to the IURD, its "Neo-Pentecostalism," has been adopted by its own spokesmen. And the IURD, a "social hybrid" like the "sects" in France, according to Giumbelli, continues to share the social space of religions and to prosper in it, while in France their space is reduced by their negative image.

48. Jacob et al., *Atlas da filiação religiosa e indicadores sociais no Brasil*, 105.

49. Number according to Jacob et al., *Atlas da filiação religiosa e indicadores sociais no Brasil*, 103; Pierucci, "Bye bye, Brasil," 20 has higher numbers, although based on the same census. Even so, he counts the Umbanda among one of the three groups that are most clearly losing members, together with the Roman Catholic and the Lutheran churches.

50. Cf. Giumbelli, O fim da religião; Montero, "Religião, pluralismo e esfera pública no Brasil."

religions of their own, many of those who belong to them would declare themselves to be Catholics, which is safer and usually not perceived as a contradiction. African Brazilian religions are the most attacked religions, mainly verbally, but also physically, which has sometimes resulted in what was called a "holy war."[51] It is here that religious violence becomes a most burning issue and calls for legal intervention, a theme that has been taken up by ecumenical initiatives both nationally and internationally. Thus, the census' numbers related to these religions are certainly too low. A strong indicator of this is that the numbers suggest a higher percentage of African Brazilian religious followers in the European impregnated state of Rio Grande do Sul than in the state of Bahia, the foremost port of entry for Africans from the slave ships, where till today African culture is visible and tangible all over the place. The same probably occurs with indigenous religions, which only 17,000 persons declared that they followed. Again, what is to be defined as "indigenous religion" is unclear, being oral, diverse, and usually not organized. And many live multiple religious identities, not least as a strategy of survival.[52] In general, though, indigenous peoples, estimated between 450,000 and 770,000 strong, show an astounding growth rate.[53]

Jews have notable communities in some cities, like São Paulo and Rio de Janeiro, but amount to only 87,000 according to the census. Henry Sobel,[54] the long-standing chief rabbi of the São Paulo congregation, has become known since the military regime for his defense of human rights and for his promotion of inter-religious dialogue. He dared to provide a proper funeral service for Vladimir Herzog (see above, IA1b), killed by the military who alleged he had committed suicide. By burying him as someone who died not of his own hand, Sobel was publicly defying the suicide version. He intensely collaborated with Dom Paulo Evaristo Arns and other authorities in São Paulo (cf. below, IIC2). Muslims, mainly immigrants from Arab and African countries, summed up 27,000 in the 2000 census, marking presence mainly in São Paulo and in Foz do Iguaçu, with strong commercial activities.[55] Both Jews and Muslims are well above average in terms of income, education, and professional status, mainly in services and administration or in commerce.

Oriental religions include Asian immigrants, mainly Buddhists from Japan and Korea (some 215,000), who are also spreading in different ways among the urban middle class, either as new religions like the World Messianic Church and Seicho No-Ie (together 151,000), or more broadly—and thus uncountable—as ways of thinking, viewing the world, and living spirituality.[56]

One of the constant claims made by Pentecostal and Neo-Pentecostal churches, and notably by the IURD, is "religious liberty," which, as they suggest, is not fully implemented and, *de facto*, usurped by the Roman Catholic Church which continues to have a strong influence on the public

51. Cf. Silva, *Intolerância religiosa*.

52. The issue of multiple identities is increasingly discussed worldwide (cf. Bernhardt and Schmidt-Leukel, *Multiple religiöse Identität*), although in the West it tends to focus on individuals, "religious virtuosos," while here we are speaking of general trends.

53. The lower number is from the government's agency National Foundation of the *Índio* (*Fundação Nacional do Índio*— FUNAI), of 2005, the higher from the IBGE 2000 census. It is noteworthy that the census' numbers, based on self-identification, have more than doubled since 1991, which seems to indicate a stronger self-esteem of indigenous peoples; cf. Azevedo, "Diagnóstico da população indígena no Brasil."

54. Sobel, *Um homem: um rabino*.

55. Jacob and alii, *Atlas da filiação religiosa e indicadores sociais no Brasil,* 102.

56. Two centers of Tibetan Buddhism are attracting people from the region, beyond national borders, at Três Coroas and Viamão in Rio Grande do Sul. The former was founded by a Tibetan Lama, Chagdud Tulku Rinpoche (1930-2002), who came to Brazil in 1991 via the U.S. and remained there from 1995 onwards. The founder of the latter, a former professor of physics, became a disciple of Rinpoche and was ordained by him as Lama Padma Samten, in 1996. See http://www.chagdud.org/pt/index.html, http://www.caminhodomeio.org and http://www.bodisatva.org, accessed on 4/24/2007.

authorities and administration. It is, therefore, appropriate and necessary to assess the legal status of churches and religions in Brazil.

2. *The Status of Religions in Legal Terms*

There is a remarkable void in terms of religious legislation in Brazil.[57] This has been so since the formal separation of church and State in the Decree number 119-A, of 7 January, 1890, which affirmed

> Art. 1. It is prohibited for the federal authority, as well as the federated states, to make laws, regulations, or administrative acts, establishing some religion, or prohibiting it, and create differences among the inhabitants of the country, or in services sustained by the budget, for reasons of belief, or philosophical or religious opinions.
>
> Art. 2. To all the religious confessions pertains the equal right to the faculty of exercising their worship [*culto*], governing themselves according to their faith and not being hindered in private or public acts, which touch on the exercise of this decree.
>
> Art. 3. The freedom hereby established comprehends not only the individuals in their individual acts, but also the churches, associations and institutes in which they find themselves aggregated; inhering to all the full right to constitute themselves and live collectively, according to their creed and their discipline, without intervention of public authorities.
>
> Art. 4. The *padroado* is extinct with all its institutions, resources and prerogatives.
>
> Art. 5. To all the churches and religious confessions is being recognized legal personhood, to acquire goods and to administer them, under the limits set by the laws regarding property of dead hand [*mão-morta*], each one maintaining dominion of its actual properties, as well as its buildings of worship.
>
> Art. 6. The Federal Government continues to provide the *congrua*, the livelihood of the current servants of Catholic worship, and shall subsidize for one year the chairs of the seminaries; remaining at the discretion of every state to maintain the future ministers of this or another cult, without prejudice of the disposed in the previous articles.
>
> Art. 7. The dispositions to the contrary are revoked.[58]

This article of the then so-called "United States of Brazil" clearly reflects the First Amendment of the U.S. Constitution, which states that "Congress shall make no law respecting an establishment of religion, or prohibiting the free exercise thereof. . ."[59] It shows a strong commitment to the lay character of the State, first of the executive, then of the legislator, as the 1891 constitution confirmed what was stated above: The separation between religion and the State, and the freedom of worship and religious association. It adds the invalidity of religious criteria for the exercise of civil and political rights, civil marriage, the secularization of public cemeteries, and the lay character of (public) education. These principles were maintained in the following constitutions.

57. The ground-breaking work of Giumbelli, *O fim da religião* has been serving as my main source in this section.

58. As all legal texts quoted (unless stated otherwise), this one is available at http://www.senado.gov.br (accessed on 4/27/2007). The "property of the dead hand" refers to donations of land made to the church which are permanent and exempt from taxation.

59. As found at http://www.law.cornell.edu/constitution/constitution.billofrights.html (accessed on 4/27/2007).

Art. 72, §3 of the 1891 constitution guarantees that "all the individuals and religious confessions can publicly and freely exercise their worship, associate to this end and acquire goods, observing the dispositions of common law." Law number 173 of September 10, 1893, regulated the cited article, widening its scope to include "the associations that are founded for religious, moral, scientific, artistic, political purposes or of simple recreation," thereby equating religious and other associations (Art.1). The law also foresaw that all "associates" had the right to vote in the general assembly, and the association had to account to them annually (Art. 7, §§3 and 4), which resounds rather oddly for hierarchical organizations like the ICAR. Already at the time, there was a heated debate as to the latter's status, which many argued had to be of a "dead hand corporation." "Dead hand" refers to a property based on donation that is continuous and, on principle, not alienable, given that it is not the property of the sum of the church's members who could dispose of it. However, it was questioned to what extent the laws of "dead hand" were still valid. In any case, there was recognition that the ICAR would not fit the character of an association like any other. There was a suggestion to provide a status of public law to religions (beyond the ICAR), but it was defeated. Instead, the Civil Code of 1917 included them among the legal persons of private law, being "the civil, religious, pious, moral, scientific or literary societies, the associations of public utility and the foundations" (Art. 16, I), separated from the "mercantile societies.[60] Indeed, from here religions and civil society—even under such name of "civil societies"—are, necessarily, negatively defined as non-profit organizations (see also above, IB).

The 1934 constitution, in a phase of rapprochement of the (Roman Catholic) church and the State, permitted "mutual collaboration in favor of the collective interest" (Art. 17, III).[61] It also recognized the civil effects of marriage "before a minister of any religious confession, whose rite does not contradict public order or good customs" (Art. 146), and introduced religious education on all levels (Art. 153). Later constitutions introduced an alternative military service for clergy, religious public holidays and tax exemptions, not present in 1891.[62] But, essentially, the line drawn up by the first republican constitution is still valid today as Giumbelli[63] clearly showed. Never has there been a definition of "religion" for the purposes of jurisdiction, although the exigency of acquiring legal status as an association[64] obliged hitherto unorganized religions to adopt such a kind of organization, lest they be considered against "public order." It is, thus, plain that the ICAR served as model for what was to be considered a religion, presenting the issues connected to it (such as matrimony and religious education).[65] Others, mainly the religions based on mediums (*religiões mediúnicas*), like African Brazilian religions and spiritists, were often judged as "magic" rather than "religion,"

60. Giumbelli, *O fim da religião*, 273.

61. The Protestant churches gathered in the Evangelical Confederation of Brazil (CEB) were critical of the new constitution and commented the draft in the sense of granting that "religious societies [. . .], which through their constitution and the number of their members guarantee continuity, can become corporations of public law," which would then be recognized to provide religious education and fill chaplaincies, safeguarding them against the dominant position of the ICAR; Prien, *Evangelische Kirchwerdung in Brasilien*, 573. The IECLB, which at the time was not a member of the CEB, made a plea in that direction in 1939, Prien, "Lateinamerika," 198.

62. The 1988 Constitution, Art. 150, VI, b prohibits the federation, the states and municipalities to levy taxes on "temples of any worship," and c includes in this prohibition "patrimony, income or services. . .of the non-profit institutions of education and social assistance, if fulfilled the requirements of the law," which includes such institutions run by churches, provided they have their own legal register.

63. Giumbelli, *O fim da religião*.

64. The only requirement is that the founding board of directors elaborate and publicly register their status, thus acquiring legal personality; Paes, *Fundações*, 74f.

65. Montero, "Religião, pluralismo e esfera pública no Brasil", 51.

and thus had to prove they were really "religions" and not "charlatans," especially when it came to issues of healing and health.[66]

Like its predecessors, the 1988 Constitution has some scattered mentions, but does not establish a religious legislation properly speaking. Like them, however, it reiterates the principle of the separation of church and State, albeit leaving open cooperation of "public interest": "It is prohibited for the union, the states, the Federal District and the municipalities [. . .] to establish religious worships [*cultos*] or churches, subsidize them, obstruct their functioning or maintain with them or their representatives relationships of dependency or alliance, being safeguarded, in legal terms, cooperation of public interest" (Art. 19).

Three items of the 5th article, in the fundamental rights section (see above, IC2), speak about religious liberty:

> vi —the freedom of conscience and belief is inviolable, being safeguarded the free exercise of religious cults and guaranteed, within the form of the law, protection to the places of worship and their liturgies;
>
> vii —religious assistance to civil and military entities of collective internment is safeguarded, within the terms of the law;
>
> viii —nobody shall be deprived of rights for reasons of religious belief or philosophical or political conviction, except if invocating them to exempt oneself of a legal obligation imposed to all or refuse to perform an alternative service, as fixed by law.[67]

The latter item refers not least to military service, to which all citizens except, "in times of peace," women and "ecclesiastics," i.e., religious ministers and friars, are obliged (Art. 143); an alternative service to those who allege an "imperative of conscience" is to be provided "in times of peace" (Art. 143 §1), but has in fact never been implemented.[68] According to some experts of the constitution, like Mendes, Coelho, and Branco,[69] the recognition of religious liberty "contributes

66. Montero, ibid., 53 argues, based on other studies, that "it was the regulating mechanisms themselves, created by the republican State, that constituted religious arrangements like Umbanda," rather than a specific kind of "urban, of class and individualist" society, which is a common hypothesis on Umbanda's emerging from the 1920s. On discrimination against African Brazilian religions see also Scherkerkewitz ("O direito de religião no Brasil."). These had to ask for permission or, at least, registration prior to exercising their religion (which includes the beating of drums). The Supreme Court sustained the constitutionality of a law of 1966 in the state of Paraíba, justifying this violation of the principle of isonomy stating that the African "cults" were "destitute of any written order [*ordenamento*] [. . ., and] do not count on priests or ministers installed by hierarchical authorities which preside over and direct them, and do not possess proper temples for the practice of their rituals" (quoted ibid., 12). Another case refers to the discrimination of a dissidence of the Roman Catholic Church, who wanted to maintain the rites, vestments, processions and the like, but declined to obey the Roman hierarchy. The Supreme Court was asked to protect such celebrations, but ruled, in 1949, that they may be lawfully impeded by public authorities, following the wish of the Roman Catholic Church. This shows how the very definition of what can be considered a religion was dominated by the ICAR's model and influence.

67. Brasil, *Constituição da República Federativa do Brasil*, 6f.

68. The National Council of Churches (CONIC) had pressed for what it called a "patriotic" or "alternative civil service" prior to the constituent assembly, which was obviously successful in providing the named clause. Law number 8,239 of October 4, 1991 is installing such a service and foresees in its 3rd article that it "will be performed in active military organizations or in formative organs of the Armed Forces' reserve or in organs subordinate to civil ministries, provided there is mutual interest and, also, the specific capacities of the conscript be taken into account," text available in http://www.senado.gov.br. According to information from the SERPAZ in São Leopoldo, a group committed to peace and non-violent practice, and confirmed to me by a former army chaplain in the rank of Lt. Col., those who have serious problems with military service, like Jehova's witnesses, are simply dismissed. They did not know of anyone who had actually performed an alternative service. Thus, Brazil seems to have missed a chance to engage citizens in an alternative civil service as existing in Germany, Switzerland and other countries where conscription is in place.

69. Mendes, Coelho, and Branco, *Curso de direito constitucional*, 409f.

to prevent social tensions," as it allows for pluralism. "Moral formation" also contributes to "mold the good citizen." But these reasons are not sufficient to explain the reason of religious liberty. "The constitution guarantees the liberty of believers because it takes religion to be a valuable good in itself, and wants to protect those who seek God of obstacles so that they may practice their religious duties."[70]

As we have seen, religions are treated like other associations of private law. The new Civil Code, introduced in 2002, included under the "legal persons of private law" associations, societies and foundations (Art. 44),[71] however without specifying their purpose as in the 1917 Civil Code.[72] This gave rise to considerable debate, with pressure namely from Pentecostal churches. Only a year later, a new law altered the cited article to now specify "religious organizations" and "political parties," and an extra paragraph (§1) read: "The creation, organization, internal structuring and the functioning of religious organizations are free, the public authorities being prohibited to deny recognition or register of the constitutive acts necessary for their functioning." At the same time, religious organizations and political parties were exempted of adapting to the rules of the new Civil Code, different from the other three types of organizations previously mentioned in the Code.[73] Thus, any interference by the State into religious affairs is, by law, prohibited. Even so, of course, religious organizations are subject to constitution and law and can come under scrutiny should there be evidence that either is being violated.[74] An interesting and worrying new factor are lawsuits against the IURD, which was condemned in the first and second instances to give back 2,000.00 Brazilian Reais to a faithful who had given this sum to the church after selling his only property, a car, but then wanted the money back.[75] It seems that the promise of material improvements in exchange for the payment of tithes is backfiring on the church—after all, if promises against payment are not attended, the "religious consumer" has the right to get his money back. This might be inimical to a highly questionable theological construction, the prosperity gospel. But what if such lawsuits should be extended to other churches, even it they do not hold such theology? This is the worrying part, as all of them live on tithes—there is no church tax system as in Western Europe, nor payment from the State.

Giumbelli concluded that, differently from France, "in Brasil, the definitions which accompanied the development of debates on 'religious liberty' at the beginning of the Republic resulted in an arrangement which did not juridically define 'religious associations.'"[76] This means that "an

70. They furthermore conclude that because of the liberty to "profess faith in God," its demonstration in public cannot be hindered with recourse to religious liberty. Thus, as the State, which is not atheistic, can live with symbols which are part of its cultural heritage and express something dear to an "expressive part" of its population, "it is not due to prohibit the exhibition of crucifixes or sacred images in public places" (Mendes, Coelho and Branco, *Curso de direito constitucional*,410).

71. Brasil, "Código Penal," 23.

72. Legal persons of (internal) public law are the union, the states, the municipalities, the "autarchies" (bodies created by the State administration) and other entities created by law (Civil Code, Art. 41). Thus, "public" here is practically identical with "State" (*staatlich*).

73. Law 10,825 of December 22, 2003.

74. Cf. Paes, *Fundações, Associações e Entidades*, 73f.

75. "STJ condena Universal a devolver doação a fiel," in *Zero Hora* of March 4, 2009, 34.

76. On this see also Scherkerkewitz ("O direito de religião no Brasil"), a law professor and state attorney in São Paulo, who affirmed: "I believe that the criterion to be used in deciding whether the State should protect the rites, customs and traditions of a specific religious organization cannot be tied to the *name* of the religion [i.e. its claiming to be one], but to its goals. If an organization has as its goal the aggrandizement [*engrandecimento*] of the individual, the search for his improvement in favor of the whole of society and the practice of philanthropy, it should enjoy the State's protection." As this article was available to me only through the internet in html-format, the page number is according

arrangement has been maintained which favored the possibility of 'collaborations,' always justified in more generic terms, between religious groups and State apparatuses."[77] Although reactions were mobilized against the IURD as not respecting even the minimal restriction on religious institutions, i.e., its non-profit character, their failure to prevent the IURD's proliferation shows that the mechanisms of defining what can be legitimately called "religion" has succumbed to the religious "market." Giumbelli adds that social scientists engaged in the study of religion tend to become "theologians of their society" (as medical doctors in other phases), which decide on what is religion, Protestantism, Pentecostalism, and the like. As they are supposedly objective as social scientists, they dispense the theologians' opinion and are exempt from an evaluation of their truth claims. Giumbelli, in turn, affirms that "what I systematically did was to take the category 'religion' in its effects of truth, refusing to use it as a heuristic instrument."[78] He thus pleads that we take seriously the religious character of IURD and the "sects," rather than reducing them to their going after money. Quite radically, then, he argues that the State should indeed be a "State without religion," and freely allow "religion without the State" to live out whatever it believes as its religious truth.

This, of course, denies any normativity of the category of "religion" and takes religion radically into the private realm, although it does allow for its self-propagation in the public sphere.[79] But what about interfaces like religious education in schools, guaranteed by federal constitutions since 1934?

In a later article, Giumbelli[80] analyzes this in a, as he himself says, "provisional" way. The 1988 Constitution fixed that "religious education, with facultative matriculation, shall constitute a subject matter of the normal schedule of public schools of primary education [i.e., during the 9 years of 'fundamental education']" (art. 210). The basic law for educational matters defined, in 1996, that such religious education shall not be paid by the public treasury, and that it could be given in a confessional or inter-confessional way, according to the preferences of students or those responsible for them.[81] That is, the State made space for the religions to formulate the content and designate those who should teach those willing to follow religious education in public schools. However, a law issued the following year changed the respective article (33), where the part on payment was left out, implying the State was indeed responsible for payment of the teachers of such education, and somehow also for its content: "Religious education [. . .] is an integral part of the citizen's basic formation [. . .], safeguarded the respect to cultural-religious diversity, [being] prohibited any forms of proselytizing."[82] Furthermore, the new law delegated the concrete shaping of religious education to the states and municipalities ("school systems," *sistemas de ensino*),

to my printout after having copied the html-Text into a Word-Document, so that it becomes p. 6.

77. Giumbelli, *O fim da religião*, 424.

78. Giumbelli, *O fim da religião*, 427.

79. Mendes, Coelho and Branco, *Curso de direito constitucional*, 407 define, with reference to the U.S. First Amendment and its understanding (including the examination of what is to be religion having in mind a "paradigmatic religion") that "Doubtless shall be a religion the system of beliefs which relates to a divinity, professes life beyond death, owns a sacred text [sic!], involves an organization and presents rituals of prayer and adoration." This excludes, implicitly, the African Brazilian religions, which do not have a sacred text — although there is the implicit reservation that they might still be a religion, even if not "doubtless." Explicitly, the authors consider commercial activities to be irreconcilable with the concept of religion.

80. Giumbelli, "Religião, Estado, modernidade."

81. Brasil, *LDB: Lei de Diretrizes e Bases da Educação*, 43, footnote.

82. Note that at least knowledge of religion is considered as contributing to citizenship here. "Proselytizing" means to actively propagate a specific religion or confession among those who do not already belong to it and try to bring them in.

which however should "hear a civil entity, constituted by the different religious denominations, for the definition of the contents of religious education."[83] The consequence was, as Giumbelli shows, that four different options were discussed and some of them implemented: 1) As the State cannot dispense with caring for issues of "citizenship" and "morality," there has to be a *confessional* model of religious education, to safeguard the plurality of religious options, while asking churches to issue credentials to their respective teachers—a model implemented in Rio de Janeiro by the Legislative Assembly and sanctioned by governor Anthony Garotinho, an *evangélico*.[84] 2) The second is an *inter-confessional* model, whose pluralistic content would be decided by an inter-denominational consulting body. It was adopted by the Rio Legislative Assembly but vetoed by governor Rosinha Mateus, Garotinhos wife, also an *evangélico*. 3) The third model is similar to the second, but does not include religious representatives; rather, religious education should be taught by teachers of history, philosophy, and social sciences, to guarantee a *non-confessional*, pluralistic information on the "phenomenon of religion." This was suggested by a group of historians from the Campinas University in the state of São Paulo. 4) The fourth model distinguishes sharply between universal science and intimate religion and, given that it would be difficult to find a common denominator for religious education, *discourages it altogether*, stating that its contents of human rights and ethics should be taught in other classes. This was suggested by a professor from the São Paulo University. As Giumbelli rightly highlights, none of the options denies the lay character of the State and public education, nor pluralism. In my view, the second model (or a variant of it) is the most appropriate, doing justice both to acquiring knowledge about religions and to religious practice within specific communities. It is favored by the (informal) Permanent National Forum for Religious Education (*Forum Nacional Permanente de Ensino Religioso*—FONAPER).[85] The interconfessional model is also the most challenging one, because it forces the churches and religions to sit together and work out a curriculum both faithful to religious engagement and wide enough to present, with justice, religious pluralism. This, in itself, would be a positive achievement.

Today, given the historical experiences of Roman Catholic dominant influence on politics and religious freedom (or the lack thereof), the tendency is understandably to avoid as far as possible any judgment on the value and validity of any religion. The result of this, however, is that there is a complete lack of criteria on how to restrict or to channel religious influence, giving way to all kinds of impositional projects of public religion (cf. below, IIIB2). Thus, it increasingly happens that a variety of religions is invited to an "ecumenical" event, on public holidays, inaugurations, or at graduation ceremonies, for instance. There is no recognizable criterion in choosing which religions should be present. Such inclusion is certainly a positive move, as in earlier times only Roman Catholic priests or bishops were invited to such public acts. However, invitations seem to be sent out at random, and there is no time for proper preparation among the participants. In the worst case, this results in every religion being granted, say, two minutes to speak, and some do use this as a platform for propagating their own religion. In the best case, representatives are sensitive to the event as such and to the other religions, and might even suggest a common religious language, like the Afro-Brazilian representative who invited all to pray the "Our Father," which they did.[86] There is

83. Law number 9,475 of 20/12/1997, in Brasil, *LDB: Lei de Diretrizes e Bases da Educação*, 90.

84. Law number 3,459 of September 14, 2000, available at http://www.alerj.rj.gov.br/processo2.htm; cf. Giumbelli and Carneiro, "Religião nas escolas públicas."

85. See http://www.fonaper.com.br.

86. While some religious communities, notably the Pentecostals and Neo-Pentecostals, but also many historical Protestants and a good number of Roman Catholics, as well as many Muslims tend to adopt an exclusive religious discourse and feel uneasy with the presence namely of African Brazilian religions, the latter, as other religious groups

an urgent need for constituted bodies which legitimately represent the religions and foster internal dialogue and articulation. This is certainly not an easy task, but a necessary one.

3. RELIGION IN THE PUBLIC SPACE

Today, the major issue seems to be the "pulverization"[87] of the "religious field," the "marketization" of it and, thus, a strong competition mainly between Christian denominations. Theologians and social scientists alike reflect on whether there should be limits to this development, at least a kind of "defense of the religious consumer."[88] Conversely, in other times, the question was raised as to what extent the State was unduly running religious matters. The separation of church and State in the republic was seen also and not least by the Roman Catholic Church as a relief, as it allowed for much more freedom in its self-organization than it had before.[89] The Empire, which had taken on itself the full responsibility for religion in its understanding of the *padroado,* was in constant conflict with the church Rome was trying to get an effective hold on all along the 19th century. This resulted, most prominently, in the so-called "schism of Feijó" (1827–38), when the Vatican and liberal forces, represented by the deputy and later regent of the Empire, Diogo Antônio Feijó (1784-1843), himself a priest, struggled over moves to abandon celibacy for priests by imperial decree. Another moment of conflict was the "religious question" (1872-75) over the influence of freemasonry, which at the time was widely spread among Protestants and Catholics, and was one of the promoting forces toward the Republic.[90]

As shown, religious freedom was fully introduced by the law in 1890, when church and State were separated and the *padroado* formally abolished. However, such separation never fully worked, and during the first decades of the 20th century, a clear rapprochement between the State and the Roman Catholic Church took place in what came to be known as "Neo-Christendom." Emblematic for this was the inauguration in 1931, on October 12, the day of the national patron saint, *Nossa Senhora da Conceição Aparecida* (something like Our Lady of the Conception who Appeared, cf. below, IIC1), of the famous *Cristo Redentor* (Christ the Redeemer) statue on Corcovado Hill, 38 meters high and overlooking Guanabara Bay.[91] In the midst of fifty bishops and archbishops, Cardinal Sebastião Leme (1882–1942) boldly stated that "either the state [. . .] will recognize the God of the people or the people will not recognize the State."[92] He said this in the presence of the head of the provisional government, Getúlio Vargas, who indeed learnt to respect and construct a close partnership with the Roman Catholic Church.[93] Leme was the architect of the renewed

(like Spiritists and Baha'i) and a good number of Roman Catholics, tend to build on the presupposition that "we all have the same God" and adopt an inclusive discourse. The concrete example is taken from a forthcoming brochure of the IECLB on inter-religious celebrations; see also Sinner, "Inter-religious Dialogue."

87. Campos, "Historischer Protestantismus."

88. Pierucci, "Liberdade de cultos."

89. Scampini, *A liberdade religiosa nas constituições brasileiras*; CNBB, *Rumo ao Novo Milênio*, 52.

90. Cf. Vieira, "Protestantism and the Religious Question in Brazil."

91. This day is also Columbus' day on the whole continent, remembering his arrival in the Caribbean, in 1492, as Della Cava, "Catholicism and Society," 13, recalls. On October 12, 1717, fishermen are reported to have found the statue of Our Lady in the waters of Guaratinguetá, Minas Gerais. In 1929, Pope Pius XI declared her "Queen of Brazil" and the national patron saint. On the occasion of Pope John Paul II's visit to Brazil in 1980, the military regime declared 12 October a national holiday.

92. In Della Cava, "Catholicism and Society," 14, who takes the quote from Margaret Patrice Todaro, 'Pastors, Prophets, and Policitans: A Study of the Brazilian Catholic Church, 1916-1945' (Ph.D. dissertation, Columbia University, New York, 1971).

93. Bruneau (*Political Transformation*, 40) states that "Oswaldo Aranha, one of Vargas' most important aides, indi-

massive influence of his church on the State and public space, usually called Neo-Christendom. This is public religion (cf. below, IIIB2).

Historian Thales de Azevedo spoke of a "Brazilian civil religion" in relation to the State's instrumentalization of religion.[94] While he analyzes public religious discourse throughout the 19th and 20th centuries, the most recent case in his book is especially interesting for the purpose of the present study: the compulsory "moral and civic education," introduced in 1969 by the military junta which had assumed the presidency following President Costa e Silva's serious illness and consequent resignation. The law decree affirmed that such education had as its goals:

> a) the defence of the democratic principle through the preservation of the religious spirit, the dignity of the human person and the love of freedom with responsibility, under the inspiration of God;
>
> b) the preservation, the strengthening and the projection of spiritual and ethical values of nationality;
>
> c) the strengthening of national unity and the sentiment of human solidarity;
>
> d the cult to the Fatherland, to its symbols, traditions, institutions and the great figures of its history;
>
> e) the enhancement of character, with support in morality, dedication to the family and the community;
>
> f) the comprehension of rights and duties of the Brazilians and the knowledge of the socio-political organization of the country;
>
> g) the preparation of the citizen for the exercise of civil activities with its fundament in morality, patriotism and constructive action, in view of the common good;
>
> h) the cult of obedience to the Law, fidelity to work and integration into community[95]

Some of this would be worthwhile to think of in the line of a theology focused on citizenship, were it not imposed by an illegitimate, undemocratic, and repressive State which indeed instrumentalized religion. It was precisely this part of "moral and civic education" that became an object of criticism in the IECLBs *Curitiba* manifest (see below, IID1c). The government even created a National Commission of Morality and Civility (*Comissão Nacional de Moral e Civismo*—CNMC), which issued a "Prayer for Brazil":

> O almighty GOD, principle and
> End of all things,
> Infuse in us, Brazilians,
> The love for study and work,
> So that we may make of our FATHERLAND

---

cated the impact of the events on the provisional government: 'When we arrived from the south [Rio Grande do Sul] we tended to the Left! But after we saw the popular religious movements, in honor of Our Lady of Aparecida and of Christ the Redeemer, we understood we could not go against the sentiments of the people!"

94. He refers to Jean-Jacques Rousseau's notion of *religion civile*, and Luiz Alberto de Boni's apparently first use of it in the Brazilian context in 1977/78 (Azevedo, *A religião civil brasileira*, 28, note 40). He also mentions the U.S.-American debate as initiated with Robert N. Bellah in 1967 (cf. Breitenberg, "To Tell the Truth," 56; below, IIIB1), highlighting that it is different from the Brazilian case in that it does not hypostazise "the State as a goal in itself," where an authoritarian system in "its laws of [National] security put the State above the nation and the person" (Azevedo, *A religião civil brasileira*, 42).

95. Law-Decree number 869 of September 12, 1969, Art. 2; cf. Azevedo, *A religião civil brasileira*, 128–38.

A land of peace, order and greatness,
Watch, LORD, over Brazil's destinies![96]

Already in 1889, at the foundation of the Republic, "voluntarist positivism of the Religion of Humanity" was present, which, as mentioned, gave the Brazilian flag its motto: "Order and Progress." Azevedo continues:

> in 64/68, [sc. military and technocrats incline themselves towards] a rational humanism in its functionality as an organ of social control, like in Rousseau's utopian thinking, to obtain a 'general will' which secures, together with the instruments of external coercion, the abidance to the exercise of power without contestation.[97]

This thinking constitutes a kind of natural religion, above and before all positive religions, which reminds one of the conflict in Nazi Germany that gave rise to the Barmen Confession, and the similar conflict in Apartheid South Africa, from which emerged the Belhar Confession, the first largely written and the second influenced by Karl Barth.[98]

The State continues to have links to the churches, perhaps even more strongly since Lula came to the presidency, who had maintained strong relationships with the progressive church. However, official encounters are slowly becoming more reflective of religious pluralism. When President Lula attended Pope John Paul II's funeral in Rome, in April 2005, he took with him representatives of ecumenical bodies and non-Christian religions. During the travel, they had an ecumenical celebration, and national TV interviewed some of these representatives after the funeral. "Ecumenical" celebrations are becoming more common throughout, as mentioned above (IIB2), as are "ecumenical" rather than just Roman Catholic spaces for prayer in airports, shopping centers, tourist resorts, and even legislative chambers. Although such spaces still tend to emphasize the altar for mass and the tabernacle for preserving the Eucharistic host, they do so in a much more modest way in order to allow for other religious expressions.

But beyond church or State governed religion, there is now increased awareness of a presence of religion or religiosity in public space, which harvests on church and/or civic principles, but is not controlled or even accompanied by their representatives. In sports events, the sign of the cross has been common for a long time. More recent, presumably under *evangélico* influence, are prayer circles like the one performed in Seoul after Brazil conquered its fifth world championship in soccer (2002; the team captain and some players were confessed *crentes*). After the Olympic Gold Medal in Athens (2004), the male Volleyball team showed a Brazilian flag with the title "God is faithful."[99]

There is also a kind of "civil society's religion," as movements like the Landless Workers' Movement (MST), which was born with the help of the Pastoral Land Commission (CPT), linked to the Catholic Church (see below, IIC2a), use religious symbols in their fights without reference to any church.[100] Regina Novaes affirms that in today's Brazil, besides the biblical inspiration present in the admitted constitutive 'mysticism' of the Movement of Landless Workers, the Bible is also

96. Quoted in Azevedo, *A religião civil brasileira,* 134.

97. Ibid., 136.

98. Cloete and Smit, *A Moment of Truth.*

99. Giumbelli, "Religião, Estado, modernidade," 47.

100. On examples of the public presence of religion outside the churches see Birman, *Religião e espaço público*, especially the contributions in Part I, 25–46; on the MST's *mística* Burdick, "Das Erbe der Befreiung," 19–22, who concludes: "Man kann häufig hören, die MST sei eine rein weltliche Bewegung. Aber diese wenigen Bemerkungen sollten ausreichen, um anzudeuten, dass unter der Oberfläche eine tiefe Quelle fortschrittlicher christlicher Ideologie verborgen ist, von der Führer ebenso wie einfache Mitglieder der MST nach wie vor zehren."

present in another important space of social critique: the Hip-Hop movement [. . .]. . . .the fact that the Bible is a source of religious knowledge socially recognized, yesterday and today, by Catholics, *evangélicos*, African Brazilians, in the country and the city, by bandits and police officers, by dwellers of the center and the periphery, by politicians and voters, is not exempt of an analysis of the configuration of the so called public space, for the virtualities of politics . . .[101]

These and other examples show how diversified are both the religious field as such and the scientific analysis of it. As stated earlier, there is a wide interest in religious phenomena in Brazil, both nationally and internationally. Theologians are, generally, on the fringe of this discourse, even if they do religious studies. Public authorities would normally refer to the social sciences or philosophy for advice, understanding that they are more "objective." While such "neutrality" is questionable, as indicated above, it is also questionable whether it should not be precisely the theologians, who are rooted in their churches and to a certain extent can represent them, who should take part in such reflections. I do believe that the fostering of thorough theological formation would force today's religious competitors to contemplate other forms of Christianity and other religions and relate them to their own understanding of faith (cf. below, IIIB2b). More specifically, installing local, state, and federal councils on religion would bind religious actors into policy making, assuring both their full participation and forcing them to formulate commonly acceptable principles for the treatment of religions.

101. Novaes, "Crenças religiosas e convicções políticas," 94f.

C. The Roman Catholic Church (ICAR)

Os pobres são os juízes da vida democrática de uma nação.

CNBB[1]

THE ROMAN CATHOLIC CHURCH is the oldest and largest Christian church on the continent, having arrived together with colonial forces in the "New World." Despite this long history, it is mainly in the 20th century that the church became organized so that it could effectively reach its members and strengthen its public influence, be it in close co-operation with the State, as in the phase called "Neo-Christendom," or in tension with the State, as under the military regime. There can be no doubt that the legal separation from the State in 1889 (see above, IIB2) has done the church much good. Just to give some structural examples of the tremendous changes that have taken place: If by 1900 there were a mere 20 dioceses in Brazil, there are now 269 (2001/2).[2] Although nearly 100 of them are *emeriti*, Brazil has 400 bishops, including 37 active archbishops and seven cardinals, among them two *emeriti* (2003).[3] The number of clergy, although still small in relation to the number of Catholics according to the statistics—and even in absolute numbers already smaller than the number of the *evangélicos'* ministers—has increased and continuously become more autochthonous. There were 17,976 priests in 2005, 1,557 permanent deacons, 4,003 brothers and 34,697 nuns, and 9,410 parishes.[4] If, in 1970, 41 percent of the priests were foreigners, being a majority among the clergy belonging to religious orders (53 percent), this rate has been diminishing constantly over the years until reaching a mere 18 percent in 2001/2, 9 percent among the diocesan clergy and 29 percent among the orders.[5] In any case, Brazil is today the country with the largest Catholic population in the world, despite the losses shown

1. "The poor are the judges of a nation's democratic life," CNBB, *Exigências éticas da ordem democratica*, 72.

2. http://www2.ceris.org.br/estatistica/caicbr/quadro_01.asp (accessed on 4/3/2007).

3. Numbers assembled from the list of bishops in CERIS *Anuário Católico*, 30ff. The number of cardinals seems rather small for this size of a church and episcopate.

4. http://www.guiacatolico.com/blogs/guiacatolico/?p=31 (accessed on 3/12/2007).

5. http://www2.ceris.org.br/estatistica/caicbr/quadro_14.asp (accessed on 4/3/2007). Naturalized foreigners are counted as Brazilians, which certainly contributed to the diminished numbers, as a good number of foreign priests and bishops decided to stay in Brazil for life. On the other hand, the numbers show a fortified system of diocesan seminaries with a relatively high number of seminarians (5,625 in 2001/2 against 885 in 1964) and novices and temporary professed friars (4,502 in 2001). However, female vocations show a decreasing tendency (8,465 in 2001/2, including temporary professed, novices and pre-novices, while novices alone decreased from 3,109 in 1961 to 1,516 in 2001/2), and while the number of professed nuns remained virtually stable, with some oscillations over the years (35,039 in 1961, 35,589 in 2001/2, with a peak of 41,988 in 1969), the number of priests has grown by 31 percent from 13,092 in 1970 to 17,167 in 2001/2. The diocesan clergy accounts now for 56 percent of the priests, against 38 percent in 1970.

above (IIB1), summing up some 125 million people who declare themselves Catholic. Church attendance, however, is much lower.[6]

Beyond these numbers, there are a variety of movements that characterize today's Roman Catholic Church (ICAR) in Brazil. In the previous chapter, I have dealt with religious pluralism as if the ICAR were a homogenous entity. After all that has been said on diversity it will hardly come as a surprise that it is present also within the ICAR. I have mentioned various times the Church Base Communities (CEBs), whose number is estimated at around 80,000, with a total of around 1 million members. The larger movement, however, is the Catholic Charismatic Renewal (*Renovação Católica Carismática*, RCC), with 8 to 10 million members, possibly half of all active Catholics.[7] While the former unites mostly lower middle class and poor persons—although not the very poor— the latter is clearly middle and upper middle class based, although expanding among the poor.[8] Similarly to the CEBs, to whom the RCC is contemporary, it seeks to promote itself as "'the' new model of being the church."[9] If the quoted numbers are correct, they might have an argument there, and might indeed be more present to the believer in the pew than the Bishop's Conference: "The average Catholic, nowadays, will probably not know the name of the CNBB president, but all know who is Fr Marcelo [Rossi],"[10] the RCC's shooting star.[11]

The RCC arrived in Brazil in the early 1970s through missionaries from the United States, among them Jesuit Father Edward Dougherty. There, the movement had originated at the "Duquesne Weekend," a spiritual retreat led by two professors, baptized in the Holy Spirit under Presbyterian charismatics' direction, at the Catholic Duquesne University in Pittsburgh, in February 1967.[12] Initially, they called themselves "Pentecostal Catholics." Indeed, they resemble the Pentecostals in many respects, insisting on baptism in the Holy Spirit, by which they receive the gifts of the Spirit like speaking in tongues and healing. They also hold, although to a lesser degree than classical Pentecostals, a relatively strict morality. While they were, initially, ecumenically open, they now distinguish themselves quite clearly from Pentecostals through their unconditional obedience to the pope and a strong Marian devotion. More recently, there is also a Neo-Pentecostal tendency, with a less strict morality, faith shows, "liberation masses," i.e., exorcism celebrations, and "tithers' masses," visible in Fr. Marcelo Rossi's activities.[13] Rossi (born in 1967) has sold millions of CDs with his devotional songs, some of which rendered him awards, has written a number of well sold books

6. For numbers from a survey in six major capitals, see Fernandes, "Prática religiosa e participação social," 98–104. 78.6 percent of Catholic informants affirm to go to mass or other church events, but when it comes to regular participation in these, numbers drop to less than 50 percent, and 36 percent participate only fortnightly or less.

7. Cf. Chestnut, "A Preferential Option for the Spirit," 62; Prandi, *Um sopro do Espírito*; Carranza, *Renovação carismática católica*; Valle, "A Renovação Carismática Católica"; Novaes, "Crenças religiosas e convicções políticas," 71 speaks of a presence of the RCC in far over half of the existing parishes.

8. Novaes, "Crenças religiosas e convicções políticas"; Chestnut, "A Preferential Option for the Spirit."

9. Carranza, *Renovação carismática católica*, 23–83; Valle, "A Renovação Carismática Católica," 102.

10. Valle, "A Renovação Carismática Católica," 103.

11. Carranza, "Catolicismo midiático" calls the tendency spearheaded by Marcelo Rossi "media Catholicism," part of the process of recatholization in Brazil and aligned with the media-friendly personalism of pope John Paul II. The influential weekly magazine *Veja* wrote on November 4, 1998: "He is a star at the altar: handsome, strong, blue eyes [. . .] factors which are so easy to explain as they are difficult to be united in a single person. He is beautiful. He sings well. He is joyful. He speaks in the name of faith [. . .] attracts masses and renews the country's Catholic Church" (in ibid., 80).

12. Chestnut, "A Preferential Option for the Spirit," 62; Thigpen, "Catholic Charismatic Renewal."

13. Fr. Marcelo acknowledged that "it was Bishop Edir Macedo [of the Neo-Pentecostal IURD, see above, IIB1], who woke us up," as quoted in Chestnut, "A Preferential Option for the Spirit," 72, who takes it from an article published in the Brazilian weekly magazine *Veja* of April 8, 1998, 3.

and produced two films so far. He is more of an animator than a traditional liturgist—a former sports teacher, he does "faith aerobics," while the celebrant in the traditional sense is usually a bishop. Huge celebrations have become a common feature on the main national TV network, Rede Globo, much more publicly visible (and technically attractive) than what is shown on the ICAR's own channel Rede Vida. The hierarchy is somewhat at odds with this phenomenon: While it keeps Catholics active and within the flock, the movement's theology is neither entirely traditional nor progressive. In 1994, later than anywhere else on the continent, the Brazilian episcopate officially approved the RCC.[14]

The so called "Progressive Church" is not a unified movement, but a tendency in a variety of parishes (through CEBs, for instance), dioceses and pastoral sectors like the African Brazilian Pastoral Action (*Pastoral Afro*).[15] It is also present in the "spearhead" organizations dealing with land reform (CPT, see below IIC2b) and indigenous' rights (CIMI). As I shall show below, the CNBB is still supporting this line of social engagement, at least as long as it does not imply any critique of the church's own hierarchical organization. It can draw easily on Catholic Social Teaching as compiled in the recent compendium published by the Pontifical Council for Justice and Peace (PCJP).[16] But when it comes to moral issues linked to reproduction and gender, like abortion, contraception, and homosexuality, the ICAR in Brazil is as restrictive as worldwide Catholicism, somewhat ironically in line with most *evangélico* churches (except for the contraception and slightly more moderate positions on abortion) and its own most conservative sectors. Both positions, socially progressive and conservative in sexual morality, are rooted in Catholic Social Teaching and, not least, in the strong position of Pope John Paul II on both ends.[17]

In this chapter, I shall show the church's positions and practices since 1985. In order to understand the *locus* of the ICAR in the Brazilian context, I start with a section on history, identifying the various stages in the church's self-organization and its relationship to the State and civil society (1). Then, I go through documents that show aspects of the church's positioning in the public space (2), followed by a description and analysis of the theological grounding of this position (3).

14. CNBB, *Orientações pastorais sobre a renovação carismática*; Chestnut, "A Preferential Option for the Spirit," 75; Valle, "A Renovação Carismática Católica," 101.

15. Cf. Burdick, *Legacies of Liberation*.

16. PCJP, *Compendium of the Social Doctrine of the Church*.

17. Pope Benedict XVI has been reinforcing this position during his visit to Brazil in May 2007, with chastity, contraception, and abortion among the main issues. As Souza, "Catolicismo em tempos de transição," 11 states, already the year 1968 stands for both the progressive Medellín conference of the Latin American episcopate, and Pope Paul VI's encyclical *Humanae Vitae*, highly restrictive on reproductive issues.

PART II: THE CONTRIBUTION OF THE CHURCHES TOWARD CITIZENSHIP

1. BRIEF HISTORICAL SURVEY

Let us always defend the Catholic Church
and we will be defending Brazil.

Fr. Agnelo Rossi[18]

Quem não crê, brasileiro não é!

Catholic Hymn[19]

In its programmatic document on evangelization, "On the Way to the New Millennium," the CNBB indicated three high points of its public influence in the 20th century: "in 1934, with the New Republican Constitution; in the [19]70s, with the defense of human rights, during the regime of exception; and immediately after, with the 'opening' that prepared the return to democracy."[20] In fact, it was the separation of church and State in 1890 which, after a long period of State tutelage in the *padroado* system, facilitated the autonomy of the church. From there, the ICAR was able to both extend its outreach to its own base and link itself more closely to Rome. The CNBB recognizes this, saying that "the separation of Church and State created the conditions for the strengthening and renovation of Catholicism, utterly weakened at the end of the colonial regime and during the empire."[21] Presumably because the 1891 Constitution was fairly secular (cf. above, IIB2), the document highlights the 1934 Constitution which brought back State privileges for the ICAR, without however bringing back State tutelage. The next step, the 1970s, indicates already the turn towards a critical stance over against the State, interrupting a centuries-long partnership. Finally, the process of "opening" (see above, IA1b) made possible a renewed partnership, even if it continued to be a critical one.

But let us see more precisely how these stages followed each other, not merely in a historical but a systematic perspective, i.e. looking at the different ways of relating to the State and society. First, the church was a colonial church, somewhat an extension of the State (a), but was able to strengthen its own position over against the State in the phase of Romanization and Neo-Christendom (b). In the 1970s, the ICAR became arguably the main space for opposition under the military regime (c) and is, today, still redefining its role after transition (d).

a) The ICAR as Colonial Church

On April 22, 1500, the Portuguese seafarer Pedro Álvares Cabral (1460-1526) landed near today's Porto Seguro in North-Eastern Brazil, with a fleet of 13 ships and some 1,200 men. The first mass on Brazilian soil was held on April 26, first Sunday after Easter, by Franciscan Friar Henrique de Coimbra (d. 1532), one of the seventeen priests who came with the expedition.[22] "With the

18. In Mainwaring, *The Catholic Church and Politics in Brazil*, 32.

19. "Whoever does not believe, is not a Brazilian," in Azzi, *A neocristandade—um projeto restaurador*, 23. This was part of the official hymn, intoned at the II Eucharistic Congress, in Recife (in fact in Belo Horizonte, Barros, "Gênese e consolidação da CNBB," 23).

20. As in official documents paragraphs are usually numbered, facilitating its exact localization, I quote the paragraph and not the page number.

21. CNBB, *Rumo ao Novo Milênio*, 53.

22. Matos, *Nossa história*, 24.

sword went the cross," as Bruneau rightly states,[23] and indeed the formal occupation of the land was sealed with the erection of a huge cross on May 1, with the royal coat of arms, while the second mass was celebrated. The land became called "Island" and later "Land of the True (or Holy) Cross" (*Terra da Vera/Santa Cruz*).[24] The newly conquered land became a colony under the Portuguese Crown, adopting its typical system of *padroado*, by which the crown was responsible not only for the material, but also for the spiritual "well-being" of its subjects. In recognition for its efforts against the Moors in the 12th and 13th centuries—Portugal completed the reconquest already in 1249, more than 200 years before Spain—and against the Turks in the 15th century, the popes gave the Portuguese Crown virtually total control over the church in its territory—"from the most basic issues of building the first churches to such matters as paying for the clergy, nominating bishops, approving documents, selecting sites for convents and to almost all areas of Church concern."[25] Included in this was also the right to recourse to the Crown in matters of ecclesiastical discipline, and the right of the Crown to censorship of ecclesiastical documents prior to their publication in Brazil, which meant they all passed through Lisbon before arriving in the colony. The State also disposed of the tithes' revenue at its discretion, mixing it with the royal treasury. As was the case for all Latin America, "when they were first set up, the Latin American churches had closer relationships with the Iberian states than they did with the papacy and this situation continued up to the turn of this [20th] century."[26] Rome had virtually no say in matters of the Brazilian church. But different from the Spanish colonies, the church remained much longer in a very fragile position. By 1750, only eight dioceses had been created for a country of continental size, and two were under control of Lisbon rather than the Archbishopric of Bahia. Only in 1739, a seminary for the secular clergy was established, so that the "training of priests was [. . .] rather *sui generis*" as Bruneau notes.[27] Priests in the parishes functioned as civil servants and were regarded as such. As payment was low and the laity did not feel responsible for the priests, they looked out for other means to top up their salary, which rendered them very low esteem among the population. Brazil was a rural society with

23. Bruneau, *The Political Transformation of the Brazilian Catholic Church*, 12.

24. On the name, see Matos, *Nossa história*, 27f. In this section, I follow mainly Bruneau, *Political Transformation* with occasional other references as indicated. Thomas Bruneau is a political scientist from California and taught at McGill Unversity in Montreal from 1969 to 1987, when he became Distinguished Professor of National Security Affairs in the Naval Postgraduate School's Department of National Security Affairs in Monterey, California. From 2000–04 he was the director of the Center for Civil Military Relations; http://www.ccc.nps.navy.mil/people/bruneau.asp (accessed on 5/10/2007). The quoted book is based on his doctoral thesis.

25. Bruneau, *Political Transformation*, 13, who also cites J. Lloyd Mecham, *Church and State in Latin America*, rev. ed. (Chapel Hill: University of North Carolina Press, 1966), 36: "Never before or since did a sovereign with the consent of the Pope so completely control the Catholic Church within his dominions" (ibid., note 6). The legal basis of this system rests on four papal bulls: *Romanus Pontifex*, issued by Pope Nicholas V on January 8, 1455, to King Alfonso V; *Inter Coetera*, granted by Pope Calixtus III to the same king on March 13, 1456; *Dum Fidei Constantiam* of June 7, and *Pro Excellenti*, of June 12, 1514, both signed by Pope Leo X, for King Emanuel; see Bruneau, *Political Transformation*, 13f. Technically, the patronage was bestowed upon the Order of Christ, a lay religious association of noblemen with military goals; by the bull *Praeclara Charissimi* of 1551, Pope Julius III acknowledged the Portuguese King as the Grand Master of this order, whereby the monarchs of Portugal "come to exercise, simultaneously, the civil and ecclesiastical power over all Lusitanian [i.e. Portuguese] dominions" (Matos, *Nossa história*, 101). The bull *Super Specula Militantis Ecclesiae* of February 25, 1551, established the diocese of São Salvador da Bahia, the first independent Brazilian diocese, reinforces the *padroado* and explicates the Crown's right to present the candidate for the bishopric to be nominated by the pope; Matos, *Nossa história*, 113.

26. Bruneau, *Political Transformation*, 5.

27. The expression is from Paulo Florêncio da Silveira Camargo, *História Eclesiástia do Brasil* (Petrópolis: Vozes, 1955), 284, as quoted in Bruneau, *Political Transformation*,16.

low control by State and church alike. There were no great urban centers as in other Latin American countries. It was the rural family which held effective power:

> The family and not the individual, much less the State or any commercial company, was from the sixteenth century the great colonizing factor in Brazil, the productive unit, the capital that cleared the land, founded plantations, purchased slaves, oxen, implements; and in politics it was the social force that set itself up as the most powerful colonial aristocracy in the Americas.[28]

The priests were part of the family, and it was not considered unusual that they should enjoy a woman's companionship. In the few important cities (Salvador, Rio, Ouro Preto), the brotherhoods (*irmandades*) became the backbone of religious life, although they could also function as professional guilds. Some administered the main colonial hospitals, the *Santas Casas de Misericórdia* ("Holy Houses of Mercy").

The church worked best through the religious clergy, with a strong presence of the Benedictines, Franciscans, Carmelites, Capuchins, Oratorians, and, above all, the Jesuits. The so called Jesuit "reductions," namely in what was then Paraguay and now is known as the "missions" region, where indigenous peoples were agglomerated in the 16th and 17th centuries, have become known worldwide. They were torn apart in political negotiations between Spain and Portugal, and by the economic interests of the landlords. But the severest blow to the Jesuits—as to the whole church in Brazil—came in the 18th century through the powerful acting of the Marquis de Pombal (1699–1782) in Portugal, who achieved the suppression of the Jesuits and left the already weak church in Brazil without leadership through breaking temporarily with Rome. He fostered the teaching of regalism and Jansenism, both anti-papal, at the University of Coimbra, the only place for Brazilians to study in Portuguese as no university had as yet been established in the colony—again a difference to Spanish Latin America (cf. also below, IIIB2b). Liberalism also made its way into Portuguese university, which made some priests open to revolutionary moves and republicanism, to the point that the 1817 Pernambucan republican revolt came to be called "the Padres' Revolution."[29]

b) Romanization and Neo-Christendom

Brazilian independence from Portugal resulted in an empire under an emperor from the Portuguese royal house. The emperor was also the head of the church and thus responsible for nominations and expenses. As statesmen and abolitionist Joaquim Nabuco (1849-1910) affirmed, "For this the legislator constituted the Emperor as the first ecclesiastical authority of the country in the sense that to him belonged not only the choice of personnel—the formation of the church hierarchy—but also the supreme judgment of all the laws and decrees of the Popes and councils."[30] No concordat was established, and while Rome simply tolerated the continuation of the *padroado* as a *modus vivendi*, the emperors took it for granted. Especially emperor Dom Pedro II (in office 1840–89) had great reservations over against religion and was more interested in reason and science. He resisted the attempts of Rome to gain more influence over the church in Brazil and created only three new dioceses during his long reign. The orders, which did not have to submit to the State-dominated episcopacy, were also targeted, and in 1855 were forbidden to receive novices in the country. The

28. Gilberto Freyre, as quoted in Bruneau's *Political Transformation*, 17.

29. Bruneau, *Political Transformation*, 22.

30. Joaquim Nabuco, O Partido ultramontano: suas invasões, seus órgãos, e seu futuro, in *Reforma* (Rio de Janeiro, 1873), p. 9, as quoted in Bruneau, *Political Transformation*, 22.

secular clergy continued weak and quite worldly, amounting to a bare 700 by the end of the empire, with a population of 14 million in an enormous territory.[31]

In 1874, the so-called "Religious Question" (*questão religiosa*) exploded as a conflict between the church and the State. Pius IX (pope from 1846–1878), anti-modern and centralist, tried to get a better hold on the Brazilian church, while the emperor refused to implement, for instance, the "Syllabus of Errors" published in 1864, seeing ultramontanism as a threat to his sovereignty. As D. Pedro II had high intellectual standards, he chose intellectually apt bishops, who in turn adhered, however, to Rome's centralism. Two of them, Dom Vital de Oliveira (1844–1878), bishop of Olinda and Recife, and Dom Antônio de Macedo Costa (1830–1891), bishop of Pará, laid an interdict on the *irmandades* that had freemasons among its members. An *irmandade* appealed to the government and won the case, but the bishops refused to repeal the interdict, and so they were convicted and imprisoned until being granted amnesty the following year. In a pastoral letter issued in 1890, shortly before the formal separation of church and State, the bishops stated in a pastoral letter that "among us, the oppression exercised by the State in the name of a pretended patronage was a main cause of weakness in our Church and almost led to its destruction."[32] Even so, however, the bishops resisted the separation of church and State "in the name of social order, of public peace, of harmony among the citizenry, in the name of the right of conscience," demanding "the union of the two powers." While the bishops wanted independence from State tutelage, they felt that disestablishment would undermine the church's influence on the population, fearing a "Nation without religion and without God" and an "atheistic government."[33] In any case, the church was now free to institutionalize on its own terms, and the number of dioceses and seminaries started to increase constantly. With a strong influx of foreign priests, mainly of the religious orders, and with Rome's tendency to centralize which was now no longer impeded by the State, the Brazilian church was modeled largely along the European features, with worship, schools for the middle classes, and a variety of associations "aimed at a bourgeois society." Also, "a fortress mentality against Socialism, Protestantism, Masonry and the like" became the dominant orientation, somewhat strange in a Brazilian context where these forces were much less influential than in Europe at the time.[34] The church also pressed for an increased influence on the State as it felt it should be recognized as the representative church of the vast majority of Brazilians.

Other churches had been, for the first time, recognized in their right to exist, albeit in a clearly inferior status. The first Brazilian constitution was promulgated in 1824, and its Fifth Article stated: "The Roman Catholic Apostolic Religion shall continue to be the religion of the Empire. All other religions shall be permitted with their domestic or private worship, in houses destined toward this purpose, without any outward appearance of a church."[35] Apart from restrictions as to the appearance of their temples, Anglicans, Lutherans (with United and Reformed mixing in) as immigration churches, and later Congregationalists, Presbyterians, Methodist and Baptist, as churches of (North American) mission, had to slowly conquer their full citizenship, among others against discrimination in the acceptance of marriages and for the availability of cemeteries for burying Protestants.

31. Ibid, 24.

32. João Dornas Filho, *O Padroado e A Igreja Brasiléia* (Rio de Janeiro: Companhia Editora National, 1937), 289, cited in Bruneau's *Political Transformation*, 29.

33. Ibid., 290, in Bruneau's *Political Transformation*, 32.

34. Bruneau, *Political Transformation*, 34.

35. Reily, *História Documental do Protestantismo no Brasil*, 48.

The Republic granted full religious liberty, which benefited, as indicated, also the Catholic church. Albeit abolishing privileges, the separation of church and State freed the ICAR to steer and organize itself, and gave momentum to a thorough restructuring in what came to be called Neo-Christendom, especially from 1922 onwards. The main figure here was Cardinal Sebastião Leme (1882–1942), Archbishop of Olinda and Recife (1916–21), coadjutor (1921–30) and then Archbishop of Rio de Janeiro until his death. His conception was clearly outlined in a 1916 pastoral letter addressed to (the people of) Olinda:

> In fact, as Catholics, we are the majority in Brazil, and yet the principles and organs of our political life are not Catholic. The law that governs us is not Catholic. [. . .] Lay are our schools, lay the teaching. In the Republic's Armed Forces, there is no care of religion. Finally, in the administration of official Brazil we don't see one single manifestation of Catholic life.[36]

By the 1920s, people had become uneasy with the low levels of development and social unrest became manifest, delegitimizing the government. It went to the church for help, and Leme was the key figure to provide it. However, the State was not yet prepared to give the church official recognition by naming the "Catholic religion" as the faith of the people, nor did it permit religious education in its schools. This was to happen only in the next decade. But Leme prayed at the 1922 Eucharistic Congress in Rio de Janeiro that "the Lord may give his hand to my Brazil, elevating it to the level of a great Christian State, preserve it and sustain it in the faith which presided at the birth and the development [*desdobramento*] of our civilization."[37]

Leme played a crucial role at the end of the 1930 "lieutenant's" revolution, when he convinced President Washington Luís Pereira de Souza (1869-1957, in office since 1926) to step down and hand over power to the revolutionaries, sparing the revolution of major bloodshed. Getúlio Vargas became the leader of the provisional government and was looking for support. Cardinal Leme provided it, but on his own terms. This became most evident on October 12, 1931, day of *Nossa Senhora da Conceição Aparecida*, who had been declared "Queen of Brazil" and national patron saint by Pope Pius XI only two years earlier. As mentioned above (IIB3), on that day, the 38m statue of Christ the Redeemer (*Christo Redentor*) on Corcovado Hill in Rio de Janeiro was inaugurated, and a new, close collaboration between the ICAR and the State began. Leme resisted the creation of a Catholic political party, presupposing that the ICAR represented all Brazilians; thus, what was needed was a pressure group beyond parties, and thus the Catholic Electoral League (*Liga Católica Eleitoral*) was founded in 1932.[38] Its strategy of organizing the Catholic electorate worked very successfully for the election of the constituent assembly in 1933, and for implementing its proposals during the assembly's work. Thus, the 1934 Constitution included a number of achievements: An invocation of God in the preamble, recognition of State-church collaboration "in favor of collective interest" (Art. 17, III), chaplaincies for the military and other State establishments, civil effects of religious marriage and religious education in public schools on all levels, as well as possible subventions for Catholic schools (cf. above, IIB2). The authoritarian regime of the *Estado Novo* under Vargas' dictatorship drafted a new constitution but did not effectively interfere in the good

36. Quoted in Azzi, *A neocristandade*, 25.

37. Ibid., 60.

38. The Brazilian Catholic hierarchy consistently resisted the creation of a Christian Democratic Party, different from what was happening in neighboring countries like Chile and Venezuela. In 1948 such a party was founded, the *Partido da Democracia Cristã*—PDC, but it never received the episcopacy's support, nor would the progressives joint it later. Even so, it became the fourth largest party in Brazil in 1962; Bruneau, *Political Transformation*, 100–102.

relationship with the ICAR. "On the whole, the Church approved of the Vargas system, because of its order, anti-Communism and stability."[39]

Another important aspect of Leme's strategy was to foster the laity's religious formation and engagement. This included attracting intellectuals around the "Center Dom Vital" in Rio de Janeiro, founded in 1922 and initially led by Jackson de Figueredo (1891–1928), followed by Alceu Amoroso Lima (1893–1983), both of them recently converted laymen.[40] The latter was more liberal than Figueredo and introduced the Christian humanist thinking of Jacques Maritain (1882–1973) and Georges Bernanos (1888–1948) to Brazil.[41] Alceu Lima affirmed that "the influence of Jacques Maritain came to be of another type in me, an influence characterized by the democratic and liberalizing tendency of Catholic thinking, which was seen by the rightism (*direitismo*) as heterodox and even apostatic."[42]

In 1935, the Catholic Action was founded, based on the Italian centralist and hierarchical model. It was quickly successful, but lost momentum when the State took over its fight against communists and the clergy became again dominant in the parishes. The church as a whole was still very much focused on the middle class, visible in its prioritization of higher over primary education, and the much better ratio of people per priest in the more developed South and Southeast regions compared to the Northeast, with nearly three times as many people per priest.[43]

Another tendency, more radical but short-lived, was the Brazilian Integralist Action *(Ação Integralista Brasileira)*, founded in 1932 by the Catholic writer Plínio Salgado, which looked to Portuguese Salazarism for inspiration.[44] Alceu Amoroso Lima initially supported the movement, but then distanced himself, as did Fr. Hélder Câmara. An offspring of Northeastern sugar cane producers, Plínio Corrêa de Oliveira (1908–95) founded, in 1929, the Student's Catholic Action *(Ação Católica Universitária)*, created the weekly *O Legionário* and the monthly *Catolicismo*, and in 1960 the ultra-conservative Brazilian Society for Defending Tradition, Family and Property (*Sociedade Brasileira de Defesa da Tradição, Família e Propriedade* – TFP).[45]

Hélder Câmara took over as National Assistant of the Catholic Action in 1947, which under French, Belgian and Canadian influence mutated into the Specialized Catholic Action, primarily for young people as the rural (*Juventude Agrária Católica* – JAC), student (*Juventude Estudantil Católica* – JEC), independent, i.e., middle class (*Juventude Independente Católica* – JIC), workers' (*Juventude Operária Católica* – JOC) and university student's Catholic Youth (*Juventude*

39. Bruneau, *Political Transformation*, 43. Communism grew in those years, with one of its leaders being Luiz Carlos Prestes (1898–1990), who strongly opposed Vargas, heading the anti-fascist and anti-imperialist National Liberating Alliance (*Aliança Libertadora Nacional*—ALN).

40. 1922 was a crucial year in Brazil, with the "Week of Modern Art" and the consequent movement of "anthropophagism," pointing to a syncretistic culture that swallows everything.

41. Souza, "As várias faces da Igreja Católica," 86 highlights both Maritain's ambiguous proposal of a "New Christendom" and the (much more positively viewed) distinction between "act like a Christian" (individually as Christians in politics) and "act as a Christian" (as the Church itself).

42. In Azzi, *A neocristandade*, 132.

43. Bruneau, *Political Transformation*, 48.

44. Souza, "As várias faces da Igreja Católica," 78.

45. See http://www.tfp.org.br/fundacao.asp (accessed on 5/11/2007). Oliveira, a lawyer, politician and historian, published, in 1959, a book on "Revolution and Counter-Revolution," confirming the anti-communist and anti-revolutionary thrust of the movement, which consequently opposed Liberation Theology and the upcoming progressive line of the Roman Catholic Church in Brazil. Oliveira was portrayed in a biography by Roberto de Mattei as the "crusader of the 20th century," in a book translated into German and Polish; http://www.pliniocorreadeoliveira.info (accessed on 5/11/2007).

Universitária Católica – JUC). These movements were responsible, in the 1950s and 1960s, for a "strong dynamism"[46] in the church, with an evident presence of Catholic laity in the public sphere. The JUC was especially radical, launching, in 1960, a utopian "historical ideal" for Brazil, which rendered it criticism among the episcopate. It gave birth to a democratic socialist movement in 1962, the Popular Action (*Ação Popular* – AP), no longer linked to the church, and influenced by the thought of Emmanuel Mounier (1905–1950).[47] Later, the AP turned into a clandestine Marxist movement.[48]

Some Bishops started to formulate statements on social issues in the 1950s. The first statement on the need of rural reforms came from Bishop Dom Inocêncio Engelke of Campanha (Minas Gerais), who affirmed publicly, in 1950: "With us, without us, or against us will be made the rural reform."[49] Especially strong were statements coming from the Northeast, understandably so as it has always been the poorest region in Brazil. The bishops there also met with the political leadership and their influence was decisive in the creation of the Northeast Development Agency (*Superintendência de Desenvolvimento do Nordeste* – SUDENE).[50]

In 1952, the CNBB was founded, giving the church a national structure, having Bishop Hélder Câmara as its first general secretary. As Souza[51] highlights, this happened in a phase of nation-building under Getúlio Vargas' second presidency (1950–54) and especially Juscelino Kubitscheks (1955–59) bold development program, which included the construction of a new national capital, Brasília. In the early 1960s, a treaty of cooperation between the CNBB and the Ministry of Education made possible the Base Education Movement (*Movimento de Educação de Base* – MEB), which promoted alphabetization and basic education through "radio schools," inspired by Paulo Freire's campaigns. "These were years of intense social and political activity, and the presence of the Church, through its movements and lay people, was strongly being felt. However, it was also a time of ideological and political polarizations, which had its effect on the institution,"[52] where a division between progressives and conservatives became accentuated, dividing, inclusively, the episcopate. Casanova[53] recalls the CNBB's 1962 Emergency Plan, which defined secularization, Marxism, Protestantism and Spiritism as the four main threats facing the ICAR. On the other hand, the bishops were able to call, in a 1963 message, for "profound and serious transformations" and quote agrarian and other reforms like those of business, taxation, administration, voting, and education.[54] The papal nuntio from 1954–64, Dom Armando Lombardi, supported the churches' new

46. Souza, "As várias faces da Igreja Católica," 78.

47. Souza ("As várias faces da Igreja Católica," 86) cites his *Oeuvres* (Paris: Seuil, 1961); while Mounier did not make a direct link between the Christian faith and a specific political system, his type of socialism was oriented by the faith, together with the instruments of the social sciences and concrete life experiences. In the same line, Brazilian Jesuit Henrique C. de Lima Vaz played a decisive role, still according to Souza. Vaz, in turn, affirmed that Mounier was "(the author) who most influenced Brazilian Catholic Youth" in the 1960s (in Löwy, *A guerra dos deuses*, 53).

48. Souza, "As várias faces da Igreja Católica,"; Kadt, *Catholic Radicals in Brazil*; Antoine, *Church and Power in Brazil*.

49. Bruneau, *Political Transformation*, 66.

50. President Kubitschek acknowledged in a 1959 speech to the bishop's meeting in Natal (Rio Grande do Norte) that "this initiative of the Federal Government [. . .] is due to the inspiration of the Church and the energetic dedication of the Northeastern Bishops, ever since the first meeting in Campina Grande [in 1956], to save our courageous fellow countrymen from destitution and misery" (cited in Bruneau, *Political Transformation*, 78).

51. Souza: "As várias faces da Igreja Católica," 79.

52. Ibid.

53. Casanova, *Public Religions*, 120.

54. Souza: "As várias faces da Igreja Católica," 79.

social stance and was influential in the renewal of the episcopate, as Bruneau[55] highlights. Again on the conservative side, 1964 saw the emergence of the "Marches with God for the Family and Freedom," with the help of U.S.-American Fr. Peyton. While one part of the church strove toward social transformation, the other strongly opposed what it saw as the subversion of order.

c) The ICAR and the Military Regime

As cited above (IA1a), the ICAR initially welcomed the coup as it reestablished order and seemed to contain the communist forces. However, it also cautioned in its message of May 27, 1964, that "we do not accept, nor can we ever accept unjust and generalized accusation, cheap, subtle or explicit, by which bishops, priests, faithful or organizations like, for example, the Catholic Action and he MEB, are said to be communists or sympathizers of communism [*comunizantes*]."[56] Although the church kept largely silent on political issues in the following years,[57] it was predictable that the church would react inasmuch as persecution turned against it, which was to happen soon. The Institutional Act number 5 gave the government virtually unlimited power and led into the "years of lead" (*anos de chumbo*), the climax of political repression. The church itself became the object of persecution due to its critical voices against political and economic oppression. Except for relatively small groups, however, the church still complied with the State and disciplined the sectors it considered too radical.[58] But slowly, even conservative bishops were drawn into resistance, in order to protect their own church. Following the death of guerilla leader Carlos Marighella, in 1969, seven Dominican friars (among them Frei Betto, Frei Tito, and Frei Ivo Lesbaupin) were imprisoned and tortured, as they had allegedly adhered to Marighella's movement. The CNBB rejected the accusation and then Archbishop of São Paulo Dom Agnelo Rossi, a conservative, denounced all types of violence. Decisive for a change in the church's attitude was also the death of Fr. Antônio Henrique Pereira Neto in Recife, in the same year, as part of State pressure against D. Hélder Câmara.[59] Pereira Neto had worked with youth and was threatened prior to his assassination.[60] Such persecutions, as well as the church's protest against them, continued well into the period of transition. The church issued excommunication sentences as it had no other way of reacting[61]. Furthermore, it celebrated masses remembering repression against itself or persons like Jewish journalist Vladimir Herzog (in an ecumenical celebration, cf. above, IA1b, IIB1) and steelworker Manoel Fiel Filho, which attracted thousands of people. Only in 1973 was the first collective pastoral document issued which criticized the military regime, but individual bishops had been speaking out much earlier.[62] A clear sign of the danger the regime saw in the church is that, according to a report on repression against the church based on official sources and the media: "The STM ('Supreme Military Court') consid-

55. Bruneau, *Political Transformation*, 117.

56. Ibid., 81.

57. Mainwaring, *Catholic Church and Politics*, 83.

58. Antoine, *Church and Power in Brazil.*

59. Pereira Neto, 28 years old, was a JOC assistant and the first clergyman in Brazil to be assassinated, on May 25, 1969. His assassins were not tried, nor a serious investigation made. The bishops of the CNBB Northeast 2 Region issued a statement strongly condemning torture; Mainwaring, *The Catholic Church and Politics*, 99f.

60. CEDI, *Repression against the Church in Brazil*, 22.

61. Ibid., 38.

62. Adriance, *Opting for the Poor*, "Brazil and Chile," 289; Mainwaring, *Catholic Church and Politics.*

ers the pulpit to be 'an instrument of mass communications subject to committing offenses of an adverse psychological war.'"[63]

The tone of the conflict can also be measured with the following statement by TV Globo's director Edgardo Erichsen in 1977, who attacked Dom Pedro Casaldáliga, an outspoken defender of indigenous rights, land reform and social justice in general. In a national TV programme, Erichsen said

> It seems that the bishop has exchanged his crucifix and rosary for the hammer and sickle, his prayer book for the thoughts of Mao Tse-tung, his priestly piety for violence and that he is only waiting for the right moment to exchange his cassock for a guerrilla's uniform. Of some left-wing priests it can be said that they light one candle to God and the other to the devil. But for bishop Dom Pedro Maria Casaldáliga, the least can be said is that he lights both candles to the devil.[64]

In Bruneau's assessment,

> [. . .] the Church's role was important in delegitimating the military regime; in creating a network of organizations and informal contacts that provided an umbrella for political action and encouraged a variety of individuals and groups to become involved; in the mobilization and political education promoted through the CEBs; and in the specific statements on participation and democracy.[65]

The church, more and more critical of the State, received support from the Vatican and Catholic agencies abroad, as well as from ecumenical organizations like the WCC, who made possible the famous research in State documents on torture, published as "Brazil: Never Again!" (*Brasil: Nunca mais!*). Had it not been for this work, mainly executed by Cardinal Arns and Presbyterian Pastor Jaime Wright (1927–1999) with support from the WCC, such documentation would have disappeared for ever when the military destroyed their records at the end of their regime.[66] Indeed, torture became one of the central issues in the church's pressure on the State, and was helped by the fact that the military regime felt embarrassed by the international press' allegations on torture in the country. The "Bipartite Commission" between the government and the ICAR, co-steered by Catholic layman and general secretary of the Brazilian Section of the Pontifical Justice and Peace Commission, Candido Mendes de Almeida (b. 1928), held secret talks with the government between 1970 and 1974. It included a delegation of generals and, on the church's side, senior bishops, both conservative and progressive.[67] In those most repressive years under General Médici's

63. CEDI, *Repression against the Church in Brazil*, 13. The CEDI report lists defamatory attacks, invasions, imprisonment, torture, death and death threats, abductions, indictments, summons, expulsions, censorship, prohibitions and falsifications, based on official and media sources, including church newspapers and bulletins (9f.). Given censorship, especially strict in the years of the strongest repression (1970–74), with often imprecise ("Father X was arrested with several peasants," ibid., 19) or no information at all, the report is necessarily incomplete. The ecumenical organization CEDI, today Koinonia (http://www.koinonia.org.br), could count on the support of the WCC in its work.

64. As quoted in Sader and Silverstein, *Without Fear of Being Happy*, 58. They describe how Casaldáliga "covered much of his huge 150,000 square-kilometer diocese (almost the size of Portugal) by bus and on foot, and his support for landless peasants was largely responsible for the seven threats of expulsion he received from the generals, and the innumerable death threats he received from the region's landowners." (ibid.).

65. Bruneau, "The Catholic Church in the Redemocratization of Brazil," 90.

66. On Wright, see Oliveira, "Jaime Wright (1927–99)." Jaime's brother Paul, who had been state deputy in Santa Catarina and a leading figure in the AP, had his mandate cancelled by the military in 1964, went to Mexico into exile, returned secretly, was captured, tortured, and killed. His body never appeared. Doubtlessly, this event marked Jaime's life and engagement profoundly (ibid., 177).

67. Cf. Serbin, *Secret Dialogues*. Candido is the brother of Dom Luciano Pedro Mendes de Almeida (1930–2006),

government, the commission worked to prevent human rights violations, on the one hand, and to contend the revolutionary tendencies among the clergy, on the other, in an attempt to maintain the traditionally strong links between the State and the church, prevent the country from the threat of "communism" and promote the return to democracy. President Geisel dissolved the commission as he understood that the State's partner for negotiation was not the Bishops' Conference (CNBB), but the Vatican as a State and, thus, its nuncio.

At the same time, the church's contribution went far beyond its own boundaries. I have already highlighted its role as a protecting umbrella for the nascent civil society (cf. above, IB2). Ralph Della Cava comments:

> Clearly, however, this uncommon transference of secular tasks to a religious institution was neither instantaneous nor inevitable. In the final analysis, it was part of a process of trust. Increasingly, churchmen demonstrated that their defense of human rights went beyond that of Catholicism's own immediately threatened cadres. In the early seventies, the national Peace and Justice Commission appealed to the regime on behalf of all the imprisoned, tortured and disappeared – regardless of their religious or political affiliation.[68]

It was in this same period that the Church Base Communities (CEBs) came to the fore, organizing the Catholic flock into groups led by lay people, gathered around the Bible and articulated locally focused projects for healthcare, water and power supply, sanitation, education, and the like. Such communities had been created already in the 1950s by conservative bishops like Dom Agnelo Rossi, then in Barra do Piraí (Rio de Janeiro), and Dom Eugênio Sales, then bishop of Natal (Rio Grande do Norte), not least to prevent, given the accentuated shortage of priests, Catholics falling prey to the communist Rural Leagues or the advancing Pentecostal churches.[69] Dominique Barbé, a French priest of Charles de Foucault's Little Brothers of Jesus living and working in Brazil, indicated 1968 as the "birth" of the progressive CEBs, when priests and religious stood before the decision to

> either join the guerrilla forces and the clandestine subversion, as urged by certain Marxist and even Christian elements of the middle class, or attach themselves, more seriously than before, to a pastoral labor at the base, in order to get close to the worker militants and peasants and form communities with them.[70]

Azevedo[71] underlines that the CEBs did not "arise spontaneously out of the base," but were "the result of the consciousness-raising activity of clergy and religious, who were helping the people to see real elements of their life and historical situation." We could say that in a specific

---

who became general secretary and president of the CNBB in 1979 and 1987, respectively. Among the Catholics were some of the most conservative members of the episcopate, like Eugênio Sales and Lucas Moreira Neves, as well as some of the most progressive bishops like Aloísio Lorscheider, Ivo Lorscheiter, and Paulo Evaristo Arns.

68. Della Cava, "A Vision of Short-Term Politics and Long-Term Religion," 18.

69. On the history and characteristics of CEBs, see Barbé, *Grace and Power*; Azevedo, *Basic Ecclesial Communities*; Teixeira, *A Gênese das CEBs no Brasil*; Dawson, *The Birth and Impact of the Base Ecclesial Community*. The line of argument stressing the "use" of CEBs to strengthen the ICAR's institutionality and hegemony is maintained by Adriance, *Opting for the Poor*, "Brazil and Chile"—although recognizing the movement then went on its own ways, not being reduced to such function—, Bruneau, *The Church in Brazil*, and especially by Liehr, *Katholizismus und Demokratisierung* and Gill, *Rendering unto Caesar* (based on rational choice theory), while being contested by Azevedo, *Basic Ecclesial Communities in Brazil*, 39–41, who says that CEBs cannot be regarded as part of "any overall, programmatic, strategic view" (ibid., 41). In any case, he agrees with Bruneau that CEBs became "the most important transformation in the Brazilian church" (ibid.).

70. Barbé, *Grace and Power*, 92; Azevedo, *Basic Ecclesial Communities*, 27f. takes the First Join Pastoral Plan of 1965–70 as the "official launching of Basic Ecclesial Communities in the Brazilian Church" (emphasis omitted).

71. Azevedo, *Basic Ecclesial Communities*, 35.

historical situation, CEBs became, for many, a meaningful way of being the Church under pressing circumstances, lay in character but supported by pastoral agents, priests, bishops, and the mood of Vatican II. From there, the CEBs became the birthplace of civil society and, not least, a training place for its leaders.[72]

In Mainwaring's[73] assessment, the period from 1974–82, which coincides with the beginning of decompression and the gradually opening space for other movements and institutions of civil society being formed, was the high point of the ICAR's "importance in international Catholicism," when it "became the most progressive Church in the world." As CEBs and other sectors of the "popular church" remained tied up with the hierarchy and emphasized more consistently their ecclesial character—albeit with political consequences[74]—and as the church continued to suffer repression against its representatives, even conservative bishops came out in its defense, thus closing the ranks of the ICAR in considerable harmony. The church right, including the above mentioned conservative TFP-movement, lost ground as the left became more moderate. In fact, "even progressive Church leaders felt that the Church's work must change as civil society developed the capacity to articulate its own political mechanisms."[75] After 1982, with the continuation of *abertura*, the importance of church support for civil society diminished, as did internal support for them, and if the papal nuncio was crucial in providing progressive bishops in the decade 1954–64, the current one did everything to ensure that more conservative bishops were nominated. Pope John Paul II followed a clearly conservative policy in episcopal nominations, which had its slow, but thorough effect on the Brazilian episcopate. In Porto Alegre, Dom Ivo Lorscheiter did not become the archbishop in 1981, despite his high prestige, and Dom José Cardoso Sobrinho, nominated in 1985 as successor of Dom Hélder Câmara in Olinda and Recife, made sure he thoroughly changed the progressive line his predecessor had adopted, among others by closing the diocese's seminary. Cardinal Arns had his archdiocese dismembered, with three new dioceses being created to reduce his influence. The virtual consensus on the church's progressive stance in the 1970s had gone.

d) The ICAR after Transition

After transition, as was to be expected, the prominence of the Catholic church in civil society diminished.[76] For one, as opening proceeded and other forms of opposition and free organization become possible, amnesty brought exiled leaders back and parties were allowed to form, the church's protective umbrella was no longer needed. On the other hand, it had urgent internal matters to attend to, not least to see how to react to the continuing loss of members to Pentecostal churches.

72. Cf. Liehr, *Katholizismus und Demokratisierung*; Mainwaring, *Catholic Church and Politics*, "Grassroots Popular Movements"; Hewitt, *Base Christian Communities*.

73. Mainwaring, *Catholic Church and Politics*, 145.

74. Cf. Mainwaring, *Catholic Church and Politics*, 204: "The charge of the conservatives that the CEBs are deeply political has little to do with the reality of the vast majority of base communities in Brazil, but their perception that CEBs affect political life is clearly correct."

75. Ibid.

76. Already in 1978, Della Cava stated ("A Vision of Short-Term Politics and Long-Term Religion," 20): "At this moment, the Church's leadership in the struggle for freedom and justice is both unprecedented and unrivalled. But its duration is very much predictable: it must and will come to an end at the moment in which Brazilian civil society is reconstituted in all its fullness and under the scrutiny of an irradicable and inalienable rule of law"; cf. Bruneau, *Political Transformation*, 226. A decade later, Bruneau ("Catholic Church in the Redemocratization of Brazil," 88) wrote, highlighting a meeting of the pope with CNBB leaders and the Brazilian cardinals during their visit to Rome in March 1986: "It is my hypothesis that the political role defined and implemented by the Church during the military regime will change. At the same time the Church will not disappear from the social and political scene in Brazil."

Archbishop Dom Eugênio Sales of Rio de Janeiro put it bluntly:

> A new period for the Brazilian Church is beginning. The Church had a very active role in the period when Brazil was becoming a closed society. It was 'the voice of those who had no voice'. Today the parliament, press and parties are functioning fully. They should speak, and the Church should take care of its own affairs.[77]

Even progressive bishops like Dom Ivo Lorscheiter conceded that "from now on, in a situation of greater freedom and popular organization, although the hierarchy will not become silent, it wants the laity to speak more."[78] As we shall see in the second section (IIC2), this did not mean that the hierarchy would no longer speak out on social issues. But there was a much lower sense of urgency now. On the grassroots level, the CEBs suffered an exodus both into other social movements and NGOs, by those who held a mainly political interest—without necessarily leaving their faith behind—and into other religions by those searching for a stronger spirituality. Burdick[79] has argued that this was due to the heavy load of ethical responsibility laid on the shoulders of humble people, while those other "cults of affliction" attributed evil in both its individual and collective bearings to external evil forces. Another strain on the CEBs was the reluctance of newly appointed bishops, most of them conservative, to support them. While a kind of basic democracy could be exercised within the CEBs, the Roman Catholic Church's hierarchical structure was not changed through it, and so their work continued to depend heavily on the priest's and, especially, the bishop's support.

Even the existing CEBs did not provide univocal support for the Worker's Party, supposedly "their" party, as expected in the 1982 elections.[80] Bruneau contended that

> it is likely that the CEBs will remain important, even a defining characteristic of the Brazilian Church, but [. . .] it is unlikely they will have the momentum to provide the orientation for the institutional Church. More likely they will be but one element of the pastoral [action], one that is appropriate for the lower class in the rural areas and the periphery of the larger cities.[81]

One of the reasons for such feeble support was that, according to Margaret Keck, both churches and trade-unions, the main supporters of the PT,

> mistrusted political mediation and conceived the party's role as one of linking and spreading (but not organizing and transforming) the demands of unions and movements. At the same time, however, they felt that party members should participate in and help to fortify unions and movements (without, however, subordinating them to the party). Their view of democracy was one of direct democracy, involving delegation rather than representation, reiterating a tradition which goes back to Rousseau and has recently given rise to intense debate about the possibility of recombining institutions of representative and direct democracy [. . .].[82]

If this reading is correct, it brings us back to the problem of the relationship between different actors in civil society, as indicated above (IB3). The discussion continues, with a prominent position represented by Marilena Chauí who judged the main problem of the PT as having lost its binding relationship with the social movements.[83]

77. *Jornal do Brasil* of July 7, 1983, in Mainwaring, *Catholic Church and Politics*, 240.
78. *Estado de São Paulo* of December 30, 1984, in Mainwaring, *Catholic Church and Politics*, 240.
79. Burdick, *Looking for God in Brazil.*
80. Cf. Maclean, *Opting for Democracy?*, 76f.
81. Bruneau, "Catholic Church in the Redemocratization of Brazil," 105.
82. Keck, *The Workers' Party and Democratization in Brazil*, 243.
83. Chauí et al., *Leituras da crise.*

Still, it is true that "in many cases, the first people to adhere to the new party [i.e., the PT] were local Church and peasant activists who were already involved in the struggle to form unions and defend squatters (in numerous cases there was—and is—almost no difference between membership lists at the union, the Base Community, and the PT)."[84] Keck also admits that in some places, there was strong support for PT in CEBs, namely in São Paulo.[85]

The Boff case (cf. above, ID1a), precisely in the first period of the new civil government, brought him and the Brazilian church back into the limelight of the world's stage. He received support from some of the most senior bishops, namely Cardinals Arns and Lorscheider, who themselves, however, had been looked upon suspiciously by the curia for a while. The presidency of the CNBB went to Rome in 1985 to deal with the Boff case, and a year later a delegation of all the cardinals and the bishops in charge of the 14 CNBB regions and the national conference spent five days in Rome for their *ad limina* visit. According to Bruneau, the message was that "the Church in Brazil is part of the Universal Church and the role of the Church is primarily religious unless conditions are such that the Church is called upon for a suppletive role. These conditions have now passed in Brazil."[86] Apparently, the pope was satisfied with the bishops' position, or wanted to show his goodwill; in any case, Boff's "obsequious silence" was revoked very soon thereafter.

The church sought to continue its political influence, but more indirectly. According to Azevedo, "the commitment of the Church in Brazil to democracy and the constitutional State [*Estado de Direito*] and its option to support a democratic model, politically sovereign and participatory, economically inclusive and socially just has to be registered."[87] At the same time, such a position was not to change the church's structure itself, despite the noteworthy attempts at giving the laity more space in the church. The conservative bishop of Petrópolis (state of Rio de Janeiro), Dom Manoel Pedro da Cunha Cintra, affirmed in the early 1980s that "the Church should not be democratic because the quality of opinions is more important than the number of opinions."[88] It becomes clear that, while the "popular church" has been important in empowering people to speak up in CEBs and social movements, the church made sure it would not itself be lastingly influenced by such democratization, thus widening the gap between political and ecclesiastical citizenship (see below, IIC3c/d).

While there is ample agreement that the church has been making a difference and had influence on the political process, especially under the military regime and during transition, there is disagreement as to the effective degree of such difference when it comes to the level of members. In their interpretation of surveys carried out in 1982 and 1984, Bruneau and Hewitt concluded that "the church, at present, is only weakly tied to the population" and "its ability to influence the current process of political and hence social change will be severely limited."[89] This conclusion stems from the analyzed data, which show "that practicing Catholics do not distinguish themselves as the standard-bearers of the social justice theme articulated by the institutional church."[90] Even

84. Sader and Silverstein, *Without Fear of Being Happy*, 59.

85. Keck, *The Workers' Party and Democratization in Brazil*, 78f., 97f.

86. Bruneau, "Catholic Church in the Redemocratization of Brazil," 101.

87. Azevedo, "A Igreja Católica e seu papel político no Brasil," 118.

88. Mainwaring, *Catholic Church and Politics*, 250.

89. Bruneau and Hewitt, "Patterns of Church Influence in Brazil's Political Transition," 40. If Mainwaring (*Catholic Church and Politics*) is right in seeing the beginning of the politically progressive stance's erosion from 1982, this coincides with the period of the quoted surveys. The broad "consensus," then, faded, while the "progressive" or "popular church" remained as one tendency among others, losing its hegemony.

90. Ibid., 44.

more: "[. . .] where church involvement in political issues generally and strikes in particular are concerned, practicing Catholics are slightly less supportive than their nonpracticing counterparts," while they "much more strongly uphold the value of traditional church teaching on family matters (for example, divorce, use of birth control) and morality (for example, abortion)."[91] Of course, empirical data are always limited in their reach, methodology and interpretation, and later data indicate other directions.[92] But it is significant that the firm commitment of the church's leadership to social justice—which continued even under conservative CNBB presidencies—did not directly materialize in the attitudes of the active church members, not even in progressive dioceses. Thus, "the church has largely been unable to cultivate a mass following of committed progressives, even among its closest adherents. It would seem that in the frankly elitist society that is Brazil, the church has had much more success in dealing with other elite institutions, civil and military, including the media."[93]

While the church has maintained a relatively progressive line in social matters, as we shall see, it has at the same time maintained a conservative line in matters of sexual morality, in this reflecting Pope John Paul II's position. Apparently, the majority of active and practicing Catholics (not of all nominal Catholics) is inclined to more strongly support the line of sexual morality than the socially progressive stance, and the RCC is precisely advocating such a position.

Summing up these findings, we can then say that the ICAR has found its own structure and identity in, first, coming closer to Rome and being freed from the State's tutelage. It then tried to re-approach the State in order to construct a new Christendom, but now on the church's terms. This worked for some time, especially under President Vargas, but gave way to more progressive thinking and to concrete social action through movements and leaders that emerged since the 1930s but came to the fore in the 1950s. When the coup happened in 1964, the church had already organized itself as a national church under a quite progressive CNBB leadership, linked to Rome but with a considerable degree of autonomy, a tendency that found support—as did the stance on social issues—in the Second Vatican Council. Pressed by the State and the growing general repression and social inequality, the ICAR further strengthened its commitment for the poor, not least through supporting the creation of CEBs in many places, becoming a kind of incubator for civil society. After transition, this role was lost, as was to be expected, but the CNBB continued to speak out strongly on social issues, even if moral issues also came to the fore, reflecting Pope John Paul II's strong convictions on both issues. The church itself is today much more diversified than it was, and is facing serious challenges from the rising number and influence of Pentecostals, the emptying of CEBs—which still exist, but only as one grouping among many— the stronger grip of Rome on the CNBB and an uneasy partnership with a party which came out, in many respects, of the progressive church, but is now in a different position as government.

2. DISCOURSE AND PRACTICE

In this second section, I shall explore the church's discourse after transition, i.e., after the takeover of a civilian president in 1985. As sources, I have used both theological and sociological literature. For the present section especially, the monthly (sometimes two-monthly) bulletin (*Comunicado Mensal*), in existence since the CNBB's foundation in 1952, records declarations of the CNBB, dio-

91. Ibid., 46.

92. CERIS, *Desafios do catolicismo na cidade: pesquisa em regiões metropolitanas brasileiras*; Medeiros, "Orientações ético-religiosas."

93. Bruneau and Hewitt, "Patterns of Church Influence in Brazil's Political Transition," 60.

ceses, and institutions (like the Pastoral Land Commission), but also of the pope, foreign bishop's conferences, ecumenical bodies, and related churches, thus giving a fairly broad view of ICAR positions and reflections and of what was being considered relevant by the official church.[94] I have also used major documents and some studies of the CNBB. Although it might be rightly questioned whether such documents are really read and made known among the clergy and laity, they still provide the main references in specific dioceses, regions or the national church, and have certainly to be seen as important guidelines issued by the leadership of a hierarchically organized church. They are elaborated for and adopted by the episcopate, who exercises a decisive influence in his diocese.[95] Whatever the bishop tolerates or even fosters, will grow; whatever he may reject or even combat, will have no place in parish life and might, at most, survive at the fringes or in independent organizations.

For good or bad, such documents are meant to be binding in a much stricter sense than in other churches like the IECLB. Although all documents were considered, only exemplary quotes are made to show tendencies, formulations and lines of thought. As in any selection, different quotes might have been chosen; I tried to bring those that most clearly speak to the issues of citizenship.

In general, we can say that the CNBB has maintained its discourse adopted in the 1970s, with elements of it present locally and regionally since the 1950s. This is especially evident in the continuous general critique of poverty and social inequality, and the more specific statements on land reform and indigenous' rights. In these issues, it maintained harmony with ecumenical collaborators who, although small in number, could mobilize international support, both financial and moral, for instance through the WCC and agencies of international cooperation like Bread for the World. On the other hand, the church also consistently defended traditional values like the family and matrimony, and of late accentuatedly chastity, the prohibition of abortion, contraceptives, and euthanasia, and opposition against the legal recognition of homosexual relationships. Pope Benedict XVI, during his visit to Brazil in May 2007, has harped strongly on all these issues, which had already been central for John Paul II. Except for the contraceptives, the ICAR is in these matters in good and somewhat ironical consensus—given their strong competition—with most Pentecostal and Neo-Pentecostal churches, against ecumenical and liberal circles. With the latter, in turn, the ICAR has much in common on the side of social transformation. While CNBB documents which stress, at the same time, social transformation—where it appears progressive—and moral values—where it appears conservative—are the fruit of compromises between different tendencies in the episcopate, not rarely both are defended by the very same bishop. In any case, both tendencies are well grounded in Catholic Social Teaching and reflect Pope John Paul II's line,

94. For this section, I could count on the invaluable assistance of Daiana Ernest who spent two weeks at the CNBB headquarters in Brasília in July 2005 and, during a year of undergraduate research assistance, went through a number of recent publications and all the issues of the *Comunicado Mensal* from 1985 to 2005 in order to spot relevant themes and texts for the purpose of this study. I would also like to thank Fr. Gabriele Cipriani and Sr. Delci Maria Franzen for their help as Daiana stayed in Brasília. —Differently from books and official CNBB documents, I shall quote the full references of the texts quoted from the *Comunicado Mensal* (abbreviated as CM) in the footnotes, without listing them again in the bibliography. On the ICAR's communication between 1962 and 1989, see Della Cava, "A Conferência Nacional dos Bispos do Brasil."

95. An important element of the yearly assemblies of the CNBB are the fairly extensive "analyses of conjuncture" (*análises de conjuntura*) which present the social, economic and political context, at the time, as well as ethical considerations. These are also reproduced in the CM, but have not been taken into account here, as they constitute subsidies and not adopted positions. As an example see the 1999 analysis, formulated by Fr. Virgílio Leite Uchôa, political consultant to the CNBB, and Francisco Whitaker Ferreira, executive secretary of the Brazilian Commission on Justice and Peace and one of the founders of the World Social Forum (the first was held in 2001, in Porto Alegre), CM 48/530 (1999), 799–848.

who has consistently spoken out both on issues of social justice and traditional values in matters of family and sexuality. Both also frequently use the terminology of the protection or defense of life. It is noteworthy, however, that the tone in which the two lines of argument are sustained is relativizing in the first case—the laity are encouraged and oriented towards action—and absolute in the second—those supporting liberal abortion laws might have excommunicated themselves.[96]

Let us now see what issues stand out in the named documents after 1985, namely citizenship (a), land reform (b), indigenous rights (c), other pastoral action (d), political participation (e), and moral issues (f). My analysis is based, mainly, on documents and thus on discourse, but practice is included through sociological data from surveys and data from Catholic social work. Especially the major, official documents use as sources both data and analysis of the situation and biblical and magisterial foundations for arguing their practical conclusions, quite clearly following the tripod of "See – Judge – Act" (cf. above, ID). They are elaborated by a commission and then submitted to the bishops for discussion, changes and voting, a process which is likely to reflect, as indicated, compromises among tendencies in the episcopate. But though the language might be more radical or more moderate at times, the arguments itself are remarkably consistent.

a) Focus on Citizenship

Right in 1985, progressive sectors of the church formulated what they understood to be the church's mission:

> The church has a transforming function in the humanization of the world. This function is exercised
>
> a) through concrete action in the structures of the world, inserting itself into the intermediary social structures [i.e. civil society];
>
> b) through the word, thinking, reflection, the Church seeks to be the world's conscience on its way towards full humanization.
>
> The Church in Brazil, over the last twenty years, has opened large space for the organization of the popular, trade-union, and political movement, was the voice of whom was silenced, defended life, physical integrity, the rights of many. The hierarchical church must invest its charism and its power to challenge Catholics themselves so that they may assume concretely, with seriousness and competence, their role in the structural changes. One more severe problem of the Church in Brazil, today, is the formation of the laity: to capacitate them so that they might assume their role in the Church and in society, as responsible for the transformation of earthly structures. There is a lack of improvement in the formation which should include, beyond the knowledge of Doctrine and religious practices, as well as theology, the deepening

96. A recent case shook the country in March 2009. A nine-year old girl had been raped by her stepfather and became pregnant. Abortion in case of rape is foreseen in the Brazilian penal code as legal. Furthermore, the doctors said abortion had to be carried out in order to prevent risks for the mother's life. Dom José Cardoso Sobrinho, the Archbishop of Olinda and Recife, however, after trying to convince the grandmother not to give her consent, announced the excommunication *latae sententiae* for the grandmother (a child cannot be excommunicated) and the doctors. Reactions on all sides were highly critical of the ICAR, both because the public agreed with the abortion, and because Dom José did not excommunicate the stepfather, saying that such sin did not incur in excommunication and that the killing of an innocent life (the fetus) was worse. See, for instance, *Zero Hora* of March 7, 2009, 4–5, and further editions. The CNBB's presidency, at the time on visit to the Vatican, downplayed the rejection of the abortion (although, of course, upholding it) and emphasized its repudiation of the rape (http://www.cnbb.org.br/ns/modules/news/article.php?storyid=1124 accessed on 3/12/2009). Furthermore, it supported the declaration of the CNBB's Northeast 2 Regional, who did not even mention excommunication, but stressed its defense of life, both of the raped child and of the fetus, with explicit reference to the Church's defense of "life and the dignity of people, defending human rights of persecuted, tortured and political refugees" under the military regime (http://www.cnbb.org.br/ns/modules/news/article.php?storyid =1125 accessed on 3/12/2009).

> of the concept of citizenship (rights and duties), concepts of ethics which include the love of truth, personal, professional and social responsibility.[97]

As mentioned above (IC3), the church played an active role during the constituent process and made a considerable number of proposals, which are well documented.[98] Some of them were articulated in cooperation with ecumenical bodies, mainly the National Council of Churches (CONIC), whose president at the time was Gottfried Brakemeier, also Pastor President of the IECLB. One of such declarations, issued by the diaconal institution CESE with support from CONIC, affirmed that "despite all announced and foreseeable distortions [i.e., mainly the distance between the constituent congress and people's movements and aspirations], the constituent moment is highly significant, because it is the moment when the principal laws of the country can be changed."[99]

Before the actual constituent process, the CNBB had laid out its principles in the pastoral declaration "Toward a New Constitutional Order" (*Por uma nova ordem constitucional*), a statement approved by the CNBB's 24th General Assembly in April 1986. There, the bishops affirmed that

> the new constitution should not restrict itself to the reorganization of the State and its relationship with society. It shall translate the search for a new model of society in its social, political, economic, cultural and international dimension. A model that shall be based on the ethical demands of human society and on the extension of effective citizenship to all Brazilians without exception. Within this new model, it inheres to all citizens to participate co-responsibly in the effort toward social improvement and to the State to promote the common good, featuring an organic and participatory democracy.[100]

"Citizenship" is quite frequent (9, 10, 84-86, 99) and even more so the "citizen" (8, 10, 26, 66-7, 84, 90, 92, 127, 139, 141), not least in the rich quotations of other relevant documents in the endnotes. Quite in the line of what has been said above (IB and IC) on the relationship between civil society and the State as seen by those related to social movements, the document insists in an inversion of roles, putting the State at society's service rather than vice-versa. Society is to use the State as a mediator "so that democratic life may be deepened and justice may prevail more and more on social relationships." (11). The CNBB insists on society's participation in drafting the constitution, mindful of proposals for direct intervention like referendums.

The church's participation is grounded in faith, which "shall illuminate the Christians' actions [. . .] in permanent fidelity to Christ, the Church and human being." (18). Through its pastoral action, the church can contribute with a specific pedagogy: "The pedagogy of its pastoral action, characterized by the effort to open spaces for the poor to come together in communities, in the light of a faith profoundly embedded in life seeks to overcome the separation between faith and life, named among the gravest errors of our times by the Second Vatican Council."[101] The church shall collaborate in the constituent process as part of society, not in order for the Constitution to be confessional, but "in coherence with its action till date, it [the Church] works towards the incorporation of democratic mechanisms and instruments—means [*alavancas*] of social transformation—

97. CPT; Ação Católica Operária; Comissão Brasileira Justiça e Paz et al. Missão da Igreja no processo de transformação sócio-política no Brasil, CM 34/394 (1985), 1390f. As the text speaks of the church's "charism and power," it is certainly resounding Leonardo Boff's book "Church, Charism and Power," for which he had been condemned, some months earlier, to "obsequious silence" by the Vatican.

98. CNBB, *Participação popular e cidadania*.

99. CESE/CONIC, "As Igrejas no debate da constituinte," CM 35/401 (1986), 906–9, at 909.

100. CNBB, *Por uma nova ordem constitucional*, 10.

101. Ibid., 20 with a reference to *Gaudium et Spes,* 43 All documents of the Second Vatican Council, quoted here as commonly known by their Latin names, are to be found on the Vatican's Website http://www.vatican.va.

which shall permit the population's active participation in the decisions of collective interest" (23). The document makes clear that the church is, in these matters, acting through "the Christians," i.e., the laity, but with support from the church. Indeed, as the documentation shows,[102] it has been doing this through an intensive circulation of news and assessment of the constituent process, has made "popular amendments" for the family, education, religious freedom and the economic order, and has supported amendments put forward by the Missionary Council for Indigenous Peoples (CIMI), and the National Campaign for Land Reform, among others.[103] Especially remarkable is the emphasis given to religious liberty,[104] which is to be given to all religions "as long as they do not infringe upon the rights of others or the common good."[105] It includes the right to religious education respectful of the pupil's conviction and that of those responsible for him,[106] and religious assistance to the armed forces and those in custody. While this reinforces what pre-military constitutions already guaranteed, there's now also an emphasis on the "right and duty of religious groups to exercise a critical function in society, in relation to the behavior of groups, institutions or even the public power, whenever they disrespect religious convictions or ethical values based on them" (68), which can be read as a kind of right to resistance, growing out of the experience under the military. And the CNBB also suggests a civil service for conscientious objectors (69), a proposal supported by the National Council of Churches (CONIC; cf. above, IIB2). Finally, symbols, rites, and other characteristic features of any religion should be protected in their dignity and against imitation (70).

According to then CNBB president Dom Luciano Mendes de Almeida, the "possibly most complete document of the CNBB" was approved by its 26th Assembly in 1988 and published under the title of "Church, Communion and Mission in the Evangelization of the Peoples, in the World of Labor, Politics and Culture."[107] Mission is seen as mission "in the present historical moment" (paragraph 1) and "in our country" (2), assuming it clearly as a contextual mission. Citizenship is mentioned fairly soon:

> The same challenge [sc. as on the economic level] presents itself on the political level. It has not been possible yet to integrate into the effective exercise of citizenship the great parcel of the population which are at the margins of the process of democratic participation, even though new legal and political instruments have been created for making popular participation viable.[108]

The issue comes back in describing the political moment of the new constitution's finalization[109] and the role of popular participation, as well as in describing the church's role in politics, when it is said that the church is driven to provide documents on the political situation and the demands of social justice, to create institutions of solidarity which value the people's contribution, denounce the violations of human rights, encourage the "evangelical option for the poor" and suffer, where necessary, the martyrium in its "prophetic mission," to "accompany" Christians in politi-

102. CNBB, *Participação popular e cidadania.*

103. Ibid., 22f.

104. CNBB, *Por uma nova ordem constitucional*, 67–70.

105. Ibid., 67.

106. This seems to imply indication of a preference for confessional rather than interconfessional or interreligious religious education (see also below, IIIB2a).

107. CNBB, *Igreja, comunhão e missão na evangelização dos povos, no mundo do trabalho, da política e da cultura.*

108. Ibid., 10.

109. Esp. CNBB, *Igreja, comunhão e missão*, 197–202.

cal office and to "contribute towards political education in order for Man [sic] to be the subject of his own history and exercise with responsibility his political citizenship."[110]

Another important CNBB document on issues of democracy and citizenship was published as a follow-up to the constituent process, in 1989, as "Ethical Demands of the Democratic Order" (*exigências éticas da ordem democrática*). Right in its first paragraph, it states that

> The new Brazilian democratic order will only consolidate when the nation commits itself decidedly in a profound transformation, which shall modify social relationships and guarantee the effective participation of all citizens. Stable forms of democracy presuppose conditions in which citizens can fully exercise their rights and responsibly carry out their duties.[111]

Again, the notion of the citizen[112] and citizenship (explicitly only in paragraph 5) permeates the whole document, which is a clear indication that the new constitutionally based democracy is a legitimate starting point for what is due to the country's citizens. Paragraphs 5-22 highlight positive and negative aspects of the new Constitution. Among the former, the CNBB cites measures of popular participation (referendum, collective legal action etc.), fundamental rights for all, the equality of women and, in general, the (re-)establishment of a constitutional State, among others. As to the latter, the bishops highlight deficiencies in terms of land reform (the guarantee of property is considered too strong) and the lack of a clear affirmation of the "right to life from the conception" (19), the downgrading of matrimony and the facilitating of divorce. In general, the document affirms a qualitative shift from "a situation founded, principally, in privilege and force to a situation where, within the universe of law, citizenship emerges" (5). Democracy is affirmed as the "adequate form" of the "organization of the conviviality [*convivência*] of men [sic] among themselves," explaining that "democracy consists in the simultaneous realization and valorization of the freedom of the human person and of the participation of all in the economic, political, social and cultural decisions that concern the whole of society" (66). It goes on to name restrictions to democracy in a situation of economic inequalities, highlighting the importance of work for participation in society and the priorization of work over capital. While all power emanates, ultimately, from God, in a democracy power emanates from the people, as the Constitution rightly states. The State, in this system, is to use this power to serve the people, eradicate misery and serve the common good (71). It is "the poor" who are "the judges of a nation's democratic life" (72).

Quoting the 1979 Puebla (III Assembly of the Latin American Episcopate) document, the ICAR recognizes that it has to give a good example and to undergo itself the conversion it is proposing. However, it states clearly that

> although in the Church of the Lord Jesus power does not come from the people, nor is it exercised in the name of the people, we want to work generously that in our dioceses and in our communities the spirit of communion, the climate of co-responsibility, mutual respect, the attitude of service and the flourishing of adequate mechanisms of participation (cf. Mt 20,25-28) may consolidate, being excluded all forms of arbitrary authoritarianism.[113]

Furthermore, the CNBB recognizes that it is not for the church to propose an "alternative model of society's organization," nor "guidelines of economic and social policy," but hearing the

110. Ibid., 214.

111. CNBB, *Sociedade, Igreja e Democracia*, 1.

112. CNBB, *Exigências evangélicas*, 1, 5, 8, 30, 37, 66, 70, 96, 101 and in various footnotes.

113. Ibid., 107. Subtly, but still clearly, Clodovis Boff ("Fé cristã e democracia," 101) indicates that this should mean, in order to be credible, that the church should not only be "living the democratic spirit, but strive to endow itself with structures which would be effectively democratic."

"clamor of the people," the church can call the State's attention to specifically urgent issues (108). Among them, the document cites land reform, a just distribution of urban space, the preservation and renovation of the environment, social justice and rights for workers, insistence on the social function of businesses, the public auditing of external debts, the defense of the liberty and veracity of the media, the elaboration of laws to effectively apply the Constitution and discernment in the election of the president, assessing candidates according to the issues stated and the "guarantees they offer through the coherence of their testimony of life" (118). The document ends on a note of trust, both in God and in the people:

> Invoking, through the intercession of the Virgin Aparecida [i.e. the national patron saint], God's blessing without which 'those who build it [sc. the house] labor in vain' (Ps 126 [127],1), we trust that the Brazilian people can realize also their Easter, passing through the suffering of the cross to a new life, in solidarity, in justice and in peace.[114]

Another important document is "Towards the New Millenium" where, again, the theme of citizenship has a central place, namely in the more practically oriented section of the document.[115] "The proposed activities of service and participation in societies are centered around the axes of the conquest of citizenship and the construction of democracy. The striving for citizenship becomes concrete in the conquest of civil rights (life, integrity, freedom, security); social rights (education, health, culture, information, environment); and economic rights (land, food, work, habitation)." Here as elsewhere, it is noteworthy that the CNBB focuses on civil and social rights, while political rights seem to be taken for granted.[116]

In all documents, the church leadership clearly recognizes that it has a limited role to play in politics, but it does recognize a continued role as it has, for instance, continuously encouraged electoral participation under ethical criteria:

> The main duty of politics is to promote a just order of the State and society. Evidently, in this task, the Catholic Church recognizes the 'autonomy of the temporal realities', according to the affirmation of the II Vatican Council (cf. *Gaudium et Spes* 36); it is not for her to, as an institution, substitute the State, nor does she pretend to take into her hands the political battle to realize the most just society possible. This is the duty of all citizens and organizations of society.
>
> At the same time, however, the Church has the duty to offer her specific contribution, through the ethical formation and coherent criteria of discernment, so that the requirements of justice become comprehensible and politically realizable in the diverse historical and social circumstances. The Church cannot remain at the margin of the struggle for justice.[117]

The issue of citizenship in a new political order, then, is plain, as is the necessity of the formation of the laity to be able to exercise this citizenship concretely and in a discerning way. The apparent self-restriction in the limited role the church can play and in the "duality (not dualism) between the religious and the political instances,"[118] mentioned with reference to Luke 20.25: "Then give to the emperor the things that are the emperor's, and to God the things that are God's," can be seen as a consequence of the Vatican's pressure on the Brazilian church to stay away from party involvement (namely the PT), and its increasingly conservative episcopate. In fact, the documents show a strong "church" tendency, insisting on evangelization and a concentration on the church's

114. Ibid., 120.

115. CNBB, *Rumo ao Novo Milênio*, 125, 135–6, 210.

116. Ibid., 125.

117. CNBB, *Eleições 2006*, 3.

118. CNBB, *Igreja, comunhão e missão*, 210.

"own business," while it is also plain that the more progressive tendencies—which still held the CNBB presidency, until 1995—tried to safeguard the achievements of the more militant times. In any case, the indicated duality, but not dualism between church and State, religion and politics seems healthy at least for a Protestant reader (it is in line with the Lutheran position, see below IID and IIIA5) in a time of an increasing religious plurality and a critical-constructive cooperation without imposition (cf. below, IIIB4).

Let us now see how concrete issues have been treated in the ICAR during the period under analysis.

b) Land Reform

Land reform has been one of the most continuous issues in the Roman Catholic Church. Since the 1950s, it has been an issue of critique and declarations by bishops.[119] Then, land reform was considered "one of the indispensable policies to foster the country's development [. . .] motivated by the need to create better conditions of life for many Brazilians and, on the other hand, to avoid the advance of revolutionary proposals of a socialist kind."[120] However, a minority of bishops contested this position as an attack on the right to property which they considered grounded in natural law and, thus, originating in God.[121]

At the time, Brazil was still a largely agricultural country, but the estates' poor productivity appeared as a brake to industrialization, for supply of food for urban workers was needed. The times seemed ripe for an agrarian reform, with rural workers mobilizing and president Goulart beginning to talk about dividing the big estates, being himself a landowner.[122] However, rising anti-communism, both nationally and internationally, made land reform look dangerous. The military regime repressed the forming guerrillas early and massively and left them without a chance. It promoted a huge land settlement program, shifting families into the Amazon region[123]—under the slogan of "no people's land for people without land" (*terra sem homens para homens sem terra*), disregarding the prior presence of indigenous peoples in those lands. As Branford and Rocha state, however, "these colonisation projects [. . .] were intended to guarantee a pool of labour for the ambitious mining, ranching, farming and logging projects that the military planned for the region."[124] They had the settlers clear the way for the big companies, who bought up the land and expelled or employed the farmers as day-laborers.[125]

119. Souza, "As várias faces da Igreja Católica," 79.

120. Poletto, "A CNBB e a luta pela terra no Brasil," 335.

121 *Reforma Agrária—Questão de consciência*, published by the TFP (see above, IIC1b) in 1960, cited in Poletto, "A CNBB e a luta pela terra no Brasil," 335.

122. Branford and Rocha, *Cutting the Wire*, 4.

123. On the land conflicts about land in the "legal Amazon," i.e., the Amazon region made up by the states of Acre, Amazonas, Pará, Amapá, Roraima, and Rondônia (the latter three were not yet states then, but federal territories), and parts of Mato Grosso, Goiás, and Maranhão, between small occupants and big landowners and agricultural companies, see the study published as CNBB study, carried out by the Brazilian Institute of Development (*Instituto Brasileiro de Desenvolvimento*—IBRADES); CNBB, *Pastoral da Terra*.

124. Branford and Rocha, *Cutting the Wire*, 5.

125. In his master's thesis, Antônio Carlos Teles da Silva (*As origens do movimento ecumênico*), himself from the North, described this massive capitalist take-over of the Amazon region and showed how the ecumenical movement in this region (namely in the state of Pará) came about through an articulation of solidarity following the imprisonment of two French priests in 1981 who had said mass for peasants and were charged with directing them against the police, cf. Mainwaring, *Catholic Church and Politics*, 162.

While in some regions, as in the Northeast, big landowning has always been in place, notably in the plantations of sugar, relying highly on the work carried out by slaves, it was a novelty for others as in the South, where European immigrants were placed in the 19th century precisely to work their own land in small farming lots. Now, in the name of development and the rise of agro-technology, large lots were said to be more productive.

The vast and little populated lands in the North and the Northeastern backlands were fervently protected against intruders, rural unions or leagues and criticizers of all colors, either through the influence exercised over the judiciary and the police or directly through hired gunmen. Violence against land occupations or unliked voices became a common feature. It even worsened after the end of the military regime: In the first five years of the New Republic, far more people were killed in the land than during an equivalent period of time under the military: some 800 persons, according to Sader and Silverstein.[126] For the period of 1985-2003, the CPT reports the killing of 1,349 persons, including dozens of children, in rural conflicts.[127]

Even today, church people are being threatened of death in the Amazon region, which remains in the hands of landowners and managers, with their political allies and their gunmen. According to the (conservative) journal *O Estado de São Paulo*, there is a "death list" of ten names from the Amazon region, namely from the states of Pará, Rondônia, and Mato Grosso, including three bishops. One of these, Dom Erwin Kräutler, an Austrian, has been bishop in the Altamira (Pará) area since 1980 and outspoken on issues of land reform and rights of indigenous peoples. Threats have become so strong that he has to be accompanied by policemen during his pastoral visits.[128] And the announced assassination of Sr. Dorothy Stang, a nun from the United States, in 2005 was a clear sign that such threats are not hollow. Due to the international repercussion, at least in this case the (federal) police was effective, and the murderers and one of those who ordered the crime were convicted.[129]

While land reform is one of the old, unresolved problems of Brazil, it is no longer perceived as such by everyone. Comblin stresses that it is somewhat anachronistic to insist so much on rural life, given the stark urbanization,[130] while Weyland mentions that "whereas agrarian reform was ranked as the second or third most important 'problem confronting Brazil' in the early 1960s [. . .], it did not appear at all among the fifteen most frequently mentioned problems in 2000 [. . .], despite the continued agitation of the Movement of Landless Rural Workers, which grew tremendously in the mid-1990s."[131] Still, the ICAR and, as we shall see, also the IECLB (cf. below, IID2), have consistently had it on their list of burning issues, visible in a recent joint document, called "The Poor Shall Own the Land" (*os pobres possuirão a terra*).[132]

126. Sader and Silverstein, *Without Fear of Being Happy*, 69.

127. Carter, "The Landless Rural Worker's Movement," 11.

128. *O Estado de São Paulo* of April 7, 2007, available at http://txt.estado.com.br/editorias/2007/04/07/pol-1.93.11.20070407.7.1.xml (accessed on 4/13/2007).

129. According to the journal *O Globo Online*, one of the orderers was convicted to 30 years in prison on May 15, 2007. Relatives of Sr. Dorothy and others who know the area, including Bishop Kräutler, speak of a "consortium of crime" in the region; http://g1.globo.com/Noticias/Brasil/0,,MUL37024-5598-7794,00.html (accessed on 5/18/2007).

130. Comblin, *Called For Freedom*. This is seconded by Dom Luciano Mendes de Almeida, who said that in his archdiocese in the state of Minas Gerais, ever more people were migrating to the cities and did by no means want to return to the land—"all appreciated the land, but don't put their salvation there" (as quoted in Poletto, "A CNBB e a luta pela terra," 352).

131. Weyland, "The Growing Sustainability of Brazil's Low-Quality Democracy," 102.

132. *Os pobres possuirão a terra*. The document, presumably written by the CPT in 2006, was signed by 86 Roman Catholic bishops and archbishops (about 28 percent of the active episcopate), twelve bishops of the Episcopal Anglican

As I have stated above (IB, IIC1), the ICAR became a birthplace for civil society. Thus, under the aegis of the Pastoral Land Commission (*Comissão Pastoral da Terra* – CPT), the Movement of Rural Landless Workers (*Movimento dos Trabalhadores Rurais Sem Terra* – MST) was founded in 1984 in the city of Cascavel (Paraná). It has became one of the most visible, organized and feared social movements, in any case remarkable in its persistence.[133] The ICAR has been giving considerable support to the MST, considering it "a legitimate popular movement born of the conscience of the suffering people, which is not of the Catholic Church, but has its total support, for being a manifestation of the fact that the people are finally sensing that faith has a political dimension"[134] Other texts underline that the CNBB understands itself as supporting the people (*o povo*), saying that "earlier, the CNBB spoke *for the* people, now it follows [*acompanha*] closely and speaks *with* the people," namely on land reform.[135]

It was out of a meeting of pastoral agents in the Amazon region in 1975 that the CPT was founded, which acknowledged and coordinated, on a national level, proposals and pastoral action that had been brought forward by a number of dioceses.[136] The CPT became a semiofficial organization, pastorally related to the CNBB with a bishop overseeing its work, but autonomous in its organization and administration which allowed, for instance, for a significant collaboration of Lutheran and Methodist pastors in this work.[137] The CNBB saw the CPT as an "evangelizing agent," concretizing the church's social doctrine, and came to see in the various organizations of land workers "the expression of the citizens' active conscience and the primary instrument of its struggle

Church of Brazil (about 80 percent), nine Synod Pastors of the IECLB (50 percent) and five bishops (including the one woman bishop) of the Methodist Church (63 percent). Among others, it denounces that "the advance of the predatory, excluding and demobilizing domination of agro-business has increased violence against the environment, nature, public patrimony and people" (paragraph 53), and commits the assigned to continue "faithful to our mission of denouncing the sin of idolatry of property, of richness and power" (131). The document was issued on the date of commemoration of the 25 years of the CNBB's "Document 17," published in 1980 under the title of "Church and Land Problems" (*Igreja e problemas da terra*). With it, the 2006 document holds that there is a difference between "land of work" (i.e., to be worked for subsistence) and "land of business."

133. On the MST see Brandford and Rocha, *Cutting the Wire*, who explicitly highlight the citizenship "hopeless cases" like "drug addicts, emotionally disturbed street kids and violent criminals" can find there, who are turned "into productive, fulfilled citizens" (ibid., XII). According to Carter ("The Landless Rural Workers Movement"—this publication is still forthcoming, but the author kindly provided me with his manuscript, in 2007), who has done extensive and recent study on the movement, specific conditions in the Southern regions, like immigration (mainly German and Italian), small farmlands, the threat posed by huge dam projects and the help of religious agents, plus the ongoing national process of political opening made the birth of this new movement possible. Shortly after my first arrival in Brazil, in April 1996, 19 MST members were killed by the police as they blocked a road near Eldorado do Carajás (Pará). Needless to say that the MST is a highly polemical movement, but this massacre rendered it considerable goodwill among the population. Today, however, media in Rio Grande do Sul state and elsewhere promote a violent and chaotic MST which they say has lost any credibility, extensively citing its earlier supporters and now critics like sociologists Zander Navarro and José de Souza Martins. Both supporters and critics are not free of ideological restrictions in their analysis.

134. D. Antônio Possamai, [Bishop of Ji-Paraná/Rondônia], "Diocese fiel ao povo," CM 34/387 (1985), 208f.

135. CNBB [Northeast 4 Region]. "Romaria sobre Reforma," CM 36/414 (1987), 1259f.

136. CPT 2002; Poletto, "A CNBB e a luta pela terra no Brasil."

137. Cf. Sauer, *The Land Issue as a Theological Problem*; Branford and Rocha, *Cutting the Wire*. Today, on the CNBB's website, the CPT is listed under "other related [*relacionadas*] Catholic organizations," http://www.cnbb.org.br/index.php?op=menu&subop=15&sublinha=03 (accessed on 4/4/2007) in a status more remote from the CNBB than the CIMI, which is an "organism related [*vinculado*] to the CNBB," with a stronger relationship than the former (see below, IIC2b). On the ecumenical character, the CPT site informs in its historical section that "during the military regime, its links with the CNBB helped the CPT to carry out its work and to maintain itself. But already in its first years, the organ acquired an ecumenical character, both in the sense of the workers it supported, and in terms of the incorporation of agents of other Christian churches, namely the Evangelical Church of the Lutheran Confession in Brazil—IECLB."

to make its rights effective."[138] From 1980 onwards, the land issue has been recurrent in many public statements and documents issued by the CNBB. The 1986 Lenten Campaign was entitled "Fraternity and Land" and had as its motto "Land of God, Land of Brothers." Bishops emphasized that "the land created by God to serve all is, now, being a cause of much violence, carrying the responsibility for the death of thousands who do it for its cause."[139]

In view of the upcoming Constituent Assembly, Cardinal Lorscheider affimed that

> there is not only an individual right to property, but also a collective right to property. All that exists was given by God for the use of all and must serve all. [. . .] We, human beings, must organize our living together [*convivência*] in a way that everything serves to all [. . .] The fundamental basic principle is not the one of private property, but of the universal destination of goods. [. . .] 'Not to steal', 'not to covet your neighbor's house' exhort us that we are not allowed, in [good] conscience, to concentrate goods, accumulate them in a way that our brothers find themselves impeded to live honestly. Such accumulation, such concentration of goods constitutes stealing; it is, in fact, coveting of others' goods.[140]

In the same line of argument, Lorscheider invoked the prophet Isaiah (5.8): "Ah, you who join house to house, who add field to field, until there is room for no one but you, and you are left to live alone in the midst of the land," saying that "the exaggerated ownership of houses and rural properties is clearly condemned by God here."[141] On the grounds of the rebuttal of such accumulation in God's Word, Lorscheider justified the church's speaking out through the bishops and, indeed, the pope, against those who question whether this issue could be a "subject-matter for the Church": "All that is in God's Word is a subject-matter for the Church."[142] In an earlier text, he had insisted that civil law was not above God's law, which served as a basis to affirm that "what the Church, in Brazil, wants is that God's plan is respected, that the rights legitimately acquired by every human person are respected."[143] The CNBB underlined this argument by insisting that

> The Church, as it fulfils its mission to contribute toward the respect of the dignity of the human person and the promotion of social justice on the fields cannot be accused of exceeding its pastoral task: it is being faithful to the exigencies of the Gospel, and this action cannot in any way be confused with communist ideological practices or other inspirations which do not comply with the Gospel.[144]

In a later statement, Cardinal Lorscheider underlined that the church in Brazil did "enjoy the esteem and trust of ample sectors of Brazilian society [precisely] because it does not hesitate to defend with intrepidity the just and noble cause of human rights" and its support for a "courageous"

138. Poletto, "A CNBB e a luta pela terra no Brasil," 337.

139. D. Miguel Fenellon Câmara, [Archbishop of Teresina/Piauí], "A terra que Deus criou," CM 38/434 (1989), 1474f.

140. D. Aloísio Lorscheider, [Cardinal and Archbishop of Fortaleza/Ceará], "Constituinte e Reforma Agrária," CM 34/390 (1985), 733f. Cf. also D. Orlando Dotti, [Bishop of Vacaria/Rio Grande do Sul], "Direito da propriedade e à propriedade," CM 35/406 (1986), 1645; Bispos do Maranhão [Bishops of Maranhão], "Carta ao Povo de Deus," CM 34/395 (1985), 1743–44.

141. D. Aloísio Lorscheider, [Cardinal and Archbishop of Fortaleza], "Reforma Agrária é assunto da Igreja," CM 35/400 (1986), 754f.

142. Ibid.

143. D. Aloísio Lorscheider, "2ª Romaria da Terra," CM 34/394 (1985), 1426–28.

144. D. José Ivo Lorscheider [CNBB president] et al., "Reforma Agrária é compromisso democrático," CM 35/400 (1986), 670f.

land reform.[145] The CNBB affirmed that "the Church does not have a technical project for Land Reform, but it must be faithful to its mission of promoting ethical exigencies which must preside over Land Reform."[146]

Apart from the rights to property and property's social function, rural violence was a central issue. In 1985, the CPT affirmed that "violence against rural workers is generalized violence, selective violence, of class, and unpunished violence. It is impunity that has guaranteed and stimulated this violence."[147] Bishop Itamar Vian from Bahia said that "one can count with only one hand's fingers the judges which, really, do justice here."[148] Bishops frequently called for the investigation of cases of violence against land dwellers (*posseiros*).[149] A Northern regional group of the CNBB stated that

> We feel all the violence in the country, a fruit of unjust structures which deprive the majority of our people of a place worthy to live, work and remuneration which supplies the basic needs of the family, a school which attends to the education of the children, an efficient health program, land to plant. . . It is from injustice that violence flourishes. We hail the launching of the '*mutirão* against violence', but find ourselves in duty to alert all about the silence in relation to the violence in the rural area because of the lack of a vigorous action of the judicial power in the elucidation of the crimes and the punishment of the criminals and their sponsors. We are worried by the impunity of landowners who cold-bloodedly contract gunmen to practice selective murders, trying to disperse efforts in defense of human rights. We affirm our support for land reform proposed by the government as a beginning of the implantation of justice on the land. [150]

Citizenship comes in as an implicit argument with reference to Brazilian citizens, as does the idea of subsistence:

> [. . .] we appeal to the authorities of our land to assume the responsability of helping the campers, who are peaceful Brazilian citizens with the right to live, to eat, to have a school, health and acquire, with their honest work, the indispensable piece of land so that it may produce the necessary for sustaining the family.[151]

The bishops affirmed that "Land reform is a democratic commitment, and there is no democracy without effective promotion of social justice for the rural workers. Without just life conditions for all, one cannot speak of democracy."[152] In the same line, the "democratization of the land"

145. D. Aloísio Lorscheider, "Missão da Igreja no mundo, hoje," CM 35/402 (1986), 1026–27.

146. D. Ivo Lorscheider, "Reforma Agrária é compromisso democrático," CM 35/400 (1986), 670–72.

147. CPT, "A violência contra os trabalhadores rurais," CM 34/395 (1985), 1602.

148. D. Itamar Vian, [Bishop of Barra, Bahia], "Terra, violência e impunidade," CM 38/432 (1989), 1093–95.

149. Diocese de Marabá, CPT, Associação dos Professores de Marabá, Associação dos Moradores dos Bairros da Cidade Nova, Movimento de Educação de Base e outras entidades, "Chacina de trabalhadores rurais," CM 34/389 (1985), p. 747–49; D. Paulo Lopes de Faria, [Bishop of Itabuna, Bahia], "Chacina de posseiros em Sarampo," CM 34/391 (1985), 902.

150. Os Bispos do Regional Norte 1 da CNBB, "Carta ao Povo de Deus," CM 34/392 (1985), 1213–15. A later statement, issued by religious leaders from the South, called clearly for an end to violence from all sides, but specifically the one "which violates the dignity of land workers." Bishops, friars [and nuns], priests, and lay people at the Meeting of Pastoral Organizations of the CNBB South 3 Region, 18–19 March 1993, "Reforma Agrária sem violência," CM 42/469 (1993), 288–89.

151. Pedro Fedalto, [Archbishop of Curitiba, Mato Grosso], "Bispos socorrem acampados," CM 38/428 (1989), 271–72.

152. D. José Ivo Lorscheider, [CNBB president] et al., "Reforma Agrária é compromisso democrático," CM 35/400 (1986), 670f.; cf. also Bispos nordestinos do Rio Grande do Norte, Paraíba, Pernambuco e Alagoas [Bishops from the

was considered "an indispensable step toward political democratization. Without social democracy there is no real political democracy."[153] And the CPT stated that "the land must not remain concentrated in the hands of a class of parasites that does not use it productively, but for speculative purposes. The land, stricken by hunger, must guarantee its workers the necessary land to live and produce the aliments necessary for the population. Faithful to the orientation to be at the workers' service, in accordance with the documents of the CNBB, we reaffirm here our disposition to continue the struggle for the democratization of Brazil's land property structure."[154]

It was with particular intensity that the ICAR insisted on land reform in this early period of the New Republic. In the years 1985 and 1986 alone, it issued some 50 statements on land reform, either through the CNBB or bishops and organisms, while the same number of statements applies to the whole period of 1987 to 2002.[155] One reason for this I see in the pressure for the inclusion of land reform in the 1988 constitution, so the CNBB was building up a lobby. In part, the concentration of statements was also a reaction to the National Plan for Land Reform (*Plano Nacional de Reforma Agrária* – PNRA), issued in October 1985 by President Sarney, which generated a heated polemic. The CPT wrote a text entitled "Vision and Reaction of Society in Relation to the PNRA," identifying interests of landowners (and now also banks, industries, and businesses) and government instances to suppress Land Reform. Among the arguments in favor of the plan, as denounced by the document, were that large properties were more productive and would create more jobs; to give land to all would be a return to feudalism of the Middle Ages and to negate industrialization, and that land reform would be very costly, difficult to be paid by a country in crisis.[156] The CPT, for its part, called it a "no land reform plan" and stated that among the land workers the opinion was strong that "we shall do the land reform. You don't receive land, you conquer it."[157]

In 1995, the CPT published a document under the title "Manifest for Land and Life," in which it affirms that "the transition to the democratic regime has not reached the fields" and that "land reform will be the solution,"[158] an idea repeatedly stated over the whole period. They criticize, at the same time, that the government was collaborating too much with the "ruralist bench and the most backward [i.e., outdated, conservative] sectors of Brazilian politics," following the system "give here, take there."[159] A CNBB Region pleaded in a document "that the rulers remain on the side of the humble and suffering people, as there were many people who 'wished' to stay on the side of the powerful."[160] Some alerted about the danger of "this very grave phenomenon of the commencement of social convulsion" as "our people of the land [are] already tired, disillusioned and hopeless of all this waiting for solutions that never come, despite illusive promises."[161] Land occupations, a common act of civil disobedience, especially since the creation of the MST, are interpreted as

named Northeastern states], "Apelo à nação em favor da Reforma Agrária," CM 34/387 (1985), 189–91, where they affirm that there will not be democracy in the New Republic without a true land reform.

153. Pe. Mário Aldighieri, [CPT], "CPT e política agrária brasileira," CM 34/389 (1985), 592–94.

154. CPT, "CPT e Reforma Agrária," CM 34/390 (1985), 708–10.

155. Among others, some of which are cited elsewhere in this chapter, see D. Ivo Lorscheider, [CNBB president], "Moção ao Presidente da República sobre os planos regionais de Reforma Agrária," CM 35/398 (1986), 517f.

156. CPT, "Visão e reação da sociedade frente ao Plano de Reforma Agrária," CM 35/398 (1986), 240–42.

157. Ibid., 242.

158. CPT, "Manifesto pela terra e pela vida—A CPT e a Reforma Agrária hoje," CM 44/493 (1995), 1513–16.

159. Conselho Diretor da CPT, "Reforma Agrária e justiça para o campo," CM 45/504 (1996), 2008–10.

160. CNBB: Regional Sul 3, "Romaria reflete problemas da terra," CM 44/488 (1995), 312.

161. Frei Humberto Pereira de Almeida, "Questão agrícola," CM 41/463 (1992), 1360f.

> the expression of a grave social problem which is the result of a lack of political will to realize land reform, as it is incomprehensible that the government remain insensible in view of the suffering of thousands of families without land, without taking the necessary measures for their definitive settlement. The Church has taken position uncountable times in favor of Land Reform, without which the solution of land conflicts and the production of the necessary aliments for the population is impossible. We lament profoundly to have to come back to this issue. Without an ample Land Reform and without an adequate agricultural policy, the rural exodus, misery, urban violence will grow and the population's insecurity will increase. In the name of Christian conscience, we demand that the government [*poderes públicos*] take the immediate measures to make viable the settlement of all the camped families and we call on the population that it manifest its effective solidarity with those who suffer the violence of a concentrating and excluding agrarian system.[162]

In 2001, the ICAR published a manifesto on the issue of genetically modified organisms, accompanying attentively the public debate through its Justice and Peace Commission. "Scientifically qualified opinions suggested caution in relation to the first results of the application of the new technology. The big multinationals, on their part, engaged to rapidly adopt this technique so that they may gain the control of a market which seemed promising to them." The church insisted that "ecological values be respected and the environment be preserved," and that "because of the enormous difficulties posed to small farmers, one must act in order to harm them as little as possible, to avoid that existing inequalities increase even more."[163] This shows that, while land concentration is still a problem, new themes like the fostering of organic production, strongly promoted by the MST and its supporters, and its resistance against transgenic plantations have come up, keeping the land issue on the agenda.

Some statements of solidarity were formulated ecumenically, like a CONIC document that said, in 1986: "Finally, as Christians, we cannot remain apart from the actual moment of the nation. We seek to show to our people that their hopes make sense, because they point to a higher hope: the one of a fully installed fraternity among the sons [and daughters] of the same Father who is in Heaven."[164] Another example is the declaration of Cabo Frio (Rio de Janeiro), which was issued jointly by Catholic priests and Methodist pastors.[165]

Overall, it is clear that the CNBB, mainly through the CPT, has played—and continues to play—an important role for keeping land issues on the agenda of social movements, the churches, and wider society. At the same time, it has to be said that, even on its own accounts, its impact was restricted due to only partial adherence of the dioceses, as its first and longstanding (1975-93) executive secretary and consultant, Ivo Poletto, admits.[166] Poletto deplores the lack of unity among the bishops as it came to concrete actions in their dioceses, beyond mere documents, the fact that CNBB documents did not generally and satisfactorily reach the faithful, that mobilization has been low and dialogue with other churches and society (too) weak. Partially, this can be ascribed to divergences over concrete actions and the very urgency of the land issues, as well as the growing unrest over land occupations, which many consider not only illegal, but illegitimate (cf. above, IB).

162. A manifesto elaborated by bishops, friars [and nuns], priests, and lay people at the Meeting of Pastoral Organisms of the CNBB South 3 Regional Conference, held March 18-19, 1993, CM 42/469 (1993), 288f.

163. Raymundo Damasceno Assis, [Secretary-General of the CNBB], "A propósito dos transgênicos," CM 50/553 (2001), 1170.

164. CONIC, "CONIC e atuais medidas governamentais," CM 35/398 (1986), 286–88.

165. Presbitério Católico da Igreja em Duque de Caxias e Colegiado da Igreja Metodista na Região da Baixada Fluminense, "Solidariedade aos Sem-Terra de Cabo Frio," CM 37/421 (1988), 1034–35.

166. Poletto, "A CNBB e a luta pela terra no Brasil," 342–48.

And, of course, it is much easier to issue a statement than to do concrete follow-up *in loco*. Others might say the land issue was so prominent because the ICAR was more likely to keep its members there within its flock, as a strategy to keep up its membership. There is some truth in this, but given the CPT's radical statements on the issue and its alignment with Lutherans and Methodists on this, as well as the fact that landowners are powerful, wealthy, and normally also belong to the church, makes it not very likely that this was the main element in the church's engagement. In any case, the consistency and continuity with which the CNBB, CPT dioceses and other groups and persons have been claiming land reform is remarkable and continues to serve, even if only potentially, as a reference for the church itself, but also for other churches, movements, agencies (including international), and the State. While for some this is a nuisance, it has given the church credibility among many small farmers or those who would like to be it.

c) Indigenous Peoples

The struggle for the rights of indigenous peoples[167] is another of the most continuous engagements of the ICAR, which predates transition but has been intensified in the debate leading up to the constituent assembly, and continued ever since. The organ responsible for CNBB policy in this area is the Missionary Council for Indigenous Peoples (*Conselho Indigenista Missionário*—CIMI), founded in 1972. At the time, the integration of indigenous peoples into society was the authoritarian State's sole policy, while "the CIMI sought to favor the articulation between villages and peoples, promoting the great indigenous assemblies in which the first contours of the struggle for the guarantee of the right to cultural diversity were drawn."[168] The CIMI's founding principles are to respect the right to be different of the indigenous in their ethno-cultural and historical plurality and to value their traditional knowledge; to respect also the protagonism of indigenous peoples, to whom the CIMI wants to be an ally in their struggle for the guarantee of rights; and the option for the indigenous cause in the wider perspective of a democratic, just, solidary, pluri-ethnic, and pluri-cultural society.[169]

The defense of the indigenous peoples presupposed on the side of the church to assume the historical guilt:

> Unfortunately, our history is stained by gravest crimes against the *índios*, who were expelled, enslaved and massacred. These brothers [sic] have the right to live and develop their cultural patrimony. The issue of the land is central for the survival of the indigenous peoples. It is not only a source of alimentation. It is cultural soil, the place of their myths and traditions. Thus, to take the land away from them amounts to destroying their lives.[170]

The ICAR issued a considerable number of statements on the matter, directed in the first place to the government,[171] in defense and demand of the rights of the indigenous peoples, which were

167. "Indigenous peoples" is the appropriate translation of *etnias* (literally "ethnic group") or *povos* ("peoples) *indígenas*, but many church documents and even institutions still use *índios* ("Indians"). In order to avoid the colonialist sound this has in the English language, I use the Portuguese *índios* in these cases without translation, which for some time has been used abroad as a designation of indigenous peoples.

168. Barros, "Gênese e consolidação da CNBB," 66.

169. Ibid., 67.

170. D. Luciano Mendes de Almeida, [CNBB secretary general], "Em defesa dos povos indígenas," CM 34/386 (1985), 100f.; cf. Assembléia Diocesana de Ji-Paraná [Rondônia], "Protesto contra exploração dos índios," CM 36/414 (1987), 1301f.

171. Julio M.G. Gaiger, [Legal Counsel to the CIMI], "A respeito da questão indígena em nosso País," CM 36/412 (1987), 872–74; D. Aparecido José Dias, [CIMI president], "Carta aberta ao Presidente da República," CM 42/475

being threatened both by the landowners and their gunmen,[172] by the big mining companies,[173] by the illnesses brought in through invasions, either because the police did not do their job[174] or because government policies and agencies failed to protect the indigenous' rights.[175]

> The Church, in its mission to evangelize, has to strive towards all having a life worthy of God's children. Hence her engagement with the poor whose rights are most violated: the *índios*, land workers, day laborers, abandoned youth, workers and unemployed. It is just, then, that the Church associate herself to other voices of the nation so that the identity of the indigenous peoples be respected. [. . .] The words of John Paul II to the *índios* in Manaus, in 1980, remain alive and strong among us: 'I entrust to the public powers, and others responsible, the plea I make with all my heart in the name of the Lord, that to you, beloved *índio* brothers, whose ancestors were the first inhabitants of this land, obtaining over it a particular right along the generations, be acknowledged the right to live on it in peace and serenity, without fear of being driven out for the benefit of others, sure of a space that will be the base not only for their survival, but for the preservation of their identity as a human group, as a people.'[176]

Another important manifestation was made on the eve of the Constituent Assembly, when the CIMI said that "the democracies that function with the majority of votes will always threaten their minorities, in this case the Indians, with democratic defeat,"[177] thus pointing to the important aspect of minority protection in a democracy. The church also organized talks between indigenous persons, government agencies and its own, but they often did not yield—at least not immediate—results.[178]

As in the case of land reform, violence is a central issue. Many have died in conflicts like the Calha Norte, and invariably those most affected were the indigenous.[179]

> We express our solidarity with the indigenous peoples. Threatened in their survival, they cry out for the urgent demarcation of their lands. We denounce that indigenist politics which, at the discretion of the interests of politicians, entrepreneurs and landowners, has been permitting the robbery of indigenous territories by landowners, rubber extractors, wood traders and mining and hydroelectric companies. Furthermore, we renew our support to the CIMI and to the groups which fight for the defence of the indigenous peoples, and we reject the ongoing campaign to discredit them. We assume our positions motivated by our faith in Jesus Christ, the liberator of his people.[180]

(1993), 1770–72.

172. D. Izidoro Kosinski, [Bishop of Três Lagoas, Mato Grosso do Sul], "Índios vivem sob tensão," CM 37/421 (1988), 1065.

173. Presidência da CNBB, "Compromissos com a causa indígena," CM36/413 (1987), 1074f.; CIMI, "Situação dos índios Makuxi," CM 40/451 (1991), 901f.

174. D. Erwin Kräutler [CIMI President], "Sobrevivência indígena está em risco," CM 36/409 (1987), 595f.

175. Conselho Permanente da CNBB, "Que fizemos de nossos irmãos?," CM 42/473 (1993),1303; II Assembléia Nacional dos Organismos do Povo de Deus (Itaici, São Paulo, 7- 12/10/93), "Pela vida dos povos indígenas" CM 42/475 (1993), 1768; D. Aparecido José Dias, [CIMI President], "Situação dos povos indígenas," CM 44/491 (1995), 994–98; CIMI, "Assassinato de índio Kakriabá," CM 35/400 (1986), 737.

176. D. Luciano Mendes de Almeida, "Em defesa dos povos indígenas," CM 34/386 (1985), p. 101.

177. D. Erwin Kräutler [CIMI president], "A causa indígena às vésperas da Assembléia Nacional Constituinte: Desafios e Perspectivas Pastorais," CM 35/399 (1986), 518–25.

178. Felisberto Ascenção Damasceno [Legal counsel of the CIMI], "Situação indígena no Brasil," CM 35/398 (1986), 233–37.

179. CIMI, "A luta continua e a mata guardou o segredo," CM 36/412 (1987), 942; CIMI, "Índios assassinados em 1993," CM 42/477 (1993), 2159–61.

180. CNBB Regional Norte 1, "Carta ao Povo de Deus," CM 34/392 (1985), 1213–15.

> On the threshold between an authoritarian regime and a democracy to be constructed, we hope that also the indigenous question will receive a democratic treatment in the formulation of the official indigenist policy, as well as in the selection of staff who should execute this policy. Staff with anti-indigenous practices in the past must be dismissed from the indigenist agency in the New Republic. Nobody will be better than the *índios* themselves to help in the composition of the new executive staff body. The trust in the indigenist policy of the incipient democracy depends on the reliability of the persons that execute it.[181]

Violence is extended also to priests and missionaries. Bishop Jorge Marskell said that "the lords of power and wealth determine the death, the tears and the disgrace of the people. They persecute all those who fight for the defense of the life of the people."[182] Among the prominent priests was Josimo Moraes Tavares, of African descent, murdered by a hired gunman in May 1985 when he served as the CPT's regional co-ordinator. Over 3,000 people, including peasants and 120 priests and bishops, attended the funeral service.[183] He knew he was going to die, and two weeks before his murder he said:

> I die for a just cause. . . All that is happening is a logical consequence of my work, in the struggle and defense of the poor, on behalf of the gospel, that leads me to assume responsibility up to the final consequences. My life is worth nothing in view of the deaths of so many peasants, who have been assassinated, violated, thrown off their land, leaving women and children abandoned, without love, without bread, without a home.[184]

Specifically delicate are cases of conflicts between indigenous and (small) farmers over lands at the time allotted to the settlers against the norms in place.[185] Sometimes, the problem was solved by taking the land from the settlers and giving it to the indigenous.[186] But this is a highly difficult issue for the ICAR (as for the IECLB), because it fights both for the indigenous and for small farmers.

Not surprisingly, there were campaigns against the church and its siding with the indigenous fought out in the media. Accusations included suggesting that there was a "conspiracy" against Brazil's sovereignty, spearheaded by the World Council of Churches with the CIMI's involvement.[187] This still echoes the military regime's terminology, although it happened under the already installed civil government. They resented what the CIMI in fact was pressing for: what they saw as "restricting sovereignty," the CIMI understood as a necessary transformation in policy:

> to substitute—in a new Constitution—the figure of 'incorporation', which imposes to the *índios* a 'relative incapacity for the practice of certain acts of civil life', by the acknowledgment of the otherness of the indigenous micronations, which guarantees the territorial unity of the

181. CIMI, "Igreja missionária e Estado," CM 34/396 (1985), 1729.

182. D. Jorge Edward Marskell [Bishop Prelate of Itacoatiara in the state of Amazonas], "Defesa de missionários indigenistas", CM 36/415 (1987), 1490; Bishops of the Amazon present at the Assembly of the CNBB North 1 Region (Manaus, September 21–27, 1987), "Bispos defendem índio e Igreja", CM 36/415 (1987), 1434–36; D. Moacyr Grecchi [Bishop of Rio Branco in the state of Acre], "Pastoral Indígena," CM 37/423 (1988), 1205.

183. Sader and Silverstein, *Without Fear of Being Happy*, 63ff.

184. Ibid., 74.

185. Conselho Diocesano de Pastoral da Diocese de Chapecó, CPT, CIMI, "Denúncia da Diocese de Chapecó," CM 34/392 (1985), 1237f.

186. Couto, Ronaldo Costa [Minister of the Interior], "Decisão de Governo sobre Chimbangue," CM 34/392 (1985), 1235f.

187. Julio M.G.Gaiger, "A campanha contra o CIMI e a Igreja," CM 36/413 (1987), 1099–1102, at 1099.

> Brazilian State and the difference of the social, economic, political and religious organization of indigenous peoples.[188]

Another accusation, specifically against the CIMI, was that it was receiving money from international mining companies to "help" them in their work, because they would like to see Brazilian production diminish.[189] Adversaries also alleged that the religious were inciting indigenous peoples to commit crimes, such as stealing wood, setting landowners' residences on fire while they were sleeping, sending and leading indigenous communities in the destruction of fences, among others.[190] Notwithstanding, the CIMI reaffirmed its commitment with the cause of the indigenous:

> We must continue with our presence among the indigenous peoples in the daily life of their struggles and hopes, of its aspirations and anguish, in a truly evangelical dimension of solidarity, in listening, in love and in justice. We must thank the missionaries who throughout Brazil dedicate themselves 'religiously' to the work of a global evangelization.[191]

Another aspect often highlighted was the omission of the competent State agency, the National Foundation of the *Índio* (*Fundação Nacional do Índio*—FUNAI), which is responsible for the demarcation of indigenous lands.[192] Not rarely, it was seen rather as part of the problem than of the solution.[193]

> The National Foundation of the Indigenous has only sporadically striven for the well-being of the *índio* and has sought a solution for the indigenous' problems. The FUNAI has normally stood for the landowner, as its staff are constantly being threatened and suffer pressure from the landowners. Before the FUNAI, the *índio* has always lost against the white. The *índio* has always been obliged by the FUNAI to retreat because of the claims of the landowner, who increased his lands and improvements.[194]

More concretely, the ICAR insisted on finding ways for the FUNAI to consult the indigenous communities themselves, redefining the relationships between the State and the indigenous peoples. It should also become more agile, follow a constant policy in harmony with all the organs involved, and seek to remove the legal obstacles that hinder a new policy.[195] Nearly ten years later, the CIMI affirmed that "for the indigenous peoples, the self-demarcations are the only alternative to guarantee the rights conquered in the Constitution."[196]

Whenever a small victory could be celebrated, the church publicly manifested its satisfaction and thanked those who brought it about, as when federal justice decided to take the gold miners out of the area of the Yanomami in 1989, a struggle that had been strongly supported by the

188. CIMI, "Igreja missionária e Estado," CM 34/396 (1985), 1729. This paradigm shift in fact occurred in the 1988 Constitution.

189. Julio M.G.Gaiger, "A campanha contra o CIMI e a Igreja," CM 36/413 (1987), 1100. The accusation was based on false or non-existing documents, according to the CIMI's lawyer, Julio Gaiger.

190. D. Moacyr Grecchi [President of the CNBB North 1 Region], "Denúncia à campanha contra Igreja em Roraima," CM 35/398 (1986), 243–46.

191. D. Erwin Kräutler, "Os Povos Indígenas e a Pastoral Indigenista no atual momento histórico," CM 34/388 (1985), 414–19.

192. See http://www.funai.gov.br.

193. CIMI, "Genocídio de indígenas na Bahia," 35/402 (1986), 1006–1007.

194. D. Aldo Mongiano [Bishop of Roraima], "Questão indígena," CM 35/398 (1986), 275–78.

195. Antônio Brand [National secretary CIMI], "Dívida Indigenista para a Nova República," CM 34/387 (1985), 180–82.

196. CIMI, "Governo brasileiro corta verba," CM 43/478 (1994), 120.

church.[197] Conquests are intermingled with setbacks; in 1991, then-President Fernando Collor decided for the demarcation of the Yanomani people's lands, saying this was a "historical decision."[198] However, the process was not as smooth as expected, and in 1993 the ICAR had to write, again, to the president, worried about the missing demarcation.[199] Government spending cuts left clear that demarcation ranked low in its priorities.[200]

Another typical problem were the huge construction projects, mainly for hydroelectric plants. In 1995, the government decided to construct one in the area of the Macuxi and Cotingo peoples.[201] This aroused violent clashes after protests did not yield any result. There were numerous protests by the indigenous and the ICAR.[202]

In 2002, indigenous peoples were the focus of the Lenten Campaign, under the motto of "Towards a Land without Evil!" alluding to an ancient Guarani myth of the *terra sem males*. Once again, it highlighted the centrality of the land to the indigenous peoples. Much more than just a utility for growing food, the land carries myths and traditions. Despite possible religious differences, the ICAR, mainly through the CIMI, has consistently supported the indigenous' struggle for land and the effective right to be different. It has tried to carry out its mission in this sense, not measuring success in terms of converts, but of a strengthened citizenship. Its 2005 Assembly stated:

> Impelled by our faith in the Gospel of life, justice and solidarity and in view of the aggressions of the neoliberal model, we have decided to intensify the presence and support to the indigenous communities, peoples and organizations, and to intervene in Brazilian society as allies of the indigenous peoples, strengthening the process of autonomy of these peoples in the construction of an alternative, multi-ethnic, popular and democratic project.[203]

This means that the CIMI's mission is mainly a mission of listening, supporting, and advocacy with the indigenous peoples, motivated by faith but not concerned with church growth. This has become known as a pastoral of *convivência*, a mutually supporting and respecting living-together.[204]

d) Other Pastoral Action

The ICAR has a number of other pastoral action sectors, among them for workers (*pastoral operária*), children (*da criança*), prisoners (*carcerária*), health (*da saúde*) and African Brazilian (*afro*). Such areas of action have been successively themes of the yearly Lenten Campaigns, which after 1973 have taken on more clearly politically relevant themes.[205] While their actions vary re-

197. CIMI, "Yanomani: apoio à decisão da Justiça Federal," CM 38/435 (1989), 1607–08; see also Apparecido José Dias [CIMI President], "Ano de lutas e conquistas," CM 44/497 (1995), 2668–70.

198. D. Aldo Mongiano, [Bishop of Roraima], "Demarcação das terras Yanomani," CM 40/457 (1991), 2177.

199. Apparecido José Dias [President of CIMI], "Carta aberta ao Presidente da República," CM 42/475 (1993), 1770–72.

200. CIMI, "Governo brasileiro corta verba," CM 43/478 (1994), 120. See also, on the problematic of demarcation, Apparecido José Dias [President of CIMI], "Situação dos povos indígenas," CM 44/491 (1995), 994–98; Orlando Dotti [CPT President], "Nota da CPT" [on the discontentment with the slow pace taken by the government to take measures and solve the problems], CM 44/492 (1995), 1224.

201. CNBB [North 1 Region], "Cotingo e povo Macuxi," CM 44/488 (1995), 138.

202. D. Aldo Mongiano [Bishop of Roraima], "Demarcação de terras," CM 44/488 (1995), 183–84; Idem, "Urgência da demarcação da área única Raposa-Serra do Sol em Roraima," CM 44/488 (1995), 184–85; see also CIMI, "Área indígena Krikati," CM 44/488 (1995), 129.

203. See http://www.cimi.org.br/?system=news&action=read&id=247&eid=224 (accessed on 3/19/2009)

204. Cf. Zwetsch, *Missão como com-paixão*; cf. IIIA2c.

205. CNBB, *Campanha da Fraternidade*.

gionally and according to the diocese, some have become very powerful national organizations, effective in fund-raising with the help of the country's main media, namely the Pastoral Action for Children (*Pastoral da Criança*).[206]

In a situation of continuously pressing social problems, *hunger and misery* have been constant preoccupations of the ICAR, and it has repeatedly spoken out against it.[207] In a relatively recent document, called "Evangelical and Ethical Demands of the Overcoming of Misery and Hunger,"[208] the bishops reinforced the preferential option for the poor, calling it "evangelical" in the sense of stemming from the Gospel. This has to have consequences beyond charity: "We know that, beyond the immediate help and compensatory measures, it is necessary to promote the citizenship of every person and guarantee dignified life conditions, as inheres to God's children."[209] It explicitly refers to the 1988 Constitution, finding that even 13 years after its promulgation, and despite some real advances, still much has to be done, namely in the area of social rights. Positively, the bishops emphasize that much social work is being done in dioceses and through Caritas. While it is, primarily, the State's task to ensure food for all (paragraph 55), it needs partnership with society, including "the most suffering." Once again, the CNBB harps on the importance of people's participation. Concretely, the document suggests to implement locally the [CNBB's] National "mutirão" (common action) for Overcoming Misery and Hunger (58). Ending, the CNBB reinforces that it is part of a wider movement: "To win such enormous challenge, associating ourselves to all persons of good will of the Catholic Church, of other Christian churches and religious groups, of popular movements, trade-unions, institutions and Public Powers, we ask for God's blessing and the protection of Mary" (67).

The issue of *violence* was taken up more generally, not only in terms of land conflicts and violence against indigenous, but also violence against the population in general and people living on the streets in particular, especially after 1990.[210] The church stated that it was "impossible to combat [sic] violence without getting to the causes that generate it." Efficient action was needed, capable of attending to the clamor of the people.[211] As this generalized violence is affecting all people in society, notably in the megacities, even conservative bishops spoke out against it. Rather than looking for the deep causes in society, however, they spotted non-specified "tentacles of evil" and a "dangerous moral anesthesia," as "one coexists more and more with violence, in a natural way, as part of daily life." Cardinal Sales added that "a society which is capable of getting used to evil, without the sentiment of rejection and indignation, is accessory to it, ill in that it passively accepts the negation of fundamental values of human dignity."[212] An aggravating factor of violence has been

206. See http://www.pastoraldacrianca.org.br/ (accessed on 3/19/2009). The website is, quite unusually, available in six languages, which indicates how well it is known even outside the country, and receiving donations from all over the world.

207. For instance Comissão Pastoral Operária (CPO),"Mãe, este povo passa fome," CM 37/424 (1988), 1428; Itamar Vian [Bishop of Barra in the state of Bahia], "O sertão vai florir," CM 41/459 (1992), 307–8.

208. CNBB, *Exigências evangélicas e éticas de superação da miséria e da fome.*

209. Ibid., 7.

210. Let us remember that this was the period when a number of massacres happened (cf. above, IA3b).

211. Pastoral Social Seminário sobre violência, "Sociedade violenta, raízes e lutas (16–18 March in São Paulo)," CM 39/438 (1990), 242–43.

212. D. Eugênio de Araújo Sales [Cardinal Archbishop of Rio de Janeiro], "Tentáculos do mal," CM 39/438 (1990), 288–89.

the impunity of some in relationship to the imprisonment of others, mainly poor persons, generating great discredit for the Judiciary and, not least, for the police.[213]

The CNBB has spoken out on various forms of *discrimination*, not least against the discrimination of *women*. In 1990, the Lenten Campaign was held under the motto of "Woman and Man: Image of God," which gave an occasion to comment on the issue and also to the pope to comment on it in his traditional greeting at the beginning of the Campaign.[214] Five years later, Pope John Paul II wrote his "letter to women," which was reproduced in the *Comunicado Mensal*,[215] together with other texts on the issue, committing the ICAR to women. A Lenten Campaign was dedicated to *African Brazilians* in 1988 under the theme "Fraternity and the Black Person" *(A Fraternidade e o Negro)*, and a African Brazilian pastoral sector was formed.[216] The 15th Biennial Plan of Activities of the CNBB's National Secretariat (2000-2001) affirmed:

> The national movement of the black people, oriented towards the affirmation of their cultural identity, has become an important reference for the evangelizing action of the Church. Pope John Paul II, during his visit to Brazil in 1997, called to the attention that: 'These Brazilians of African origin deserve, have a right and can, with reason, ask for and expect the utmost respect to the fundamental aspects of their culture which continue to enrich the culture of the nation, as citizens in their full right'.[217]

The lack of habitations,[218] the specifically risky situation of youth[219] and the droughts in the Northeast[220] are other aspects highlighted in statements of the ICAR. The CNBB, its regional councils and many bishops and related organizations have consistently taken up burning issues of poverty, famine, discrimination, and the like. Although authors of documents might diverge on the reasons for the situation—more personal, natural (droughts), or structural— and on the best remedies, they leave no doubt that society, and within it the church, and especially the State have to take on their responsibilities in answering the situation.

213. Bispos da Província Eclesiástica do Espírito Santo, "Carta Pastoral contra a violência, a favor da vida," CM 40/448 (1991), 156–63; the CM reprinted also a manifest of the IECLB "in Favor of the Respect to Life," which had been sent to the state governments and also to the CNBB: IECLB, "Manifesto em favor do respeito à vida," CM 40/452 (1991), 1220f.

214. Papa João Paulo II, "Mulher e homem: imagem de Deus," CM 39/438 (1990), 7f.

215. Papa João Paulo II, "Carta do Papa João Paulo II às Mulheres," CM 44/493 (1995), 1298–1305.

216. Cf. http://www.cf.org.br/temas.php (accessed on 3/20/2009); CNBB, *Pastoral Afro-Brasileira*. Although forced—it essentially meant throwing a bucket of water over the Africans on landing in Brazil, before they were sold as slaves—baptism is taken as a theological point of departure for affirming Christian black identity. Christ the liberator is also emphasized, as a figure for identification in the struggle for their own liberation (ibid., paragraph 10-15.37). The CNBB also published a note in support of the Third UN World Conference against Racism held in Durban, in 2001: CNBB, "Nota de apoio à 3ª Conferência Mundial contra o Racismo," CM 50/553 (2001), 1171.

217. CNBB, *15º Plano Bienal de Atividades*, 40; cf. *Pastoral Afro-Brasileira*, 8.

218. D. Olívio A. Fazza, [Bishop of Foz do Iguaçu, Paraná], "Declaração sobre demolição de casas," CM 37/421 (1988), 1038–39; Pontifical Commission for Justice and Peace [International Year of the Homeless], "Que fizeste do teu irmão Sem Teto?" CM 37/418 (1988), 30f. The Propriá diocese in the Northeastern state of Sergipe went ahead and, not seeing another solution, bought land and distributed it to families for them to construct their houses and have a place to live, while insisting that this was still the State's task; D. José Brandão Castro [Bishop of Popriá], "Diocese distribui lotes," CM 34/389 (1985) 625f.

219. D. Serafim Araújo [Archbishop of Belo Horizonte, Minas Gerais], "O menor e o dever de todos," CM 40/453 (1991), 1527–28.

220. D. Marcelo Carvalheira, "A seca do Nordeste," CM 41/463 (1992), 1290; "A seca continua matando," CM 40/449 (1991), 324–25.

e) Political Participation

The ICAR has been consistently building up a process of political conscientization before elections. The vote is seen as a kind of procuration, endowing the elected with powers to act in the name of the citizens.[221]

As an institution, the ICAR clearly states that it has no right to back a specific candidate or party.[222] However, it has the duty to guide the people in their electoral responsibilities. Thus, it establishes criteria to assess the candidates so that people may choose somebody committed to the struggle for the people's rights. The "principal criterion to choose a candidate is that he strive for the common good."[223]

> The Church does not have a party. The Church does not support, as its own, specific candidates. However, it is seriously interested in strengthening the democratic parties, with proposals that correspond to the Christian exigencies. It wishes that the best among the most capable and with the best intentions may be elected from the different parties. It feels, thus, having the right to define the profile of the trustworthy candidates, who merit the votes of the Brazilians, Catholics or Non-Catholics.[224]

Such orientation has been exercised through seminars, lectures, and courses, but principally through publications, many of which are reprinted in the *Comunicado Mensal*, in texts with titles such as "Pastoral Orientation for Elections"; "Message on Municipal Elections," "Open Eye in the Elections,"[225] and "The Voter's Ten Commandments." The latter might be the most interesting not only for its content, but its name and style:

1. Believe in the force of your vote to change your municipality. If many vote correctly, good candidates will be elected and more just laws will be approved.
2. Vote freely, without fear. The vote is secret. Nobody knows whom you voted for.
3. Vote for candidates that have already proven they are on the side of the people and defend the interest of all.
4. Don't vote for those who visit the people only in view of the election.
5. Don't vote for those who offer money, a job or presents in exchange for your vote. Whoever buys votes is corrupt.
6. Don't vote for those who are against land reform and against the struggle of the people for the holding of land on the fields and in the city.
7. A fox does not represent a chicken. A rural worker does not vote for the landlord, nor for his candidates. An [industrial] laborer does not vote for an entrepreneur.
8. Wolf and lamb do not yet eat together. Don't vote for those who have already expelled workers from their lands, who have already dismissed employees without a just cause, or who have already persecuted and ordered murders.

221. D. Silvestre Luis Scandian [Archbishop of Vitória in the state of Espírito Santo] and D. Geraldo Lyrio Rocha [Auxiliary Bishop in the same diocese], "Orientações pastorais para eleições," CM 37/421 (1988), 1026–28.

222. D. Clemente José Carlos Isnard [Bishop of Nova Friburgo/Rio de Janeiro], "A propósito das eleições," CM 35/406 (1986), 1635–36.

223. D. Affonso Felippe Gregory [Bishop of Imperatriz/Maranhão], "Hora de grande decisão," CM 43/484 (1994), 1777f.

224. Clemente José Carlos Isnard, "A propósito das eleições," CM 35/406 (1986), 1635–36.

225. D. Henrique Froehlich [Bishop of Sinop/Mato Grosso], "Olho aberto nas eleições," CM 37/425 (1988), 1693–94.

9. The government's money belongs to the people. Don't vote for those who spend the people's money for their own benefit, for propaganda, for political campaigns, for works that do not serve the people.
10. Your responsibility does not end on the day of the election. Don't ask personal favors from the elected, but watch their activity and press them on the commitments they made for the people.[226]

In the same line, other bishops stressed that the vote must be free, conscious, and responsible, and that the vote must be neither bought nor sold, not bargained for, or exchanged for favors.[227] Another text published by the (conservative) Archbishop of Salvador, then also president of the CNBB, established as the five primary criteria for a candidate that he be decent, competent, experienced, coherent, and efficient, and that he make alliances not with the powerful, but with those who serve the people and the common good.[228]

Apart from criteria for the decent candidate, bishops exhorted the faithful not to nullify their vote. Although voting is compulsory in Brazil, a good number of voters express dissatisfaction by either not turning up or by casting a blank vote. As "faith has a political dimension," those who "don't vote, or cast a blank vote, sin by omission."[229] In the same line, another document stated that whoever "did not vote, does not have the right later to claim his rights or even to state them should things not work out the way he expected." Much is expected of the "Christian conscience of the Catholics."[230] "Nobody can evade the right to vote which is the exercise of citizenship";[231] "to vote with liberty and responsibility is, at the same time, a grave obligation and a noble right";[232] "to vote well is to vote with conscience and responsibility. The vote is an instrument of participation, of the conquest of the rights of citizenship and the construction of a true democracy."[233] "It is through the art of politics that a society can configure itself as just and participatory."[234]

At the same time, bishops stressed that the voters' responsibility does not end with voting; to the contrary, voters should continue to act in a committed way everyday, in all places and environments.[235] Indeed, against critics from the in- and the outside, it texts stressed that "the Church cannot become like the mute dogs: it has to shout, to act, to suffer for the new social, economic

226. The Permanent Commission of Political Education, under the orientation of the Archbishop of Paraíba, D. José Maria Pires, updated a flyer produced in 1986 on the "The Voter's Ten Commandments," which in 1988 was circulated in the whole state following a decision of the bishops of Paraíba, CM 37/425 (1988), 1881–83.

227. D. Silvestre Luis Scandian and D. Geraldo Lyrio Rocha, "Orientações pastorais para eleições," CM 37/421 (1988), 1026–28.

228. D. Lucas Cardeal Moreira Neves, O.P., "Votar responsavelmente," CM 45/502 (1996), 1404–05.

229. Diocesan Commission of Political Pastoral Action of Apucarana in the state of Paraná [the bishop, D. Domingos Wisniewski, and the Council of Presbyters approved the document], "Cartilha de educação política," CM 37/423 (1988), 1316–18.

230. D. Serafim Fernandes de Araújo [Archbishop of Belo Horizonte/Minas Gerais], "Os cristãos e a política," CM 37/421 (1988), 1000.

231. D. Miguel Fenelon Câmara [Archbishop of Teresina in the state of Piauí], "Mensagem aos fiéis sobre eleição," CM 35/405 (1986), 1442–43.

232. D. Bonifácio Piccini [Archbishop of Cuiabá in the state of Mato Grosso], "A propósito das eleições à Constituinte," CM 35/405 (1986), 1437–38.

233. Conselho Arquidiocesano de Presbíteros da Arquidiocese de Manaus, "Cristãos, eleições e candidatos", CM 37/425 (1988), 1661–63.

234. D. Fernando Antônio Figueredo [Bishop of Teófilo Otoni in the state of Minas Gerais], "Orientações para ano eleitoral," CM 37/421 (1988), 1063–64.

235. D. Benedito de Ulhoa Vieira [Archbishop of Uberaba in the state of Minas Gerais], "Os cristãos e a constituinte," CM 35/402 (1986), 1030–31.

and political order."[236] This is, admittedly, a quite stark statement that not many dioceses would formulate. That there has been a good deal of resistance against open political engagement is shown by the following quotation: "To the eyes of many, the Church appeared intolerant when it showed itself in issues that had not only to do with the sacristy."[237]

f) Moral Issues

Once the strong conflict and division of the military regime was over, the above mentioned issues received wide acceptance. Although some might still question the church's positioning, the debate is not as heated as in earlier times. Land rights and indigenous claims are highly conflictive for those directly involved, but public opinion tended to recognize the basic problems implied, and even the MST had, at times, as indicated, a favorable press. The "watchdog" role of the Catholic church, it seems to me, is widely accepted on these issues even if, as indicated, there might be divergences over root causes and concrete remedies. At the same time, Catholic Social Teaching[238] and not least Pope John Paul II's personal commitment to issues of social justice gave ample worldwide support to this role.

On moral issues, the church has also been remarkably consistent, speaking out on the importance of the family and against divorce, abortion, contraceptives, and homosexual relationships. This double consistency on social transformation and moral conservation seems to reflect, not least, Pope John Paul II's intransigent position against contraceptives and abortion,[239] which resonated much more conflictually both within the church and, even more so, in wider society. Defending a "culture of life,"[240] the CNBB could at the same time speak out against abortion and reject the death penalty,[241] in both cases going against the majority of public opinion. In the same line, the church also spoke out against euthanasia.[242] While the "culture of life" and its defense are used both for social and moral issues, a "culture of death" is diagnosed, again, in both the social and the moral realm linked to sexuality and human reproduction. The 45th Fraternity Campaign, in 2008, was dedicated to "Fraternity and the Defense of Life." Its poster showed an elderly man with a baby on his arm, making evident that the campaign was directed against euthanasia and abortion,

236. Bispos da Província Eclesiástica da Paraíba, "Momento político no Estado," CM 35/405 (1986), 1439–40.

237. Fr. Virgílio Leite Uchoa [Member of the commission accompanying the constituent process], "Participação da Igreja na Constituinte," CM 35/417 (1987), 1733f.

238. Cf. PCJP, *Compendium of the Social Doctrine of the Church.*

239. CNBB, "Despenalização do aborto," CM 42/471 (1993), 753; D. Eugênio Araújo Sales, "Aborto é crime," CM 42/474 (1993) 1625–27; "A pílula do dia seguinte," 50/556 (2001), 1730.

240. Setor Família, "Um novo sim à vida," CM 38/430 (1989), 528f.; idem., "Seminário sobre a vida humana," CM 39/441 (1990), 899–901.

241. Bispos da Província Eclesiástica da Paraíba, "Não à morte," CM 40/453 (199), 1538–39. The bishops combine here opposition to abortion, hunger (which also kills), killings, and the death penalty, with emphasis on the latter, stating that "nobody has the right to conduct anybody to an irreversible situation." See also D. Aloísio Lorscheider [President of the Northeast 1 Region], "A ninguém é permitido matar," CM 40/451 (1991), 915–16.

242. In CNBB, *Por uma nova ordem constitucional*, these items are all combined together: "Unacceptable, as attacks on human life, are directly provoked abortion, genocide, suicide, euthanasia, torture and physical, psychological or moral violence, as well as any kind of unjust mutilation" (ibid., 55). Furthermore, also unacceptable are "permanent situations of hunger, malnutrition, subhuman conditions of existence and the impossibility of access to health services" (56). The death penalty is considered "unjustifiable" with reference to the human condition, values of the Gospel and the "recognized pacific mentality of the Brazilian people" (57) —the latter featuring a common notion in and on Brazil, but in blatant contrast to widespread daily violence and a majority of the people being in favor of the death penalty (cf. above, IA3).

even if it sought to go beyond this into an affirmation of the dignity of life in all its phases.[243] Life, as is invariably being emphasized, is sacred and to be protected from its conception.[244]

There are groups of "Catholic Women for the Right to Choose" in Brazil and other Latin American countries. The Vatican, represented by former CELAM president and outspoken critic of Liberation Theology, Colombian Cardinal Alfonso Lopez Trujillo, prefect of the Pontifical Council for the Family, left no hints of doubt on its position: that group "went about confusing people's heads and generating polemics in society, while the ICAR is totally against abortion and any other practice which constitutes an attack against life."[245] The above mentioned silencing of Ivone Gebara and the excommunications around the abortion of the fetus of a nine-year old girl that had been raped by her stepfather are cases in point, where the ICAR consistently stands up to public opinion—and seems to lose.

A more recent discussion touches on issues of *biotechnology*,[246] namely when embryos are involved. The church positioned itself clearly against the law of biosecurity (Law nr. 11.105), passed by Congress in March 2005, which allowed both genetically modified organisms to be planted under specific conditions, and embryos, produced in processes of assisted reproduction but not implanted, to be used for embryonic stem cell research, again under specific conditions. Many, not least the media, condemned this position as outdated, conservative, fundamentalist, anti-scientific, and the like.

It seems significant to me that at a debate held on March 2, 2005, the day of the voting, on the much listened to "Polêmica" programme of Radio Gaúcha (AM 600) in Porto Alegre, no Catholic priest had been invited, presumably because everyone knew what he was going to say. The doctor and two biologists present were, however, Catholics. Two of these, members of the Bioethics Commission of the Pontifical Catholic University of Rio Grande do Sul (PUCRS), were contrary to embryonic research, as is their institution to date, while it invests heavily in adult stem research. The Lutheran pastor present also spoke against embryonic research, but none spoke in an absolutizing way. The public, however, sent e-mails and phoned the radio station, overwhelmingly in favor of embryonic research, alleging that the (Catholic) church was imposing its opinion on the public—in a blatant contradiction to the debate itself. This shows that the opinions had already been made and there was no openness to dialogue and possible meaningful arguments.

The church subsequently supported a Direct Action of Unconstitutionality, which held up official support for stem cell research for some years; in July 2008, the Supreme Court declared the law constitutional. Another subject-matter caused polemics more recently: the abortion of anencephalous fetuses, who usually die within hours, days or weeks from their birth—if not stillborn—because they lack brain (except for the brain stem) and the upper part of the skull. Again, the ICAR is consistently against abortion even in this case, and once more against public opinion and, of course, the majority of the scientific community, but also other churches, like the Methodists.[247] So

243. http://www.cf.org.br/index.php?link=news/read.php&id=58 (accessed on 3/21/2009).

244. See, for instance, CNBB, *Ética*, 170, with reference to the Congregation for the Doctrine of the Faith's Document *Donum Vitae* (1987). It has to be said, however, that "personal ethics" comes after "public ethics" and "professional ethics" in the document, which might be an indication of priorities.

245. Alfonso Cardenal López Trujillo, "Católicas com direito de eleger," CM 43/487 (1994), 2267.

246. For instance Frei Antônio Moser, "Biotecnologia e genômica: algumas reflexões bioéticas," CM 50/554 (2001), 1347–49.

247. Cf. Anis, *Anencefalia*; Igreja Metodista. *Pronunciamento do Colégio Episcopal—Questão do Aborto.* June 5, 2007. Available at http://www.metodista.org.br/arquivo/documentos/download/Pronunciamento_03_07.pdf (accessed on 12/16/2010).

far, such abortions need a court's authorization. The decision as to whether it should be generally allowed, is currently being discussed in the Supreme Court.

3. THEOLOGICAL ELEMENTS

Having gone through the history and documents of the ICAR, mainly its bishops and namely the CNBB, as registered in official and semi-official documents in separate publications and the *Comunicado Mensal,* it is now time to ask about the theological grounding of the churches stance on democracy, citizenship, the State, society and specific public issues. I shall first look into the foundations of democracy and citizenship (a), followed by the grounding of the relationships to the State (b) and society (c), and finally ask about the relationship between political and ecclesial citizenship (d).

a) Foundations of Democracy and Citizenship

In the previous section, we have seen that there is a clear acceptance of democracy as the desirable and appropriate political system, but that, beyond being a system, it is a process, something to be constructed and shaped, utopian—or ideal—in character.[248] In this context, citizenship is what makes democracy concrete for the citizens, not only in terms of rights and duties, but beyond it in terms of the well-being of all and social justice necessary to empower all people to be able to live "full" or "effective" citizenship. This also includes an "ethical attitude by the citizens who are the sovereign in this [sc. democratic] regime," grounded in "the Word made flesh."[249] The Constitution is an important element, first in the participatory nature of its confection, then in the fundamental rights guaranteed by it, and finally in its implementation, which is the part that is most in need of improvement.

The church sees itself clearly as part of society and is conscious of its not being a political party, thus not being entitled to give direct instructions on how the State, society, and politics should be. It understands its role as a watchman and educator, giving orientations to the laity and being a critical partner of the State and society in calling attention to people's needs and, not least, watching over the due place of religion—not without, in my interpretation, presupposing that being Brazilian and Catholic are still close to synonymous, or should be.

One of the often cited, although rarely elaborated theological groundings for a democracy is the doctrine of the Trinity, and it seems plain to me that the thinking of Leonardo Boff, who had written extensively on the matter precisely in the final period of transition (1985), the very year he had been silenced, has given new dynamic to this argument, although it had been present already in the Second Vatican Council and then at the III General Assembly of the Latin American Episcopal Council (CELAM) in Puebla 1979.[250] Boff's book "Trinity and Society," published in 1986, was

248. C. Boff, "Fé cristã e democracia," 85 changed an otherwise virtually identical reprint of a text published in 1989 at this term: while he spoke, then, of "utopian," he now speaks of "ideal," apparently avoiding to evoke a philosophical debate which might sound too human an expectation to church leaders. The original text was presented as a commentary on CNBB, *Exigências éticas*, and was printed in the seminar documentation which accompanied the process (CNBB, *Sociedade, Igreja e Democracia,*113–38).

249. Still, the emphasis lies on the State: "The citizens, living the ethics of respect towards the law, their own rights and those of others, towards civic solidarity, will be the support [sic!] of a State that by its efficient action may produce the Common Good. . ." Menezes, "Democracia e exigências éticas," 68.

250. Kirche Lateinamerikas, 184f. (paragraphs 211–19 of the Puebla Document), quoting *Lumen Gentium* 50; cf. PCJP, *Compendium of the Social Doctrine of the Church*, paragraph 34, where the human person's vocation to love, his/her personhood as existence-in-relation is founded on the "communion of the Father, of the Son and of the Holy Spirit," with reference to John 17.20–22 and *Gaudium et Spes* 24. See also C. Boff, "Bases teológicas do ideal democrático,"

reflected in the 6th inter-ecclesial encounter of the CEBs in Trindade ("Trinity") in the state of Goiás, held in and around a sanctuary dedicated to the "Eternal Divine Father" (*Divino Pai Eterno*) in July of the same year, in its final document and also in banners that said "the Trinity is the best community."[251] Although one can barely say the participants had really internalized this notion (there is no other sign of it in the reports from the meeting), and although even the sanctuary has as its image the coronation of the Virgin Mary by the Trinity rather than an image of God the Father alone or of the Trinity, it was visibly present.

Boff's insights have been taken up, at least in the early phase of the New Republic, by other theologians and bishops. The CNBB document refers to it when it says:

> The experience the first Christians had of the divine revelation led them to recognize in God the Holy Trinity: The Father, the Son, and the Holy Spirit. God appears, then, as a community of persons perfectly solidary among themselves, who realize themselves in the communication and love that unite them. This communion reveals itself, also, as the ultimate reason of creation and History: humanity is called to realize itself as People of God, as communion of persons, which in communication and love among them and with Godself encounter the plenitude of their being.[252]

Boff himself has applied this trinitarian theology to democracy in a—deliberately—vague way, and others have taken it up in that very same vague way, in order to avoid direct analogies and the reduction of the Trinity to a political model.[253] He affirms:

> It is not the theologian's task to devise social models that best approximate to the Trinity. Nevertheless, if we take basic democracy in the sense that the ancient Greeks (Plato, Aristotle and others) took it, as not so much a definite social structure as the principle underlying and providing inspiration for social models, then we should say that the values implied in this constitute the best pointers to how to respect and accept trinitarian communion. Basic democracy seeks the greatest possible equality between persons, achieved by means of progressive development of processes of participation in everything that concerns human personal and social existence. And beyond equality and participation, it seeks communion with transcendent values, those that define the highest meaning of life and history. The more such ideas are put into practice, the more will divine communion be mirrored among men and women.[254]

For Boff, the Trinity is a "critique" of authoritarian society and also of an authoritarian church, as well as an "inspiration" for a community that seeks to make space for both communion and difference. While the critique becomes quite concrete with authoritarian structures pointed to, the inspiration stays vague—but it is not without possibly interesting consequences. I shall mention some of them in the concluding part of this study.[255]

125–29.

251. Cf. Sinner, *Reden vom Dreieinigen Gott*, 136; Boff, *Trinity and Society*.

252. CNBB, *Exigências éticas*, 90. See also Tepe, "Igreja e democracia," 94. —As I have argued elsewhere, in relation to Boff's thinking, there is a double relationship between the triune God and humanity here: an ontological (God as foundation and goal of humanity, from where humanity comes and to which it strives) and an analogical relationship (God as a model for society); Sinner 2003:117–42, 168–82.

253. C. Boff, "Fé cristã e democracia," 92f.; Bento, "Cristianismo e democracia," 31.

254. L. Boff, *Trinity and Society*, 151f. Without being able to discuss this here, I just point to the fact that it is questionable if Plato and Aristotle are adequate references here, given their very critical view of democracy, outrightly rejected by Plato and relativized by Aristotle.

255. IIIb1c; Sinner, "Trinity, Church and Society in Brazil."

As Catholic theologian and sociologist Fábio Régio Bento outlines,[256] there is a problematic contradiction in the Roman Catholic position over against ethical pluralism and, thus, democracy. The double insistence on "life" and its protection and preservation in social matters, on the one hand, and moral matters, on the other, has repeatedly been pointed out. What is of central importance here, however, is that the degree of freedom of decision attributed to the individual's conscience is utterly asymmetric. "From Pius XII onwards, the Roman magisterium came to accept ethical pluralism and the methodology of democracy for issues of political and economic morality, but it does not yet accept the methodology of democracy and ethical pluralism in other moral areas of communitarian interest."[257] In John Paul II's encyclical *Veritatis Splendor* (1993), for instance, ethical pluralism appears as "ethical relativism," and the "power of decision on good and evil" is reserved "not to Man, but to God alone," with the implicit understanding that its authoritative interpreter is the magisterium.[258] While it is certainly correct to insist on values, needed in democracy and not implicit in the system as such, it is questionable why this would apply to some matters more than to others, or rather, why some ethical demands are straightforward, like the absolute protection of the embryo and fetus, and others form more general principles, like human rights based on human dignity. As Bento rightly points out, the Catholic position on a variety of ethical and moral issues has changed through the centuries, sometimes dramatically, as has the church's position in relation to democracy itself. The absolutistic tone in the affirmation of "life" in relation to embryos and fetuses appears, therefore, as a strange certainty within the history of changing positions. The church, thus, tends to lose credibility as a moral authority rather than gain it. And the element of subsidiarity, one of the four central dimensions of Catholic Social Teaching, becomes one-sided, if it starts from the person via the family and mediating corporations (civil society) to arrive at the State, attributing freedom of decision in some, but not in other matters.[259]

In general, the CNBB is in line with Catholic Social Teaching's (CST) main principles, based on the *dignity of the human person* from his/her conception, with his/her rights and corresponding duties, the *common good, subsidiarity,* and *solidarity,* oriented by the values of *truth, freedom, justice,* and *love.*[260] CST has, in turn, adopted the "preferential option for the poor."[261] Although the notion of "poverty" is extended here to "cultural" and "religious" poverty, it does start with "material" poverty. As we have seen, the CNBB, individual bishops and CNBB Regions or other related groupings might have been more radical than CST in many aspects, for instance in their critique of property and their insistence on its social function (see above, IIC2b), but the restriction of

256. Bento, "Cristianismo e democracia."

257. Ibid., 22; cf. Libânio, *Olhando para o futuro.*

258. See also Congregation for the Doctrine of the Faith, *Doctrinal Note on some questions regarding the Participation of Catholics in Political Life*, where "cultural relativism" is criticized, as well as the notion that "ethical pluralism is the very condition for democracy." Quite to the contrary, the document reminds readers of the Christians' (sic!) duty "to exert a greater effort in building a culture which, inspired by the Gospel, will reclaim the values and contents of the Catholic Tradition." Concretely, when "the essence of the moral law, which concerns the integral good of the human person" is at stake, it is the duty of Catholics to oppose laws that attack human life. The document cites, in this order: laws concerning abortion and euthanasia have to be opposed, and there is a duty to protect the human embryo, the family, to promote education of children and protect them, to fight modern forms of slavery (among which are cited "drug abuse" and "prostitution"), and the right to religious freedom and the development of an economy at the service of the human person and the common good are to be safeguarded.

259. On freedom PJCP, *Compendium of the Social Doctrine of the Church,* paragraph 200, reads "The fullness of freedom consists in the capacity to be in possession of oneself in view of the genuine good, within the context of the universal common good."

260. PCJP, *Compendium of the Social Doctrine of the Church*, paragraphs 160ff.

261. Ibid., paragraphs 182ff.

property in terms of its social function and its submission to God's reign and the development of all humanity has become part of CST, not least (and quite explicitly) through the influence of Latin America like the Puebla Assembly.[262] The "social function of any kind of private ownership" and the "equitable distribution of land" receives a special emphasis here[263] and resounds well with the CNBB's consistent defense of land reform.

As the Brazilian church has had considerable support from Rome in social matters, and indeed has clearly influenced Rome's thought on these matters, there was no need of a reformulation. This support might also explain why even under conservative leadership—since 1995, when Dom Lucas Cardinal Moreira Neves (1925–2002) assumed the presidency—the church continued to speak out clearly on matters of social justice. On the other hand, the church has also adopted Rome's stance on moral issues, possibly partly as a price to be paid for its support in social issues, but also because of a strong pressure in this line within its own episcopate, including socially progressive bishops. But many Catholics do not follow the church in this regard, including many clergy and teachers of theology, although they tend not do so openly.[264] It is here that the dominant Roman Catholic position, including the CNBB, appears most abstract and in its rigidity and inflexibility seems unable to communicate with people in any helpful way. Rather, these are left to themselves without official, effective support from their church.

b) Church and State

As we have seen, the relationship between the church and the State in Brazil has changed considerably since the 19th century. Having been a colonial and established, but dependent and poorly organized church with very limited outreach to its nominal members, the republican separation has done the church much good in fostering its self-organization, as well as the spreading out of its doctrine to the people. In the first half of the 20th century, this resulted in a renewed approximation between church and State in Neo-Christendom, seeking to secure the church's influence and power as *the* church of the Brazilians, linking up both to the State and to the laity. From the 1950s onwards, revolutionary effervescence diffused in church lay movements, with a strong setback at the beginning of the military regime, but with a very notable transformation in the 1970s to a socially and politically critical church that drifted away (partly pushed, partly pulled) from the State and aligned itself with the poor and social movements fighting for them.[265]

262. Ibid,, paragraphs 177f. and footnotes.

263. Ibid., paragraphs 178, 180.

264. Cf. Ribeiro, *Sexualidade e reprodução*. According to Medeiros, "Orientações ético-religiosas," 250, the majority of Catholics (in six Brazilian capital cities) are in favor of family planning, contraceptive methods, sex before marriage, second marriage and divorce, and thus against their church's teaching. They support, however, the church's position on same-sex relationships, extramarital adventures, adultery, euthanasia, genetic manipulation and the death penalty. Catholics are divided over celibacy for priests and religious, and generally prefer a "dialogical and pedagogical" (ibid., 251) attitude of their church, rather than an imposing one. The latter aspect was especially strong in Rio de Janeiro, as noted the religiously most plural city in Brazil (see above, IIB1). And, not surprisingly, the church should be, if so, imposing on issues where Catholics and their magisterium are in concord; where the Catholics disagree with their church's teaching, they prefer a dialogical, contributive attitude.

265. Based on rational choice theory and an economic model of church-State relations, Gill, *Rendering unto Caesar,* believes that "the Church opposition to authoritarianism is a function of religious competition" (ibid., 15 and chapter 3, 47ff.). For him, it was "Luther's Shadow" through Pentecostal growth (sic!) that drove the ICAR to such reaction, in order to keep its flock at bay. As indicated, there are elements of truth in this hypothesis, but it is certainly insufficient to declare the dedicated engagement of hierarchy, clergy and laity, under threat of death, towards the safeguarding of a faith opting for the poor, and social and political transformation. On the problematic of rational choice theory and an economic model of religion see now Mariano, "Usos e limites da teoria da escolha racional da religião."

Today, the ICAR has come closer again to the State, not least because the last two presidents have come out of the same resistance against authoritarianism. But while Cardoso's privatization policy met with considerable resistance from the church, and he remained a laical intellectual, even if he recognized the church's important role in society,[266] Lula has been a long-standing ally of the progressive sectors in the ICAR. He has great respect for the church to which he confessedly belongs and from which he received support when he was a trade-union leader. Still, as he became the president, the church has not given up criticizing him—as it would have, indeed, to criticize any president, given that its main demands, as shown above (IIC2) are still only very partially attended to.

As clear by the documents analyzed and well grounded in the Second Vatican Council,[267] the church holds that all power emanates from God, and that from there all power is given but also restricted and can be legitimately criticized or even encounter resistance and civil disobedience. But the documents and the Council recognized the legitimate autonomy of the "temporal order." Referring to the principles that oriented the first Christians, the CNBB affirmed that "they integrate the social *convivência,* and submit to the civil authorities (Romans 13.1–7; 1 Peter 2.13–17), even when they courageously affirm their faith and claim the liberty of 'obeying God rather than men.'"[268]

The church, then, understands itself as a sentinel, a watchdog over the State, in a critical-constructive way. The documents make clear that it does not think of itself as giving concrete instructions to the political system or civil society. Its role is to educate and to give general orientations.[269] As we have seen, this balanced line is not totally kept up when it comes to moral matters; but despite the more heated discourse at least of some bishops and certainly of Rome, at least in theory the church seems to have clarity with respect to its own restricted role in a pluralistic society. Certainly, as the church to which the vast majority still lays claim, the government's ears are more open to it than to other churches, and the president's door is more frequently open to it than to other denominations. But the ICAR seems to recognize that it has to take into account that other churches are also being heard and, not least, courted by politicians for assistance with government programs and electoral support.

Still, reading historical overviews like Barros'[270] that seem to be able to draw a straight line from Cardinal Leme's Neo-Christendom to the Church Base Communities—something which to the more distant reader appears as a contradiction—one wonders whether not even progressive Catholics still kindle the idea of a Catholic Brazil.[271] This is visible, for instance, in Leonardo Boff's

266. Cardoso, *A arte da política*, 508.

267. E.g. Brighenti, "Pessoa – comunidade – sociedade," 166.

268. CNBB, *Exigências éticas*, 96. The document gives as a reference to the latter quotation Acts 4.19: "But Peter and John answered them, 'Whether it is right in God's sight to listen to you rather than to God, you must judge,'" while the text reflects rather Acts 5.29: "But Peter and the apostles answered, 'We must obey God rather than any human authority.'"

269. Antoniazzi ("Igreja e democracia," 105) observes a shift between CNBB, *Exigências cristãs* and CNBB, *Por uma nova ordem constitucional.* While the former still rehearses "the authoritarian scheme of the magisterium, by which politics is subject to morality," a morality defined by the hierarchy of the church, the latter shows the bishops as "defenders of the popular will" that "make of 'participation' (another name for democracy?!) the central axis of their text." Of course, times were others: Neo-Christendom was not so far away, and the church, who in 1977 directed itself much more to the State (in the state of exception) than to the people, might have thought that such recourse on its moral power might have an effect on the military.

270. Barros, 'Gênese e consolidação.'

271. Also the (Catholic) Sociologist José Casanova (*Public Religions in the Modern World*, 118) seems to see this in a line without rupture, in that intellectuals and church leaders "began in the 1940s to adopt a more progressive form of social and political Catholicism, thus anticipating and influencing the progressive turn the entire Brazilian church

theology, with the difference that after his rupture with Rome, the cosmos takes the place of the church,[272] re-establishing the "catholic" harmony. On the political level, the recent agreement between the Vatican (as a sovereign State) and Brazil appears to return to direct influence methods in order to strengthen the church's position, namely, by insisting on confessional religious education (cf. below, IIIB2a).

c) Church and Society

The ICAR has by now a long-standing history of cooperation with civil society. In fact, as we have seen, it has been the birthplace of civil society during the long process of transition. And it appears, today, clear in its own role as part of civil society, in partnership with other churches, ecumenical organizations, and social movements. While the ICAR has lost its monopoly as the "voice for the voiceless," as was to be expected and, in fact, is a good sign for a democratic society, it is still in many instances the dominant voice on a variety of social issues. While it is in line, here, with other churches and organizations of civil society, this is different where moral issues are implied. There, official position and lay opinions (and practice!) lie often in contradiction. Still, the fact that the church today reaches many more people than it has ever done, necessarily through many lay people, gives it an important and, indeed, unique role in reaching out to the poor. The Pentecostals are especially strong among the poor, as we have seen and shall again see (above, IIB, and below, IIE) but still much smaller in numbers.

One of the important aspects of the church seeing itself as part of civil society is that it comes to define its identity no longer in a complete identity of the believer and the citizen, but rather in a model of concentric circles, similar to Karl Barth's famous *Christengemeinde und Bürgergemeinde*, from person to community to society.[273]

While every person is co-responsible for the common good in society, the church relates to it through *service*,[274] *dialogue*,[275] i.e., co-operation with other religious groups and civil society in an "ecumenical and citizen spirit,"[276] and as proclamation,[277] where coherence of faith and life is sought and religion, namely Christianity, is seen as the ferment of liberation and the transformation of society. Warnings are expressed for religion not to become a marketed good in an excluding and consumerist society. Finally, the church relates to society through *witness*,[278] where the Christian community ought to show "an authentic and sincere interest for the problems of society,"[279] and

would later take." Even if those decades prepared what was to come, there is a quite considerable difference, theologically and politically, between a Neo-Christendom model or a "prophetic" church acting in society without an alliance with the powerful (although, historically, still with personal and structural influence, via high-level secret talks and mass mobilization).

272. Sinner, *Reden vom Dreieinigen Gott*; "Leonardo Boff."

273. CNBB, *Diretrizes gerais da ação evangelizadora*; Brighenti, "Pessoa – comunidade – sociedade." Tepe, "Igreja e democracia", 95 refers to *Evangelii Nuntiandi* 15 (Paul VI, Apostolic Exhortation *Evangelii Nuntiandi*), where it says: "She [sc. the Church] is the People of God immersed in the world . . .," and Tepe adds: "immersed in democracy." Alberigo, "Eclesiologia e democracia," 34ff. precisely draws analogies, as Barth had done in his time, and focuses on the doctrine of the Trinity, although recognizing that "the dynamism of trinitarian origin is much more radical and far more complex than the one of a democratic kind" (ibid., 35).

274. CNBB, *Diretrizes gerais da ação evangelizadora*, 176–85.

275. Ibid, 186–92.

276. Brighenti, "Pessoa – comunidade – sociedade," 169.

277. CNBB, *Diretrizes gerais da ação evangelizadora*, 193–98.

278. Ibid., 199–203.

279. Brighenti, "Pessoa – comunidade – sociedade," 170.

foster formation on "faith and politics," solidarity and other burning issues through its own organizations and events like Caritas, Justice and Peace Commissions, and "Clamor of the Excluded",[280] among others. Through celebrations, especially on particular dates relating to society, the church commits itself to foster the practice of solidarity and the reinforcement of a citizen consciousness.

d) Political and Ecclesial Citizenship

The most problematic aspect, in my view, of the ICARs position on democracy and citizenship is that it has rejected significantly altering the traditional hierarchical relationships in its own ranks. To a certain extent, the progressive or popular church in the ICAR was also not exempt from this, as the clergy continued to exercise considerable and often decisive influence over the laity, even within CEBs.[281] Even where priests worked hard to involve the laity respecting their own opinion, contribution and responsibility, the situation easily swung back to the traditional relationship with the priest in charge of all decisions.

I could accompany with my own eyes a community I have known for over 10 years now. For 20 years, and still when I came to know the parish in 1996, it had worked on decentralizing the church's life and the power of decision making, insisting on presence in the poverty stricken areas themselves rather than in the main church. Often, these small communities built a small chapel with their own hands, using any material they could find with a minimum of financial investment. Lay celebrations were frequent and the laity present in the sanctuary; the youth were active and found open ears among the priests. When the priests changed, some years of a transition followed that were difficult for all, and eventually a traditional, centralized parish life came back into practice, with the laity still active, but in a clearly subordinate role, and expelled from the sanctuary. From what I hear from other persons involved, lay, clergy, and theologians, this is by no means an isolated case.

Representatives of a progressive or popular church have long insisted on a more democratic church. Leonardo Boff had brought up this issue early and very clearly in his famous *Church, charism and power* (1981). There, he clearly criticized the "pathologies" of the hierarchical structure and the "institutional sclerosis" of the ICAR, which made it centralist and authoritarian. While not questioning the hierarchy as such, he insisted on their character of service and addressed the exclusion of women from the priesthood as a matter of human rights.[282] Boff's is not only an ecclesiology of the people, i.e., the laity (*laos*), but it is also a people based ecclesiology in the sense of Liberation Theology, being built up by and from the poor. It is an ecclesiology aimed at the concrete context of life, mainly that of the poor; therefore, Boff speaks of an "ecclesio-genesis" through the self-organization of this people of God, especially in the Ecclesial Base Communities (CEBs). [283] He does not only defend "a new way of being Church" [*um novo*

280. The *Grito dos Excluídos* is a manifestation spearheaded by the ICAR's pastoral sectors, in partnership with other organizations of civil society, held yearly on September 7 (Independence Day) to recall, in the midst of military marches, the voice of those at the margins of society. It was founded in 1995.

281. This is shown quite concretely, from his own experience while working in Brazil, by Martin, in "The Call to do Justice," who distinguishes six models of being a priest and doing priestly work, testing discourse against the reality.

282. Cf. Sinner, *Reden vom Dreieinigen Gott*, 67–70. One of the criticisms brought forward against him was that he had protestant leanings and was quoting Protestant authors, to which Boff responded, by his own record, "absolutely, it is the evangelical side of protestantism, and we have much to learn with Luther. So, I do not accept that it is the Protestant side; it is the healthy side of theology that perceives the excess, the abuse of power by the Church, its arrogance, and it is up to theology to have a critical word about this," quoted and commented in Sinner, "Leonardo Boff—a Protestant Catholic."

283. At the time, he had full support in this by his brother C. Boff ("Bases teológicas do ideal democrático," 115),

modo de ser Igreja] but also "a new way for the whole Church to be" [*um novo modo de toda Igreja ser*].[284] As we have seen, his and other's expectations of what CEBs could become as the new model of the church were thoroughly frustrated.

Boff and other theologians, also radical in their reading, could defend such a democratic church based on Vatican II's ecclesiology and its theology of the laity, which—in their view—"recognizes the sovereignty of the Catholic citizen also in the ecclesial community."[285]

It is of course true that faith, as such, is not subject to a majority vote. But if faith is the base for the citizen's acting in society, and the church, there, clearly supports democracy, why should this be different in the church itself, where all are baptized into the royal priesthood of believers, joined as the people of God, as members of the body of Christ?[286] Alberigo well formulated that the church "is" not a democracy, as it never made sense to say it was a monarchy or an aristocracy. It is, however, possible to "introduce into the Church aspects of the democratic method," characterized by participation and co-responsibility.[287] As is to be expected and we shall see below (IID3), this question is much easier to be answered in a Protestant than in a Roman Catholic ecclesiology. Still, as many in the ICAR in Brazil ask this question, and have indeed tried to live other, co-operative forms of the exercise of authority in the church, there remains an open question for the church to answer and explain—or to change, lest it may further lose credibility, especially among the educated. In this context, the dimension of gender and ethnic belonging has to be raised. Women have been consistently excluded from the priesthood in the Roman Catholic Church. This, it has to be said, is not different in other Brazilian churches, including most Protestant and Pentecostal churches. But there, changes are more easily possible, and do happen as in 1999, when the Independent Presbyterian Church agreed to ordain women to the ministry. Furthermore, many Presbyterian churches have gone this way worldwide, which has paved the way for change.

At the same time that the ICAR excludes women from the ordained ministry, they form the majority of believers and are the most active parts of the church. While their important contribution is being recognized in official documents, much remains to be done to do justice to the enormous amount of time and energy women are dedicating to the church, with a minimal degree of visibility and the virtually total exclusion of formal power. Also the presence and role of black believers and priests, as well as of indigenous clergy and laity are still to be fully recognized and, moreover, fostered.

---

who described democracy as lived in the CEBs ("seminaries of democracy") as a democracy of the oppressed (subjects), a social democracy (object), and a base democracy (participation).

284. L. Boff, "CEBs."

285. Bento, "Cristianismo e democracia," 39.

286. Cf. Alberigo, "Eclesiologia e democracia." Antoniazzi, "Igreja e democracia," 108 raises the historical point that "It is true that, in history, the Church adopted in his internal organization institutional forms derived from the society in which it found itself inserted. Why, now, not adopt democratic forms, as it has already done in various historical circumstances?" He further refers to Ratzinger and Maier, *Demokratie in der Kirche*. In his epilogue to the new edition, Ratzinger sees the danger of submitting issues of faith to a majority vote (as a negative example, he uses the decision of the Anglican Church to ordain women), and that "to believe" would be replaced by "to think"/"to be of the opinion" (*meinen*). Issues brought forward by lay people are dismissed as "standard claims" and "*Schlagwortpastoral*": celibacy, women's ordination, communion for the divorced and newly married, and the like (ibid., 84). Maier, in his epilogue, recalls his criticism against the "ghetto of the emancipation," when he reproached the 1968 revolutionaries of caring too much for abstract concepts and too little for the concrete business of democracy. On the other hand, he asks whether in the ICAR one could not more clearly distinguish between "unchangeable" and "changeable" things (like constitution and law in politics) and, furthermore, questions the "in today's world unique" (ibid., 98) melting together of powers (judiciary, executive, and legislative), which makes a system of "checks and balances" unlikely to develop.

287. Alberigo, "Eclesiologia e democracia," 33.

D. The Evangelical Church of the Lutheran Confession in Brazil

[O] povo da igreja [é o] chão em que
um agir público responsável deve ter
suas verdadeiras raízes

Lindolfo Weingärtner[1]

THE EVANGELICAL CHURCH OF the Lutheran Confession in Brazil (*Igreja Evangélica de Confissão Luterana no Brasil*—IECLB) is the second largest single Protestant historical church in Brazil today, with some 720,000 members enrolled, behind only the Seventh-Day-Adventists.[2] It began to form communities in the early 19th century, organized into synods from 1886, created a federation of synods in 1949 and, finally became a national church in 1968. Thirty years later, it was reorganized internally into 18 synods.[3]

Other Protestants had come to Brazil before this. One of the first, German Lutheran Hans Staden (1525–79), became well known for having narrowly escaped being eaten by the Tupinambá people by, among other factors, he says, singing Luther's hymns.[4] He wrote the first eyewitness book about Brazil, published in 1557.[5] Followers of Calvin from Geneva and French Huguenots came with a detachment to create the "Antarctic France" in Guanabara beach, a shortlived experience (1555–67) that resulted in the first martyrdom of Protestants in Brazil by their own French leader, the ambitious and ambiguous Villegaignon, and eventually defeat by the Portuguese governor-general, Mem de Sá, but also provided an ample description of Brazil[6] and the first Protestant confession of faith on Brazilian soil, the *Confissão Fluminense* of 1558.[7] From 1630–54, the Dutch

1. "The people of the church [are] the soil in which responsible public action must have its true roots," Weingärtner, *A responsabilidade pública dos cristãos*, 6.

2. The WCC (World Council of Churches, *Handbook of Member Churches*) informs 715,959 members, 18 synods, 471 parishes, 1,812 congregations, 1,160 (additional) preaching points and 1,041 pastors and catechists. Although the Baptist churches, taken all together, have more than triple that figure in members, they are highly autonomous and organized in a variety of conventions (cf. above, IIB1).

3. For information on its present life and structure, see http://www.luteranos.com.br.

4 Fischer, "Luther in Brasilien," 6.

5. "Warhaftige Historia und Beschreibung eyner Landtschafft der wilden, nacketen, grimmigen Menschfresser Leuthen in der Newenwelt America gelegen"; Staden, *Brasilien*.

6. Léry, *History of a Voyage to the Land of Brazil*.

7. Although barely known, it has its place among the early Reformed Confessions worldwide, even before the Gallican (1559), Scots (1560) and Belgian Confessions (1561). It is interesting to note that natives could be negatively branded by the conquerors and missionaries as "Jews, Muslims or apostate Christians ('Lutherans')," and those accused by the Inquisition received the statement that "they left this Kingdom to become Lutherans" (Westhelle, "O tamanho do paraíso," 240f., 249f. n. 7).

West-Indian Company occupied the coastal area from Pernambuco to Sergipe in the South and Maranhão in the North, and brought with it the Reformed Confession. Under the apt leadership of Johann Moritz von Nassau-Siegen-Dillenburg (1604–79), "the Brazilian," Duke of Orange, who gave his name to "Mauritsstad" (today Recife), the area saw a considerable economic development, and a certain tolerance was exercised in relation to Catholics and Jews.[8] After this, *acatólicos* ("non-Catholics") were strictly forbidden (as were foreigners in general). Only in the early 19th century, when the British fleet protected the Portuguese court as it fled Napoleon's troops by coming to Brazil, were Anglicans allowed to practice their faith, founding a community of foreigners in Rio de Janeiro in 1810.

Other Lutheran churches include the Evangelical Lutheran Church of Brazil (*Igreja Evangélica Luterana do Brasil*—IELB), founded in 1904 through the activity of Missouri Synod missionaries among the German immigrants and their descendants in Brazil, which today has some 200,000 enrolled members, and a number of free communities. Interestingly, the total number of declared Lutherans counted by the 2000 census,[9] 1,062,144, is about 100,000 higher than the sum total of the official figures given by the churches, so that more people feel that they belong to the Lutheran tradition than are actually enrolled in the churches.[10] Still according to the census, this amounts to 0.6 percent of the total population and 4 percent of the Protestants. Despite its relative stability in terms of membership, the slow growth of the IECLB does not keep up with the population's growth rate. While its birth and baptism rates are below, its number of funerals is above Brazilian average, in a striking contrast to the 1940s and before, when there was above-average growth in the Lutheran population.[11] In part, this can be explained through the growing urbanization of a traditionally rural church, although the IECLB still maintains an urbanization rate well below average, at 64 percent.[12]

By the fact that the IECLB largely consists of immigrants and their descendants, it has a specific position in the Brazilian context. Right from the beginning, this resulted in its being called "the German church," a designation still common today.[13] The church has maintained this ethnic profile till today. In fact, in 1987, 92.5 percent of the IECLB's members were of German origin (even if this dates back many generations) and, according to data of 1991, 94.6 percent were white.[14] It functions much as a "Volkskirche," similarly to its German counterparts, i.e., a church one belongs to as a descendant of a family that already belongs to it, without requiring an especially profound knowledge, fervent piety, missionary activity, constant presence at worship, or the like.[15]

8. Cf. Fluck, *Basler Missionare in Brasilien*, 49–60.

9. IBGE, *Censo demográfico 2000*.

10. Altmann, Walter, *Quem é membro da IECLB?* Pastoral Letter from the Presidency, IECLB nr. 131806/07, Easter 2007, 1. As in the previous chapter, references for documents, unless published as books, are given only in the footnotes. Part of the problem is that the church's own statistics don't give much certainty—in a good number of communities, people are counted as "families" or else per contributing member only, and there are serious problems in keeping up the registers. Annual fluctuations are so high (upward or downward) that they are likely to be based on problems with registering rather than real changes.

11. Kliewer, "O Declínio do Crescimento Natural."

12. Kliewer, "Effervescent Diversity," 317.

13. Cf. for instance Fischer and Jahn, *Es begann am Rio dos Sinos*, 9; Fischer, "Geschichte der Evangelischen Kirche," 162; Dreher, *Kirche und Deutschtum*, 10. In some periods of time, communities and synods called themselves "German," but this ended definitively with World War II.

14. Kliewer, "Effervescent Diversity," 320.

15. Cf. Altmann, Walter, *Quem é membro da IECLB?* Pastoral Letter from the Presidency, IECLB nr. 131806/07, Easter 2007, 2f.

In fact, as we have seen, "Germanity" and belonging to the church that would come to be the IECLB was interchangeable at times. This has meant that the IECLB had to find its identity as an immigrant church in often hostile lands, conquering its citizenship and becoming lawfully and consciously Brazilian. Its generally good relationship with the Roman Catholic Church, especially with Catholic fellow immigrants, has rendered it suspicious among the Protestant churches, which arrived through mission with a generally strong anti-Catholic position. One of the classical studies on Protestantism in Brazil barely mentions it.[16] Among others, there is also a regional divide: While the IECLB took roots mainly in the Southern states of Rio Grande do Sul (first and foremost), Santa Catarina and Paraná, and the Southeastern state of Espírito Santo—although it is present today in virtually all states, and has contributed considerably to the migrant population in the North of Mato Grosso and in Rondônia—Presbyterians and Methodists have their centers in São Paulo and Rio de Janeiro, respectively, while Baptists and Adventists have a strong presence also in the Northeast and Northern region.[17]

One of the strong aspects has been, since its beginning, the value given to education and its efficient system of community schools. The high standard of Lutheran high schools and faculties is widely recognized today, and certainly one of the factors that contributed to a public impact beyond its relatively modest membership.[18]

In this chapter, I follow the same pattern as in the previous one: First, a brief historical survey will situate the church in its historical development and specific context (1). The second section will analyze documents from the IECLB and historical and sociological studies on it (2). Finally, theological readings describe and assess the theological grounding of the churches' position on democracy and citizenship, church and State, church and society and the relationship between political and ecclesial citizenship (3).

1. BRIEF HISTORICAL SURVEY

Auch wir vertrauen feste auf Gott, sein heilig Wort,
So gehen wir von dannen jetzt nach Brasilien fort.

Emigrants' hymn[19]

As indicated, the 19th century became the century of Protestantism in Brazil, first with a tiny congregation of Anglicans in Rio de Janeiro, then with Lutheran, Reformed, and United "German" immigrants—in a wide cultural and linguistic, not political sense—and later with Congregationalists, Presbyterians, Methodists, Baptists and, again, Anglicans.[20] What would become, after World

16. Léonard, *O protestantismo brasileiro*. This is also true for Bastian, *Geschichte des Protestantismus*. Prien, *Die Geschichte des Christentums in Lateinamerika*, 8, to the contrary, worked extensively on immigration churches and, specifically, cites the IECLB (ibid., 759–67); see also Prien, *Evangelische Kirchwerdung in Brasilien* and *Das Christentum in Lateinamerika*, 308ff.

17 Jacob et al., *Atlas da filiação religiosa*, 69–99.

18. Gertz, "Die Lutheraner in der Gesellschaft und Kultur Brasiliens," 165f.; Kliewer, "Effervescent Diversity," 320.

19. "We, too, trust firmly in God, in his holy Word, so we now leave for Brazil," in Prien, *Evangelische Kirchwerdung in Brasilien*, 30. Other hymns were more secular: "Wir ziehen in ein anderes Land. Da finden wir Gold wie Sand. Wir wandern nach Brasilia, Hurra, hurra. Nur Schulden lassen wir da" (ibid.).

20. Cf. Mendonca and Velasques Filho, *Introdução ao protestantismo no Brasil*. On the confessionality of the immigrants, all of which were not Lutherans, but also Reformed or United, see Wachholz, "Luterano? Reformado? Unido? Evangélico!"

War II, the IECLB, began with small groups of immigrants that came to the hinterland of Rio de Janeiro (then the capital of Brazil) and founded the colony of São Leopoldo at the Sinos river in the Southern province of Rio Grande do Sul. In this section, I shall show how this developed into today's IECLB, focusing on its three "struggles for citizenship" and its relationship to the State and society.[21]

a) The IECLB as an immigrant Church: Struggling Towards Citizenship

In 1824, when the Imperial Constitution allowed certain religious freedom, immigrant communities were founded by Protestant Germans in the originally (predominantly Catholic) Swiss colony of Nova Friburgo (Rio de Janeiro), and in São Leopoldo (Rio Grande do Sul).[22] Migrants came mainly from Germany, but also from Switzerland, Austria, Luxemburg, and Russia.[23] At the time, there was widespread poverty and population growth in those lands, and the named countries were eager to send people out, never to return, and sometimes supported their one-way travel. Religious interpretations followed migration, like the hymn that compared them to Abraham and his calling by God to go to a new land, which ends in the words cited at the beginning of this section: "We, too, trust firmly in God, in his holy Word, so we now leave for Brazil."

The Brazilian State, in turn, was interested in receiving immigrants for mainly two reasons: One was to replace African slaves, given that the slave-trade was becoming dangerous and very costly, namely in the coffee plantations of São Paulo state.[24] The other reason was the fear of the African population seeking to seize power, as had happened in Haiti (1804) and in the *malês*-Rebellion in Bahia (1807–10).[25] There were considerably more African than Portuguese descendants at the time.[26] Thus, the Brazilian government sought to pursue a politics of "whitening" the popula-

21. On the history and identity of what is now the IECLB, see Schröder, *Brasilien und Wittenberg*; Fischer, "Geschichte der Evangelischen"; Dreher, *Kirche und Deutschtum*, *História do povo luterano*, "Heutige Situation der Lutherischen Kirche in Lateinamerika," esp. 196–207; Prien, *Die Geschichte des Christentums in Lateinamerika*, *Evangelische Kirchwerdung in Brasilien*; Gertz, "Die Lutheraner in der Gesellschaft und Kultur Brasiliens."

22. Prien, *Die Geschichte des Christentums in Lateinamerika*, 759 states that the congregation in Nova Friburgo, founded in May 1824 by Pastor Friedrich Oswald Sauerbronn (1784–1867) with immigrants from the Hunsrück (partly from Sauerbronn's own community in Germany) and some Swiss Protestants, "is the oldest Protestant congregation in Latin America which has existed uninterruptedly," with the exception of the Anglican community of expatriates in Rio de Janeiro; see also Prien, *Evangelische Kirchwerdung in Brasilien*, 68f. Fluck, *Basler Missionare in Brasilien*, 67–110 holds that the formation of a congregation happened before the Germans arrived among the group of Swiss Protestants that arrived in Nova Friburgo in 1819; see also Spliesgart, *"Verbrasilianisierung,"* 167–74, who speaks of a "Protestantische Untergrundkirche." As to São Leopoldo, Emperor Dom Pedro I, who was married to an Austrian, had invited specifically Germans to come to Brazil, who in turn named their colony after the empress, Leopoldine of Habsburg.

23. According to Prien (*Evangelische Kirchwerdung in Brasilien*, 27), of the roughly 10 million emigrants from Germany in the 19th century, relatively few migrated to Brazil: 15,000 from 1815–48, 15,815 between 1850–59, and 63,370 between 1860-95, although effective numbers might be higher, as Brazilian statistics restricts itself to Germany within the borders of 1871. A number of factors, including wars, interrupted or restricted immigration at various points in time.

24. Minister Pedro de Araújo Lima affirmed: "Brazil has to see the number of its sons growing, at least in the same measure as in the United States of North America. . . The slave trade is dwindling, and we face the necessity to close this gap. . . Brazil needs arms, industrious and hard-working," as quoted in Fischer, "Geschichte der Evangelischen Kirche," 87; cf. Prien, *Evangelische Kirchwerdung in Brasilien*, 36. The São Leopoldo colony indeed came to be nicknamed as "laboriosa Colonia allemã" (industrious German colony), ibid., 38. See also, for Swiss immigrants and their fate in the coffee plantations of São Paulo Hasler, *Ibicaba*; Ziegler, *Schweizer statt Sklaven*.

25. Prien, *Evangelische Kirchwerdung in Brasilien*, 35, n. 36, questions the importance of this aspect in the mind of the monarch and believes that he was more interested in "filling" the scarcely populated Southern province of Rio Grande do Sul to secure the borders.

26. Fischer, "Geschichte der Evangelischen Kirche," 87 gives 2.7 million black and 920,000 white people, while Prien,

tion, by inviting Europeans to settle in small farms—a new system over against the huge coffee and sugar-cane plantations. As they were forbidden to hold slaves, they were forced to have more children to work the land, thus enhancing the white population. Companies like the *Hamburger Colonisationsverein* advertised something near paradise on earth awaiting the colonists, an expectation which was very soon sobered by the wild and often damp lands, where hard work, illnesses, and animals took lives daily.[27] Even so, the number of immigrants and, thus, the immigrant population grew rapidly. As they came to as yet unworked lands, their contact with "Brazilians," i.e., those who spoke Portuguese, was restricted and they created virtually homogenous settlements. Still, there was no idea of "Germanism" then, but rather the struggle to survive, having to count on the solidarity of those who were in the same situation. The new communities soon organized schools for their children, and the teachers often exercised the spiritual leadership, as pastors were rare and had to travel far to attend to the scattered communities. The first pastors came as immigrants and were paid by the State to cater for the immigrant communities, others were called and paid by the colonization companies. Later, churches and missionary societies in Germany and Switzerland sent out pastors in higher numbers. Others, especially in Rio Grande do Sul, acted as pastors out of need but lacked theological training and formal ordination, were thus labeled by the proper pastors and institutions as "pseudo-pastors."

The immigrants were separated from the existing population geographically and linguistically. This was true also for the Catholic immigrants. But Protestants, the majority among the German speaking immigrants, were restricted in their citizenship, as they could not bury their dead on public cemeteries, nor was their blessing of marriage accepted—their children were thus considered bastards.[28] Neither did their baptisms receive public recognition, which was highly problematic in a time when there were no civil birth registers. Throughout the 19th century immigrant Protestants had to fight for their citizenship,[29] which I see as their *first struggle for citizenship*. Partial conquests could be celebrated along those years, but it was not until 1890 that religious liberty was fully granted,[30] and Protestants were, thus, recognized fully as citizens and allowed to perform their religious rites publicly.

It was only from 1871 onwards, with the creation of the German Reich centered in Prussia and the nascent idea of pan-germanism, that a more conscious ethnic identity linked to the German motherland was formed and, not least, directly promoted by Germany.[31] The church, present as it was among the immigrant population and with constant links to Germany, became one of the primary vehicles of this Germanization. The shameful culmination of this became the adoption of Nazism by a considerable part of the Germans and their descendants in Brazil, including the

Evangelische Kirchwerdung in Brasilien, 33 cites 1,987,000 blacks and 628,000 mestizos (which, taken together, amount to about the number quoted by Fischer) and 845,000 whites, besides about 1 million of "not integrated" indigenous.

27. Cf. Cunha, *Das Paradies in den Sümpfen*.

28. They were also not naturalized automatically on arrival, differently from what had been promised, and could not become deputies in the Legislative Assembly; Fischer, "Geschichte der Evangelischen Kirche," 105.

29. Kunert, "Aspectos da relação IECLB," 219–22; Prien, *Evangelische Kirchwerdung in Brasilien*, 47f.

30. Cf. above, IIB2.

31. Dreher, *Kirche und Deutschtum*, 72.

churches and their leadership.[32] Not few maintained that "for us, *Volkstum* and church, Germanity and Gospel belong tightly and non-detachably together."[33]

After a first failed trial to organize the scattered communities in 1868, it was not until 1886 that the first Synod was founded: The *Rio Grande Synod.* In 1905 followed the *Evangelical Lutheran Synod of Santa Catarina, Paraná, and other South American States*; in 1911, the *Evangelical Synod of Santa Catarina*; and in 1912, the *Evangelical Synod of Central Brazil.* Only the Lutheran Synod had a binding confession. The others had more open formulations, given their mixed constituency. There were, however, no different confessional statuses from congregation to congregation as in united churches in Germany, and overall the Lutheran confessions tended to be emphasized, without being exclusive.[34]

b) The IECLB after World War II: Towards a Truly Brazilian Identity

With State measures during the world wars (especially during World War II under Getúlio Vargas' dictatorship) against the German language, German nationals working in Brazil, and the Protestant schools where German was spoken, a phase of repression and discrimination in relation to the German immigrants and their descendants commenced. While this created much suffering, severed ties to Germany, and made personal and financial support from there impossible, it facilitated a new phase of consciousness in the church of their Brazilian citizenship, which became evident through the increasing use of the Portuguese language.[35] I would call this the *second struggle for citizenship* in the church's history: becoming not only legally, but also consciously Brazilian and, without denying their German origins, diminishing their centrality and exclusivist tendency.

Pastors, most of whom had come from Germany to serve the Brazilian communities, were imprisoned and deported. The small number of Brazilian pastors, all of them trained in Germany, was unable to attend to the large and scattered Germanic population. Training had to be done in Brazil, henceforth, which led to the creation of the School of Theology (today EST) in 1946. The church also organized itself to be able to survive and, also, to assume consciously its Brazilian identity, joining together the four existing synods in the Federation of Synods, created in 1949

32. Cf. Prien, *Evangelische Kirchwerdung in Brasilien*, 299–462. The church, especially the Rio Grande Synod, was well aligned with the German Evangelical Church, of which it was dependent for support and especially the formation and sending of pastors; with the *Estado Novo* (from 1937 onwards, cf. above, IA1a), such links ended and the church had to rethink and reorganize itself standing on its own feet. Under these new circumstances, members of the church were among those who fought, towards the end of the war, with the allied forces in Italy as part of the Brazilian Expeditionary Force. One of them was pastor, theologian, activist and ecumenist Bertholdo Weber (cf. Jahn, "Porto Alegre im Juni 1970," 28, without mentioning the name). There were small and episodic signs of a Confessing Church in 1937, with a group meeting around vice-president Gustav Reusch, who had had contact with the Confessing Church and with Karl Barth on a visit to Germany; ibid., 436–61.

33. Fischer, "Geschichte der Evangelischen Kirche," 163. Spliesgart, "*Verbrasilianisierung*," has presented a differentiated account for the imperial period (1822–89) and identified a constant process of acculturation since the first immigrants arrived. To be "deutsch-evangelisch," for him, was not only a consequence of German nationalism, but also of a composition of identity in the process of a "confessional reajustment" ("konfessionelle Neujustierung") in Brazil at the time. "Deutschtum" was mainly an effort during the Republic, while acculturation occurred during the whole period of the Brazilian Empire (ibid., 566f.).

34. Cf. Wachholz, "'IECLB'"; Fischer, "Identidade confessional."

35. For Dreher (*História do povo luterano*, 57), this is the third phase of the IECLB's history, after the migration (1) and the Reich periods (2). I have joined together the first two, as the main watershed between the immigration origins of the church and its formation properly speaking is after World War II. In terms of citizenship, 1890 (full religious liberty in the Republic) and not 1871 (the beginning of the Reich) would be the date of reference.

under Pastor President Herrmann Dohms' and his deputy Ernesto Th. Schlieper's apt leadership.[36] The first General Council of the Federation was realized in 1950, in São Leopoldo, and affirmed that "the Federation of Synods is Church of Jesus Christ *in Brazil* with all the consequences that might result from this for the preaching of the Gospel in this country and the co-responsibility for the formation of the political, cultural and economic life of its people."[37] While the church sought to affirm its Brazilian citizenship, it also affirmed its international and ecumenical insertion into the church worldwide, joining the World Council of Churches (WCC) in 1950 and the Lutheran World Federation (LWF) in 1952.[38] Nationally, it joined the Brazilian Evangelical Confederation (*Confederação Evangélica Brasileira*) in 1959. It was only at the time of the Federation that the Augsburg Confession and Luther's Minor Catechism were adopted as binding confessions for all communities.[39]

In 1954, the church adopted the name of "Federation of Synods. Evangelical Church of the Lutheran Confession in Brazil"; in 1962 it dropped the "Federation of Synods," using only the latter name, and in 1968 reshaped itself as a truly national church, with its center in Porto Alegre, organized in regions, districts and parishes. The Theological Faculty in São Leopoldo, until the late 1960s staffed predominantly by Germans and still using the German language (although Portuguese was becoming more common), changed dramatically. In 1968, the first Brazilian with a doctorate in theology became a professor (Brakemeier), and by 1986 Brazilians were the majority among the teaching staff, using exclusively Portuguese.[40] Also among the pastors, the ratio of foreigners dropped from 57.82 percent in 1965 to 20.52 percent in 1976, while the total number of pastors rose from 230 to 341 in the same period.[41]

Given the new structure and the will to be truly Brazilian, it is understandable that the church tended to avoid clashing with the State, although some groups were already pressing in this direction.[42] As cited above (IA1a), the Brazilian Evangelical Confederation had given a moderate

36. Schlieper had gone to Germany in 1927 to become a pastor, in order to preserve German ethnicity in Brazil. There, he underwent an experience of conversion while studying under Karl Barth in Bonn, in 1931, and joined the Confessing Church before returning to Brazil in 1937. Dohms, for his part, was against Barth, whom he felt to do "Calvinist politics," but was able to recognize his positive contribution in the *Kirchenkampf* and accepted the importance of the Barmen Declaration in the post-war synodal assemblies of the Rio Grande Synod; cf. Prien, "Identity and Problems of Development," 213f.; Dreher, *Kirche und Deutschtum*, 215–27.

37. In Dreher, *História do povo luterano*, 57, emphasis mine.

38. Dreher, "Heutige Situation der Lutherischen Kirche in Lateinamerika," 205 says 1950, but the LWF site informs "joined: 1952": http://www.lutheranworld.org/Directory/SAM/Ev-ChurchLuthConfBrazil-EN.html (accessed on 3/20/2008).

39. On the ecumenical insertion of the Federation of Synods and the confessional status see Prien, *Evangelische Kirchwerdung in Brasilien*, 544–75.

40. Cf. Schünemann, *Do gueto à participação*, 60f.; cf. Kirst, "A reforma do estudo—marca registrada da última década." Important scholars and church leaders have come out of their teaching at São Leopoldo in the 1960s and later: Hans Eberhard von Waldow (later professor in Pittsburgh), Joachim Fischer (who remained in Brazil), Harding Meyer (later professor at the Institute for Ecumenical Research, Strasbourg), Hans Jürgen Prien (later professor in Marburg and Köln), Erhard Gerstenberger (later professor in Marburg), Hermann Brandt (later professor in Erlangen), and North Americans Richard H. Wangen (a college pastor, professor and peace activist, who remained in Brazil) and Peter Nash (now professor at Wartburg College, Iowa), among others. Among the Brazilians related to the Faculty who have become well known internationally, I mention Gottfried Brakemeier (who became church president and LWF president), Walter Altmann (church president and moderator of the WCC Central Committee), later Vitor Westhelle (now professor at the Lutheran School of Theology at Chicago), Wanda Deifelt (now professor at Luther College in Decorah, Iowa), and João Biehl (an alumnus who became professor of Anthropology at Princeton University).

41. Schünemann, *Do gueto à participação*, 65.

42. Cf. Brandt, "Die Evangelische Kirche lutherischen Bekenntnisses in Brasilien," 44; Schünemann, *Do gueto à*

statement on the military regime after the "revolution," but made clear its expectations as to human rights and social justice, among others. The IECLB itself did not issue a statement, being represented by the CEB and reprinting the message in its own official organ. Then Pastor President, Karl Gottschald (in office 1969–78), was reluctant to embrace public issues and critical comments against the government. Even so, the Church Council asked the Theological Commission to elaborate theses on the issue of "the use of violence and the right to resistance," following the 1966 Geneva Conference on "Church and Society," where revolutionary moods had come to expression.

On behalf of the Commission, Rev. Lindolfo Weingärtner, at the time principal of the Faculty of the Theology in São Leopoldo, elaborated theses in the form of questions to the government and the opposition, pressing the former on its responsible use of power "which has been given to it [by God]," being that it will have to "answer for its acts before God and that any power used beyond this responsibility is usurped power." He further questioned the government on its efforts to create a better social order, the political inclusion of the larger population, the law's protection for all, the need for a "police State," corruption, land reform, and the permission for an authentic opposition to exist. The latter was questioned as to its representing the "alive conscience" of the government, its criteria for being opposition, its realistic program rather than "ideological utopia," the danger of "political anarchy," and, finally, the opposition's readiness to assume power were it given to it. These questions-theses, in Portuguese, were published preceded by theological theses in German on the "service of the Christian in today's world," and an introduction that insisted that Weingärtner's questions had to be read in the light of these theses. The main difference is that this text, although not negating the Christians' responsibility to serve and even resist in the "social, political and economic context" in which he or she is situated, insists much more clearly—and with a more theological and less concrete language, avoiding direct references to the actual government or opposition—that this must not be done in a revolutionary perspective, much less as a "theology of revolution." God must not "be degraded from the Lord of history to an immanent principle of history"; he operates in history through human beings. The Christian will "resist wherever his neighbor is subjected to powers [*Gewalten*] which obscure the love of God in Christ to his human beings," but he will never do so in a way that "his 'violence' [*Gewalt*] shall obscure this love."[43]

In the same year (1968), a committee for the preparation of the 5th Assembly of the LWF, to be held in Porto Alegre under the theme of "Sent Into the World," was formed. Politically, the fatal Institutional Act number 5 (AI-5, see above IA1a) was decreed, which inaugurated the highest accumulation of power in the hands of the regime and the fiercest period of repression. The LWF and many of its European member churches were very worried by these developments and especially by the fact that according to custom and the IECLB's insistence they would have had to welcome the head of State, President General Emílio Garrastazú Médici, at the Assembly. After a difficult, belated debate over the political feasibility of an Assembly in Brazil, with heated arguments from both sides (a sign of support for the military regime vs. a sign of support for the Third World), the LWF finally decided (on June 5, 1970, only) to hold its Assembly in the resort of Evian on the French

participação. Prien ("Identity and Problems of Development," 219) states that "the middle class Protestants belong economically to the sector that benefits from the existing regime, and thus they support its principle of 'law and order,'" defending the "strict separation of church from political life," thus, "probably unconsciously" supporting "the notion that each of the different spheres of existence was autonomous."

43. Text published in the *Órgão Oficial* of the IECLB n. 14, July 15, 1968, 7-11. I would like to thank my colleague Roberto Zwetsch and Wilfried Hasenack, director of the IECLB's historical archive in São Leopoldo, for providing me with this text. This archive is located in the EST's library and open for consultation on request. Schünemann, *Do gueto à participação*, 101 also refers to this text.

side of Lake Geneva.[44] In the IECLB, who had not shunned efforts to make this Assembly happen, the move created nothing less than a shock, emblematically evident in the title of a text published in reaction: "They cancelled our [sic] 5th Assembly!"[45] The IECLB held back its delegation, only two attended the Assembly in Evian, and President Gottschald read a statement from the church's council,[46] which stated that the relocation "was received with deep regret and with displeasure by the ECLCB [IECLB] and by the Brazilian public."[47] It affirmed that "if the church feels itself called upon to fulfill its task of political guardianship, knowledge of the matter and an unprejudiced attitude are two prerequisites which are absolutely necessary."[48] The church regarded the relocation as a lack of trust and a consequence of misinformation. In fact, delegations from Germany, Holland, and Scandinavia had felt the IECLB was being complacent in view of the incoming news of tortures in Brazil, while the latter judged these to be biased. In hindsight, both sides have part of the truth on their side. The IECLB (as many sectors in Brazilian society at the time) did underestimate the State's repression, but the concrete reports were apparently exaggerated.[49] The LWF's move resulted, to some extent, in an even stronger solidarization of the IECLB with its country, and of other churches—like the Pentecostal Church "Brazil for Christ," then a member of the WCC and an observer at Evian—with the IECLB, and some argued that the church's insistence (against the LWF) in inviting the country's president to Porto Alegre was the real birthplace of an authentic, Brazilian IECLB,[50] which could demonstrate autonomy.

On the other hand, this public and international scolding of military Brazil and, thus, of the host church, made space for the critical sectors of the church, namely from the Faculty of Theology (today's EST). Already in 1968, the church had formed a commission on social and political affairs.[51] The 1968 Church Assembly in São Paulo, which sealed the merger of the three synods (two of the four original synods had combined in 1962) to a national church, declared that it understood itself "co-responsible . . . for the shaping of public life in our country."[52] According to Fischer, in

44. LWF, *Sent Into the World*, 9. See Knirck-Wissmann, "Kontextualität und Partikularität der Kirche"; Jeziorowski, "Gesandt in die Welt"; Jahn, "Porto Alegre im Juni 1970"; Schünemann, *Do gueto à participação*, 81–95; Schørring et al., *From Federation to Communion*, 382-389.

45. Hasenack, Johannes, "Cancelaram nossa 5ª Assembléia," *Folha Dominical* 85/26 (1970), 1.8; cf. Schünemann, *Do gueto à participação*, 92. Then LWF president Fredrik A. Schiotz (USA) recognized that "we have brought only pain and sorrow to the Brazilian church" (in LWF, *Sent Into the World*, 21) and suggests that the decision had to be taken to avoid the absence of major delegations who had affirmed they would not attend were the Assembly held in Brazil. Schiotz, while taking full responsibility, recognizes that "the change of location has forfeited a great opportunity" (ibid., 22).

46. LWF, *Sent Into the World*, 123–25.

47. Ibid., 123.

48. Ibid., 124.

49. In LWF General Secretary André Appel's account, the Brazilian church delegates' meeting in Blumenau in preparation for the Assembly were "particularly grateful to it [sc. the present regime] for having put an end, in 1964, to political and economic stagnation, which could have led to a disaster. Of course, the return to democracy seemed to be taking its time, but since the government affirmed that its intentions were good, it was necessary to trust and support it." They also rejected, according to Appel, any comparison with the "pre-war Nazi situation" as "completely out of place." But the conference did present a motion to the church's leadership to install a "commission of inquiry [. . .] to look into the question of the tortures" (LWF, *Sent Into the World*, 112). This commission, according to Schünemann (*Do gueto à participação*, 98), visited victims and heard those who had more direct contact and knowledge, mainly of the ICAR, and found out what came as a "bomb" to the IECLB's leadership, i.e. the "systematic practice of torture on political prisoners." Some had known about this before, and some supported the generalized opinion that "Communists indeed have to be tortured"!

50. Jahn, "Porto Alegre im Juni 1970," 38f.

51. LWF, *Sent Into the World*, 123.

52. Fischer, "Geschichte der Evangelischen Kirche," 186.

his history of the IECLB meant as an introduction for those who would come to the Fifth LWF Assembly in Porto Alegre, the status of an immigrant church had restricted the church's action to its boundaries, but now, "community members strive much more strongly today to put into practice their 'co-responsibility for the environment' and to go beyond the boundaries of earlier times."[53]

A group from the Faculty of Theology in São Leopoldo who manned the church's Theological Commission, as well as the newly established "Commission of Political, Economic and Social Issues" had prepared a document that would be adopted by a clear majority at the church's General Council in Curitiba (state of Paraná).[54] Lindolfo Weingärtner was a central figure in this process, as was Gottfried Brakemeier (later church, CONIC and LWF president), who "applied the assembly's motto—'Sent Into the World'—to his own church."[55] Among others, he said that

> if Jesus Christ said to his disciples to be salt of the world, he attributed to them, among other things, a function which is comparable to Man's conscience. This accuses and bewares of errors and false practices. Therefore, we ask the organs [sc. of the State] and society in general that they accept the Churches as critical partners for an open and sincere dialogue, and that they do not expect from the Churches an exclusive support. . .[56]

Pastor President Gottschald represented more the other side, critical of a major political engagement by the IECLB, when he affirmed, in his report to the Curitiba Council:

> The whole Church is, today, threatened by influences and movements which seek to engage it in a unilateral manner for their goals and ideals, be they noble or dubitable. Therefore, it is essential that the Church, obedient uniquely to its Lord, and without giving in to pressures, wherever they may come from, fulfill in freedom its genuine mission to take the liberating and saving message of Jesus Christ to today's man, knowing in detail his real needs.[57]

Already before the Council, when Gottschald called on congregations to celebrate the week of the Fatherland with worship services, preferably in ecumenical celebrations, on September

53. Ibid.

54. There is a debate among historians and church leaders as to the exact role the relocation of the LWB Assembly played in prompting the church to be more critically outspoken on public issues, as the text of the Curitiba Manifest had already been written at the time of the LWF's decision (Dreher, *História do povo luterano*, 59; Schünemann, *Do gueto à participação*, 81–95; Schørring et al., *From Federation to Communion*, 386). On the other hand, the controversy among LWF member churches, mainly in Germany and Finland, had also already been known at the time, and the document might have been thought at least in part as an answer to that. In any case, the relocation event can be said to have served as a catalyst. There had also been a manifest of pastors, professors and students of theology, in which they called for the church to exercise a stronger role of sentinel (Prien, *Lateinamerika*, 200).

55. Bachmann and Bachmann, *Lutheran Churches in the World*, 473; cf. Schünemann, *Do gueto à participação*, 100f., for whom Brakemeier tried to pacify the stirred moods and to prepare the way for he Curitiba Manifest. Jahn ("Porto Alegre im Juni 1970," 40) concludes that "the Fifth Assembly of the Lutheran World Federation has been a burden for the Evangelical Church of the Lutheran Confession in Brazil, but eventually turned to its benefit." In an interview with the author, granted in December 2004, Gottfried Brakemeier opined: "I don't know whether the relocation of the Assembly to France [. . .], was a help or an impediment in the development or the taking on of a political consciousness of the IECLB. Perhaps there were both things: it was an impediment, as it naturally provoked protests and closed doors. [. . .] And it was a help, in the sense that it alerted the IECLB for a reality many did no want to see. Now, it is absolutely wrong to say that it was this relocation that awakened the IECLB. This is not true [. . .] In 1968, I was already a professor at the Escola Superior de Teologia [then, in fact, called "Faculty of Theology"]. We were very attentive to the news of torture in Brazil and the violation of human rights. And the 'Curitiba Manifest' was prepared by a group of which I was a part, but who more [directly] formulated it was Rev. Lindolfo Weingärtner. So there was a preparation, inclusively by the initiative of the faculty, and the [IECLB's] theological commission, etc."

56. Schünemann, *Do gueto à participação*, 101.

57. Ibid.

7 (Independence Day), various pastors refused to do so. They also refused to place flags in the churches and debated the compulsory discipline of "moral and civil education" (see above, IIB3) in schools. These subjects, together with the issue of torture, would give the Curitiba Manifesto its content.

c) Assuming a Public Critical Stance: Citizenship for All

The Curitiba Council is generally taken as the starting point or, rather, the necessary catalyst for a change in policy: It set the foundation stone for the IECLB to comment more regularly on public issues, in an increasingly critical form, accompanying in this to some extent the ICAR, although with different language and arguments, as we shall see, and different positions in some aspects. This is not to say that there had not been any social sensibility before. Quite to the contrary, diaconal work was carried out in many places, as Christoph Jahn, pastor in Brazil from 1956 to 1965, well describes.[58] Together with other Protestant churches, out of the CEB, the ecumenical organization *Diaconia* was founded in 1967, with its headquarters in Rio de Janeiro (later Recife). But there was no national position on public issues until the Curitiba Manifesto, and some felt that even the church's social projects were merely "assistencialist," a judgment certainly in the mood of the contemporary questioning of developmentalism.[59]

The Curitiba Manifesto was handed over to the presidency by a delegation under Pastor President Karl Gottschald on November 5, 1970. The delegation was received the next day by President Médici in audience, and the following evaluation added to the document:

> The very frank and cordial dialogue established between Mr. President of the Republic and the representatives of the IECLB made evident, in a clear and unmistakable manner, the disposition of the men responsible for our government to dialogue with our Church about the problems that preoccupy us. The way in which the manifestation of our Church was received, shows the openness of our government for suggestions and constructive criticisms.[60]

58. Cf. Fischer and Jahn, *Es begann am Rio dos Sinos*.

59. Schünemann, (*Do gueto à participação*, 96) also judges that "till 1970, the typical faithful of the IECLB, just as the majority of pastors, was collaborationist." It seems to me both questionable what this precisely meant at the time and to what extent the attitude of church *members* (not of the leadership, and many pastors, which certainly changed their stance and for which we have clear indications, see below IID2) really changed. There are no major empirical studies that could shed light on the facts and thus the matter remains in speculation. The survey carried out by Kliewer ("Uma comunidade evangélica") is based on 60 questionnaires of one middle class urban congregation and points, despite a strong conservatism and an emphasis on the individual as responsible for his/her situation, a more open position towards a critical socio-political activity of the IECLB. Purper ("Religião e desenvolvimento") interviewed pastors throughout the IECLB and was able to work on a sample of a bit more than half of all active pastors. They were divided into two groups: the "verticalist" (A Group) and the "horizontalist" (B Group), directed towards the individual's relationship with God or to the practice of faith in society, respectively. Not surprisingly, young ministers who had studied at the Faculty of Theology in São Leopoldo were strongly represented in the B Group. Purper established that "the theological concept of Church defines the relationships Man-God, Man-Man and Man-society. From there, we conclude that the concept of Church has socio-political implications, be it in an attitude of indifference, of omission or conscientious engagement" (ibid., 248), which has bearings also on the pastors' ecumenical attitude and activity. As to the "assistentialist" and, moreover, often inefficient and unsustainable character of projects developed in the church and their relationship to donor agencies see Sobottka, *Kirchliche Entwicklungsprojekte in Brasilien*. He comes to a more favorable assessment of CESE's work, while he attests to the Service of Project Development of the IECLB that, generally and with exceptions, ideas of social transformation and matters of (ideological) attitude prevailed over empirical data and measurable objectives. I add that, in 2000, the 34 year old project service was totally reformulated, reorganized and professionalized into a foundation with its own legal personality, in the Lutheran Foundation for Diaconia (*Fundação Luterana de Diaconia*—FLD); see http://www.fld.com.br.

60. Schünemann, *Do gueto à participação*, 170.

While, in hindsight, this judgment sounds exaggeratedly positive, it probably was the case that both the church was keen on stating its success in the meeting, and the presidency, who had certainly followed the debate in the LWF, was eager to show itself open to constructive dialogue. As stated earlier, the government wanted to preserve a good reputation abroad, which gave the leadership of this minority church which, though, was inserted in a considerable international network, a special weight.

At this point, as it was published before the present study's focus period, I cite the first part of the Curitiba text nearly in its entirety, italicizing the aspects and arguments used:

> [. . .]
>
> 1. Theses on the relationship between church and State
>
> 1.1 —The message of the Christian Church envisages the salvation of Man, a salvation which goes beyond the human possibilities, including the political. *It is a message of God—not of this world. But it is destined to this world* and wants to witness Jesus Christ as Lord and Savior of the world. Therefore, the Church *cannot live a sectarian existence*, keeping for itself the message which has been entrusted to it. It has the ministry to witness the word of God, a ministry which it cannot eschew, except at the price of disobedience to its Lord.
>
> The Church's message is *always directed to Man as a whole*, not only to his 'soul'. Thus, it will have *consequences and implications in all spheres of his life*—including physical, cultural, social, economic and political. It will tend not to regulate only the relationships between Christians, but will envisage equally *dialogue with other citizens or groups*, on all issues related to the common good.
>
> 1.2 —*The 'public' message of the Christian church, in regard to the problems of the world, cannot be divorced from its 'internal' testimony*, as the latter has implications for the former. Therefore, the Church cannot condition its public message according to the interests of political ideologies in evidence at a particular moment, or to groups and factions which aspire or maintain power. In its public witness, it may not use methods which are incompatible with the Gospel.
>
> 1.3. —In principle, *Church and State are separate instances*, as defined also by the Constitution of our country. But due to the consequences of Christian preaching which become manifest in the secular sphere, and *due to the fact that Christians are disciples of Christ and simultaneously citizens of their country, it will not be possible to separate totally the areas of responsibility of the State from those of the Church, despite the need to distinguish them*. Where the respective areas overlap, the Church, which in turn needs the critique of the world, will perform a *critical function*—not of a controller, but of a sentinel (Ezekiel 33.7), and of a conscience of the Nation. It will alert and remind the authorities of its responsibilities in specific situations, in a non-partisan spirit, and always with the intention of finding a just and objective solution.
>
> 1.4. —The Church seeks the *sincere and objective dialogue with the State in an atmosphere of openness, of freedom and authentic partnership—a dialogue which has as its purpose finding solutions for the problems which afflict society*. As a co-responsible partner of the secular government, it obeys the precept of the Lord who says: "Give to the emperor the things that are the emperor's, and to God the things that are God's" (Mark 12.17). Based on this fundamental premise, it feels called to cooperate with the governmental authorities in a wide range of tasks, such as, for example, the education of the new generations, the alphabetization of adults, the support of social actions of the government, the fight against illnesses, poverty, Man's marginalization, and in other activities which are not of a purely technical character. This cooperation implies the constant effort destined to *eliminate the causes* which eventually provoke the evils mentioned.
>
> 1.5. —As a consequence from the Church's public preaching, *tensions* with the governmental authorities could emerge, be it for human errors, be it for reasons of fundamental character.

> The Church, in such cases, will not seek to contest the State's power, as if it were a political party, but will proclaim the power of Christ. Where it feels compelled to counter governmental measures, *it will seek, before taking any public stand, to dialogue* with the respective authorities. In all the cases it will act without being demagogic—making clear that it knows itself called to *advocate on behalf of all men who suffer.*[61]

This way of arguing sets the line that would be used in most subsequent documents. I summarize and explain it as follows:

(1) While salvation and history (or "the world") are not to be confused, and while the priority is always to be given to God, witness to him is destined to the world. Speaking to the world is thus part of the church's mission. (2) The church's proclamation is directed to the welfare of human beings as a whole, and thus includes social, economic, political, cultural, and physical aspects. In seeking to contribute to this welfare, the root causes have to be seen and "eliminated." (3) In its seeking to build up relationships oriented by ethical principles stemming from its proclamation, the church cooperates with other parts of civil society and also with the State. (4) There is a kind of doctrine of the two kingdoms or regiments at the basis of the argument that while church and State are to be distinguished, they are not separate, independent blocks.[62] Both realms are under the power of Christ, which the earthly rulers cannot arrogate for themselves (cf. Mk 12.17). Believers are "disciples of Christ" and "citizens of their country," a formulation that recalls Barth's *Christengemeinde und Bürgergemeinde.*[63] (5) The church has, therefore, a critical role to play, as a "sentinel" and "conscience of the Nation," in a "co-responsible" partnership, in order to find solutions for society. It entered, thus, what I call its *third struggle for citizenship:* This time not (only) in its own interest, but in favor of the whole of society, a tendency that would grow in expression, both by the leadership's declarations and the initiatives of individuals, groups, and bodies, often with financial, logistic, and moral support from outside.

The second part of the Curitiba Manifesto takes up three concrete issues that "preoccupy" the church: *Worship*, which is to be preserved from an excessive presence of patriotic symbols; *Christian Education*, which is not to be supplanted by "moral and civic education" (cf. above, IIB3); and *Human Rights*, namely their violation through torture ("inhuman methods"), "be it in the treatment of common prisoners, or of political terrorists, or of suspects of subversive activities." "As a Church, we understand indeed that not even exceptional circumstances can justify practices that violate human rights."[64]

It is noteworthy that in this moderately phrased,[65] but unequivocal way, courageously brought before the military President in person, the IECLB's council marks the critical (and constructive)

61. Translated by the author from Schünemann, *Do gueto à participação*, 168f. (identical with IECLB 1970), and checked against the translation given in Lissner and Sovik, *A Lutheran Reader on Human Rights*, 38f.; emphasis mine.

62. As Prien, "Lateinamerika (Brasilien/Argentinien)," 195 noted, this doctrine has not played "any significant role in theological discussion up to the present time." He is correct in terms of the lack of an explicit doctrine, be it in church documents or in theological publications; I still see it implicitly present in many church documents, as I shall show.

63. Indeed, Barth has been an important influence on the progressive sectors of the IECLB, but also—and from the mid-1960s onwards even more so—Bonhoeffer (especially the letters from prison which became "our book to be left on our pillow"), Richard Shaull, and Moltmann, cf. Dreher, "Reflexões sobre os Sessenta Anos," 61.

64. Schünemann, *Do gueto à participação*, 170.

65. In Schünemann's interpretation (*Do gueto à participação*, 103), the "inoffensive and moderating character made it possible for the Council's plenary, composed in its majority by Lutheran citizens [note the ironic tone of "citizen" here, as a "good citizen" who obeys the authorities in an uncritical way] which possess a great esteem for the present regime, to approve the manifesto."

stance of a national church even before the CNBB did so in all clarity (from 1973 onwards),[66] despite its much higher vulnerability as a minority church considered "foreign" by many. As in the case of the ICAR, the fact that an international church body (the LWF, in this case, but also the WCC) looked critically on the government, might have given it a certain protection. On the other hand, as the IECLB was a small and regionalized church, and shunned too revolutionary a position, it was unlikely to create major problems for the regime. Still, it is significant that the Curitiba Manifesto was "the only public statement of a Protestant church criticizing the regime."[67]

As we shall see, from Curitiba onwards, the national church has with certain continuity been speaking out on public issues. This does not mean that everything changed immediately, and indeed this new stance remained controversial, an ambiguity well noted by Hermann Brandt,[68] who had come from Germany to serve as a professor at the Faculty of Theology in São Leopoldo and had, thus, both the views of an out- and an insider. He comments on the problematic celebrations for the 150th anniversary of Brazil's independence, on September 7, 1972, which created a controversy as to how to react to it as a (minority) church. Schünemann mentions the fact that the IECLB did not join at the time the Ecumenical Coordination of Service (*Coordenadoria Ecumênica de Serviço*—CESE), founded in 1973 following a WCC sponsored conference in Salvador/Bahia on the situation in the particularly poor Brazilian Northeast.[69] As mentioned, the IECLB had cofounded *Diaconia* in 1967, but Gottschald avoided joining CESE because of its outright progressive stance, and alleged that membership in *Diaconia* was sufficient. Only in 1982 would the IECLB join CESE, where it has remained to date. In 1974, a number of initiatives by pastors lead to the document "Permanent Discipleship—Permanent Catechumenate," which stated that

> it inheres to the Church to be a kind of society's conscience, criticizing and warning, wherever it may be necessary, and collaborating where the good of Man is promoted. The Church will not be satisfied with the cure of society's and individuals' infirmities; it will engage also in the elimination of the roots of the actual castigations.[70]

But as Schünemann bluntly claims, this proposal "was not implemented,"[71] despite its having been supported by the 9th General Council of the IECLB in Cachoeira do Sul in 1974, "because it lacked support of the base of members." He argues that a new phase began properly speaking with the document "Our Social Responsibility" (1975/76),[72] as the leadership did not make any efforts to put the Curitiba Manifesto into practice or continue explicitly the line taken there. This was done, instead, by individual pastors, who tried to create groups and networks and encourage the laity to share in parish work so that they would have some freedom to work on public and social issues. In some places, groups similar to CEBs were created, although they did not receive this name. Some church intellectuals created the semi-clandestine "Curitiba Group," which pondered further on the church's public responsibility, but protected itself against both the dominant—and, then, conservative—church leadership and the State's persecution. In the IECLB as in all churches, denunciation to the State authorities of some members by others also occurred.

66. Cf. above, IIC1c.
67. Freston, *Evangélicos na Política Brasileira*, 27.
68. Brandt, "Die Evangelische Kirche lutherischen Bekenntnisses in Brasilien."
69. Schünemann, *Do gueto à participação*, 107.
70. In Burger, *Quem assume esta tarefa?* 87–105.
71. Schünemann, *Do gueto à participação*, 113.
72. For the text in English translation, see Lissner and Sovik, *A Lutheran Reader on Human Rights*, 41-45.

While the increasingly progressive leadership could count on intellectual support from its theological school, which was soon to undergo a profound reform of its curriculum,[73] and on international support from politically sensitive development agencies, confessional bodies, and ecumenical bodies, its stance remained controversial among its members. Based on two empirical studies, one of which included about half of the active pastors at the time,[74] Schünemann concludes that only a minority of pastors and lay people adopted a critical stance towards "the socio-economic structure, attributing to the IECLB the task to conscientize in an active and participating way the marginalized and to denounce the injustices."[75] There are indeed no comprehensive empirical studies among the members of the church that could prove in a satisfactory way what their position was. But there is, except for the restricted statistical representativity of the studies, no reason to believe that the reality was different from what the partial studies show.

A word still on the country's first Lutheran president, Ernesto Geisel, who commenced the process of transition.[76] While he was always called *Alemão*, "the German," and had quite a Prussian posture in his appearance and attitudes, his being Lutheran does not seem to have had any decisive influence on his politics, and he did not maintain close contacts with the church.[77] In fact, little is known about his religious beliefs—Prien has called him "a distant Protestant,"[78] who would not deduce his political credo from "the" Lutheran doctrine of the two kingdoms, but "from the military doctrines of 'interdependence', 'continental' and 'national security','" protected by cooperation with the USA and the consequent fight against all tendencies seen as communist.[79] In any case, he had been baptized and confirmed by the IECLB, and his matrimony was celebrated by Rev. Ernst Dietschi in Estrela (Rio Grande do Sul), in 1940, his wife being the daughter of a Lutheran pastor.[80]

73. The reform, as indicated by Kirst ("A reforma do estudo—marca registrada da última década"), had as its goal to make the study more accessible to students with a Brazilian public formation, rather than a German-type classical training as offered by the church's "Pre-Theological Institute," and to allow for a more profound interaction with the context through "auxiliary disciplines" like sociology and psychology, through a practical semester and seminars of intensive study. The latter's themes and the whole reform was done in intensive collaboration between students and teachers, while student numbers rose steadily from 52 in 1965 to 125 in 1975, and 257 in 1985 (Schünemann, *Do gueto à participação*, 58). In his evaluation after ten years, Kirst concludes that the reform was "well succeeded" and that it "equipped the Faculty of Theology with a highly creative system of study, well based theologically, pedagogically, and ecclesiologically, adequate to the educational reality of the country, and apt for a theological formation at the same time solid and contextualized" (Kirst, "A reforma do estudo—marca registrada da última década," 59).

74. In Burger, *Quem assume esta tarefa?* 219–49.

75. Schünemann, *Do gueto à participação*, 118.

76. His father, Wilhelm August Geisel, had migrated to Brazil in 1883 and took roots in Estrela in the State of Rio Grande do Sul, an agricultural village where German was spoken and virtually all were Protestants. He later became a Brazilian citizen, changed his name to Augusto Guilherme and joined freemasonry. His mother was a daughter of the Lutheran pastor in the community. Ernesto was born in 1907, when they had already moved to Bento Gonçalves, to live in the midst of Catholic Italian immigrants.

77. Glauber Rocha, the famous filmmaker from Bahia, then exiled, had hope in Geisel, saying—to the Brazilian left's dismay—that "I think that Geisel has everything in his hand to turn Brazil into a strong, just, free country" and "The facts that Geisel is Lutheran [which probably is to be read as "German," i.e., well-organized, dedicated to work], and my birthday is on 14th March [in 1974, the eve of Geisel's inauguration as president], when I turn 35, make me absolutely certain that it is for Him [sic] to respond to the questions of Brazil speaking to the world. . ." in Gaspari, *A ditadura derrotada*, 402.

78. Prien, "Präsident General Geisel."

79. Ibid., 5. Geisel identified such tendencies in the IECLB's Faculty of Theology: "In a seminary in Rio Grande do Sul, in São Leopoldo, there was a lot of leftist infiltration, fostered by German pastors. Like many Catholic priests, they also exploit the problem of land reform, distribution of land and poor settlers," quoted in Dreher, "Reflexões sobre os Sessenta Anos," 64, without quoting the source.

80. Information related to me personally by Wilfried Hasenack, responsible for the Historical Archive of the IECLB

But Geisel seems to have assimilated values typically fostered in the German Protestant immigration community: hard work, commitment, honesty, and a Spartan lifestyle.[81] His father moved upward to become a clerk, and his two brothers, Henrique and Orlando, became Generals like Ernesto. Pastor President Karl Gottschald, who had baptized Geisel's daughter Amália, had a number of meetings with Geisel after 1974.[82] Regional Pastor Augusto Kunert, who would succeed Gottschald as Pastor President in 1978, appealed to Geisel in a statement to, as a Lutheran, "make his the church's preoccupation for the mass of the Brazilian people" for "peace, employment, sufficient livelihood and school education."[83] Literally, he said that

> we trust that General Ernesto Geisel will lead a government which is oriented wholly towards the Brazilian interests, so that history may in the future record the joy of the evangelical community, to have had one of their own in the Brazilian presidency, who did not deny his origin, but given to the Brazilians the good luck of an upright and respected office bearer.[84]

An ecumenical celebration with Regional Pastor Heinz Ehlert and Diocesan Bishop D. Gregório Warmeling was held on May 1, 1975 during Geisel's visit to Joinville.[85]

d) The IECLB today: Surviving in the Religious Market

The church's own summary of its position, as in the 2004 General Council, on celebrating the 180 years of the church's emergence with the first congregations being formed, is very positive:

> After 180 years since the emergence of our first congregations [. . .], we celebrate and emphasize that we are a Church of Jesus Christ in the country, inclusive, solidary and citizen [*cidadã*]. We have made our way engaged in favor of peace, justice and the integrity of all creation, practicing in our congregations mission, diaconia and public responsibility in favor of social inclusion and the overcoming of poverty and misery.[86]

Thus, the church is affirming that it has conquered its own citizenship and is engaged in solidarity for the citizenship of others, implicitly confirming the existence of the three struggles of citizenship mentioned above. But it is certainly exaggerated to state that it simply is so—although the debate over public issues might be less ideological and heated nowadays, not least because internal matters and indeed the struggle for survival in a competitive and ever more pluralistic religious market have come to the fore, it cannot be taken for granted that members agree on the church's political role, nor that the IECLB is overall really "inclusive" and "solidary."[87] We can, however,

in São Leopoldo.

81 Dressel, *Brasilien*, 181 calls him, apparently quoting a common saying, an "'authoritarian, Protestant-Prussian workmachine'; typically Protestant and ruler."

82. Schünemann, *Do gueto à participação*, 106. I could not find any precise information on these meetings. A document in the IECLB's Historical Archive in São Leopoldo (APGo 6/9) contains the reflection on Gal 6.2 given by Rev. Gottschald, who had long retired, at the celebration of the golden marriage anniversary of the Geisel couple on January 10, 1990, in Teresópolis (Rio de Janeiro). I would like to thank Wilfried Hasenack for his generous help in tracing this and the following archive documents.

83. Prien, "Präsident General Geisel," 5.

84. Ibid.

85. Document APGo 11/1/164 contains the program. The classification "APGo" refers to Gottschald's personal archive.

86. IECLB, *Mensagem do XXIV Concílio da IECLB*, Boletim Informativo [BI] 185/2004, 1.

87. Schmidt studied two socially rather different congregations in Rio Grande do Sul, Erval Seco and São Leopoldo, which identified a "preference for a more traditional parish life, although not without a certain openness toward the problems of the world around" (*Quand nous joignons notre voix au chant de la liberation*, 112), being that the poorer

notice a considerable consistency in the church's public statements, as we shall see, and certainly a clear retreat of "Deutschtum" since World War II.

Religious pluralism is not only a reality in society at large, but is reflected within the IECLB. There are different tendencies that compete with each other for members, theology students, the leadership's attention, and the like. In 1927, a pietistic mission started among German immigrants and their descendants, who had asked for help from the *Evangelische Gnadauer Gemeinschaftsverband* under the often used phrase from Paul's vision in Acts 16.9: "Come over [. . .] and help us." Thus, the "Evangelical Mission Christian Union" (*Missão Evangélica União Cristã*—MEUC) was founded and later started its own seminary in São Bento do Sul (Santa Catarina), meanwhile recognized by the IECLB for ministerial formation and also by the Ministry of Education for its Bachelor of Theology.[88] Under U.S.-American missionary influence, the 1950s saw the emergence of the "Encounter Movement" (*Movimento Encontrão*—ME), an evangelical (in its English and North American sense) tendency, which also maintains its own theological school in Curitiba (Paraná), recognized by the IECLB and in process of recognition by the Ministry of Education.[89] On the other side of the spectrum, the "Popular Lutheran Pastoral Action" (*Pastoral Popular Luterana*—PPL) maintains a progressive, socially and politically aware line. Somewhat in the middle is the "Martin Luther Community" (*Comunhão Martin Lutero*), which cares especially for the heritage of the Lutheran tradition. The most recent movement is the "Movement for Spiritual Renewal," commonly called the charismatic movement, which finally led to a schism in an otherwise fairly pluralistic and non-schismatic church, namely over the issue of rebaptism.[90]

The church's leadership has been giving increasing space to these movements, expanding freedom, but also depriving itself of a stronger influence and clearer theological leadership. Two factors were of central importance here: The structural decentralization in the fusion of regions and districts into 18 synods with a considerable amount of autonomy, implemented by the General Council in 1998, and the pluralization of theological formation by recognizing three schools rather than just one, with their specific profile, creating competition and dispersion over students in a church which has, at this time, ever fewer pastorates to staff. After a long period of growth, when many parishes were left unattended and graduates in practical training had to take care of the parish alone, there is now a saturation and stagnation that is reducing job offerings and, thus, student numbers.

Under the presidency of Huberto Kirchheim (1995–2002), who also saw through the restructuring, the church made an option to turn to the congregations and strengthen them or create new ones, under the "Church's Plan for Mission" (*Plano de Ação Missionária*—PAMI), whose motto reads

congregation (Erval Seco) tended to speak more freely about public issues, while "some persons of the PI [the Paróquia do Imigrante, in São Leopoldo] were visibly embarrassed by these questions." Another survey, based on 200 questionnaires from parish members in Porto Alegre, levied doubts whether it was really the members of the congregations who were more conservative or rather the clergy, contrary to what one would expect (Bobsin 2001). A more recent and more representative survey among 1,123 young Lutherans (14-24 years), was quite positive in its conclusion: "We understand that the influence exercised by the IECLB in the co-formation of youth identity, even if creating instable, diffuse and provisional relationships of interaction—competing with other cultural references and being situated in strongly pluralist and increasingly segmented contexts—are defining modalities of an emancipatory theological praxis and, thus, point to modalities of a critical conscience which foster the insertion and participation of the youth in social life, in ethical commitment towards the other, in the elaboration of social criticism and the transformation of human being" (Bobsin et al., "Sociabilidade juvenil").

88. Cf. http://www.meuc.org.br; http://www.flt.edu.br (last accessed on 7/28/2011).

89. Cf. http://www.me.org.br (last accessed on 7/28/2011).

90. IECLB, *Unidade*; *Batismo*.

"no congregation without mission—no mission without a congregation."[91] In this understanding of mission, diaconia and solidarity, but also evangelism, ecumenism, formation and administration are seen as intrinsic dimensions. Kirchheim also maintained a network of communication with a number of persons in congregations to better connect the church's leadership to them; it was called the Support Network for Mission (*Rede de Apoio à Missão*).[92] The missionary efforts continued under the presidency of Walter Altmann (2003–10), who also became the Moderator of the WCC's Central Committee in 2006. A special advisory group looks into the church's missionary action, together with a newly appointed mission secretary, and a National Forum on Mission was held in July 2006, in Florianópolis (Santa Catarina), which issued the "Campeche Document" as a report. Quoting the opening lecture by Altmann, the document considers the IECLB as a church in transition, where ethnic and regional arguments do not suffice, but persons need "reasons of conviction and passion to be and remain in the IECLB." The "face mission will have with the IECLB's confessional proposal" should be "propositional in its witness to the Gospel of Jesus Christ," rather than "anti-pentecostal" or "anti-catholic," which implies, if I read correctly, to seek being an alternative to most actors in the religious market: Not to be competitive, but missionary.[93] One of the main problems, clearly identified in the document, is the high dependency of missionary projects on overseas financing—which, of course, is not only a material problem, but indicates flaws in missionary theology and, not least, missionary engagement among the church's members. In my experience, confirmed by informal exchanges with ministers of various theological tendencies, the mobilization of human and material resources is much higher in evangelical than in more traditional, liberal, or even progressive congregations. It is, thus, not only or even primarily a result of the members' financial resources, but much more an issue of mobilization and commitment.

One of the certainly unusual—for the IECLB, probably less unusual for the general religious arena—but interesting fruits of the church's missionary efforts has been the creation of a new congregation in the Northern city of São Luís (Maranhão), of people who have no German ancestry, nor come from the South, but who were weary with their Pentecostal church(es) and looked for an ecumenically open church, finding the IECLB through the internet and making contact with its leadership, eventually joining the church, which sent two ministers to attend to the new congregation.[94]

2. DISCOURSE AND PRACTICE

For this part, the following documents are being taken into account: Normative and orienting documents, manifestos and declarations of General Councils, pastoral letters from the presidency and articles in the church's national monthly newspaper, *Jornal Evangélico*.[95] The order given here

91. IECLB, *Recriar e criar comunidade juntos*.

92. It would be interesting to research this material and see how these contacts worked and what the issues and positions were.

93. http://www.ieclb.org.br/noticia.php?id=8101 (accessed on 7/7/2007). Another minister, from the *Encontrão* movement, cited by the document, mentioned explicitly a concept of "integral evangelization which joins faith, diaconia, and citizenship."

94. See http://www.luteranos.com.br/articles/6885/1/Sao-Luis-Maranhao-a-proposta-evangelico-luterana-e-atraente-sim/1.html. The congregation was officially founded on December 11, 2005; http://www.luteranos.com.br/articles/6982/1/Nasceu-a-Comunidade-de-Sao-Luis-do-Maranhao/1.html (accessed on 3/27/2009).

95. This section was elaborated based on research carried out by Rodrigo Gonçalves Majewski, a member of the Assemblies of God and former student at our faculty (EST) in São Leopoldo, Bachelor of Law by the Federal University of Rio Grande do Sul (UFRGS) and now a Federal Prosecutor. He was my research assistant from 2003-4, on a scholar-

follows the hierarchy of documents as indicated by the document on "Unity: Context and Identity of the IECLB," adopted by the 24th Council in São Leopoldo in 2004,[96] with the addition of the newspaper articles. This document reminds the ministers (*obreiros/obreiras,* literally "workers"), who can currently be ordained for the pastoral, diaconal, catechetical, or missionary ministry, of the normative document on the ministry,[97] which suggests that they take the church with them as they act publicly for it: "installed in the field of work, the minister, in his pronouncements and attitudes, shall consider the Church as a whole, striving for its unity."[98] Although this was not said specifically as to statements on the issues under consideration in this study, but rather of potentially schismatic tendencies as from the charismatic movement, it is a way of linking up the ministers to the national church and its leadership, which then also has implications for the latter's pronouncements on public issues.

Since 2003, the church has also regularly issued "motives for intercession," explaining the issue at stake and suggesting a short formula for inclusion in the intercessory prayer, thus exploring a new way for the leadership to share issues of common concern with the whole church. The document on unity calls them "small pastoral letters of the presidency on diverse issues at stake in the life of the Church."[99]

A word is needed on the *Jornal Evangélico* (JOREV), which has been researched in the period 1980–2002.[100] It was planned to use this journal's articles to catch more voices than just those of

ship grant by the faculty. I am very thankful to him for his most competent research and for his helpful explanations on the Brazilian legal system. Much of the research material used here has been published in Portuguese as Sinner and Majewski, "A contribuição da IECLB." I would also like to thank the IECLB and the responsible person in the General Secretariat, Ms. Cerise Pahl, for their generous help in finding material from the archives. Along these years, a growing number of documents from the Presidency and the Councils have been published on the church's website, http://www.luteranos.com.br. Some texts by Pastor Presidents have been published as books: Brakemeier, *Por Paz e Justiça*; Kirchheim, *Novo jeito de ser igreja*.

96. IECLB, *Unidade,* 177f.

97. IECLB, *Estatuto do ministério com ordenação,* art. 27.

98. IECLB, *Unidade,* 178.

99. Ibid., 180. The majority of its themes touch on public issues: the war against Iraq (March 2003), the end of violence (April), the (political) reforms in the country (August), for the children (October) and the equality between men and women on the International Day of Non-Violence against Women (November), safety in traffic and the respect of laws (January 2004), Mission in Moçambique, after the cruel assassination of the IECLBs missionary there, Sister Doraci Erdinger (February), conflicts between farmers and indigenous "with respect to the rights of both" (June), the Olympic Games, for "peace and solidarity among the nations" (August), the (ecumenical) Decade to Overcome Violence, Elections (September), HIV/AIDS (November), the Tsunami victims (January 2005), the Ecumenical Lenten Campaign on the overcoming of violence (February), the Mission of the Church in Moçambique and the investigation on Sister Doraci's assassination (February), the drought in the South (March), for ethical and political integrity in public life (June, after the corruption scandal in the PT government became known), for persons with disabilities (August), reconciliation with truth and justice (September), the referendum for the prohibition of arms trade (October), the promotion of affirmative action (November), the assassination of the president of an IECLB community (April 2006), the promotion of a culture of peace and non-violence (May), the production of healthy food (June), the citizen participation of the church's youth (July), health matters (August), Persons with disabilities (August), peace and justice on the World Day of Prayer for Peace (September), and the elections in 2006 (September and October), "for a project for Brazil." See IECLB, *Motivos de intercessão da IECLB 2003-2006* for a full list. In Pastor President Altmann's second mandate (2007–2010), such "motives of intercession" have become much less frequent. The website lists only eight of these for 2007–2009 (January): http://www.luteranos.com.br/categories/Servi%E70s--%252d-IECLB/ Recursos/Vida-Celebrativa/Motivos-de-Intercess%E30/ (accessed on 3/28/2009).

100. The terminus a quo is given by the works of the master's thesis of Schünemann (*Do gueto à participação*), who researched the period from 1960-1975, and the bachelor's thesis by Weimer (*Aspectos da inserção da Igreja Evangélica*), who looked into the Councils and the *Folha Dominical/Jornal Evangélico* between 1968 and 1980. Although the focus of our study is on the period from 1985 onwards, it was necessary to fill the gap left open by these previous researches. A

the church's leadership. But this has been possible only in a restricted way, as shall follow from the journal's history as given by Fiegenbaum.[101]

> The JOREV was founded in 1971 as a result from the fusion of two earlier newspapers, the weekly *Folha Dominical* of the Rio Grande do Sul Synod, and the monthly *Voz do Evangelho* of the church in the state of Santa Catarina. Both had started to make their own newspapers by the end of the 19th century, when synods became organized and larger church units were, thus, formed, making communication a necessity. The Curitiba General Council (1970) had decided to install a Press Council (*Conselho de Imprensa*) to facilitate a better communication between the national church and the ecclesiastical regions, their districts and parishes, approved the fusion of the said newspapers and indicated the need to have a full-time professional working as the editor, to be paid by the income from subscriptions. The newly installed Press Council decided to issue a common newspaper every two weeks, with eight pages dedicated to the national church, four regional pages and four pages in German. Pastor Jost Ohler, a missionary from the Evangelical Church in Germany, would exercise the editorship, located in São Leopoldo at the domicile of Church Region IV, not too far from and not too close to the national church headquarters. According to Fiegenbaum, from the outset a number of conflict factors were implicit in the project: Regional differences (Rio Grande do Sul vs. Santa Catarina), historical differences (an 86-year-old vs. a 25-year-old newspaper), confessional differences (a more united and a deliberately Lutheran theology), economic differences (financing the journal), differences of professional competence (pastoral vs. journalistic) and, of course, struggles of power over this new medium of communication. A number of conflicts on journalistic independence, both in relation to the church leadership and the readers, many of which cancelled their subscriptions because of discontentment with the paper's progressive and political rather than "edifying" and "evangelizing" editorial line, followed in the late 1970s and early 1980s. In 1985, the Church Region that followed the Santa Catarina synod began to make its own newspaper again, called "The Way" (*O Caminho*), which exists till date. Not least due to an ever increasing financial crisis, the JOREV moved closer to the church headquarters and asked to be supported by it. In 1989, it became clearly the national churches' paper, using the church symbol in its logo, and in 1992 moved its offices to the church headquarters in Porto Alegre.

The crisis is not over yet, and one cannot say that the JOREV has truly become the recognized national church newspaper. Subscriptions are still on a low level, despite various attempts to increase its readership. Competition with *O Caminho* continues, as it does, since the churches' reorganization in 1998, with the synods' own newspapers. There is also a more journalistic magazine, *Novo Olhar*, published by the church's main editing house *Editora Sinodal* since 2004, which continues the JOREV's more progressive line and counts on many of the latter's authors. Still, between 1985 and 2002, which was the focus of the documentary research that could be executed for this study, the JOREV is the church's most national communication vehicle, and certainly the most outspoken on issues of politics and citizenship. Different from what I originally expected, though, it cannot be said to generally reflect the opinions of church members; rather, it reflects the strong opinions of a progressive intellectual elite in the church.

In what follows, I shall present and analyze statements on democracy and citizenship (a), land reform (b), economic and social criticism (c), human rights (d), and participation in public life (e).

---

database was mounted with all the relevant articles, registering a total of 874 files.

101. Fiegenbaum, *Midiatização do campo religioso*, 100–34. Ricardo Zimmermann Fiegenbaum is a church journalist, who defended this study as a master's thesis in the department of communication science at the Jesuit University (UNISINOS) in São Leopoldo.

a) Democracy and Citizenship

The IECLB spoke of citizenship already in its Christmas message in 1978, when it called for an amnesty—which was to be granted the following year (see above, IA1b). In a fairly bold language for the time—repression was still in place!—it said:

> In the last years, deep and painful ruptures have occurred in Brazilian Society. [. . .] Many citizens have suffered prosecution, imprisonment, been stripped of their mandates or banished, without the possibility of appealing to their legitimate right of defense. Multiple forms of violence have been unleashed, culminating in hijackings, torture and even assassinations. Their victims still today bear the physical, moral and professional consequences of the sufferings they had to endure. Thousands of fellow citizens are impeded to practice their citizenship, with all the rights and duties that stem from it.[102]

Understandably, the church has insisted more clearly on citizenship and democracy in the difficult period of consolidation after 1985, when Gottfried Brakemeier was in the church's presidency (1985–94). The relationship between church and politics was explained as follows in a pastoral letter of 1988:

> It is known that we find ourselves in a particularly difficult and decisive political moment. The Church of Jesus Christ is also affected by it. It cannot stay aloof of what is happening. It is inherent to it that it motivate the members to assume the share of responsibility which belongs to them. Political engagement, striving towards the common good, the defense of justice are mandates of God and a way to serve the people and the Creator. The attempt to shun this significant task to become culpable against the commandment of love, which has in political action one of its most efficient instruments. I believe that this should be a common premise of every Lutheran Christian. Injustice, corruption, violence and hunger in our country challenge Christian conscience and must necessarily translate into action for the victims of our society and a more just social order. As Lutherans, we are impeded to separate faith and politics. They are not separate, incommunicable things.
>
> In the same way, however, we must not confuse. This means, in the first place, that as Church and congregation, we cannot identify with a specific party. At the common base of the commitment to justice and the promotion of good, there must be space for adherents of all parties in the same community. There must be space for political discussion and the good competition of programs and proposals. This is what the democratic rules claim and what all want to see respected. [. . .] For this very reason, the Church must not be tied to a specific ideology, either. [. . .] In theory, neither capitalism nor socialism are bad systems; in practice, however, things are different. This is because the Church must claim ethics from all systems and all ideologies.
>
> The Lutheran position to neither separate faith and politics nor to confuse them, is difficult to practice. But it is the only way of preventing abuses. The separation, beyond its being a fiction, collaborates with the corruption of the political institutions and favors arbitrariness. The confusion, through ideological exclusivisms, destroys community and leads, ultimately, to a theocratic, authoritarian and legalistic regime. We should learn from Luther himself: he did not hesitate to raise his voice, pointing to the evils of his time. He was calling the attention of authorities and claiming structural changes. Luther was in no way an a-political person, but remained free in relation to the parties of the time, resisting the transformation of the Gospel into a political-social project. He knew how to distinguish between Church and State. He certainly committed errors. Even so, his proposal of avoiding both mixing faith and politics and divorcing them remains exemplary.

102. Boletim Informativo (BI) 57/1978, 1. As in the corresponding section of the previous chapter (IIC2), I shall cite documents only in the footnotes, unless they have been published specifically as books. For the BI, as the IECLB's official organ, its authorship is presupposed. For other texts, whenever possible, the author is indicated.

> In our Country, we need a new way of understanding and doing politics which has credibility, which prioritizes ethics and democracy and is based on competence. The Christian community has much to contribute to this.[103]

The message is very clear: Faith and politics are neither separate nor to be mixed, but distinguished, reflecting a moderate form of a "Two-Kingdoms Doctrine," in a use more in line with Luther's position as developed in his "Temporal Authority: To What Extent it Should be Obeyed" (1523) and "Whether Soldiers, Too, Can Be Saved" (1526), than with early 20th Lutheranism, which tended to a separation of the two with the consequence that obedience to secular authorities went virtually unquestioned.[104] At the same time, the Pastor President also seeks to steer clear of criticisms that pastors confuse the pulpit with a stage of political propaganda.[105] He thus seeks to preserve the church's proprium while at the same time stimulate its engagement in the world. The letter, in fact, leaves no doubt that such engagement is part of the Christian's and, thus, the church's calling, in fulfillment of God's commandment of love. The categories used to describe political engagement are quite similar to the Roman Catholic discourse: The "common good" and "justice" as main principles for its political ethics.[106]

This line of argument is being continued by general statements contained in a letter written in 1989, in view of the first direct presidential elections since 1960. The statement again—without naming it—recalls the "Two-Kingdoms Doctrine," and in a rather bold way at that: "Also politics is under the divine claim. It is not a neutral field, alien to faith, even though the Church cannot constitute itself as a political party or an ideologically defined group, but it inheres to it to publicly recall the will of God, valid for Christians and non-Christians [!]."[107] Further, the letter states that democracy in Brazil is frail and threatened, but that

> the democratic regime deserves a special commitment by Christians today. It offers the best chances to correct the social distortions and to overcome injustice. It values the citizen and simultaneously holds him responsible. Thus, it fulfils what the Bible says about the dignity of the human being in his quality of a creature loved by God. The democratic spirit [. . .] makes a bet on the maturity and responsibility of the voters. It does not subject them to ecclesiastical tutelage.[108]

Thus, democracy is clearly affirmed as the currently best and most adequate political system, valuing human dignity as attributed by God, which includes human responsibility. Again, this is in line with Roman Catholic thinking as shown above. It insists on the freedom of voters, with the church only generally orienting voters on their responsibility and the ethical and democratic qualities of a candidate to be voted on, but free of the tutelage of the church—a constant fear especially of the more educated in both churches.[109]

103. Brakemeier, Gottfried, *Relação entre Igreja e Política,* Carta Pastoral no. 9845/88, August 16, 1988; reprinted in Brakemeier, *Por Paz e Justiça*, 16–19.

104. LW 45,75–129; LW 46, 87–137; cf. below, IIIA5.

105. In those years, a good number of Lutheran ministers stood for political office, cf. JOREV 6/1990, 1; 11/1990, 16.

106. "Peace with justice" was also a current formula, see for instance the news on Pastor Carlos Möller's lecture to the XV General Council in Rio de Janeiro, JOREV 19/1986, 10. He developed the theme in connection with the WCC's conciliar process on Justice, Peace and the Integrity of Creation (JPIC); cf. Niles, "Justice, Peace and the Integrity of Creation."

107. Brakemeier, Gottfried, *Eleições,* Carta Pastoral no. 11229/89, August 24, 1989.

108. The latter affirmation probably refers, critically, to the Pentecostals' politics of indicating candidates; see Freston, *Evangélicos na Política Brasileira*, and below, IIE2.

109. Less educated and less socially privileged members would rather just do what they think is best than voice a

After the failure and impeachment of the first directly elected presidency after the military regime, at the end of 1992, in view of the upcoming plebiscite of October 1993 on the form of government (cf. IA1c), the pastoral letter called "Law and Power" states that

> the critical moment [. . .] demands the responsible exercise of citizenship and democratic mobilization.
>
> 2. The Church of Jesus Christ performs an important role in this process. It confesses itself heir to the prophetic tradition of the Bible, profoundly committed to peace and justice, which puts it at the service of society. The grave threats which hover over the Brazilian people cannot leave the Churches apathetic. They owe them their alert and appeal to reaction. 'God is a God not of disorder but of peace' (1 Cor 14.33). To collaborate in the perception and implantation of whatever serves peace (cf. Lk 19.42) constitutes the noble and inalienable political mandate of Christians, by the way in partnership with all persons of good will. [. . .]
>
> 7. For the good of society, then, it is urgent to retrieve the primacy of law over power. [. . .] It is inherent to the State to strive for every citizen to have the support [*amparo*] of the law and to be a fulfiller of the duties implied in it. To such end must power serve. It is the only way of legitimizing it. Power becomes useful only when it submits itself to law and lends itself to it as an instrumental arm.
>
> 8. [. . .] We invite the congregations of the IECLB and her sister churches to unite with corresponding movements. We mention, particularly, the 'Movement for Ethics in Politics', the 'Action of Citizenship Against Misery and Hunger and for Life', among other initiatives.[110]

The text ends on a bold note: "To ally itself with this [sc. movement] and to collaborate in the re-establishment of law and justice—indispensable presuppositions for social peace —is a commandment of Christ Himself." [111]

In his report to the 18th General Council in Pelotas (Rio Grande do Sul), in 1992, Pastor President Brakemeier had already insisted on the relationship between faith and politics, stating that "the Church is co-responsible for the good of society. [. . .] The Christian Congregation is called to contribute for peace in society."[112] While it does not follow a specific party or ideology, it must "be in solidarity with whoever is suffering injustice." But it shall do so according to its "primary mandate, which is the witness to the work of God and the learning of faith, hope, and love."[113] Here there is a clear affirmation that the church's action in public space comes from the inside out and not vice-versa, i.e., it is a task derived from the church's primary calling.

Finally, a pastoral letter written in 1994 for the federal and state elections is perhaps the best summary of the church's position on citizenship, in the line already indicated. It stated:

> The exercise of citizenship is a right and duty given to human being by God. It documents his or her dignity and is derived from it. This is why democracy deserves the absolute preference among the political systems. It is the only one to guarantee to the members of society the full participation and co-responsibility for political issues. [. . .] The thesis of political incompetence of the Christian community must be rejected. [. . .] Political issues have religious relevance, and the Church and its believers have a political mandate.[114]

---

critique of the church's supposed or real tutelage.

110. Brakemeier, Gottfried, *O direito e o poder,* Carta da Presidência no. 17817/93, November 23, 1993; reprinted in Brakemeier, *Por Paz e Justiça*, 50–52.

111. Ibid.

112. Brakemeier, Gottfried, *Relatório do Pastor Presidente,* XVIII Concílio Geral, 1992, 6.

113. Ibid.

114. Brakemeier, *Por Paz e Justiça*, 42. See also Kunert, "Aspectos da relação IECLB e estado," 226, quoting Pastor

It is striking that, to some extent, such statements are even bolder than the CNBB's official statements, as they do not shun away from stating that "the Church" also has a political mandate, not "only" its believers—in a apparently different emphasis from a report in 1992, when the Pastor President stated that "it does not inhere to the Church to strive for political power. It inheres to the lay member to assume the political cause."[115] Given that the Lutheran tradition defines the church as the community of believers (CA VII), however, this appears more as a kind of explication than the postulation of two different actors. Still, the tone is not only clear, but authoritative, with a lot of prescriptive elements like "the only one," "deserves absolute preference," "must be rejected," and the like. This seems to be reflecting both the personal style of the Pastor President at the time, who invested in theological clarity and discipline, and a politically insecure situation, with great disparities of opinion among the church members, seeking to steer a clear line and giving direction to the church's profile. In any case, theses statements leave no doubt on the church's political role, although it must not adhere to a particular party or undertake party politics.

Another element that comes forth with clarity is the ecumenical dimension, mentioning the sister churches as well as social movements. It is important to remember here that the IECLB had joined CESE in the 1980s, an ecumenical body reaching out to social movements and channeling funds from abroad to their small projects; Pastor President Brakemeier had been the CONIC president from 1986 to 1990, as well as LWF president from 1990 to 1997, and a long-standing member of the bilateral dialogue commission with the Roman Catholic Church. Thus, ecumenism and confessional identity always went together for him, which made the presidency a link between the inter-confessional and international dimensions of being the church and its internal matters. In this period, the IECLB was probably more clearly an ally of the ICAR and the Brazilian ecumenical movement than ever, which rendered it respect and recognition among them.

b) Land Reform

Being a church formed, traditionally and still to a large extent, by small farmers, the IECLB has always been aware of the difficult situation these settlers lived in. Schünemann mentions the "Evangelical Academy,"[116] which existed in the IECLB from 1963-67 and followed the model of German lay formation, in order to "orient, inform and assist, so that the members would become conscious members which knew themselves responsible as Christians for the world in which they live, contributing in this way toward the congregation's understanding itself as a community in the world and for the world."[117] One such academy functioned—in a decentralized way, through meetings in different places—in the Rio/São-Paulo area, geared more towards issues of the urban-industrial society, and another in the South, centering on communitarian work. In the rural areas, it brought together a good number of farmers in the "Settler's Days" (*Bauerntage*), and sought to develop projects among farmers, stimulating the formation of co-operatives, the improvement of farming techniques and the modernization of work methods, and the construction of rural schools. In this, it paralleled the "Gaucho Agrarian Front," promoted by the ICAR, also in its rather developmentalist proposal and the objective of neutralizing the activity of the politicized rural unions and the "Movement of the Landless Farmers" (*Movimento dos Agricultores sem Terra*—MASTER),

Rodolfo [Rudolf] Saenger's dictum: "A democracy working badly is ten times better than any dictatorship working well."

115. Brakemeier, Gottfried, *Relatório do Pastor Presidente,* XVIII Concílio Geral, 1992, 6. This formulation recalls starkly the CNBB's position.

116. Schünemann, *Do gueto à participação*, 77–81.

117. Ibid., 77.

which is not to be confounded with the Landless Workers' Movement (MST), created in the early 1980s. In the midst of the more and more heated revolutionary trends of the time, initiatives like the rural boarding school in Teófilo Otoni (state of Minas Gerais), funded by agencies from Europe and the USA, were meant to give a technical formation to the sons of small farmers, not to transform society, but to "set up a signal in a society which is in full process of transformation."[118] Based on research, the principal problems of underdevelopment—like high mortality, high birthrate, insufficient nutrition, analphabetism, and fatalism as an attitude—were identified and tackled by courses provided by centers like the "Rural Center Dr. Albert Schweitzer" in Boa Vista do Herval (state of Rio Grande do Sul), whose founder was a German missionary doctor who wanted to create a kind of "mini-Lambarene." Another project was the "Indigenous Mission of Toldo Guarita" in Tenente Portela (also in Rio Grande do Sul state), which created a bilingual education and health project, later expanded to train farming instructors. If I read the data given in Schünemann correctly, I can conclude that at that time there was a certain openness among Brazilian Lutheran businessmen to support such projects personally and financially, as long as they did not embrace "communism" and did not have a too outrightly political, transforming, or even revolutionary agenda. The later more political stance of the church resulted in a polarization and considerably restricted such support, making projects even more dependent on outside funding—a situation that persists till this day.

In 1978, the Center of Support for the Small Farmer (*Centro de Apoio ao Pequeno Agricultor*—CAPA) was founded and started its work in Santa Rosa (Rio Grande do Sul) in 1979, funded till today by German church aid agencies, continuing the high dependency on outside funding for social work.[119] Its goals were to help farmers stay on the land rather than moving to the cities, stimulate their participation in activities that would improve their conditions of life, such as creating cooperatives and joining unions; create awareness for farmers' rights; and give technical support.[120] According to one of its promoters, Rev. Werner Fuchs, the CAPA became a good example for combining technical assistance and socio-political organization.[121] Increasingly, resistance against the use of agrochemicals and the promotion of ecological production has become a pillar of CAPA's work. CAPA took on a work of mediation between the farmers and their ecclesial, political, and economical environment, not restricting itself to a "theology of contestation," but believing that "creating conditions favorable for the transfer of knowledge and techniques (in a perspective of solidarity), personified in an exercise of citizenship, may lead to an emancipatory, autonomous and anti-excluding social practice."[122]

Another aspect to be mentioned is that, when the waves of migration started, promoted by the military government to populate the vast areas in the Amazon region and to have workers for the huge projects it pursued there, Lutherans also migrated from Rio Grande do Sul to the North and from Espírito Santo to the West, mainly to the state of Mato Grosso and to Rondônia, then a federal territory. In Rondônia, where the IECLB's presence has recently been studied,[123] the first migrants arrived in 1967. It brought with it conflicts with indigenous peoples, unknown during the immigration to Espírito Santo from Germany, as that land had already been "cleared" of

118. Schünemann, *Do gueto à participação*, 79n83.

119. Vanderlinde, *Entre dois reinos*, "CAPA: o jeito luterano."

120. BI 59/1979, 5.

121. Vanderlinde, "CAPA: o jeito luterano," 150f.

122. Vanderlinde, "CAPA: o jeito luterano," 155. In his generally very critical evaluation of the IECLB's projects, Sobottka, *Kirchliche Entwicklungsprojekte in Brasilien*, gives good marks to some of CAPA's projects.

123. Link, *Luteranos em Rondônia*.

indigenous. From 1972-78, the IECLB sought to attend to the migrants by sending ministers and creating social projects, funded by agencies abroad. From 1979 onwards, as Rogério Link shows in his Master's dissertation, a new "brand" of ministers went to the new areas of colonization on their own wish, seeking to live out a new way of being the church, quite in line with the CEBs' project.[124] They recognize, in hindsight, that this created tensions with the congregations (as with the church's leadership). The new ways sought by the ministers, which created a new liturgical vestment, the *bata* (a beige vestment which went down only to the knees, in exchange for the common black *talar*), insisted on having all services in Portuguese (they refused to hold any in German), sought to implement a social awareness geared towards transformation and worked on issues of land reform (with the CPT) and indigenous peoples (with the newly created COMIN, see below, IID2c). Central theological terms were "service" and "emptying."[125] All these clashed with the migrants who were seeking continuity rather than change in order to settle in new, unknown, and hostile lands. One church member wrote to his pastor complaining about what he saw as a wrong way of being the church, and I reproduce it here as it is one of the unfortunately few testimonies by a church member I could get hold of:

> Forgive me to say that but our church together with the Catholic is giving false witness against the neighbor. She [sc. the church] does no longer preach the Gospel of Peace and joy and love to the neighbor it only preaches destruction and death and hunger disheartening for the workers but of what we live and if we want to speak only of authority as the money of the poor, then let us look also to our Church which lives in the same way than all people it helps to pay the studies of the pastors and a car to drive and the maintenance and travels and little work we see. They come together 2-3 times to study how to speak badly of the rich and governments, and the work for God is little. Our children don't learn anymore the Christian living as it should be that if we cease to preach the Gospel of the Good news and only dishearten the people how and whom will receive salvation.[126]

Another experience of this kind was the engagement of a Lutheran pastor from Germany, Rosa Marga Rothe, who was in charge of the IECLB's small community in Belém (state of Pará). She played a decisive role in the ecumenical movement, which emerged precisely around the imprisonment of two French Catholic priests in the early 1980s because of their stance on land conflicts.[127] Rothe later left the congregation to dedicate her work to the defense of human rights, acting in social movements, and became an *ouvidora* (a kind of ombudsman) in the state government of Pará.[128]

124. This was noted by the Center for Migratory Studies (grown out of the ICAR, according to Rogério Link's information related by an e-mail received on 5/31/2007), which stated that "for those who believe in the force of the little ones, Rondônia offers a hope which flourishes from the birth of a new church and the seeds of organization which many migrants carried with them. In the prelature of Ji-Paraná, [. . .] the CEBs are a priority. And within them, the CPT, the work in the area of health, etc. United in this work are both Catholics and Lutherans (IECLB)" (in Link, *Luteranos em Rondônia* 146).

125. Link, *Luteranos em Rondônia*, 158.

126. In ibid., 150f. I have reproduced the style by leaving out commas as does the original, but have not attempted to reproduce the spelling errors. They show the difficulties of a humble farmer with restricted schooling to express himself in ways considered correct, but the message becomes very clear.

127. Silva, *As origens do movimento ecumênico na Amazônia paraense*.

128. She has retired in the meantime and has been replaced in this function by her third successor as pastor of the congregation, Cibele Kuss.

In 1979, the IECLB talked about land reform as a preferential activity, affirming that the issue had been mobilizing the church for a good number of years.[129] Some pastors of the IECLB had already been working with the CPT at the time.[130] But it was in the 1980s that the theme came to receive its highest emphasis, especially when "Land of God, land for all" (*Terra de Deus, terra para todos*) became the church's yearly theme in 1982.[131] At the end of the 13th General Council, the IECLB adopted a document and a letter to the congregations in which it defended the popular associations, the CAPA, movements in the spirit of non-violence, the Land Statute, the CPT, a model of simple life, land reform and the continuation of debates on the subject within the IECLB.[132] At the same time, the incipient construction of the hydroelectric of Itaipu, where settlers were dislocated, gave rise to serious concern.[133]

There were specific proposals on the table to limit the size of property. Werner Fuchs, at a panel during the 13th General Council in Hamburgo Velho (Rio Grande do Sul), considered it "anti-evangelical and immoral, when someone had a profession or his living guaranteed, to also be a landowner or even have a manor [*sítio*] for leisure."[134] At the 15th General Council, in 1986, a motion was put forward to orient the members of the IECLB not to own any rural propriety beyond 500 hectares or beyond a size sufficient for the subsistence of them and their families.[135] This motion, however, which had the CAPA's support, was not adopted by the Council, who felt that it was sufficiently attended to by the sending of a popular amendment to the Constituent Assembly (see above, IC3), which claimed land reform and, in a generic way, the "social" use of land.[136]

All along the 1980s and at the beginning of the 1990s, the JOREV published articles on the land issue, mainly on land reform and the MST, clearly defending both of them.[137] A number of pastoral letters were written by the presidency. In 1985, Pastor President Gottfried Brakemeier manifested his preoccupation with the conflict between settlers and indigenous in Chapecó (Santa Catarina),[138] and in 1987 he wrote a letter to reject a report published in the (conservative) daily

129. BI 59/1979, 8.

130. Cf. above, IIC2b.

131. The church began to have yearly themes in 1976, inspired by the ICAR's Lenten campaigns, which had begun in 1964 and turned to highlighting public issues in 1973. In the IECLB, more theological and public issues alternated, with an emphasis on public issues between 1976 and 1993. On the specific theme on land reform, the IECLB was earlier than the ICAR, who dedicated the Lenten campaign to this issue only in 1986. For the IECLB with its predominately agricultural base and the challenge of the rural exodus to the cities, where many members were lost ("the big cities are the IECLB's cemetery," as many said), this was a particularly pressing issue. Conscientization and mobilization of congregations, apparently till this day the most difficult element of the yearly campaigns prepared by specific interdisciplinary teams, whatever the issue at stake, were a constant goal of the themes of the year (some of which were valid for two years). I would like to thank Silvio Schneider, former communication secretary of the IECLB and now executive secretary of the Lutheran Foundation for Diaconia (e-mail of June 1, 2007), for his valuable information, and Carlos G. Bock, advisor to the IECLB's Presidency, who kindly sent me the list of themes.

132. IECLB. *Atas do XIII Concílio Geral*, 1982, annex 53, 1-2; mensagem às comunidades, ibid., annex 54. A survey carried out during the Council shows how divided opinions were among those present, in Vanderlinde, *Entre dois reinos*, 237-43. The outcome is, thus, a kind of middle, negotiated position.

133. Rui Bender, "Agricultores pedem um preço justo por suas terras," JOREV 3/1980, 6f. The article criticizes the poor compensation paid by the company for taking the farmer's lands.

134. IECLB, *Atas do XIII Concílio Geral*, 1982, annex 34, 4.

135. BI 100/1987, 7f.

136. BI 102/1987, 7.

137. Sinner and Majewski, "A contribuição da IECLB," 35–39.

138. Gottfried Brakemeier, *Jejum de solidariedade em Florianópolis/SC*, Carta da Presidência, s.n., September 30, 1985.

newspaper *Estado de São Paulo*, which claimed that the church was financing an allegedly armed movement (the "Regional Commission of the Afflicted by Dams"), saying that the accusations were false, while the support for the movement was necessary. He clearly stated that the IECLB would not support violence of any kind.[139] A declaration by the Directing Council of the IECLB on the struggle for land, published in 1989, affirmed that "never will violence be the means capable of bringing about social peace," and stated that it never "fostered the occupation of lands or armed resistance. It has, however, drawn attention to the despair of those which have grown weary of empty promises and see themselves thrown into abandonment." The declaration also affirmed that "this is not about an ideological or political-partisan option. It is love, the supreme commandment of Jesus Christ, which demands the inconformity with evil and the search for solutions that guarantee the daily bread for all people."[140]

In another pastoral letter, of 1991, Pastor President Brakemeier communicates that the IECLB is to support land reform "with new vigor." This followed up on a motion approved by the 17th General Council in Três de Maio, held in 1990, which insisted that the IECLB should, again, press for land reform, which indicates that statements and action on the matter had somewhat "cooled down." The letter sought to demonstrate the land situation in the country, and to inform and exhort the members, calling them to join the struggle for this issue, in constant debate with other sectors of society, including the MST.[141]

In 1999, finally, the presidency wrote a letter on transgenic plants, seeking to alert its members about the potential dangers inherent in this type of alimentation, raising objections as to their potential damages to the environment, and the economic domination of seeds patented by multinational companies, among others.[142]

In sum, the IECLB has consistently sought to awaken its members' conscience and consciousness on the situation of land in Brazil, and has stimulated their participation in, prayers and engagement for this cause. It (morally) supported social movements like the MST, but always defended non-violence. Through these manifestations, it has contributed towards a struggle for citizenship of farmers, both of their own flock and beyond, and has sought to intervene concretely with actions through its CAPA.

c) Economic and Social Issues

In relation to the economic and social situation in Brazil, a great number of declarations are to be found in the JOREV[143] and the reports of the Pastor President, especially under Brakemeier's presidency (1985–94). Rather than concrete proposals—except for land reform, as mentioned, which was also seen in this wider context of the economy—these were critical analyses of the situation, especially as it created and maintained poverty in large sectors of society and promoted the rural exodus and migration, contributing to the rapid process of urbanization. Among others, the presidency's declarations criticized capitalism as unjust, but also recognized dangers in socialism.[144]

139. Gottfried Brakemeier, *Sem-terra têm aula de guerrilha*, Carta Circular no. 13.516/87, December 11, 1987.

140. BI 111/1989, annex.

141. Gottfried Brakemeier, *Reforma agrária*, Carta Pastoral no. 16462/91, December 2, 1991.

142. Huberto Kirchheim, *Alerta sobre transgênicos*, Carta da Presidência, no. 19721/99, August 18, 1999.

143. During the 1980s, this occurred regularly in the column "Black in the White" (*Preto no Branco*), which no longer exists; previously, p. 2 of the JOREV was dedicated to such issues; Sinner and Majewski, "A contribuição da IECLB," 39.

144. Gottfried Brakemeier, *Relatório do Pastor Presidente*, XVI Concílio Geral, 1988, 5.

Together with CESE and CONIC, where the IECLB had become a member and even was a co-founder (CONIC), the presidency also mentioned the external debt issue and the policies of the Bretton-Woods-Institutions, the International Monetary Fund (IMF), and the World Bank.[145]

Throughout the 1980s and 1990s, the JOREV printed reports on the situation of workers, especially the formally employed. Many were published in May, around Worker's Day. Capitalism was also a constant issue of criticism, with titles like "capitalism imposes itself with violence on the people."[146] More specifically, the planned—and meanwhile stranded—Free Trade Area of the Americas (FTAA–ALCA) became an object of strong criticism, both in the JOREV and the 23rd General Council in Santa Maria do Jetibá (state of Espírito Santo), where a motion was put forward and carried

> which proposes that the IECLB, together with CONIC and CLAI, conduct seminars and forums of debate in the sense of taking to the population the interests under discussion for the creation of ALCA, and that the IELCB, together with CONIC and CLAI, conduct seminaries and forums of debate with authorities and institutions which are involved in the issue of the Amazon region and the knowledge in the sense of safeguarding the Brazilian patrimony, during the negotiations for the creation of ALCA.[147]

The already mentioned pastoral letter on transgenic plants, although speaking on an issue related to the land, in fact carries a mainly economic preoccupation because of the patents of seeds and related pesticides being in the hands of U.S. firms like Monsanto, thus further enhancing the economic dominion of the U.S.A. Although public and environmental health are mentioned, the main emphasis is on the economic aspects rather than on health and, indeed, biodiversity is not seen in its own right.[148]

Finally, the *Manifesto of the Chapada dos Guimarães*, drafted by the Synodal Pastor of the Southeast Synod (São Paulo, Rio de Janeiro and Minas Gerais), Rolf Schünemann, and adopted by the church's 22nd General Council in Chapada dos Guimarães (Mato Grosso) in 2000, forms a major document on the social and economic situation in Brazil and the world, and provides a theological foundation for this critique.[149] In the first part, the world economic system is being criticized, with data on the flow of capital, foreign debt, migration, violence, degradation of working conditions, and the like, under the heading of Romans 12:2 "Do not be conformed to this world." In what follows, the church confesses its hope ("always ready to . . . account for the 'hope that is in you,'" 1 Peter 3:15), and goes on to founding its critique theologically based on its belief in the Trinity. Under the heading of 1 Peter 4:10 "serve one another with whatever gift each of you has received," the manifesto concludes by rejecting ideologies that support accumulation and concentration of riches, adoration of capital, economic models that are not sustainable, individualism that

145. Ibid., 40; the same issue comes up in the Pastor President's report to the Councils in 1990 and 1992.

146. This was the theme of the XV Camp on Sharing Together (*Repartir Juntos*), an initiative which emanated from the WCC's El Escorial Conference, held in 1987.

147. IECLB, *Atas do XXIII Concílio,* 2002, Décima Segunda Sessão, 10.

148. This was confirmed as I served as an adviser on bioethics in 2005 for the seminar of a group of ministers from one of the synods of the IECLB in Rio Grande do Sul. An agronomist, who has been working for CAPA for a long time, exposed the dangers for the soil and biodiversity, but the debate focused on the economic domination of the (foreign) multinationals and the economic marginalization of Brazil—despite the latter's economically strong position, when looked at as a whole. It struck me that the environment and biodiversity did not come up as an argument in its own right.

149. IECLB, *Manifesto da Chapada dos Guimarães.*

is concerned solely with self-satisfaction, proselytism between the churches, and religious intolerance, here also attributed to a capitalist market ideology.

The line adopted by the IECLB's leadership is similar to the language and content of civil society in general, as with the ICAR. This, however, says little about the member's position on the matter, which one would expect to be quite controversial, especially among businessmen. What is more worrying, however, than this very fact, is the apparent absence of any major dialogue with them, although there are initiatives to change that, and certainly local dialogues, similar to the assistance some projects received already in the 1960s from Lutheran businessmen.[150] A perception of the changed context, both politically and economically notwithstanding the enduring and appalling misery of large portions of society—should also inform the language of statements, which still tend to reflect a dualistic perception of dependency and exploration.

d) Human Rights, Violence, and Ecology

The IECLB has spoken out on a variety of occasions against the violation of human rights. This goes well together with IID2a, as citizenship and human rights mutually imply each other. Here, I refer to specific human rights violations, of specific groups of society. Among the principal preoccupations we can cite discrimination against women, black people, indigenous, and homosexuals; and (non-)violence, the environment, and peace. Usually, these declarations were published through pastoral letters and reports in the JOREV. They tended to alert for the present situation in the country, to offer an adequate Christian position, theologically grounded, and making suggestions for members to act.

The IECLB has, thus, defended the liberation of *women* from oppression in a *machista* (sexist) and conservative society. The JOREV has been giving wide space to this issue since the 1970s, including reports on feminist theology. A recent text affirmed that

> we want our women alive, making their own choices, being attended to with dignity and quality. We don't want to weep over violated bodies, silent and killed by the public policies of a neoliberal government which defends a so-called 'humanitarian capitalism'. What we really need is a lot of politicized mother-fraternity [*mater-fraternidade*], which begins in our groups, congregations, parishes, co-operatives and which wants to enter into partnership with whomever also struggles for life and justice.[151]

According to reports from women and youth, they suffer social, physical, economic, and emotional violence; more precisely, low salaries, low quality of life, and submission to husbands and to the *patrão* [employer]; they are subject to unwanted flirting and harassment, bad treatment, and exclusion, among others. They are exploited by society when they execute the same work as men, but at a lower salary. In rural areas, apart from caring for the household, women accompany their husbands in their productive activities, while it is the men who mediate between the family and the external world.

150. Cf. Schünemann, *Do gueto à participação*, 78. There is a group of Lutheran businesspersons (*Grupo de Empreendedores Evangélico-Luteranos de Porto Alegre*—GEELPA) meeting monthly for lunch and discussion in Porto Alegre, to which preliminary results of the present research were presented in May 2004 at their invitation. Among some, resistance against he IECLB's statements and the political line taken therein, especially against the support expressed for the MST, was still very noticeable, while others, especially younger businessmen seemed to be more laid-back, and one affirmed he liked the new emphasis given to "negotiation. I had said that it seemed a new phase in the IECLB's struggle for citizenship had begun, in which new alliances and negotiation between former adversaries would be possible and necessary.

151. Cibele Kuss, *Consolidando nossos direitos e insistindo na vida,* JOREV 653/2002, 13.

Not only in the world, but also in the church, women are discriminated against. They often sustain life in the congregation, but are excluded from leadership offices.[152] Explicitly, the issue of citizenship is raised:

> In Genesis 2.23 we are shown that woman is made of a piece of Man and thus likewise "created in the image of God" as man. If, then, women and men are partners before God and in relation to creation, this cannot mean that this partnership is restricted to the area of faith, but that it is a total partnership which implies citizenship. In the light of the Gospel, there is no space for discrimination. Before God and society we have the same value.[153]

The church has also spoken on the situation of *black people* in Brazil. In 1988, a pastoral letter spoke out against discrimination, and the church exhorted to be "a pioneer" in this field "of a mentality that corresponds to our being in Jesus Christ":

> In the same way we should be worried by the discrimination of which the black person is a victim in our society. Even if overcome by law, this discrimination is still a reality. Jesus Christ requires non-conformism with a mentality which violates the black person's dignity. School, health and other public services are rights of the black person, as they are of every Brazilian citizen. The same goes for salaries, employment and leadership offices. In God's world we are partners one of another. It is necessary to put this into practice.[154]

Four years later, in 1992, a resolution of the 18th General Council affirmed:

> 2. The identification of this horrible tendency has the Evangelical Church of the Lutheran Confession in Brazil, by resolution of its 18th General Council, make public a declaration of its inconformity and alert. It inheres to the Church of Jesus Christ, committed to the service of life and engaged in widening the spaces of faith, hope and love, to denounce what destroys peace and violates the rights of God. Among the great threats of these times is, not least, racial obsession. . .
>
> 9. The Evangelical Church of the Lutheran Confession in Brazil invites its congregations and institutions, its sister churches and all segments of Brazilian society to combat the racial expressions present in its own ranks. Fraternal partnership between races, cultures and ethnic groups also in Brazil remains a goal to be pursued, despite the undeniable successes achieved in the complex process of the integration of differences. As Christians and citizens, we have the duty to oppose the signs of racist thinking and to collaborate with the elimination of factors which produce it or make it opportune. The Bible says: 'God saw everything that he had made, and indeed, it was very good' (Genesis 1.31). Human being is forbidden to despise what God has clothed with such dignity.[155]

It is probable that this document reacted, on the one hand, to the memorials of the 1992 arrival of Columbus in what became Latin America, beginning a period of violent cultural clashes and a strong sense of superiority among the invaders. Indigenous peoples, but later also Africans

152. In principle, however, all offices are open to women, as is the ordained ministry, with the first woman studying in the regular course in 1966 (Dreher, "Reflexões sobre os Sessenta Anos da Escola Superior de Teologia," 65), and the first being installed in congregation in 1976 (Reily, *História Documental do Protestantismo no Brasil*, 394f.). While about half of the students of theology are female today, they are still in a minority in the ministry; cf. Kliewer, "Ex-alunos e ex-alunas da EST."

153. *Cidadania é compromisso dos dois sexos*, JOREV 606/1998, 13.

154. Gottfried Brakemeier, *Carta às comunidades contra a discriminação racial,* Carta Pastoral no. 4689/88, May 3, 1988.

155. Gottfried Brakemeier, *Deus não é racista,* Declaração da Igreja Evangélica de Confissão Luterana no Brasil, no. 18386/92, December 9, 1992.

brought over to the continent as slaves by the Portuguese, were the main victims of this attitude. A reference to South Africa, which at the time was finally opening up and headed towards free and comprehensive elections and the end of the apartheid system, might also be heard in the text ("also in Brazil").

In the same line, the manifesto "500 years of Brazil: Public Manifestation of the Evangelical Lutheran Churches," issued on the occasion of the memorial of 500 years of Brazil's "discovery," in 2000, the IECLB speaks of slavery as a tragic episode in Brazil's history and of forgiveness and confession of sins.[156] This confession became explicit in the declaration of the 24th Council, held in São Leopoldo in 2004, when the church remembered the 180 years since the first German settler's arrival in Brazil: "We have to recognize [. . .] that in many places a sentiment of cultural superiority over other ethnic groups emerged and prospered, especially over the indigenous and African [Brazilians]. We are till today victims and constructors of prejudices against whomever is different."[157]

The defense of *indigenous people* also became an important issue, covered widely by the JOREV, not least to diffuse the work carried out by the Council of Mission among *Índios* (*Conselho de Missão entre Índios*—COMIN). As indicated earlier, also the IECLB suffered with conflicts between settlers and indigenous, given that it had made it a point to defend both of them, and thus had to be very careful in not to take sides easily. The church's general vision was that the indigenous peoples were "under the serious threat of extinction by the aggressiveness of our society, which restricts, more and more, their physical and cultural space, which is indispensable for their survival."[158] The issue was constant in the biennial reports of the Pastor President to the General Council during Brakemeier's tenure, and the IECLB apparently joined the ICAR's fight for the Yanomami people against the gold miners,[159] issuing a manifesto in favor of the Yanomami people at its 17th Council, in 1990.[160]

On *homosexuality*, one of the most difficult issues, with generally negative statements by churches as to ordination and same-sex unions, the IECLB took a moderate line, seeking to stimulate debate and reflection. Following a seminar on the issue, a pastoral letter published in 1999 recognized the existence and the discrimination against homosexuals was a reality, within and outside the church. What is new is that the debate has come into the public only recently. A consensus was stated as to the justification by faith, which is needed by all persons regardless of their sexual orientation, and that the love of God is extended to all. At the same time, the letter identified a strong antagonism between those who considered homosexuality to be condemned by the biblical texts, and thus advocating "correction" for homosexuals, while others said that those texts should be read in the light of their specific context, and that homosexuality was immutable. The letter left the matter open, but called for dialogue, being that "the theme must not be treated under pressure,

156. BI 170/2000, annex, 5f.

157. IECLB, *Unidade*, 187f. The text also recognizes, explicitly, that "in the year in which the Jewish community commemorates its 100 years of immigration in the state of Rio Grande do Sul, we acknowledge with deep regret that in the period when National Socialism reigned in Germany, we were not totally immune against the influences of the ideology of Arian racial superiority," a rather understating affirmation, but possibly as far as the Council felt it could go to have the text accepted.

158. Gottfried Brakemeier, *Jejum de solidariedade em Florianópolis/SC*, Carta da Presidência, s.n., September 30, 1985.

159. Cf. IIC2c, in 1989.

160. IECLB, *Atas do XVII Concílio Geral*, 1990, annex 59.

but in solidarity, love and fraternal dialogue."[161] A study group was installed and, based on its findings, the presidency issued a statement in 2001 on the possibility of the ordination to the ministry of homosexuals. While it stated, again, that the matter was highly controversial within the church, it called for "pastoral sensitivity" in relation to homosexual persons, pointing to their situation of great suffering and discrimination. This should not happen in the congregation. But given the importance of "a special care in sexual behavior" of ordained ministers, seeking to avoid scandals and divisions in the congregation, a person (hetero- or homosexual) who gives reason for such unrest could not exercise a meaningful ministry in the church. Thus, under the present circumstances, while not negating the gifts God gave them and their profitable use for serving the Gospel, "there are no conditions for a *practicing* homosexual person to assume the public exercise of the ecclesiastical ministry in the IECLB."[162] Within the Brazilian church context, this is a moderate statement, as it leaves open the possibility of a future change in policy. But since it distinguishes—as do other churches—between practicing and non-practicing homosexuals, essentially calling for chastity, it reinforces the tendency for homosexuals to hide their sexual identity and practice, and prevents them from having positive models of ethically sound sexual behavior.[163]

The issue of *violence*, already mentioned in relation to land reform and indigenous rights, has also been a constant preoccupation of the IECLB, including its 17th Council in 1990, which issued a statement on the Yanomani people. Generally, violence was seen as a social problem, resulting from the socio-economic situation and its disparities. In 2002, a manifesto on "Violence in the Country" described the reality of violence in Brazil and suggested actions to overcome it, like the "retrieval of the conscience of the dignity of life," the "construction of peace and social justice," the "correct and efficient combat of criminality," envisioning the qualification of police, avoiding the use of (meaningless, aggressive) violence to combat crime, and the end of impunity.

> The prophet [Habakuk 1.2-4] spoke more than two thousand years ago, but he seems to have thought of the situation we are experiencing in Brazil today. [. . .] The cases of assaults and assassinations are piling up and hit even bearers of political mandates. In addition, there is the frequent lack of training and incapacity of the police forces to inhibit violence, to disclose the crimes committed and to arrest the criminals. [. . .] There is corruption on all levels and in all sectors. The population feels unprotected and does not trust the authorities. Like the prophet, they cry to heaven: 'We can't bear the violence any more! How long, Lord?' [. . .] In this context, the IECLB raises her voice in view of the growing violence against human dignity and life. We are convinced that it is necessary to retrieve the fundamental notion that, because of being the image of God, all and every human being is inviolable and has the right to live in a dignified and secure manner.[164]

Such statements were encouraged both by the continuously precarious situation of violence, both criminal and police, in Brazil, and the ecumenical decade to overcome violence, called by the World Council of Churches from 2001–10, parallel to the UN Decade for a Culture of Peace and Non-Violence for the Children of the World.[165] As indicated, among the reasons cited in the

161. Huberto Kirchheim, *Acolhei-vos uns aos outros, como também Cristo nos acolheu para a Glória de Deus (Rm 15.7)*, Carta da Presidência, no. 16844/99, May 19, 1999.

162. BI 173/2001, annex 5, 17, emphasis mine.

163. Cf. Musskopf, *Homossexuais e o Ministério na Igreja*.

164. Huberto Kirchheim, *A violência no país. Um manifesto em favor da vida e dignidade humanas*, manifestação da Presidência e da Conferência dos Pastores Sinodais, São Bento do Sul/SC, March 22, 2002; http://www.luteranos.com.br/articles/8201/1/A-Violencia-no-Pais---2002/1.html (accessed on 6/6/2007).

165. See http://www.overcomingviolence.org (accessed on 6/6/2007). In Brazil, the campaign is coordinated by the

manifesto for this situation are, besides the consumption and trafficking of illicit drugs, poverty, unemployment, and the "extremely unjust" distribution of income, which is associated with "economic policies" that favor capital, profit, and "not rarely, external interests." Furthermore, "consumerism" was creating a notion of "having" as the main goal and spreading envy among the people. The text insists that, contrary to the mainstream where one has to "merit" one's image, being created in God's image is a gift given to all, irrespective of their merits. This does not mean that the person is free to sin, but, rather, reconciled to God and to humans, being able to come out of their heart's being *incurvatus in se*, as Luther had described it in his commentary on Romans.[166]

On the worldwide level, the church had spoken out against the use and production of antipersonnel landmines, and joined the national campaign in this line to sound the church bells in 1999.[167] In 2003, the church joined the worldwide critique of the war against Iraq, in a joint declaration with the Evangelical Lutheran Church of Brazil (IELB), the church linked to the Missouri Synod, which was accompanied by a pastoral letter for the communities of the IECLB, calling them to prayer for peace.[168]

The preoccupation for a balanced *environment*, the preservation of the forests and a sustainable development have been an issue for the IECLB since the 1970s. Often, it has been linked to the way of agrarian production in large land holdings with the use of synthetic fertilizers and pesticides and the infliction of damage to the environment. Many reports on this were published in the JOREV in the 1980s and 1990s. The issue entered the church's guidelines for development programs, where they recommend considering the ecological dimension in the process of approval.[169] In 1988, the 16th General Council of the IECLB in Brusque (Santa Catarina), following the burning of enormous rainforest areas, issued a "Manifesto in Defense of the Amazon Region." Initially, the church, "fulfilling its public responsibility," reminds the State that there are "constitutional determinations" to be fulfilled by "legal means which halt the destructive process in the Amazon and other ecologically vital regions," including educational campaigns, the promotion of social justice, the protection to the habitat of indigenous peoples and the sensitization of the international public opinion for its co-responsibility for the destruction of region, namely "through foreign debt, the cause of the need for exportation at any price." The manifesto also remembers that "ecological crimes are equivalent to crimes against Godself. God's creation is sacred, a life condition for human being. It is important to learn anew that we are part of this creation: With it we live or perish."[170] The mentioned "public responsibility" is included in the church's "missionary and evangelizing responsibility," ecumenically inserted, as the document calls on "our sister churches in the country and abroad." In the same line, the "Manifesto against Deforestation" was issued by the Presidency in May 2000. This very short document speaks out against the "ecocide" in a law proposal that would permit deforestation to an even higher extent, and calls on the politicians to reject it and, instead, to adopt the proposal of the National Council on the Environment. The church describes itself as "partner in the dialogue

---

CONIC, whose longtime executive secretary was a Lutheran, Rev. Ervino Schmidt (in office 1992-2006), http://www.conic.org.br (accessed on 6/6/2007).

166. LW 25:291.

167. Huberto Kirchheim, *Manifestação da IECLB contra o uso e a fabricação de minas terrestres antipessoais,* Carta da Presidência, no. 12274/98, December 22, 1998; Walter Altmann [Acting President], *Felizes os que trabalham pela paz. . .! (Mt 5.9a)*, Carta da Presidência , no. 20667/99, September 17, 1999.

168. Walter Altmann, *Carta Pastoral às comunidades da IECLB*, no. 66185/03, March 27, 2003.

169. BI 150/1996, annex.

170. "Manifesto em defesa da Amazônia," in IECLB, *Atas do XVI Concílio Geral*, realizado nos dias 18–23 de outubro de 1988 em Brusque/SC, annex 55.

on issues that concern the well-being of the Brazilian people and the preservation of the environment, and moved by the theme of the Ecumenical Lenten Campaign 2000, adopted by our church: 'Human Dignity and Peace. . .'" thus linking up with other churches and with its own theme, which I suppose was meant to render it recognition both inside and outside its boundaries.[171]

e) Participation in Public Life

The church's action in politics was done through letters sent to authorities (the president, governors, mayors, city councilors, the judiciary, etc.), asking for justice, the fulfillment of the government plans, and formulating expectations to the newly elected while congratulating them, among others. As an example, I cite the letter sent by the Pastor President to the newly elected President Fernando Henrique Cardoso, congratulating him on his election and announcing that the church would be praying for his government, which includes the church´s expectations from government and committing it to its promises.[172] A letter sent by the Pastor President to the mayors and city councilors elected in 1996 wished them well on their victory and called them to a responsible mandate, which should bring development to society and to the municipality.[173] The 22nd General Council, held in Chapada dos Guimarães (Mato Grosso), in 2000, called on the government to intensify actions to promote dignity and peace for the Brazilians.[174]

Another common way of acting was through pronouncements and official declarations, be it on the Councils, or through the Pastor President in a pastoral letter, where the church would position itself on issues of social interest, as we have seen in the previous sections. It is interesting to note here the period of "flexible moratorium" imposed on the church by then Pastor President Augusto Kunert in 1983/84, attending to criticism voiced against the church's progressive position.[175] This is one of the few moments when the more conservative voices of the IECLB are becoming public through the leadership's reaction, showing that the leadership's position was not shared by all.[176] Kunert, himself quite progressive, affirmed that it was necessary to allow for self-questioning. This implied asking whether the congregations were able to take on the church's public responsibility at the same pace as the Presidency and if the church was really equipped to give opinions and contribute in social, political, and economic issues. The church should, thus, be protected from being weakened, preventing people from thinking that the church had a negativist attitude of the matter and leaving the 'experts' to have more space in the church's media. This did not mean that the church stopped its pronouncements altogether. But their frequency, especially under Brakemeier's presidency, shows how controversial the issue continued to be, and some phrases make this explicit: "There has been an awakening in our Church with regard to the political responsibility of

171. Huberto Kirchheim, *Manifesto contra o desmatamento*, Carta da Presidência no. 29240/00, May 17, 2000.

172. Huberto Kirchheim, *Carta ao Presidente da República Sr. Dr. Fernando Henrique Cardoso*, Carta da Presidência no. 19369/94, December 23, 1994.

173. Huberto Kirchheim, *Felicitações e votos de bênçãos*, Carta IECLB, no. 3867/97, April 30, 1997.

174. Carta destinada ao Presidente da República Sr. Dr. Fernando Henrique Cardoso, in IECLB, *Atas do XXII Concílio Geral*, 2000, annex 24.

175. Augusto Ernesto Kunerto, *Relatório do Pastor Presidente*, XIV Concílio Geral, 1984, 6f.

176. About a decade earlier, a similar conflictive situation becomes visible in professor Walter Altmann's inaugural lecture on October 14, 1974, where he mentions the tensions between (as extreme positions) those who say the church has its own task to foster faith, and to stay away from political engagement, and those who dissolve faith into politics. Aware of the contemporary stalling between evangelicals (in the Anglosaxon sense) and ecumenicals, marked by the 1973 Bangkok World Mission Conference for the latter and the 1974 Lausanne Conference for the former, he called for a "technical stop" rather than a fervent activism, in order to "locate ourselves where God really wants us, at the foot of the cross and within the world"; Altmann, "A crise da identidade eclesial e a inconformidade de Cristo," 293.

Christians, hailed by some, deplored by others. In some cases, this has led to flagrant tensions, a reason not to stop working on this important question."[177]

Pastoral letters suggested that congregations make space to discuss "the political commitment of Christians," and to invite political candidates, namely Protestants, in order to hear their proposals and the dialogue among them, and transmit to them the "congregation's expectations and the exigencies of Godself."[178] The 1992 letter on elections affirmed that "ethical duty imposes the need to cast a responsible vote," namely:

1. To privilege candidates of proven moral integrity and administrative competence.
2. To reject the purchase of votes through personal favors and mere electoral gifts.
3. To insist on the presentation of programs and measures by whomever aspires to a public office.
4. To examine the credibility, the authenticity, as well as the commitment to social justice on the side of the people who dispute the offices.
5. To claim from whomever was elected the fulfillment of promises and the good exercise of the mandate. We judge that to cast a blank vote is no solution. Neither are apathy or political disinterest. Under the Evangelical-Lutheran perspective, to assume responsibility for the public cause is a demand of God and a way of worshipping Him.[179]

Pastor President Walter Altmann's letter on elections in 2006 is particularly significant, as its author assumed the presidency precisely when Lula became president of the Republic, and stood for reelection in the same year, each representing the progressive sector in the church and society, respectively, and had to show they could represent the whole church or country. Thankfully, different from Lula, Altmann did not have to face charges of corruption and mismanagement. Joining the critique of many, Altmann, who does not only speak of elections, but of a "project for Brazil," started affirming that "a great part of the Brazilian people's hopes in a government and democratic institutions committed to social justice and human dignity have been frustrated. A grave ethical crisis is hovering [*se abala*] over the Nation."[180] He perceives that mistrust against politics and its institutions is strong and can easily lead to abstention or casting a blank vote. Against this, he reminds the Lutheran voters that "elections are part of the history of our congregations," and *a fortiori*, important for the country, thus linking up internal and external, ecclesial and political elections. The act of "voting consciously" is described as part of Christ's discipleship, so voting is mandatory, albeit in a critical way, examining candidates, their reliability, programs and financing. Apart from voting, the Christians' task is to participate "in popular movements, trade-unions, NGOs, municipal councils (on health and education, for instance)," motivated by the promise of "new heavens and a new earth, where righteousness is at home" (2 Peter 3.13).

The JOREV regularly published articles on public issues, related also to the elections. A series of articles in 1982 (decisive elections, as seen above, IA1b), brought information on the parties' programs, giving emphasis, in the case of the PT, to its program of land reform—of course always a decisive issue for the IECLB.[181] In 1983, a number of articles explored Luther and

177. Brakemeier, *Por Paz e Justiça*, 16.

178. Ibid., 18.

179. Gottfried Brakemeier, *Eleições*, Carta Pastoral no. 13136/92, September 4, 1992.

180. Walter Altmann, *Por um projeto para o Brasil,* Carta Pastoral no. 121, January 7, 2006, 1.

181. JOREV 16/1982,1.6f.

politics.[182] According to an article in 1984, the church council pronounced itself favorably to the "diretas já" campaign.[183]

Thus, the IECLB has been speaking out regularly and consistently on public issues and sought to foster the political participation of its members, based on its clear affirmation of citizenship and democracy, Christ's commandments and discipleship, the eschatological promise and, not least, the alignment of internal and external democracy.

3. THEOLOGICAL ELEMENTS

In order to present the IECLB's history of conquering its own citizenship and becoming engaged in the struggle for the citizenship of all, I have gone through documents, mainly from the leadership of the IECLB, that is the General Council, the Directing Council and the presidency, as well as articles in the JOREV. I have also cited the few empirical studies and evaluations available. On this basis, I shall now take up the theological elements contained therein and present them according to the items already used in the previous chapter (IIC3): The theological foundations of democracy and citizenship (a), the relationship to the State (b), to society (c), and between political and ecclesial citizenship (d).

a) Foundations of Democracy and Citizenship

As seen in the previous section (IID2a), democracy and citizenship are clearly affirmed in their importance and—in the case of democracy—declared to be the best and most appropriate political system. The main theological elements are human dignity, the common good, and then discipleship and "Christ's commandment" or "God's mandate," in a generic sense *(Gebot)*. Although the content of such commandment and mandate is seldom made explicit, it grounds human action in God's will and Christ's example and his commandments to love and serve. Such service is understood as being for all, not only for oneself or the church's members, and the church thus cannot and must not eschew its public responsibility. Pastor President Kunert[184] based such service in the central concept of Lutheran theology, justification by faith, a faith that "seeks communion" and "knows itself involved with the brothers." Christ came precisely to save the lost (Luke 19.10), "God so loved the world that he gave his only son" (John 3.16), that faith becomes concrete in love for the neighbor (Matthew 22.37–40) and that faith is responsible according to the new commandment (John 13.34). This is to live out the Gospel contextually, given that "the person's life is interconnected with the lives of other persons," which should orient the church's preaching. Throughout his text, he maintains that Christ is Lord over all, the human being in his/her totality and also church and State, so that "the State, the Government, Politics belong to the responsibility of the evangelical [in the sense of *evangelisch*] citizen."[185]

182. JOREV 22/1983, 1; citing, among others, Luther's saying that politics is everything from shoes to good government. More precisely, Luther said, in his Small Catechism, on commenting the fourth petition of the Lord's prayer: "What then does 'daily bread' mean? Answer: Everything included in the necessities and nourishment for our bodies, such as food, drink, clothing, shoes, house, farm, fields, livestock, money, property, an upright [*frumm*] spouse, upright children, upright members of the household [*Gesinde*], upright and faithful rulers, good government, good weather, peace, health, decency, honor, good friends, faithful neighbors, and the like." Book of Concord, *The Confessions of the Evangelical Lutheran Church*, 357.

183. JOREV 8/1984, April 15, 1.

184. Kunert, "Aspectos da relação IECLB e Estado," 228f.

185. Kunert, "Aspectos da relação IECLB e Estado," 242. In a strong affirmation, broadly covered by the JOREV (22/1983, 1.6-8), Church Historian Martin Dreher (1984) spoke on "Lutheranism and Political Participation" in a Cycle

"Political engagement, striving towards the common good, the defense of justice are mandates of God and a way to serve the people and the Creator. The attempt to shun this significant task is to become culpable against the commandment of love," said Pastor President Brakemeier in his 1988 letter on the Church and Politics.[186] There, church or faith and politics are seen in the same way dialectically inter-related as church and State.[187] This is certainly a somewhat reduced view, as it does not take into account the difference between the State and society, namely as represented through civil society, probably a consequence of the earlier dual antagonism under the military regime.[188] Later, however, as we have seen and shall cite again (IID2a; IID3c), the church declares itself an ally of other churches and movements.

Another important element is the value given to freedom. Kunert, speaking during the *abertura* under President Figueredo, stressed the importance of a growing conscience of the democratic regime among the church's members "because democracy is the system which contains respect for the human person, for the freedom of the person and of society itself. [. . .] In its prophetic task, the Church must announce to the Christian congregation, to the world and to the State that freedom is a feature of the 'Regnum Dei.'"[189]

Although freedom is not named in the 1989 pastoral letter, democracy is affirmed as the currently best of systems because "it values the citizen and simultaneously holds him responsible."[190] This is only thinkable presupposing freedom of action and decision as given to an adult citizen, and indeed the letter mentions a "bet on the [sc. voters'] maturity and responsibility." This goes well into the need for interpersonal and institutional trust, including trust in the voters (see below, IIIA1). It also echoes the Protestant principle of the priesthood of all believers, where there is no ontological difference between Christians and citizens, nor between lay people and their ordained ministers. More on this will be said in chapter IIIA below, based mainly on Lutheran insights.

b) Church and State

The Christological emphasis mentioned above can be seen both in Luther and in Karl Barth, whose theology had influenced church leaders and theologians such as Gustav Reusch, Ernesto Th. Schlieper, Augusto Kunert, and Walter Altmann. Although Barth had strongly criticized the "Two-Kingdoms Doctrine" because of its submission by some to the political ideology of the Nazis—abuses that were rejected in the formulations of the Barmen Declaration—they saw no need to reject it altogether.[191] Kunert affirmed, in his programmatic lecture at the Faculty of Theology in São Leopoldo:

> They [sc. church and State] are different entities, but simultaneous for the person. [. . .] We cannot . . . separate the relation church and State in a spiritual and a political (earthly) sphere,

of Discussions on Luther promoted by the Federal University of Rio Grande do Sul (UFRGS), in 1983, 500 years after Luther's birth. He recalled Luther's writing to the *Christian Nobility of German Nation* (LW 44:115-217), claiming the need for *Besserung*, which for Dreher is more than reform. After stating that the Lutherans who came to Brazil were "a-political," he concludes that they are so no longer, citing some of the documents presented above, IID2. Such engagement is not only the believers', however, but the church's.

186. Brakemeier, *Por Paz e Justiça*, 16.

187. Cf. below, IID3b.

188. Cf. above, IB3.4.

189. Kunert, "Aspectos da relação IECLB e Estado," 227.

190. Gottfried Brakemeier, "Eleições", Carta Pastoral no. 11229/89, August 24, 1989.

191. See Kunert, "Aspectos da relação IECLB e Estado," 224f.; Altmann, *Luther and Liberation*, 69–83. On the doctrine and Barth's critique, see below, IIIA5.

> as if there were not, for the citizen, a communication between the two spheres. [. . .] Luther, to use today's language, within a contextual reality, protested against the State's totalitarianism, protested and raised his voice against the State's intention to want to dominate all spheres of human life, in pretending to totally dominate Man.[192]

He concluded that, whenever the State reaches its limits, the church must protest in exercising its "prophetic" role. However, it must not forget that it also must know its own limits. He based his argument on CA XVI and XVIII, which preach subordination to the magistrates and the laws (limited by the *clausula Petri*, Acts 5.29), and the use of the free will. Furthermore, he cited Luther's writing on secular authority.[193] In a self-critique, he affirms that the IECLB had "enclosed" itself and stayed away from "Brazil's public and political life" because of a false interpretation of CA XXVIII, unduly separating the sacred and the profane and living a "real quietism."[194]

According to Prien, writing in 1977, "the activity of the ECLCB was not determined by any explicit reflection on Luther's thinking concerning the church's place in secular structures."[195] The doctrine was, thus, not used explicitly, not even in a separating way and stressing the State's autonomy as in Germany. But if the church did not actively follow such a theology, it followed it by implication, in a way that had it lack any strong element of criticism, be it against the German or the Brazilian State at the respective time. Rather, such criticism was provided to those who held it by Barth's theology and the Barmen Declaration. A reading of the Two-Kingdoms Doctrine through Barth's theology, then, as well as referring to Luther's writings enabled Altmann[196] to affirm that "the so-called two kingdoms can be distinguished regarding their tasks and their means, but they overlap in time and space. Furthermore, they have a common foundation—God is the Lord of both—and a common goal—human well being."[197] Like Gottfried Brakemeier in his pastoral letters, and the leadership in general in the period analyzed, Altmann tends to refer to Scripture and to Luther with his practice rather than to Lutheran doctrines developed in the confessional tradition. The reference, then, is more Luther than Lutheranism, possibly in an attempt similar to the one practiced by Liberation theologians to return to the sources rather than their magisterial or confessional interpretation.[198]

Liberation theologians have tended to understand the doctrine as useless or even antagonistic, but as "an essential part of the task of theology is to reflect dialectically on this historical process [sc. marked by antagonisms, conflicts, and transformations, in which Christians participate through

192. Kunert, "Aspectos da relação IECLB e Estado," 224f.

193. LW 45:75-129.

194. Kunert, "Aspectos da relação IECLB e Estado," 228.

195. Prien, "Identity and Problems of Development," 192.

196. Altmann, *Luther and Liberation*, 71.

197. At the already mentioned event at the UFRGS, in 1983, where Martin Dreher held his lecture, Altmann spoke on "Reign of God in the Church and in Politics," and said that "the so called 'two kingdoms' differ in attribution and means, but cover each other in space. [. . .] The State limits [. . .]the Church as a social institution (for instance in issues of property). The Church proclaims God's will to the State (for instance criticizing its arbitrariness or calling it to political, economic and social transformations)." JOREV 22/1983, 7. Altmann's view is based, to a large extent, on Duchrow's seminal work (*Christenheit und Weltverantwortung*).

198. It is, in this view, Lutheranism that lost Luther's political drive and courage; while returning to his *ipsissima vox* makes it possible to retrieve his critical stance, even if one has to avoid, then, some of Luther's more problematic positions, as in the peasant's war; see for instance Dreher, "Luteranismo e participação política"; Fischer, "Luther in Brasilien." An important sign of this interest for Luther is the excellent edition of his works, translated from the *Weimarana*, with introductions and helpful historical footnotes, which has by now reached ten volumes. It is edited jointly by the IECLB and the IELB's Commission on Luther's Works.

their experience and faith] and on the political praxis of Christians within it," a dialectics that finds a grounding precisely in Luther's work.[199]

One of the important aspects here is that the two kingdoms (or, rather, regiments, *Regimente*) are to be distinguished, but not separated precisely because God in Christ reigns over both of them. This is the reason why Brakemeier could say that "also politics is under the divine claim. It is not a neutral field, alien to faith [. . .] it inheres to it [sc. the Church] to publicly recall the will of God, valid for Christians and non-Christians."[200] This is, of course, the church's perspective, where respect for non-Christians and their differing view seem to be understated. Even more so, the IECLB could be accused here of implying a vision of Christendom. Of course, Luther was thinking in such terms, but he had paved the way for a more restricted action of the church by not allowing that it should surpass its proper tasks. At the same time, the State was to guarantee the free exercise of religion, which, as is well known, resulted historically in the rulers' decision on the religion of their people and not (yet) in a real religious freedom.

Ironically, the ICAR is less bold in their statements at this point. But the mentioned document correctly states that from a Christian perspective, Christ is Lord for both regiments, and they are thus more of a distinction in the attribution of tasks than a real separation. Although Luther presupposes Augustine, his distinction does not totally correspond to Augustine's two *civitates*, as Luther's distinction is less sharp and underlain with theological value than the *civitas dei* vs. the *civitas terrena* or *diaboli*. For Luther, Christians indeed belong to both regiments, and the distinction is not used to separate those who love God from those driven by *superbia*.[201] Again, it is in this sense compatible with Barth's concentric view of the Christian community and the citizens' community, where Christians are also citizens, while the contrary is not necessarily true. And, as we have seen, the church indeed defines its action from the inside out: It contributes to "peace in society" and is "in solidarity with whoever is suffering injustice" precisely because it does so according to its "primary mandate, which is the witness to the work of God and the learning of faith, hope, and love."[202] In this sense, the churches' action in the public sphere is also seen as part of its mission, as indicated already in the Curitiba Manifesto and made very clear by the PAMI missionary plan.[203]

Thus, the relationship to the State can be called a "critical-constructive one."[204] In a situation with legal separation of church/religion and State, and a growing religious pluralism, one cannot think of the two kingdoms or regiments as if one were still in a situation of Christendom. But it seems to me also exaggerated to submit the church to the State as does Pauly.[205] It is true that the State sets the legal framework for the action of churches and organized religions—which it does with extreme reserve, as we have seen, seeking to impose only a minimum of demands.[206] But as the churches, with their specific Christian motivation, come forward to contribute to politics in

199. Altmann, *Luther and Liberation*, 71. The same question was posed by Roman Catholics in the SOTER Congress, in my view grounded on a misunderstanding of the said doctrine; cf. my exposition in Sinner, "Religião e transformação no Brasil."

200. Gottfried Brakemeier, *Eleições*, Carta Pastoral no. 11229/89, August 24, 1989.

201. Cf. Lienemann, "Zwei-Reiche-Lehre," 1410.

202. Gottfried Brakemeier, *Relatório do Pastor Presidente*, XVIII Concílio Geral, 1992, 6.

203. IECLB, *Recriar e criar comunidade juntos*.

204. Cf. 82, who at the time did not believe the time in Latin America had come for such a type of relationship. In a personal statement to the author twelve years later, however, he conceded that the situation had changed sufficiently to make it possible.

205. Pauly, "Sociedade civil e igreja."

206. Cf. above, IIB2.

a critical and constructive way as part of civil society, there is no simple submission, but mutual relationship, as is the case with civil society as a whole, expressed more and more in partnerships (cf. IB). What remains, however, as a challenge to all churches from the "Two-Kingdoms Doctrine" is that it implies restriction also on the churches' part—not to interfere unduly with its power into politics, an important reminder especially to churches holding a lot of power and those seeking it.

c) Church and Society

While it seemed, initially, to position itself simply vis-à-vis the State, the IECLB has later made clear its insertion into the ecumenical movement, by quoting its "sister churches" and institutions like CONIC and CESE. The 1993 Pastoral Letter on "Law and Power" clearly states that "we invite the congregations of the IECLB and her sister churches to unite with corresponding movements. . ."[207] The church also declares herself at the service of society, as "heir to the prophetic tradition of the Bible, committed to peace and justice," in a "partnership with all persons of good will," echoing an expression common to the ICAR. The church is "co-responsible for the good of society" as the president's report to the 1992 General Council states. [208]

Thus, the critical-constructive position mentioned earlier is here inserted into a network of churches and movements with similar goals. Although there were and are Lutheran politicians, the church has never supported them as such, even if it called to invite them and accompany them. It has also, more clearly than the ICAR's progressive sectors, shunned away from supporting any party, even indirectly through its electoral criteria, although a good number of ministers and theologians have joined the PT. As stated earlier, others have joined the land struggle together with the CPT. It is also in this area that the IECLB has probably most effectively contributed to social transformation, through the CAPA, in a practice that went beyond mere *assistencialismo* (paternalistic welfare creating dependency)and also beyond mere statements. More recently, the Lutheran Foundation for Diakonia (FLD) is also seeking to maintain a professional and effective support for concrete, transforming projects, in collaboration with similar organizations like CESE and DIACONIA, where the IECLB is a full and participating member. A serious problem—as for many NGOs in Brazil—is the continuing dependence on overseas funding, which is difficult to overcome when domestic donations are not easily made, both through excessive bureaucracy[209] and restriction among donors for lack of funds or other priorities for their destination.

The fact that there are persons from the IECLB and related institutions representing civil society today, like the president of the National Council for Social Assistance, who won the election against the CNBB candidate and remained in office until 2008, is a sign of trust over against a church that has never had power in overall society, but is also not proselytizing like the Pentecostals and, furthermore, stands for a high level of education and professional competence. It also tends to be well organized, as proven recently in holding the 9th Assembly of the WCC in Porto Alegre, where most local executive posts were held by Lutherans.

207. Gottfried Brakemeier, *O direito e o poder,* Carta da Presidência no. 17817/93, November 23, 1993.

208. Gottfried Brakemeier, *Relatório do Pastor Presidente,* XVIII Concílio Geral, 1992, 6.

209. To make a donation, the donor must not only make a bank deposit, but also send in a copy of the confirmation slip so that the donation can be traced by the church—an element inherent in the banking system, although improvements are slowly being made. There are also restrictions as to the possibilities of tax deduction, another lack of incentive for donors.

d) Political and Ecclesial Citizenship

Of the churches analyzed in the present study, the IECLB most directly views ecclesial and political structures as having a very close relationship, both being organized democratically. Given the royal priesthood of all believers (1 Peter 2:9) through baptism and the church's constitution as the congregation of believers, there is no reason for more than functional differences between them. While it is true that faith matters cannot be subject to majority votes, it is still true in the IECLB that even procedures to verify doctrinal correctness of ministers are democratically organized, i.e., through lawful and accountable processes with inclusion of lay people at all stages. There is no reason why, on principle, the citizen should act differently as a church member and as a member of society, even if the two citizenships are by no means identical. Quite to the contrary, the church insists that faith orients all areas of life, while the church's message has to be credible to the inside as to the outside. In 1981, Pastor President Kunert stated that "the IECLB must maintain presently [for itself] that its public action cannot be different from its internal action. It has the duty to announce the Gospel of Jesus Christ, valid for the Christian congregation as for the whole of society."[210] The 2006 letter on elections and the country's "political project," issued by Pastor President Altmann, begins with referring to the experience of voting acquired in the church, and extending from there into voting in municipal, state and federal elections. In fact, historically, the IECLB has had a long experience in democratic organization, given that the immigrant communities had no other way than to organize themselves and provide for their schooling and pastoral assistance, even if through so-called "pseudo-pastors" without theological training. This does not mean that authoritarian elements were always absent, or that the church has not become quite pastor-centered in the meantime, but there are still democratic and lawful procedures to be followed, and presbyteries have a sometimes strong notion of their power in decision-making. Since it is the congregation that pays the minister, it has a direct means of power over him or her. The structure as a whole is bottom-up, with a great deal of autonomy in the congregation or parish, passing through the synod up to the General Council and the church's executive. Thus, it has a high potential to contribute to the formation of citizens conscious of their rights and duties and able to stand up for them. On the other hand, it remains de facto an exclusive church in that it has not been able to overcome its restriction to the German immigrants and their descendants, remains largely white, middle-class, well educated, and "Southist," or forms fairly homogenous rural communities. While it has never had a mass appeal, and is unlikely to achieve one, it can make an important difference in specific key positions, and its traditional moderation could be useful in an ever more competitive religious arena.

210. Kunert, "Aspectos da relação IECLB e Estado," 242.

E. The Assemblies of God

The Pentecostals do not have a social policy,
they are a social policy.
Jeffrey Gros[1]

Religion should not be used for politics.
Cardinal Paulo Evaristo Arns[2]

PENTECOSTAL CHURCHES ARE PART of the most remarkable shift in Christianity in the 20th century: While the center of gravity of Christianity has moved to the "South," namely Africa and Latin America, it has also changed its face: From a tiny minority, Pentecostal churches have grown to become a considerable part of World Christianity, and together with charismatic movements in historical churches and African Independent Churches—which have similar features, but are to be differentiated— they sum up an estimated quarter of the world's 2 billion Christians today.[3] It is, thus, no wonder that this remarkable shift and growth is what might be shaping, in the words of Philip Jenkins,[4] the "Next Christendom." According to the World Christian Database, Brazil is now considered the country with the highest Pentecostal population in absolute numbers, estimated at 24 million in 2006.[5] Thus, if Brazil is the "most Catholic country" in terms of numbers, it is also the "most Pentecostal country" in the world today. And this includes merely those who belong to Pentecostal churches. But the phenomenon of speaking in tongues, experiencing healing and other gifts of the Spirit goes far beyond and reaches into the historic churches. In relative numbers, the Pew Forum's comparative survey estimates 15 percent of Pentecostals and 34 percent of Charismatics, totaling 49 percent of Christians in Brazil.[6]

1. Jeffrey Gros, "Confessing the Apostolic Faith from the Perspective of the Pentecostal Churches," in *Pneuma: The Journal of the Society for Pentecostal Studies* 9/1 (1987), 12, cited in Stewart-Gambino and Wilson, "Latin American Pentecostals," 234.

2. This rather surprising statement of an outspoken defender of human rights and the churches' involvement in that defense was made on television as candidates sought the "Evangelical vote" in the 1994 elections, cited in Freston, *Evangelicals and Politics*, 43.

3. Cited in Pew Forum, *Spirit and Power*, 1.

4. Jenkins, *The Next Christendom.*

5. Leandro Beguoci, "Brasil é o maior país pentecostal," in *Folha de São Paulo* vol. 86, no. 28,425, of 1/29/2007, available at http://www1.folha.uol.com.br/fsp/brasil/ fc2901200708.htm (accessed on 2/2/2007).

6. Pew Forum, *Spirit and Power*, 2. The Pew Forum defines believers as "charismatics" if "(a) they describe themselves as 'charismatic Christians'; *or* (2) they describe themselves as 'pentecostal Christians' but do not belong to pentecostal denominations; *or* (3) they say they speak in tongues at least several times a year but they do not belong to

Although this is certainly a global movement, it is by no means uniform, much less uniformly organized. It has, thus, not the hierarchical universal structure of the ICAR, nor the federation-like interaction of the IECLB with its sister churches worldwide. To take the Assemblies of God (*Assembléias de Deus*—AD) in Brazil, the plural is justified by the fact that it is essentially congregationalist—more precisely, the "central temple" (*templo-sede*) or "mother church" (*igreja-mãe*) with its dependencies, led by a pastor-president (*pastor-presidente*), also called "ministry" (*ministério*) is virtually autonomous—and thus made up of (local) assemblies rather than one assembly under an overarching structure.[7] The other reason is that there is a diversity of AD conventions that bring those ministries together. As the General Convention (*Convenção Geral das Assembléias de Deus no Brasil* - CGADB) is the oldest (founded in 1930 and legally registered in 1946) and largest of them (having 58 state and regional conventions among its members in 2006, in Brazil in the United States, Japan, and Europe), we concentrate on it for the purpose of this study.[8] It is subdivided into state and regional conventions and ministries (*ministérios*), the most important being the *Ministério do Belém* with its headquarters in the Belenzinho city district in São Paulo, whose presiding pastor, José Wellington Bezerra da Costa, also heads the CGDAB.[9]

But there is also the Madureira Convention, which goes back to Paulo Leivas Macalão's (1903-1982) ministry in the Madureira city district of Rio de Janeiro. Following discordances with the CGADB leadership, it constituted itself as an independent Convention in 1988, called the *Convenção Nacional das Assembléias de Deus no Brasil—Ministério de Madureira* (CONAMAD), and since 1999 has its national headquarters in the national capital Brasília, headed by Manoel Ferreira who ascended to the office of bishop. There are also other, minor autonomous groupings like the *Assembléia de Deus Betesda,* the *Assembléia de Deus do Bom Retiro,* the *Assembléia de Deus Ministério da Plenitude,* among others.[10] Altogether, 8,418,154 persons[11] have declared themselves members of the AD, which makes them the largest church in Brazil after the ICAR. The CGADB's interpretation of the growth of Pentecostalism in Brazil and worldwide is that it shows three "truths about the Pentecostal Movement": (1) that it came to stay and is not just a momentous and short-lived "straw fire"; that (2) "baptism in the holy Spirit [. . .] continues to be one of the most powerful factors to dynamize the evangelization of the Church," and it is (3) "a proof that the Coming of the Lord Jesus is near," elements that show some of the most important features of the AD: Emphasis

pentecostal denominations" (ibid.). As an overarching term, including Pentecostals and charismatics, the Pew Forum survey uses "renewalist."

7. The new "Dictionary of the Pentecostal Movement," published by the General Convention's Publishing House, also uses the plural; see Araújo, *Dicionário do Movimento Pentecostal*, 34–104.

8. On its history, see Araújo, *Dicionário do Movimento Pentecostal*, 207–19. Although there was no intention of schism, it was felt like that by the Swedish missionaries; in fact the Brazilians sought more autonomy (ibid., 208). The Publishing House (CPAD) is an association whose members are the ministers (pastors and evangelists); in 2006, 25,000 ministers were registered as members (ibid., 212).

9. Bezerra has been in the presidency with only one interruption (1993–95) since 1990, the first to create a kind of perpetual government, together with a strengthening of the CGADB's structure, cf. Araújo, *Dicionário do Movimento Pentecostal*, 213f.

10. The Wikipedia-article quotes another eleven such ministries, see http://pt.wikipedia.org/wiki/Assembl%C3%A9ia_de_Deus (accessed on 6/13/2007).

11. These are the 2000 census numbers (IBGE 2000), the most reliable number available. AD leaders claim between 12 and 15 million, of which 75 percent (9-10 million) would belong to the CGADB (Soares Filho, *Assembléia de Deus na política brasileira*, 5f.).

on Baptism in the Holy Spirit (and the receiving of the gifts of the Spirit), evangelization, and a (pre-millennial) eschatology.[12]

The AD are generally anti-ecumenical and particularly anti-catholic. It does, however, allow for a certain proximity with other churches. The website set up by the CGDAB and its publishing house (*Casa Publicadora das Assembléias de Deus*—CPAD) for the centenary of the AD (in 2011) includes the Madureira Convention and mentions "other denominations," like the Seventh Day Adventists, Baptists, Presbyterians, and even the Universal Church of God's Kingdom (IURD, cf. above, IIB1).[13] At the same time, the Roman Catholic Church is considered a "sect," together with the African Brazilian Candomblé, the Mormons, and the like, in a terminology that certainly reflects the AD's rejection of having been called a sect itself by the ICAR for so long.[14]

For long, it had been normal for AD believers to think of themselves as alien to politics, and so they were considered. *Crente não se mete em política*—"the believer does not mix with politics," and *política é coisa do Diabo*—"politics belongs to the Devil" were common slogans.[15] However, since transition and especially the constituent process in 1987–88, this has changed radically and the church now has a considerable number of federal and state deputies, mayors and city councilors, and even a government minister, although numbers dropped in the last elections (2006) due to the probable involvement of AD federal deputies in a corruption scandal. The church's monthly newspaper, the "Messenger of Peace" (*Mensageiro da Paz*), noted the remarkable reduction of the number of *evangélico* congressmen from 60 to 15, and among the AD members from 22 to 5, and quoted the leader of the church's Political Council as saying that there had been a "media massacre" against the accused and that they have "the right to defend themselves." But the paper concludes, rather laconically, that the church's members "have already made their decision at the ballot."[16] The AD have their specific ways to name and support their candidates, and are courted by candidates for executive offices to gain their support. Since the 1990s, the evangelical sociologist Paul Freston, a pioneer in research on Pentecostalism in Brazil and arguably one of its best connoisseurs, critical and empathic at the same time, has affirmed that

> evangelical religion is arriving at a series of social instances where it had only a timid existence previously, or none at all. The best known example is television [. . .]. Other examples are sportsmen and—women [e.g. the "Athletes" and "Surfers" of Christ], businessmen and—women, the police, criminals and gypsies. A mass Protestantism is forming, which assumes functions of popular religiosity: churches in the place of *terreiros* [i.e. African Brazilian houses of worship] in the slums, Pentecostals with the gift of healing rather than *rezadores* [i.e. prayer

12. "Pentecostais já são 28 milhões no Brasil segundo pesquisa," in *Mensageiro da Paz*, vol. 76, no. 1,458, of November, 2006, 4f. A pre-millennial theology expects the coming of Christ to establish the "thousand years" mentioned in Revelation 20:1–7, which precedes the final reign of Christ. This moment is expected as coming in the near future, and only Christ himself can establish it, which sheds a negative light on the present world, from which nothing good can be expected. According to Araújo (*Dicionário do Movimento Pentecostal*, 592), however, while they share this view with many others, Pentecostals are unique in "seeing the pouring out of the Spirit as, in itself, the fulfillment of the prophecy on the end of the times." Cf. Bauckham, "Chiliasmus IV," 742f.; Dayton, *Theological Roots of Pentecostalism*, 143–71.

13. http://www.assembleiadedeus100.org.br/htm/denominacao/denominacoes4_1.htm (accessed on 6/13/2007).

14. http://www.assembleiadedeus100.org.br/htm/seitas/candomble.htm (accessed on 6/13/2007). The text itself, however, is a fairly adequate summary of the history of the church and its doctrine, based on Roman Catholic sources.

15. According to an empirical research carried out fairly recently by Schuler (*Pfingstbewegungen in Brasilien*, 161) among 200 Pentecostals in Recife (state of Pernambuco), 54 percent still denied that a Christian should get involved in politics, against only 12 percent in the IURD.

16. *Mensageiro da Paz* vol. 76, number 1,458, of November 2006, 3.

women and men] and *curandeiros* [i.e. healers] [. . .]. The new political presence is part of this ample process of evangelical expansion.[17]

Freston aptly highlights the ambiguity of this process, as he was writing just after a big budget scandal in which many Pentecostal politicians were involved—according to Freston a clear sign of their lack of preparation for the new tasks.

It is important not to reduce the Pentecostal potential for social change to formal politics and, namely, the election of "brothers" to the legislative. Such concentration is prone to presuppose, as did the critics who called Pentecostalism *eo ipso* "alienating," "that social change happens only in the realm of politics, and that the stage of history is set exclusively in the political world."[18] As Mariz rightly insists, "poverty is above all experienced as a daily problem in the lives of individuals."[19] Already at the beginning of the 1990s, presenting the ample and relevant sociological study carried out among *evangélicos* in Rio de Janeiro, Rubem César Fernandes distinguished between "*evangélico* politicians" and "the politics of *evangélicos*," emphasizing that direct questions on "religion and politics" would be in vain given that this relation is not made explicitly. However, indirectly, "we encounter issues that open ways of communication with the problem of citizenship: processes of individualization, associative practices, diversification of language, approximation between rite and ethics etc."[20]

It is here that the main contribution of the AD to citizenship lies, as I shall try to show: to give believers a sense of dignity and capacity, to empower them to change and reorganize their lives, and, thus, to feel and act truly as citizens, even with a conservative, indeed fundamentalist—in the sense of the 1910 U.S. "fundamentals"—theology and little discourse on what it could mean to be a citizen.[21] Even so, as Freston states,[22] "in the AD, there is more theoretical conscience of citizenship and the universalism of Christian ethics than in the majority of Pentecostal churches. But practice often stays behind." He does not explain this further, but only gives the negative examples of support for specific candidates. What follows will provide data to assess Freston's statement.

17. Freston, *Evangélicos na Política Brasileira*, 15. This book was written for an "evangelical" audience, here meaning evangelicals in the Anglo-Saxon sense of a specific way of believing, within historical Protestant churches, a group to which Freston himself belongs, not least via the Latin American Theological Fraternity (*Fraternidade Teológica Latino-Americana*—FTL), a continental, progressive evangelical movement founded in 1970 in Cochabamba (Bolívia), linking up to the Lausanne Evangelical Movement (1974), but with a stronger social and political engagement in what came to be called "integral mission"; see Zabatiero, "Um movimento teológico." Freston's book is based on his doctoral dissertation on *Protestants and Politics in Brasil: From the Constituent to the Impeachment,* defended in 1993 at the University of Campinas (São Paulo). Today, Freston is Professor and Chair in Religion and Politics at Wilfrid Laurier University in Ontario, Canada.. See also Freston, "Breve História do Pentecostalismo Brasileiro," *Evangelicals and Politics, Religião e Política, sim*; *Evangelical Christianity.*

18. Mariz, "Pentecostalism and Confrontation," 133. Reacting to this common prejudice, Couto, *Lições Bíblicas: Mestre*, 92 insists that the necessity of apologetics and a Christian counter-culture [which implies, in the Brazilian context, being both contrary to common "Brazilian" culture, and to Roman Catholicism, given their presumed unity] does "not imply in social [or cultural] alienation," because "it is possible to be faithful in a pagan and secularized world."

19. Mariz, "Pentecostalism and Confrontation," 133.

20. Fernandes, "Governo das almas," 164.

21. Lehmann (*Struggle for the Spirit*, 217) points to the following indicators for Pentecostalism's political impact, rather than to "explicit political programmes or statements": "the symbolic and imaginary world which it [sc. Pentecostalism] is projecting, and also to its impact on the broader political theatre of these countries, taking into account the 'scandals' provoked by the neo-Pentecostal Churches, the media, and also the possible effects on the world-view of their followers." He sees their impact especially in a "radical cultural change" as they "attack the culture of the people, even while speaking the language of the people" (*Struggle for the Spirit*, 228).

22. Freston, *Evangélicos na Política Brasileira*, 121.

As in the previous chapters, I start with a short historical overview (1), then go on to analyze documents and activities by the church (2), and finally evaluate the church's contribution theologically as I describe what emerges as position in the terms established for the three case studies (3).

1. BRIEF HISTORICAL SURVEY

É tempo de agir, pois esta pode ser a
última Constituição antes da volta de Cristo.

João de Deus Antunes[23]

It is an old prejudice that Pentecostalism is a foreign religion, induced by the U.S. to expand its influence in Latin America and to use Pentecostals as yet another bulwark against communism.[24] As we shall see, the AD did serve to some extent in this sense during the military regime—as did most Protestant churches—and they were indeed founded by foreigners. But there was only a very indirect, and not political, U.S. influence, and the church has for long been run by Brazilians. The movement started in the North, in the city of Belém ("Bethlehem"), the capital of the state of Pará, and then migrated along with its members southward. From a tiny movement the AD have risen to become the largest church grouping in Brazil after the ICAR, and one of the largest in the world, and has become a notable political force. I shall first describe the pre-history and founding of the AD (a), then its position under the military regime (b), and finally after transition (c), when a considerable turnaround happened and the church started to engage actively in parliamentary and executive politics.

a) The Assemblies of God: The Arrival of Pentecostalism in Brazil

What became the AD was the second arrival of Pentecostalism in Brazil. As stated above (IIB1), the Italian Luigi Francescon (1866–1964) was the first to arrive and found a Pentecostal church, the Christian Congregation of Brazil (*Congregação Cristã do Brasil*—CCB), in 1910 in the Brás city district of São Paulo, among Italian immigrants. Originally a Roman Catholic, he had migrated to the U.S.A. in 1890 and worked as an artist specialized in mosaics in Chicago. He converted and founded the Italian Presbyterian Church in 1892, but left it when he was baptized by immersion in 1903. He came into contact with Pentecostalism through the same W.H. Durham which would be instrumental for the Swedes that founded the AD, and received Baptism in the Holy Spirit in 1907, as well as a prophecy that he should take Pentecostalism to the Italian colony. [25]

Similarly, the Swedes Gunnar Vingren (1879–1933) and Daniel Berg (1884–1963) had gone through the U.S.A. before coming to Brazil. Already back in Sweden, as Baptists, they had experienced being among a tiny minority in the environment of an established Lutheran church. They held a high esteem for the Bible, but a low esteem for erudition; they also came from a very modest background in what was then a poor and emigration country, factors that would favor their mission among the poor in Brazil.[26] In 1902, Berg went to the United States, and Vingren the year after. The

23. "It is time to act, as this could be the last Constitution before Christ's return," as quoted in Freston, *Evangélicos na Política Brasileira*, 38. Antunes was an AD candidate to the Constituent Assembly, to which he was elected with the highest vote in his party (PDT) for the Rio Grande do Sul state; ibid. 49f.

24. E.g. Lima, *Os demônios descem do norte* ; critically on this for instance Rolim, *Pentecostalismo*, 131–53.

25. Freston, "Breve História do Pentecostalismo Brasileiro," 100f.

26. Ibid., 79.

latter took up theological studies at the Swedish Baptist Theological Seminary in Chicago from 1904-08, and served a number of Baptist congregations as intern and then as pastor. He was to go to India as a missionary, but eventually declined.[27] He received Baptism in the Holy Spirit at the 1st Swedish Baptist Church in Chicago. Berg worked as a steel founder and returned to Sweden in 1908, where he discovered that his best friend from childhood, Lewi Pethrus, had become Pentecostal. Pethrus was influential in Berg's return to the U.S., and also on the AD in Brazil.[28] Apparently, Berg received the Holy Spirit while still on the ship.[29] He met Vingren at a conference in Chicago in 1909, and the two convinced each other they should be missionaries. A Pentecostal brother told them he had seen them in a dream, together with a strange name: Pará. Vingren counts:

> Another brother, Adolfo Ulldin, received one day, by the Holy Spirit, wonderful words and hidden mysteries, which were revealed. Among other things, the Holy Spirit spoke through this brother that I should go to *Pará*, where the people for whom I would give testimony of Jesus were of a very simple social level. I should teach them the first rudiments of the Lord's doctrine. We also heard through the Holy Spirit the language of that people, the Portuguese idiom. We should eat very simple food, but God would give us all which would be necessary. The Holy Spirit also said that I would marry a person called Strandberg, which happened later, as I married Frida Strandberg. This prophecy occurred much before I knew her. God also said other things which I had later the opportunity to verify that they were truths. God had now spoken and I understood that I had received a divine calling for my future missionary field. Glory to Jesus![30]

In Vingren's account, Berg was called in the same way, but apparently a little later, to accompany him.[31] He (they?) went to a library and checked out where "Pará," apparently a place, was located, and found the Brazilian state under that name. "They had little money, only $90.00, but even this proved to be of divine consequence, for the trip to a place called Pará cost exactly that amount."[32] As common in Pentecostal accounts, all necessary factors came together to confirm that this was really the mission God had entrusted to them. Schuler[33] quotes literature which allows for a broader interpretation: Pará state had already been known to the people in South Bend (Indiana) where Ulldin received his audition. The pastor of the Baptist church in Belém, where Vingren and Berg arrived on November 19, 1910, Erik Nilsson, was a Swedish missionary who had emigrated to the United States before coming to Brazil. Since 1897, he had been founding churches all over the Amazon region so that reports must have told about mission in Pará. It was also an important and well-known place for exporting rubber, not least to Chicago, then a rising industrial center. Even South Bend had a car factory that used rubber from Pará.

So Vingren and Berg started in Belém, capital of Pará, in Nilsson's Baptist church. Other missionaries arrived, most of them from Sweden or the United States. The first person to receive

27. Almeida, *História das Assembléias de Deus no Brasil*, 14

28. Pethrus had been a sheep pastor and shoemaker before going to the Baptist seminary in Stockholm, where he lost his faith in Christ's divinity, a paradigmatic experience for the AD as to the study of theology. He became Pentecostal in Norway, then Pastor of a Baptist church in Stockholm, which was excluded by the denomination in 1913. The church started a mission to Brazil, supporting Berg and sending out other missionaries; Freston, "Breve História do Pentecostalismo Brasileiro," 80.

29. This is claimed by Berg in his *Enviado por Deus*, 3rd ed. (Rio de Janeiro: CPAD, 1973), 27, apud Reily, *História Documental do Protestantismo no Brasil*, 369 and 436; cf. Almeida, *História das Assembléias de Deus no Brasil*, 16.

30. Vingren, *O diário do pioneiro*, 25f.

31. Ibid., 26f.

32. Oliveira, *The Assemblies of God in Brazil*, 34.

33. Schuler, *Pfingstbewegungen in Brasilien*, 54f.

Baptism in the Holy Spirit was Celina Albuquerque (1876-1966), on June 2, 1911. Before, she had been healed of an "incurable illness" (cancer?) on her lips through prayer; the effect made her pray for receiving the Holy Spirit, according to Vingren's account.[34] Women had indeed a central place in the church in those days, namely but not exclusively pastor's wives. As there is little official writing valuing women's historical contribution, a small excursus is in place here. Women have been acting since the beginnings "in the works of prayer, evangelism, use of the spiritual gifts (prophecies, cure and others), preaching, biblical teaching (mainly in Sunday school), music and praise, missions, social work, women's union and even as leaders of churches," admits Araújo[35] in his *Dictionary of the Pentecostal Movement,* officially printed and, thus, approved by the CPAD. Of the first group which left the Baptist church in 1911, more than half were women. As mentioned, the first one to be baptized in the Holy Spirit was a women, and so also the second one, Maria de Jesus Nazaré (life dates unknown),[36] who became an important missionary. Frida Maria Strandberg (1891-1940) was sent as a missionary to Brazil from Sweden and wed Gunnar Vingren there. She was a "nurse, poet, composer, musician, editor, researcher, preacher, and teacher,"[37] and effectively led the church during Gunnar's absences and frequent infirmities. She was the only woman to write commentaries in the Sunday school review, *Lições Bíblicas*, and also a frequent collaborator with the *Mensageiro da Paz.* Her husband defended women's ministry and "separated" as the first deaconess Emília Costa, in Rio de Janeiro. There was, however, strong opposition against women's ministry among the fellow AD leaders. It became a matter of debate at the first General Convention in 1930. It was felt that women should testify and teach, if necessary, but not be pastors unless in cases of need, based on Matthew 12:3–8.[38]

After having attended to the church in Rio de Janeiro, the Vingren couple returned for the last time to Sweden in 1932 and Gunnar passed away the following year. Berg went into the hinterland to evangelize as soon as he was fluent enough in Portuguese. In fact, he never learnt it well. He worked as a founder to sustain the two and to pay a U.S.-American (!)[39] teacher of Portuguese for Vingren, who in turn passed on what he had learnt to Berg.[40] During his visit to Sweden, he married Sara, in 1920. He would still see the church's golden jubilee before he passed away in Sweden, in 1963.

There soon occurred a breach with the Baptist church over Baptism and the gifts of the Holy Spirit.[41] Expelled from that church, the group created the "Apostolic Faith Mission" *(Missão da Fé Apostólica)* on June 18, 1911, 19 persons (12 of them women, if I interpret the names correctly) and the two missionaries. This became the birthdate of the AD in Brazil. On January 11, 1918, the new church was registered as "Assemblies of God." The name was chosen by unanimity, after Vingren had come to know that this name had been adopted in the U.S.A. Oliveira[42] emphasizes that "It was not, however, affiliated to any foreign mission. The birth was genuinely native, a characteristic

34. Vingren, *Diário do Pioneiro Gunnar Vingren*, 40; Araújo, *Dicionário do Movimento Pentecostal*, 7f.

35. Araújo, *Dicionário do Movimento Pentecostal*, 492.

36. Ibid., 501f.

37. Ibid., 903.

38. Ibid., 494. The 1983 General Convention rejected women's (ordained) ministry unanimously; the vast majority opted for the same position in the 2001 General Convention.

39. Vingren, *Despertamento apostólico no Brasil*, 11.

40. Almeida, *História das Assembléias de Deus no Brasil*, 25.

41. Cf. Reily, *História Documental do Protestantismo no Brasil*, 370–74.

42. Oliveira, *The Assemblies of God in Brazil*, 59; cf. Almeida, *História das Assembléias de Deus no Brasil*, 27.

they have always sought to maintain." Even so, up to about 1950, Swedish missionaries were a common feature in the AD, and they occupied the General Convention's presidency till 1951. But the mission's property, the churches and meeting rooms were handed over to the Brazilian churches already at the first General Convention, in 1930, which 11 Swedish missionaries and 23 Brazilian leaders attended.[43] The convention's newspaper, the "Messenger of Peace" (*Mensageiro da Paz*), was launched at the same convention meeting.

Later, U.S.-American missionaries also came to Brazil (the first one in 1934), but were seen negatively as rich and morally relaxed: "The Swedes have the doctrine [*doutrina*, i.e., the code of behavior] and the Americans have the dollars."[44] In later, more revolutionary times, some Pentecostals were also active in social movements, like Francisco Julião's Rural Leagues. Julião sought the support of "the Bible folk" *(os Bíblia)*, as they were called, affirming that

> You are the oppressed religion. The farmers also are being oppressed. Why don't you join us? You can sing your hymns, recite your extracts from the Great Prophets and we work together. Take a Bible and I'll go with the Civil Code.[45]

Julião's call was answered by some Pentecostals, many of which were sugarcane cutters; individuals, of course, not churches.[46] One of them says that "Suffering and poverty are produced by the proprietors of the sugar cane farm. [. . .] God wants us to remove this injustice from our lives, sin [. . .] The pastors, they don't like it, no."[47]

b) The Assemblies of God and the Military Regime

Not much study has been done on the AD under the military regime, as we also lack major studies in the case of historic Protestant churches. The church's own historians do not give the period specific attention. The recent *Dictionary of the Pentecostal Movement* just says that "many *evangélicos* participated in the military government, which commanded the country from 1964 onwards, and some were even deputies. The churches [. . .] maintained relations with the public authorities."[48] At the same time, the whole period from 1951 to 1970 is considered the church's "golden" period, of considerable growth.[49] The following period, however, is described as still one of expansion, but also of loss of doctrinal and moral consistency. Works by non-Pentecostal scholars provide us with some, albeit restricted, data and reflections.[50] Rolim, although admitting that there are Pentecostals contributing to social movements, concludes that

> Pentecostal churches gave their support, not publicly, but veiled, in the sense that they not only did not talk about politics in the temples, but watched that their members would be totally

43. Freston, "Breve História do Pentecostalismo Brasileiro," 83.

44. Ibid., 85.

45. In Rolim, *Pentecostalismo*, 68.

46. Rolim, "Pentecostalismo, governos militares e revolução," 336. Rolim, *Pentecostalismo*, 67 deplores the absence of a thorough study of the *evangélico* participation in the Rural Leagues; Julião himself mentions in an interview published in the oppositional magazine *Pasquim*, in 1979, that the movement counted on "Baptists and adepts of other sects [probably Pentecostals] which I couldn't identify" (quoted ibid.).

47. In Rolim, *Pentecostalismo*, 69.

48. The entry on politics (Araújo, *Dicionário do Movimento Pentecostal* , 703-712) is largely an apologetic of the churches' candidates and its project *Cidadania AD Brasil* (see below, IIE1c), and otherwise based on sociological literature on the subject (e.g. Mariano, *Neopentecostais*).

49. Ibid., 50-52.

50. Kliewer, *Das neue Volk der Pfingstler*; Chesnut, *Born again in Brazil*, 1999.

> submissive and obedient to the norms and procedures dictated by the military government." On the side of the government, "for the first time in the history of Brazilian governments, Pentecostalism is seen with sympathy, although in a veiled and camouflaged way" because of their "social conservatism it implemented among the poor stratums which had adhered to it."[51]

In 1970, the AD were already the largest church in membership according to a government report,[52] with 746,400 members, i.e., 28.5 percent of all Protestants, before the Lutherans (16.4 percent) and Baptists (12.6 percent). Overall, the historical Protestants still held a slight majority (50.6 percent). The third wave of Pentecostalism (see above, IIB1) was still to come.

While the relationship between the regime and the ICAR became much more distant than it had ever been, and even hostile, Protestant and Pentecostal churches stepped in for it in many instances, being courted as allies to provide legitimacy for the regime, in turn receiving better chances for State benefits and privileges, not least broadcasting concessions for radio and television. Kliewer[53] noted the fact that Pentecostals were discovered and courted by politicians as an important electoral group even before the military regime. The AD's golden jubilee in 1961 was attended by the governor, high military and congressmen. Almeida[54] stresses that "many authorities, and even members of National Congress took part in the inauguration of various temples. They recognize the most valuable contribution of the AD for the Brazilian nation." The AD felt honored and respected by such signs of attention. Some Protestant congressmen at the time received Pentecostal support, although there was by no means a unified policy as there would be later. The most politically (and ecumenically) active Pentecostal leader at the time was Manoel de Mello, the founder of the "Brazil for Christ" church. He created the "Movement of National Redemption" (*Movimento de Redenção Nacional*), represented by the Pentecostal deputy Levy Tavares, elected to the Chamber of Deputies in the early 1960s. The movement's goal was to "turn every church into a school" and mobilize the *evangélico* forces "for a frontal and indefatigable struggle against right or left extremism, for freedom and democracy according to Christian principles."[55] According to Kliewer, it became common already in that period to recommend, from the leadership, specific candidates to the faithful. The criteria given for such recommendation included social elements like healthcare, the struggle against homelessness and land reform, as well as fighting corruption, prostitution, gambling, and alcoholism, the naming of streets after *evangélico* personalities, and the restriction of State support for the ICAR. Similarly to what is true for the wider population, there is a certain pragmatism in such political support, but it resounds especially well with "Pentecostal ideology, which values concrete deeds and behavior more than doctrines"[56]

While, thus, Pentecostals were not socially insensitive, and indeed stress they always maintained social works,[57] they stuck to strict moral values and the maintenance of order, both

51. Rolim, "Pentecostalismo, governos militares e revolução," 337f. 346.

52. In Reid and Ineson, *Brazil 1980*, 23.

53. Kliewer, *Das neue Volk der Pfingstler*, 160ff.

54. Almeida, *História das Assembléias de Deus no Brasil*, 353.

55. In Kliewer, *Das neue Volk der Pfingstler*, 162.

56. Ibid., 163.

57. Almeida (*História das Assembléias de Deus no Brasil*, 352) mentions literacy and language courses and that "every mother-church provides for the needs of members that are part of it and persons of its community [sympathizers? Persons outside the church?], providing food, housing, clothes, medical assistance. [. . .] They have schools and conduct, with efficiency, a multi-ministry blessed by God, which cares for the old and children, students and heads of families, abandoned youth and housewives. The secretary of the Ipiranga ministry, São Paulo, expressed himself as follows: 'God cares for our souls, therefore we must care for the bodies.'"

represented by the military regime. They were also totally in accordance in terms of the fight against communism. In this way, Pentecostals, not least from the AD, became effective allies for the regime and substituted the former Catholic allies, as Chesnut[58] has shown for Belém and the Pará state. Political scientist and member of the Movement of Progressive Evangelicals (*Movimento Evangélico Progressista* – MEP) Robinson Cavalcanti, in his *Christianity and Politics*, used the following allegory to say what was happening:

> If the movement of 31 March, 1964, could be compared to a railway composition which is forced to continue by a deviation (in 1968 [the year of the AI-5, see above, IA1]), we could say that the majority of the Roman Church's leadership decided to get down at the first station after entering the deviation. They had been occupying the first class coaches, and the *evangélicos* the second class coaches. When the former got off, the latter were invited to move into the first class coaches (with access to the restaurant) and did it with pleasure, immensely grateful for the consideration. The voyage via the deviation lasted over a decade. Despite the discomfort of some parts of the journey, including attacks by Indians, the crew did not stop their efforts to treat the passengers well. There were few who decided to get down and continue their journey by another way and other means of transport.
>
> Enchanted by 'development' and 'security', as well as 'religious liberty', the *evangelicals* were becoming, from the decade of the [19]70s, together with the freemasons and kardecists [see above, IIB1] civil tentacles of the regime. Understanding the loss of progressive Catholic passengers, the regime sought to invest as much as possible in the Protestants: courtesy visits, employment opportunities, partnerships, nominations for important offices, invitations for pastors to do courses at the ESG [i.e. the Superior War College, *Escola Superior de Guerra*], and the like. [. . .] The *evangélicos,* in the past a discriminated minority, which for so long a time had been praying for liberation, gladly welcomed the new situation, a real 'blessing', and continued obliviously their way of constantinization.[59]

In the military period, there was a slightly higher Protestant representation in Congress, but still very modest, with a number between 11 and 17 in the period between 1963 and 1987, including proxies who came to substitute the elected on resignation. Until 1975, these congressmen were mostly Presbyterian, but from 1975 to 1987, Baptists took the lead.[60] Pentecostals were still a tiny minority, holding only 5 percent of all seats occupied by Protestants between 1946 and 1987.

While the AD's leadership, as other Pentecostal churches, adopted a submissive and apolitical line, which probably corresponds to the majority of its followers in that period, this was never true for all its followers. As indicated, some indeed became leaders of rural unions,[61] but also of neighborhood associations.[62] But overall, obedience and submission prevailed, as well as opportunistic collaboration. Still in 1991, it is clear that the church does not have a problem with its past under the military regime, and cites freely its slogans: "Do not damage the Assembly of God, love it or leave it [*ame-a ou deixe-a*],"[63] which was precisely the military regime's slogan to enhance patriotism: "Brazil: love it or leave it."

58. Chestnut, *Born Again in Brazil*; "The Salvation Army or the Army's Salvation."

59. Cavalcanti, *Cristianismo e política*, 228f.

60. Freston, *Evangélicos na Política Brasileira*, 29f.

61. Ibid., 110.

62. Ireland, *Kingdoms Come*; Burdick, *Looking for God in Brazil.*

63. Apud Freston, "Breve História do Pentecostalismo Brasileiro," 76

c) The Assemblies of God after Transition

The end of the transition process and the return to a civilian government would bring a fundamental change to the AD's political engagement. Emblematic for this considerable reversal of the old principle that *crente não se mete em política*, was the slogan "brother votes for brother" (*irmão vota em irmão*).[64] Although not completely new—already in 1978, the *Mensageiro da Paz* had affirmed that "believer votes for believer"[65]—it was around the constituent process that it took much more weight. The AD's main paper remained silent as to the 1984 *Diretas Já* campaign, but started to speak about politics frequently from 1985 onwards, following the new policy: "Our church has sufficient potential to put a representative in parliament in every state... The church's commitment, in this case, does not presuppose a political-partisan involvement, as our security is in God, but it represents an effort of the church to manifest its beneficial influence in the highest spheres of public life."[66] Such pretensions were criticized by more progressive evangelicals, like the future president of the Brazilian Evangelical Association (*Associação Evangélica Brasileira*—AEVB), charismatic Presbyterian Caio Fábio de Araújo Filho. He said it was not enough to simply vote for "brothers," but criteria for candidates should include "a past of militancy with the causes of justice and right, parties' principles, defense of land reform and opposition to the Law of National Security."[67]

Following the 1986 elections, an "Evangelical Bench" *(bancada evangélica)* was constituted, made up of 32 deputies elected to the Constituent Assembly-cum-Congress, the largest group being from the AD, with 14 congressmen. Apart from the AD, the system of appointing official candidates was adopted by the IURD and the Foursquare Gospel Church, while the Christian Congregation of Brazil and the God is Love Church, both morally very rigorous, maintained their apolitical stance. As Freston[68] states, the candidates generally represented what Pentecostals were striving for: coming from a poor background, but economically successful and providing religious leadership: "they are poor who did well and are elected for their religious and/or financial prestige." Many of them were evangelists, singers, or media persons, often also related to pastor-presidents, and they represent both the commoner and the "brother," but not union leaders or leaders of social movements.

In Congress, they stood for a variety of parties, freely moving from one to the other if that promised better eligibility in the next election. Before, Protestants in Congress had been positioned slightly to the left of the center. Now, Pentecostals were to be found mainly in center-right parties. Their activity was (and is) marked by a pragmatism and, as Freston argues, the change from absence from politics to engagement in party, legislative, and executive politics was not undergirded by theological changes. Theology remains dispensationalist and pre-millennial, i.e., awaiting the imminent return of Christ, and maintains the strict dualism between good and evil.[69] Also, whatever

64. Sylvestre, *Irmão vota em irmão.*

65. In Freston, *Evangélicos na Política Brasileira*, 40

66. Statement from a meeting of the presidents of the AD's state conventions, published in the *Mensageiro da Paz*, May 1985, 1, in Freston, *Evangélicos na Política Brasileira*, 43.

67. In Freston, *Evangélicos na Política Brasileira*, 44

68. Ibid., 47.

69. On pre-millennialism see above; dispensationalism essentially assumes that "God deals with the human race in successive dispensations." Usually there are seven dispensations, all containing a beginning, a testing of obedience to God and a judgment: "innocence, conscience, civil government, promise, law, grace and the kingdom"; see Arlington, "Dispensationalism," 585. The current dispensation, since Jesus Christ's coming, would be the dispensation of grace. Soares Filho, *Assembléia de Deus na política brasileira*, 34 also mentions, quoting Freston and one of Freston's students, Claudirene Bandini, that the obligatory theological formation for pastors in biblical courses rather than seminaries

they are fighting for in content are a restricted set of predominantly moral issues linked to family and sexuality (cf. below, IIE2), and of course whatever will benefit the church directly, like media concessions, tax exemption and public *evangélico* holidays.[70] As for the Constituent Assembly, in Frestons' account,[71] the AD leadership was reasonably satisfied. "God's name was included in the Charta [i.e., the Constitution], religious freedom amplified, religious education maintained in the curriculum. 'Sexual orientation' [i.e., as a feature against which discrimination would be forbidden], death penalty and district vote were rejected. On the other hand, the Pentecostals were defeated as to abortion, artistic censorship and divorce."

A constant item has indeed been "religious freedom." Justified on principle in view of the Catholic hegemony, it repeatedly served as an argument to arouse believers' fear that such and such candidate or policy would strengthen rather than weaken Catholic hegemony and restrict space for Pentecostal evangelism, and thus became a political token rather than a honorable claim. In this game, as Freston rightly highlights,[72] the AD and other churches, especially the IURD, do actually adopt the Catholic model, although in their discourse they fight the Catholic church.[73] Thus, "religious freedom" is not simply about space for a minority over against Catholic hegemony, but seeking proper hegemony, relying on the fact that there are more Pentecostals than active Catholics, and many more pastors than priests. To hold huge gatherings and marches in public places, stadiums and enormous temples, competing architectonically with the Roman Catholic churches and shopping centers in size and refinement, are among the most visible signs of such pretension. The huge buildings in public spaces are the IURD's specialty, consciously called "Faith Cathedrals." The AD are less blunt and, indeed, ethically bound by their doctrine, and have a less hierarchical structure of command, but they share the basic project of making Brazil *evangélico*.[74]

All other issues are left to the individual's discretion. This has not changed till this day, as we shall see, but there is an interesting dynamics between the church leadership's policy and the behavior of the "brothers," who do by no means just follow their leaders' appointments, and continue to apply the church's high standard of morality to their "brother" politicians, punishing them by not casting a vote in their favor. This is a clear difference from the IURD, where appointments of candidates are made top down and their election (very effectively) enforced through massive propaganda also in worship, something the AD has refrained from to date. In fact, AD members have a great deal of freedom over against their leaders when it comes to following their convictions.[75] Although they are much more exposed to the church's discourse than others, due to their regular

---

resulted in a centralization of theological formation around the mother-churches, which, thus, could control it better and avoid too critical a theological thinking from developing, as it would in seminaries with a wider and more critical formation.

70. Like the Day of the Bible (December 9) and the Day of the Evangelical, cf. Mariano, "Secularização do Estado, liberdades e pluralismo religioso," 19; Soares Filho, *Assembléia de Deus na política brasileira*, 67.

71. Freston, *Evangélicos na Política Brasileira*, 84.

72. Ibid., 66.

73. This is stated ever more bluntly by the IURD, see Macedo and Oliveiro, *Plano de poder* in their "Plan to Power," and below, IIIB2a.

74. Freston (*Evangélicos na Política Brasileira*, 67) calls this a "dispute over space in *civil religion*," although I fear they would head rather towards a theocracy.

75. I myself encountered AD members at an ecumenical gathering in July 2002, who were members of the progressive Movement of Homeless Workers (*Movimento de Trabalhadores Sem Teto*—MTST). They recognized they were at odds with their pastors, but were not bothered by that: What had to be done, had to be done. Personal conversations at the 2nd Ecumenical Journey in Mendes (Rio de Janeiro), July 11–14, 2002, cf. http://www.projornada.org.br/2jornada (accessed on 6/15/2007).

presence at church events and their restricted consumption of media products, and show that the church does serve as a source of political guidance, this is by no means the only or even the most important element in voting. Although nearly 19 percent of Evangelicals stated that they consider voting for the party that has the religious authorities' support, the criterion "to be a party of honest people" fares much higher at 51.8 percent.[76]

There was indeed reason to scold the AD's politicians. While *evangélicos*, due to their high standards, have generally been renowned for their honesty, correctness, punctuality, and hard work—still today, they are better liked in some businesses for these qualities—the generality of this prejudice came to an end through the actions of the *bancada evangélica* during the Constituent Assembly. Possibly because of their political inexperience, but certainly for their customary patriarchal and clientelist modes of relationships, they became, indeed, "models" of corruption, bargaining and *fisiologismo*,[77] which some of them acknowledged openly: "Indeed I am *fisiologista*. But who is not? Everybody who goes to National Congress already knows what it means to practice *fisiologismo*. It's just that I do it with my morals high."[78] Thus, while they pretended to change the country in bringing it under Jesus' command, they in fact continued the worst parts of Brazilian political culture and were at odds in developing a critical attitude towards it.[79]

The AD's politicians were central in reviving the still existing, but inactive Brazilian Evangelical Confederation (CEB), which once had been founded to represent Protestants in the 1934 constituent process and played an active role in the following thirty years, but lost it under the military regime because of its insistence on social justice and transformation. It was used to channel public funds into the politicians' and their churches' patrimony. After massive public criticism, the CEB was dissolved in late 1990.[80] The *evangélico* politicians' public image was seriously damaged, and came to worry the believers, who were uncomfortable with their leaders and the politicians they

76. Bohn, "Evangélicos no Brasil," 333. Interestingly, although Evangelicals tend not to have any party preference, the largest minority opted for the Worker's Party (PT) in 2002, which was actually the case across all religions surveyed (ibid., 331). I have no data to say whether the same situation still held true in 2006—although Lula was clearly reelected, the party had losses and the corruption scandals are prone to have diminished the Evangelicals' support.

77. One of the standard dictionaries for Portuguese, Ferreira, *Novo Aurélio século XXI*, 909 defines *fisiologismo* as "attitude or practice (of politicians, civil servants etc.) which is characterized by striving for gains or personal advantages, rather than having public interest in sight." It recalls the image of an organic functioning of politics, where "one hand washes the other" and people use their relationships in order to exchange favors, following the principle of *toma lá dá cá* ("take there—give here"). See also above, IA3c.

78. In Freston, *Evangélicos na Política Brasileira*, 50.

79. On this see also Baptista's study (*Cultura política brasileira*) on Brazilian political culture and Pentecostal practices, where he concludes that Pentecostalism has been only partially innovative in terms of ways of doing politics in Brazil. Its own model, although to a certain degree based on the universal priesthood of believers and entrusting a good number of activities and, especially, direct access to divine power, is still authoritarian and concentrated in the figure of the pastor (president). While efforts were democratized, power was centralized (cf. also Alencar, *Assembléia de Deus*). Such authoritarian structure, without proper checks and balances, "becomes a favorable field for the abuse of power and practices of corruption and scandals" (Baptista, *Cultura política brasileira*, 447). One of the problems identified by Baptista is the lack of ethical, critical reflection, as what they practice is moralism based on "behavior and not on principles." They prohibit smoking and alcohol, which is considered sin, but "it is not sin to legislate in favor of bankers, as happens in Brazil, and to evade resources for food, accommodation and health, which would benefit multitudes of people in need. In the ethical sense, to participate in a corruption scheme is not so condemnable, if it benefits the church with ambulances or radio concessions, for example, because this expands its capacity to 'win souls for Christ'" (ibid., 448).

80. In its stead, the Brazilian Pastors' Council (*Conselho de Pastores do Brasil*—CNPB) was founded in 1993, mainly from among the IURD and the CONAMAD, in opposition to the more historic AEVB and in clear pretension to be an equivalent to the CNBB, even by its virtually identical name and acronym.

had appointed. The official church media, however, tried to make it all look like a concerted assault on "religious freedom," an old trick to talk away one's own faults by pointing to the other's.

The interesting thing is that the process would be virtually repeated 20 years later. For a number of elections, the AD lost its hegemony to the IURD. It then realized that appointments should be made on a clearer basis, strongly discouraging the vote for other candidates, even if AD members. At the same time, the project "Citizenship AD Brasil—Valuing the *Evangélico* Vote" (*Projeto Cidadania AD Brasil—A valorização do voto evangélico*) centralized the policy and imposed a strict system for appointing candidates, including a process of consultation of ministries, in this sense more democratic than the IURD's top down appointments. The strategy was immediately successful. In 2002, 21 AD deputies were elected, 19 of whom were linked to and appointed by the CGADB. Again, in 2004, about 1,000 city councilors, 100 mayors, and 60 vice-mayors from the AD were elected, a considerable result. But while they made their "greater ethics" a point of advantage over other parties, in their typically triumphalist language, the Pentecostal voters did not forgive that their politicians would fall over precisely this pretension. They steered clear of the *mensalão* scam in 2005 (cf. above, IA1), but 13 of the CGADB's deputies where cited in the Federal Police's "bloodsucker" (*sanguessuga*) raid, which identified a huge bribery scheme in the purchase of ambulances in Mato Grosso state. In the 2006 elections, only 15 of the Evangelical Parliamentary Front, which had consisted of 60 members in the outgoing legislature, were re-elected, among them only 5 of the AD. For the whole group, this gives a re-election ratio of barely 36 percent, against the Chamber's general 61.66 percent.[81] In both democratic and ecclesiastico-theological terms, this seems to me an excellent result, as it indicates moral coherence and a certain independence from the leadership among the Pentecostal electorate.[82] The AD, in turn, admitted that culprits would be punished, but only if their fault was proven, and again harped on the victimization discourse, saying that "the National Political Council perceives [. . .] a clear intention of certain political segments to use the episode to denigrate the image of the parliamentarians linked to the evangelical church."[83] The electorate punished them beforehand, and the damage could set back the CGADB's ambitions for some time. The IURD, conversely, withdrew its support for the implied politicians immediately and thus preserved its image, although it did not have any deputy re-elected in 2006.[84]

Two left wing AD members made it into the federal government ministry, both as PT members: Benedita da Silva, a black woman from a Rio de Janeiro *favela*, who made her way up the ladder starting as a domestic employee and becoming a federal deputy, senator, vice-governor, and governor of Rio de Janeiro, and eventually a minister for social issues in 2003.[85] Harvey Cox, gener-

81. Soares Filho, *Assembléia de Deus na política brasileira*, 87.

82. As indicated, the AD mix what could be called a "democratization through the Spirit" with a highly authoritarian structure. But ministers and politicians are not beyond the moral rules they themselves preach, which shows that this is not a totally personalized authority; the rules stand for themselves and can be applied against their promoters. It has, however, to be stated that this is much more viable in a electoral plea, were ballots are secret, than in a direct confrontation within a congregation.

83. Official note of the CGADB's Political Council, of September 4, 2006, http://www.cpad.com.br/cpad/noticias%20antigas/noticias_02_20-09-06.htm (accessed on 6/22/2007).

84. Soares Filho, *Assembléia de Deus na política brasileira*, 87f.

85. In his *Calendar of Power*, which relates and documents his activity as special advisor during the first two years of the first Lula government (2003-2004), Frei Betto (*Calendário do poder*, 172) reproduces a letter which he wrote to the president on August 13, 2003, to protest against Benedita da Silva's nominations of *evangélicos* to her ministry, which he sees as a violation of the "secular, non-confessional" State—"God keep us." He further critizes, indirectly, the creation of a working group with representatives of fifteen *evangélico* churches in order to map their social projects and elaborate a program of co-operation. However, he apparently sees no problem in celebrating mass with employees at

ally very enthusiastic about Pentecostalism, said "this woman could out-preach every liberationist priest I have ever met, and she was a member of the left opposition party."[86] In early 2004, however, she had to step down following a trip to an *evangélico* meeting in Buenos Aires, a trip she paid for with public money. The other one is Marina Silva, from the state of Pará, who had been a senator (elected in 2002) and became minister of the environment in 2004 until she stepped down in 2008 over differences within the cabinet on policy for the Amazon region. Although AD members, both were not supported nor appointed by their church, and only referred to by their church leaders when deemed beneficial.[87]

2. DISCOURSE AND PRACTICE

Não somos apenas cidadãos da pátria celeste;
também o somos da terrenal. Como tais, temos
direitos e deveres a serem cumpridos.

Claudionor de Andrade[88]

More heavily in this chapter than in the previous (IIC, IID), I have to rely on secondary sources to show the AD's discourse and practice. Access to original material proved more difficult than expected, and a number of studies have been carried out recently that provide the necessary documentation, like the monograph of Edson d'Avila on the *Mensageiro da Paz*,[89] the CGADB's monthly newspaper with a wide distribution among church members, Soares Filho's work on the "Citizenship AD Brazil" project and Rodrigo Majewski's analysis of the AD's Sunday School Lessons.[90] In any case, as explicit, official discourses in the AD on issues common in the ICAR and IECLB (citizenship and democracy, land reform, indigenous rights, women's rights, black people's rights, poverty, and the like) are scant, with the exception of electoral mobilization and some moral issues like abortion and homosexuality, but quite consistent, I have taken into account mainly the church's self-presentation on its website as well as material on doctrine and theology widely distributed or used in theological formation. Besides, books published by the CPAD publishing house were used if written by Brazilian authors, and of course a selection from the abundant sociological literature on the AD.

---

the presidential palace, although some celebrations were ecumenical (e.g. ibid., 371). Employing Catholics is probably not seen as opposing secularity, because being Catholic and being Brazilian is, implicitly, still considered synonymous. Catholics are the primarily citizens, while *evangélicos* are seen, primarily, as *evangélicos*. This is not to say, of course, that da Silva's employment policy was beyond criticism; in fact, she had to resign in 2004 because of the loss of trust in her after she paid her participation at a Buenos Aires *evangélico* meeting with government money.

86. Cox, *Fire from Heaven*, 165.

87. Soares Filho, *Assembléia de Deus na política brasileira*, 60f.

88. "We are not only citizens of the heavenly, we are also [citizens] of the earthly fatherland. As such, we have rights and duties to fulfill." Andrade, *Lições Bíblicas: Mestre*. 77.

89. D'Avila, *Assembléia de Deus no Brasil e a política*.

90. Hênio Santos de Almeida, research assistant in 2004–05, was helpful in mapping the literary field of AD authors, providing summaries and commenting with his own experience as a former minister in the AD, who came to study at EST. Soares Filho (*Assembléia de Deus na política brasileira*) provides data from the CGADB's political commission's website, consulted in 2006, but deactivated in 2007 (http://www.cpnad.com.br). Rodrigo Majewski ("Pentecostalismo e reconciliação", *Assembléia de Deus e teologia pública*), who was my research assistant for the IECLB's documentations (see above, IID2), has just finished his master's thesis on public theology in the AD under my supervision.

a) Democracy and Citizenship

The leading principles of the church's relationship with the authorities are laid out in the following text, taken from the Belém ministry, which is led by Pastor José Wellington Bezerra da Costa, who is also the president of the CGDAB. It reads as follows:

> The Church respects all constituted authority and teaches its members to be faithful fulfillers of their duties, and to obey the laws of the country. The Church collaborates with the authorities by restoring lives through the preaching of the Word of God. Among the Church's members, there are a great number of ex-vicious, ex-addicts to all kinds of drugs, ex-criminals of all kinds of crimes, who were reached by the Gospel message and became decent and honorable persons.
>
> Obedience and submission to the authorities are commandments of God. Romans 13:1-7. (The Church obeys the laws of the country provided these are not contrary to the laws of God Acts 4:19, Acts 5:29).[91]

Differently from the previously cited churches, the AD's text does not refer to a specific system of government—it only states that the authority has to be (legally) constituted. It also does not only recognize the authorities' rights to loyalty, but speaks of "obedience" and "submission," something the other two churches studied here have carefully avoided, given the illegitimacy of the military regime and their resistance against it. In this, however, the AD represent the common position of most historic Protestant and Pentecostal churches.[92] They complied under the military regime, why should they not do it now? However, it is to be noted that submission and obedience are not total. They are restricted by "God's laws," quoting Peter and John who told the Sanhedrin: "Whether it is right in the sight of God to listen to you rather than to God, you must judge; for we cannot but speak of what we have seen and heard" (Acts 4:19), and Peter and the apostles, who stated before the same organ: "We must obey God rather than men" (Acts 5:29).[93] This seems to suggest a possibility of civil disobedience should it come to such contradiction. What are, then, possible issues that might make it necessary? The statements that show the AD's position show what the burning public concerns are: Divorce, abortion, homosexuality, and euthanasia.[94]

The above cited text on the authorities does not speak of rights, but only of duties, which seems to contradict the most important aspect of citizenship, i.e., to have and be able to enjoy rights. This aspect is reinforced by the following statement, made by the CGADBs National Political Council:

> *evangélicos* in general have become conscientious that the commitments with the church do not exempt them from the commitments as citizens. To the contrary, the more firmly rooted they are in their faith, the more responsible must they be in their duties to the State. [. . .] Like

91. http://www.ad.org.br/ad/a_nossa8.asp (accessed on 6/22/2007). Unfortunately, as is the case with other websites used in this chapter, this link is no longer valid.

92. Cf. Cavalcanti, *Cristianismo e política*, 228ff.

93. As seen, both texts are also quoted by the ICAR and the IECLB as binding for Christians and restricting obedience to the State authorities.

94. These issues, apart from ecclesiastical matters including the denial of women's ordination, are cited as the CGADB's position at http://www.cgadb.com.br/sobreCgadb/posicaoSobre.html (accessed on 6/22/2007). See also Majewski, *Pentecostalismo e reconciliação*, 18, note 58, where this issue is discussed and the "motifs for intercession for the fatherland" are listed, highlighting again the main preoccupations of the AD: "the valorization of life against abortion, euthanasia, preservation of Christian values, against the civil union of homosexuals, conservation of democratic liberties, combating corruption, promoting the common good, and maintaining individual and civil liberties and the coming of a great awakening."

> other influential sectors in Brazilian society, we also want to contribute to the improvement of public life, of the institutions and of the State.[95]

The text speaks of "citizens" and, thus, of citizenship, but highlights duties and not rights. The fact that responsibility as a believer is in a direct way correlated to responsibility as a citizen, again recalls Barth's "Christian community and civil community," but is meant mainly for supporting the AD appointed politicians and defending the church's interest, which uses its numerical power and national expression for legitimating its political pretensions, boasting, in the same text, to have a by far exaggerated "22 million members in the country."[96] Still, the Church is also to "conscientize the believers on their role in society and to offer them, through biblical teaching, the opportunity to have a Christian and healthy formation for the exercise of citizenship."[97]

What follows from the first quotation a specific way of fostering citizenship: Through "restoring lives." As indicated, this refers mainly to persons addicted to drugs and alcohol and to prisoners, indeed groups largely unattended to by the State.[98] The AD are, in this sense, a very inclusive church. This leads us to an apparent, striking contradiction that I have already alluded to. Although pastors and especially the pastor presidents hold much power in their local church, and are thus likely to reinforce traditional patronage and clientelism,[99] they lead, at the same time, churches that proclaim the most democratic distribution of the Holy Spirit: Everybody, regardless of color, gender, ethnic origin, profession, or wealth, can receive the Holy Spirit, without any mediation.[100] Furthermore, once the person belongs to the flock, there are numerous offices where women and men—albeit the latter with considerably more career opportunities, since the church rejects women's ordination[101]—can acquire communication and leadership skills and hold a position of authority from which they tend to be excluded in secular society.[102] The believer passes through a radical conversion, a spiritual transformation that has an immediate effect on his or her life. The moral rigor of the Assemblies of God (see below, IIE2e) tends to be criticized and ridiculed from outside, but it certainly helps to reconstruct families and boost the budget: Men take more care of their families and bring home the little money they receive rather than spending it all on drinking. Pentecostal policemen fulfill their duties even under difficult circumstances:

95. http://www.cpnad.com.br, as quoted by Soares Filho, *Assembléia de Deus na política brasileira*, 51, given the current unavailability of this website. See also Gilberto, *Lições Bíblicas: Sal e Luz*, 16f.21; cf. Majewski, *Pentecostalismo e reconciliação*, 9f.

96. Soares Filho, *Assembléia de Deus na política brasileira*, 51

97. Couto, *Lições Bíblicas: Igreja*, 59.

98. This is the result of a current research in the Rio do Sinos region in Rio Grande do Sul state (which includes São Leopoldo) on "spaces of citizenship" among the "crazy," executed by psychiatrist and historian Nádia Maria Weber Santos as post-doctoral research with my supervision. Further research, specifically on the method and effectiveness of the so called "therapeutical farms," often run by AD-related staff, is being planned.

99. Cf. Chesnut, *Born Again in Brazil*, 129-144 ("Authoritarian Assembly: Church Organization"). Chesnut denominates the paradoxical organizational model as "participatory authoritarianism" (130).

100. This paradox has been noted already in the first studies on the phenomenon in the 1960s: While Lalive D'Epinay (*Haven of the Masses*) stressed the role of the pastor as the new patron, reproducing the old hierarchical order despite pentecostalism's radical break with the existing society, values, and class structure, Willems (*Followers of the New Faith*) conversely argued that pentecostalism was "a symbolic subversion of the traditional social order," and attributed to it an indirect political influence by shaping the political culture and personal values; cf. Dodson, "Pentecostals, Politics and Public Space," 26f.

101. Cf. http://www.cgadb.com.br/sobreCgadb/posicaoSobre/ordenacaoPastoras.html (accessed on 6/22/2007).

102. Cf. Chesnut, *Born Again in Brazil*, 135–41.

> What changes [sc. on knowing Jesus and converting] is behavior and responsibility. Because we have to submit ourselves to local authorities, because in this way we are submitting ourselves to God. [. . .] The word of God says: 'For the eyes of the Lord are upon the righteous' [1 Pt 3.12]. Every step, he is observing. [. . .] And we cannot live in hypocrisy. Thus, if an order is given to us, in our office, it has to be carried out, independent from whoever is around us.[103]

While their insistence on obedience in a "Prussian" manner is certainly ambivalent and might, under authoritarian circumstances, even be dangerous for its lack of analysis of the order's legitimacy, it is most vital in a context where many policemen are themselves involved in crime and do not necessarily execute orders nor abide by the law (cf. above, IA3b).

One of the most famous physicians in Brazil, Drauzio Varella, who worked for some time in the São Paulo Carandiru prison, says that the Assemblies of God represent, most probably, the only real project of re-socialization existing in the prison.[104] This is because those who convert in prison are exempted from the rigid law imposed by the inmates and are protected from their violence. In addition to that, they might find a stable network of relationships when they leave the penitentiary that can help them into a non-criminal life. Thus this testimony, as well as scientific research, proves what the church itself claims: It restores lives in transforming women and men from the margins of society, who become visibly "decent and honorable" persons.[105] While discourse on issues of citizenship might be scarce, although not totally absent—this transformation makes a difference in people's lives. They often show it by using formal clothes, giving them the typical outlook of *crentes* (believers): Suits and ties for men, sleeved blouses and long skirts for women. Persons feel dignified in their new clothes, and are clearly distinguishable from potential robbers or prostitutes, which gives them some measure of protection. Thus, they find support for feeling and acting like citizens, partake of citizenship, even if they do tend not to take part in social movements that seek to transform society.[106]

Thus, the absence of a (critical) discourse is not to be too simplistically understood as "alienation." Certainly, Pentecostalism provides support primarily for the problems of everyday life, which is precisely what many poor people are desperately looking for. However, as they discover their dignity and recover their self-esteem, they are empowered to change their lives practically, not only in terms of faith, and thus do make a contribution "from below" to citizenship. This has been shown clearly by Mariz,[107] and I agree with her basic assumption that to see the poor merely as victims of a social structure can be as damaging to the poor as to blame them for their own poverty. "The poor are not passive and powerless victims of society."[108] They might use unexpected

103. Interview with the Military Policeman Francisco, of Rio de Janeiro, in Mafra and Paula, "O espírito da simplicidade," 73.

104. Varella, *Estação Carandiru*, 117–20.

105. Mariz, *Coping with Poverty*, 1995; also Shaull and César, *Pentecostalism and the Future of the Christian Churches*.

106. Some counterexamples, however, have been mentioned above, IIE1. Burdick, *Looking for God in Brazil*, 206-20, emphasizes, with good examples, that Pentecostals are far less apolitical than generally assumed and might in fact take part or even the lead in neighborhood associations (as long as they are not dominated by Catholics), and be an important and credible, non-violent backbone of strikes. See also Bobsin, "Fuga do 'mundo' e participação popular" who affirms that "for the *evangélicos*, society and the 'world' are not equivalent realities. The [sc. politically engaged in neighborhood associations and the like] Pentecostals have retreated from the world, but not from the unions, parties and other movements" (ibid., 37). According to him, "worldly" things are related to moral issues, not to politics as such.

107. Mariz, *Coping with Poverty*; "Pentecostalism and Confrontation with Poverty in Brazil."

108. Mariz, "Pentecostalism and Confrontation with Poverty in Brazil,"134.

and unspectacular ways to attain their citizenship, and never use the word nor concept, but still enhance it, in the sense exposed above.[109]

More specifically, what is central is the "belonging to a group, the experience of power, and the creation of a new identity."[110] As indicated above, believers are easily recognized by their unfashionable, formal dress, and they would rush to their worship place with a Bible under their arm. This might seem odd in the subtropical heat of many places in Brazil, and not rarely are they ridiculed for it. But for them, the public rejection only confirms that they are on the right way, with suffering and sacrifice, but supported by Christ through the Holy Spirit, the strongest power of all. "The search for distinction, though it may seem to the poor as a negation of class origin, appears to be more a rejection of the negative stereotypes associated with poverty."[111]

Mariz also notes that by entering networks of mutual support, believers are provided with "an alternative to family and neighborhood ties."[112] This is corroborated by the Pew Forum's recent comparative survey,[113] which shows an especially high trust among renewalist church members, in a situation where interpersonal trust is generally very low (cf. above, IA3c; and below, IIIA2). As families become ever more denominationally plural, family loyalty still provides some cohesion beyond church boundaries, but is also strained by antagonistic positions, especially between Pentecostals and Roman Catholics.

Another important aspect Mariz brings to the fore is that believers encounter "lawfulness": "The sense of power and control over one's life remains [. . .] when they also are endowed with something Antonovski (1979) calls 'lawfulness', that is, when meaning is attributed as much to a miracle as to the absence of one, and people believe that 'things will be how they should be.'"[114] This refers, of course, to a strong notion of God's providence.

Faith and life are seen in direct coherence, something similar to the experience in the CEBs and Liberation Theology, although in a much more individualistic and "micro" sense: "Although Pentecostal ideology is conservative, Pentecostalism fosters a new political culture that is more egalitarian and participative, and therefore more compatible with the interests of those less favored socially."[115] This culture-transforming aspect, highlighted already by Willems,[116] is contrasted by those who, since Lalive d'Epinay,[117] see the pastoral hierarchy as a conservative element, reinstating the paternalism and patriarchalism of the rural *caudillo* in an urban setting. It is of course true that the AD have a strongly hierarchical system, and that access to power is strictly controlled by the pastor-presidents of the mother churches. Even so, as we have seen in relation to the AD's politicians and Pentecostals acting in social movements, believers are not simply submissive to their

109. The fact that Pentecostal politicians can be as corrupt as anybody else, as we have seen above (IIE1c), and that there is a great deal of political opportunism among them and the churches' leadership does not undo this important contribution to citizenship among the laity, indirect as it may be. Already in 1975, Ronald Frase in his PhD dissertation, *A Sociological Analysis of the Development of Brazilian Protestantism,* defended at Princeton University, affirmed, as non-literally quoted by Martin, *Tongues of Fire*, 65, that "Pentecostalism offers the fruits of honesty and thrift and a surrogate family, as well as the chance of participation, and a sense of worth, meaning and empowerment."

110. Mariz, "Pentecostalism and Confrontation with Poverty in Brazil," 135.

111. Ibid.

112. Ibid., 136.

113. Pew Forum, *Spirit and Power.*

114. Mariz, "Pentecostalism and Confrontation with Poverty in Brazil," 136, referring to A. Antonovsky, *Health, Stress and Coping.*

115. Ibid., 138.

116. Willems, *Followers of the New Faith.*

117. Lalive d'Epinay, *Haven of the Masses.*

leaders, and they can submit them to the scrutiny of the churches' moral law. Pastors can, at least in theory, be held accountable to their flock by being subject to the very same law. In the anomic situation many poor people are living in, being guided by clear rules that apply even to superiors is certainly an advance in citizenship.

Surely, submission to this law is also questionable; it can become highly repressive[118] and easily support authoritarian regimes, as indeed happened during the period. But it does narrow the distance between leadership and members by adopting a universally and equally valid law in a way that has never been in place for the *caudillos* or *coronéis*, who act precisely as if there were no law, except for the one they themselves impose on their subjects. As Mariz states,[119] there is a "depersonalization of power by attributing greater power to the 'word' and the law than to people," which signals a change in political culture. The factual practice of Pentecostal politicians, however, as Baptista has shown in his recent study,[120] is by no means free from the general ambiguities of Brazilian political culture, which obliges the researcher to be cautious in terms of expectations for effective transformation.

Thus, according to Mariz,[121] the new ethic adopted upon conversion "reinforces rational [sic!] option over tradition and cultural inheritance. Emphasis on the word and the study and systemization of the faith encourage attitudes and abilities that are useful to poor people in modern capitalist societies." To read and interpret the Bible is training reading skills, but also "seems to encourage verbal competence and an ability to argue, fundamental skills in democracy and modern societies."[122] They same type of training, it is worth remembering, also occurred in CEBs. As to pastors, they are offered a proper profession with little theoretical training but vast practical experience. But also musical skills can be learned and enhanced in the church which can help people professionally.

b) Social Transformation

Pentecostals are primarily concerned with individual salvation and sanctification, and there is a strong distinction between the church, as the community of the faithful, and the world.[123] Liberation Theology is repeatedly rejected for falsely suggesting that human beings could change themselves and the world effectively, among other aspects.[124] There are, however, glimpses of an instance on a "full gospel," caring and catering for the whole human being and not only his or her soul, even if

118. Cf. Alves, *Protestantism and Repression.*

119. Mariz, "Pentecostalism and Confrontation with Poverty in Brazil," 138.

120. Baptista, *Cultura política brasileira, práticas pentecostais e neopentecostais.*

121. Mariz, "Pentecostalism and Confrontation with Poverty in Brazil," 137.

122. Ibid., 139.

123. Araújo, *Dicionário do Movimento Pentecostal*, 357, in his summary of Pentecostal identity, mentions the following aspects, of which I highlight those most relevant for our theme: "1—emphasis on spirituality and power in the believers' lives [. . .]; 2—resistance against the worldly system and withdrawal from worldly things, expressed in an rigorous ethics and in the uses and customs; 3—social change of its adepts through the transformation that comes from the gospel; [. . .] 5. Abomination of sin and emphasis on the sanctification of body, soul and Spirit; [. . .] *7. Strong identification with the poor, the sufferers and the marginalized in society, making it a popular movement;* [. . .] 9. Emphasis on the universal priesthood of believers; 10. Emphasis on the centrality of the Bible [. . .]."

124. See Araújo, *Dicionário do Movimento Pentecostal*, 55; Gilberto, *Lições Bíblicas: Sal e Luz*, 63f., cf. Majewski, *Pentecostalismo e reconciliação*, 10; and extensively Almeida, *Teologia contemporânea*, 201–362.

the "preaching of the Gospel, for the salvation of the sinner, comes first."[125] Soares,[126] in his Sunday school lessons on God's justice in Romans, reinforces this, stating that "the activity of the Church is oriented towards two directions: vertical—adoration, spiritual activities; horizontal—to serve one's neighbor, philanthropic and social activities." Practicing charity is important given that most of the AD's members come from among the poor, although there is less emphasis on this aspect than in other churches. Love of the neighbor is emphasized in Sunday school, for instance while focusing on the parable of the Good Samaritan (Luke 10:30–36).[127] A book published in 1996 insists that "Man lives in the dimension of here and today [. . .] A true revival will bring back to the Brazilian believer love for the nearly 50 million of compatriot brothers who live in absolute poverty."[128]

Tithing is central and can also be interpreted as empowering, because to give money for others is to have power, and thus contradicts the situation of being poor, as Mariz argues.[129] But such charity is usually restricted to the church's members or else combined with evangelistic work, and thus not without a specific interest involved in it.

Participation in non-religious associations is low among Pentecostals,[130] but this is the case for Brazilians in general, as we have seen (IB). On the other hand, believers fervently go to church (85 percent against 17.6 percent of Catholics),[131] not only to Sunday service, but other meetings as well. Thus, Pentecostal churches are those who best mobilize people as compared to any other association. And compared with other Latin American countries, Brazilian Pentecostals show a relatively high (up to 13 percent) engagement in associations like social and cultural associations, community action and women's groups, although less so than their counterparts in Africa, Asia and the U.S.[132] However, it seems probable that many if not most of these associations are run by the church, so such engagement appears to be acceptable only when done within the churches' outreach and not in secular organizations.

In terms of specific issues, Pentecostals might or might not support them. In any case, as Political Scientist Simone Bohn's analysis[133] of the data on voters in 2002 has shown, there is no evidence to support the hypothesis that they would form anything like a "New Right." They are to be found across the party spectrum and, although morally conservative, support a variety of issues usually counted more on the left, among them State provision of services like transport, health,

125. Gilberto, *Lições Bíblicas: Sal e Luz*, 63, cf. Majewski, *Pentecostalismo e reconciliação*, 10. "Full gospel" normally refers, in the Pentecostal realm, to the gifts of the Spirit whose rediscovery restored the full gospel; see Araújo, *Dicionário do Movimento Pentecostal*, 325; Dayton, *Theological Roots of Pentecostalism*, 19–21; it here is used to include also social works. This resounds the Latin American evangelical (in the Anglo-Saxon sense) emphasis on an "integral mission" (explicitly called so in Gilberto, *Lições Bíblicas: Mestre*, 53), already mentioned above (IIE introduction). Cf. Zwetsch, *Missão como com-paixão*, 146-263 on two of this position's representatives: René Padilla and Valdir Steuernagel (the latter is a minister of the IECLB and directed, for some time, the works of World Vision in Brazil).

126. Soares, *Lições Bíblicas*, 62

127. Gilberto, *Lições Bíblica: A parábola do bom samaritano*. It has to be remembered that Sunday school, both in most historic Protestant and then in the Pentecostal churches, is for all ages and not just for children, and therefore serves as continuous education for the believers. As Majewski, Pentecostalismo e reconciliação, 2 (with reference to Araújo, *Dicionário do Movimento Pentecostal*, 35f.; 165-178; 207-214) highlights, the AD's Publishing House CPAD is highly censured and, thus, whatever is published has passed through doctrinal scrutiny and can be regarded as the church's official position.

128. Címaco, *Um grito pela vida da igreja*, 87f.

129. Mariz, "Pentecostalism and Confrontation with Poverty in Brazil."

130. Cf. Fernandes, "Governo das almas," 176ff.; Carneiro, "Cultura Cívica e participação política entre evangélicos."

131. Fernandes, "Governo das almas," 179

132. Pew Forum, *Spirit and Power*, 49.

133. Bohn, "Evangélicos no Brasil."

education and the like. As mentioned above, Pentecostals can be found in social movements, urban and rural, in unions and neighborhood associations. But they do so on an individual basis and are not supported by their church in such activities. Among the politicians, social issues are cited as necessary, as stated by the "Citizenship AD Brazil" project, which considers that there is a "need to stimulate the conscience of a stronger preoccupation with socio-political questions, fostering behavior directed by ethics, respect for the human being, the institutions and, above all, the Christian principles" and that "the existing crises in the world which involve hunger, poverty, violence, lead to claim from the constituted authorities and organized society more concrete initiatives, committed to human solidarity and the spirit of fraternity." It then also cites the "moral crisis" the Brazilian nation was passing through, visible in the low quality of Brazilian TV and other media.[134]

The practical result is certainly ambivalent. During the Sarney government, the first civil government after the end of the military regime, the AD dominated *bancada evangélica* was decisive in toppling a constitutional amendment on land reform, apparently after they received payment from the Ruralist Democratic Union (*União Democrática Ruralista*—UDR).[135] On the other hand, a survey on "issues of interest to workers" attributed a positive mark (above average) to the Pentecostal politicians in these matters (ibid.). Two AD deputies participated in the Organ Traffic Investigation Commission, and two others were involved in constitutional amendment projects on slave labor.[136] The CGDAB also supported the Referendum against the arms trade in 2005, and even sought to complement the law, prohibiting the production and sale of all arms toys, not only of those which could be taken for real arms (cf. above, IA2b).

Another important aspect is highlighted by Marco Davi de Oliveira,[137] the son of a black Pentecostal minister, who quite rightly calls Pentecostalism "the blackest religion of Brazil" (*a religião mais negra do Brasil*).[138] Of course, in absolute numbers, more black persons are Catholics than anything else. But in the Pentecostal churches, according to the 2000 Census, there are nearly as many blacks as whites: 8,690,931 whites and 8,676,997 blacks (including the *pardos*, of mixed color). Considering the error margin in statistics like these, this is a 50/50 situation. Specifically in the AD, there is a slight majority of blacks (54.54 percent or roughly 4.5 million),[139] probably because of its Northern and Northeastern origins, where black people are much more strongly present than in the South, and have indeed migrated with their belief to the Southeast, namely Rio and São Paulo. However, the AD and other Pentecostals tend to maintain the common myth of "racial democracy" (cf. above, IC), as if there were no racism, and indeed contribute to discrimination as they explicitly fight against the African Brazilian religions.[140]

Finally, while the right to property and prosperity is recognized, there is a considerable amount of reflection given in theological writings to *mordomia* (stewardship): God is Lord of all creation, and humans are to be its stewards, which means that they are to use their goods in a responsible

134. In Soares Filho, *Assembléia de Deus na política brasileira*, 54f.

135. Soares Filho, *Assembléia de Deus na política brasileira*, 40.

136. Ibid., 65.

137. Oliveira, *A religião mais negra do Brasil*.

138. On a worldwide scale, Walter Hollenwerger (*Charismatisch-pfingstliches Christentum*, 31-164) has repeatedly insisted on the "black oral root" as one of the main features of Pentecostalism and Charismatism, next to the catholic, evangelical, critical and ecumenical roots.

139. Oliveira, *A religião mais negra do Brasil*, 34.

140. Ibid., 92.

way and also to care for the environment. Believers are to care for body, soul, and spirit in a holistic stewardship.[141]

c) Family and Sexuality

Similarly to the ICAR, the *family* is of central importance to the AD. According to their literary reading of the Bible, they insist on the man as head of the family. But while doing that, the man is called not only, and maybe not even primarily, to exercise authority in the family, but to assume responsibility for it. The number of single parent families is high in Brazil, which invariably means that women have to care for the family and work for the income to support it. Thus, men who are present at home and care for their family do effectively contribute to women's liberation, even as they do it under a patriarchal biblical discourse.[142] Mariz and Machado affirm that "Pentecostal women no longer see men as masters they must obey. Nor, however, do they view them as oppressors they must rebel against. Rather, men are seen as victims of evil as they once were themselves, and therefore women feel responsible for their husbands and try to help them."[143] As men stop drinking and look out more actively for jobs, they are better received by their families and behave in a much more controlled way. As their drinking problem is also being attributed to the devil, their own responsibility is reduced, which facilitates forgiveness and reintegration into the family.

The importance of such reintegration can be illustrated by a meeting I attended with adolescent girls of about 15 years of age in a Catholic Church in Salvador (Bahia), who all spoke very badly of their fathers—either they are absent, or else when they are present they beat their wives and children and in any case do not contribute at all or very little to the household's well-being. I was struck by the extremely bad image these girls had of their fathers, and it came out in such a definitive way that our (the leader's and mine) attempts to awaken understanding for their father's behavior—without, of course, condoning it—were in vain. There was no sign of understanding for their father, nor any—at least apparent—wish for his reintegration into the family. Having been victims of their fathers' emotional and physical explosions, they seem to prefer his absence to his presence.

In comparison, Brazilian Pentecostals are relatively progressive on gender issues, as they quite readily accept women in jobs and politics. Agreement with the statement "a wife must always obey her husband" is relatively low among Brazilian Pentecostals (61 percent) as compared to their counterparts in Africa and Asia (except South Korea).[144] Even for the possibility of female clergy, there is an approval of 64 percent among Brazilian Pentecostals, although they lag behind the "other Christians" and are less pioneering in this respect than Pentecostals in all other countries surveyed by the Pew Forum.[145] The AD in Brazil, however, leave no doubt that women cannot be ordained as ministers, because they do not see any biblical resources for such practice. Paul "never separated, nor ordained, nor mentioned deaconesses, women pastors, women bishops, women apostles, etc., although he affectionately emphasizes women workers of the Gospel, whose names are eternalized on the Bible's pages because of their dedicated and loving efforts in the Lord's service."[146] The

141. Cabral, "Mordomia cristã"; Majewski, *Pentecostalismo e reconciliação.*

142. Cf. Machado, *Carismáticos e pentecostais*; Mariz and Machado, "Pentecostalism and Women in Brazil"; Mafra, "Gênero e estilo eclesial entre os evangélicos."

143. Mariz and Machado, "Pentecostalism and Women in Brazil," 52.

144. Pew Forum, *Spirit and Power*, 42.

145. Pew Forum, *Spirit and Power*, 40.

146. http://www.cgadb.com.br/sobreCgadb/posicaoSobre/ordenacaoPastoras.html (accessed on 6/22/2007).

document then tries to show that Phoebe (Rom 16:1) was exercising a merely provisional function, as an exception and not the rule.

As to *homosexuality*, the *bancada evangélica*, during the constituent process, managed to get "sexual identity" off the Constitution among those aspects for which discrimination would be forbidden. The CGADB leaves no doubt about its rejection of such sexual orientation, which it considers sin and an "abomination" (cf. Leviticus 18:22).[147] The text adds prostitution to homosexuality, apparently seeing them as belonging together, and repeats the common prejudice that "still today it can be seen that the greatest number of homosexuals is to be found in the afro-brazilian cults," thus combining rejection against sexual orientation with the rejection of another religion. Also the change of sex by surgery is condemned and should be reverted, as God has created humans "male and female" (Genesis 1,27). If such reversal was not possible, the persons concerned should "assume the condition of a eunuch."[148] The Belém ministry explains that "Like any addict or criminal abandons his life of sin and becomes a servant of God, so also the homosexual abandons his sinful practices and assumes his real identity (1 Corinthians 6.10; Romans 1.18–32)," thus considering homosexuality as a morally wrong behavior, not accepting its probably genetic origin.[149] Consequently, the CGADB is against homosexual civil unions (called *casamento*, "marriage"), as "we are absolutely convinced that the solution for homosexuals, bisexuals and lesbians is not public recognition [*oficialização*] of civil marriage, but repentance for and complete abandonment of these practices, and in the acceptance of salvation in Christ."[150]

While most Protestants and certainly Pentecostals are in line with the ICAR's position on family and against homosexuality, they diverge, as Protestants have done traditionally in Brazil, on the issue of *divorce*. The CGADB's 32nd General Assembly ruled, in 1995, that they, in light of the current legislation and biblical witness (Matthew 5.31f. and 19.9), would "welcome divorce only in cases of conjugal infidelity and repugnant crimes, duly proven, admitting, in these cases, a new matrimony, when all resources for reconciliation are ineffective." "Conjugal infidelity" is defined through "the practice of adultery," and "grave crimes" are given on drug trafficking or consumption, the practice of terrorism, homicide and "sexual deviation." Divorce and remarriage may, however, be the end of a pastor's career, at the discretion of the regional Convention or Ministry, in case the ex-wife is still alive.[151]

There are some interesting aspects to be seen in comparing Brazil and Latin America with other regions of the world, according to the Pew Forum's 2006 survey. Despite the fact that 76 percent of Brazilian Pentecostals are against homosexuality, they lag behind Guatemala and Chile, and even behind the United States in this respect, and the three Latin America countries seen together are far behind their fellow believers in Africa (99 percent among Pentecostals in Kenya!) and Asia.[152] Latin Americans generally also do not agree with the phrase that AIDS is "God's punishment for immoral sexual behaviour": only 37 percent of Pentecostals in Brazil agreed, against 42 percent in Chile, 51 percent in Guatemala, and 77 percent in South Korea.[153]

147. http://www.cgadb.com.br/sobreCgadb/posicaoSobre/homossexualismo.html (accessed on 6/22/2007), 2.

148. Ibid., 3.

149. http://www.ad.org.br/ad/a_nossa8.asp (accessed on 6/22/2007).

150. http://www.cgadb.com.br/sobreCgadb/posicaoSobre/casamentoHomossexual.html (accessed on 6/22/2007).

151. Resolution nr. 001/95, of January 29, 1995, http://www.cgadb.com.br/sobreCgadb/posicaoSobre/divorcio.html (accessed on 6/22/2007).

152. Pew Forum, *Spirit and Power*, 36.

153. Ibid., 37.

Even as to extra-marital sex, despite 63 percent of disapproval among Pentecostals in Brazil (but only 26 percent among Charismatics and 21 percent among other Christians), Latin America as a whole seems more tolerant of it than Africa and, even more so, than Asia.[154] Also in terms of prostitution, Latin America fared significantly lower than Asia and Africa, despite Brazil's 81 percent rejection among Pentecostals (but 97 percent in South Korea!). Thus, it seems possible to conclude that Latin American Christians, even Pentecostals who are the most restrictive among them, are more tolerant in sexual matters than are their Asian and African counterparts, although their ratio of disapproval is still well above 50 percent. This is valid except for the AIDS question, which is generally not understood as God's punishment, and such position may allow for a more pastoral approach towards people with AIDS. Finally, on divorce, the Pew Forum's survey confirms what has been said above: Only 37 percent of Brazilian Pentecostals say that "divorce is never justified," against far higher numbers in all other countries except the United States (84 percent in the Philippines, the highest score). The survey report states that "interestingly, in most countries, drinking is viewed as less acceptable than getting a divorce."[155]

d) Abortion, Stem Cells, and "Euthanasia"

Again quite in line with the ICAR, the AD is opposed to *abortion*, which they consider a "grave crime" and "grave sin." Only in one case it is permitted, i.e., if the mother's life is in danger.[156] During the Constituent Assembly, *evangélicos* and particularly Pentecostals were in favor of a text that would guarantee legal protection of life from its conception, with a 93 percent approval over against 46 percent of historic Protestants and 22 percent general average.[157] Deputies also spoke out against the decision by Supreme Federal Court minister Marco Aurélio Mello, which allowed the abortion of fetuses with anencephaly, and the new norm of the Health Ministry, which dispensed with the presentation of a police report when requesting abortion following rape.[158] Seen comparatively, while the rejection of Brazilian Pentecostals to abortion is very high (91 percent say it is "never justified"), a considerable percentage (41 percent) also affirm that the "government should not interfere with obtaining an abortion," much higher than in Kenya (19 percent) or the Philippines (21 percent).[159] One could speculate that the Pentecostal believers are more pragmatic here than their leaders, but it is also possible they understood such interference as supporting abortion.

Like the CNBB, the CGDAB's deputies opposed the Biosecurity law, which would allow embryonic *stem cell research*. However, the rationale given in the AD's political journal was more pragmatic, stating that "science has not yet clarified whether the used embryos do already constitute human life—and because of the absence of proof of concrete and positive results of [embryonic] research where it is permitted."[160] This can be considered a quite balanced statement on the ethical issues implied. However, the CGADB has spoken out against such research on principle, and its main ethicist, Elionaldo Renovato, expressed a clear opposition against embryonic stem cell research, given that "the Bible" (Psalm 139:13-16) considered the human being as initiated from

154. Ibid., 36.

155. Ibid., 39.

156. http://www.ad.org.br/ad/a_nossa8asp (accessed on 6/22/2007).

157. Soares Filho, *Assembléia de Deus na política brasileira*, 39.

158. *Jornal AD Brasil* 5/2, 7, and 9/3, 6, respectively, in Soares Filho, *Assembléia de Deus na política brasileira*, 66.

159. Pew Forum, *Spirit and Power*, 38.

160. *Jornal AD Brasil* 2/6, 3, cited in Soares Filho, *Assembléia de Deus na política brasileira*, 65.

the moment of fertilization, and that "the embryo is a person and needs to be respected as such in its condition of a defenseless human being [. . .] so that the sacredness of life be valued as a gift from God."[161] This is indeed the Roman Catholic position, which, surprisingly given the church's fervent anti-Catholicism, is quoted in the book.[162]

A number of issues are included under "euthanasia," starting from the principle of the sixth commandment: "you shall not kill" (Exodus 20:13).[163] On *capital punishment*, the CGADB argues that although the death penalty is not mandatory from the biblical witness, it is recognized and the State can institute it (cf. Romans 13:1-6, especially 13:4). Still, the document says that "we are against the death penalty because it was not God's original proposition." While the Bible recognizes the penalty's existence, the New Testament—differently from the Old—does not prescribe it, and in his death Jesus fulfilled the law and abolished capital punishment:

> Thus, such practice violates the spirit and the essence of Christianity, which preaches love and pardon. We repeat that we are against the death penalty, [. . .] this highest penalty will not resolve the problem of violence and criminality and can, furthermore, strengthen corruption. The solution is in the transforming message of Calvary.[164]

The second issue under this heading is *war*, where the CGADB's document says that the sixth commandment is never used in reference to war. While Christianity stands in the "dispensation of grace and [. . .] is pacifist," with reference to the Sermon on the Mount (Matthew 5:9), the notion that Christians are not only "citizens of heaven (Philippians 3:20), [but] also of the earth (Matthew 22:21)" is used precisely to insist on their submission to government. But this is followed by the argument that God's will has to prevail over the State, and thus both obedience and resistance are licit if the war is "unjust": "There are just and unjust wars, and everybody has the right to defend what is his; in this case the Christian does not sin. In the same way, he also does not sin if he refuses to go to an unjust war.[165] Renovato[166] mentions the wars against drug traffic, organized crime, and against a tyrant (like Hitler, explicitly mentioned), as well as UN peace missions as situations for legitimate participation by Christians.

The next issue here is *suicide*, which the CGADB declares sin, as here the sixth commandment is disobeyed against oneself. The text mentions that the "highest rate of suicide is in the rich countries," "among university students, of the middle class upwards and professionals," as a "result of spiritual failure." There is a certain triumphalism in such formulations, as the AD know they are composed primarily of poor people with low education, so they declare that suicide is not only sin, but a problem of the others, who are spiritually weak, while the AD are considered spiritually strong.[167] The Pew Forum[168] survey gives a similarly high rejection to suicide ("never justified," 96 percent) than in all other countries surveyed except for the United States, a fact prone to confirm the AD's prejudice against the rich and educated.

161. Renovato, *Células-tronco*, 8.

162. See, however, the favorable position of Renovato (*Lições Bíblicas: Ética cristã*) toward the donation of organs for transplants, which is considered an "act of love and solidarity" (ibid., 45).

163. http://www.cgadb.com.br/sobreCgadb/posicaoSobre/eutanasia.html (accessed on 6/22/2007).

164. Ibid., 2.

165. Ibid.

166. Renovato, *Lições Bíblicas: Ética cristã*.

167. http://www.cgadb.com.br/sobreCgadb/posicaoSobre/eutanasia.html (accessed on 6/22/2007).

168. Pew Forum, *Spirit and Power*, 38.

Finally, the document comes to what is commonly called *euthanasia*. Based on the argument that "only God can give and take life," the CGADB positions itself against euthanasia, namely any active form of it. But passive euthanasia is also considered wrong if it implies switching off machines that keep the patient alive, which here is considered active euthanasia. However, in some cases, where a "vegetative" status of the person is factual or probable and "no hope" is left, suspending or, rather, not applying a medicament is thinkable.[169] The Belém ministry is more categorical and says no to any kind of euthanasia, as God can still interfere directly "by the prayer of his servants."[170]

e) Personal Behavior

Personal behavior is certainly an important aspect in the "restitution of lives" claimed by the AD (cf. above, IIE2a), given that conversion and personal transformation lie at the heart of their proclamation, repeated in all worship services, where people are called forward to accept the Lord as their savior. The rigid rules do give a clear orientation as to how life as a convert is supposed to be, and church discipline reinforces it, especially when it comes to issues related to family and sexuality. The so called "uses and customs" *(usos e costumes)*[171] are seen as linked to doctrine. According to Antonio Gilberto, the main CGADB theologian, as paraphrased by Araújo,[172]

> biblical doctrine, when ministered under the unction of the Holy Spirit and lived by the believer, in practice, through the 'love of the Holy Spirit' (cf. Romans 15:30), produces in the believer and the congregation *holy and good customs* which, on their part, confirm biblical doctrine (cf. 1 Corinthians 15:33; Titus 2:10).

Such customs, by many believers simply called "doctrine" because of the connection just shown, are seen as distinctive of the AD, as they are of other churches. Thus, a taxi driver in São Paulo who was from the AD explained that they could not commune with believers from the Brazilian Christian Congregation because the latter insisted that women came veiled to church. Apparently, such "custom" of women (not) using a veil during worship is considered "doctrine" and so distinctive that it becomes exclusive. Mariano, on describing the liberalization of such customs by the Neo-Pentecostal churches, remembers that, due to their distinctive outfit, the *crentes* ("believers") were (and are) immediately spotted, and called names like *bíblias* ("Bibles"), *glórias* ("glories"), *aleluias* ("alleluias") or even *bodes* ("bucks").[173] The Brazilian population holds a stereotype of the beliefs and practices of Pentecostal believers, while largely reflecting the same outlooks themselves. To be against alcohol, smoking, dancing, sensual clothing, and other worldly things had already been practiced in many historical Protestant churches in their countercultural attitude, but this became radicalized in the classical Pentecostal churches.[174]

169. http://www.cgadb.com.br/sobreCgadb/posicaoSobre/eutanasia.html (accessed on 6/22/2007), 3.

170. http://www.ad.org.br/ad/a_nossa8.asp (accessed on 6/22/2007).

171. Araújo, *Dicionário do Movimento Pentecostal*, 879-891.

172. Ibid., 879.

173. Mariano, *Neopentecostais*, 187.

174. An interesting detail is brought up by Schuler, *Pfingstbewegungen in Brasilien*, 46f., who quotes Francisco Cartaxo Rolim, *O que é pentecostalismo?* (São Paulo: Brasiliense, 1981): although both the Catholic and the Pentecostal churches did not engage with the workers' movement at the beginning of the 20th century, they shared these values with them: the Pentecostals because they considered these practices sin, the workers' movement because they saw them as expressions of a corrupt and oppressive bourgeoisie. However, while Pentecostals complied, the workers did not.

There is an ongoing debate in the AD whether such customs can and should be altered.[175] Already at the 1946 General Convention, it was a matter of debate due to clothing, hairstyle, and makeup rules for women introduced in the São Cristóvão AD in Rio de Janeiro, considered exaggerated by the Convention. Swedish missionary Samuel Nyström (1891–1960) responded insisting that the "Dispensation of the Law is over" and that "faith works through love." He also mentions that there are different clothing costumes around the world and different climates, which have to be taken into account. The thrust of the argument is that the Spirit would work in women and man so that they would seek to live a decent life. Not to the least, Nyström recalled to the AD that

> there are many other things that are equally dangerous for the Lord's work, which can only be removed by the Holy Spirit, like love of money, which [. . .] is the root of all evils. The man who exposes his own justice, criticizing everything and all, is a dangerous individual for the advancement and the unity of the Lord's work.[176]

Of course, the 1968 student and sexual revolution stirred up the AD and led to discussion on miniskirts and long-haired males. A typical authoritarian principle was used to end the discussion: "If the pastor cannot govern his house, he should also not govern the church."[177]

The 22nd General Convention of the AD in 1975 had reaffirmed eight such "healthy principles established as doctrine in God's Word—the Holy Bible—and preserved as customs since the beginning of this Work [i.e. the AD] in Brasil."[178] A Commission preparing the 5th meeting of AD leaders (ELAD), held in Rio de Janeiro in August 1999, insisted, however, on the difference between "doctrine" and "customs." While the former were seen as divine, general and unchangeable, the latter would be human, local and temporary.[179] The commission thus changes the 1975 wording by leaving out "as doctrine," now reading only "healthy principles established in God's Word—the Holy Bible—and preserved as customs," moderating the language and inserting biblical references. The changes are shown in the following table:

AD churches [i.e., their members] are to abstain from:

22nd General Convention—1975	*Commission for the 5th Meeting of AD leaders—1999*
1. The use of grown hair by members of the male sex;	1. For men to have grown hair (1 Corinthians 11.14), as well as to make extravagant cuts;
2. the use of male dress by members or congregants of the female sex;	2. women using clothes which are typical for men and indecent and rude, or without modesties (1 Timothy 2.9,10);
3. the use of paintings on eyes, nails and other facial organs;	3. the exaggerated use of painting and make-up—nails, tattoos and hair— (Leviticus 19.28; 2 Kings 9.30);

175. Some texts go as far as to contrast the customs debate with social justice and the need for a "prophetic" role of the church: "It brings us no further to combat uses and customs, when one closes the eyes and remains silent in relation to the injustices and the oppression of the rich over the poor. God makes us preachers of justice" (Renovato, *Lições Bíblicas: Mestre*, 77); see also Gilberto, *Lições Bíblicas: Mestre*, 53.

176. The whole text is reproduced in Araújo, *Dicionário do Movimento Pentecostal*, 881f. See also Andrade, *Lições Bíblicas: Não terás outros deuses diante de mim*, 14–16, who argues against the "worship of money" and calls for investing excess money into philanthropy.

177. Araújo, *Dicionário do Movimento Pentecostal*, 883.

178. http://www.cgdab.com.br/sobreCgadb/posicaoSobre/usosCostumes.html (accessed on 6/22/2007), 1.

179. http://www.cgdab.com.br/sobreCgadb/posicaoSobre/usosCostumes.html (accessed on 6/22/2007), 2.

4. [sc. short] haircut by sisters (members or congregants);	4. the use of short hair against Biblical recommendation (1 Corinthians 11.6,15);
5. altered eyebrows;	
6. the use of mini-skirts and other clothes against the good testimony of Christian life;	
7. the use of television—one should abstain from it, in view of the bad quality of the majority of its programs; abstention which is justified, inclusively, for leading to possible health problems;	5. a bad use of the means of communication: television, internet, radio, telephone (1 Co 6.12; Phil 4.8);
8. the use of alcoholic beverages.	6. the use of alcoholic and intoxicating beverages (Proverbs 20.1; 26.31 [sic!]; 1 Corinthians 6.10; Ephesians 5.18).[A]

A. Proverbs 26.31 does not exist; they probably refer to Proverbs 23.31.

Source: CGDAB Website

This "aggiornamento" in terms of behavior is accompanied by an interesting argumentation that wants to steer a path between losing the AD's identity—which is precisely expressed through its "customs"—and absolutizing it. Thus, the document separates salvation by faith (alone!) from such customs, while it recognizes that "religious convictions are personal" and, if there are different denominations with different customs, it is because God wanted it so. This sounds surprisingly ecumenical—although it only refers to a debate among Pentecostals and between them and Neo-Pentecostal churches—and, at the same time, very Protestant with its emphasis on salvation (justification) by faith alone. Not without boldness, the document emphasizes, using the sociologists' terminology in their self-denomination: "We are classical [sic!] Pentecostals, i.e., we are models for others, [and] it is they who should learn from the Assemblies of God and not we from them inasmuch as Pentecostal doctrine is concerned," which refers critically to AD pastors who think the IURD's techniques should be copied and that doctrine and customs prevented the church from growing.[180]

The rejection of drinking is a common feature among Pentecostals anywhere in the world, but lower in Brazil (72 percent) in relation to other countries (86 percent in Guatemala, 88 percent in Kenya, 84 percent in Nigeria and in the Philippines, although South Africa, Chile, and the U.S. are still lower—all of them, *nota bene*, important wine producers).[181]

Mariz highlights the importance of the concept of "liberation" in Pentecostal practice and theology, which precisely reflects such personal transformation.[182] Without explicitly citing him, but certainly referring to DaMatta's distinction between "person" and "individual" (cf. above, IA3c), for Mariz Pentecostalism leads the believer to conceive of himself as an "individual" with a certain degree of autonomy or power of choice, and to reject the concept of "person," i.e., the subject that restricts itself to the traditionally prescribed roles. Thus, for her, Pentecostalism is not exclusively, not even primarily "magical," but "the idea of 'liberation' would permit [. . .] a transition between the magical universe of 'person' to the ethical-rational of the 'individual.'"[183]

180. http://www.cgdab.com.br/sobreCgadb/posicaoSobre/usosCostumes.html (accessed on 6/22/2007), 4; also Araújo, *Dicionário do Movimento Pentecostal*, 884–86.

181. Pew Forum, *Spirit and Power*, 39.

182. Mariz, "Libertação e ética."

183. Ibid., 205.

It is, then, the concept of liberation that bridges the magical and the ethical, the personal and the individual. Indeed, in comparison to the IURD, where the magical clearly prevails over the ethical,[184] the AD seeks to maintain both aspects in a balance. It is precisely this fact, if I interpret correctly, that prevents the AD believers from blindly following their leaders or condoning corruption among their politicians. The "law" is, at least in principle, above everybody, and all have to measure themselves and others against it.

While this is indeed about personal behavior and not a project of social transformation, it does have a bearing on the latter. This has been the object of considerable debate. While a good number of social scientists defend that Pentecostalism has a far stronger bearing on politics than one normally sees and expects,[185] others hold there would be no evidence to prove such a bearing.[186] It is certainly correct to say that empirical literature "gives us no particular reason to believe that Protestants [read: Pentecostals] intrinsically constitute a cultural or organizational opposition to patterns and structures of traditional, authoritarian political and social domination in the democratic era," although they in any case "contribute to post-authoritarian pluralism."[187] Especially in view of Pentecostal politicians, the result is at the least ambiguous.[188]

But the problem of such arguments, in my view, is to tendentiously narrow politics to formal politics in electing or elected roles, or to participation in civil society, and also to expect a direct coherence between discourse and practice—which, as we have seen, is not the case on the political level. Such coherence exists only for personal behavior on the micro-level. There, abidance is controlled and sanctioned by (formal and informal) church discipline, but generally restricted to matters of sexual and family morals.

My argument is that precisely the fact that such coherence does not exist on the political level can be seen as a signal for an enhancement of individual decision-making, on the one hand, and a referral to common rules, on the other, which are applied indistinctively to all, believers and leadership alike.[189] This should, of course, not serve as an excuse to critically analyze the rules, the "law" itself, nor say that a higher direct engagement in social transformation would not be desirable and, indeed, theologically perfectly justifiable, even in the AD's own terms. In fact, as we have seen, many documents do state such transformation as a goal of the AD's political project. The problem is that this project seems to have been used primarily in terms of getting more *evangélicos* into elected offices to enhance the church's influence. Thus, the church itself points to its politicians as the main political contribution. But it was proven wrong by its own constituency, which did not re-elect its representatives allegedly linked to a corruption scheme. Thus, customs or "doctrine" provide a restricting anchor and a recognizable identity, which, if more clearly amplified to include social issues apart from family and sexuality related issues, could be a promising basis for concentrating the already existing, but dispersed efforts.

184. Cf. Mariano, *Neopentecostais.*

185. Willems, *Followers of the New Faith*; Martin, *Tongues of Fire*; Ireland, *Kingdoms Come*, "Pentecostalism, Conversions, and Politics in Brazil," "Popular Religions"; Burdick, *Looking for God in Brazil*; Mariz, *Coping with Poverty*, "Libertação e ética," "Pentecostalism and Confrontation with Poverty in Brazil"; Dodson, "Pentecostals, Politics and Public Space."

186. Prandi, "Perto da magia, longe da política"; Gaskill, "Rethinking Protestantism.."

187. Gaskill, "Rethinking Protestantism," 86f.

188. Baptista, *Cultura política brasileira.*

189. In practice, however, it is a rare case to denounce pastors, who often are seen and treated as untouchable in the sense of a category distinct of and above the believers; I thank Rodrigo Majewski for this information taken from his own AD member experience and knowledge, cf. also Alencar, *Assembléia de Deus.*

Another aspect is the related debate as to whether Pentecostalism is in continuity with Latin American, Catholic, patron-client relationship based culture, or in discontinuity with it—the debate opened already in the 1960s by Lalive D'Épinay on the one hand and Emilio Willems on the other, and reinforced recently by Baptista.[190] But it is highly questionable to maintain an either-or outlook, because there have been and still are different tendencies, cultures, and sub-cultures at work that are not to be decided in an either-or way, lest one fall into essentialisms that post-colonial studies have rightly questioned,[191] or disregard the contradicting evidence on Pentecostals taking part in different ways in formal and informal politics, both in conservative and progressive ways.

3. THEOLOGICAL ELEMENTS

. . . o aprendizado e a postulação de direitos civis e sociais
[. . .] farão do grupos dos irmãos um elemento
de vanguarda na luta pela plenitude cidadã.

Carlos Lessa[192]

Having gone through some of the CGADB's official documents as well as literature published by the CPAD and some of the sociological literature available, the result can be called ambiguous. Based on considerable sociological research, available to a relatively higher degree than on the ICAR and, even more so, the IECLB, we can say that the AD's discourse is highly conservative, often in line with the ICAR on moral issues, but, different from the ICAR, remarkably silent on social issues. This has not prevented it, since the early 1980s as *abertura* progressed, from increasingly sending "brothers" to political bodies, nor has it been thorough enough to prevent individuals and small groups from engaging in social movements, neighborhood associations, and the like. Like the CEBs, the AD's congregations have worked as catalysts for the formation of citizens, who discovered themselves as human beings with dignity and were able to show this in their form of belief and worship, but also in their attitudes, practices, clothing, and respected activity, up to assuming leadership in their congregations and church related associations.

As in the previous case studies, I shall now take up the theological elements contained in both discourse and practice, on democracy and citizenship (a), the relationship to the State (b), to society (c), and between political and ecclesial citizenship (d).

a) Citizenship and Democracy

As we have seen, the AD's contribution to citizenship and, thus, to democracy is much less theoretical and indeed counts on little explicit discourse. But sociological data supports the hypothesis that they are making an extremely important indirect contribution. First, believers are enabled to discover and recover their sense of dignity. Second, they are empowered by the Holy Spirit and can be, regardless of color, gender, social location, or other distinctive factor, receivers of the Spirit's gifts. Third, they can learn to exercise leadership in their church, in ways that may benefit their professional activity. Fourth, they take more responsibility for their own lives and their families and are often able to escape drug or alcohol addiction, as well as crime. Fifth, they submit to a

190. Lalive D'Épinay, *Haven of the Masses*; Willems, *Followers of the New Faith*; Baptista, *Cultura política brasileira*.

191. Cf. Costa, *Vom Nordatlantik zum "Black Atlantic."*

192. ". . .the learning and the claiming of civil and social rights will make of the brothers [i.e., Pentecostal believers] an element of vanguard in the struggle for citizen plenitude," Lessa, *O Rio de todos os Brasis*, 443.

principle of lawfulness rather than to hierarchy—although the latter exists and clearly concentrates and controls power—to the extent that failing pastors and church appointed politicians are equally subject to such law as the believers and are effectively held accountable for their behavior.

More specifically, in his book on ethics, Oliveira states that the Christian has rights and duties.[193] However, only the duties are emphasized and specified: the Christian has *civil duties*, that is to respect the Fatherland and the authorities and to pay taxes (Matthew 22:21), and *social duties*, to act for the well-being of one's neighbor. To be saved does not put the Christian outside the world, and thus he has a commitment to help others in an appropriate way. Among the examples quoted are Sunday school, which gathers children, and the Salvation Army, which combines spiritual and social work.[194] For whatever the Christian has done or not, he will have to account for it on the day of God's judgment.

It is true that Pentecostals in general and the AD in particular follow a dualistic contraposition between the church and the world, certainly in a more Augustinian than Lutheran sense (cf. below, IIIA5). Their pre-millennial expectation of the imminent return of Christ seems to discourage political engagement. But a closer look at the sociological evidence shows that this is not so. Pentecostals are indeed engaged in social issues, mainly on the micro- but also on the macro-level. They are to be found across the party and ideological spectrum. The appointed politicians follow a pragmatic line. The only themes reasonably predictable in their voting and engagement are the above named moral issues, such as the family, abortion, opposition to homosexuality, divorce, as well as the broad field of "euthanasia," where they hold relatively balanced views (for instance against the death penalty and supporting opposition against an "unjust" war, as well as the possibility of passive euthanasia in some cases) and, more recently, bioethics. They certainly tend to hold clear views, similar to the ICAR on moral issues, rather than giving the decision back to believers as is the tendency in the IECLB. But they take care to argue their case, as is shown by the CGADB's statements, and on some points signal that another position would be thinkable.

Fernandes affirms that "the democratic bias according to which there is no salvation outside citizenship must be relativized by the Christian maxim 'render to Caesar the things that are Caesar's, and to God the things that are God's.'[195] With it, the theme of the coexistence of distinct totalizing spheres of socialization open up, as well as the intersection and dynamic which could be gained between them." Certainly, the quoted biblical principle can be read towards a more critical or a more submissive relationship with the State, but it holds open a potentially healthy tension.

b) Church and State

The AD have never been an established church, nor come from a place where they had been an established church. To the contrary, from the outset they were founded by persons and among persons who were a tiny and disliked minority over against a Lutheran (in Sweden) or Roman Catholic Church (in Brazil), established *de iure* or *de facto*, respectively. The very fact that religious pluralism came about mainly through this strongly growing segment of Christianity is a gain in terms of religious freedom and independence of the State from religion and religion from the State.

The AD theologian Oliveira insists both on the separation of and relationship between church and State.[196] While there should be no official church or even a concordat between the church and

193. Oliveira, *Ética cristã*.

194. Ibid., 105.

195. Fernandes, "Governo das almas," 180.

196. Oliveira, *Ética cristã*.

the State, since they have distinct responsibilities, the church should be the State's "conscience," calling it to "act with legality," and it should evaluate the State's actions according to God's commandment. At the same time, the church has duties with respect to the State and must fulfill them, with reference to Romans 13:1-7, 1 Peter 2:11-17, and 1 Timothy 2:1-3. But there are voices that insist that Romans 13 is a generic text and "does not speak of the legitimacy or not of the instituted government," thus opening up the possibility of resisting illegitimate governments, without, however, defining them.[197] Renovato affirms that "as citizens of heaven, Christians already have their legitimate representative, who is the Holy Spirit. As Christians of the earth, we need to influence the nation's destinies."[198] How exactly this is to be done, or what would be the criteria to resist a government, is unclear, but the whole spectrum of themes highlighted in the ICAR and the IECLB are also present, interestingly with the exception of indigenous peoples and land reform, which have not found specific repercussion. As with black people, there is no specific valuing of indigenous culture as such; so called "transcultural" missions use cultural knowledge merely in order to come close to indigenous peoples, through the translation of the Bible and the formation of native leaders, seeking to "reach" as many peoples as possible.[199] Furthermore, Pentecostalism, although not totally absent in the countryside, is largely an urban phenomenon.

While this view comes near to a sound Two-Kingdoms-Doctrine, the tendency has in fact been to insist more on submissiveness and obedience to the "constituted authorities" than criticism of them. Moreover, the copying of many of the latter's non-democratic habits among the AD's leadership is an obstacle to a critical relationship. As we have seen, during the military regime, the AD did not only practice quietism, but enjoyed the authorities' courting to substitute the ICAR where it had become critical of the State and thus had withdrawn its support for particular politicians. Even under democracy, the AD's politicians sought personal (!) and corporative advantages and fell twice (in 1986 and 2006) over corruption scandals, in contrast to their preaching of morality in politics. IURD's supreme bishop Edir Macedo's "Plan to Power"[200] seeks to mobilize all *evangélicos* (under his leadership, of course) to make their electoral weight being felt. It seems a good sign for Brazilian society that this is by no means considered an acceptable plan for all *evangélicos*, and they are in many respects as heterogenous as anybody else, which makes a religious cleavage that could endanger democracy highly unlikely.[201]

c) Church and Society

Although they, in principle, affirm the social responsibility of the church and believers for the "neighbor's well-being,"[202] the AD tend to be very much focused on their own institutional interests, and then how best to be a client of the State's representatives, rather than seeking cooperation with other organizations of civil society. There were and are certain networks like the *bancada evangélica* and the CEB, later the "Evangelical Parliamentary Front" and the Brazilian National Pastor's Council (CNPB), but they remain partial and are virtually exclusively geared towards parliamentary politics. Even the "Citizenship AD Brazil" project, although focusing on citizenship and social issues, was mainly an articulation of the CGADB's interest to make it more efficient. Different

197. Lira, *Lições Bíblicas: Mestre*, 69.

198. Renovato, *Lições Bíblicas: Ética cristã*, 60.

199. Cf. Almeida, "Tradução e mediação."

200. Macedo e Oliveira, *Plano de poder*.

201. Cf. Burity, "Religião, voto e instituições políticas," 197–202.

202. Oliveira, *Ética cristã*, 105.

from Catholics and Lutherans, then, who explicitly seek to interact with other sectors of society, the AD tend to trust only their own organizations. This does not, however, exclude the possibility, as we have seen, of individuals or small groups joining associations of civil society to press for specific issues.

Indeed, the AD themselves and institutions created by them provide opportunities for civil society engagement, which might potentially become more open to cooperation with others by focusing on issues that are critical for all (like health care, education, employment, and transportation). In this way, a sense of being accepted rather than a victim of persecution might come to the fore. Dodson affirms:

> What I have argued [. . .], more in the spirit of Willems than in that of Lalive d'Epinay, is that the high degree of participation Pentecostal membership encourages is a necessary attribute of civil society. The increased senses of personal efficacy that conversion and membership bring can help to overcome the alienation that is so threatening in a state of increasing equality of condition. The finding of one's voice in the context of an association has the potential to take members of Pentecostal churches beyond the cultivation of the spiritual life alone. It can, although there is no guarantee that it will, lead to participation in the wider activities of civil society—fostering education, creating structures to find or deliver health care, seeking legal protection for their churches and religious activities, and so on. To the extent that this happens, Pentecostalism will become a companion to freedom in a democratizing Latin America.[203]

As has been pointed out by Gaskill[204] and others, this remains a potential rather than a clear reality. But if there is no evidence that Pentecostalism fosters political engagement necessarily or even more strongly than others, there is also no evidence to the contrary, despite the *fuga mundi* theological discourse. It is probably inadequate to expect a clear position here given that Pentecostals are still seeking their place in society in the midst of a society in which the Catholic Church is dominant, and in the face of competition with other rapidly growing churches, and their own ambiguity towards rational theological argument. What is important, then, is to remain attentive to small signs here and there that might be indicative of a new or strengthened tendency.

d) Political and Ecclesial citizenship

In its internal structure, the AD stand for both democratic and hierarchical elements. While believers recover their sense of dignity and are empowered as bearers of the Spirit, and get concrete opportunities to exercise and improve their skills, when it comes to offices in the church, they are submitted to a strict hierarchy. Power is organized in a top down way, and while the process of political appointments, for instance, is more participatory than in the IURD, it is still not democratic in the sense of consultations with the whole flock. Believers do, however, have indirect power in terms of moral pressure, when members or leaders infringe the moral law imposed on all.

The Christian is clearly seen as a "civil citizen," defined as a "free citizen" with reference to the 1988 Constitution's famous 5th article.[205] A certain coherence between the two citizenships is claimed from *crente* politicians: they must stay faithful to the church and follow their respective party's philosophy with a "Christian conscience." There is a tension between party militancy and Christian witness, stated with reference to 1 Corinthians 2.2: "For I decided to know nothing among you except Jesus Christ, and him crucified."

203. Dodson, "Pentecostals, Politics and Public Space," 37.

204. Gaskill, "Rethinking Protestantism."

205. Oliveira, *Ética cristã*.

But nowhere is the democratic principle applied to themselves, to a critique of the church as such or its pastors' practices. When the new Civil Code was introduced, Pentecostals were very keen to reestablish a specific category for churches in order to avoid having to adopt an association's structure, where a General Assembly could be called by members and a pastor's usually fairly autocratic decisions could be overruled (cf. above, IIB2). Clientelism within the church is also not uncommon, and, as seen in the case of the president of the CGADB, there is a tendency towards perpetuating oneself in office, as well as putting one's family in key positions.[206] As long as these practices prevail, and the democratization of the Spirit does not reach the church's own structure and functioning, the AD will only partially operate as schools for citizenship and democracy.

206. Cf. Baptista, *Cultura política brasileira*.

F. Concluding Remarks

On concluding the case studies, before heading into the development of a public theology focused on citizenship, it is appropriate to provide a comparative summary.

The *Roman Catholic Church* has stood out as the one that tackles contemporary issues, namely human dignity, human rights, citizenship, social justice, land reform, and rights for indigenous peoples most consistently, far beyond the return to civilian government. Catholic Social Teaching has provided the grounds for this, having grown stronger especially since the Second Vatican Council, and having incorporated insights from Latin America, like the preferential option for the poor. The ICAR is able, through its own communication network as well as the media in general, to communicate its position both to its members and to the public in general, so that its position is easily identifiable. Being a hierarchically structured church, the bishops, the CNBB and the pope, and to a minor degree the theologians, intellectuals, and church-related movements and institutions, are those looked to for the church's profile. The ICAR's continuous influence on the State, albeit informal, is palpable. Through its pastoral work, movements and many individuals, a good number of which have migrated from a church centered or CEB activity to action in civil society or even the political system, the church is present among the population in general and civil society in particular. While it no longer serves as the umbrella for civil society, as had been the case in the 1970s and 1980s, it still maintains a high degree of credibility and influence, and Catholics in civil society and politics up to president Lula will respect, to a large extent, its position. Even if what Catholics in fact think and do shows, in some respects, considerable differences from official positions, the authority of those who represent such positions goes largely unquestioned. Liberation Theology's questioning of the church's hierarchical structure and the striving for an ecclesiogenesis "from below" has had only modest results. While the ICAR fully accepts and seeks to contribute to democracy in the public sphere, it does not find it acceptable within its own ranks, even if some adjustments have been made to enhance lay participation in the church's administration. While a great deal of liberty and responsibility is attributed to the believing citizens with respect to social issues, this is not the case with moral issues. This asymmetry between social and moral issues is in line with the world church, namely under the pontificate of John Paul II (1978–2005), which covers most of the period treated here. The ICAR's transnational dimension has given both invaluable support and a certain protection during the military regime, and imposed restrictions on the church's position and freedom of theological discussion towards its end and, especially, into the new democracy.

The *Evangelical Church of the Lutheran Confession in Brazil* has had to conquer its own citizenship first, then to define it clearly as citizenship in Brazil, detached from a nationalist Germanism, and then to expand it to a participation in the struggle for citizenship for all. The documents have shown a growing public positioning since the Curitiba Manifesto in 1970. As is the case with the

ICAR, a broad spectrum of themes is treated in official documents (manifestos, pastoral letters from the presidency, Council resolutions) and echoed in the church's main newspaper, the *Jornal Evangélico*. The JOREV and the Faculty of Theology in São Leopoldo can be seen as places where more radical thinking was developed and socialized. It has drawn on the theology of Luther, Barth, and Bonhoeffer, Liberation Theology and Ecumenical Social Thought, and gained from interaction with the national and continental ecumenical organizations (namely CONIC, CESE, and CLAI), the Lutheran World Federation, and the World Council of Churches. Alumni and alumnae have joined the ICAR's struggle for land reform and indigenous rights, collaborating in the CPT and with the CIMI in the church's own missionary council (COMIN), and the church has created the CAPA to work with its specific traditional constituency, the small farmer. Such articulation and reflection had a great deal of influence on the church's leadership. Its reach, however, was limited among the church's members and the public in general, and became even more limited as the JOREV saw a considerable drop in subscriptions. Due to its still being seen by many as a foreign or at least ethnic church ("church of the Germans"), its concentration in the South of the country and its modest size, public repercussion of the IECLB's statements has been much more restricted than is the case with the ICAR. Among its members, the church's position is not always known and, if it is, does not necessarily influence their own position and behavior. From what can be said based on the very restricted empirical research, church members have remained largely conservative and skeptical towards social transformation. This is, of course, also a consequence of the Lutheran tradition of the priesthood of all believers and the church's democratic structure, which does not impose a position on its members, but seeks to assist and orient them in their own decisions. The IECLB grew up as a participatory, democratic church and continues to have a high degree of internal plurality. It is probably the church that fosters citizenship most through its own practice and insistence on the believer's responsibility, and in this has been able to appeal to some, namely well educated people. The church's plea for social justice, combined with personal freedom, ecumenical openness, and low level of moral prescriptions is attractive for them. The IECLB has not been able, however, to reach out to the poor beyond its traditional rural membership, which includes people with very modest income. It has also been unable to overcome its low profile in the public sphere, especially on a national level. For many, Lutheranism is still a great *incognito*.

Conversely, the *Assemblies of God* represent a remarkable phenomenon of church growth, especially among the poor. Their discourse on issues of citizenship is scant, and centered much more on duties and obedience than on rights and a critical stance, which has led to quietism, compliance, and even subservience during the military regime, rewarded by excellent conditions for further growth—these were the "golden years" according to Araújo.[1] It is timid on social issues, different from the ICAR, and outspoken on morals, in this respect maybe ironically close to its principal adversary, the ICAR. Still, the AD are probably the church that has most been able to "restore lives," giving back a sense of dignity to those who have lost it in drug addiction, prison, or poverty. Here lies the AD's main contribution to citizenship. But it retains an ambivalence between the democratization of the Spirit and the priesthood of all believers, and an authoritarian, pastor-centered structure that copied rather than modified personalistic, hierarchical, and clientelist structures present in traditional Brazilian society—especially in the North and Northeast regions, where the AD came from and where they are particularly strong. Since the 1980s, the church has been politically active, mainly in providing representation within the political system through voting for brothers. In contrast to their moralist discourse, they have not proven to be any less corrupt than

1. Araújo, *Dicionário do Movimento Pentecostal*.

other politicians; but at least some paid for this by not being reelected. The "law" is for all, even if it is not applied to all in the same way—pastors are largely untouchable and run their churches like fiefdoms, practicing nepotism and clientelism as they find fit. The AD's profile is clearly detectable and known both by its members and the wider public through its publicity and a rigid code of behavior that makes it easy to detect on the street who is a *crente*. Internal discipline is maintained among its members and avoids too much distance between the leadership and believers, different from the other two churches. Still, such control is not totalitarian, and has not prevented individuals from joining social movements or from voting for other candidates rather than those supported by the church's leaders. Theological reflection, initially developed on a minimum scale in a church that is largely composed of people with little formal education, and centered on religious experience and a literalist understanding of the Bible, appears to be growing and may provide the grounds for a more explicit and critical positioning on social issues.

Based on the case studies in Part II and the summary given here, I have organized the most important aspects of each case in a table. I admit that the categories do not follow a clear-cut quantifiable categorization as in a sociological or politological study, but are indicative of tendencies identified from documentary, theological and empirical research.

	ICAR	*IECLB*	*AD*
military regime	opposition	moderate opposition	compliance
democracy	affirmed	affirmed	affirmed (implicitly)
citizenship	strong in discourse and practice stress on rights	strong in discourse, moderate in practice stress on rights and duties	strong in practice, weak in discourse stress on duties
civil society	strong collaboration	moderate collaboration	weak collaboration
political influence	strong through direct contacts moderate in paritative councils weak through parties	moderate through participation in paritative councils and civil society, some elected members weak through parties	moderate through elected members weak through parties
public influence	strong	weak	moderate
clarity of position	strong	moderate, delegated to believers, allows for pluralism	strong
members' compliance	moderate in social issues disparate in moral issues	moderate—controversial, but supportive in governing bodies like the Council	moderate in social issues strong in moral issues

theological foundation	strong principles of Catholic Social Teaching church as watchdog option for the poor God's Kingdom has signs in society	moderate human dignity and rights justice, love and peace two differentiated, but not separate kingdoms	weak or counter-productive submissiveness Romans 13 with slight limit in Acts 5:29 separation of religion and politics, pre-millennialism
international support	strong, formative	moderate	weak
ecumenical articulation	moderate	strong	weak
internal democracy	weak hierarchical with participatory elements	strong participatory	weak hierarchical, authoritarian

With these results and distinctions in mind, I can now go on to part III.

PART III

TOWARDS A PUBLIC THEOLOGY FOCUSED ON CITIZENSHIP

After having gone through the Brazilian situation and theological discussion (I), focusing on the challenges and possibilities of citizenship and the activities of citizens in the public sphere through institutions of civil society, among them the churches, and having analyzed the position of three representative churches in Brazil as to issues relevant to citizenship (II), I am now in a position to venture into theological references for a public theology focused on citizenship. All along the present study, issues to be tackled by theology and specific references have been mentioned, according to the official church positioning and some of its main bodies and related institutions, where possible counterbalanced with empirical data on the opinion of church members. What can, then, be said from a theological reflection on being a citizen in Brazil today? How can it react to the challenges outlined earlier—social inequalities, disjunctions between democracy as a system and democracy as lived, ambiguities in relationships, lack of trust? In what way can the identity and practice of human beings in general, and Christians in particular be defined as a citizen's? An answer is sought for the challenges and developments outlined in chapters IA-IC, and an effort is made to fill in the gap left open by Liberation Theology by, despite being the theology *par excellence* of social transformation, only timidly taking on board the issues of citizenship, despite their being so widely debated today in Brazilian society (cf. ID).

Although this part will engage with the theological foundations outlined by Liberation Theology and identified in the churches' positions in part II, it is not simply a synthesis of all, nor does it adopt one particular church's position. Of course, the Lutheran tradition as lived and thought in Brazil will be particularly visible, being the one in which I have been moving, congregating, and ministering while in Brazil. It will also be evident that I believe, with Gottfried Brakemeier, that Christianity in general is a "difficult religion," and Lutheranism in particular is "one of the most ambitious varieties of Christianity."[1] This is certainly contrary to a mass appeal, and it is indeed not likely that Brazilian Lutheran churches will attract new members in great numbers. Still, it can make a difference by showing its qualities rather than hiding them, precisely as a church with a low degree of ambition to compete, but a high degree of quality in terms of education, theological and other, and diakonia. Furthermore, it seems to me to be worthwhile to bring to a wider, international public a Lutheran reflection on citizenship with reference to Brazilian authors, because it

1. Brakemeier, *O ser humano em busca de identidade*, 27. This can also be said about the CEBs, which for researchers like Burdick (*Looking for God in Brazil*) is a reason for their loss of members; cf. Drogus, "Review: The Rise and Decline of Liberation Theology," 470.

is a genuine contribution to a tradition that has been repeatedly questioned, and rightly so, as to its submissiveness and lack of critical posture in relation to the State and society.

In any case, even as to this tradition, what I shall propose is meant to be a constructive as well as critical contribution. The kind of reflection offered here follows the line of mediating between contextuality and catholicity, as lined out in earlier publications.[2] Both dimensions, which guarantee the contemporary relevance (contextuality) and the time- and space-transcending identity of the Christian Faith (catholicity), are dynamically interrelated and find their expression in human language, with all the restrictions that necessarily entails. What follows is, therefore, neither a dogmatic tract of a specific *locus* in its own right, nor the sealing of a specific situation or "historical project" (see above, ID1). It tries, however, to offer reflections for the churches and seminaries to rethink and strengthen their efforts towards citizenship for all, and thus to make a theological contribution to one of the central debates in Brazil's public sphere today.

The first chapter of this part shall reflect on elements for a theology focused on citizenship (IIIA). The second will focus on public theology, as it is deemed relevant for Brazil and Latin America, in comparison to public theology in other contexts, namely in other emerging countries with similar difficulties, like South Africa (IIIB).

2. Sinner, "Ecumenical Hermeneutics for a Plural Christianity," *Reden vom Dreieinigen Gott in Brasilien und Indien*, 34–53.

A. Elements of a Theology Focused on Citizenship

But our citizenship is in heaven, and it is from there that we are expecting a Savior, the Lord Jesus Christ.

Philippians 3:20

But when they had tied him up with thongs, Paul said to the centurion who was standing by, "Is it legal for you to flog a Roman citizen who is uncondemned?"

Acts 22:25

One of the features of the "religious field's" transformation in Brazil has been the discovery of the Bible. This is true not only for Pentecostals, *os Bíblia,* which can be spotted at least on Thursdays and Sundays heading towards their respective church, decently clothed and with a Bible under their arm, but also for Roman Catholics, namely in the CEBs, and of course in the IECLB, traditionally a church of the Word. So one would naturally look there first for elements of a theology focused on citizenship. Explicit references to citizenship, however, are rare. The above cited passage taken from Paul's letter to the Philippians is the only place in the Bible (except for 2 Maccabees in those editions that have the apocrypha) where πολίτευμα is used, and then in relationship to the believer's citizenship in heaven. The first Christians' strong expectation of Christ's second coming did not dispose them to spend much time thinking of how to be in the world, although they had to realize that they would have to do this as the *parousia* was delayed. They were a tiny minority, threatened both from the Roman colonizers and the Jewish Sanhedrin, and had to slowly constitute their own identity as a religion.[3] Their hope in martyrdom could only come from the city they were heading for, and not from the one they were living in. It is through their inclusion into God's household only that Jews and Greeks would be able to be συμπολῖται, co-citizens, as formulated by the deuteropauline letter to the Ephesians (2:19). Within the Christian flock, no differences are made between Jew and Greek, slave and free, male and female, because all are "one in Jesus Christ" (Galatians 3:28). It is a matter of debate to what extent this is to be extended beyond the Christian congregation—for instance, whether Paul's letter to Philemon is advocating the abolition of slavery or just declaring that it is not applicable among Christians, where Onesimus would be "more than a slave, a beloved brother [. . .] in the flesh and in the Lord" (Philemon 16). Even if the emphasis is on relationships between brothers (and sisters), Paul refers to his own being a (Roman)

3. Cf. Theissen, *Die Religion der ersten Christen.*

citizen (πολίτης) in order to be spared flogging and to be able to appeal to the Emperor (Acts 22). Concrete elements of citizenship do come into the picture, then, even if rarely explicitly so.

In the Old Testament, Israel comes into being through its liberation from bondage in Egypt. On its way, it is given commandments on its relationship to God and to the other, with the ten commandments being the central ones (Exodus 20:1–17). Love to the neighbor is grounded in God's own being: "you shall love your neighbor as yourself: I am the LORD" (Leviticus 19:18). The Torah calls the Israelites repeatedly to care for and cater to widows, orphans, and strangers (Exodus 22:22; Deuteronomy 10:17–19, 24:21). Israel becomes a State with a king (1 Samuel 8ff.). But there is always a tension, and no identification is made between God and the king as was the case in Egypt.[4] Prophets call the kings constantly to abide by God's commandment, to keep to justice and the law, and proclaim judgments on them if they do not. Even in exile, however, the people of Israel should seek "the welfare of the city" (Jer 29:7).

In the New Testament, the double commandment of love is reinforced (Luke 10:27) and radicalized in the Sermon on the Mount to even include love for one's enemy (Matthew 5:44). Jesus's witness is to care for the poor and the socially marginalized. Mission sends the disciples to proclaim the good news of the kingdom ecumenically, "throughout the world" (ὅλῃ τῇ οἰκουμένῃ, Matthew 24:14), and shows the connection of peace and *convivência* (cf. below, IIIA2c), service, witness, and proclamation (Luke 10:1–9). Significantly, one of the first converts is an African (Acts 8:26–40).

A central passage of Paul's notion of the authorities is, of course, Romans 13:1–7. It is significant that this text, too often misused to accept any "governing authorities" (ἐξουσίαις ὑπερεχούσαις), is bracketed by calls for love (12:9f.; 13:8–10).[5] That these authorities "have been instituted by God" (13:1) both legitimates and limits them: they are not absolute, but subject to God. It says that Christians should fulfill their duty and, thus, not eschew their responsibility as citizens in this world under a civil government.[6] Verse 7 states "pay to all what is due them—taxes to whom taxes are due, revenue to whom revenue is due, respect to whom respect is due, honor to whom honor is due" and recalls the famous dictum of Jesus: "Give to the emperor the things that are the emperor's, and to God the things that are God's" (Mark 12:17par.). So if some things are due to whom they are due, others are not—whatever can be expected from the Christian citizen is limited. All the cited churches, including the AD, limit it by Acts 5:29, the *clausula Petri.* Throughout Christian tradition, then, there is a tension between being in this world but not be "conformed to" it (Romans 12:2), between the city that is to come and the city that they find themselves in. The heavenly citizenship indicated in Philippians 3:20 is a metaphor of salvation[7] and maintains, again, a tension. No earthly city can be confused with the one that is to come: "For here we have no lasting city, but we are looking for the city that is to come" (Hebrews 13;14). However, this does not foreclose action in this city, but is rather an incentive and orientation for it. But it reserves a constant critical distance to all existing States, societies, and other human constructions.

It is not possible to do justice to the rich biblical witness and its different interpretations here.[8] These few strokes of a brush just served to show that although little is said explicitly about citizen

4. Cf. J. Assmann, *Herrschaft und Heil.*

5. See on this text Schrage, *Ethik des Neuen Testaments,* 226–30; Dunn, *The Theology of Paul the Apostle,* 674–80.

6. See also below, IIIA5.

7. Dunn, *The Theology of Paul the Apostle,* 328

8. It would be especially interesting to analyze the biblical arguments of Brazilian theologians on citizenship, which, however, is beyond the scope of this study. I at least mention Tamez, *Contra toda condena* (on justification by faith and its bearings on the excluded); Schmitt, *A cidadania da fé* (on citizenship from justification by faith in Romans); Schneider, *Paulo de Tarso* (mainly on Paul at the service of Jesus Christ's Gospel in an urban context); Correia and Oliva,

and citizenship (more references can be found on city, but not all are relevant), there are ample grounds to justify the Christians' action in any given society, under any State, in any public sphere. I shall come back to some of these references as I proceed.

In this first chapter, my intention is to show five elements that are essential to the citizen. These aspects refer to central elements of a theological ethics for citizenship, but are at the same time taken from the challenges identified in the Brazilian context, taking up what I see as the main problems of citizenship in Brazil, as shown in parts I and II. (1) There is a deplorable lack of awareness of one's citizenship and its implications, both rights and duties and an attitude towards society and the State. This goes namely for those who have been too humiliated to see themselves as citizens, and for them or others who think of themselves as not being (fully) part of society. The gratuity of justification and the attribution of dignity without conditions by the creator are the emphasis here. (2) While interpersonal and institutional trust are indispensable for any democracy, they are alarmingly absent or restricted in Brazil. The churches, at the same time, are among the most trusted institutions, which gives them a high potential and responsibility. The fact that their faith means trust in God goes far beyond such trust necessary for the functioning of democracy, but can strengthen and renew it. (3) To live in this world is to live in an ambiguous situation. This becomes especially palpable in Brazil, where social relations, politics, and sexuality, but also religion are being lived in highly ambiguous ways by the population. At the same time, some churches try to wipe out such ambiguity, either by pointing to Christ who is the only one who can bring change—and then the world is wholly evil, a tendency present in the AD— or by offering a total, immanent solution for one's problem in a realized eschatology as preached by the IURD. Furthermore, moralist legalism also can be seen as an attempt to overcome ambiguity rather than, with love and realism, to see oneself and others as *simul iusti et peccatores*. This also means that trust as exposed above cannot be a naïve trust, but must be cautious and informed. For Christians, there is always a distrust of human beings, both themselves and others, due to their conscience of the power of sin. (4) The issue of motivation towards a citizenship is also central, a motivation that does not only take into account one's rights, nor only one's duties. Such motivation, for which Christians have specific theological foundations, falls neither into autonomy misunderstood as mere individual interest, nor heteronomy as blind subservience, but seeks the free service in liberty. Through justification by faith, Christians become new creatures, free from bondage to evil, while in a position to serve, in the midst of sin and evil. (5) Some Christians and churches have the tendency to separate religion and politics, Church and State in a way that dispenses them unduly of their responsibilities in relation to the whole of society. Others tend to confuse them and seek to impose their belief and church on others. Both tendencies and temptations are to be overcome by the Christian citizen seeing him- or herself as serving one God under two regiments.

The experiences laid out in this sequence are, I believe, not restricted to Christian citizens, certainly the first to fourth. The theological grounding is certainly Christian and seeks to demonstrate how references found in Scripture and Tradition—the latter understood as the great treasure of the interpretation of Scripture through time and space—can, and indeed should, orient the Christian citizen in his ecclesial and secular citizenship. Still, I hope that the following insights might be a helpful challenge also to those who do not share the Christian faith, but seek to transform the current situation in order to foster citizenship for all based on the responsibility of all.

Bíblia e cidadania (a collection of articles on the subject).

1. TO BE A CITIZEN: DIGNITY AND RIGHTS

All human beings are born free and equal in dignity and rights.
UN Universal Declaration of Human Rights[9]

Only a suffering God can save us.
Dietrich Bonhoeffer[10]

To be able to exercise citizenship, persons need first to realize that they truly *are* citizens, being entitled to rights and obliged to duties. As we have seen, this is less self-evident than it seems at first sight, given the deficiencies in Brazilian citizenship.[11] Following Roberto DaMatta's diagnosis of a double system of references as to citizenship, the "person" as over against the "individual," the "house" as over against the "street," a "citizen" would be somebody lost, left alone to the cold and abstract law, which works to his detriment rather than benefit. Of course, there are changes, as Almeida[12] showed in his survey, which both confirm and relativize DaMatta's theory. Against critics like Souza,[13] the diagnosis of a double system of references embedded in culture is not to be understood in an essentialist or culturalist way, as if one were affirming that Brazilians will always be as they have been because of their colonial heritage. It is only to say that there are deep roots for people's behavior and language, in which the *jeitinho* is contrary to full citizenship because it skirts the law. At the same time, it is, for many, the only way to get what would be due to them. To the extent that habits, not least as practiced by the administration and public services, change to follow a more egalitarian pattern, and the law is being effectively applied to all, rich and poor, powerful and powerless, people will be able to be persons in a network of relationships without disregarding or contradicting their fundamental equality before the law. These are slow, but hopefully steady movements. Almeida has shown that the main changing factor is education.[14] As formal education reaches nearly all Brazilians, and the number of years they effectively spend at school increases, one can be cautiously optimistic. To be sure, education is not to be seen as something abstract, but molded by concrete curricula, teachers, and installations, and public schools especially have much to improve here. In higher education, the percentage of students is still low in comparison to many other countries. But affirmative action opening public universities (where tuition is free) for students from discriminated ethnic backgrounds (black and indigenous) and from public schools might bring improvement here. And, of course, Paulo Freire's[15] advocacy of an education that is not like a bank—depositing knowledge as on a savings account—but that involves both teacher and student in a common, emancipating process of learning continues to be an indispensable reference.

9. Available at http://www.ohchr.org/EN/UDHR/Pages/Language.aspx?LangID=eng (accessed on 12/16/2010).

10. Bonhoeffer, *Letters and Papers from Prison*, 360f.; this affirmation has found prominent reception in Latin America, cf. Tamez (*Contra toda condena*) and the works of Jon Sobrino, on these see Stålsett, *The crucified and the Crucified*, 393, 430.

11. Cf. above, IA3.

12. Almeida, *A cabeça do Brasileiro*.

13. Souza, *A modernização seletiva*.

14. Almeida, *A cabeça do brasileiro*.

15. Freire, *Pedagogy of the Oppressed*.

Churches, and in a special way Pentecostal churches, reach the poor population particularly well and have proven quite effective in "restoring lives" and democratizing faith by proving all faithful to be bearers of the Holy Spirit—regardless of gender, ethnic background, or social class. This is claimed both by the churches themselves and by sociological studies.[16] But all churches have a discourse of God's love and salvation that comes to the believer's rescue and changes his or her life, making him or her a new being (2 Corinthians 5:17) in whom Christ lives (Galatians 2:20) and who has been baptized into Christ's death and resurrection (Romans 6, esp. 3–5).

Human rights, to which every human being is entitled by his or her mere belonging to the human species—in the language of the UN Universal Declaration of Human Rights' Preamble, "the human family"—have roots, at least to some extent, in the believer's direct relationship with God as proclaimed by the Reformation.[17] It is also there that lie the roots of universal school education, defended by Martin Luther on the basis of the universal priesthood of all believers, striving to educate Christians to receive and preserve the Gospel and for them to be good citizens.[18] Even where such theology is not explicit, the intrinsic value of each and every human being is affirmed by all churches. Recent Roman Catholic social teaching,[19] as well as other theologies giving support to human rights, have insisted on the importance of the *imago Dei,* that (all!) human beings have been created in the "image and likeness" of God, as affirmed by Genesis 1:27, further supported by Galatians 3:28, where Paul claims that there are no differences in gender, ethnicity, or social status before God. While this has been long recognized in Christian theology, it has taken a long time for the church to deduce, from there, that this would endow each and every human being with equal value.

According to Huber,[20] three factors relativized human dignity: first, sin was understood to have taken all rights of humans before God, and thus there was also no human dignity to protect them in an absolute way before secular and ecclesiastical power. Secondly, dignity was understood as a privilege of Christians over against heretics, Jews, and pagans. Thirdly, Christian anthropology was understood within a frame of estates (in society) and hierarchy (in the church), thus adopting a differentiating rather than an equalizing understanding of dignity. Italian renaissance-humanism, Spanish late scholastics, and the German Reformation, according to Huber, reinstated the importance of equal dignity of human beings. The first found in Pico della Mirandola (1463–94) its main formulator, followed by Thomas More (1478–1535) and Erasmus of Rotterdam (1466/69–1536). Pico understood the human being to be a microcosm, analogous to God, with an indefinite wealth of possibilities, from which the human being had to choose in freedom. The second, with Francisco

16. Cf. above, IIE.

17. Among others, this is affirmed by Comparato, *Ética*, 167-83. The emancipatory character of the Lutheran Reformation had already been highlighted by Marx in his *Zur Kritik der Hegelschen Rechtsphilosophie—Einleitung*, in Comparato, *Ética*, 169 n. 1.

18. See *To the Councilmen of All Cities in Germany That They Establish and Maintain Christian Schools (1524)*, LW 45:347-378; *A Sermon on Keeping Children in School* (1530), LW 46:207-58. This is recognized as an important advance by (agnostic) political philosophers like Ribeiro, "Religião e política no Brasil contemporâneo," 103. As Altmann (*Lutero e libertação*, 202) states, theology and citizenship go together in Luther's emphasis on education for all, which he saw as a mandate from God, and indeed a political task, to be carried out by the local councils and to be free of fees and compulsory: ". . .for this reason of the preservation of the gospel, the interest and preoccupation of the Reformer with the issue of education is demonstrated. Luther, however, equally emphasized the importance of the formation of good citizens for society." For a contemporary reflection on Lutheranism and Education in the context of the IECLB's Synodal Network of Education, see Goldmeyer et al., *Luteranismo e Educação*; also Pauly, *Ética, educação e cidadania*.

19. PCJP, *Compendium of the Social Doctrine of the Church*, 96ff.

20. Huber, *Gerechtigkeit und Recht*, 228.

de Vitória (1483–1546) among its main advocates and preparing the way for an European law of nations, would be especially important for the "New World." The indigenous peoples who had been living there long before the Portuguese and Spanish colonizers arrived, came to be understood as capable of reason and social beings, the two criteria to prove them fully human and, thus, entitled to elementary rights. The third leads to the center of Reformation Theology: the doctrine of justification by faith, from which follows that dignity is attributed to the human being without any merit, as a gift of grace, to which faith may freely respond. Thus, freedom of faith and conscience is a correlate of such understanding of human dignity. Calvin and Calvinism take this further to insist on the practical consequences of justification in sanctification, the "practical functioning of Christian existence and true worship,"[21] where the ethical component of human rights and the need for the legal constitution in State and church become paramount and found expression, for instance, in the presbyterial-synodal system of church government. The biblical figure of the covenant, echoed by Calvin and his followers, has become influential in later philosophical reflection on politics and rights, finding its equivalent in the contractual theories of Locke, Rousseau, and others. But far from being a consensus and implemented in legal systems, human rights needed another four centuries to become the world charter through the United Nations; and, obviously, the debate is continuing, both as to the foundation and to the practice of human rights.[22]

Methodist Elsa Tamez insists that justification by grace through faith empowers people to recover their dignity.[23] However, the usually underlying concept of sin as hubris has to be criticized. Under a situation of poverty and oppression, the issue here is not that persons have to be forgiven because of *their* sin, but because of *somebody else's* sin. The poor and excluded are not responsible for their situation, but victims of oppression.[24] Tamez pleads against the devaluation of human beings in a classical interpretation of justification, focused on the individual sinner, who is unable to contribute to his salvation.[25] Justification, then, gives the oppressed their right: "it frees not only from *deserved condemnation,* but also, and especially, from *imposed social condemnation,*"[26] as Brakemeier sums up Tamez' thought.[27] She takes up earlier Latin American interpretations of

21. Ritschl, "Der Beitrag des Calvinismus für die Entwicklung des Menschenrechtsgedanken," 311.

22. On Protestantism, Law, and Human Rights see further the important works of Lutheran law scholar Witte, *Law and Protestantism*; *God's Joust, God's Justice*; *The Reformation of Rights.*

23. Tamez, *Contra toda condena.*

24. In view of the importance of citizenship, it is unfortunate that Tamez (*Contra toda condena*) sees the "law" as oppressing force of death. While this is understandable if referring to law corrupted by an authoritarian regime, or considering Jesus' critique of the specialists of law which fail its main content, his own death at the hands of the law, and Paul's struggle for liberation from the law's bondage, it does not do justice to the width of the biblical understanding of law, nor to the need for law as an instrument of the powerless to get their rights respected. Although Tamez does speak of laws "captivated by the logic of sin," leaving some space for the existence of other laws, what she points to in contrast is God's judgement, and not other laws. For her, the excluded are condemned by the laws of supply and demand, of national security, and of the "waiting for improvement" (ibid., 180).

25. Indeed, a Methodist interpretation of justification can speak much more freely of a synergism between God and human beings in their salvation than can Lutheran theology, which is always preoccupied in safeguarding salvation from human subjectivity or attributing it to some human merit. This has prompted Methodist theologian Helmut Renders (*A soteriologia social de John Wesley*), a German living and teaching in Brazil, to elaborate on Wesley's "social soteriology" in his doctoral dissertation. Despite the Brazilian Methodists' recent anti-ecumenism, it is a sign of hope and joy that the World Methodist Conference has signed the Joint Declaration on the Doctrine of Justification in July 2006, indicating that differences in their understanding are no longer obstacles to unity.

26. Brakemeier, *O ser humano em busca de identidade*, 103.

27. Feminist critique of the classical understanding of sin as hubris has pointed into the same direction, as Deifelt recalls ("The Relevance of the Doctrine of Justification," 34), namely pointing to Judith Plaskow's *Sex, Sin and Grace* (Lanham, 1980). Sin for women would, then, be precisely what classically has been advocated as Christian virtue: self-

justification, which insist on God's justice and human justice as the two sides of the same reality within a relationship of covenant,[28] on justification as bestowing dignity,[29] and as offering "spaces of freedom in a society that strangles life."[30] Passing through justification by faith in Paul, she arrives at justification as affirmation of the life of all, which creates solidarity. This, she emphasizes, goes against any idea of merit, because

> the work of grace (or faith) originates in the free commitment [*entrega*] of the sons and daughters of God to their calling for giving life, live it and celebrate it in gratuity. [. . .] whoever acts for love of God, to accumulate merits, denies the free justification, because he continues subject to the regime of the law and not of grace.[31]

As does Tamez, Wanda Deifelt insists on the link between justification and (human) justice.[32] This is, on principle, supported by Brakemeier who, however, asks how to relate the beatitudes for the poor (Luke 6:20) to forgiveness for the guilty. "Justification always frees from both, from guilt and from insignificance in human community," he affirms and "all for whom society has no room remain God's creatures for whom Christ died on the cross."[33]

---

sacrifice and obedience. It is evident that for oppressed of all kinds, these terms must sound cynical. Their "sin" would rather be dependency, lack of self-esteem, giving themselves up and the like (ibid., 35).

28. José Miguez Bonino, "The Biblical Roots of Justice," in *Word and World* 7/1 (1987), 15, quoted in Tamez, *Contra toda condena*, 38; Westhelle, "O desencontro entre a teologia luterana e a teologia da libertação."

29. Cf. Altmann, *Luther and Liberation*, 41; Hanks, "El testimonio evangélico a los pobres y oprimidos."

30. Meincke, *Justificação por graça e fé*, 230. For Meincke (*ibid.*, 229), "trust in justification by grace and faith, justification which does not depend on our achievements and our perfection, is an encouragement for us to run the risk of creating, innovating, looking for more efficient forms, also improvising and even making errors, when our action is motivated by the Gospel." He departs from the importance of "being accepted," formulated in a seminal way under the ambiguities of modernity by Tillich, *The Courage to Be*, whom Meincke, strangely, does not cite; but see Altmann, *Luther and Liberation*, 93, who, however, locates this problem [only] in an "affluent and secularized society." I would think that great parts of urban, middle class Brazil today would reflect this problem in a modified way: Not only in terms of a lack of meaning of life, but also as being lost and insecure vis-à-vis the exigencies of today's highly competitive society, which, of course, hits the poor in a much more excluding way; cf. Brakemeier, *O ser humano em busca de identidade*, 82-87.

31. Tamez, *Contra toda condena*,156f. In affirming this, she contradicts what Segundo (and with him many Catholic theologians till today, as I could verify in SOTER congresses) said on the importance of merit. According to him, "the disappearance of the notion of *merit* from Protestant theology, dating from the time of the Reformation, seems to have undermined the possibility of any theology of history," criticizing the "depoliticization" of the doctrine of justification through Luther's doctrine of the two kingdoms (*The Liberation of Theology*, 142). Quoting Moltmann, Alves, and Shaull, he sees them refraining from identifying God's action in history through human hands. Shaull's three positive attitudes of hope, freedom, and service do not serve, according to Segundo, for a revolutionary option. This example shows how, despite many levels of practical cooperation, namely under the military regimes, inter-confessional theological divergences and misunderstandings remain to be tackled. Against this interpretation see also Altmann, *Luther and Liberation*, 37ff. Westhelle ("O desencontro entre a teologia luterana e a teologia da libertação," 52) sees the main problem arising around a possible, but complicated third use of the law as in the Reformed Tradition and in Melanchthon, which for him would mean either to abandon Lutheranism in terms of social ethics (saying there is none), or resulting in an essentially conservative social ethics centered on the preservation of order in line with creation. If I understand correctly, this would be the case because God's action were tantamount—Westhelle quotes Niebuhr's "Christ transforming culture," and Althaus' concept of mandate—to the detriment of human action, or else restricted action to believers (usus in renatis). As a concrete example of social ethics in Luther, he cites the latter's treatise on *Trade and Usury* of 1524 (LW 245–310, *Von Kaufshandlung und Wucher*, WA 15:294–322), as well as his earlier *Sermon von dem Wucher* (1519/20, WA 6:3–8.36–60) and the 1540 admonition *An die Pfarrherrn, wider den Wucher zu predigen* (WA 51:331-424); cf. Rieth, "Luther on Greed."

32. Deifelt, "The Relevance of the Doctrine of Justification," 35.

33. Brakemeier, *O ser humano em busca de identidade*,103.221. For a recent German position on the centrality and implications of the doctrine of justification, with an outlook on issues of human dignity and justice, prompted

One might add that although poverty must not be considered either a sign of God's punishment, nor of personal guilt, this does not exempt the poor from personal responsibility[34]—which is where they are placed namely by the Pentecostal churches. The latter use a moralist discourse, as we have seen, but do in fact make believers aware of their intrinsic human dignity and worth. And if they are capable of steering their lives through all the dangers that haunt it with responsibility for themselves, their families and their churches (and, as it should be added, the world, see IIIB3), this in itself is a sign of worth and dignity.

Human beings, then, are dignified not through any quality intrinsic to their human nature (it's not in their genes), nor through their merit (it's not in their works, either), but because God attributes dignity to them. In its secularized version, this means that human dignity is "untouchable," the highest good to be protected, as the German constitution (*Grundgesetz*) affirms in its first article: "the dignity of the human being is untouchable. To respect and protect it is the obligation of all public power."[35] More generally, but also in itsfirst article, the Brazilian Constitution names among its fundamentals "the dignity of the human person" (Art.1, III), which is shown concretely through the long catalogue of fundamental rights and duties, political and social rights (Art. 5). It is seen as a "pre-constituent" and "super-constitutional" character, with its basis beyond the Constitution and positive law.[36]

Human dignity in its modern conception, both secular and Christian, implies human freedom as fundamental, being free from bondage and tutelage—by the State, society, the church, or any other person or institution— and being free for his or her own life in creativity, within the constraints of the other persons' freedom, a justice that looks at those who most suffer in society.[37] Such freedom, however, has to be not an individualized freedom, but a "communicative freedom,"[38] as Bedford-Strohm has called it following impulses from philosopher Michael Theunissen as taken up by Heinz Eduard Tödt, Wolfgang Huber, and Jürgen Moltmann, joining both liberal and communitarian pleas, based on reciprocity in love. It is to serve human beings both individually and socially. From a Christian point of view, freedom involves not only acceptance and respect of the other's freedom, but the willingness to serve others even where no (direct) return is to be expected.[39] The law is to guarantee such freedom and protect, especially, those who for some reason are not able to exercise it fully, be it for restrictions of health, intellectual capacity, gender, social status, economic power, or other. Justice is the principle that has to give concrete shape to the law, as its normative content. Justification is a presupposition of and calls for justice and the law, as Karl

---

by the controversy on the Joint Declaration of the Doctrine of Justification 2000, see Jüngel, *Das Evangelium von der Rechtfertigung*, esp. 221–34.

34. As Hugo Assmann has affirmed in his more recent writings (cf. above, ID), Vitor Westhelle ("O tamanho do paraíso," 247) also warns of a "romantisation of the victims."

35. "Die Würde des Menschen ist unantastbar. Sie zu achten und zu schützen ist Verpflichtung aller staatlichen Gewalt" (Grundgesetz der Bundesrepublik Deutschland, art. 1); cf. Vögele, *Zivilreligion in der Bundesrepublik Deutschland*, 266-412. The Swiss Federal Constitution of April 18, 1999, states, in its 7th article, somewhat more pragmatically: "The dignity of the human being is to be respected and protected" ("Die Würde des Menschen ist zu achten und zu schützen").

36. This becomes evident in Mendes et al., *Curso de direito constitucional,* 140 who cite philosophical and theological works at this point; Böckenförde's famous theorem comes to mind here which says that "the liberal [*freiheitliche*], secularized State is based on presuppositions that it cannot itself guarantee," citing explicitly the Christian faith as a factor of motivation and social cohesion ("Die Entstehung des Staates als Vorgang der Säkularisierung," 93).

37. Cf. Rawls, *A Theory of Justice*; Bedford-Strohm, *Vorrang für die Armen*, esp. 204ff.

38. Bedford-Strohm, *Gemeinschaft aus kommunikativer Freiheit.*

39. Cf. below, IIIA4.

Barth famously formulated.[40] The Western tradition of law has been decisively influenced by this Reformation principle.[41]

As I have stressed throughout this study, explicit doctrine is not a guarantee that it is actually believed, perceived as present in practice, or even known. Thus, the fact that the doctrine of justification by faith is the central element of Lutheran theology, and central to proclamation in the Lutheran church, does not mean that people in fact assimilate it. Wanda Deifelt describes from her parish ministry experience in a working class environment, that persons who had financial or family problems simply didn't come to church anymore as they felt it was "embarrassing, indeed shameful."[42] This is not a proof against the importance of the doctrine of justification by faith, but rather against the lack of its assimilation in the parishes, where it appears to be superseded by an ethics of work and merit. Apart from German heritage with its high value of work (cf. above, IID1), the adverse circumstances during much of the immigration most probably also contributed to such an attitude in which surviving, let alone success did not come by itself, but had to be conquered. Once achieved, the conquerors could be proud of their success, which was of their own making.[43] On the other end, the prosperity gospel in Neo-Pentecostal churches suggests that God has to give something in return for the faith (and, as a visible sign of it, tithe) invested in him.[44] Evil is a consequence of Satan and his demons, but the possibility (and responsibility) to change this lies with the believer, who invests in God and has, then, the right to ask from him whatever he wants. Should it not work, faith (or tithe) was not sufficient. In both cases, dignity is dependent on merit. There are understandable sociological reasons for such positions, which I cannot deal with here. In any case, they avoid a pre-ethical, aprioristic notion of dignity attributed by God to human beings as such, and, thus, inevitably measure dignity in terms of performance. But what about those who, for internal or external reasons, are unable to perform (well)?

Dignity comes, this subchapter contends, as a gift from God. This is a theo-logical argument based on creation and the Word: "let us make humankind in our image, according to our likeness" (Genesis 1:26). The first creation narrative installs humankind's often criticized *dominium terrae*, as the quoted verse continues: "and let them have dominion over the fish of the sea, and over the birds of the air, and over the cattle, and over all the wild animals of the earth, and over every creeping thing that creeps upon the earth." In the second creation narrative, God "took the man and put him in the garden of Eden to till it and keep it" (Genesis 2:15), when "to keep" (שָׁמַר) implies watching and guarding over it, to take care of it.[45] Both texts read together show that "dominion," in the first place, involves being a good steward, a care taker, to care for what has been entrusted by God to

40. Barth, "Rechtfertigung und Recht"; cf. Huber, *Rechtfertigung und Recht*.

41. Cf. Witte, *Law and Protestantism*.

42. Deifelt, "The Relevance of the Doctrine of Justification," 29.

43. In his interesting and relevant course monograph, based on long-standing experience and a questionnaire applied to a sample of 142 (95 lay leadership and 47 members of a traditional congregation), Synod Pastor Nilo Christmann ("A prática do perdão") showed how the distance between theology and practice in Lutheran communities is an obstacle to forgiveness. Rather than justification by faith and the consequent gratitude for God's gift, fulfilling the ten commandments seems to be what believers most recall from confirmation class. Once they feel they indeed do comply with this life-rule ("I don't steal, I don't kill and I'm honest," ibid., 46), they see this as achievement rather than as a gift, and thus as having acquired a right rather than something received by grace.

44. Cf. Mariano, *Neopentecostais*, 147–86.

45. Cf. Link, *Schöpfung*, especially 391–99. For a recent overview in ecumenical perspective see Bedford-Strohm, *Schöpfung*, and the commentary on Genesis by Westermann, who, among others, states that "[dominion] always in some way includes existence for the dominated"; in the Old Testament, the dominator does never only benefit from his subjects (*Genesis 1–11*, 227); also the more recent works of Leonardo Boff (*Ecology and Liberation*; *Cry of the Poor*).

humankind. It is precisely this idea of care (*cuidado*) that has become an important concept in pastoral care and counseling in Brazil, and made an essential concept of humanity by Leonardo Boff, based on Heidegger.[46]

As shown above (IIE), it is the Pentecostal churches that most effectively are able to transform even the poorest people's lives so that they do feel a sense of worth and dignity. Although this translates only in a limited way into a plea and commitment for democracy, be it in the church or in the State, it does provide a most important ground for concrete citizen activity in a democracy. Lutherans are, apparently, not sufficiently effective in transmitting their theology even to their members, let alone to others, but this theology offers rich reflections for the strengthening of human dignity. Roman Catholics affirm human dignity as a fundamental pillar of their social teaching, based on the *imago Dei* argument, and are able to articulate this loudly through their strong national structure and international support and visibility. Here is a way in which the churches have achieved a certain strength and effectiveness, which is important to continue. They are also, both theologically and practically, prone to foster trust—as long as they don't limit it to their own church or even destroy it through sowing mistrust in competing with others.

2. TO LIVE AS A CITIZEN: TRUST IN THE CONTEXT OF DISTRUST

Wer nach dem Schlüsselwort in der Orientierungskrise der Gegenwart sucht, wird bald fündig. ' Vertrauen' heißt dieses Schlüsselwort.

Wolfgang Huber[47]

In dem doppelten Verhältnis des Glaubens zu Jesus Christus—indem er auf ihn als seinen Gegenstand ausgerichtet und indem er von ihm als seinem Gegenstand her begründet ist—geschieht in ihm die Konstituierung des christlichen Subjektes.

Karl Barth[48]

As stated in IA3c, the lack of interpersonal trust is one of the main challenges of today's society. This is especially so in Brazil, where only 6 percent affirm to generally trust other persons.[49] But also in other countries like in Germany, trust is in danger of being lost, despite much more favorable

46. Boff (*Saber cuidar*, 45f.) quotes Heidegger's *Being and Time* (Heidegger, *Sein und Zeit*, 197f., cf. the whole paragraphs 41 and 42, 191ff., on the interpretation of "Sein des Daseins als Sorge"), which reproduces the fable of care (Cura), recalling, to Christian ears, the second creation narrative: Cura takes a piece of earth and shapes it, and then asks Jupiter to blow spirit into the new creature. There follows, however, an argument over who had the right to name him. Earth later joins the argument, and they decide to ask Saturn to serve as an arbiter. He decides that, after death, the spirit will stay with Jupiter and the body with Earth, but Cura would care for him during his lifetime. He also ruled that he should be called human (homo) as he was taken from humus, fertile earth (ex humo). From this narrative, Boff constructs a whole argument about the fundamental importance of care, which is widely used and quoted, and has an immediate appeal to students and beyond.

47. "Whoever seeks for the keyword in the contemporary crisis of orientation will find it easily. This keyword is 'trust.'" Huber, *Rechtfertigung und Recht*, 9; see also the chapter on "renewing trust," ibid. 107-127.

48. "In the double relationship of faith to Jesus Christ—in that it is oriented towards him as its object and is founded in him as from its object—occurs the constitution of the Christian subject." Barth, *Die kirchliche Dogmatik IV,1*, 837 (KD IV,1).

49. Latinobarómetro 2007, 93.

economic conditions.[50] Then President Johannes Rau said in his 2004 Berlin address that "if we want to shape this future [in peace, freedom, recognition of achievement, justice and solidarity], if we want to shape it in a human way, then we need two things: trust in those who bear responsibility for us, and the willingness to assume responsibility ourselves."[51] For the United States, Jean Elshtain characterized the situation in the mid 1990s as a "culture of mistrust."[52] Wolfgang Huber affirms that in "the crisis of trust which we currently live through, nothing is more important than the relationship, intrinsic to it, between trust in God and trust in oneself" and, as Protestant Bishop of Berlin-Brandenburg and Chairman of the Council of the Evangelical Church in Germany, commits his church on that basis to "contribute towards the overcoming the crisis of trust in our time."[53] Rau, a confessed Protestant Christian, called for the renewal of necessary virtues, besides the coherence of word and deed, "truthfulness, authenticity, but also a sense of duty and decency."[54]

The specific challenge in Brazil, as explicated above (IA3c) is to go beyond restricting interpersonal trust to family, friends, and brothers and sisters of one's church, and extend it, on principle, to all with whom one coexists in a certain context, aiming at *convivência* (communal interaction, see below, IIIA2c). As such trust bases itself on rules and values accepted by all, whether in writing—in the constitution and in laws—or by common habit, it will become safer to trust. It is basically this generalized trust that is lacking in Brazil. And it is not so just by chance. Bad experiences with authorities and with a variety of people and institutions have accumulated. These experiences, together with cultural factors as described by DaMatta, have left the impression that only those who have "friends," "sponsors," or "godfathers" in the right place can expect to be given due attention. One lacks trust in the reliability of people and institutions, and this constitutes a serious threat to the process of democratization.

It is generally accepted that trust is fundamental not only for interpersonal relationships as such, but for life in society, as "social capital."[55] From there, trust is fundamental both for democracy[56] and the economy[57] to function properly and foster democracy as well as prosperity.

50. Rau, "Vertrauen in Deutschland"; Huber, *Rechtfertigung und Recht*. Brazilian political scientist Moisés, *Os Brasileiros e a democracia* 73f. cites studies on trust in public institutions and mentions a „really dramatic" variation in old democracies, like United States, England, France, Sweden, and Canada, where a systematic reduction of trust in authorities and public institutions had occurred during the last 30 years, from around 75 percent after World War II to 25 percent of satisfied and trusting citizens in the mid-1990s. For a recent conference on the issue, see Ankersmit and Te Velde, *Trust: Cement of Democracy?* with contributions of some of the authors who will be cited in what follows.

51. Rau, "Vertrauen in Deutschland," 2.

52. Jean Bethke Elshtain, *Democracy on Trial* (New York, 1995), quoted in Wuthnow, *The United States*, 61 and 430f. (note 5), among other statements in the same direction, which are, however, relativized by Wuthnow, both empirically and theoretically, i.e., considering the impact a reduction of social capital would have on democracy given that there are no absolute standards. As for Germany, Offe and Fuchs' ("A Decline of Social Capital") case study does mention the importance of trust, but does not give details or survey results.

53. Huber, *Rechtfertigung und Recht*, 115f.

54. Rau, "Vertrauen in Deutschland," 6: "Wahrhaftigkeit, Glaubwürdigkeit, aber auch Pflichtbewusstsein und Anstand."

55. As mentioned above (IC), the category of social capital has been put forward namely by Robert Putnam, in the line of Tocqueville's emphasis on the importance of associations in United States' democracy. Wuthnow, *The United States*, 63, who has done extensive empirical research and amply considered the impact of religion and religious organizations, mentions four important general categories of social capital: associations, trust, civic participation, and volunteering.

56. Warren, *Democracy and Trust*.

57. Fukuyama, *Trust*.

In Luhmann's famous definition, trust is a means of a "reduction of social complexity."[58] He differentiates between "confidence" and "trust," where the daily, common attitude would fall under "confidence," while "trust" would presuppose a "previous engagement" and a "situation of risk" that one can enter or avoid.[59] This trust is, however, not a naïve or generalized trust—indeed, a dose of mistrust is necessary not to run blindly into a situation where trust can have bad consequences, like investing money in a dubious business. There is even a *professional* mistrust, as found among police investigators, judges, and researchers.[60] Moisés, quoting Warren, Sztompka, and Offe, speaks of the need that citizens' mistrust has to be "institutionalized," that is, become permanent through rules that, once mobilized, make sure that they can compete for their interests without a risk for their freedom and their rights."[61] If that be so, then there has to be a kind of "professional" mistrust by the citizen, which reinforces the need for commonly accepted rules of the (democratic) game, and, of course, accountability of those in power.

While interpersonal and institutional trust must not be confounded, it is remarkable that those who teach and preach trust based in God are among the most trusted institutions in Latin America. According to the IBOPE survey (2005),[62] the ICAR, with 71 percent of trust, comes just after the physicians (81 percent) and before the Armed Forces (69 percent), the latter being a remarkable number just 20 years after the end of the military regime. Further down, after newspapers, engineers, TV and radio, but still before the trade unions, come the *evangélico* churches (53 percent), without further specification. The fact that this number is considerably smaller than the ICAR's could indicate that, for many, *evangélico* refers to the Neo-Pentecostal IURD, which keeps coming up in the media for its high lucrativity (cf. above, IIB1). Pentecostal and Neo-Pentecostal politicians have also been involved in various scandals,[63] which might have contributed to their inferior number. Conversely, political institutions and, even more so, the politicians fare very low: 76 percent mistrust the Senate, 81 percent the Chamber of Deputies, 88 percent the parties, and 90 percent the politicians. A similiar research carried out for *Latinobarómetro* showed that, in a Latin American average, „the church" (not specified) comes in second at 74 percent, just after the firemen (75 percent), and well above other institutions.[64]

Polish sociologist Piotr Sztompka presents six democratic practices that presuppose "a measure of trust"[65]: (1) communication among the citizens, the exchange of opinions—one could say: a public sphere with active opinion building; (2) tolerance with the acknowledgment of differences and plurality, noting that to embrace differences is easier when people feel secure through trust; (3) conflict and struggle are replaced by compromise and consensus, bound by common rules of the game; (4) a level of "civility" in public disputes, focusing on the subject rather than attacking the

58. Luhmann, *Vertrauen*.

59. Luhmann, "Vertrautheit, Zuversicht," 148.

60. Cf. Luhmann, *Vertrauen*, 124.

61. Moisés, "Cidadania, confiança e instituições democráticas," 85; Warren, *Democracy and Trust*; Sztompka, *Trust: A Sociological Theory*, and Offe, "How can we trust our fellow citizens?"

62. IBOPE, *Confiança nas instituições*, 20f. .

63. See above, IIE.

64. Latinobarómetro, *Informe Latinobarómetro 2007*, 92; *Informe Latinobarómetro 2003*, 25-26, shows that trust in "the church" fell from 76 percent in 1996 to 62 percent in 2003, with the greatest fall between 2002 and 2003, possibly due to the evident political game in harvesting support among *evangélico* churches, especially around confessed believer (Presbyterian) Anthony Garotinho's candidateship. But also the main rivals, Lula and José Serra, sought and received support from the churches.

65. Sztompka, *Trust: A Sociological Theory*, 147.

opponent; (5) participation by active citizens, which requires a minimum of trust in fellow citizens; and (6), democracy requires educated citizens, which demands information and the availability of reliable media.[66] These are helpful elements, also for the Brazilian context. Moisés[67] quotes them without much comment, but leaves out the sixth element, which to me seems to be precisely the major challenge, and a place where churches can make a difference. Also the other aspects (communication, tolerance, civilized disputes, participation) can be learned and trained in churches; but as we have seen, the churches themselves, especially the ICAR and the AD, have much to learn in this regard, to share power and value the laity.

In what follows, I shall present aspects of trust as I understand them (a), connect them to faith (b), and propose a hermeneutics of trust and *convivência* (c). I am aware that there is a certain danger here to confuse a functional, sociological view of trust with a theological one, especially as I use metaphors like "bet" and "investment." Certainly they are not to be equated. Still, it is my intention to show that trust cannot be asked from anyone, but has to be given freely, and also withheld at appropriate moments. Therefore, the motivation one has for one's trust is central, and trust cannot be reduced to an exclusively rational decision. There is a kind of daily trust (or rather confidence) which is needed to make life viable—it is impossible to consciously and constantly question everything, e.g., should I trust the car factory that my car will not suddenly exhibit a fatal malfunction. Here indeed there is a necessary reduction of complexity, and rational analysis should show whether such trust is probably justified or not. But the living together of human beings needs a much deeper dimension of trust, including a motivation to "re-invest" trust after a series of deceptions.

a) Aspects of Trust

It is not easy to define trust, as it is not a concept that, upon being adopted, will result directly in action. Instead, it is an attitude that becomes visible in action itself. It is only when we act with trust that we can identify it. Even so, we can plausibly use a general definition to have at least a vague idea of what we are talking about. I suggest defining trust as a positive expectation in relation to the other's behavior which is to lie in my or our common interest. The decisive difference is to be found in the degree of certainty I can have that my trust will not be disappointed, i.e., that the other's behavior will indeed be to my or our benefit rather than harm us. I should add that I presuppose that there is only a gradual and not a principal difference between his or her and our common benefit, and that, thus, I would not expect a behavior from the other that would be to my benefit but at his or her expense. I will try to go deeper into this in what follows, focusing on interpersonal trust.[68]

66. Sztompka contrasts trust in autocratic societies, where it is also present, but imposed, turned "into a strongly sanctioned formal demand" in relation to the dictator or the system (*Trust: A Sociological Theory,* 148).

67. Moisés, "Cidadania, confiança e instituições democráticas," 86.

68. I am using here freely an earlier text of mine which was published in Portuguese, German, and English, being slightly revised along the way as it was discussed in a number of forums in Brazil (Sinner, "Trust and convivência").

(1) In the first place trust means to "*bet on.*"[69] I invest trust when I can expect, with a certain amount of probability—but without the possibility to calculate this probability[70]—that the other will honor it. When dealing with people with whom I live on a daily basis, such as family members and work and study colleagues, I can observe their behavior over a long period of time. In this way I accumulate experience about the trustworthiness of each person, and I know in whom I can or cannot trust. However, how can I trust in people I do not know?[71] Trust always implies a risk. My experience and my knowledge can help me judge if an unknown person is trustworthy or not. If someone asks me, as I am getting on a bus, to take a bag for that person's friend who would be waiting for me to pick it up at our destination, my experience will counsel me to refuse. Should the way he or she talks and pleads, his or her appearance and treatment convince me to take the risk by doing what he or she is asking for—even though these perceptions can obviously deceive—I would at least ask for the sender's and receiver's address and check the contents to verify that I would not be taking dangerous or illegal items. It also would depend on the rationale provided by the person, if she or he gave good reasons or not that would justify why the objects could not be sent by mail. In the Brazilian context, it is not unthinkable that the person might be forced by the lack of financial means to try this way of transporting goods, while having to invest trust in me that I would indeed hand over the bag to the receiver. Asking for information to confirm my trustworthiness might indicate sincerity. Still, the possibility of carrying something illegal could not be ruled out. More complicated yet is the trust in people I will never meet. Any democratic society works in this way, presupposing a minimal level of trust among people who know nothing of the other except that they are citizens of the same State. In this case, much depends on the trust I have in the political and judicial system of the country to place my bet. Trust always means betting on the other, because one is never absolutely certain that one´s trust will be honored.

(2) Here is a second aspect. Trusting is a *prior "investment"* that I make unilaterally without certainty about the reaction or the result. With this I make myself vulnerable.[72] However, trust can generate trust precisely because it is unilaterally invested. In advancing trust, I impose a moral obligation on the other to honor it, because we both know that breaking the trust someone invests in me is the worst imaginable betrayal.[73] If someone needs my help after a traffic accident, I feel

69. Cf. Sztompka, *Trust: A Sociological Theory,* 25: "Trust is a bet about the future contingent actions of others." For Sztompka, it differs from hope ("a passive, vague, not rationally justified feeling that things will turn out to the good (or to the bad)") and confidence ("a still passive, but more focused and to some extent justified, faith that something good will happen (or not)") in that it "falls within the discourse of agency: actively anticipating and facing an unknown future" (ibid., 24f.). Luhmann, *Vertrauen,* 29, also differentiates trust from hope: "Trust reflects contingency, hope eliminates contingency," i.e., the one who trusts is aware of the possible damage that can follow from the actions of others in whom he trusts, and faces this danger. The figure of betting has also been used prominently by Blaise Pascal and John Hick for the truth of faith, cf. below, part IIIA3 of the present work.

70. Luhmann, *Vertrauen,* 29.

71. This is precisely the focus of Offe's contribution, who puts it, among other formulations, in this way: "It is not clear how civic trust emerges among the members of mass publics within a democracy, given the condition of anonymity, diversity, and pluralism" ("How can we trust our fellow citizens?" 57). The German version of the same text has some differences; it adds, for instance, the anti-Hobbesian assumption that "There is more reason for universalized trust in the judgement capacity and the benevolence of the entirety of fellow citizens than for trust in the same qualities of autocratic or party-monopolistic holders of power" (Offe, "Wie können wir unseren Mitbürgern vertrauen?" 265).

72. On the "ethics of vulnerability," developed from a Lutheran confessional tradition and, among others, an intensive exposure to Central America, see Stålsett, *The crucified and the Crucified.*

73. As others cited before, Offe ("How can we trust our fellow citizens?" 44) also distinguishes between "confidence" and "trust," even though he concedes they are often used interchangeably. In his view, whenever confidence is being disappointed, the reasons for it lie beyond my reach and "must be attributed to *bad luck,* chance, or Providence." However, if I trust someone who is not trustworthy, it is my mistake and I shall regret "my imprudent assessment of the

obliged to help the person because I would expect the same from him or her. If I am the one responsible for the accident, by law I am obliged to give immediate help.[74] Legal sanctioning, provided it is probable to be effectively carried out, which in Brazil is not always very likely,[75] is an important reference that reduces the risk of one's trust not being honored. Beyond formal law, however, it is part of the trust in the values accepted by society to be able to count on, always and quickly, first aid given by the first passing person. When we wander in the woods or walk in traffic or in many other situations that present some danger, we are advancing trust. The expectation is that someone will help me if I need it and will not let me suffer or even die without doing everything possible to save me. However, we know from experience, as paradigmatically formulated in the parable of the Good Samaritan, that this does not always happen and that the person who ends up helping may be someone from whom one least expected that reaction (Luke 10:30–35).

(3) The example of giving first aid in the case of danger shows that the expectations we have of other people's actions depend on ethical principles and moral rules that have been widely accepted. I invest trust because I presuppose that the other shares certain basic concepts with me. One widely known and accepted principle is the so-called "golden rule," which says, in its biblical formulation from the Gospel of Matthew: "In everything do to others as you would have them do to you; for this is the law and the prophets." (Matthew 7:12). This principle is the cornerstone of the *categorical imperative* of Kant and is found in many philosophical ethics or religions.[76] Besides this "minimal ethic" we have greater demands, such as indicated in the same Sermon on the Mount from which I extracted the citation of the golden rule.[77] Here is the challenge of a *greater ethic* to be followed, one that can be expected from the Christian, but not from every citizen.[78] This is the third aspect of trust, specific to those who adhere to a belief or an ideology that contains ethical demands. Upon meeting a person who follows a greater ethic, this person has the right to greater trust but is also subject to greater demands. "From everyone to whom much has been given, much will be required; and from the one to whom much has been entrusted, even more will be demanded," says Jesus in the parable on watchfulness (Luke 12:48). A church or non-governmental organization (NGO) that receives donations in money and uses it for purposes other than those intended does considerable damage not only to its relationship with the specific donor or donors. It also jeopardizes the trust

trustworthiness of the person in question and discontinue my trust relationship with him." The breach of trust, then, hurts twice: Not only do I have to presume the other had bad intentions—he wanted to harm me or gain an advantage over me for himself—but I shall also be regarded as naive because of my possibly light-minded trust. Even if a breach of trust is not attributed to the one who trusted, he or she will still ask him- or herself whether he or she could not have sensed that before.

74. In Brazil, the reference is Law No. 5,903 of September 23, 1997 (Brazilian Code of Traffic, article 304).

75. Cf. above, Part IA3b of the present work.

76. Kant, "Grundlegung zur Metaphysik der Sitten," 51; Küng, *A Global Ethic for Global Politics*; Mieth, "Interkulturelle Ethik." Lienemann, *Gerechtigkeit*, 11 takes up this principle through the mouth of Rabbi Hillel, and sees the main elements of justice running through the Bible in the golden rule and siding with the weak—in Liberation Theology's terminology, this would be the option for the poor.

77. Cf. Theissen, *Die Religion der ersten Christen*, 242–47.

78. A similarly higher pretension can be found in the Sermon on the Mount as found in Matthew's gospel, seeking "better justice"; cf. Lienemann, *Gerechtigkeit*, 12, who refers to Luz, *Das Evangelium nach Matthäus*, 244ff.; Schoberth, "Die bessere Gerechtigkeit und die realistischere Politik" assesses this "better justice" from the Sermon on the Mount in the light of the well-known criticisms of Helmut Schmidt ("you cannot make politics with the Sermon on the Mount") and Max Weber, who thought this would lead to a dangerous "Gesinnungsethik." The Sermon on the Mount, then, is not a set of rules to be followed, but virtues to be "obeyed" (Paul Lehmann). In terms of peace, this means not a principle of non-violence, but a virtue of peacemaking (cf. Matthew 5.9: "blessed are the peacemakers," εἰρηνοποιοί, *Friedfertige*), not a general ruling out of the use of force, but an opposition against the logic of violence.

and willingness to contribute of donors in general, as soon as the news spreads. People or organizations that aim at working for a just cause, such as fighting poverty, have a high probability of gaining greater trust, since they appeal to the hearts of the people who mobilize at the least a minimal sense of indignation about the millions of people in Brazil and elsewhere who live below poverty line. Should a donation be channeled to private accounts or be misused in any other way, the betrayal will be even greater, as the donors will have a sense of having been misused in a particularly bad way. The same goes for religious ministers. In general, they are considered worthy of trust due to the ethics they adopted that demand from them that they serve others. The confessional secret, for instance, is an important element protected by canon law, and in some countries also by State law. Consequently, strong disappointment and indignation are caused by the discovery that a minister has, for example, broken the confessional secrecy or committed sexual assault.

(4) A fourth aspect is that trust is a *gift*, it is something freely given, and nobody can be obliged to trust. Accordingly, it can only be given by people who give it with conviction. The voluntary and gift character of trust comes clearly to the fore considering how much time it takes to develop an atmosphere of trust, and how quickly it can be destroyed. Once destroyed, it is very difficult to re-establish it. To illustrate this with an example from another context, I recall the South African *Truth and Reconciliation Commission*. Given the atrocities committed during *apartheid*, the Commission wanted to contribute towards a new South Africa, for which a new relationship of trust is essential. Reconciliation is the presupposition for this, which in turn presupposes repentance and the acknowledgment of guilt. Those who would speak the truth on political crimes would receive amnesty. And indeed, truth came to light in its unbearable cruelty. However, only partly has it been possible to bring forth repentance and acknowledgment. Like trust, these cannot be imposed.[79] Reconciliation, which can be understood as the re-establishment of trust, is a free gift. It can only be established when at least one of the protagonists, by his or her own will, decides to once again invest trust in the other.

(5) Finally, trust must not be invested and given naively. It can be fatal to trust the wrong person at the wrong moment. Thus, it is necessary to recognize signals that could indicate danger. Here, a rational element comes into the otherwise gift-centered character of trust. Of course, it is not always possible to perceive the other's true intentions. Experience and an attentive perception may reduce the probability of a disappointment, but cannot totally avoid it. Trust remains risk, unilateral investment, free gift. To reduce risk, trust needs to be inserted into a wider value system directed towards the well being of all. These values need to be recognized by society so that the trustworthiness of the people can be promoted. To the extent that I can expect others to honor my trust, I will be more willing to invest trust myself. If I were the only one to trust and to behave in a trustworthy way I alone would have to deal with the losses. However, if I can presuppose, on principle, that all will do what is necessary to honor the trust, I will have good reasons to trust in others. But even in this case, trust is never to be given blindly, as all will not always keep to the accepted rules, and thus it makes no sense, legally or morally, to order trust in a deontological way.

b) Trust and Faith

Does faith make a difference for interpersonal trust? I shall try to answer this question first in a sociological, then in a theological way, which recalls the importance of not blurring (but still relating) a functional and a theological way of looking at it. As to the first, there is no reason to believe that, empirically, Christians trust more than others. According to the 2006 Pew Forum survey, results

79. Cf. Kusmierz, "Vom Umgang mit Schuld"; Maclean, *Reconciliation, Nations and Churches*.

for Brazil are very low (they are much better for Chile and Guatemala). The already cited general, standardized question on trust fares low in the Pew Forum's sample (only 2 percent of the general public said they trust "a lot"), and perfectly in line with what Pentecostals (3 percent), Charismatics (1 percent) and other Christians (2 percent) say. In the United States, in contrast, interpersonal trust is higher in general, and other Christians (different from Pentecostals and Charismatics) exceed the general average (41 percent against 35 percent). In South Korea, all Christians seem to trust more than average, with 35–38 percent against 30 percent among the population. It is probable that the differences have to do not only, or not even principally, with reasons of faith, but rather with the position these Christians have in society—in Brazil, they are still fighting for recognition in wider society, and are, furthermore, subject to high competition between each other, factors that are certainly not prone to enhance trust. It is also interesting to note that interpersonal trust is low in predominantly Roman Catholic countries with an iberic (Spanish or Portuguese) colonial past: Latin America and the Philippines show by far the lowest numbers.[80]

Highest trust in Brazil is invested in family members, but even there only between 49–58 percent trust "a lot," with "other Christians" highest (average of all that say they belong to a particular religion: 52 percent)—only in Kenya and Nigeria are there lower numbers. Neighbors fare very low, in line with average, while fellow church members fare relatively high, especially among Pentecostals (23 percent), which indicates, remembering the relatively strong frontiers of identity (cf. above IIE), that the in-group is seen as trustworthy, while "the world out there" is dangerous and must not be trusted. Charismatics fare much lower (7 percent), possibly because they are in tension with non-Charismatic members of the same church. As is to be expected given the strongly exclusivist discourse adopted by many Pentecostal and Neo-Pentecostal, but also historic Protestant churches, trust in people of other faiths is very low (2–4 percent).[81]

Thus, Christians seem to be as much aware of possible breaches of trust as anybody else, although they are able to relocate themselves as "persons"[82] within the church "family." At the same time, if they could be a solution, i.e., enhancing both their own trustworthiness and the donation of trust towards others, they are obviously also part of the problem in terms of their competition and exclusive discourse. They have all rights to be mistrusting themselves as well as others, given the ambiguity of being justified and a sinner at the same time. However, if the higher trust granted to fellow church members is not merely sociological and functional, it should indicate some susceptibility to the precepts of faith. Faith is no guarantee that believers really do trust. But it gives reasons why they can dare to trust.

In the first place, "trust" is closely linked to "faith." The Greek word for both is πίστις, whose verb form πιστέυω in the LXX usually translates the hiphil stem of the root אמן, הֶאֱמִין, which means "to remain firm, trust, have faith, believe."[83] The sense of trust can be seen, for instance, in the

80. Pew Forum, *Spirit and Power*, 45.

81. Ibid.

82. Cf. Part IA3c of the present work.

83. Wildberger, "אמן fest, sicher," 178. In this family of words one also finds אֱמוּנָה (faithfulness, sincerity), in Habakkuk 2.4 translated as πίστις, and אמֶת (reliability, truth). More common, however, for "trust" in the Hebrew Bible is the root בטח (πείθω in the LXX), principally in the psalms and, thus, in a cultic context; its specifically theological use occurs "where it is presupposed that only trust in JHWH is really founded and sustainable, and that no other entity can be an ultimate object of trust," which is the case for most occurrences and, thus, close to the meaning of אמן; Gerstenberger, "בטח vertrauen," 301, 303f. Haacker, "Glaube II," 287 translates האֱמִין, as confidence (*Zuversicht*), a generic concept for the "right relationship to God," which is not to be confounded with a "formal concept for religion as such, but remains [. . .] reserved for the positive relationship to the God of Israel," different from בטח, which can be used for "faith" in the idols (Isaiah 42:17; Habakkuk 2:18; Psalm 115:8; 135:18).

wordplay in Isaiah 7:9, which the New Revised Standard Version tries to translate: "if you do not stand firm (תַאֲמִינוּ hiphil, πιστεύσητε) in faith, you shall not stand at all (תֵאָמֵנוּ niphal, συνῆτε)," or else "if you do not trust, you shall not remain." Another important quote, not least for its influence in Paul, is Genesis 15:6, "And he believed the LORD; and the LORD reckoned it to him as righteousness."

In the synoptics, we can find that faith can be small or big trust, as Jesus scolds his disciples saying "you of little faith" (ὀλιγόπιστοί Luke 12:28; Matthew 6:30). On the whole, Lührmann[84] identifies two lines in the New Testament: a subjective side, mainly in Hebrews and James, where faith is "patience" and "steadfastness," and a content side, mainly in Acts, Paul, and John. Systematically, Dalferth distinguishes between the content of faith (*Glaubensinhalt*), the act of faith (*Glaubensgeschehen*), and the practice of faith (*Glaubensleben*).[85] A similar distinction can be found in Clodovis Boff,[86] who adds to the classical *fides quae*, as faith-word, dogmatics, and *fides qua*, as faith-experience, faith *fiducia*, and the *fides informata*, the practical, incarnated faith. Castro's terms also come to mind for this "citizen faith," which is based on knowing God, loving God, and serving God, i.e., confession, trust, and action.[87] A similar triplicity of dimensions can also be found in other religions.[88]

For Martin Luther, faith is strongly linked to trust. This can be seen in his proper experience, the so called "event in the tower," when he sensed that he was unable to fulfill the huge ethical demands conveyed by the Christian faith as he perceived them at the time. The great relief came when he realized that salvation was not dependent on him, but on Christ, and trusting in Christ's work no human merit could or should be useful for justification before God, which is by faith alone. Among others, he described faith as trust in the Large Catechism, while explaining the first commandment, "you shall have no other gods" (Exodus 20:3):

> A 'god' is the term for that to which we are to look for all good and in which we are to find refuge in all need. Therefore, to have a god is nothing else than to trust and believe in that one with your whole heart [*ex toto corde fidere et credere*] [. . .] For these two belong together, faith and God. Anything on which your heart relies and depends [*tui fiduciam et cor fixum habueris*] is, I say, that is really your God."[89]

Danish Lutheran theologian and philosopher Knud Ejler Løgstrup (1905–81) emphasized the importance of trust and the ethical demand that stems from there:

> Through the trust which a person either shows or asks of another person he surrenders something of his life to that person. [. . .] this trust means that in every encounter between human beings there is an unarticulated demand [. . .] one might say anonymous demand that we take care of the life which trust has placed in our hands.[90]

84. Lührmann, "Glaube 2. Neues Testament," 193.

85. Dalferth, "Glaube 3," 194.

86. C. Boff, *Teoria do método teológico*, 30.

87. Cf. above, ID.

88. In Islam, the "act of faith consist in an internal relatedness [*Verbundenheit*], a verbal expression and a fulfilment of prescriptions" (Khoury, "Glaube 4," 203). In Hinduism, the Bhagavad-Gita designs three ways (*mārgas*) to salvation: the way of action (*karma-mārga*), of knowledge (*jñana-mārga*) and of devotion (*karma-mārga*); cf. the use of this triplicity by Raimon Panikkar (cf. Sinner, *Reden vom Dreieinigen Gott in Brasilien und Indien*, 261-271).

89. Book of Concord, 386.

90. Løgstrup, *The Ethical Demand*, 18f.

An analogous relationship is constituted with God; and if the believers' relationship to God has a bearing on the believer's relationship to other human beings, then this is also true for trust, as Løgstrup affirms in closing his book: "If God's word and action concern a person's relation to God and neighbor, it is self-evident that he must rely upon that word and action; he must trust it, and interpret it in the light of that trust."[91]

What believers believe, then, is rooted in their relationship with God, where trust is an important element. The content of their faith, as revealed through the Word (Christ), to be read in Scripture and heard in preaching, is what gives them direction and identity, and binds them together with other believers. An important element here, highlighted especially, but not exclusively by the Lutheran tradition, is that salvation, and faith itself, comes from God as a gift and is not a merit, strictly speaking not involving any human effort—although it needs *assensio* (consent) besides *fiducia* (trust), as Melanchthon insisted.[92] From there, in an attitude of gratitude, flow good works as a consequence, as "faith by itself, if it has no works, is dead" (James 2:17). Faith as trust, as content and as action are thus all connected and belong together. It is, then, the believers' faith that enables and motivates them to trust, to regain integrity as Christ repaired their relationship with God, the creator of all, and to relate to others and serve others on this basis. Again, this does not exclude, but include knowledge about one's own and any others fallibility. Trust based on faith does not lead to blind interpersonal or institutional trust, but drawing on a never-ending source of trust to be enabled to extend it to others even after having been disappointed. Forgiveness and reconciliation, the "healing of memories," come in as important steps on the way to new trust. The Truth and Reconciliation Commission in South Africa, as in other countries (but, as seen, not properly in Brazil), showed well how important it is to face truth, as ugly and devastating it may be. Only on the basis of truth is reconciliation possible, although the latter does not necessarily follow the former. As nobody can be ordered to trust, likewise nobody can be ordered to forgive and reconcile.

Faith as trust is based on the promise of God. The promise is first and enables the human answer in a relationship of trust. By faith, believers are inserted into communion with God. This communion goes beyond religious, social, and gender boundaries: "There is no such thing as Jew and Greek, slave and free, male and female; for you are all one person in Christ Jesus" (Galatians 3;28). Therefore, trust also stretches beyond certain groups and seeks to overcome inequalities, creating a new *convivência* among equals. It is true that the churches, throughout history, have often reinforced inequalities and exclusiveness rather than overcoming them. But from their faith, they are constantly being challenged to an ethics of mutual trust that presupposes equality. In the words of the letter to the Ephesians:

> [. . .] live up to your calling. Be humble always and gentle, and patient too. Be forbearing with one another and charitable. Spare no effort to make fast with bonds of peace the unity which the Spirit gives. There is one body and one spirit, as there is also one hope held out in God's call to you; one Lord, one faith, one baptism; one God and Father of all, who is over all and through all and in all (Eph 4.1-6)

91. Ibid., 230.

92. "Fides est assensio, qua accipis omnes artículos fidei, et est fiducia acquiescens in Deo propter Mediatorem" (CR 23, 456), and further: "Dies ist die wahre Bestimmung des Glaubens, von der Paulus redet, wenn er sagt: 'Aus Glauben warden wir gerecht.' Und Paulus versteht es zugleich in dem Denkvermögen die Wahrnehmung *(notitia)* und die Zustimmung *(assensus)* sowie in dem Willen das Vertrauen *(fiducia)*. Dazu muß man auch wissen, daß die Wahrnehmungen ergreifende *(apprehensiva)* sind, das Vertrauen aber im Herzen und Willen eine Bewegung *(motus)* ist, durch die wir Ruhe finden in dem ergriffenen Objekt" (StA 2/2, 786, 11ff.); both quotations in Slenczka, "Glaube VI, " 325f.

c) A Hermeneutics of Trust and convivência

A *hermeneutics of trust* means to understand the *convivência* of people based on trust.[93] My relationship with other persons depends on the perception I have of them. On the one hand, my trust is going to be influenced by people's behavior. This then would be informed trust. On the other hand, I can learn to see people in a different way, as the image and likeness of God and, therefore, as holders of great dignity. This vision of people, based on faith, creates a greater ethic that guides my behavior in relationship to people. From this is born the trust that risks the "bet," makes a prior "investment" and proves itself as a gift.

While such an understanding is not exclusive to Christians, it is imperative for them, especially among each other. Competition between churches that results in mutual defamation and verbal or even physical aggression is not an improper attitude in this context. The Christian churches believe in Jesus Christ, Son of God the Father, through the power of the Holy Spirit. This faith is trust in God and unites the faithful as sisters and brothers in the communion of the church. However, as a matter of fact, instead of trust there is often mistrust among churches and Christians.[94] Even within one particular church, such as the IECLB, with its traditional, progressive, pietistic, evangelical, and charismatic tendencies, there exist tensions, separations, prejudices and, accordingly, mistrust that contradict the principle of trust based on a common faith. Instead of living in communion they live in competition, instead of equating themselves with the vision of the Kingdom of God they equate themselves with the Kingdom of the Market. In chapter IIB1 I have shown the enormous diversity of churches in Brazil. In such a competitive situation, the other is considered with suspicion and often considered less true, less "believing," less missionary, less moral. In other words, of trust, there is not a trace, although all of them invoke the same Trinitarian God and proclaim salvation in Jesus Christ.[95]

Paul spent a considerable part of his letters caring for the unity of the church. In 1 Corinthians, for example, he writes:

> I appeal to you, my brothers [and sisters], in the name of our Lord Jesus Christ: agree among yourselves, and avoid divisions; be firmly joined in the unity of mind and thought. I have been told, my brothers, by Chloe's people there are quarrels among you. What I mean is this: each of you is saying, 'I am Paul's man', or 'I am for Apollos'; 'I follow Cephas', or 'I am Christ's.' Surely Christ has not been divided among you! Was it Paul who was crucified for you? Was it in the name of Paul that you were baptized?[96]

Because of Christ, whose body is one, Christians may dare to risk the bet on the brothers and the sisters, to invest trust, to be guided by the greater ethic to which they are called, to give,

93. Ritschl, *Theorie und Konkretion*, 179–92; Sinner, "Trust and *convivência*." Hermeneutics as referred to here goes beyond the understanding and interpretation of texts to the understanding and interpretation of life, emphasizing the perception I have of other people and of that which unites us as human beings, and among Christians as faithful.

94. Cf. Santa Ana, *Ecumenismo e libertação*, 227, for whom "it is exactly the lack of trust in faith itself" that "leads to isolationist attitudes that, beyond being expressions of religious narcissism, do not correspond with the dynamics of the Christian faith."

95. U.S.-American anthropologist John Burdick (*Looking for God in Brazil*, 230) registered, throughout his field research in the Baixada Fluminense in the state of Rio de Janeiro, a "cycle of mistrust" nurtured by the prejudice between, in this case, the Catholics from the *comunidade* (base community) and the *crentes*, that even impeded their practical cooperation in (secular) neighborhood associations. Contrary to widespread opinion, the *crentes* can be very active members of such associations, provided these are not dominated by Catholics. On the other hand, Burdick noticed that the bishop, known as progressive, withdrew his permission to use church premises for the association's meetings, as soon as its leadership became *crente* rather than Catholic (ibid., 206-212).

96. 1 Corinthians 1:10–13; cf. Witherington, *Conflict and Community in Corinth*, 94–101; Theissen, *The Social Setting of Pauline Christianity.*

freely, trust as a gift, but always in an informed way, as trust of a "second naïveté"[97] or a "second innocence."[98] It is not about trusting everyone, nor accepting everything. But it is necessary to find ways of *convivência* based on our common faith that produces trust, because the witness of competition that churches and church movements are currently giving is one of incoherence, mistrust, and even lack of faith, and damages their mission. A united church—not a uniform church—will have a greater impact on society and will be, in a better and more credible way, able to "answer all who ask the reason for the hope that is in you" (1 Peter 3:15).[99] Beside this, the churches can help each other to have a better hermeneutics of trust in God, thereby deepening and correcting their faith in God. As Dietrich Ritschl says: "Our ecumenical partners are always only the potential reformers of our own doctrine."[100] This implies "to reckon with the possibility that the Spirit speaks within and through the others" and that "those who interpret the Christian tradition differently each have a 'right intention of faith,'" as affirmed in a study done by the World Council of Churches on an ecumenical hermeneutics.[101] There is no doubt that, if one does not "bet" on the other church and "advance" trust, there will never be ecumenism, nor communion in faith.

Convivência—literally, "conviviality," but better translated as "communal interaction"—is a word used in everyday language in Brazil, and has received special attention in educational and theological literature since the 1960s. On a primary level, it simply means that human beings do not live alone. It is part of our being that we coexist with other men and other women in time and space (*convivere,* in Latin). The daily contact with neighbors, study colleagues, workers of the bus company, bakery attendants, teachers, and many other people is part of our life. It belongs to the *conditio humana* that it is not only a fact that we do not live alone, but it is part of our human nature to seek community in the family and other forms of associations in society. Moreover, it is one of the most pleasurable aspects of the human condition to be in relationship with others. Therefore, it is necessary to mold and guide this coexistence for it to become *convivência*, "assumed neighborliness."[102] Inspired by reflections that evolved from a Conference in Rio de Janeiro in 1985, German missiologist Theo Sundermeier developed the concept of *convivência* (*Konvivenz*, as a German neologism) as "a community of learning, mutual support and celebration."[103] Paulo Freire had used the term in his famous "Pedagogy of the Oppressed," where he emphasized especially the need for "trust in the people." To that end, a "conversion" is needed which presupposes *convivência* with the oppressed in order to learn to understand their life.[104] What matters is the walking

97. Ricœur, *De l'interprétation*; *Le conflit des interpretations.*

98. Panikkar, *The Cosmotheandric Experience*, 50, quoting Mark 10:15 and Matthew 5:3; in another place, he refers to the *docta ignorantia* of Nicolas Cusanus (Panikkar, *La nueva inocéncia*, 34f.).

99. There is an important parallel between accountability in a political system and was has become prominent in ecumenical dialogue as "mutual accountability," described by Tveit (*Mutual Accountability*), based among others on José Miguez Bonino, as "ethical attitude."

100. Ritschl, *Theorie und Konkretion*, 191.

101. Commission on Faith and Order, *A Treasure in Earthen Vessels*, paragraphs 8 and 30.

102. This is what my colleague and former IECLB president Gottfried Brakemeier called it in an e-mail message sent to me on April 21, 2004.

103. Sundermeier, "Konvivenz als Grundstruktur ökumenischer Existenz," especially 51-59 on the origin of the term in Latin America.

104. Freire, *Pedagogy of the Oppressed*; cf. Brandt, "In der Nachfolge der Inkarnation," esp. 375–78; see also Illich, *Tools for Conviviality*. L. Boff quotes as the two "niches of experience" for *convivência* in Brazil—after having described the Little Sisters of Charles de Foucauld in their living as "midwives" among the Tapirapé indigenous people and the parable of the Good Samaritan (Luke 10:30-38) as paradigmatic narratives—Paulo Freire and the CEBs.

together, and this is not possible without trust. Where there is no trust there will not be *convivência* in the sense here described.

As mentioned in the introductory part of this section, civil virtues, prone to enhance trust if one can rely on their generalized validity, are certainly of need in Brazil as elsewhere. While they exist on a personal level and in certain groups, including churches, it is necessary to bring them into society as a whole and overcome the restriction to "persons" around their "families." The stress on the importance of Christian witness for trust is not new. Richard Shaull, then a missionary to Latin America, in an address delivered for U.S.-American students, "Encounter with Revolution" (1955), said that "the most important [. . .] is that Christians can contribute to bring a basic attitude of trust and hope, as well as creative imagination to confront the facts."[105] More, however, is to be said on the context of such attitudes and virtues, which is what shall follow in the next session.

3.TO ENDURE AS A CITIZEN: THE AMBIGUITY OF REALITY

ultra equinoxialem non peccavit

Caspar Barlaeus[106]

Muita religião, seu moço.

Joao Guimaraes Rosa[107]

Rubem Alves, in his classical "Protestantism and Repression"[108] describes and criticizes what he calls "Right Doctrine Protestantism" (*protestantismo da reta doutrina*), a kind of rigid orthodoxy imposed on the believers and controlled by a variety of disciplinary mechanisms. Purity is sought in doctrine and behavior, while correct behavior is linked mainly to sexual behavior, and all that has connotations of an uncontrolled living of impulses, like drinking alcohol, dancing, theatre. . .[109]

105. Shaull, *Encounter with Revolution*, 84f., quoted in Burity, *Os protestantes e a revolução brasileira*, 103; in the absence of the original text, I retranslate into English from Burity's Portuguese quotation.

106. Barlaeus wrote this famous aphorism in his book *Rerum per octennium in Brasilia* (Amsterdam, 1647, cf. Bitterli, *Die 'Wilden' und die 'Zivilisierten'*, 246), written at the request of Maurice of Nassau-Siegen, after the latter's return from Brazil; in Westhelle's interpretation, this means that the New World was at the same time paradise and hell, where neither sin nor redemption were possible ("O tamanho do paraíso," 242). Thus, the ambiguity the Europeans reserved for themselves was precisely denied to the natives of the New World.

107. "Lots of religion, laddie," Rosa, *Grande Sertão*, 32. This is the classical literature pointing to ambiguity in life, and namely in religion: João Guimarães Rosa's (1908–67) *Grande Sertão: Veredas,* where the protagonist Riobaldo says: "What I most think, I put into text and explain: everybody is crazy. [. . .] That's why one needs, principally, religion: to un-crazy [*desendoidecer, desendoidar*] oneself. Prayer is what heals craziness. [. . .] Lots of religion, laddie. As to myself, I don't lose any opportunity for religion. I take advantage of them all. I drink water from every river . . . Just one, for me, is little, maybe doesn't do it. [. . .] But it's all very provisional. I would like to pray—all the time."

108. Alves, *Protestantism and Repression.*

109. I have always asked myself, and frequently asked ministers and lay people of a variety of churches in courses I taught, why church discipline is virtually exclusively linked to issues of human sexuality and the integrity of the family and not to issues of honesty, anti-corruption, charity, citizenship. Nobody has, so far, contested this questioning, except for defending sexual morals as such, which of course is important. But it seems plain that there are few—if any—theological reasons to value so much sexual morals to the detriment of other moral issues, and there is a recognition that church members that do, for instance, illicit things in financial matters tend to be overlooked by church discipline (cf. also above, Part IIE of the present work). Lutherans, in general, do not fit this picture; although they maintain restrictions in sexual matters, they do drink, dance, and smoke as they find fit; Lutheran feasts are apparently a point of attraction for believers dissatisfied with their former church's rigidity (cf. Schultz, *Misturando os espíritos*, 19).

There have been numerous processes ongoing in the Presbyterian Church of Brazil's (IPB) governing bodies, which show that it explicitly seeks to maintain such orthodoxy and—as the church understands it—connected orthopraxy.[110] This is in direct contrast to what is perceived as Brazilian culture, where sensuality and sexuality, dancing, music, and so on are important elements.[111] There is always a certain ambiguity and simultaneity there, escaping any final definition.[112] Even in religion, there is, for many, an ambiguity in that persons belong to a specific confession, but seek other religions and their representatives when they feel it might help them better.[113]

There is a continuous ambiguity and simultaneity in life, as expressed in Lutheran theology by the *simul iustus et peccator*.[114] This is not meant to excuse responsibility for wrongdoing. On the level of human practice, there is sin as different from just action, and should be denounced as such.[115] Responsibility for poverty and oppression is not evenly distributed among all, although they are, to some extent, all *simul oppressus et oppressor*, to use Silfredo Dalferth's formula[116] based on his interpretation of Leonardo Boff. What is, indeed, common is the living under the power of sin, which creates an inescapable situation of sin, with structural elements as Liberation Theology has always been insisting. Christians know about this situation brought about by Adam, the first human, and from there have, as I would call it, a "confessional" mistrust in themselves and others, inasmuch as all, including the believers, are subject to the power of sin.

110. Such processes are shown in IPB minister Marcello Fontes' master's dissertation of 2004, and have driven out a good number of ministers and lay people since the closing in of the church that coincided with the military regime. In a number of churches, like Baptist and Pentecostal, orthopraxy in this sense is straightforwardly called *doutrina*, i.e., doctrine (cf. above, Part IIE2e of the present work).

111. The attempt to establish purity is not so recent in Brazil; as anthropologist Ronaldo Vainfas shows, based on a thorough analysis of the minutes of the Inquisition, Jesuits struggled, precisely in the spirit of the contemporary European Counter-Reformation, "against the advance of 'Lutheranism' on the peninsula, be it real or chimerical [. . .], [and] for the purification of popular mentalities, the demonization of religious syncretisms, the persecution of 'moral offenses' to the family and the 'abhorrent heretical longings'" (*Trópico dos pecados*,190).

112. On sexual ambiguity, see Trevisan, *Devassos no paraíso*; on ambiguity in relation to religion Schultz, *Misturando os espíritos*, based on an empirical study of religious references among a Lutheran congregation at the periphery of São Paulo which has, atypically, about a third of members from other traditions who remain, at least in part, in the new confessional environment. In Schultz' study, the church leadership and administration in Porto Alegre, in the state of Rio Grande do Sul whose patron saint is St. Peter, is interpreted as the "Peter" model, as a static, conservative model of the church, while São Paulo (St. Paul) would represent a dynamic missionary model. For Schultz, also Lutheran Protestantism is seeking purity and orthodoxy, rather than ambiguity. Although this reductive typology is certainly debatable, it points, at the same time, to existing tendencies, and is relevant as a challenge to a missionary inertia, and to the existence of a variety of tendencies and religious identities within one church. André Musskopf (*Via(da)gens teológicas*) has also been working on this in a theological reflection from a queer theory and gay theology approach. His doctoral thesis, elaborated with my supervision, was defended successfully in August 2008, and has helped me in understanding better the aspect of ambiguity, especially sexual ambiguity.

113. Cf. above, Part IIB1.3 of the present work.

114. See Luther's lectures on Romans, here on Romans 4:7, LW 25:260: "Now, is he perfectly righteous? No, for he is a the same time both a sinner and a righteous man; a sinner in fact [*in re*], but a righteous man by the sure imputation and promise of God that He will continue to deliver him from sin until He has completely cured him. And thus he is entirely healthy in hope [*in spe*], but in fact he is still a sinner; but he has the beginning of righteousness, so that he continues more and more always to seek it, yet he realizes that he is always unrighteous."

115. Westhelle ("O desencontro entre a teologia luterana e a teologia da libertação") distinguishes between a doxological dimension, where the *simul iustus et peccator* means *totus iustus et totus peccator*, and a historical, or ethical-political dimension, which refers to *simul partim iustus simul partim peccator*, a distinction which corresponds to the Two Kingdoms Doctrine, interpreted precisely in the terms of these dimensions. In another text, Westhelle in "O tamanho do paraíso," insists on the dialectic between (individual) sins and Sin (as power).

116. Dalferth, *Die Zweireichelehre*, 240.

In Neo-Pentecostalism's prosperity gospel, which is spreading out also to classical Pentecostalism, as well as the ICAR's and historical Protestants' charismatic movements, God becomes the object of requirements. This is another attempt to overcome the deep ambiguity in life, with believers trusting too much their religious leaders, as well as their own faith, and their contributions linked to it. This can lead to disastrous situations,[117] and even to lawsuits where disappointed frequenters want their money back because they alleged they had been induced to pay a large sum of money by being promised their situation would improve, but not attended in their plea.[118] While Pentecostalism and what came out of it usually was accused of looking beyond this world to the coming Kingdom, and to forget about the importance of today—which is only partially true, as I have shown—this is exactly the opposite: an accentuated immediatism, which, ultimately, wants to utilize God for felicity on earth, even if tamed by a number of behavioral rules.

It is important, then, to stress that the world has both good and bad elements, which are and remain mixed, as the parable of the weed among the wheat shows so well (Matthew 13:24–30).[119] The world in which we live is ambiguous, and we cannot escape this situation, neither by trying to be pure, nor by trying to free the world from all evil by exorcism. Both attitudes are theologically highly questionable, but beyond this also make tolerance and the acceptance of pluralism, namely religious pluralism, virtually impossible. Where there is no *deus absconditus*, no mysterious God who surpasses our understanding and is never reducible to our perception and logic, but rather a God controlled by humans, perfectly known in his features to those who believe in him, pluralism is a theoretical impossibility and practical danger to be combated.

John R. Stumme highlights that "the ethics of the two kingdoms is an ethics of realism."[120] It implies, thus, a sober analysis and judgment, acknowledging the power of evil and its appearance in human will and social and political structures. The conscience of the ambiguous character of all decisions and "historical projects," as underlined by Stumme, remembers the importance of an eschatological reserve: No historical project can represent the Kingdom of God, nor any existing situation. While ultimately recognized by all, the applicability of this principle, i.e., the degree to which human beings can and are bringing about the Kingdom of God through their actions, has been a matter of debate. Roman Catholic theologians tended to believe more in such realization, and criticized Lutheranism for having a negative anthropology and, thus, promoting a passive attitude towards transformation and a pessimist view on the future.[121] For them, it probably aroused fears of falling back into a double notion of history as preeminent in the Catholic Thomistic tradition

117. I know of a scene where a member of such a church wanted to test the power her faith had given her, and tried to "heal," in a supermarket, a lady walking on crutches due to her poliomyelitis. By coincidence, the lady is a believer herself, a Lutheran pastor. However, she never saw her disability as something to be healed, but as the burden she was to carry and had grown accustomed to. She had learnt to, in her life and faith, combine suffering and grace. Now the Neo-Pentecostal church member tried hard to convince her that she must and could be healed, but found out that neither was this what the "patient" wanted, nor was she herself able to do what she thought she must and could. The result was a totally failed attempt of "healing" in the "name of Jesus," embarrassing for all implied, but certainly the biggest blow was on the church member's faith, as she understood it.

118. There is at least one case where such a lawsuit was won in the second instance, see http://oglobo.globo.com/sp/mat/2007/09/10/297664069.asp (accessed on 2/21/2008).

119. The dangers of dualisms in a theologically undergirded Brazilian theocracy and messianism (of the dominating and the dominated, respectively) become evident in philosopher Marilena Chauí's (*Brasil*) book on Brazil's "Founding Myth."

120. Stumme, "Algumas teses sobre os dois reinos," 263.

121. See, for instance, the previously quoted Juan Luis Segundo, *The Liberation of Theology*, 139; other authors are quoted and discussed in Altmann, *Lutero e libertação*, 307-334, a chapter unfortunately not translated in the English version, Altmann, *Luther and Liberation*.

of distinguishing between the natural and the supernatural, against which Gutiérrez and others wanted precisely to stress the unity of history.[122] Lutherans have held against this criticism that theirs was not a pessimistic, but a realistic view of humanity, and that the church "*constitutes* itself over the forgiven sin, however, it is *committed* with help and solidarity to the poor. Both are important. . . ."[123] Lutherans refuse to confuse salvation with human action. There is no human merit as to salvation, which underlines its gratuity[124] and facilitates trust in God through Christ (IIIA2). This, however, does not mean that service (IIIA4) does and must not flow from this gift, nor does it underestimate human capacity, as both Luther and Calvin highly valued reason, even the one existing outside the Christian fold.[125] Love, as such a gift, must seek efficiency, as Brakemeier emphasizes with a reference to Miguez Bonino.[126] Stumme highlights that

> The only actor for salvation is God in Jesus Christ, while in creation, action is understood as God's gift and human beings' task. Such attitude affirms human dignity, because it supplies the foundation for basic trust in reality, which is indispensable for human freedom.[127]

A certain ambiguity is defendable in religious matters, where we should not too easily adopt an exclusive stance. Not only because there is, as a matter of fact, a great deal of syncretism in Brazilian religiosity.[128] But also because we should not claim more unambiguousness in faith than the Gospel itself transmits to believers—and there are many open aspects there. This is not to say churches should not have a recognizable doctrinal and practical identity, but it need not be exclusive beyond a type of *satis* as defined in CA 7: "And to the true unity of the Church it is *enough* to agree concerning the doctrine of the Gospel and the administration of the Sacraments" (my emphasis). However, when it comes to citizenship and rights, there is no place for ambiguity. The law does not work with such lack of clarity, and despite the *jeitinho* being a means of "social navigation" (DaMatta) for poor people, the great danger is that it serves the powerful in keeping power and dealing with public issues as if they were private. From both sides, an unequivocal rule of law is indispensable. The difference between the latter and the former position is echoed in the combination of the *simul* and the Two Kingdoms Doctrine: in relation to God and under the circumstance of a disputed world, where both God and the devil are at work, the secular regiment has to provide protection, peace with justice for all, Christians and Non-Christians. Although fiercely criticizing the Two Kingdoms Doctrine—in the form he encountered it in the 1920s and 1930s in Germany—and insisting on God's sovereignty in Christ, Karl Barth[129] is after all not so far from such a position. Metaphorically, rather than suggesting a dialectics between the secular and the spiritual regiment as in the Lutheran tradition, Barth describes concentric circles, where the Christian belongs to both the Christian community and the civil community, from the inside out, whereas the inverse is not true. But both types of thought concur in the fact that Christian citizens are located in the world and both citizens in an ecclesial and a political sense. They cannot, indeed must not evade this double citizenship. While this is, on the whole, a highly ambiguous situation, which has its effects in both the State and

122. I.e., the unity of profane history and the history of salvation, see especially the chapter "liberation and salvation" in Gutiérrez, *A Theology of Liberation*, 83–105.

123. Brakemeier, "Pobres e pecadores na ótica de Jesus," 58.

124. Cf. above, IIIA1.

125. Cf. Lohse, *Luthers Theologie in ihrer historischen Entwicklung*, 214–18.

126. Miguez Bonino, *Doing Theology in a Revolutionary Situation*.

127. Stumme, "Algumas teses sobre os dois reinos," 253.

128. Cf. Brandt, *Die heilige Barbara in Brasilien*.

129. Barth, "Christengemeinde und Bürgergemeinde."

the church, where sins are practiced and human dignity is being attacked, it needs, precisely for this reason, a clear law and organization. To invoke ambiguity, factual as it is, must not serve as an excuse not to preserve peace with justice. But it is a means to avoid an excessive search for purity and exclusivism, and a way to regain confidence in a situation where mistrust seems to be the only trustworthy attitude, both for sociological and for theological reasons.

Following the above indicated line of a deeply rooted trust, which endures ambiguity, but does not content itself with it, it should be possible to find a basis for the *convivência* also of different religions and the necessary dialogue among them. There are good reasons to "bet" on the depth of trust even in inter-religious dialogue.[130] Along this line, I find the reflections of the Hispano-Indian Raimon Panikkar helpful, an author who is himself rooted in different religions and engaged within himself in a, as he calls it, "intra-religious" dialogue.[131] He can rightly be counted among the pluralistic theologians of religion, although he occupies a particular position there. This can be seen, for instance, in his modification of the well-known river metaphor—according to which the different religions would be like rivers that meet in a common ocean—to affirm that the rivers of religions will only meet in the clouds.[132] Another metaphor points "downwards": religions meet in the depth of the "cosmotheandric" or "theanthropocosmic reality." In relation to the theme of trust and *convivência,* it is important that the uniqueness of religions and, thus, the respect for their alterity is not being dissolved; religions are not being melted into a universal "world religion" or "world theology." At the same time, they are also not simply being juxtaposed as self-satisfied semiotic systems. There is a meeting point, high above in the "clouds" or down below in the "depth," that is in the perichoretic Reality of the interrelatedness of God (*theos*), World (*kosmos*) and Man (*aner, anthropos*).[133] From the constant conversion to this Reality, as it is practised by the different religions in their respective ways, follows "cosmic confidence."[134] Panikkar's main contribution towards dialogue—and thus towards the *convivência* of religions—seems to me to lie in his ability to combine an irenic attitude of "fundamental openness,"[135] a close look and open ear, a thorough restraint in judgment over people of other faiths and the respect in relation to their being different,

130. John Hick uses the Pascalian idea of the bet to convince Western skeptics of the specific rationality of religion as such (*Religion*, 231): "Pascal [. . .] recognized the crucial point that the justification of theistic faith does not lie in an argument which leads directly to the conclusion that God exists, but, rather, in an argumentation in favor of the rationality of such faith *despite* the fact that it cannot be proven [. . .] The adequate argument must show that it is reasonable that religious persons try to live *trustfully* on the basis of their own religious experience and, thus, the wider stream of such experiences in which they participate," re-translation from the German and emphasis mine. See also my reflections on the ecumenical dimension of Raimon Panikkar's thinking, which focuses on inter- and intra- (i.e., within the same person) religious dialogue, from which I take up elements in this section (Sinner, *Reden vom Dreieinigen Gott in Brasilien und Indien*, 316–28; "Trust and *convivência*," "Inter-religious Dialogue").

131. Panikkar, *The Intra-Religious Dialogue.*

132. Panikkar, "The Jordan, the Tiber, and the Ganges," 92: "'They' [sc. the rivers] meet in the form of clouds, once they have suffered a transformation into vapor, which eventually will pour down again into the valleys of mortals to feed the rivers and the earth. Religions do not coalesce. . .they meet once transformed into vapor, once metamorphosized into Spirit, which then is poured down in innumerable tongues."

133. Panikkar insists in using "Man" for human being, and prefers the greek *aner* (male) rather than *anthropos* (human), opting for traditional terminology and stating that this does not mean to fall into sexism. In any case, I follow his terminology here as it shows more clearly the elements of his "cosmo-the-andr-ism."

134. Mainly in Panikkar, "The Invisible Harmony." For a critique from an ethical-political perspective see Knitter, "Cosmic Confidence or Preferential Option?" , and Panikkar's response ("A Self-Critical Dialogue," 276–84). "Cosmic" confidence is not confidence *in* the cosmos, but the confidence (or trust, as I prefer here) *of* the cosmos, to which we belong through our being; "it is the awareness of our being in and of the universe," ibid., 282.

135. Cf. Ahlstrand, *Fundamental Openness.*

with trust in the (tri-)unity of Reality.[136] To speak in the language of the Christian faith: it is the same trust in God that makes possible Christian ecumenism, with the difference that it has a much vaguer conceptual basis. It parts from trust in a God who is *semper maior* than what I can perceive of Godself through biblical witness and my lived faith. This also means that it is necessary to have a modest perception of one's own religion. Trust as a bet and prior investment becomes even more obvious here than in Christian ecumenism. If inter-religious dialogue is to be more than the double monologue of two persons which defend their particular view, if it is to be thinkable that I can learn from the other, if I am to have more than the option of staying with my own or convert to the other's religion, then there must be "something deeper" which enables such mutual "learning." To trust in this makes dialogue and also *convivência*, which is more than mere coexistence, a viable option. Any worthwhile dialogue must build on this fundament.

For the Brazilian context, these reflections are highly relevant, because there is a widespread mistrust not only between churches, but also between different religions. This effects especially the religions brought to Brazil by people traded as slaves from Africa, which have developed a significant—in part syncretistic—existence as African Brazilian religions. Under the Portuguese *padroado*, they were forbidden and their practices had to be disguised as Roman Catholic ones: their feasts were made to coincide with the Catholic saints to avoid censure. As a consequence of this longstanding symbiosis with the Catholic Church, it has become common for many faithful to identify themselves as belonging to both, in a situation of religious ambiguity. This fact and the difficulty of getting in-depth information on these religions—they do not have a sacred book, and the oral tradition is passed on only to initiated persons, only partly and over a long period of time—probably contributed to the mysterious nimbus that surrounds them and leaves many Christians, Protestants and Catholics alike, mistrustful. These religions are being demonized and rejected by many, and not rarely their installations or members are being attacked verbally or even physically. The opposite position, which does not see any essential difference between African Brazilian religions and Christianity and preaches complete harmony between them, although politically understandable and certainly more prone to foster *convivência* than the former, exclusivist attitude, is also not helpful as it tends to rule out the understanding of difference, so crucial for dialogue. Considering these arguments, I believe that trust in a possible unity in "depth"—to take up Panikkar's metaphor again—could foster a real dialogue while accepting difference. This reminder goes, in the first place, to Christians, as they are to blame for the widespread fear, prejudice and discrimination.

136. "Openness" and fragmentarity are positive ways to understand "ambiguity" and "simultaneity": Rather than seeking uniformity and combating ambiguity for drifting away from a firm doctrinal basis, acceptance of it would be an asset to Christian mission, Schultz argues (*Misturando os espíritos*, 103ff.). While these are certainly important elements of life under this *aion*, it is problematic to make it a virtue in itself. Luther, while speaking of the simultaneity of being just and a sinner, certainly did not value both in the same way; moreover, whenever he speaks of ambiguity, it is in a negative way, often attributed to the "Sophisten." At least eschatologically, the factual ambiguity is seen as ending (cf. 1 Corinthians 13), as something to be overcome.

4. TO SERVE AS A CITIZEN: LIBERTY AND SERVICE

Also ist die welt vol von Gott. In allen gassen, fur deiner thur findest du Christum. Gaff nicht ynn himel.

Martin Luther[137]

For where there are no laws, the poor, the widows, and the orphans are oppressed.

Martin Luther[138]

Once the dignity of a citizen is established, trust in God has empowered citizens to trust each other, and the ambiguity of reality has been acknowledged, another basic impulse of the Christian faith comes to its bearing: love, which finds its most noble expression in service. If parting from justification by grace through faith relieves the believer from being responsible for his or her salvation, he or she is then freed to serve others.[139] As Luther highlighted in his famous statement: "A Christian is perfectly free lord of all, subject to none. A Christian is a perfectly dutiful servant of all, subject to all," operating with the distinction between inner (free) and outer (servant) human, works being not the condition for, but the consequence of justification.[140] While Melanchthon and Calvin defended a third use of the law—besides the first, political, and the second, pedagogical, showing human being's enlacement in sin, being unable to fulfill the law— a "*usus in renatis*," which gives especial weight to sanctification (also underlined by Wesley), Luther did not use the language of law for this element. But he certainly emphasized the importance of works following faith, and the fact that Christians are to serve others—not only Christians, but all humans in need, and the State that seeks to organize their coexistence.[141] Good works are certainly not restricted to Christians, but, again, it is not my task here to speak for others, but to seek grounds for Christian activity in the world. Non-Christians have their own motivations for doing good, and can share with Christians their views on what "good" is. But it is impossible for Christians, I contend, not to see the importance of love and service for their doing. Freedom is a "communicative freedom."[142] Jesus' own practice is showing this clearly, as is Paul's central place given to love not only, but prominently in 1 Corinthians 13. In history, such practice has become evident in hospitality, a Christian specificity,[143] in numerous

137. Quoted in Westhelle, "The Word and the Mask," 178: "Thus the world is full of God. In every alley, at your door you find Christ; stare not at heavens" (WA 20:514, 27f.).

138. LW 13:53, quoted in Lindberg, "Luther on Poverty," 151.

139. This is highlighted by L. Boff as one of the important contributions of Luther towards Liberation Theology: "Luther helps us all to understand that liberation starts from God's gift, who before any historic act, on the part of human beings, takes the initiative" (*Ética e eco-espiritualidade*, 146)

140. LW 31:344 and the whole treatise 343–77. Dalferth (*Die Zweireichelehre*), who in his doctoral thesis provides a dialogue between Luther's Two Kingdoms Doctrine and Leonardo Boff's theology of liberation, mentions that L. Boff (*Vida Segundo o Espírito*, 89f.) refers to this phrase in his book on the Holy Spirit, while dealing with the three evangelical councils [*evangelische Räte*], namely obedience, quoting 1 Corinthians 9:1 and Romans 13:8, but not mentioning Luther.

141. Cf. Mau, "Gesetz V. Reformationszeit"; Peters, "Werke IV," 636–40.

142. Cf. Bedford-Strohm, *Gemeinschaft aus kommunikativer Freiheit*. For a comprehensive study of freedom as used by Liberation Theologians, brought into dialogue with Martin Luther and Huldrych Zwingli, see Dahling-Sander, *Zur Freiheit befreit*.

143. Cf. L. Boff, *Virtudes para um outro mundo possível*, vol. 3; Hiltbrunner, *Gastfreundschaft* esp. 157–207. The

acts of *diakonia*, which is itself one of the elements of Christian self-definition: The *koinonia* of the Church as *kerygma, martyria, diakonia*, and *leitourgia*—as proclamation, witness, service, and worship. In Romans 12:1f. Paul clearly sees together the aspects of faith and action in worship:

> I appeal to you therefore, brothers and sisters, by the mercies of God, to present your bodies as a living sacrifice, holy and acceptable to God, which is your spiritual worship. 2 Do not be conformed to this world, but be transformed by the renewing of your minds, so that you may discern what is the will of God - what is good and acceptable and perfect.[144]

Love also implies the aspects of forgiveness and reconciliation, and of compassion. From a lawyer's point of view, writing on the Third Sector, Eduardo Paes states that "in all religious traditions, there is, deeply rooted, the notion that to give and to serve are among the highest manifestations of the human spirit, like the idea of forgiveness or, furthermore, of compassion."[145] Roberto Zwetsch constructed his Protestant theology of mission on the concept of compassion (*com-paixão*, highlighting the implication of passion as love and suffering), which has nothing of a condescending, patronizing assistance, but of a walking and living together, precisely in *convivência*.[146] Freedom, implied in the concept of liberation, is both freedom *from*, i.e., emancipation and independence, and freedom *for*, i.e., readiness and capacity to accept obligations in relation to God and our fellow human beings.[147] As trust in God enables trust in other human beings, so love for God empowers to love fellow human beings in a clear interconnection of the two, evident from Leviticus 19:18 via Matthew 19:19 and Luke 10:27 to Romans 13:9 and James 2:8, taken to be the sum of the law. As Luther concludes in his treatise on freedom, "a Christian lives not in himself, but in Christ and in his neighbor. Otherwise he is not a Christian."[148] It is adequate to remember here the interpretation of Liberation Theology as "*intellectus amoris*," as mentioned earlier (ID1). This is certainly not a naïve, harmonious love, in the same way as service cannot mean uncritical obedience or simple submission. Rather, as Liberation Theology or, as they called it in these regards, "liberation spirituality" has stressed, "evangelization [. . .] is to help 'non-persons' to the awareness that God is their

---

latter quotes, among others, Ambrosius of Milan, who, in reference to Matthew 25:36, says: "Whence can you know that not you also, when you receive a human, receive Christ? It is possible that Christ is in the foreign sojourner, because Christ is in the poor, as he himself says" (ibid., 176, original in italics). See also Hebrews 13.1: "Do not neglect to show hospitality to strangers, for by doing that some have entertained angels without knowing it."

144. The second part served as the motto for the IECLB's yearly theme in 2006, whose main title was—in line with the WCC's 9th Assembly in Porto Alegre—"God, in your Grace, transform the world."

145. Paes, *Fundações, Associações e Entidades*, 129.

146. Zwetsch was among those whom Sundermeier met in Rio de Janeiro and had helped to formulate the concept of a mission of *convivência* from his eight year experience among the Madihá indigenous people in the state of Acre. —Compassion is reflected in Jon Sobrino's "principle of mercy [*misericórdia*]" (cf. Mueller, "Um balanço da Teologia da Libertação," 42) and Boff's "principle of compassion and care [*compaixão e cuidado*]" (L. Boff, *Princípio de compaixão e cuidado*, which is mainly a collection of texts from different traditions and religions, and was, interestingly, first published in German, under the title "Das Prinzip Mitgefühl").

147. Brakemeier ("Justification by Grace and Liberation Theology," 220) insists on this, which goes against the critique by Segundo and others who suspect Lutheran theology to only insist on "freedom from." Against similar suspicions in this line, it is plain that economic matters were not alien to Luther (cf. Rieth, *'Habsucht' bei Martin Luther*; "Luther on Greed"; Lindberg, "Luther on Poverty"). Latin American theologians tend especially to highlight the common chest provisions in Leisnig and other cities, as common by 1523; cf. LW 45:159–94; Pauly, *Cidadania e pastoral urbana*; Altmann, *Luther and Liberation*, 103–12.

148. LW 31:371, cf. Mueller (*Teologia cristã em poucas palavras*, 84), who translates this into the metaphor of two hands: "We can imagine the Christian with the right hand extended upward, towards Christ, and the left to the side, towards the neighbor," and makes it the point of departure for his grounding of Christian ethics in a Lutheran perspective.

father."[149] Miguez Bonino emphasizes the importance of concrete communities where this is being lived "in the common appropriation of the scripture and the church, the sharing of the sorrows and joys of everyday living, and the commitment to and organization for the solution of the problems and needs of the larger community."[150] Of course, he points at the CEBs, but this seems an adequate description of how any church community could and should work. Following this line of thought, Miguez characterizes in broad, and precisely therefore useful, terms the "historical project," which "could be characterized as a humanized, participatory society in solidarity."[151] Even under changed circumstances, this seems still a valuable description of what Christians should strive and serve for.

Duchrow, in his interpretation of Luther's Two Kingdom's Doctrine, which has become influential in Brazil and Latin America,[152] emphasizes the importance of human cooperation with God. In this context, the worldly regiment, where Christians and Non-Christians cooperate, serves to protect from evil, but also to sustain creation.[153] In "this omnipotent work of God related to creation and sustention, members of both civitates collaborate,"[154] a collaboration grounded in the *imago Dei*. No sign, then, of a *fuga mundi* in Luther, nor of a parallelism of two separate kingdoms with a private-public or private-office distinction, and also not a strict division into Christians and Non-Christians in terms of acting in the world. It has to be said, though, that the complementarity of the human being's relationship with God and the relationship to the world is certainly asymmetric,[155] with a clear bias towards the former, and Luther did not foresee pluralism, namely religious pluralism as we know it today, in 16th century Germany. Still, there is an intimate connection between the human's relationship with God and the relationship with the world in Luther, which is helpful as an incentive namely to Brazilian Protestants and Pentecostals for acting in the world, while not taking it over.

There are concrete consequences from this view on an active love and service in the world. For one, Christians must not withdraw from the world, but act within it. This includes politics, the economy, civil society, arts—whatever area there is in human society. For Pentecostals, this should be an encouragement to engage in politics not only in terms of voting for "brothers," but to engage more freely and co-operatively (both with fellow Christians and with secular movements) with society's well-being. There is no need for them to disguise their being Christians, or Pentecostals for that matter. But they should see their labor as being for the good of all, not only as obedience towards the authorities, but out of love and service for God and the other. For Lutherans, who have numerous theological references and church positionings to refer to, the challenge might be to listen anew to their specific confessional identity, not to close up in it, but precisely to be in society as Lutherans, and not separate the public from the private as if the former were the secular and the latter the spiritual realm. The Two Kingdoms Doctrine, understood as a distinction without separation, and as a double citizenship of the Christian, can precisely avoid this kind of separation.[156]

149. Miguez Bonino, "Love and Social Tansformation in Liberation Theology," 122.

150. Ibid., 123.

151. Ibid., 124.

152. Cf. Duchrow, *Os dois reinos*;Westhelle, "O desencontro entre a teologia luterana e a teologia da libertação,"; Altmann, *Lutero e libertação*; *Luther and Liberation*, 69-83; Dalferth, *Die Zweireichelehre*; Baum, "Lutherische Theologie des Widerstandes heute."

153. Duchrow, *Christenheit und Weltverantwortung*, 512–22; cf. Dalferth, *Die Zweireichelehre*, 70ff. Duchrow refers mainly to LW 33:242f. (*The Bondage of the Will*, 1526).

154. Duchrow, *Christenheit und Weltverantwortung*, 515.

155. Duchrow, *Christenheit und Weltverantwortung*, 520.

156. As Dalferth (*Die Zweireichelehre*, 143) affirms: "Luther's positive attitude toward politics, that is, that Christians

Secondly, Christians cannot opt to serve just their own brothers and sisters, and have to respect those who might or might not wish to opt into the church that is providing the service. As they are, also all others are God's creatures and, thus, God's image, endowed with dignity. As Protestants and, especially, Pentecostals and Neo-Pentecostals are quick in claiming religious liberty, they should grant this also to others. Luther's logic in his treatise on freedom is that Christians would not need to claim rights if they were among themselves, or can indeed renounce their rights for themselves. But they cannot leave out on others, for whose well-being they have a duty to struggle.

Third, in giving to others, even beyond national borders, it is important not to reproduce a patronizing assistentialism, but a mutuality in giving and receiving. As a common Brazilian church hymn goes, "don't say we have nothing to offer." To be able to give and not only to receive is a visible sign of dignity and responsibility.[157] This is true both on the intersubjective level, between persons, and on the structural level. Thus, the reduction of foreign dependence for churches and church-related NGOs is a fundamentally important aspect to gain freedom and autonomy and to guarantee viability. And to increase South-South help is another important aspect, practiced by all studied churches in one way or another. Missionaries from Brazil work especially in the Portuguese speaking countries of Africa, Angola, and Moçambique, where the IECLB had, sadly, its first martyr: deaconess Sister Doraci Erdinger was killed in Moçambique in 2004, possibly by a Lutheran pastor. Other examples were the spontaneous offerings for the Tsunami victims, in 2004, and for the victims of the Peruvian earthquake, in 2007, recognizing that the IECLB is, by Latin American standards, in a privileged position, for its structure, its size, and its international contacts.

Virtues are central in Christian morality; this is widely recognized. As I have mentioned earlier (IIE1c), *evangélicos* are taken to be more honest and hard-working than others. This might not be statistically true, much less for Pentecostal politicians, but it is an obstinate prejudice held both inside and outside the fold, and indeed covers virtues in line with the ten commandments, Jesus' words and deeds, and Paul's exhortations, to just cite the most influential. The "law" as in vigor in the AD is applied to all, and contains such virtues with more rigor than the other two churches. Such virtues concern, primarily, the individual believer, even if they have social consequences. Virtues as claimed by Leonardo Boff[158] to be necessary for "another possible world" (the World Social Forum's motto) are relational qualities that only arise between human beings: hospitality, *convivência* (with respect and tolerance), and commensality (to eat and drink together and live in peace). Clovis Pinto de Castro, one of the few to venture into a theology of citizenship (cf. above, ID2) rightly points to the interconnectedness of confession, trust, and action in a "citizen faith,"[159] or else: knowing God, loving God, and serving God belong together, as mentioned above (IIIA2b). There are without doubt ample grounds for Christian theology to insist on the importance of service and to call Christians to serve others. But this has to be brought to bearing concretely, in theological grounding, ecclesial positioning, and concrete action, both by churches as institutions and the believers, wherever they may act. Again, education is central, because solidarity—and even more service, which expects nothing in return—is something to be learned and trained.[160]

are called upon by God to exercise love precisely in the secular regiment, is a motivation for the Lutheran churches in Latin America to stand up for the neighbor within society." See also above, Part IID3 of the present work.

157. These two aspects were, in an ecumenical perspective which includes—critically, but with interest and openness—the CEBs and, especially, Boff's theology of ecclesiogenesis, treated under the aspect of the "universal priesthood" of believers by Hans-Martin Barth's (*Einander Priester sein*) "Being priests to each other."

158. L. Boff, *Virtudes para um outro mundo possível*.

159. Castro, *Por uma fé cidadã*.

160. Cf. Assmann and Sung, *Competência e sensibilidade solidária*.

5. A CHRISTIAN CITIZEN: SERVING ONE GOD UNDER TWO REGIMENTS

How long will you judge unjustly and show partiality to the wicked?
Give justice to the weak and the orphan;
maintain the right of the lowly and the destitute.
Rescue the weak and the needy;
deliver them from the hand of the wicked.

Psalm 82:2–4[161]

The doctrine of the two kingdoms or regiments has been having a skeptical reception in Brazil and Latin America, or none at all. As Prien states,[162] very little had been said about it until the mid-1970s (except Schuurmann),[163] and even afterwards there are only relatively few texts on the matter, both in Argentina[164] and in Brazil.[165] The reason might be that Brazilian Lutheran theology, in its progressive strand, has been strongly influenced by Bonhoeffer and Barth, both of which are critical towards such a doctrine.[166] The sovereignty of God, as highlighted by Barth and in the Barmen declaration, seemed to be a stronger argument for political action than the Two Kingdoms Doctrine (*Zweireichelehre*), which had been so discredited through their use in conservative Lutheran theology up to World War II.[167] Conservative Brazilian Lutheran theology in that time does not appear to have made ample use of the doctrine.[168] Prien observes that many church members defended—probably unconsciously—"the notion that each of the different spheres of existence was autonomous,"[169] especially the members of the (exclusively male) Protestant Legion (*Legião Evangélica*). As I have shown, however, official church documents do use it, indirectly, in

161. This Psalm was interpreted politically by Luther in 1530 (LW 13), as a critique of secular power; God is judging the authorities: "God has taken place in the divine council; in the midst of the gods he holds judgment" (Psalm 82.1). The above cited verses should be written "in his [i.e., every ruler's] room, over his bed, at his desk, and also on his clothes" (LW 13:51); Altmann, *Luther and Liberation*, 78f.

162. Prien, "Identity and Problems of Development."

163. Schuurmann, "A doutrina dos dois reinos."

164. Stumme, "Algumas teses sobre os dois reinos."

165. Westhelle, "O desencontro entre a teologia luterana e a teologia da libertaçãos"; Altmann, *Lutero e libertação*, 159-182; *Luther and Liberation*, 69-83.

166. The drawing of a line of ancestors from Luther via Frederic the Great and Bismarck to Hitler in this regard is attributed to Karl Barth, see Lienemann, "Zwei-Reiche-Lehre," 1417; Stümke, *Das Friedensverständnis Martin Luthers*, 196.

167. If used generically, I will speak of the Two Kingdoms Doctrine, which was probably first mentioned in Karl Barth ("Grundfragen der christlichen Sozialethik," 156; cf. Stümke, *Das Friedensverständnis Martin Luthers*,196) and first systematically analyzed by Harald Diem ("Luthers Lehre von den zwei Reichen"). It has since become a common expression; otherwise it will be specified whether I mean the two kingdoms or *civitates* (from Augustine), the two swords (from the middle ages), or the two regiments (in Luther).

168. There was a certain antagonism between Hermann Dohms, the articulator of the union of the synods (realized in 1949) and founder of the Theological School in São Leopoldo, in 1946, and Ernesto Th. Schlieper, the future church president, Barthian and member of the small Confessing Church in Brasil. While the latter promoted Barth's theology and the Barmen declaration, Dohms, albeit having studied Barth's writings and acknowledged his theological significance for the Rio Grande Synod, rejected it "because he had the impression that Barth rejected the Lutheran two kingdoms doctrine and was conducting a 'Calvinist policy,'" Prien, "Identity and Problems of Development ," 215, with reference to Dreher, *Kirche und Deutschtum*. Schlieper, on his part, had strongly rejected all talk of "orders of creation" (*Schöpfungsordnungen*), as they referred to "a creator other than the Father of Jesus Christ" (ibid.).

169. Prien, "Identity and Problems of Development ," 219.

that they insist on distinguishing, while not separating between secular and ecclesial powers and their specific tasks (above, IID2).[170]

Of course, nearly five centuries separate the period analyzed in the present study and Luther's time, with differences on the political, ecclesial, economic, cultural, social, philosophical, and theological levels.[171] Wolfgang Lienemann declared that "the Two Kingdoms Doctrine does not serve as a basis for a timeless doctrine on the relationship between church and State already because it always presupposed, in the models of the 16th century, a corporative order and patriarchal forms of dominion [*Herrschaftsverhältnisse*],"[172] pointing to new ways of ordering society in a constitutional State's democracy. A different reservation was made by John Stumme, then a professor at the Protestant Superior Institute of Theological Studies (*Instituto Superior Evangélico de Estudos Teológicos*—ISEDET) in Buenos Aires:

> Luther's concept of secular authority cannot serve as a basis for a concept of State in the 20th century. Luther's answer to the question: 'Who should govern?'—'The one who is governing'—has been inadequate, at least for the last 200 years. The rejection of any revolution, the absence of democratic tendencies, the lack of an idea of illegitimate government, the acceptance of medieval structures, the end of the subject's duty in obedience, the excessive fear of chaos, the predominantly negative understanding of the function of secular authority, the lack of a social analysis, the concept of politics limited to the state, and so on, show that the concrete concept of Luther has only a negative proposition for our days.[173]

These lines were written still under a military regime in an Argentina where, differently from Brazil (*cum grano salis*), both Protestant *and* Catholic churches tended to stay away from politics or more or less directly supported the *status quo*. However, they seem to be useful also under democratic circumstances, even more so with respect to a democracy that is still looking for its shape, citizenship, and the specific role of the churches. Stumme does not stop at his reservations with Luther's concept, but goes on to name eleven positive, useful aspects, among which I highlight that the State has its function from God as a means of fighting evil; that the State is free in relation to the church, but itself limited in matters of faith; that the Christian can and must serve others in political institutions; that leaders be guided by moral considerations; that there is an ambiguity in concrete decisions and there are difficulties in establishing justice; that order is better than chaos; that the use of Gospel language in politics must be mistrusted and that political activity is fundamentally secular—while it is still God who gives the good in politics. Without discussing these aspects in detail, they are useful in that they trace the way in terms of a distinction, but not separation between the Two Kingdoms. Such a position is important in that it tries to avoid either

170. This is already true for the 1970 Curitiba Manifesto, but strangely not mentioned by Prien ("Identity and Problems of Development," 219f.) in his study on the Two Kingdoms Doctrine in Brazil.

171. For thorough analyses of Luther's doctrine of the two kingdoms in its tradition history and systematic structure see the still classical study by Duchrow, *Christenheit und Weltverantwortung* (for a comprehensive treatment since biblical roots via Augustine and the Middle Ages to Luther), and more recently Mantey, *Zwei Schwerter* (focusing on Luther against the back drop of the late Middle Ages' doctrine of the two swords, as it had been decisive since 1300 for the relationship between church and State). A summary of Duchrow's research and systematization is to be found in the introduction and conclusion of *Lutheran Churches* (1977), texts which were translated and published into Portuguese ten years later, in the midst of the Constituent Assembly (*Os dois reinos*, in 1987).). With the eye firm on Luther's writings, but rich references to secondary literature, in order to find grounds in his theology for a contemporary ethics of peace, see Stümke, *Das Friedensverständnis Martin Luthers*, especially 196–271.

172. Lienemann, "Zwei-Reiche-Lehre," 1416.

173. Stumme, "Algumas teses sobre os dois reinos," 257. Stumme's theses are the result of a seminar in Systematic Theology held at ISEDET on the Two Kingdoms, in 1978.

confusing them, or giving one the priority over the other, or still condoning the emigration from the world, which would give rise to a theocracy.

It seems that precisely this was Luther's intention: To reformulate the now antagonistic, now complementary relationship between (the Catholic) church and State, in place since the 11th century. Prompted by the State's prohibition, motivated by the church's pressure, of the distribution and possession of "certain books," i.e., his books, Luther wrote on the reach and limits of secular ("temporal" in LW's translation) authority.[174] While he affirms that both the secular and the ecclesial regiment are used by God and stand under God's authority, they have separate tasks, and only the secular regiment may use the sword, in order to defend peace with justice for all.[175] In Altmann's words: "the so-called two kingdoms can be distinguished regarding their tasks and their means, but they overlap in time and space. Furthermore, they have a common foundation—God is the Lord of both—and a common goal—human well-being."[176] It is more precise to speak of "two regiments" than of "two kingdoms," although Luther uses both concepts and conceptions. To speak of the two kingdoms seems to lead too straightforwardly to Augustine's antagonism between the *civitas terrena* or *diaboli* and the *civitas Dei*, respectively.[177] This distinction is important for their conceptual and, of course, contextual differences: In Augustine's time, Christendom as the official religion of the Empire, supported and guided by the Emperor, was only beginning to be established, and under constant threat from the pagans. When the Visigoths conquered Rome in 410, Christians were blamed for the defeat, which was particularly dangerous, as Christians themselves had joined very closely together the unity of the Empire and the unity of religion in a "imperial theology."[178] *De civitate Dei* was, then, both an apologetic to the pagans and a critique of Eusebius' too worldly imperial theology, and not—despite medieval understandings in that direction—a relation between State and church, or secular and spiritual regiment. The two *civitates* are two modes of knowledge and will, two modes of leading one's life.[179]

For Luther, the two kingdoms (or *civitates*) are the ultimate horizon for understanding the fight of good and evil in the world, the "eschatological situation of struggle" (*eschatologische Kampfsituation*)[180] to which all are exposed. The two regiments, secular and spiritual, in contrast, are located within this struggle situation, with specific areas of action. However, although both regiments (and also the kingdoms!) are under God's power, such complementarity is asymmetrical, as God's Kingdom—brought about by Godself—will ultimately prevail, and also because the head of the spiritual regiment is not the pope or any church leader, but Christ.

174. *Temporal Authority: To What Extent it Should be Obeyed*, LW 45:75–129.

175. As Stümke, *Das Friedensverständnis Martin Luthers*, 228 emphasizes, only once in *Temporal Authority* does Luther speak of a "spiritual sword" (LW 45:101), to identify it immediately with the Word of God (cf. the metaphorical use of the sword in relation to the Spirit in Ephesians 6:17: "Take the helmet of salvation, and the sword of the Spirit, which is the word of God").

176. Altmann, *Luther and Liberation*, 70.

177. See Schindler's ("Augustin/Augustinismus I," 682) important comment: „auch wenn *civitas diaboli* und *civitas terrena* synonym verwendet werden und im Einzelfall einen bestimmten Staat meinen, ist doch der *Staat (res publica)* als solcher nicht eine Ausgeburt des Teufels." While *civitas dei* is synonymous with the true church, as sum of those beings capable of reason who love God above all (represented by Abel), *civitas diaboli*, as the sum of those characterized by their self-love (represented by Cain), is not as such the State.

178. Lienemann, "'Eschatologik' als Antipolitik?," 414f.; cf. Sinner, *Reden vom Dreieinigen Gott in Brasilien und Indien*, 108f.. Only in the East was it possible, for another thousand years, to live the "symphony" between church and State, otherwise called "cesaropapism," for ultimate power over both lay with the Emperor.

179. Lienemann, "'Eschatologik' als Antipolitik?," 417.

180. Stümke, *Das Friedensverständnis Martin Luthers*, 199.

Thus, Christians are under both regiments, the spiritual and the temporal. Both are instituted by God, and both are under God's judgment. This means that Christians must obey the secular power, along the lines of Paul in Romans 13:1–7 and Jesus in Matthew 22:21, but are entitled to resist it in the line of the *clausula Petri* in Acts 5:29.[181] To the latter, Luther says: "Thereby, he [Peter] sets a limit to the temporal authority, for if we had to do everything that the temporal authority wanted there would have been no point in saying, 'We must obey God rather than men.'"[182] As concrete examples, Luther cites "if your prince or temporal ruler commands you to side with the pope, to believe thus and so, or to get rid of certain books,"[183] which for him are clear examples of the secular power interfering with spiritual power. The well-known counterexample is the peasants' war, where order had to be preserved by all means, even though the peasants' claims should be taken seriously by the authorities.[184] While Luther could think of a quite democratic organization for the church, increasingly deconstructing the Catholic hierarchy based on priesthood as sacrament in favor of offices held by some from among the universal priesthood of all believers, he did not apply this to the secular *Obrigkeit*, nor did he support revolution.[185] Both aspects led to criticism within Liberation Theology who tended to favor Müntzer's heritage as a revolutionary.[186] Luther did, however, as Altmann highlights, use stark words against the princes, and called them to fulfill their duties, namely to guarantee the "free, critical and prophetic preaching of the gospel, to defend law and justice and to guarantee peace, especially in regard to the rights of the poor and their protection."[187]

The space for relating to secular power, then, spans between Romans 13 and Acts 5:29. Matthew 22:21 stresses the aspect of distinction: To Caesar what is Caesar's, to God what is God's. For Luther, of course, such relationship and distinction was located with Christendom, religious pluralism not being a part of his mind. Once confessional separation became inevitable, it would be territorially organized, thus presumably best preserving peace. The Turks, as the danger coming from the East, received very bad evaluations by Luther, and secular power had the task to protect their subjects and, not least, the Christian faith from the Turks' onslaught.

181. Lienemann, "'Eschatologik' als Antipolitik?," 410, calls to attention that Romans 13 did not serve as a reference for justifying serving the army or the occupation of political offices by Christians until the 4th century; in fact they occurred very rarely, and Christians were critized (by Celsos, for instance) precisely for not serving in the army.

182. LW 45:111.

183. Ibid.

184. Naturally, this is one of the most polemical elements about Luther, and made necessary explanations on the part of Brazilian Lutherans. For Dreher ("Luteranismo e participação política," 124), the fact that the secular authority was then put in charge for the Reformation, leading to the "Summepiskopat" of the territorial lord, was "fatal" in two senses: Lutheranism was becoming "provincial," and the territorial lord assumed control of all the elements formative of opinion: "the school, the pulpit and the [teaching] chair." More balanced is the evaluation of Altmann, *Lutero e libertação*, 241–58. He explains Luther's position in the peasant's war by his preoccupation that the "cause of the gospel" was threatened, and, even if his position was "shameful" (even in language: *Wider die räuberischen und mörderischen Rotten der Bauern*), he laid the ground for new, creative positions based on his "intensive solidarity [. . .] with persons in need" (ibid., 256).

185. Cf. Stümke, *Das Friedensverständnis Martin Luthers*, 237f., who argues that Luther held only "passive" resistance to be legitimate, recommending suffering disobedience, penitence, prayer, protest and suggestions by word, and emigration.

186. See Hugo Echegaray, "Lutero e Müntzer," in *Utopia e reino na América Latina* (São Paulo: Loyola, 1989), 78–105, quoted and discussed in Altmann, *Lutero e libertação*, 310f.; Echegaray's reading was strongly influenced by Ernst Bloch's view of Müntzer as a theologian of revolution.

187. Altmann, *Luther and Liberation*, 78f. For instance in his interpretation of the above quoted Psalm 82 (1530), LW 13:41–72; see also *To the Christian Nobility of the German Nation* (1520), LW 44:115–217, the *Magnificat* (1521), LW 21:297–358, and the third part of *Temporal authority*, LW 45:118ff.; cf. also Altmann, *Luther and Liberation*, 85–93.

On the political level, I agree with Stümke that the State has the task of guaranteeing peace with justice, for which its monopoly on coercion is an important element. Christians and churches have great interest in the State exercising this task, which guarantees, not least, the freedom to exercise one's religion.[188] From there, what seems especially important in present-day Brazil is the recognition of religious pluralism, which makes it necessary to go beyond a dualistic thinking between "the" religion and the State. Although the *padroado* and Cardinal Leme's Neo-Christendom are no longer in place,[189] there is still a strong tendency of the Catholic Church to consider itself *the* religion of the Brazilians. Its presence in the media is much stronger than any other religion's, and the CNBB has a fairly direct (although no longer exclusive) access to the government. Neo-Pentecostal churches, namely the powerful IURD, try to compete with the Catholic Church precisely on this level, and would simply substitute it, were they to gain a numerical majority. While this is unlikely to happen, they already have and might in the future consolidate their considerable force in politics, as we have seen.[190] Historic Protestant churches have little numerical weight, although they can gain some visibility, namely locally, through politicians, scientists or other powerful representatives, and through the media if they manage to use them well. The Assemblies of God have awoken in terms of securing political influence, but still have a tendency (like some of the historic Protestants) to rather stay out of politics, either by separating the two realms, granting each of them autonomy (even if relative), or by considering life in the "world" a necessary evil, escaping it wherever they can into church events and Gospel music.

A dialectic relationship between church and State, or rather, avoiding a perspective of Christendom, Religion, and Politics, as Freston[191] rightly claims, is appropriate to avoid falling into either of the two main traps: To try to conquer the State for Christ (in fact, for a specific church) and try to influence it from there, or else to retreat into the spiritual realm and abandon all critical and constructive interaction.[192] The fact that civil society has come in as a media-

188. Stümke, *Das Friedensverständnis Martin Luthers,* 256, n. 623, based on Baum, "Lutherische Theologie des Widerstandes heute," cites Latin American Lutheran liberation theologians who were now struggling to preserve the State against neo-liberalism and globalization for its negative consequences on State activity in education, health and other social areas. He notes that Baum does not mention any reference to Luther's two regiments; in his concentration on the German situation and German literature, he is not aware of Prien, "Identity and Problems of Development" and the LWF studies conducted by Duchrow and others on the Two Kingdoms Doctrine in other contexts; neither is Baum, who concentrates on more recent publications, especially the LWF studies on justification. More recently, Westhelle has taken up the issue again, defending that the "two-kingdoms doctrine is not a doctrine. It is an epistemic principle that teaches the faithful that to know Christ is to know justice. And, conversely, where justice cries out, there we find Christ" ("The Word and the Mask," 178). He even seems to propose a new kind of epistemological rupture (cf. above, ID1) stating that "it [i.e., the justice of Christ] entails the grace of God toward us in the midst of our condition, although it does so not by supplementing or even mending the systems in the world. It does this by disclosing the fissures in the systems of knowledge and power. The new justice, the knowledge of Christ, is indeed foolishness. The power of Christ is indeed weakness" (ibid., 175). And he goes on to say: "Luther's insight brings into question the relation between revelation and the regimes that control knowledge, establish rationalities, norm the market, and rule the church (the visible church is an earthly regime, just like the state or 'economy'). This reading of the two-kingdoms doctrine suggests that knowledge of Christ can emerge only when we understand that it is in the fissures and ruptures in the order of things that a new justice can be shaped" (ibid., 176). He, thus, insists on a qualitative difference of the spiritual and the secular regiment, which correspondingly cannot correspond to church and State, but is rather a different kind of power, subversive to powers in State and church(es): "Luther's spiritual governance is a difference, a counterpoint in the order of things: it is another régime in the sense of being a different régime and not an alternative one." (177)

189. Cf. above, Part IIC1 of the present work.

190. Cf. Part IIB of the present work.

191. Freston, *Religião e Política, sim.*

192. Cf. also Altmann (*Luther and Liberation,* 81f.) who concludes that "the fundamental choice is not between church and state, spiritual or political power, but between justice and injustice, truth and lies, liberty and oppression,

tor between the political system and the lifeworld, to use Habermas' terminology, and uses the public sphere to act, is a major achievement over the church-State antagonism in Luther's times. The churches can, and indeed should, make an important contribution here. The Pentecostals' and other Christian's fixation on constituted power, either executive or legislative, is exaggerated and misleading. Not that a Christian politician, as such, must be bad. Ideally, Christian values will help to exercise an honest and dedicated mandate, free of corruption and full of initiatives to improve citizenship. However. once elected he or she must act as in the secular realm, not as a representative of his church, but as an elected representative of the citizens, to whose totality he is responsible. That is why the distinction between the realms is so important.[193] On the other hand, while the State (the polity as a whole) must be lay, there is no reason why Christians should not exercise their citizenship and bring forward issues and suggestions as any other citizen. This presupposes both the acceptance of the rules of the game and a humility not to impose, nor try to impose, specific religious convictions on those who do not share these beliefs. This is one of the challenges to be taken up in the next chapter.

Thus, the churches can give orientation, but those who live in the "world" are lay people, individual citizens, even if they are not alone, but inserted into a network of relationships where people share certain common convictions. This is what Freston calls the "communitarian model"[194] without, however, developing what this exactly means beyond its difference from an institutional (IURD) or an "auto-impulsed," individual model, where individuals seek to benefit from church support without any commitment. He gives only very rough features of this model, saying that "evangelicals should be involved politically not in the name of their churches or institutions, but in groups of persons which think politically in the same way, inspired by their understanding of the Christian faith."[195] The main idea seems to be that such candidates are accompanied by a group to whom they respond and from where they are supported and criticized.[196] Taking this idea further, one could confirm the role of the churches as places of education for citizenship, where theological and practical orientation can be given and individual conscience forged, and where such support groups can be formed, both confessionally and ecumenically, but where churches as such restrict themselves to orientation rather than orders, and would not serve as electorates for specific candidates. Such well educated and informed Christian citizens would be responsible to exercise their citizenship according to their conscience, which implies that they cannot blame anybody else than themselves for their position and action.

---

life and death. The gospel confronts both the church and the state with this option" (ibid., 82).

193. Here I differ from Altmann's (*Luther and Liberation,* 82) evaluation that "the problem is not to defend the state from the interference of the church nor to protect the church from the control of the state," as the first part is indeed an ongoing and growing problem since more churches, and not just one, are trying to get influence on the State. I agree however, with what follows, which is that "it is rather to participate in the struggle for justice and human rights, democracy and popular participation, whether it is in the order of the state or within the churches themselves."

194. Freston, *Religião e Política, sim,* 12.

195. Ibid.

196. He might think there of a group like the Movement of Progressive Evangelicals (*Movimento Evangélico Progressista*—MEP), founded in 1991, to which Freston himself belongs, which has links to the Latin American Theological Fraternity, an evangelical (in the U.S. sense) movement; cf. Zabatiero, "Um movimento teológico."

B. Public Theology in Brazil: Contribution without Imposition

Gott will aus grosser Barmherzigkeit gegen dem menschlichen geschlecht, im für und für ein Heuflin sammeln, das jn und den Heiland Jhesum Christum recht erkenne und anrufe. Unb wil darumb, das seine lere öffentlich gepredigt werde, wie im Psalm geschrieben ist, jn alle Land is jre Stim ausgegangen.

Philipp Melanchthon[1]

Religion is the prime animating and destructive force in human affairs.

Philip Jenkins[2]

As exposed in the introduction, the public dimension of religion is coming back forcefully into the academic discourse, deplored by some, hailed by others, more soberly evaluated by yet others. There can be no doubt that religion has not left the public sphere, although it has certainly lost the influence it used to have centuries ago, especially in Europe. The separation of church and State, or more precisely religions and the State, is irrevocable and the condition for the possibility of religious freedom and plurality. Furthermore, in those countries, privatization of faith has indeed largely occurred, but the main churches as institutions of public law (as in Germany and Switzerland) still maintain a strong voice in controversial issues like stem-cell research, genetic engineering, and euthanasia, and in some (predominantly Catholic) countries also on abortion and homosexuality. Islam is being felt as a new force, in some cases by now the third largest—although quite heterogeneous—religious group in traditionally Christian countries, arousing fears due to the authoritarian behavior of Islamic states like Iran and terrorist activities like those promoted by Al Qaeda. Secularization has only partly occurred; religious influence in the public sphere has not vanished, it has even increased in some cases. Religious pluralism has been on the rise in virtually all places, both through internal differentiation, like in Brazil, and through migration, as in Europe. Pluralism, respect for other opinions and negotiation are essential elements for a democratic society and its public discourse. Thus, a public theology that is to reflect on the contribution churches can make in public space towards the common good or weal, has both to encourage such contribution among those who tend to see the world as evil and close themselves up in their churches as the community of those who await Christ's second coming, and restrict it among those

1. In "Examen Ordinandorum," CR 23, LXXV, quoted by Huber, *Kirche und Öffentlichkeit*, 54. Melanchthon also spoke of a "publica Ecclesia" (CR 13,1210, Comentarii in Psalmos), see ibid., 53.

2. Quoted in *In God's Name*, 2. This special report of *The Economist* was wholly dedicated to "religion and public life," significantly with Adam wondering whether he should eat the apple from the forbidden tree as its cover illustration.

who want to impose their belief, values, corporate interests, and power on the whole of society. Both phenomena are present in Brazil, as we have seen in parts I and II. Theological resources for a meaningful content of a public theology in Brazil focused on citizenship have been explored in the previous chapter (IIIA), and some possible consequences will be drawn in this chapter and in the conclusion. What, then, is to be understood by public theology, and what could it mean for Brazil, where the concept is virtually unknown?[3] In what follows, I shall first explore public theology in an ecumenical perspective (1.), tracing its origins in the United States and its present diffusion among other English speaking countries, namely South Africa, as well as refer to possible theological references for it. Second (2.), I analyze the factual public presence of religion in Brazil and possible contours of a conscious public theology, focusing on the rising importance of academic theology, not only for inter-disciplinary interaction with other sciences, but for the necessary clarification of the self-understanding of the churches, which has to include self-critique. Finally (3.), I shall comment on the common weal as an indispensable category for the public discourse and action for the churches, overcoming (merely) corporate interests, isolations and competition.

1. PUBLIC THEOLOGY IN AN ECUMENICAL PERSPECTIVE

In this section, I shall present the contours of public theology as currently developed in the United States (a), where the term comes from, and then in the recently founded Global Network of Public Theology (b), further focusing on theological references (c) and the different publics of a public theology (d). The literature is growing and cannot all be taken into account here. I have included those works most cited by theologians linked together in the Global Network, and given special attention to South Africa due to its contextual similarities with Brazil. While in Brazil reflection on the concept is only beginning, South Africa has been working on it for a some years now and found it helpful in redefining the theological task after the end of Apartheid.

a) Public Theology in the United States of America

The term "public theology" was used for the first time in an article published by Martin E. Marty on Reinhold Niebuhr (1892–1971) as "the century's foremost interpreter of American religious social behavior."[4] Marty further referred to Presbyterian Jonathan Edwards (1703–1758), Congregational Horace Bushnell (1802–1876) and Baptist Walter Rauschenbusch (1809–1865), the father of the "social gospel," as representatives of "what might be called public theology from the churches' side,"[5] and to U.S. politicians Benjamin Franklin (1706–1790), Abraham Lincoln (1809–1865), and Woodrow Wilson (1856–1924), who "used specifically deistic or theological materials in order to make sense of the American experience," being "statesmen-philosophers who served as public

3. Cf. above, Part ID3 of the present work.

4. Marty, "Reinhold Niebuhr," 334. On the history and different definitions of public theology see Breitenberg, "To Tell the Truth"; further Smit, "Notions of the Public and Doing Theology." Among Niebuhr's works, Marty mentions *Does Civilization Need Religion?* [1927]; *Moral Man and Immoral Society* [1932]; *Reflections on the End of an* Era [1934]; his Edinburgh Gifford Lectures, *The Nature and Destiny of Man: A Christian Interpretation,* 2 vols. [1942-43]; *The Children of Light and the Children of Darkness* [1945]; *The Irony of American History* [1952]; *Man's Nature and His Communities: Essays on the Dynamics and Enigmas of Man's Personal and Social Existence* [1965]; *Faith and Politics: A Commentary of Religious, Social and Political Thought in a Technological Age* [1968]. It is worth noting that, like a good number of Public Theologians after him, (e.g., Duncan Forrester, William F. Storrar, Elaine Graham), he came from Practical Theology and not from Systematic Theology to Ethics.

5. Marty, "Reinhold Niebuhr," 333.

theologians."[6] Niebuhr, according to Marty, brought these strands together as he "moved progressively away from seeing the churches as the repository of religious conviction and practice in America," more and more "seeing the *nation itself* in this role."[7] Consequently, Niebuhr designated Abraham Lincoln and not a church leader as "America's greatest theologian."[8] "He took the behavior of his people, and, reflecting on it in the light of the biblical, historical, and philosophical positions, offered the ensuing generation a *paradigm for a public theology*, a model which his successors have only begun to develop and realize."[9] However, while Niebuhr was looking for the bearing of the Gospel on the nation, and thus "responsive to what some have come to call a civil religion,"[10] he at the same time was well aware of the dangers of idolatry of a national God. In a more programmatic book, published in 1981, Marty advocated a "public church," composed of the three Christian "constituencies" of mainline Protestantism, evangelicalism, and Roman Catholicism in an "ecumenical model [. . .] in symbiotic relations,"[11] which was to form a "communion of communions," in analogy to Johannes Althusius' political concept of a "community of communities." This should overcome the common tendencies of religions to organize in a "totalist," "tribalist," or "privatist" way, with openness to other forms of Christianity and also other religions. In such a public church, "people would learn to combine religious commitment with civility, spiritual passion with a public sense.[12] The first sentence of his book defines the public church as "a family of apostolic churches with Jesus Christ at the center, churches which are especially sensitive to the *res publica*, the public order that surrounds and includes people of faith."[13]

As Breitenberg showed, Marty's definition of public theology and Robert N. Bellah's earlier description of civil religion coincide to a considerable degree.[14] Despite stating a distinction, Marty's affirmation indeed comes near to Bellah's: "*Public theology* is in my view an effort to interpret the life of a people in the light of a transcendent reference. The people in this case are not simply the church but the pluralism of peoples with whom the language of the church is engaged in a larger

6. Ibid., 333f.

7. Ibid., 354, emphasis mine.

8. As quoted by June Bingham, *Courage to Change: An Introduction to the Life and Thought of Reinhold Niebuhr* (New York: Charles Scribner's Sons, 1961), 310, quoted in Marty, "Reinhold Niebuhr," 355n60. Marty further notes a "general agreement" with Niebuhr's colleague Paul Tillich's contention that religion is the soul of culture and culture the form of religion, even though Niebuhr "saw America as a problematic concretization of a spiritual reality" (ibid.).

9. Ibid., 350, emphasis mine.

10. Ibid.

11. Marty, *The Public Church*, 14.

12. Ibid., 8.

13. Ibid., 3.

14. Bellah ("Civil Religion: The American Case," 14) confirms this, when he says that "from the point of view of the national community, still largely religious in its self-consciousness, such elaboration [sc. of religious symbolism] was public even though lacking in any legal status. Here we can speak of public theology, as Martin Marty has called it, in distinction to civil religion. The civil millennialism of the revolutionary period was such a public theology and we have never lacked one since." Bellah quotes Nathan Hatch (*The Sacred Cause of Liberty*, 1977, esp. chapter 1) who claimed that from the Great Awakening arose a "civil millennialism," which included, namely, "the providential religious meaning of the American colonies in world history" (ibid., 13). He further states that also "enlightenment religion and ethics" can be seen "as a form of public theology" (ibid., 14). And he affirms that "most of what is good and most of what is bad in our history is rooted in our public theology. Every movement to make America more fully realize its professed values has grown out of some form of public theology, from the abolitionists to the social gospel and the early socialist party to the civil rights movement under Martin Luther King and the farm workers' movement under Caesar Chavez. But so has every expansionist war and every form of oppression of racial minorities and immigrant groups" (ibid., 15).

way. The *public church,* then, is a specifically Christian polity and witness."[15] Just before this quote, Marty stated that the public church was a "partial Christian embodiment within *public religion,*" a term taken from Benjamin Franklin.[16] He affirmed that this term fitted "the American pluralist pattern better than does Rousseau's 'civil religion,' because it took into account the particularities of faith that would not disappear or lightly merge to please other founders of the nation" and goes on to say that "these churches could, however, contribute out of their separate resources to public virtue and the common weal."[17] The nuance, then, seems to be that public religion and public theology are more specific (not detached from real religions) and pluralist (not unified) than civil religion.

For his part, quoting Rousseau, Bellah affirmed that "there actually exists alongside of and rather clearly differentiated from the churches an elaborate and well-institutionalized civil religion in America."[18] He identified in presidential speeches, mainly Kennedy's inaugural address of January 20, 1961, an unspecific, God-centered religion that served to guarantee national identity and cohesion as well as giving legitimacy to the office of the president—who could even be a Roman Catholic as in Kennedy's case, but hardly an agnostic. American civil religion derives, according to Bellah, from Christianity, but is independent of it and has its own rituals like Memorial Day, Thanksgiving Day and the pledge of allegiance under the flag: "One Nation under God."[19] It constantly invokes its foundations, given by God and stemming from the founding fathers. As governments recognize a superior, transcendent power, they can by the same referral be questioned, even be deposed or opposed by acts of civil disobedience. For Bellah, civil religion has, thus, a critical element to it and is not legitimatory of any government or any of its actions, as evident at the time

15. Marty, *The Public Church,* 16.

16. Bellah, "Civil Religion: The American Case," 23, note 2, remembers that Benjamin Franklin spoke in this sense of "Publick Religion" in a pamphlet called *Proposals Relating to the Education of Youth in Pensilvania* (1750).

17. Ibid.

18. Bellah, "Civil Religion in America," 168. Rousseau (*Vom Gesellschaftsvertrag oder Prinzipien des Staatsrechtes*), in Book IV, Chapter 8 of his *Contrat Social* first advocated a *religion civile* with the following features (in the absence of an available English version I quote the German translation): "Die Glaubenssätze der bürgerlichen Religion [religion civile] müssen einfach sein, gering an Zahl, klar im Ausdruck, ohne Erklärungen und Auslegungen. Diese positiven Sätze sind: Die Existenz einer mächtigen, vernünftigen, wohltätigen, vorausschauenden und vorsorglichen Gottheit; das künftige Leben; die Belohung der Gerechten; die Bestrafung der Bösen; die Heiligkeit des Gesellschaftsvertrages und der Gesetze. Es gibt nur einen negativen Satz: Unduldsamkeit." (Ibid., 207). As Stackhouse ("Civil Religion, Political Theology and Public Theology," 280) notes, Rousseau refers to Cicero (*De Legibus*), who "treats the kinds of religious beliefs and practices that should be accepted or forbidden by political authority to insure the sacred solidarity of the citizenry, so that loyalty to Rome should not be undercut by the worship of any non-native or trans-national deities." Varro's political theology *(teologia civilis),* mentioned in the introduction to this study, also comes to mind (as recorded and criticized in Augustinus, 413ff. *Vom Gottestaat, De Civitate Dei* VI,5ff.), but is not mentioned by Rousseau. For Rousseau, Christianity is unfit to serve as a national, civil religion for two reasons: It is exclusivist in its soteriology (*extra ecclesiam nulla salus*) and thus intolerant, which cannot work in a time when an exclusive national religion is no longer thinkable. Furthermore, it is by definition supra-national and, indeed, otherworldly. The priests, globally united in one body, are dangerous to any government, but their invention is "a political masterpiece" (Rousseau, "Vom Gesellschaftsvertrag oder Prinzipien des Staatsrechtes," 199, note k). What Rousseau saw as negative and anti-national seems, however, to be an asset in a globalized world. As Tipton ("Globalizing Civil Religion," 50) rightly remembers, Durkheim, on the verge of World War I, also saw religion as an important bond of social cohesion. In the 1950s, Jewish sociologist Will Herberg (*Protestant – Catholic – Jew*) noted that "The American system is one of stable coexistence of three equi-legitimate religious communities [i.e., Protestant, Catholic, Jewish] grounded in the common culture-religion of America. [. . .] Americanism [. . .] has its religious creed, evoking the appropriate religious emotions; it may, in fact, be taken as the *civic religion* of the American people," something he criticizes as "incurably idolatrous" because it is merely legitimatory and not critical. (274.279).

19. Cf. Kleger and Müller, *Religion des Bürgers,* with texts on the US (by Bellah), the Netherlands, Italy, Great Britain, Switzerland, and France, as well as by German thinkers Niklas Luhmann and Hermann Lübbe. The latter also served as main reference for Vögele's (*Zivilreligion in der Bundesrepublik Deutschland*) study on civil religion in Germany.

in the "civil rights movement and the opposition to the Vietnam War," in Henry David Thoreau's advocacy of civil disobedience.[20]

In a recent study, Mark G. Toulouse[21] has distinguished four different modes of (U.S.-) American Christianity's relationship to public life. On the one hand, there are the iconic cultural faith (similar to civil religion) and the priestly faith (which confuses the nation with the church). In both cases, public life prevails over faith. On the other hand, there is the public Christian (where the church is for salvation, differentiated from the nation, but Christians are encouraged to engage in public life) and the public church (where the church raises a prophetic voice for others, not only for itself, and respects religious pluralism). Here faith prevails over public life.[22] Although I am critical of any kind of prevalence, and see church(es, and indeed religions) and nation in a dialectical interaction, my intention here is to define public theology "from the inside out," i.e., from within a faith perspective to be offered as a contribution to debate in the public sphere. This goes both for the believer and for the church as an instituted community of believers. In the U.S., such perspective also means to emphasize Bellah's critical, but also Marty's specific and pluralist elements, rooted in the free exercise of religion in what is at the same time a "religiously resonant republic that depends on the participation of public-spirited citizens for its shared self-government" and "a liberal constitutional democracy that pledges to secure the individual rights of self-interested citizens who pursue wealth and wisdom through free markets for economic and intellectual exchange."[23] According to Tipton, then, "public theology [. . .] has always unfolded as an argument and a conversation within communities of faith as well as among them, and in their relations to public dialogue in the polity."[24] This, of course, does not determine what content such a public theology is to have—it can imply a struggle for social justice or against abortion, or even both as seen in the case of the Roman Catholic Church in Brazil (above, IIC). Like civil religion, also public theology is, as such, ambiguous. Nazism had theological support and religious undergirding, and even more clearly so the South African Apartheid system. Similarly to what arises around the concept of civil society,[25] public theology also has to contain a normative element in order not to remain a barely descriptive category and say everything and nothing. I shall come back to this important point.

First, however, it is important to stress that public theology is being *distinguished* not only from civil religion, as indicated above, but also from *political theology*—with its roots in Aristotle and leading up to Hobbes, Machiavelli, and Carl Schmitt, on the right, and Müntzer, Marx, and Ernst Bloch, on the left, but having as its main reference the *new* political theology of Metz and

20. Bellah, "Civil Religion in America," 185.

21. Toulouse, *God in Public*.

22. In this line, Charles Mathewes (*A Theology of Public Life*) has developed a "theology of public life," rather than a "public theology," in order to clearly indicate its root in the Christian faith, based namely on Augustine, and working on the Christian citizen.

23. Tipton, "Globalizing Civil Religion," 52. Cf. Marty ("Two Kinds of Civil Religion") who had distinguished between two kinds of Civil Religion: 1) The nation "under God," in a "priestly" or a "prophetic" mode (here he quotes Jonathan Edwards, Abraham Lincoln, and Reinhold Niebuhr and suggests they might rather "be thought of as critical public theologians as opposed to votaries of civil religion," ibid., 148), and 2) an emphasis on "national self-transcendence" without reference to a transcendent deity, again in a "priestly" or a "prophetic" mode, the latter including advocacy of a "world civil religion" and approaches to Christianity by former Marxists like Roger Garaudy: "faith [sc. whether in God or in the human task] imposes on us the duty of seeing to it that every man becomes a man [. . .] one who has experienced, day by day, the creative surpassing of himself" (quoted in ibid., 155). According to Marty, the future belongs to both (ibid., 156).

24. Ibid.

25. Cf. above, IB.

Moltmann—for its being wider than the political system and more pragmatic than utopian and revolutionary, without necessarily missing out totally on such visions. For Stackhouse,[26] public theology is geared first of all towards "inner political convictions, the communities of faith, and the associations that they generate in an open society," while "the principles and purposes they advocate [. . .] do not stay in the religious community or in private associations."[27] It goes from the inside out. I shall take this feature further within its recent global setting, where Public Theology is being discussed in a number of countries from Brazil to China.

b) Global Explorations of Public Theology

It is nearly a tautology to say that all theology, and certainly Christian theology, is public. But what precisely can be said about this dimension? Such definition, of course, is subject to contextual variations both in time and space. I seek to link up here to a new global wave, the "explosion of interest"[28] in public theology, as now articulated within the *Global Network for Public Theology*, founded in May 2007 in Princeton (New Jersey, U.S.A.), and its organ, the *International Journal of Public Theology*, launched the same year.

The first issues of the journal have dealt explicitly with the overall project and implications of the concept. Various authors, namely from the Southern hemisphere with its postcolonial suspicion of all universalist claims, affirm that here is "no uniform, monolithic public theology,"[29] "no single and authoritative meaning of public theology and no single normative way of doing public theology,"[30] "no universal 'public theology,' but only theologies that seek to engage the political realm within particular localities," although there is an emerging "ecumenical public theology" to be tested in specific contexts.[31] However, "the very notion of a public theology has the capacity to 'bring together and address a number of disparate and related issues.' It has indeed an 'integrative power,'" affirms the Australian Clive Pearson,[32] quoting Linell Cady. He goes on to say that it is "more of an ethos, a commitment to the public sphere rather than a particular platform or agenda."[33] I would call it an *aggregating concept,* that is, a way of expressing a dimension intrinsic to the church while incorporating a diversity of aspects and foci. It is, in this sense, similar to Liberation Theology that has successively aggregated all kinds of themes, subjects, and theological references.[34] For this reason, the plural has come to be used: liberation theologies of women (in different contexts: e.g., feminist, womanist, *mujerista*), black people (as in the U.S., in South Africa, in Brazil), indigenous peoples (as in Brazil, Paraguay, the Andine region, Mexico), gay/lesbian persons, and so on. Public theology, however, is more generalizing than liberation theologies, and for this very reason is more of a dimension than a specific line of thought. In fact, liberation theologies are public theologies, and indeed are an important point of reference in the Global Network of

26. Stackhouse, "Civil Religion, Political Theology and Public Theology," 291.

27. Pfleiderer, "Politisch-religiöse Semantik," 55ff. freely combines the two and advocates a "öffentliche Politische Theologie in etablierten demokratischen Gesellschaften," combining public and political in a "public political theology."

28. Pearson, "The Quest for a Glocal Public Theology," 55.

29. Ibid., 159.

30. Smit, "Notions of the Public and Doing Theology," 443.

31. Gruchy, "From Political to Public Theologies," 45.

32. Pearson, "The Quest for a Glocal Public Theology," 156; Cady, "H. Richard Niebuhr and the Task of a Public Theology," 108.

33. Ibid., 157.

34. Cf. above, ID1.

Public Theology.[35] In any case, while public theology is more "neutral," i.e., does not have to explain immediately what it seeks to liberate from and what to liberate for, it is also more vague and open to all kinds of approaches. For this very reason, it makes sense to continuously use the singular. Due to its vagueness, in the context of the present study, I insist on the focus on citizenship. Without such a focus, public theology runs the danger of remaining a rather amorphous dimension, too wide, too generic. But it would be too narrow if simply replaced by a theology of citizenship, and too one-sided to subsume it under liberation theologies. The advantage of public theology is that it is more open to a critical *and* constructive approach, seeking to put into place, in a democratic society, citizenship for all.

Due to its contextual closeness to Brazil—a recent transition, an important and recognized participation of churches on both sides, but eventually prevailing on resisting Apartheid, and the need to reformulate a liberative theology after transition—a look to post-Apartheid South Africa is especially interesting for this study.[36] More than in Brazil to date, public theology has come to serve as a kind of aggregating, overarching term for the redefinition of theology in a not only prophetic and oppositional, but increasingly also in a constructive and participatory way. Thus, Nico Koopman insists that "Public theology [sc. as different "from liberation, political, black, feminist, African and other particularistic theologies"] has more of a dialogical, cooperative and constructive approach,"[37] without, however, being naively too positive about democracy and, indeed, neo-liberal capitalist market economy.[38] According to John De Gruchy: "By its very nature, Christian witness is public not private, but public theology is not simply about the church making public statements or engaging in social action; it is rather a mode of doing theology that is intended to address matters of public importance."[39] Thus, if I read him correctly, he inserts public theology in a contextual methodology as formulated by liberation theologies, where public issues go to the heart of the faith rather than staying at the surface.[40] Both in this liberation heritage, and in the need for reformulating theology under new circumstances, where not only resistance but also constructive collaboration are needed, South Africa and Brazil have much in common. They are among the champions of social inequality[41] and maintain a hegemonic position within their respective continents.[42] Other

35. See on this Martinez, *Confronting the Mystery of God*, who draws a line from Karl Rahner to political (Metz), liberation (Gutiérrez) and public (Tracy) theologies, all of which seek to be consciously and explicitly contextual (in this regard they go beyond Rahner) and dialogue with modernity, deepening at the same time their spirituality, encountering "the mystery of God in history."

36. Cf. the doctoral dissertation on public theology in South Africa by Kusmierz (*Theology in Transition*, forthcoming). Exchange with her on the topic has been very helpful, enabling me to test my perception of South Africa.

37. Nico Koopman, "Some Comments on Public Theology Today," 7.

38. Cf. Kusmierz and Cochrane, "Öffentliche Kirche und öffentliche Theologie," 220.

39. Gruchy, "Public Theology as Christian Witness," 40.

40. Gruchy, "Public Theology as Christian Witness," 39f. formulates in seven theses what a "good public theological praxis" is to be: (1) it "does not seek to preference Christianity but to witness to values that Christians believe are important for the common good"; (2) it "requires the development of a language that is accessible to people outside the Christian tradition, and is convincing in its own right; but it also needs to address Christian congregations in a language whereby public debates are related to the traditions of faith"; (3) it "requires an informed knowledge of public policy and issues"; (4) it "requires doing theology in a way that is interdisciplinary in character and uses a methodology in which content and process are intertwined"; (5) it "gives priority to the perspectives of victims and survivors, and to the restoration of justice," highlighting its prophetic task; (6) it "requires congregations that are consciously nurtured and informed by biblical and theological reflection and a rich life of worship in relation to the context"; and (7) it "requires a spirituality which enables a lived experience of God, with people and with creation."

41. Cf. above, IA3a.

42. For this reason, a common research project under the auspices of the Global Network of Public Theology be-

key terms used in post-apartheid South African theology are "a theology of reconstruction"[43] and, more recently, a "theology of transformation."[44] The former stresses the constructive contribution of theology and, not least, its contribution to lawmaking as key for reconstruction. In this line, he takes up the early ecumenical thought of the Oxford Conference on Life and Work (1937), when Joseph H. Oldham called for "'middle axioms' to facilitate social construction."[45] For Villa-Vicencio,

> the unique task of the church is to keep alive the revolutionary spirit that has fired the oppressed people in South Africa to rise in rebellion against apartheid, as a tentative approximation of what is involved in translating the eschatological vision into political action in a given place at a given time. It is at the same time to temper, shape, redirect, and challenge that spirit in the long march to the emergence of a new nation.[46]

Thus, Villa-Vicencio sees such a theology of reconstruction, i.e., democratic nation-building after Apartheid, in continuity with liberation theology as taught and practiced in South Africa with its insistence on resistance against oppression. However, after the exodus, a "post-exilic theology" is needed. The new times offer the opportunity and claim a more constructive type of theology, with concrete contributions towards the nation, "learning to say theological 'yes,'"[47] a "thoughtful and creative 'Yes' to options for political and social renewal"[48] and, not least, helping oneself and others to repent and reconcile. The famous Truth and Reconciliation Commission, led by Archbishop emeritus Desmond Mpilo Tutu, is certainly a clear example for the trust deposited in the churches and the need for their mediating role, as well as their religious and symbolic resources for repentance and forgiveness—although truth has not always been followed by these two.[49] Another important aspect is that Villa-Vicencio seeks to overcome the "more or less comfortable divide between First and Third World theologies that has in recent years simply come to be accepted by theologians on both sides of the divide," all needing "to learn from the other."[50]

The latter, a "theology of transformation," stems from a critique of Villa-Vicencio's proposal as elaborated by H. Russel Botman. He first refers to Dirkie Smit's works and appropriation of H. Richard Niebuhr towards the transformation of culture, as well as to David Bosch's hermeneutic of transformation. He further draws on John de Gruchy, who saw the role of the church as "acting as a midwife to the birth of our democracy,"[51] and to N. Barney Pityana, who stresses lawmaking and an ethic of responsibility within "the development of a human rights culture."[52] All these are

tween the Beyers Naudé Center of Public Theology at Stellenbosch University and the Lutheran School of Theology's (EST) Institute for Ethics and Contemporary Issues (in formation) is in course. Similarities are striking, and there is considerable potential in this pioneering South-South collaboration, which can benefit from the political networking between Brazil, South Africa and India.

43. Villa-Vicencio, *A Theology of Reconstruction*, "From Revolution to Reconstruction."

44. Botman, "Theology After Apartheid."

45. Villa-Vicencio, *A Theology of Reconstruction*, 9, quoting W.A. Visser't Hooft and J.H. Oldham, *The Church and its Function in Society* (Chicago: Willet, Clarke and Co, 1937), 210. He further refers to Karl Barth and Dietrich Bonhoeffer, as well as nation-building in India through the thoughts on Christian participation developed by M.M. Thomas and P.D. Devanandan.

46. Villa-Vicencio, "From Revolution to Reconstruction," 266.

47. Ibid., 255.

48. Villa-Vicencio, *A Theology of Reconstruction*, 1.

49. Cf. Kusmierz, *Vom Umgang mit Schuld*.

50. Villa-Vicencio, *A Theology of Reconstruction*, 15.

51. In Botman, "Theology After Apartheid," 41.

52. Ibid., 41.

called "public theologies" by Botman. He then presents Villa-Vicencio's proposal and criticizes it for, in Bonhoeffer's terms, remaining in the penultimate rather than seeking to be oriented "to the ultimate obedience to God."[53] Echoing a criticism also made by Tinyiko Sam Maluleke, Botman stresses that new structures "do not form new humanities," which, however, is the "essential promise of Christianity." At the same time, transformation also "suggests a paradigm of growth and formation rather than of engineering and mechanization."[54] Botman, like other South African theologians, lays emphasis on Christology, with an emphasis on Jesus' practices and discipleship, as well as the "form of Jesus Christ which is present in the church as the embodiment of the narratives and practices which go by the name Christian."[55]

Following James Cochrane and Klaus Nürnberger at Pietermaritzburg, John De Gruchy's son Steve speaks of "social theology" rather than public theology because "its primary locus is the church rather than the public square." In a less secularized environment than in the West, Steve De Gruchy is reported to defend, there needs to be a "much greater reliance on biblical, theological and church language." For John De Gruchy, there is no contradiction, because "Public Theology is [. . .] engaged in all three publics—academy, church and society—while the strength of social theology is to be found in the fact that it does precisely this."[56] This latter point can also be seen as a difference in theology in Brazil today, as visible in SOTER and other congresses,[57] as well as my own work at a well developed and long-standing Faculty of Theology. Here, dialogue with the social sciences seems to be stronger, but these tend to be agnostic or even outrightly anti-religious, which brings with it a certain "reduction" of religious language.[58] In South Africa, if I see well, a more direct religious language is possible and a doctrinal basis sought for, possibly because many of the articulators of a public theology in that country come from the intra-church struggle on the theological justification or rejection of apartheid. There does not appear to be such a strong rejection of religious and theological language in the universities as in Brazil.

Another, albeit not unrelated direction in public theology is represented by U.S. ethicist Max Stackhouse, the *Nestor* of the Global Network, who has taken special interest in a public theology for a globalized civil society. Together with renowned colleagues, mainly from the U.S., he developed a three year project (1999–2001) sponsored by the Center of Theological Inquiry at Princeton on *God and Globalization: Theological Ethics and the Spheres of Life.* Its findings are published in three volumes, the fourth volume being a summary and theological foundation of such a global public theology by Stackhouse himself, under the title of *Globalization and Grace.*[59] "In brief, God is in globalization; and that is why theology must be public and interested in global issues."[60] Stackhouse insists that public theology is to be an apologetic theology which "must show that it can form, inform, and sustain the moral and spiritual architecture of a civil society so that truth, justice and mercy are more nearly approximated in the souls of persons and in the institutions of the common life."[61] Theology is "to provide a reasonable proposal with regard to the moral and spiritual

53. Ibid., 47.

54. Ibid.

55. Ibid., 49.

56. All quotes from Gruchy, "Public Theology as Christian Witness," 37.

57. Cf. above, ID1b.

58. Cf. below, IIIB2b.

59. Stackhouse, *Globalization and Grace.*

60. Stackhouse, "Public Theology and political economy," 179.

61. In "Public Theology and political economy," 191, note 2, Stackhouse distinguishes between a "confessional"

architecture and the inner guidance system of civilizations," and "necessary in order to account for how and why humanity can debate such ultimate matters and give reasons as to why one account is more adequate than another.[62] In terms of method, public theology is to be "interpretive-diagnostic," "critical-evaluative" and "prescriptive-practical." In terms of content, Christian theology's distinctive contribution to public life is

> the concept of a gracious God who created the world and made humanity in the very image of the Creator, who providentially gave humanity the spiritual resources to form and sustain a viable civil society in history, and who promised to save humanity from our betrayals of that image and those resources by pointing to possibilities beyond creation and history that we cannot ourselves accomplish.[63]

Protology, providence, and eschatology are then presented as foundations of public theology, and compared to "the offerings of other religions."[64] For Stackhouse, religion lies at the heart of any society, and it has not only a faith to offer for believers to act in society, but for a specific comprehension and indeed the functioning of society as a whole. For a global society, then, global religion is needed. Although Stackhouse is careful not to confound this religion simply with Christianity, but listens carefully to the contribution of other (world) religions, he leaves no doubt that he sees in Christianity the most suitable religion to serve as the center of a globalized (civil) society.[65] While Stackhouse's venture certainly deserves a more thorough analysis than can be offered here, it seems to me to be too bold a proposal for a fruitful discussion of public theology in Brazil. It is one thing to offer a theological interpretation of today's world as one specific, in this case a Christian interpretation of it, but quite another to localize God in the world and suggest the central place of religion in society as best suited for humanity, in history as today. Is Stackhouse not heading here more for public religion, i.e., one religion being present and influential in public, even if stressing the inter-religious dialogue and dimension, rather than public theology, i.e., a humble, specific, contributing reflection? In any case, these reflections have already shown the importance of *theology* for a public theology, which I shall now explore further.

c) Theological References of a Public Theology

Like other terms used here, namely civil society and citizenship, public theology is, then, more of a field and a dimension of theology than a clear-cut concept. This does not mean, however, that it

definition of public theology, which proclaims its own position but holds it incommensurable to others; a "dogmatic" or "social-ethical" definition, which proclaims its dogmas in public forums, combined with "selected reading of the issues before public life"; and a an "apologetic" definition, which "can be shown to be, as reasonable, as ethical, and as viable for authentic, warranted commitment as any other known religion or philosophy and, indeed, indispensable to other modes of public discourse." Here is a bold statement of a theological interpretation of the world offered to public discourse which claims to go beyond its specific, confessional, or dogmatic presuppositions.

62. Ibid., 84, 113.

63. Ibid., 115.

64. Ibid., 116.

65. He underlined this as he presented his thoughts to a Brazilian audience during a week-long graduate seminar in June 2008. It was precisely this confidence that was constantly being questioned. Postcolonial discourse, conscientious of this denominator or not, is suspicious of all universalist claims, and it is difficult not to identify such a claim in Stackhouses's proposal. More specifically, discomfort is created by what seems to reemerge here as heir to the specifically U.S.-American tradition of a nation's vocation in parallel to Israel's chosenness, applied to the whole world. Edir Macedo (and Oliveira, *Plano de poder*), the Brazilian world church leader whose residence is in Chicago, is treading along the same line, as we shall see (IIIB2a), although in a much less sophisticated way and certainly not open to any inter-religious dialogue.

simply stays as a black box, meaning everything and nothing at the same time. I have already shown (IIIA) what contents it could have with its specific focus on citizenship, in my case with special emphasis on resources from the Lutheran tradition. Authors have made links with a number of notions from various specific or common traditions(s). Smit names the Calvinist notion of *common grace*,[66] as developed by Dutch theologian and politician Abraham Kuyper (1837–1920), on whom Stackhouse and others have drawn.[67] Another line takes up the *third article* of the creed and speaks of the "Spirit in Public Theology" or the "public person of the Spirit."[68] Common is also a reference, namely among Reformed theologians, on the *triplex munus Christi* as prophet, priest, and king, as well as other elements of the creed's *second article*.[69] *Obedience* and *discipleship* are also reasons for a public theology, with all the imperfections and ambiguities common to life under sin from which the church is not exempt:

> The church of Jesus Christ is indeed a human church of failure and unfaithfulness, and, therefore, being public church and doing public theology may be called for, not because the church is perfect, but because it is obedient; a living witness to the goodness and loving kindness of the living Lord, who became flesh for us and for our salvation.[70]

From here, we can go on to essays on *trinitarian theology*, among them Nico Koopman, who takes up Sallie McFague's planetary theology, insisting on the "public dimension of Trinitarian faith," holding together God and the world.[71] Lesslie Newbigin spoke of "The Trinity as Public Truth," insisting that "Christian doctrine, with its prime model in the doctrine of the Trinity, ought to be playing an explicit and vigorous part in the public debate that makes up the life of the public square."[72] However, opposing theses of ecumenical thought indicating a shift to a more Trinitarian thinking (Konrad Raiser), he takes the church to task, as "the Trinity cannot be public truth except in the measure that the Church is faithful in its mission to the world."[73]

I myself have ventured into reflections on bearings of trinitarian theology on citizenship, seeking to avoid, however, simple analogies. As features of God as Trinity that are fundamental for human beings not only to coexist, but to interact in communion (*convivência*), I identified otherness, participation, trust, and coherence.[74] A first central aspect is *otherness*. Plurality implies diversity, and community in a democracy is unthinkable without recognizing the uniqueness of each member of society. Therefore, respect to otherness, the acknowledgment of difference and the right to be different is essential. In Latin American theology, this originated among those who were in close contact with indigenous peoples, but has received wider attention in recent times. A sensitive hermeneutics of the other is necessary to preserve each person's uniqueness and her

66. Smit, "Notions of the Public and Doing Theology," 450ff.

67. Cf. Lugo, *Religion, Pluralism, and Public Life*.

68. Bacote, Vincent E., *The Spirit in Public Theology* (Grand Rapids: Baker, 2005); cf. Welker, *Gottes Geist*, 259-313, namely 289: "Der Heilige Geist ist zunächst zu verstehen als die vielgestaltige Einheit der Perspektiven, der Beziehungen auf Jesus Christus und der gesprochenen und gelebten Zeugnisse von ihm. In dieser Hinsicht ist der Geist eine Einheit, an der wir teilhaben, die wir mitkonstituieren können. Er ist der Resonanzbereich Christi. Er ist die öffentliche Person, die dem Individuum Jesus Christus entspricht."

69. Cf. Stackhouse, *Globalization and Grace*, 93.

70. Smit, "Notions of the Public and Doing Theology," 454.

71. Koopman, "Public Theology in South Africa,"205; cf. McFague, *Life abundant*.

72. Newbigin, "The Trinity as Public Truth," 1.

73. Ibid., 8.

74. Sinner, "Trinity, Church and Society in Brazil."

right to difference, including religious difference.[75] It preserves mystery and seeks understanding, as happens in theology trying to unveil and, at the same time, respect the mystery of God as tri-une, unity in difference. A second aspect is *participation*. This concept is central to the discourse on civil society and the struggle for citizenship. In terms of trinitarian theology, the aspect of participation well describes the idea of interpenetration, *perichoresis*. A third aspect is the need for *trust*, as already dealt with extensively above (IIIA2). God seen as Tri-une can give good reasons to invest trust in democracy even where it is "disjunctive"; Godself preserves continuity in the midst of different, highly ambiguous historical situations where he manifests Godself, most centrally in the cross at Golgatha, and empowers persons to live their lives seeking to be just while knowing they are inescapably sinners (see also above, IIIA3). Finally, a fourth necessary element is *coherence*: to have a project for the whole of society and not just for oneself or one's peer group or even for one's church. This shall be dealt with more extensively below (IIIB3). Theologically speaking, insisting on God as Trinity could help to prevent restrictive misunderstandings, as if God were only Holy Spirit and not also Son, made human in Jesus Christ, and Father, as creator. This balance of a unity and diversity in God is prone to foster *koinonia*, the ecumenical key word for community among the different members of the body of Christ.[76] In terms of society as a whole, such integration of unity and diversity could, if well succeeded, be an important contribution of churches to a pluralist society.

This presupposes that Christians and churches do not primarily seek to gain advantages for themselves, but see their mission as a testimony of service (diakonia) to the whole of society. The public dimension of the church is part of its mission, its proclamation of the Gospel through *koinonia, kerygma, martyria, diakonia* and *leitourgia*, whose belonging together can be made evident in missionary texts like Luke 10 (the sending of the 70) and Acts 8 (the baptism of the Eunuch) (see above, IIIA4).[77] The two stories mentioned are, in my reading, among the most intriguing for finding out about the purpose and mission of the church. In the Eunuch's story, Philip draws near (*martyria*) and explains the Scriptures (*kerygma*), resulting in the Eunuch's baptism (*leitourgia*) and his inclusion into the church (*koinonia*). In the sending out of the 70 in Luke, Jesus stresses the risk of mission as he describes the disciples as they are being sent like "lambs into the midst of wolves" (*martyria*), and being forbidden to take anything with them. They are to wish peace to the house they enter, share any food they will be served (*koinonia*), to cure the sick (*diakonia*) and, then only, proclaim that "the kingdom of God has come near" (*kerygma*). Whatever defines the church, defines its mission, and whatever defines mission, defines the church. Thus, a church is missionary not as something additional to its nature, but as intrinsic to it. As says the Faith and Order document on the Nature and Mission of the Church: "The mission of the Church is to serve the purpose of God as a gift given to the world in order that all may believe (cf. Jn 17:21)" and "mission [. . .] belongs to the very being of the Church."[78] And as indicated in the initial quotation from Melanchthon: out of his mercy, God wills that his doctrine (*lere*) be preached publicly, "*wie im Psalm geschrieben ist, jn alle Land is jre Stim ausgegangen*."

75. I have tried to explain this further in Sinner, "Inter-religious Dialogue." German literature tends to describe the "other" as "stranger," not in a derogatory way, but in order to safeguard the always remaining difference which cannot—and must not—be completely overcome, and also to indicate the difficulty in understanding the other; see for instance the contributions in Schultze, Sinner and Stierle, *Vom Geheimnis des Unterschieds*.

76. Cf. Tillard, "Koinonia."

77. See also Sinner, "Ökumene im 21. Jahrhundert."

78 Commission on Faith and Order, *The Nature and Mission of the Church*, paragraphs 34f.

d) Publics of the theologian

A further aspect to be highlighted in terms of the *publics* of theology or, more precisely, the publics the theologian responds to, namely, Society, the Academy, and the Church.[79] He presupposes that "every theologian, by the very acts of speaking and writing, makes a claim to attention," that is,

> a claim to public response bearing meaning and truth on the most serious and difficult questions, both personal and communal, that any human being or society must face: Has existence any ultimate meaning? Is a fundamental trust to be found amidst the fears, anxieties and terror of existence? Is there some reality, some force, even some one, who speaks a word of truth that can be recognized and trusted? Religions ask and respond to such fundamental questions of the meaning and truth of our existence as human beings in solitude, and in society, history and the cosmos.[80]

In describing the different publics, i.e., audiences the theologian responds to, Tracy explicitly refers to Marty's texts on public religion and public theology. He speaks of society, the academy, and the church. *Society* is further subdivided into three realms: the technoeconomic structure, the polity, and culture. For Tracy, "whether or not particular theologians are explicitly involved in the tasks of responsible citizenship in so complex a society, they are clearly affected by specific roles in that society."[81] He discusses the claimed or real absence of religion and theology in these realms and then states his own claim that "if any human being, if any religious thinker or theologian, produces some classical expression of the human spirit on a particular journey in a particular tradition, that person discloses permanent possibilities for human existence both personal and communal. Any classic [. . .] is always public, never private."[82] The *academy* is today disputed as a locus—or not—for theology. Criticism is raised both from other disciplines in the academy and from the churches, claiming that theology is always confessional and belongs strictly to the churches and its institutions, not the secular university.[83] Conversely, Tracy believes that "theology clearly belongs as an academic discipline in the modern university."[84] Quoting Nygren, Ebeling, Pannenberg, Küng, Kaufman, Metz, and others, they have, as university theologians, "been engaged in the construction of proposals for the fully public, here integrally academic, character of theology in the context of the modern university and its internal debate on the

79. Tracy, *The Analogical Imagination*, 3-46.

80. Ibid., 4.

81. Ibid., 7.

82. Ibid., 14.

83. Among the theological critics, more recent than Tracy's book, are Stanley Hauerwas, John Milbank, and Alasdair MacIntyre. A representative of "radical orthodoxy," Milbank is also a fierce critic of Liberation Theology for its extensive and, for him, submissive use of the social sciences: "the claim of political and liberation theology that theology 'requires' secular social science always implies the displacing of the Christian metanarrative, essential for the constitution of faith, by new modern stories, which themselves arose partially as an attempt to situate and confine faith itself" (Milbank, *Theology and Social Theory*, 206–56, at 249). Recently, Gavin D'Costa (*Theology in the Public Square*) has placed an argument along this line, claiming a Christian, namely Roman Catholic University as the proper locus for a public theology. He boldly states: "If the university cannot recognize and facilitate the unique character of this intellectual discipline, indeed the queen of sciences, then the university must be called into question, not the discipline. Hence, my argument for a Christian university [. . .]. In such a university, not only can theology be theology, but also the transformation of all the disciplines can begin" (ibid., 216). For all of the cited, although of different denominations, the rehabilitation of Thomas Aquinas as main theological reference can be clearly noted, and there is a tendency to boldly argue from an internally developed church theology toward the public space. Although this is not precisely an imposition onto the public sphere, as this position is disposed to suffer and endure the world, it does not seem to be open to a really pluralistic (ecumenically Christian, inter-religious or with non-believers) dialogue.

84. Tracy, *The Analogical Imagination*, 16.

character of a scholarly discipline."[85] Like the humanities and social sciences, however, theology has to be presently content with its status as a "diffuse" or "would-be" discipline, as over against a "compact" discipline, using Stephen Toulmin's criteria.[86] In any case, theology is to meet the "highest standards of the contemporary academy. [. . .] Theology aids the public value of both academy and society when it remains faithful to its own internal demand—publicness."[87] As to the *church*, it is "sociologically [. . .] a voluntary association and one public of every theology."[88] Tracy emphasizes that both the church and the "world" are to be understood both as sociological and as theological realities, while commonly the former is understood merely as a theological, the latter merely as a sociological reality. He is aware of the different role theology plays in different church traditions, as well as in different contexts, explicitly referring to "Euro-American 'political' and Latin American 'liberation' theologies."[89] Theologians have, then, to "explicate the basic plausibility structures of all three publics through the formulation of plausibility arguments and criteria of adequacy as a general theological model for informing discussions of apparent or real conflicts on particular issues" and "continue to drive to reinterpret or retrieve the classical resources of church tradition in genuinely new applications for the present day."[90]

Max Stackhouse has stated repeatedly that the *economy* is to be included as a fourth partner, "an area [which] was historically presumed to be a matter of concern to the household [. . .] But economic institutions and practices have [. . .] begun to transcend the control of any familial or royal household and of every nation state, and are now increasingly located in the modern corporation."[91] In today's globalized world, the economy has turned out to be an "increasingly independent public realm pulling millions into the middle classes, and leaving some behind."[92] There seems to be a certain contradiction here, as he also includes the economy within civil society, herein following Hegel and Locke against Habermas—and, I add, with him, the main Brazilian line of thought.[93] It could, thus, be subsumed under "society" as a public.[94] But Stackhouse is certainly right in stating the importance of the economy for a public theology, and in pleading for a competent, critical, *and* constructive dialogue with its leaders—and I add, workers, share- and stakeholders—in order to foster effective change. Liberation theology's one-sided criticism has hindered rather than promoted such a dialogue, while evangelical business fellowships seem to have taken

85. Ibid., 17.

86. The "diffuse" disciplines lack "a clear sense of disciplinary direction" as well as an "adequate professional organization for the discussion of new results," Tracy, *The Analogical Imagination*, 18. He quotes Stephen Toulmin, *Human Understanding*, vol. 1 (Princeton: Princeton University Press, 1972).

87. Tracy (*The Analogical Imagination*, 41n74) notes here his disagreement with Liberation Theology's—at the time common—attacks on "academic theology," cf. Segundo, *Liberation of Theology*, 7–39.

88. Tracy, *The Analogical Imagination*, 41.

89. Ibid., 27; cf. Martinez, *Confronting the Mystery of God*.

90. Tracy, *The Analogical Imagination*, 31.

91. Stackhouse, *Globalization and Grace*, 110; cf. *Public Theology and Political Economy*, "Public Theology and Ethical Judgment," "Public Theology and political economy."

92. Stackhouse, *Globalization and Grace*, 110. Given the economic data quoted in IA, one tends to be less enthusiastic than Stackhouse, and would replace the "some" by "many" or, at least, a "considerable number." He is, however, right that never before have so many people ascended into the middle class.

93. Stackhouse, "Civil Society, Public Theology," cf. above, IB, IIB.

94. It is true that in "Public Theology and Ethical Judgment," 166, Stackhouse speaks of the "political public" as opposed to the "economic public," and not of society and the economy, but links the political public explicitly to civil society.

the field in Brazil. To my knowledge, a deeper engagement by Brazilian theologians not only with the economy as a subject-matter, but with those responsible for it, is still an unattended need.

Furthermore, Stackhouse goes (as does Tracy in his own way) beyond a sociological statement in correlating these four publics with holiness (the "authentic religious public"), justice (the political public), truth (the academic public), and creativity (the economic public).[95]

A public theology has, then, fairly identifiable partners for its dialogue, for its speaking and listening. As the churches are, sociologically and legally speaking, parts of civil society (although with a special status, cf. above, IIB), it is there that their main action should be situated. Both the direct dialogue with the government (as traditionally practiced by the Roman Catholic Church, but increasingly also by others, namely the IURD), and refraining from the public realm (by either retiring to separate places "out of the world" or separating the spiritual and the secular), are modes of escape from a proper public theology that neither denies its own mission nor flees from dialogue with other positions and bodies other than the churches. Let us now see how such a public dimension can be situated in Brazil.

2. THEOLOGY AND RELIGION IN BRAZIL'S PUBLIC SPACE

Não se forma para a cidadania,
sem mobilizar a alma da cidadania

Evaldo Luis Pauly[96]

I have repeatedly stated that public theology has been used very rarely in Brazil and Latin America to this date. There are, however, some sociological and anthropological works on religion in public space,[97] which are empirical analyses of public religion, i.e., the presence of religion in all its forms in the public sphere, and do not engage with or reflect on public theology. Such studies are certainly necessary for public theology not to build ivory towers without any empirical verification. They complement the reading of documents and books on the public role of the church, as they more clearly identify the churches that deliberately—although not necessarily explicitly in their discourse—compete for hegemony in public space and seek to directly influence politics through their representatives in Congress or indirect contacts and lobbying. Such analyses of public religion are also important to discover the appearance of religion in non-ecclesial environments, even if their symbols can be traced to (usually) Christian sources. Some examples of such public religion in Brazil have been cited above (IIB3).[98]

But this is only part of the story. The social sciences, as the Brazilian academy in general, tend to shun theological discourse and do not seek to engage in dialogue with theology. They remain observers and take a certain degree of delight or furor in their observation, but do not seem to find relevant the inner logic of their objects' discourse. Partly, the churches themselves are responsible for this as they have not sufficiently sought to communicate with others in the academy. Many

95. Stackhouse, "Public Theology and Ethical Judgment."

96. "You can't educate for citizenship without mobilizing the soul of citizenship." Pauly ("O novo rosto," 7) goes on to say that "There is no popular democracy without the pedagogical construction of the democratic spirit. Spirituality is, before and above any theological divergence, an attitude of the subject in relation to the world of which he or she is, at the same time, producer and product. Spirituality, in this precise and legal sense, is an attitude of citizenship.'"

97. Cf. Birman, *Religião e espaço público*; Montero, "Religião, pluralismo e esfera pública no Brasil."

98. See also Sinner, "Brazil: From Liberation Theology."

churches, especially the Pentecostals and namely the Neo-Pentecostals, are at pains with academic theology as such, visible to the extreme in Edir Macedo's call for the "liberation of theology,"[99] in the sense of getting rid of it. In what follows, I shall seek to distinguish between public religion as a phenomenon and public theology as conscious reflection (a), and then add a description of and reflection on academic theology in Brazil (b).

a) Public Religion – Public Theology

Initially, a distinction is to be made between public theology and *public religion*.[100] While public religion is a descriptive and analytical term, used for a variety of religions (mainly Christianity and Islam), public theology—as all theology—has a normative element to it and stems from a specific religious tradition, in our case the Christian faith. It is, thus, also related to the concrete praxis of Christian communities that it seeks to analyze and to provide a critical orientation for them. Public theology is not only an academic exercise, as it constantly relates and promotes action and reflection. But it is also an academic exercise, and consciously and deliberately so.

As we have seen in the case studies in part II, some churches appear more obviously as public churches and, thus, as public religion, than others. While the IECLB is generally left out because of its small size and ethnic and regional connotations, the AD have not yet conquered sufficient influence to be dealt with under the heading of public religion. Consequently, it is the Roman Catholic Church that is treated as public religion in Brazil. In Casanova's case, it is the—probably exaggerated—move towards a "people's church" that he sees as a remarkable example of a "deprivatization" of religion in the 1980s.[101] But one could just as well argue that the ICAR has never left the public scene. In Brazil, the ICAR is traditionally hegemonic and with good and direct access to the Government, as well as the IURD. For the first, such contacts are so natural that they dispense theological grounding. A recent agreement with the Vatican, with public effect but far from public opinion building, was signed by President Lula and Pope Benedict XVI on November 13, 2008. On the basis of the "historical relations between the Catholic Church and Brazil" (caput), the church's legal status is reaffirmed as a juridical personality (Art. 3), without, however, stating whether that is of public or civil law, the latter being the case for the other "religious societies."[102] Decree number 119-A of January 7, 1890 is safeguarded (Art. 20),[103] without any specification of what that precisely means. Other regulations are invariably tied to the Brazilian constitution or laws. The most polemical article, once the agreement became known to the public (only on November 12), is Art. 11, on religious education in public (i.e., state run) schools. Although the ingress underlines the "observance of the right to religious liberty, cultural diversity and confessional plurality," paragraph 1 speaks of "religious education, Catholic and of other religious confessions," while the law on education had precisely extinguished the formulation on confessionality to foster an interconfessional

99. Macedo, *A libertação da teologia*.

100. See Casanova, *Public Religions in the Modern World*. Vries and Sullivan, *Political Theologies* speak of "public religions" and "political," not "public" theologies because their interest lies more in the functioning of religion in the public sphere and its factual influence on the State and society, as well as the degree to which those institutions and spaces themselves have incorporated theological values and become a kind of religion. This is, therefore, not a dialogue with theologians (except for a text by Pope Benedict XVI), but a relatively distanced view on the role of religion in public space—even if the co-editor is a professor of world religions (but appears only as editor and in the preface).

101. Casanova, *Public Religions in the Modern World*, 113–14.

102. Cf. above, part IIB. According to the papal nuntio's explanation in Baldisseri, *O acordo entre a Santa Sé*, 11f., this refers to civil law.

103. Cf. above, part IIB.

and multireligious teaching.[104] If the agreement says materially nothing new, it sets ambiguous accents and gives the impression of secret talks unworthy of a religiously plural country with public visibility of a multitude of churches and religions, underlining the idea that the Roman Catholic Church is, at least for the government, a largely uncontested public religion.[105]

The upcoming pretender is the IURD, which is emerging with considerable efficiency. A recent hearing (August 25, 2008) called by the Supreme Federal Court on the possible liberation of abortions in case of anencephalous fetuses, had as religious representatives two from the CNBB, one from the Universal Church (of the Kingdom of God, the IURD), one from the National Pro-Life and Pro-Family Association, one from the Catholics for the Right to Decide and one from the Spiritist Medical Association.[106] The IURD in this point outrightly contradicts the CNBB, saying that "discrimination of this type of abortion must not be stopped by religious radicalism."[107] It is not the place here to discuss what this says about the IURD itself in terms of its religious position, but it shows clearly that the church is positioning itself as an alternative to the ICAR. Different from the latter, it has no doctrinal system that holds it bound to certain principles, among them the absolute defense of life as the ICAR understands it. It can, thus, adapt much more freely to public opinion and thus gain easy applause. What is possibly even more worrying is that the State's institutions, in this case its Supreme Court, appear to recognize the CNBB and the IURD as *the* representatives of the spectrum of the Christian faith. More balanced opinions of the historical Protestant fold are not welcome, nor those of the Pentecostals. It is true that many Protestant and Pentecostal churches hold similar views to the CNBB as to abortion, but apart from the fact that they still represent a segment numerically larger than the IURD (but much less visible in public), in the case of anencephaly, there are differences. The Methodist Church, for instance, admits abortion in "extreme cases," including danger for the mother's life, rape and "inviability of the survival of the fetus" as precisely in the case of anencephaly.[108] The State, then, gives right to the IURD's pretension and has

104. Baldisseri, *O acordo entre a Santa Sé*, 20 emphasizes that this means the church is defending "pluriconfessional" education (i.e., always in a specific confession, but not necessarily Catholic), and says the agreement "avoids that the constitutional right of receiving religious education in official establishments of fundamental education [i.e., the first eight years] be [. . .] diluted into the teaching of a mere sociology of religions or a comparative study of religious emphases." In its statement of November 17, 2008, the Permanent Forum on Religious Education (FONAPER), an organization of civil society, saw the constitutional separation between State and church violated, as the formulation in the agreement seems to indicate the wish to transform religious education classes into religion classes, i.e. confessional catechesis, rather than to provide ample knowledge about religion and the religions; htp://www.fonaper.com.br (accessed on 11/19/2008).

105. In his pastoral letter about the agreement, IECLB pastor president Walter Altmann affirms that, being a sovereign State, the Vatican has the right to sign agreements as it has done with other countries. He laments, however, "that the agreement has been elaborated, negotiated and, finally, signed, without a previous exchange of ideas and dialogue with other religious confessions, as well as society in general." He hopes that possible privileges contained in the agreement would be "naturally extended to the other confessions," given that the government is constitutionally bound to maintain religious freedom and equality between the religions, and wishes that "the discussion on the role of the State vis-à-vis religion and of religion vis-à-vis the State may grow for the strengthening of the common good, for which both governments and churches should always strive." Walter Altmann, *Carta pastoral referente ao Acordo Brasil—Vaticano*, no. 162444/09, February 6, 2009.

106. According to the court's own press release, www.stf.jus.br/portal/cms/verNoticiaDetalhe. asp?idConteudo=94896&caixaBusca=N (accessed on 11/19/2008).

107. "STF deve aprovar aborto de anencéfalo por 11 a 0, diz ministro," *Jornal O Povo* of August 28, 2008, www.opovo.com.br/saude/815456.html (accessed on 11/18/2008).

108. Colégio Episcopal da Igreja Metodista, *Pronunciamento do Colégio Episcopal: questão do aborto*, http://www.metodista.org.br/arquivo/documentos/download/Pronunciamento_03_07.pdf (accessed on 11/3/2010). The IECLB is preparing a statement on anencephaly as the Supreme Court is discussing a general liberation of abortion in this particular case.

it represent the whole evangelical flock, not referring, for instance, to Lutheran specialists on bioethics, albeit represented in such prominent organs as the National Research Ethics Commission (Dr. Euler Westphal).

Just before the municipal elections in 2008, IURD's supreme Bishop Macedo launched a new book called "Plan of Power," in which he openly preaches that the IURD faithful and their *evangélico* allies should head for God's political plan for them: to govern Brazil.[109] Comparing the *evangélicos* throughout the whole text to the chosen people of Israel, he insists on the importance of "strategic," well-informed, and planned political action, and insists on good relationships with the governing and a position high enough to be respected and received by them, while rejecting any "theocratic, or semidemocratic characteristics, as Brazil historically seems to have had," from which, to the contrary, "liberation" has to be sought. Macedo is, of course, hinting at the ICAR.[110] Joseph, Moses, and Daniel are quoted, having gained power and learned how to govern under the Egyptian Pharaoh or the Persian King, but in favor of their own people and loyal to their God. David and Martin Luther King, Jr. complete the list for their "achievements, attitudes and immortalized phrases" representing "the collective longing for social justice and honor."[111] Significantly, Jesus in his humbleness and kenosis is not mentioned; he only appears once as an example to be followed when he submits himself to baptism although he would not need to.

Quite coherently, Macedo's political mentors are Machiavelli[112] and Hobbes, and not, for instance, Locke, thus pointing to an authoritarian way of government, even if democratically elected. This seems to defy all references to civic participation, citizenship, and the grown level of education among the electorate that he says has become more critical. Of course, Macedo underlines the secular character of the State and religious freedom, but between the lines there is a clear hegemonic project to be detected. This project is surely anti-Catholic: only *evangélicos* are considered Christians, and Macedo is eager to position himself contrary to the ICAR in sensitive issues like embryonic stem cell research, where he says that "parts of society resist the new even though there is scientific proof of benefits for all of humanity," which is, by the way, not entirely true.[113] But the point here is that the IURD is positioning itself clearly as an alternative to the ICAR and as much more acceptable to modern society than the latter. Thus, Macedo underlines, among others, that "society, in general, is autonomous and critical in its positions, and it can by no means be underestimated in its intelligence," and that "an illuminated people is less prone to manipulation."[114] Conscious of the considerable electoral power of the *evangélicos*, a community Macedo estimates at 40 million (22 percent of the population), he boasts they could "decide any electoral bid" on all

109. Thus, Macedo and Oliveira, *Plano de poder*, 53 ask, for instance: "And you, as a Christian, which side should you be on? And further, how many readers and evaluators of the Holy Bible have already had the sensitivity to perceive that it is a manual not restricted to orientation of religious faith, but is also a book that suggests resistance, the taking and establishment of political power or of government, and goes far beyond these themes? When all or the majority of those who follow it are convinced that it is God's Word, then the realization of the great Divine dream will occur."

110. Macedo and Oliveira, *Plano de poder*, 57, cf. 10.

111. Ibid., 103.

112. See Machiavelli, *Il Príncipe—Der Fürst*, 43, using Moses as the example of a prince who, despite only executing God's commandments, was given the grace to be worthy of speaking with God; *Il Principe VI*; cf. Macedo and Oliveira, *Plano de poder*, 77f.

113. Ibid., 80. While expectations are high because of the high potency of embryonic stem cells, no therapy has as yet been successfully developed, so scientific proof is yet to come.

114. Ibid., 80f. This kind of argument, in itself correct, but populist in its intention to gather support for the IURD's political project, reminds one of the Swiss People's Party's (SVP) constant invocation of direct democracy and "the people's will" in order to gain support for its xenophobic policies.

levels.[115] This is certainly an exaggeration, as the faithful do not all vote with their leaders, as we have seen above (Part IIE). Macedo's nephew, IURD bishop Marcello Crivella, a senator who stood for election to the mayorship of Rio de Janeiro in October 2008, representing the recently founded IURD-close Brazilian Republican Party (PRB), was not elected. Still, the project is explicitly stated, and the book's intention is precisely to, as Macedo formulates it, "awaken the potential—which has been dormant—of a people with serious, progressive and innovative proposals."[116] The church feels so strong by now, it seems, that it can openly assume its pretensions.[117]

Public theology in Brazil, then, would have to provide alternative space and voices to the mentioned manifestations of hegemonic public religion that tends to occupy rather than contribute to the public sphere. The problem of Roman Catholic theological reflection is that it is doctrinally very restricted, especially in sensitive and much discussed issues like abortion, homosexuality, and embryonic stem cell research. It is here where it most clashes with public opinion, despite the fact that the vast majority of Brazilians consider themselves Catholic. The IURD is free from such bonds, but might ultimately strand precisely because of the failure to provide not only opinions of its absolute leader, Bishop Edir Macedo, but arguments biblically and confessionally grounded. There is room in Brazil—at least—for a third alternative, based on academically sound arguments and a clear commitment to the common good and religious pluralism. This is why a reflection on the status, importance and possibilities of academic theology is in place here.

b) Academic Theology in Brazil

Paraphrasing Tertullian, one could ask: What has Brasília to do with Rio de Janeiro, the headquarters of the Ministry of Education with one of the most religiously plural cities in Brazil?[118] Since 1999, there has been a renewed discussion on the academic status of theology, as it was in this year that the Ministry of Education recognized the possibility of a Bachelor's degree in Theology and Religious Studies. Graduate degrees on the master's and doctoral levels have already been recognized since the early 1980s through the Ministry's organ CAPES (Coordination of Continuous Formation of Graduate Personnel—*Coordenação de Aperfeiçoamento de Pessoal de Nível Superior*) which is responsible for the evaluation of all graduate courses in Brazil. But on all levels there is an ongoing questioning of theology and—to a lesser degree—religious studies as to their academic character and quality, as we shall see below in a concrete example. In any case, one of the central issues is who should be the teachers to teach religious education in public schools, which is mandatory by the 1988 Constitution and, by law, has to be funded by the State? Teachers working in public schools must be duly licensed, but the Ministry of Education has not authorized any licentiate course in theology to date.[119] So far, very few public universities have installed an undergraduate

115. Ibid., 25 et passim.

116. Ibid., 10.

117. It cannot go unperceived that Macedo is using the by now common language—social movements, citizenship, liberation, democracy, secularity—to position his church within it and, in doing this, suggests to be different from the ICAR. Strangely, Matthew 22:15-22 serves as basis for a clear distinction between the private and the public (Macedo and Oliveira, *Plano de poder,* 114), which seems contradictory to the evident public role of faith in God. The project itself is not so clearly stated, but anchored in faith (Hebrews 11:1-3), action (good works, James 2:18), culture (innovation) and ethics, which are the fields of "the transformations capable of a true revolution and emancipation of the human being in social and political matters, fostering his ascension, and of making him better prepared [*condicionado*] to conquer, establish, and amplify his conquests" (ibid., 117).

118. Tertullian, *De praescriptione haereticorum,* 7, said: "What has Athens to do with Jerusalem, the Academy with the Church, the Heretics with the Christians?" Corpus Christianorum Series Latina, I.185ff..

119. Such licentiate degree is normally presupposed for teachers according to Law number 9,394/96, Art. 62 (cf.

course in theology or religious studies, and only two graduate courses in religious studies are located at public universities.[120] Theology is, thus, virtually exclusively left to private, confessional institutes of higher education, including seminaries and universities like the Pontifical Catholic Universities (PUCs) in various parts of the country. There are now over 120 courses in Theology recognized or authorized by the Ministry of Education on the bachelor's level, and 16 programs for master's and doctoral studies, eight in Religious Studies and six in Theology.[121]

It is true that public universities in Brazil have a tradition of strong reservations against religion and theology, and thus a more qualified communication with them is needed.[122] The reasons for this lie in part in Portuguese centralism which would not establish a university in Brazilian lands, while Spanish America could boast six universities by the end of the 16th century. Brazilian intellectuals had to go to the University of Coimbra in Portugal (founded by papal bull in 1308) to get university training. The only university-like place in colonial times was the Jesuit *Colégio da Bahia*, where its missionaries were educated. The expulsion of the Jesuits and the secularization of education by King Dom José I's minister, the Marquis de Pombal, in the second half of the 18th century, had deep effects both in Portugal and in Brazil. The 1772 university reform defined the Faculty of Philosophy as center, understanding that its "natural philosophy" or science was to teach technicians "to explore the riches of the Kingdom."[123] From there, the university was understood as an aggregation of professional schools. Dom João VI, who fled to Brazil with his court in 1808, established military and medical schools. In the early independent Empire, what was to be two universities in the pombaline sense (the project included a course of theology) turned out to become law faculties in São Paulo and Olinda. Eclecticism, brought to Brazil from France (Maine de Biran, Victor Cousin) via Portugal, as well as Comte's positivism became influential during the independent Brazilian Empire. Representatives of the latter affirmed that "it is necessary to sacrifice theology and metaphysics and to teach exclusively science [. . .] May true houses of higher scientific instruction be created, and the maleficent dreams of University be abandoned."[124] To have a university in Brazil was to remain "an idea" well into the Republic.[125]

In 1920, the University of Rio de Janeiro was founded, but again as a conglomerate of professional schools rather than fostering critical thought and fundamental research. This only changed when the University of São Paulo (USP) was founded in 1934, where all fields of knowledge should be developed and integrated through the Faculty of Philosophy, Sciences and Arts, which was to

---

Klein and Junqueira, "Aspectos referentes à formação," 222). Models of formation differ from state to state, as the states are responsible for the organization of Religious Education at public schools (see also above, IIB3). Often, teachers already licensed in other fields take a graduate course (*lato sensu*) in Theology or Religion in order to teach this course. Four federal or state universities have now a licentiate in Religious Studies for this purpose (in the states of Santa Catarina, Pará, and Maranhão); data for courses taken from http://sinaes.inep.gov.br:8080/sinaes/index.jsp (accessed on 1/5/2007, access restricted to course evaluators selected by the Ministry of Education).

120. The first one is the Federal University of Piauí in Brazilian's Northeast, the other two are the Federal Universities of Juiz de Fora (Minas Gerais) and Paraíba.

121. All courses but three are Christian, of a variety of denominations. Data on the bachelor's level according to Rega, "As diretrizes curriculares nacionais," 2; on postgraduate courses see http://www.capes.gov.br, "cursos recomendados" (accessed on 12/12/2010).

122. This has been confirmed by philosophers during the International Symposium on Public Theology in Latin America, held from July 4–7, 2008, in São Leopoldo. On what follows, see Paviani and Pozenato, *A universidade em Debate*, 63-72; Lisbôa, *A idéia de Universidade no Brasil*.

123. Lisbôa, *A idéia de Universidade no Brasil*, 72.

124. Ibid., 70.

125. Lisbôa, *A idéia de Universidade no Brasil*.

be the center of the university. However, while philosophy was important, science was considered a conquest against the ecclesiastical tutelage of knowledge, and thus religion became *persona non grata* in the USP. Until 1979, no courses were taught even on medieval philosophy, due to fears that this would bring religion back into academic discourse.[126]

In 1961, the University of Brasília was founded as a similar project. Anthropologist Darcy Ribeiro was crucial in this process. Although an agnostic, he wanted to install a course of theology, but the military regime in power from 1964 prevented this from happening, as former government minister and now secretary-general of UNCTAD, Rubens Ricupero, recalls. Ricupero clearly advocates the study of theology at universities.[127]

On the part of the theological academy itself, there is a considerable influence of the French *laicité* and its anti-religious, namely anti-clerical tradition. At the same time, there are tendencies in the Roman Catholic, Presbyterian, and more recently also in the Methodist church to impose doctrinal restrictions in their (not only theological) schools and faculties. But even in the traditionally liberal and inclusive Lutheran (IECLB) fold, there are conflicts between students—all of them potential ministers—and their church leadership, for reasons that cannot be explored here in detail. It is certainly no mere coincidence that there is a search for the resistant, prophetic, and even heretic traditions in Christianity, read in a sociological way through the eyes of Weber, Bourdieu, and Foucault's works on power.[128] Popular and indigenous religiosity, as well as ecumenism and especially inter-religious dialogue come to the fore as an interest, and Pentecostal and Neo-Pentecostal churches are, despite all due theological critique, also seen as movements of protest. While this is understandable and an important corrective to a certain anti-ecumenical, narrow line of thought and action adopted by many church leaders, it tends to leave out opportunities to rediscover the properly theological, doctrinal tradition in a new way, something Liberation Theology had indeed undertaken (cf. above, Part ID1).[129] The danger is, thus, that theology ceases to do what is its specific "business" and, rather than being in dialogue with social sciences, simply repeats them.

Possibly an even greater challenge than conquering theology's citizenship within the Brazilian academy, however, is to ensure communication between faith communities, namely churches, among themselves and between them and society.[130] Religious competition and the strongly exclusivist character of Pentecostal and most historical Protestant churches on the one hand, and the still hegemonic behavior and self-consciousness of the Roman Catholic Church on the other, makes such communication enormously difficult. One interesting result of the recognition of theology by

126. I thank philosopher Franklin Leopoldo e Silva (USP) for this information.

127. In Neutzling, *A teologia na universidade contemporânea*, 52.

128. See, for instance, the whole number of the electronic journal *Protestantismo em Revista*, 14, September to December (2007), available at http://www.est.edu.br/nepp (accessed on 07/24/2008), dedicated to Bourdieu, as well as the doctoral theses by Adilson Schultz (*Deus está presente*) and André Musskopf (*Via(da)gens teológicas*).

129. Cf. above, Part ID1.

130. This is especially urgent as it has become common to invite a variety of religions to an "ecumenical" event on public holidays, inaugurations, or at graduation ceremonies. This is certainly a positive move, as in earlier times only Roman Catholic priests or bishops were invited to such public acts. However, invitations seem to be sent out at random, and there is no time for proper preparation among the participants. In the worst case, the result is that every religion is granted, say, two minutes to speak, which is not rarely used as a platform for propagating their own religion or denomination. In the best case, representatives are sensitive to the event as such and to the other religions, and might even suggest a common religious language, like the Afro-Brazilian representative who, at the installation of a new mayor in Porto Alegre, invited all present to pray the "Our Father" (!), which they did. I take the example from a declaration of the IECLB on inter-religious dialogue (IECLB, *Diretrizes teológico-pastorais para atos inter-religiosos*), elaborated by the presidency's advisory committee on ecumenism.

the Ministry of Education is that many ministers holding a seminary degree are now looking for booster courses to obtain a recognized diploma. It might be, thus, that academic formation can provide a more thorough mediation between the churches' clergy and wider society than church-run seminaries tend to do, and incipient higher studies undertaken by Pentecostal theologians could lead to a yet increased awareness of the churches' role and task in the public sphere. By insisting on rational, communicable, and pluralist reflection, such formation forces students to engage with colleagues from other traditions and with different positions, breaking the ghetto-like homogeneity they tend to experience in their own church. There is, of course, no guarantee of making a lasting difference, but it is a promising space for testing alternative visions on the churches, their task and activity in the public sphere.

If academic theology is, as I contend,[131] a methodologically responsible reflection on our talking of God—and not on Godself—then this will help believers and Christians to see themselves in a not neutral, but more objective way as one way of belief among many others, both Christian and of other religions. Theology is truth-seeking and thus not only descriptive, in this aspect different from Religious Studies. But it does so being conscious that it will never possess the truth, nor find it in an absolute way. Theology presents what it perceives of truth with arguments that can be discussed and questioned, not by decree. This distinguishes it from an ecclesiastical magisterium or doctrinal decisions of church commissions and leadership. Doubt is an important motor of this truth-seeking, as long as it is not destructive to faith in an endless skepticism. It saves, however, theology from falling into a self-reproductive dogmatism. As Ingolf Ulrich Dalferth well stated, these are the two dangers for any science: to fall into skepticism or dogmatism, i.e., the "denial of a sustainable differentiation between opinion and knowledge" or the "restriction of scientific knowledge solely to a very specific type of knowledge."[132]

Theology is still *fides quaerens intellectum,* as Anselm of Canterbury and many since him have expressed it.[133] This is not to say that only believers could study theology in an academic way. But there would not be any sense in doing theology were there not many concrete believers whose faith brings forth the need to reflect academically on theology. If others *can* study faith, believers and especially those responsible in their organizations, the churches, *need* to study faith. 1 Peter (3:15f.) is wise to remind believers always to be "ready to make your defense to anyone who demands from you an accounting for the hope that is in you," but also "do it with gentleness and reverence." Dalferth affirms, from the standpoint of the German context, that through being present in the framework of institutionalized science, theology "accepts the duty to account publicly for its thinking, that is to enter the critical-argumentative discourse about its themes and arguments."[134]

131. Cf. Sinner, "Teologia como ciência."

132. I. Dalferth, "Öffentlichkeit, Universität und Theologie," 61.

133. The main report that led to the authorization and accreditation of courses of theology in Brazil is CNE/CES number 241/99. It accepts this definition saying that theology was, in its origin (and nothing is said that this should be different today), "constituted as an analysis performed by reason on the precepts of faith." What has changed is the separation of church and State and the pluralisation of theological orientations, which is given as reason not to impose any specific curriculum (more on this see below). It further states that "in terms of academic autonomy which the Constitution guarantees, the State cannot [!] impede or fence [*cercear*] the creation of these courses." Text accessible at http://faculdadeunida.com.br/site/index2.php? ostion=com_content& do_pdf=1&id=89 (accessed on 12/5/2008). See also Zwetsch, "Nova situação do ensino de Teologia no Brasil."

134. Dalferth goes on to say that "all that participate in this discourse constitute together the scientific public space (Öffentlichkeit) of theology. This is by no means the only, but an essential public character (Öffentlichkeit) of theology" ("Öffentlichkeit, Universität und Theologie," 66f.), explicitly referring to Tracy, *The Analogical Imagination*, and Thiemann, *Constructing a Public Theology*, as well as Huber, *Kirche und Öffentlichkeit*, 295-379.

In discussions on the academic character of theology, however, there are contestations from both sides, both internal and external. Education Councilor and philosopher Marilena Chauí pleaded for the rejection of the accreditation of a Baptist Faculty in Feira de Santana (Bahia state), and won her case against the favorable report of one of her colleagues and the evaluation of the designated commission that had visited the Faculty. In the session of the National Council for Education's Chamber on Higher Education, Chauí asked that her opinion be registered in the report, according to which "I cannot see how a State organ of a secular republic can have whatsoever reason to analyze the request of an institution whose vocation is eminently pastoral and not academic," precisely because she was "a defendant of freedom of belief, opinion and expression."[135] From what I could detect in the published reports, she referred to a passage in the evaluators' report that stated that "various lecturers of the specific disciplines of the course in theology have only a Bachelor's diploma [. . .] there is a need to pass from an eminently pastoral preoccupation to a mentality that joins pastoral preoccupation with academic rigor."[136] In my experience, such is the case for many if not most Protestant seminaries, many of which have been accredited by the same Council.[137] The decision, thus, shows considerable lack of information on how theological seminaries in Brazil work, and casts doubt on the original decision to recognize courses in theology, where the Council explicitly stated that due to the guarantee of religious freedom and the separation of church and State, it was inappropriate to enforce specific curricular guidelines beyond the formal requirements for a higher education course.[138] It also did not sufficiently consider, in my view, the evaluation report in its entirety, but emphasized one specific statement listed under "frailties."[139] Still, it is certainly appropriate and in the interest of theology to look for ways of enforcing an academic, i.e., critical, pluralist, comprehensive, and interdisciplinary study of theology. In any case, negative and positive religious freedom clash. While the former is here being interpreted as

135. http://portal.mec.gov.br/cne/arquivos/pdf/2008/pces003_08.pdf (accessed on 11/27/2008), 8.

136. Ibid., 7. The recourse judgment, administered by the Council's Plenary (and not only the Higher Education Chamber, but with a report elaborated by one of the original opponents), highlighted this same quote and also the statement that library development was not at the heart of the institution's planning process. The recourse report stressed the institution's academic deficiency, based on its reading of the evaluation report which, according to the Council, "should not have itself recommended the accreditation"; http://portal.mec.gov.br/cne/arquivos/pdf/2008/pcp002_08.pdf (accessed 11/28/2008), 5. It has to be added, however, that evaluation commissions—since the evaluation process reform in 2006—must not recommend anything (and they indeed did not), but describe what, in their view, is to be said in relation to the rather extensive list of items prescribed for evaluation. For them, the result was satisfactory.

137. In July 2008, the Messianic Faculty (http://www.faculdademessianica.edu.br), one of the three existing Non-Christian theological schools, belonging to the World Messianic Church (cf. IIB1), a religion of Japanese origin, and its Mokiti Okada Foundation, was accredited by the Council. According to the report, a vigorous discussion preceded the finally unanimous decision. One of the councilors undertook, in this case, the task to compare the curriculum to other, already approved courses and found that it was compatible. Differently from the earlier case, coherence in the decisions was being sought—and found. As is due to the Council, the academic character of the curriculum was the main issue, and in her final (favorable) vote, Councilor Marília Ancona-Lopez recommended that "in the concretization of the referred course and disciplines, the institution develop in the student a comprehensive epistemological and historical vision, empowering him to think critically the universe of Theology from different philosophical [sic!] perspectives and work it in a methodologically adequate way, in line with scientific progress." See http://portal.mec.gov.br/cne/arquivos/pdf/2008/ pces101_08.pdf (accessed 11/28/2008), 11.

138. The formal requirements are that candidates have successfully concluded High School (in Brazil called *Ensino Médio*) and go through an entry examination. As to the institution, it has to offer the minimum of class hours, qualification of the faculty and infrastructure (i.e., namely class rooms and library).

139. Among others, the Evaluation Commission affirmed that "the Institution of Higher Education proves capable of, while respecting its confessional character, not losing sight of the indispensable academic character of the formation to be offered"; http://portal.mec.gov.br/cne/arquivos/pdf/2008/pces003_08.pdf (accessed 11/27/2008), 4.

impeding the State from recognizing degrees geared towards pastoral work, the latter prompted the National Council on Education to allow studies of theology to be of "free curriculum."[140]

Another group challenging theology as an academic study is specializing on issues of secularity, namely on religious education in public schools. The "observatory of secularity" (*observatório da laicidade*) is a research group of the Federal University of Rio de Janeiro, headed by sociologist Luiz Antônio Cunha, who specialized in issues of education. It follows three lines of interest: "Political-Ideological Socialization in the Institutions of Education," fostering "impartiality in relation to the conflicts in the religious field" and, thus, secularity (*laicidade*); "Religious Education in Public Schools," in its variety of curricula and the historical movements to suppress it for its "incompatibility with the principle of secularity of the State"; and "Religious Restrictions for the Teaching of Sciences and the Health Programmes in Schools," i.e., creationism, not only in its biblicist, but also "pseudo-scientific form of intelligent design."[141] The latter is seen as an "attempt to reconstitute symbolically, by evoking biblical images, a lost social order in today's convoluted world" that, beyond schools, interfere with health programs and education, as well as "fortify social prejudices especially in relation to sexuality and reproduction."[142] Like other groups, with their links to be found on the same site, they feel uncomfortable with the public influence of certain religious groups and opinions. It is most probable that the proposal of a public theology also gives them discomfort, at least until they come to know it in its non-impository setup. Many academics and intellectuals think this way, but there has been little explicit debate, different from the United States and, to a much lesser degree, Germany and Switzerland.[143] Academic theology could and should be precisely the place for such discussion, in order to substitute prejudice by information and comprehension. If, at the same time, academic freedom is granted by those who maintain the theological schools, namely the graduate courses, a fruitful and trustful dialogue could be established rather than a competition of apologetics, be they faithful or atheist.

This could help clarify also issues like the office of the theologian. A law project has been processed in the Senate since April 13, 2005, proposed by Senator (and IURD Bishop) Marcelo Crivella. It pretends to make "the theologian" an official professional category,[144] entering which would presuppose not only a recognized diploma, but also becoming a member of a National Council of Theology and its state sections, in analogy to other official professional categories like physicians and lawyers. Furthermore, all persons who have already been exercising the office of theologian during the five years before the approval of the law, even without recognized diploma, would be included.[145] The matter was virtually ready for voting in the plenary, having received a positive

140. Strangely, USP anthropologist Eunice Durham, one of the councilors responsible for the report 241/99 which authorized the accreditation of courses in Theology, used the same argument to vote against the recognition of licentiate courses in theology, which would habilitate for teaching Religious Education, because it would be impossible to impose a (national) "uniform curricular standard" given that Religious Education lies in the responsibility of the states. However, as the accreditation of Higher Education courses is the matter of a federal authority, it seems that (following pressures?) the National Education Council simply wanted to wash its hands in innocence. It thus contributed to the continuing confusion on who could possibly teach Religious Education. Cf. Pauly, "O novo rosto," 9.

141. According to the Observatory's website, there are two creationist associations in Brasil, the *Sociedade Criacionista Brasileira*, founded in 1972, and the *Associação Brasileira de Pesquisa da Criação*, founded in 1979. Furthermore, creationism is being taught at faculties run by the Seventh-Day-Adventists, recognized by the Ministry of Education.

142. http://www.nepp-dh.ufrj.br/ole/linhas.html (accessed 11/20/2008).

143. Cf. Grotefeld, *Religiöse Überzeugungen im liberalen Staat*.

144. The lack of such official standardization had been precisely an argument for the freedom of curricula in theology, see the above cited report CNE/CES 241/99.

145. There already exists a Federal Council of Theologians which would certainly put forward itself as a natural

report by Senator Magno Malta (a Baptist minister), when a declaration from the newly founded National Association of Graduate Programmes in Theology and Religious Studies (ANPTECRE) was received by the Senate's President and sent back to the Commission on Social Issues for further discussion. A similar project is being evaluated in the Deputy's Chamber, where it received a negative opinion from Deputy Eudes Xavier for the Commission on Work, Administration and Public Service.[146] He argues that there is an "absolute absence of public interest to sustain its [i.e., the profession of the theologian's regulation." A profession needs regulation if its undue exercise could cause "social damage or risks to safety, health and the physical integrity of the collectivity," which he says is evidently not the case. Furthermore, the regulation could unduly restrict the market for theologians and discourage the constitutionally guaranteed right to freedom of worship through the levying of annual membership fees of those who, as religious leaders, "should not seek profit, but the salvation of souls."[147] Again, public theology is a disputed field, and it is not easy to steer clear between the Skylla of occupation and imposition and the Charybdis of public inertia and retreat into the private. In any case, while it is in the interest of believers themselves to insist on religious freedom and pluralism, it is also in their interest that they can participate fully in public debate. To this end, they need not have a project to establish God's power plan on earth (in Macedo's sense), but to think of God's will as flowing through them towards others. This will be further explored in the next section.

3. THE COMMON WEAL AS GOAL FOR THE ACTION OF THE CHURCHES

. . .seek the welfare (שָׁלוֹם) of the city

Jeremiah 29:7

As stated above, one of the most serious problems of churches in Brazil is their inclination to introspection, on the one hand, or to defend their interests on different levels by imposing force, on the other. The Roman Catholic Church still uses its direct influence on the government, with ample access to its representatives. The AD tries to articulate its own political representatives in order to press for its interests. The IECLB is working on a more subtle level through its educational and diaconal experts and projects, and surely the least self-interested church agent—although this does not necessarily mean that it does so out of conviction, but possibly because of a lack of engagement and interest for the national church, or even the synod for that matter. The history of the IECLB has given priority to lay participation and leadership, and to congregational organization, which is an asset in terms of the Christian's citizenship, his or her consciousness of rights, duties, and the importance of the polity. In any case, however, this is a minority posture.

If the aim of public action is not either for corporate interests or for proselytist evangelization, then what is it for? My thesis is that it is necessary for the churches to act together, and with others, towards the *bonum commune*, the common good or weal, as part of their obedience to God's double commandment of love and, thus, their mission. ". . .seek the welfare of the city where I have sent you

candidate for the Council named "National Council of Theology" in the project; see http://www.cft.org.br (12/12/2010). It is, by the way, notable that traditionally anti-theological leaders like Edir Macedo (see Macedo, *A libertação da teologia* on "the Liberation of [= from] Theology") now boast academic titles (DD, ThD and PhD according to the back flap of Macedo and Oliveira, *Plano de Poder*—all acquired from a graduation mill with no official accreditation, the FATEBOM; http://www.bispomacedo.com.br; http://www.fatebom.com.br).

146. The text is published on http://www.soter.org.br/projetolei.doc (accessed on 11/27/2008).

147. Ibid., 3.

into exile, and pray to the LORD on its behalf, for in its welfare you will find your welfare" (Jer 29:7) says Jeremiah in his letter to the exiled in Babylon. The exile can be a good metaphor for those who see the earthly kingdom as a mere necessity to be endured. In any case, given that Christians and churches are located in this world, already for their own sake the wellbeing of the whole of society and the environment should be their goal.[148] As I have shown, Luther sees Christian service, God's love by faith flowing through believers towards all human beings, including and especially non-believers, as part of Christian liberty: "By faith we receive blessings from above, from God; through love we give them out below, to our neighbor."[149] The Gospel proclaims the extension of love to one's neighbor and even one's enemy, inverting positions and abandoning status.[150] Although sent primarily to the Jews, to which he preached publicly,[151] Jesus also attended to foreigners and non-Jews, even highlighting what they supposedly could not have: "Woman, great is your faith" (Matthew 15:28). Such task of living out discipleship in the world is of the whole "royal priesthood" (1 Peter 2:9) believers are ordained into through their "ordination" in Baptism. But as Baptism initiates into the Church as the body of Christ, the churches themselves are called to fulfill their public mission.

The churches, located above within civil society (IB), have a particularly interesting and important task within the public sphere. On the one hand, they easily fit into my rather narrow, ideal-typical definition of civil society because of their high moral standards based on their divine calling and mandate. On the other hand, they transcend even the whole of society by their reference to God as creator and redeemer, finding themselves, however, bound by human finitude and the eschatological hope and reserve. What is, is not what was to be, broken as it is through sin, and what eventually is to be is not yet here, although showing signs of its presence. In such constant tension between the "already now" and "not yet," the present and the future, the believers and their churches can see what else could be and have a notion that the present is never finished, complete, or perfect. They are, thus, both distrustful (of themselves and other humans) and trustful (of God),[152] apt for enduring the ambiguity of existence[153] just as they are for disposing of resources that allow them not drown in it, but to work for improving and transforming what can be improved and transformed.[154] They can bring such a disposition into dialogue with other groups, movements, and organizations. Furthermore, with their wide access to the population, beyond any other association in Brazil, they have the chance to include this population into discourse within the public sphere—if they so wish.

To this end, then, it is necessary to be able to see a common future for humanity without presupposing everyone would be Christian in such future—at least not inasmuch as it lies in human hands. While a Christian by his or her faith is impelled to act beyond his or her own interest, the result of a commonly constructed world is of interest to all, including the Christians'. As the churches are highly influential groups in Brazilian society, it is also in civil society's interest to have them with rather than against their struggles. Even more so, churches should cooperate

148. The central term in Hebrew is שָׁלוֹם, "welfare," "integral wellbeing," rightly put at the centre of his "citizen faith" by Castro, *Por uma fé cidadã*.

149. Martin Luther in his *Sermon on the Third Sunday after Epiphany*, quoted in Moe-Lobeda, *Public Church*, 52, 88, note 14; see also above, IIIA4.

150. Cf. Theissen, *Die Religion der ersten Christen*.

151. Cf. Stegemann, "Ich habe öffentlich zur Welt gesprochen."

152. Cf. Part IIIA2.

153. Cf. Part IIIA3.

154. Cf. Part IIIA4.

ecumenically, as a "communion of communions" to recall Martin Marty's proposal for a public church.[155] This would not only improve their testimony, but ensure that less energy is lost in mutual competition. Appropriate instruments for this would be both a strengthening of the National Council of Churches (CONIC), which already serves as a representation of non-ICAR churches in relation to government, administration and Congress, but is in the odd situation that its numerically most relevant membership is precisely represented by the CNBB, while the other churches represent only a very small part of the country's Christians. The CNBB, although a member of the CONIC, works with the CONIC as partner and not a council of which it is (only) a part; thus, the Ecumenical Lenten Campaigns (2000, 2005, and again 2010) are sponsored by the CNBB and the CONIC, not through the CONIC.

Another element would be the creation of a "National Council of Religions" to represent religious communities before the State. This would be important to discuss matters like religious education, theological education, chaplaincies in hospitals, prisons, the Armed Forces and the like, a policy on religion, and even the definition of religion itself to be as inclusive as possible and still allow for some criteria based on which privileges (such as ground tax exemption) should be granted or withheld. It is indeed a difference to allow freedom of conviction and belief and grant privileges to religious societies, which needs justification.

It is, then, necessary that a public theology develop an idea for the whole of "good life," beyond its own boundaries, because it tries to see the world with God's eyes and seeks to contribute to it from this angle. This does not mean, in my view, that Christians have, as seen in Stackhouse's proposal (above, Part IIIB1b) to make the claim that religion lies at the heart of every society, or that religion must have such a central place. More humbly, a public theology should analyze and formulate the Christian contribution to the whole of society and bring this into the public discourse, together with other religions and non-religious movements. "The whole of society" is not to be understood in the sense of a totality, but to say that Christian principles are worthy to be followed beyond those who hold the Christian faith, because they are principles of living together potentially fruitful for all human beings.

155. Marty, *The Public Church*. This is echoed in the Lutheran perspective of Cynthia Moe-Lobeda who rightly recalls, among others, the character of a communion of churches assumed by the Lutheran World Federation at its 1990 Assembly in the Brazilian city of Curitiba. This means a "movement toward deeper relationships of accountability, interdependence, responsibility, and mutuality" (*Public Church*, 34).

Conclusion: Boldness and Humility

I have spoken openly (παρρησίᾳ) to the world; I have always taught in synagogues and in the temple, where all the Jews come together. I have said nothing in secret.

John 18:20

. . .but emptied himself (ἐκένωσεν), taking the form of a slave, being born in human likeness.

Philippians 2:7

THE MAIN TASK OF this study, as set out by the Introduction, was to give an answer to the question of the public role of Brazilian churches since transition to democracy. It has done so by showing the centrality of citizenship and democracy both historically and conceptually, and situated the churches and Liberation Theology prominently in this new phase of Brazil's history, which began over a quarter of a decade ago with the installation of a civilian president. It has further shown, mainly through documentary research complemented with existing empirical studies, the specific contribution and its founding theological elements of three representative churches in Brazil. Such contribution is doubtlessly strong, although not free from ambiguities, as was to be expected. Finally, this study has tried to venture, within an ecumenical horizon, into a new aggregating concept for theology in post-transition Brazil, a public theology focused on citizenship. I end in this conclusion pointing to some contemporary challenges that show that churches should act in the public sphere both with boldness and with humility.

A public theology in general, but especially for Brazil needs a good equilibrium of boldness and humility. The first one is necessary especially for those Christians and churches who are timid or impose restrictions on the public dimension of the faith, holding a purely negative view of the world and awaiting Christ's coming in a pre-millennial way, like many in the AD. It is also for those who think the church has nothing to do with politics, a quite widespread understanding especially in Protestant churches and also the IECLB, as stated above, although there is not enough empirical data to properly prove it. Furthermore, it is for those for whom it is out of place to use religious arguments or references in public discourse.

Liberal political thinkers, particularly in the United States of America, among them John Rawls, Kent Greenawalt, and Robert Audi, have argued that, while free to believe what they want and express it in a specifically religious environment, matters of public concern argued in public have to obey to rational, empirical, theologically neutral arguments.[1] More radical, Richard Rorty has called religion a "conversation-stopper," although he later weakened this strong opinion.[2] Habermas, as already mentioned, is much more open to a religious contribution, which he thinks can indeed use religious arguments. According to him, there is no reason why specifically religiously based arguments should be restricted, a restriction usually not imposed on otherwise based arguments. However, they have to be communicable by means of reason, and refrain "*out of their own insight* from a violent enforcement of their faith truths and renounce militant coercion of their own members, even more so a manipulation towards suicide attacks." Presupposing a pluralistic society, religious conscience has to confront itself with other confessions and religions, accept the authority of sciences with their "monopoly on knowledge of the world," and finally accept the presuppositions of the constitutional state, "which are founded by a secular morality" lest they become destructive.[3] Of course, this was written under the impression of September 11, 2001, which brought forcefully back into even the most secular minds that religion has not disappeared from public space, nor lost its destructive (but neither its constructive) force. The second and third presuppositions are certainly debatable, but the first is indeed necessary and the most lasting effect of secularity: in a democratic constitutional state, no single religion can or should determine morality, much less the law. Remembering Böckenförde's famous theorem, according to which "the liberal, secular State lives from presuppositions which it itself cannot guarantee," the question is about the role of religion for the foundation of the State.[4]

Paul Weithman and Stefan Grotefeld[5] have recently both argued that there is no need to renounce religious language and reasoning altogether in public discourse. Although this discussion is yet to be developed in Brazil, I contend that a reasonably developed and expressed religious discourse could be helpful for both sides: for politicians and representatives of civil society to better understand the role of religions, churches, and religious organizations in society, its dangers and possibilities, and for the latter to be able to interact in a less naïve and more effective way. I recall Freston's critique that the "*evangélicos*" were just too little prepared for political offices in the 1980s,[6] and Macedo's recent plea for a more strategic and planned action in politics.[7] There is a need for Pentecostal ministers, especially, to better distinguish between a sermon and an academic or political speech, a distinction which for many of them, not least because of their poor formal education, is not easy. Again, academic theology will be of help here. In sum, despite its many deficiencies as seen in the Brazilian context, theology, both in the academic realm and in the churches, may and should speak out with boldness, "openly," through παρρησία, following Jesus' model which

1. John Rawls, *Political Liberalism* (New York: Columbia University Press, 1996); Kent Greenawalt, *Private Consciences and Public Reasons* (New York: Oxford University Press, 1995); Audi and Wolterstorff, *Religion in the Public Square*. The latter publication is already a controversial dialogue between philosophers Audi and Wolterstorff. Cf. Stackhouse, *Globalization and Grace*, 95–100; Maddox. "Religion, Secularism and the Promise of Public Theology," 85.

2. Rorty, "Religion As Conversation-Stopper," 168–74; cf. Grotefeld, *Religiöse Überzeugungen im liberalen Staat*, 22.

3. Habermas, *Glauben und Wissen*, 13f.

4. Böckenförde ("Die Entstehung des Staates als Vorgang der Säkularisation," 230) takes up the question from Hegel whether the secular State does not also need those "inner motivations and forces of cohesion which the religious faith of its citizens provides," not in the sense of going back to a "Christian" State, but that Christians can see this State not as something against their faith, but as a "chance of freedom, which to preserve and enact is also their task." It is to be remembered that this text was presented originally in 1964 and published in a revised version in 1967, within the Roman Catholic context of opening-up towards modernity.

5. Weithman, *Religion and the Obligations of Citizenship*; Grotefeld, *Religiöse Überzeugungen im liberalen Staat.*

6. Freston, *Evangélicos na Política Brasileira.*

7. Macedo and Oliveira, *Plano de poder.*

makes Christianity from the outset a religion with a public mission, and also one whose contents are publicly accessible for whomever wants to know about it.

Humility, on the other hand, is necessary to distinguish the spheres, to resist theocratic tendencies, and to accept both religious pluralism and pluralism about what the State and civil society are meant to be. Christianity originated in a religious plural setting, which made it possible for Paul to connect to already present ideas of "the unknown god" explaining that this is precisely the one he proclaims as the creator and Lord of all, who rose from the dead the one which is to judge the world (Acts 17). Differently from when he was persecuting the Christians, Paul now had no power to enforce on anyone what he was proclaiming, and we are told his success in this case was quite limited. Still, some say "we will hear you again about this" (Acts 17:32), as was common to do on the Areopagus. Paul contributed in the public square to religious understanding. In his letter to the Philippians, he points to another principle: the one of *kenosis*, the self-emptying of Jesus Christ who "was in the form of God" to be "born in human likeness" (Phil 2:5–11). As one of the humans, God in Christ walked on earth and died on the cross, the definitive sign that this was not a person of human power. The resurrection, of course, showed God's power over all powers, even over death. But the fact that God comes as a frail human being shows an enormous humility, exemplary for his followers. Dietrich Bonhoeffer certainly lived boldness and humility at the same time as he gave his testimony of peace against the "world in rage," but also took a clear stance against Hitler's tyranny. At the same time, he cared for his family, his fellow prisoners, his guards, and declared the world to have become "of age."[8] It is appropriate, then, that he should serve as an important reference for the Church's public task, as happened explicitly among the IECLB's theologians.

An important principle of boldness and humility in today's world would be that Christians would strive to make only such matters to be binding on all citizens that violate basic principles of human dignity. By this I mean to say that matters of life and death need more attention than matters of religious commemorations (paying homage to persons of merit or creating commemorative dates like the "Pastor's Day"). There is a hierarchy in the urgency of issues. Issues of bioethics and social justice are especially pressing, and even with different understandings of a "culture of life," with more emphasis on those already born, but living in misery, as in Liberation Theology, or on those not yet born, as in recent papal encyclicals, it is legitimate to fight for it with special intensity, based on the principle of the dignity of human life, widely acceptable today. The more such principles are in danger of being violated, the more it is legitimate to offer resistance also on religious grounds. This, however, must not mean that the discussion ends there—if it were so, religion would indeed be a "conversation stopper." Furthermore, the more normal case seems to me to be that the church would give support for arguments and general orientations, but leave polemical decisions for the conscience of the believer to take. A *status confessionis* that would only allow for a "Yes" or "No" position and put into danger the Gospel message itself in turning it into its opposite, is certainly an exceptional situation—as for instance the South African apartheid system at the time.

Such self-restriction is necessary also out of the historical consciousness that for most of their history, the Christian churches have condoned slavery, with some honorable exceptions. The same is to be said in regard to apartheid, where, thankfully, the Christian opposition against a system understood as grounded in Christian faith prevailed eventually. Other examples are easy to be cited. If churches in the West were, sometimes willingly, sometimes less so at the forefront of human rights, they also were their fiercest opposition.

8. Bonhoeffer, *Letters and Papers from Prison*.

An important consequence of such a double approach of both boldness and humility is that no aspect of public life can, as such, be decided upon without consultation, negotiation, and discussion. In the debate on abortion, to cite just one example in finalizing, the Roman Catholic Church refuses discussion, both internally and externally, as seen above (Part IIC), and is joined in this by most Protestant and Pentecostal churches, some more moderately than others. The IECLB, for instance, although it understands that abortion does violate the divine commandment not to kill, admits that "yet unborn life cannot be valued higher than the right to life of the pregnant woman," and that there can be "situations in which abortion is the minor evil."[9] The church further indicates it is favorable to abortion in cases of rape. The current legislation (Art. 128 of the Penal Code of 1940) foresees precisely these two cases, "if there is no other way to save the pregnant woman's life" or "if pregnancy is the result of rape," in which cases "abortion shall not be punished."[10] The latter is currently only permitted on special request before a court, and judges have approved about 54 percent of such requests.[11] The AD consider abortion, as seen above (Part IIE2d), a "grave crime" and "grave sin," permitting it only in the case of danger for the mother's life. The Presbyterian Church of Brazil follows suit in this, even if recognizing the problems given with clandestine abortions.[12] In what way would a public theology help in this debate? It could (1) lay open the variety of opinions present in the church(es); (2) assess in the best possible way the biological and medical implications in dialogue with experts from these areas; (3) assess the theological presuppositions as to whether they are really so unflexible, and why they should be more absolute in this case than in issues of social justice; (4) consider aspects of pastoral care and counseling in cases of abortion even if opting, on principle, against it, for the sake of human dignity, life's ambiguities and the gift of the sinner's justification; (5) maintain possibilities for counseling for women in the phase of deciding; (6) create spaces for an open discussion within the church(es), avoiding discrimination, clandestinity, and hypocrisy. Such a posture would make clear that the churches are indeed seeking the common good and not only pushing their own opinion. It would make clear the first option for human well-being and not abstract principles, and the sincere search for the best solution in such matters, without giving in their specific contribution, nor renouncing their Christian principles, which may be used in the debate. To be sure, matters of life and death, like abortion, are certainly more urgent than others, and give less room for negotiation. Still, churches could make a most constructive contribution here rather than closing up in clear-cut positions that do not do justice to human suffering. To be able to make a constructive contribution, academic theological reflection is crucial, not only to facilitate dialogue with other disciplines, but for the sake of the qualification of the churches' own understanding, biblical, historical, systematical, and practical.

9. Kirchheim, Huberto. *Posicionamento da IECLB sobre o aborto*, September 1997. http://www.luteranos.com.br/posicionamentos/aborto.htm (accessed on 11/12/2008). On this issue, I have been benefited by the research carried out under my supervision by Eneida Jacobsen for her bachelor's dissertation, which is gratefully acknowledged here.

10. Brasil, Código Penal, 358.

11. See *Estado de São Paulo* of September 1, 2008, available at http://www.estado.com.br/editorias/2008/09/01/ger-1.93.7.20080901.1.1.xml (accessed on 3/12/2009).

12. Brasileiro, "IPB manifesta-se a respeito das leis sobre o aborto e a homofobia."

Bibliography

ABONG [Associação Brasileira das Organizações Não Governamentais]. *Ações das ONGs no Brasil—perguntas e respostas*. 2005. Online: http://www.abong.org.br.

Adriance, Madeleine. "Brazil and Chile: Seeds of Change in the Latin American Church." In *World Catholicism in Transition*, edited by Thomas M. Gannon, 283–98. New York: Macmillan, 1988.

———. *Opting for the Poor: Brazilian Catholicism in Transition*. Kansas City: Sheed & Ward, 1986.

Agamben, Giorgio. *Homo Sacer: Sovereign Power and Bare Life*. Stanford: Stanford University Press, 1998.

———. *State of Exception*. Chicago: University of Chicago Press, 2005.

Ahlstrand, Kajsa. *Fundamental Openness. An Enquiry into Raimundo Panikkar's Theological Vision and its Presuppositions*. Uppsala: Swedish Institute for Missionary Research, 1993.

Alberigo, Giuseppe. "Eclesiologia e democracia: convergências e divergências." *Concilium* 5 (1992) 23–37.

Alencar, Gedeon Freire de. *Assembléia de Deus: Origem, implantação e militância (1911-1946)*. São Paulo: Arte Editorial, 2010.

Almanaque Abril. *Brasil 2003*. São Paulo: Abril, 2003.

Almeida, Abraão de, editor. *História das Assembléias de Deus no Brasil*. 2nd ed. Rio de Janeiro: CPAD, 1982.

———. *Teologia contemporânea: A influência das correntes teológicas e filosóficas na Igreja*. 6th ed. Rio de Janeiro: CPAD, 2002.

Almeida, Alberto Carlos. *A cabeça do Brasileiro*, 2nd ed. Rio de Janeiro: Record, 2007.

Almeida, Dom Luciano de, "Recentes pronunciamentos pastorais da CNBB sobre Igreja e participação política." In CNBB, *Leigos e participação na Igreja*, 9-20, São Paulo: Paulinas, 1989.

Almeida, Ronaldo de. "Dez Anos do 'Chute na Santa': A Intolerância com a Diferença." In *Intolerância religiosa: impactos do neopentecostalismo no campo religioso afro-brasileiro*, edited by Vagner Gonçalves da Silva, 171-89. São Paulo: EDUSP, 2007.

———. "Tradução e mediação: missões transculturais entre grupos indígenas." In *Deus na aldeia: missionários, índios e mediação cultural*, edited by Paula Montero, 277–304. São Paulo: Globo, 2006.

Althaus-Reid, Marcella. *Indecent Theology*. London: Routledge, 2000.

———, editor. *Liberation Theology and Sexuality*. Aldershot: Ashgate, 2006.

Althaus-Reid, Marcella, Ivan Petrella and Luiz Carlos Susin, editors. *Another Possible World: Reclaiming Liberation Theology*. London: SCM, 2007.

Altmann, Walter, "A crise da identidade eclesial e a inconformidade de Cristo: reflexões sobre a identidade da IECLB." In *Quem assume esta tarefa? Um documentário de uma igreja em busca de sua identidade*, edited by Germano Burger, 275-95. São Leopoldo: Sinodal, 1977.

———. *Lutero e libertação: releitura de Lutero em perspectiva latino-americana*. São Paulo: Ática, 1994.

———. *Luther and Liberation: A Latin American Perspective*. Translated by Mary M. Solberg. Eugene: Wipf and Stock, 2000.

Alvarez, Sonia E., et al., editors. "Introduction: The Cultural and the Political in Latin American Social Movements." In *Cultures of Politics—Politics of Cultures: Re-visioning Latin American Social Movements*, 1–29. Boulder: Westview, 1998.

Alves, Rubem A. *O enigma da religião*. São Paulo: Papirus, 2006.

———. *Protestantism and Repression*. London: SCM, 1979.

———. *A Theology of Human Hope*. Washington: Corpus, 1969.

Amaral, Nelson Cardoso, "Projeções para o financiamento da expansão das IFES no contexto de um novo PNE 2011–2021." S.l., s.d., http://www.observatoriodaeducacao.org.br/images/pdfs/estudo_nelson_3.pdf (accessed on 10/19/2011).

Andrade, Claudionor. *Lições Bíblicas: Mestre. As Disciplinas da Vida Cristã: trabalhando em busca da perfeição*. Rio de Janeiro: CPAD, 2008.

———. *Lições Bíblicas: Não terás outros deuses diante de mim.* Rio de Janeiro: CPAD, 2000.

Andreola, Balduino A., and Ribeiro, Mário Bueno. *Andarilho da esperança: Paulo Freire no Conselho Mundial de Igrejas.* São Paulo: ASTE, 2005.

ANIS [Instituto de Bioética, Direitos Humanos e Gênero]. *Anencefalia: o pensamento brasileiro em sua pluralidade.* Brasília: ANIS, 2004.

Anjos, Márcio Fabri dos. "Teologia e ciências da religião no Brasil—Balanço prospectivo da *Soter* (1985–2005)." In *Teologia e sociedade: relevância e funções.* São Paulo: Paulinas, 2006, 477–91.

Ankersmit, Frank R., and Henk Te Velde, editors. *Trust: Cement of Democracy?* Leuven: Peeters, 2004.

Antoine, Charles. *Church and Power in Brazil.* London: Sheed and Ward, 1973.

Antoniazzi, Alberto. "Igreja e democracia—enfoque histórico." In CNBB *Sociedade, Igreja e Democracia,* 97–112 São Paulo: Loyola, 1989"

———,editor. *Nem Anjos nem Demônios: interpretações sociológicas do pentecostalismo.* Petrópolis:Vozes, 1994.

Antoniazzi, Alberto, and Cleto Caliman, editors. *A presença da Igreja na cidade.* Petrópolis: Vozes, 1994.

Araújo, Isael de. *Dicionário do Movimento Pentecostal.* Rio de Janeiro: CPAD, 2007.

Araújo, João Dias de. "Igrejas Protestantes e Estado no Brasil." *Cadernos do ISER* 7 (1977) 23–31.

———. *Inquisição sem fogueiras.* Rio de Janeiro: ISER, 1978.

Arrington, French L. "Dispensationalism." In *The New International Dictionary of Pentecostal and Charismatic Movements,* edited by Stanley M. Burgess and Eduard M. van der Maas, 584–86. Grand Rapids: Zondervan, 2002.

Assmann, Hugo. *Paradigmas educacionais e corporeidade.* Piracicaba: Unimep, 1993.

———. "Por uma teologia humanamente saudável: fragmentos de memória pessoal." In *O mar se abriu: trinta anos de teologia na América Latina,* 115–30. Porto Alegre: SOTER; São Paulo: Loyola, 2000.

———. "Teologia da Solidariedade e da Cidadania. Ou seja: continuando a Teologia da Libertação." In *Crítica à Lógica da Exclusão,* 13–36. São Paulo: Paulus, 1994.

———. *Teología desde la praxis de la liberación.* Salamanca: Sígueme, 1973.

———. *Theology for a Nomad Church.* Maryknoll: Orbis, 1976.

Assmann, Hugo, and Franz J. Hinkelammert. *A idolatria do mercado: ensaio sobre economia e teologia.* Petrópolis: Vozes, 1986.

Assmann, Hugo, and Jung Mo Sung. *Competência e sensibilidade solidária.* Petrópolis: Vozes, 2000.

Assmann, Jan. *Herrschaft und Heil: politische Theologie in Altägypten, Israel und Europa.* München: Hanser, 2000.

Audi, Richard, and Nicholas Wolterstorff. *Religion in the Public Square: The Place of Religious Convictions in Political Debate.* Lanham: Rowman & Littlefield, 1997.

Augustinus. *Vom Gottestaat.* München: Deutscher Taschenbuch-Verlag, 1997.

Avritzer, Leonardo. *Democracy and the Public Space.* Princeton: Princeton University Press, 2002.

———. "Modelos de sociedade civil: uma análise da especificidade do caso brasileiro." In *Sociedade civil e democratização,* 269–308. Belo Horizonte: UFMG, 1994.

Avritzer, Leonardo, and José Maurício Domingues, editors. *Teoria social e modernidade no Brasil.* Belo Horizonte: Editora UFMG, 2000.

Azevedo, Dermi. "A Igreja Católica e seu papel político no Brasil." *Estudos Avançados* 18/52 (2004) 109–20.

Azevedo, Marcello de C. *Basic Ecclesial Communities in Brazil: The Challenge of a New Way of Being Church.* Washington: Georgetown University Press, 1987.

Azevedo, Marta Maria, "Diagnóstico da população indígena no Brasil."*Ciência e Cultura* 60/4 (2008) 18–22.

Azevedo, Thales de. *A religião civil brasileira: um instrumento politico.* Petrópolis: Vozes, 1981.

Azzi, Riolando. *A neocristandade— um projeto restaurador.* História do pensamento católico no Brasil vol. 5. São Paulo: Paulus, 1994.

Bachmann, E. Theodore, and Mercia Brenne Bachmann. *Lutheran Churches in the World: A Handbook.* Minneapolis: Augsburg, 1989.

Bacote, Vincent E. *The Spirit in Public Theology.* Grand Rapids: Baker, 2005.

Baer, Werner. *The Brazilian Economy: Growth and Development.* Westport: Praeger, 2001.

Baldisseri, Dom Lorenzo. *O acordo entre a Santa Sé e o Brasil assinado em 13.11.2008, aula inaugural do Mestrado em Teologia.* Curitiba: PUC-PR, 2009.

Baptista, Saulo de Tarso Cerqueira. "Cultura política brasileira, práticas pentecostais e neopentecostais: a presença da Assembléia de Deus e da Igreja Universal do Reino de Deus no Congresso Nacional (1999–2006)." PhD diss., Universidade Metodista de São Paulo, 2007.

Barbé, Dominique. *Grace and Power: Base Communities and Nonviolence in Brazil.* Maryknoll: Orbis, 1987.

Barcellos, Caco. *Rota 66: A história da polícia que mata* [2003]. Rio de Janeiro: Record, 2005.

Barros, Raimundo Caramuru. "Gênese e consolidação da CNBB no contexto de uma Igreja em plena renovação." Instituto Nacional de Pastoral, editor, *Presença Pública da Igreja no Brasil*, 13-69, Sâo Paulo: Paulinas, 2003.

———. "Sinais de esperança no processo histórico brasileiro." In CNBB, *Leigos e participação na Igreja*, 37-51, São Paulo: Paulinas, 1989.

Barth, Hans-Martin. *Einander Priester sein: Allgemeines Priestertum in ökumenischer Perspektive*. Göttingen: Vandenhoeck & Ruprecht, 1990.

Barth, Karl. "Christengemeinde und Bürgergemeinde." In *Rechtfertigung und Recht. Christengemeinde und Bürgergemeinde*, 49–82. Zürich: EVZ, 1970.

———. "Grundfragen der christlichen Sozialethik. Auseinandersetzung mit Paul Althaus." In *Anfänge der dialektischen Theologie*, part I, edited by Jürgen Moltmann, 152–65. München: Chr. Kaiser, 1974.

———. *Die kirchliche Dogmatik IV,1, Studienausgabe v. 23*. Zürich: Theologischer Verlag Zürich, 1986.

———. "Rechtfertigung und Recht." In *Rechtfertigung und Recht. Christengemeinde und Bürgergemeinde*, 5–48. Zürich: EVZ, 1970.

Bastian, Jean-Pierre. *Geschichte des Protestantismus in Lateinamerika*. Luzern: Exodus, 1995.

Batstone, David, et al., editors. *Liberation Theologies, Postmodernity, and the Americas*. London/New York: Routledge, 1997.

Bauckham, Richard. "Chiliasmus IV." In *Theologische Realenzyklopädie* 7, 737–45. Berlin: Walter de Gruyter, 1981.

Baum, Gregory. "Lutherische Theologie des Widerstandes heute." In *Luther zwischen den Kulturen*, edited by Hans Medick and Peer Schmidt, 530–42. Göttingen: Vandenhoeck & Ruprecht, 2004.

Bedford-Strohm, Heinrich. *Gemeinschaft aus kommunikativer Freiheit. Sozialer Zusammenhalt in der modernen Gesellschaft. Ein theologischer Beitrag*. Gütersloh: Gütersloher Verlagshaus, 1999.

———. *Schöpfung*. Göttingen: Vandenhoeck & Ruprecht, 2001.

———. *Vorrang für die Armen. Auf dem Weg zu einer theologischen Theorie der Gerechtigkeit*. Gütersloh: Chr. Kaiser, Gütersloher Verlagshaus, 1993.

Bellah, Robert N. "Civil Religion in America." In *Beyond Belief: Essays on Religion in a Post-Traditional World*, 168–89. Berkeley: University of California Press, 1991.

———. "Civil Religion: The American Case." In *Varieties of Civil Religion*, edited by Robert N. Bellah and Phillip E. Hammond, 3–24. San Francisco: Harper & Row, 1980.

Beloch, Israel, and Alzira Alves de Abreu, editors. *Dicionário histórico-biográfico brasileiro: 1930–1983*, vol. 2. Rio de Janeiro: Forense-Universitária, FGV/CPDOC, FINEP, 1984.

Bendix, Reinhard. *Nation-building and Citizenship: Studies of Our Changing Social Order*. New Brunswick: Transaction, 2005.

Benevides, Maria Victoria de Mesquita. *A cidadania ativa: referendo, plebiscito e iniciativa popular*. São Paulo: Ática, 2003.

———. "Cidadania e democracia." *Lua Nova* 33 (1994) 5–16.

Bento, Fábio Régio. "Cristianismo e democracia: da soberania dos "pastores" à soberania das ovelhas." In Fábio Bento Régio, editor, *Cristianismo, humanismo e democracia*. São Paulo: Paulus, 2005, 17-47.

———. *Cristianismo, humanismo e democracia*. São Paulo: Paulus, 2005.

Berger, Peter, editor. *The Desecularization of the World: Resurgent Religion and World Politics*. Washington: Ethics and Public Policy Center; Grand Rapids: Eerdmans, 1999.

———. "Religion and Global Civil Society." In *Religion in Global Civil Society*, edited by Mark Juergensmeyer, 11–22. New York, Oxford University Press, 2005.

Bernhardt, Reinhold. "Love like Jesus and fight like David. Religiöse Dimensionen in der politischen Kultur der USA." In *Politische Religion*, edited by Georg Pfleiderer and Ekkehard W. Stegeman, 265–87. Zürich: TVZ, 2004.

Bernhardt, Reinhold, and Perry Schmidt-Leukel, editors. *Multiple religiöse Identität: aus verschiedenen religiösen Traditionen schöpfen*. Zürich: TVZ, 2008.

Betto, Frei [Carlos Alberto Libânio Christo]. *Calendário do poder*. Rio de Janeiro: Rocco, 2007.

———. *A mosca azul*. Rio de Janeiro: Rocco, 2006.

Bevans, Stephen B., and Peter Schroeder. *Constants in Context: a Theology of Mission for Today*. Maryknoll: Orbis, 2004.

Biehl, João. "Pharmaceutical Governance." In *Global Pharmaceuticals: Ethics, Markets, Practices*, edited by Adriana Petryna, et al., 206–39. Durham and London: Duke University Press, 2006.

———. *Vita. Life in a Zone of Social Abandonment*. Berkeley: University of California Press, 2005.

———. *Will to Live: Aids Therapies and the Politics of Survival*. Princeton: Princeton University Press, 2007.

Bill, M.V., and Celso Athayde. *Falcão: meninos do tráfico*. Rio de Janeiro: Objetiva, 2006.

Birle, Peter. "Zivilgesellschaft in Südamerika—Mythos und Realität." In *Systemwechsel 5. Zivilgesellschaft und Transformation*, edited by Wolfgang Merkel, 231-71. Opladen: Leske & Budrich, 2000.

Birman, Patricia, editor. *Religião e espaço público*. São Paulo: Attar, 2003.

Bitterli, Urs. *Die 'Wilden' und die 'Zivilisierten'. Grundzüge einer Geistes- und Kulturgeschichte der europäisch-überseeischen Begegnung*. München: C.H. Beck, 1991.

Blaser, Klauspeter. *La theólogie au XXe siècle: histoires—défis—enjeux*. Lausanne: L'Age d'Homme, 1995.

Bobbio, Norberto. *A era dos direitos*. Rio de Janeiro: Campus, 1992. [English edition: *The Age of Rights*, Cambridge: Polity, 1991].

———. "Gramsci and the Concept of Civil Society." In *Civil Society and the State*, edited by John Keane, 73-99. London, New York: Verso, 1988.

———. "Sociedade Civil." In *Dicionário de política*, edited by Norberto Bobbio, Nicola Matteucci, and Gianfranco Pasquino, 1206–11. Brasília: Editora Universidade de Brasília, 1986.

Bobbio, Norberto, Nicola Matteucci and Gianfranco Pasquino, editors. *Dicionário de política*. Brasília: Editora Universidade de Brasília; São Paulo: Imprensa Oficial, CD-ROM, 2003.

Bobsin, Oneide. "Fuga do 'mundo' e participação popular." *CECA—Informação, Formação, Experiência* 1/3 (1989) 33–40.

———. "Luteranos em casa, na igreja e na política." *Estudos Teológicos* 41/1 (2001) 37–56.

Bobsin, Oneide, et al. "Sociabilidade juvenil: Contexto religioso e sua inserção social." *Protestantismo em revista* 3/3 (2004) 55-81. Online: http://www3.est.edu.br/nepp/revista/005/ano03n3_05.pdf.

Bock, Carlos G. "Teologia em mosáico: o novo cenário teológico latino-americano nos anos 90." PhD diss., IEPG/EST, 2002.

Böckenförde, Ernst-Wolfgang. "Die Entstehung des Staates als Vorgang der Säkularisation." In *Kirche und christlicher Glaube in den Herausforderungen der Zeit: Beiträge zur politisch-theologischen Verfassungsgeschichte 1957–2002*, 213–230. Münster: LIT, 2004.

Boff, Clodovis. "Bases teológicas do ideal democrático—primeiras colocações." CNBB, *Sociedade, Igreja e Democracia*, 113-38, São Paulo: Loyola, 1989.

———. "Epistemology and Method of the Theology of Liberation." *Ellacuría and Sobrino* (1993) 57–85.

———. "Fé cristã e democracia." In *Cristianismo, humanismo e democracia*, edited by Fábio Régio Bento, 77-105. São Paulo: Paulus, 2005.

———. *Teoria do método teológico*. Petrópolis: Vozes, 1998.

———. "Die Theologie der Befreiung und die Krise unserer Tage." In *Brasilien: Land der Zukunft?* edited by Rafael Sevilla and Darcy Ribeiro, 214–29. Unkel, Rhein/Bad Honnef: Horlemann, 1995.

———. *Theology and Praxis: Epistemological Foundations*. Maryknoll: Orbis, 1987.

Boff, Clodovis, et al. *Cristãos: como fazer política*. Petrópolis: Vozes, 1987.

Boff, Leonardo. "CEBs: Que significa 'novo modo de toda a Igreja ser'?" *Revista Eclesiástica Brasileira* 49/195 (1989) 546–62.

———. "The Contribution of Brazilian Ecclesiology to the Universal Church." *Concilium* (2002/3) 78–83.

———. *Cry of the Poor, Cry of the Earth*. Maryknoll: Orbis, 1997.

———. *Ecclesiogenesis: The Base Communities Reinvent the Church*. Maryknoll: Orbis, 1986.

———. *Ecology and Liberation: A New Paradigm*. Maryknoll: Orbis, 1995.

———. *Ética e eco-espiritualidade*, Campinas: Verus, 2003.

———. *Faith on the Edge: Religion and Marginalized Existence*. Maryknoll: Orbis, 1991.

———. *Igreja, charisma e poder: ensaios de uma eclesiologia militante*. Rio de Janeiro: Record, 2005. [English edition: *Church, Charism and Power: Liberation Theology and the Institutional Church*. New York: Crossroad, 1986]

———. *The Maternal Face of God: The Feminine and its Religious Expressions*. San Francisco: Harper and Row, 1987.

———. *Princípio de compaixão e cuidado*, with the collaboration of Werner Muller. 3rd edn. Petrópolis: Vozes, 2001

———. *Saber cuidar: ética do humano—compaixão pela terra*. Petrópolis: Vozes, 1999.

———. *Teologia à escuta do povo*. Petrópolis: Vozes, 1981.

———. *Trinity and Society*. Tunbridge Wells, Burns & Oates, 1988.

———. "Um balanço de corpo e alma." In *O que ficou. Balanço aos 50*, edited by Leonardo Boff, et al. Petrópolis: Vozes, 1989.

———. *Vida Segundo o Espírito*. Petrópolis: Vozes, 1995.

———. *Virtudes para um outro mundo possível*, 3 vols. Petrópolis: Vozes, 2006.

Boff, Leonardo, and Clodovis Boff. *Introducing Liberation Theology*. Maryknoll: Orbis, 1987.

Bohn, Simone R. "Evangélicos no Brasil. Perfil socioeconômico, afinidades ideológicas e determinantes do comportamento eleitoral." *Opinião Pública* 10/2 (2004) 288–338.

Bonavides, Paulo. *Curso de direito constitucional*. São Paulo: Malheiros, 2008.

Bonavides, Paulo, and Paes de Andrade. *História constitucional do Brasil*. São Paulo: Paz e Terra, 1991.

Bonhoeffer, Dietrich. *Letters and Papers from Prison*. London: SCM, 1971.

Book of Concord, The. *The Confessions of the Evangelical Lutheran Church*, edited by Robert Kolb and Timothy J. Wengert. Minneapolis: Fortress, 2000.

Boschi, Renato. "Social Movements and the New Political Order in Brazil." In *State and Society in Brazil*, edited by John D. Wirth, et al., 179–211. Boulder: Westview, 1987.

Botman, H. Russel. "Theology After Apartheid: Paradigms and Progress in South African Public Theologies." In *Theology in the Service of the Church, essays in Honor of Thomas W. Gillespie,* edited by Wallace M. Alston, Jr., 36–51. Grand Rapids: Eerdmans, 2000),

Bourdieu, Pierre. *A economia das trocas simbólicas,* edited by Sérgio Miceli. São Paulo: Perspectiva, 1974.

Boxer, Charles R. *The Portuguese Seaborne Empire 1415–1825.* Manchester: Carcanet, 1991.

Brakemeier, Gottfried. "Justification by Grace and Liberation Theology: a Comparison." *The Ecumenical Review* 40/2 (1988) 215–22.

———. "Pobres e pecadores na ótica de Jesus." *Estudos Teológicos* 25/1 (1985) 13–63.

———. *Por Paz e Justiça: manifestos da presidência da Igreja Evangélica de Confissão Luterana no Brasil, 1986–1994.* Blumenau: Otto Kuhr, 1997.

———. *O ser humano em busca de identidade: contribuições para uma antropologia teológica.* São Leopoldo: Sinodal; São Paulo: Paulus, 2002.

Brandt, Hermann. "Befreiungstheologie nach der Wende." *Theologische Literaturzeitung* 124/10 (1999) 963–78.

———. "As ciências da religião numa perspectiva intercultural: a percepção oposta da fenomenologia da religião no Brasil e na Alemanha." *Estudos Teológicos* 46/1 (2006) 122–51. [German version: 'Religionswissenschaft interkulturell: die gegensätzliche Wahrnehmung der Religionsphänomenologie in Brasilien um Deutschland', in *Theologische Literaturzeitung* 132 (2007), 611–30.]

———. "Die Evangelische Kirche lutherischen Bekenntnisses in Brasilien (EKLB) und die Feiern zum 150. Jahrestag der Unabhängigkeit Brasiliens am 7. September 1972." *Zeitschrift für Evangelische Ethik* 17/1 (1973) 43–49.

———. *Die heilige Barbara in Brasilien: Kulturtransfer und Synkretismus.* Erlangen: Universitätsverbund Erlangen-Nürnberg, 2003.

———. "In der Nachfolge der Inkarnation oder: Das 'Auftauchen' Gottes in Lateinamerika. Zum Verhältnis von Befreiungspädagogik und Befreiungstheologie." *Zeitschrift für Theologie und Kirche* 78 (1981) 367–89.

Branford, Sue, and Jan Rocha. *Cutting the Wire. The Story of the Landless Movement in Brazil.* London: Latin America Bureau, 2002.

Branford, Sue, and Bernardo Kucinski. *Lula and the Workers' Party in Brazil: Politics Transformed.* London: Latin America Bureau, 2003.

Brasil. *Código Penal.* In *Código penal, Código de Processo penal, Constituição Federal,* 2nd ed. edited by Anne Joyce Angher, 281-404. São Paulo: Rideel, 2002.

———. *Constituição da República Federativa do Brasil,* de 5 de outubro de 1988, edited by Alexandre de Moraes, 28th ed. São Paulo: Atlas, 2007.

———. *LDB: Lei de Diretrizes e Bases da Educação.* Lei 9.394/96. Edited by by Antonio de Paulo and presented by Carlos Roberto Jamil Cury, 9th ed. Rio de Janeiro: DP&A, 2005.

Brasil: Nunca Mais! Petrópolis: Vozes, 1995.

Brasileiro, Roberto. "*IPB manifesta-se a respeito das leis sobre o aborto e a homofobia.*" Online: http://www.ipb.org.br/noticias/noticia_inteligente.php3? id=808.

Brazil: Dilemmas and Challenges. São Paulo: EDUSP, Instituto de Estudos Avançados, 2002.

Breitenberg, E. Harold, Jr. "To Tell the Truth: Will the Real Public Theology Please Stand Up?" *Journal of the Society of Christian Ethics* 23/2 (2003) 55–96.

Briesemeister, Dietrich, et al, editors. *Brasilien heute: Politik, Wirtschaft, Kultur.* Frankfurt a. M.: Vervuert, 1994.

Brighenti, Agenor. "Pessoa—comunidade—sociedade: o trinômio da realização da vocação humana e cristã." In *Cristianismo, humanismo e democracia,* edited by Fábio Régio Bento, 145-71. São Paulo: Paulus, 2005.

Brinkman, Martien E., and Dirk van Keulen, editors. *Christian Identity in Cross-Cultural Perspective.* Zoetermeer: Meinema, 2003.

Bruneau, Thomas. "The Catholic Church in the Redemocratization of Brazil." In *The Politics of Religion and Social Change,* edited by Anson Shupe and Jeffrey K. Hadden, 87–109. New York: Paragon, 1988.

———. *The Church in Brazil: The Politics of Religion.* Austin: University of Texas, 1982.

———. *The Political Transformation of the Brazilian Catholic Church.* Cambridge: Cambridge University Press, 1974.

Bruneau, Thomas, and W. E. Hewitt. "Patterns of Church Influence in Brazil's Political Transition." *Comparative Politics* 22/1 (1989) 39–61.

Brunkhorst, Hauke, and Sérgio Costa, editors. *Jenseits von Zentrum und Peripherie: Zur Verfassung der fragmentierten Weltgesellschaft.* München/Mering: Rainer Hampp Verlag, 2005.

Buffa, Ester, Miguel Arroyo and Paolo Nosella. *Educação e cidadania: quem educa o cidadão?* São Paulo: Cortez, 2007.

Burdick, John. "Das Erbe der Befreiung: Fortschrittlicher Katholizismus in Brasilien." In *Religion und Macht, Jahrbuch Lateinamerika Analysen und Berichte 26,* edited by Karin Gabbert, et al., 13–35. Münster: Westfälisches Dampfboot, 2002.

———. *Legacies of Liberation: The Progressive Catholic Church in Brazil at the Start of a New Millennium,* Aldershot: Ashgate, 2004.

———. *Looking for God in Brazil: The Progressive Catholic Church in Urban Brazil's Religious Arena.* Berkeley: University of California Press, 1993.

Burger, Germano, editor. *Quem assume esta tarefa? Um documentário de uma igreja em busca de sua identidade.* São Leopoldo: Sinodal, 1977.

Burgess, Stanley M., and Eduard M. van der Maas, editors. *The New International Dictionary of Pentecostal and Charismatic Movements.* Grand Rapids: Zondervan, 2002.

Burity, Joanildo A. "Os protestantes e a revolução brasileira: a Conferência do Nordeste (1961–1964)." Master's thesis, Universidade Federal de Pernambuco, Ciência Política, 1989. Online: http://www.fundaj.gov.br/geral/textos%20 online/ciencia%20politica/ jburity11.pdf.

———. "Radical Religion and the constitution of new political actors in Brazil: the experience of the 1980s." PhD diss., University of Essex, 1994.

———. *Redes, parcerias e participação religiosa nas politicas sociais no Brasil.* Recife: Fundação Joaquim Nabuco/Editora Massangana, 2006.

———. "Religião e cultura cívica: onde os caminhos se cruzam?" *Política hoje* 7/11 (2001) 199–234.

———. "Religião, política e cultura." *Tempo Social* 20/2 (2008) 83–113.

———. "Religião, voto e instituições políticas: notas sobre os evangélicos nas eleições 2002." In *Os votos de Deus: evangélicos, política e eleições no Brasil,* edited by Joanildo A Burity and Maria das Dores C. Machado, 173–213. Recife: Fundação Joaquim Nabuco/Editora Massangana, 2005.

Burity, Joanildo, and Maria das Dores C. Machado, editors. *Os votos de Deus: evangélicos, política e eleições no Brasil,* Recife: Fundação Joaquim Nabuco/Editora Massangana, 2005.

Cabral, Elienai. *Lições bíblicas: Mordomia cristã: servindo a Deus com excelência.* Rio de Janeiro: CPAD, 2003.

Cady, Linell. "H. Richard Niebuhr and the Task of a Public Theology." In *The Legacy of H. Richard Niebuhr*, edited by Ronald F. Thiemann, 119-126. Minneapolis: Fortress, 1991.

Caldeira, Teresa P. R. *City of Walls: Crime, Segregation, and Citizenship in São Paulo.* Berkeley: University of California Press, 2000.

Campos, Leonildo Silveira. "Historischer Protestantismus und Pfingstbewegung in Brasilien: Annäherungen und Konflikte." *Zeitschrift für Missionswissenschaft und Religionswissenschaft* 81 (1997) 202–43.

———. *Teatro, Templo e Mercado.* Petrópolis: Vozes; São Paulo: Ciências da Religião, 1999.

Canclini, Nestor García. *Hybrid cultures: strategies for entering and leaving modernity.* Minneapolis: University of Minnesota Press, 1995.

Canêdo, Letícia Bicalho. "Aprendendo a votar." In *História da Cidadania*, edited by Jaime Pinsky and Carla Bassanezi Pinsky, 517-43. São Paulo: Contexto, 2003.

Cardoso, Fernando Henrique. *A arte da política. A história que vivi.* Rio de Janeiro: Civilização Brasileira, 2006.

Cardoso, Fernando Henrique, and Enzo Faletto. *Dependência e desenvolvimento na América Latina: Ensaio de interpretação sociológica.* Rio de Janeiro: Zahar, 1967. [English edition: *Dependency and Development in Latin América*, Berkeley: University of California Press, 1979].

Carneiro, Leandro Piquet. "Cultura Cívica e participação política entre evangélicos." In *Novo nascimento: os evangélicos em casa, na igreja e na política*, edited by . Rubem César Fernandes et al., 181-210. Rio de Janeiro: Mauad, 1998. [English edition: 'The Church as a Political Context: Civil Culture and Political Participation Among Protestants', paper prepared for the LASA XX International Congress, Guadalajara, Mexico, April 1997. Online: http://136.142.158.105/LASA97/carneiroeng.pdf.]

Carranza, Brenda. "Catolicismo midiático." In *As religões no Brasil: continuidades e rupturas*, edited by Faustino Teixeira and Renata Menezes, 69-87. Petrópolis: Vozes, 2006.

———. *Renovação carismática católica: origens, mudanças e tendências.* Aparecida: Santuário, 2000.

Carter, Miguel. "The Landless Rural Workers Movement & the Struggle for Social Justice in Brazil." In *Rural Social Movements in Latin America: Organizing For Sustainable Livelihoods,* edited by Carmen Diana Deere and Fred Royce. Forthcoming.

Carvalho, José Murilo de. *Cidadania no Brasil. O longo caminho.* Rio de Janeiro: Civilização Brasileira, 2001.

———. "Interesses contra a cidadania." In *Brasileiro: cidadão?* edited by Roberto DaMatta, et al., 87–125. São Paulo: Cultura, 1992.

Casanova, José. "Civil society and religion: retrospective reflections on Catholicism and prospective reflections on Islam." *Social Research* 68/4 (2001) 1041-80. Online: http://findarticles.com/p/articles/mi_m2267/is_4_68/ai_83144759.

———. *Public Religions in the Modern World.* Chicago: University of Chicago Press, 1994.

Castro, Clovis Pinto de. *Por uma fé cidadã. A dimensão pública da igreja. Fundamentos para uma pastoral da cidadania.* São Bernardo do Campo: Ciências da Religião / São Paulo: Loyola, 2000.

Cavalcante, Ronaldo, and Rudolf von Sinner, eds. *Teologia pública em debate,* São Leopoldo: Sinodal, 2011.

Cavalcanti, H. B. "Political Cooperation and Religious Repression: Presbyterians under Military Rule in Brazil (1964–1975)." *Review of Religious Research* 34/2 (1992) 97–116.

Cavalcanti, Robinson. *Cristianismo e política.* Viçosa: Ultimato, 2004.

CEDI [Centro Ecumênico de Documentação e Informação]. *Repression against the Church in Brazil (1968–1978).* Rio de Janeiro: CEDI, 1978. Manuscript.

CELAM [Conselho Episcopal Latino-Americano]. *Documento de Aparecida. Texto conclusivo da V Conferência Geral do Episcopado Latino-Americano e do Caribe, 13–31 de maio de 2007.* Brasília: CNBB; São Paulo: Paulus, Paulinas, 2007.

CERIS [Centro de Estatística Religiosa e Investigações Sociais]. *Anuário Católico 2003,* Rio de Janeiro: CERIS, 2003.

———. *Desafios do catolicismo na cidade: pesquisa em regiões metropolitanas brasileiras.* São Paulo: Paulus, 2002.

César, Waldo. "Church and Society—Or Society and Church?" In *Revolution of Spirit: Ecumenical Theology in Global Context, Essays in Honour of Richard Shaull,* edited by Nantawan Boonprasat Lewis, 133–48. Grand Rapids: Eerdmans, 1998.

CESE [Coordenadoria Ecumênica de Serviço]. *Declaração universal dos direitos humanos,* 5th edition. Salvador: CESE, 2000.

Chauí, Marilena. *Brasil: mito fundador e sociedade autoritária.* São Paulo: Fundação Perseu Abramo, 2000.

———. "Raízes teológicas do populismo no Brasil: teocracia dos dominantes, messianismo dos dominados." In *Anos 90: política e sociedade no Brasil,* edited by Evelina Dagnino, 19-30. São Paulo: Brasiliense, 1994.

Chauí, Marilena, et al. *Leituras da crise: diálogos sobre o PT e a democracia brasileira.* São Paulo: Perseu Abramo, 2006.

Chesnut, R. Andrew. *Born Again in Brazil: The Pentecostal Boom and the Pathogens of Poverty.* New Brunswick: Rutgers University Press, 1997.

———. *Competitive Spirits: Latin America's New Religious Economy.* Oxford, New York: Oxford University Press, 2003.

———. "A Preferential Option for the Spirit: The Catholic Charismatic Renewal in Latin America's New Religious Economy." *Latin American Politics and Society* 45/1 (2003) 55–85.

———. "The Salvation Army or the Army's Salvation? Pentecostal Politics in Amazonian Brazil 1962–1992." *Luso-Brazilian Review* 36/2 (1999) 33–49.

Christmann, Nilo O. "A prática do perdão em uma igreja identificada com a teologia da graça." Unpublished course monograph. São Leopoldo: EST, 2007.

Címaco, J. Armando. *Um grito pela vida da igreja.* Rio de Janeiro: CPAD, 1996.

Cleary, Edward L. "The Brazilian Church and Church-State Relations: Nation-Building." *Journal of Church and State* 39 (1997) 253–72.

Cleary, Edward L., and Hannah W. Stewart-Gambino, editors. *Power, Politics, and Pentecostals in Latin America.* Boulder: Westview, 1997.

Cloete, G.D., and D.J. Smit, editors. *A Moment of Truth: The Confession of the Dutch Reformed Mission Church 1982.* Grand Rapids: Eerdmans, 1984.

CNBB [Conferência Nacional dos Bispos do Brasil]. *Campanha da Fraternidade: vinte anos de serviço à missão da Igreja.* São Paulo: Paulinas, Estudos da CNBB 35, 1983.

———. *15º Plano Bienal de Atividades do Secretariado Nacional,* 2000–2001, 1999. Online: http://www.cnbb.org.br.

———. *Diretrizes gerais da ação evangelizadora da Igreja no Brasil.* Documentos da CNBB 71, 2003. Online: http://www.cnbb.org.br.

———. *Eleições 2006, orientações da CNBB.* Brasília: CNBB, 2006.

———. *Ética: pessoa e sociedade.* São Paulo: Paulinas, Documentos da CNBB 50, 1993.

———. *Exigências cristãs de uma ordem política,* 1977. Online: http://www.cnbb.org.br.

———. *Exigências éticas da ordem democrática.* São Paulo: Paulinas, Documentos da CNBB 42, 1989.

———. *Exigências evangélicas e éticas de superação da miséria e da fome.* São Paulo: Paulinas, Documentos da CNBB 69, 2002.

———. *Igreja, comunhão e missão na evangelização dos povos, no mundo do trabalho, da política e da cultura.* Documentos da CNBB 40, 1988. Online: http://www.cnbb.org.br.

———. *Leigos e participação na Igreja: reflexão sobre a caminhada da Igreja no Brasil.* São Paulo: Paulinas, Estudos da CNBB 45, 1986.

———. *Orientações pastorais sobre a renovação carismática.* São Paulo: Paulinas, Documentos da CNBB 55, 1994.

———. *Participação popular e cidadania: a igreja no processo constituinte.* São Paulo: Paulinas, Estudos da CNBB 60, 1990.

———. *Pastoral Afro-Brasileira.* São Paulo: Paulus, Estudos da CNBB 85, 2002.

———. *Pastoral da Terra: posse e conflitos.* São Paulo: Paulinas, Estudos da CNBB 13, 1981.

———. *Por uma nova ordem constitucional.* Documentos da CNBB 36, 1986. Online: http://www.cnbb.org.br.

———. *Rumo ao Novo Milênio: projeto de evangelização da Igreja no Brasil em preparação do grande jubileu do ano 2000.* São Paulo: Paulinas, Documentos da CNBB 56, 1996.

———. *Sociedade, Igreja e Democracia.* São Paulo: Loyola, 1989.

Codato, Adriano Nervo, editor. *Political Transition and Democratic Consolidation: Studies on Contemporary Brazil.* New York: Nova Science, 2006.

Cohen, Jean L., and Andrew Arato. *Civil Society and Political Theory.* Cambridge: MIT Press, 1999.

Comblin, José. *Called For Freedom: The Changing Context of Liberation Theology.* Maryknoll: Orbis, 1998.

———. *The Church and the National Security State.* Maryknoll: Orbis, 1979.

———. *Viver na cidade: pistas para a pastoral urbana.* São Paulo: Paulus, 1991.

Comissão Pastoral da Terra. *Os pobres possuirão a terra (Sl 37,11). Pronunciamento de bispos e pastores sinodais sobre a terra.* São Leopoldo: Sinodal; CEBI; São Paulo: Paulinas, 2006.

Commission on Faith and Order. *The Nature and Mission of the Church: A Stage on the Way to a Common Statement.* Geneva: WCC, 2005.

———. *A Treasure in Earthen Vessels.* Geneva: WCC, 1998.

Comparato, Fábio Konder. *Ética: direito, moral e religião no mundo moderno.* São Paulo: Companhia das Letras, 2006.

Congregation for the Doctrine of Faith. *Doctrinal Note on some questions regarding The Participation of Catholics in Political Life,* 2002. Online: http://www.vatican.va/roman_curia/ congregations/cfaith/documents/rc_con_cfaith_doc_20021124_politica_en.html.

———. *Donum Vitae: Instruction on Respect for Human Life in its Origin and on the Dignity of Procreation—Replies to Certain Questions of the Day,* 1987. Online: http://www.vatican.va/roman_curia/congregations/cfaith/ documents/rc_con_cfaith_doc_19870222_respect-for-human-life_en.html.

———. *Explanatory Note on the Notification on the Works of Father Jon Sobrino, S.J.,* 2006. Online: http://www.vatican.va/roman_curia/congregations/cfaith/documents/ rc_ con_cfaith_doc_20061126_nota-sobrino_en.html.

———. *Liberatis Conscientiae: Instruction on Christian Freedom and Liberation,* 1987. Online: http://www.vatican.va/roman_curia/congregations/ cfaith/ documents/rc_con_cfaith_doc_19860322_freedom-liberation_en.html.

———. *Libertatis Nuntius: Instruction on Certain Aspects of the "Theology of Liberation."* 1984. Online: http://www.vatican.va/roman_curia/congregations/cfaith/documents/rc_co_cfaith_doc_19840806_theology-liberation_en.html.

———. *Notification on the works of Father Jon Sobrino, SJ: Jesuscristo libertador, Lectura histórico-teológica de Jesús de Nazaret* and *La fe en Jesucristo. Ensayo desde las víctimas,* 2006. Online: http://www.vatican.va/ roman_curia/congregations/cfaith/documents/rc_con_cfaith_doc_20061126_notification-sobrino_en.html.

Corrêa, Darcísio. *A construção da cidadania: reflexões histórico-políticas.* Ijuí: Unijuí, 2006.

Correia Júnior, João Luiz, and José Raimundo Oliva, editors. *Bíblia e cidadania.* Petrópolis: Vozes, 2003.

Corten, André. *Pentecostalism in Brazil: Emotion of the Poor and Theological Romanticism.* New York: St. Martin's Press, 1999.

Costa, Sérgio. "Atores da sociedade civil e participação política: algumas restrições." *Cadernos do CEAS* 155 (1995) 61–75.

———. *As cores de Ercília: esfera pública, democracia, configurações pós-nacionais.* Belo Horizonte: Editora UFMG, 2002.

———. "Menschenrechte weltweit. Politisches Handeln jenseits neokolonialer Dualismen." In *Zwischen Kontakt und Konflikt: Perspektiven der Postkolonialismus-Forschung,* edited by Gisela Febel, 63–80. Trier: Wissenschaftlicher Verlag Trier, 2007.

———. *Vom Nordatlantik zum "Black Atlantic". Postkoloniale Konfigurationen und Paradoxien transnationaler Politik.* Bielefeld: Transcript, 2007.

Coutinho, Amélia, and César Benjamim. "Geisel, Ernesto." In *Dicionário histórico-biográfico brasileiro: 1930–1983,* vol. 2. Rio de Janeiro: Forense-Universitária, FGV/CPDOC, FINEP, 1984, 1450–1459.

Coutinho, Carlos Nelson. *A democracia como valor universal e outros ensaios.* Rio de Janeiro: Salamandra, 1984.

Couto, Geremias do. *Lições Bíblicas: Igreja: projeto de Deus.* Rio de Janeiro: CPAD, 1998.

———. *Lições Bíblicas: Mestre. E agora, como viveremos?* Rio de Janeiro: CPAD, 2005.

Cox, Harvey G. *Fire from Heaven: The Rise of Pentecostal Spírituality and the Reshaping of Religion in the Twenty-First Century.* Cambridge: Da Capo Press, 2001.

Crane, Ed. "Civil society and theology—the challenge of concepts, thinking and action." In *Consultation on Theology and Civil Society: God's People in Civil Society—Ecclesiological Implications,* edited by Fritz Erich Anhelm, 89–104. Rehburg-Loccum: Evangelische Akademie Loccum, 1996.

Croissant, Aurel, Hans Joachim Lauth and Wolfgang Merkel. "Zivilgesellschaft und Transformation: ein internationaler Vergleich." In *Systemwechsel 5. Zivilgesellschaft und Transformation,* 9–49. Opladen: Leske & Budrich, 2000.

Cunha, Dilney. *Das Paradies in den Sümpfen.* Zürich: Limmat, 2003.

Dagnino, Evelina, editor. *Anos 90: política e sociedade no Brasil.* São Paulo: Brasiliense, 1994.

———. "Os movimentos sociais e a emergência de uma nova noção de cidadania." In *Anos 90: política e sociedade no Brasil.* São Paulo: Brasiliense, 1994, 103–15.

———. "Sociedade Civil, Espaços Públicos e a Construção Democrática no Brasil: Limites e Possibilidades." In *Sociedade Civil e Espaços Públicos no Brasil,* 279–301. São Paulo: Paz e Terra, 2002.

Dahl, Robert A. *Democracy and its Critics.* New Haven, London: Yale University Press, 1989.

Dahling-Sander, Christoph. *Zur Freiheit befreit: Das theologische Verständnis von Freiheit und Befreiung nach Martin Luther, Huldrych Zwingli, James H. Cone und Gustavo Gutiérrez.* Frankfurt a.M.: Lembeck, 2003.

Dalferth, Ingolf U. "Glaube 3. Systematisch-theologisch." In *Evangelisches Kirchenlexikon,* 193–202. Göttingen: Vandenhoeck & Ruprecht, 1989.

———. "Öffentlichkeit, Universität und Theologie." In *Wieviel Theologie verträgt die Öffentlichkeit?* edited by Edmund Arens, 38–71. Freiburg: Herder, 2000.

Dalferth, Silfredo Bernardo. *Die Zweireichelehre Martin Luthers im Dialog mit der Befreiungstheologie Leonardo Boffs: ein ökumenischer Beitrag zum Verhältnis von christlichem Glauben und gesellschaftlicher Verantwortung.* Frankfurt a.M.: Lang, 1996.

DaMatta, Roberto. *Carnivals, Rogues and Heroes: An Interpretation of the Brazilian Dilemma.* Notre Dame: University of Notre Dame Press, 1991.

———. *A Casa & A Rua. Espaço, Cidadania, Mulher e Morte no Brasil,* Rio de Janeiro: Rocco, 1997.

———. "Introdução." In *Brasil & EUA: Religião e identidade nacional,* edited by Viola Sachs, et al., 11–26. Rio de Janeiro: Graal, 1988.

———. *O que faz o Brasil, brasil?* Rio de Janeiro: Rocco, 1998.

———. "The Quest for Citizenship in a Relational Universe." In *State and Society in Brazil,* edited by John D. Worth et al., 307–35. Boulder: Westview, 1987.

DaMatta, Roberto, et al. *Brasileiro: cidadão?* São Paulo: Cultura, 1992.

Daudelin, J. and W. E. Hewitt, "Churches and Politics in Latin America: Catholicism Confronts Contemporary Challenges." In *Religion, Globalization and Political Culture in the Third World,* edited by Jeff Haynes, 141–63. New York: Macmillan, 1999.

D'Avila, Edson. "Assembléia de Deus no Brasil e a política: uma leitura a partir do mensageiro da paz." Master's thesis, Universidade Metodista de São Paulo, 2006.

Dawson, Andrew. *The Birth and Impact of the Base Ecclesial Community and Liberative Theological Discourse in Brazil.* San Francisco: Catholic Scholars Press, 1999.

Dayton, Donald W. *Theological Roots of Pentecostalism.* Peabody: Hendrickson Publishers, 2004.

D'Costa, Gavin. *Theology in the Public Square: Church, Academy and Nation.* Oxford: Blackwell, 2005.

Deifelt, Wanda. "The Body in Pain: A Feminist Analysis of Frida Kahlo's Paintings." In *Grenzen erkunden—zwischen Kulturen, Kirchen, Religionen,* edited by Katrin Kusmierz, et al., 257–71. Frankfurt a.M.: Lembeck, 2007.

———. "The Relevance of the Doctrine of Justification." In *Justification in the World's Context,* edited by Wolfgang Greive, 33–42. Geneva: Lutheran World Federation, 2000.

Della Cava, Ralph. "Catholicism and Society in Twentieth-Century Brazil." In *Latin American Research Review* 11/2 (1976) 7–50.

———. "A Conferência Nacional dos Bispos do Brasil e os Meios de Comunicação Social: 1962–1989." In *...E o verbo se fez imagem: Igreja Católica e os meios de comunicação no Brasil: 1962–1989,* edited by Ralph Della Cava and Paula Montero, 21–129. Vozes: Petrópolis, 1991.

———. "The People's Church, the Vatican, and Abertura." In *Democratizing Brazil. Problems of Transition and Consolidation,* edited by Alfred Stepan, 145-67. New York: Oxford University Press, 1989.

———. "A Vision of Short-Term Politics and Long-Term Religion: The Roman Catholic Church in Brazil in April 1978." In *Debate on Church and Politics in Brazil,* edited by Ralph Della Cava and Paulo J. Krischke, 11–38. Toronto: Brazilian Studies—Latin American Research Unit, 1978.

Dejung, Karl-Heinz. *Die Ökumenische Bewegung im Entwicklungskonflikt 1910–1968.* Stuttgart: Klett; München: Kösel, 1973.

Demo, Pedro. *Cidadania menor. Algumas indicações quantitativas de nossa pobreza política.* Petrópolis: Vozes, 1992.

———. *Cidadania pequena. Fragilidades e desafios do associativismo no Brasil.* Campinas: Autores Associados, 2001.

———. *Cidadania tutelada e cidadania assistida.* Campinas: Autores Associados, 1995.

———. *Política social, educação e cidadania.* Campinas: Papirus, 2004.

Diem, Harald. "Luthers Lehre von den zwei Reichen." In *Zur Zwei-Reiche-Lehre Luthers,* edited by Gerhard Sauter, 1–173. München: Chr. Kaiser, 1973.

Dimenstein, Gilberto. *O cidadão de papel: a infância, a adolescência e os Direitos Humanos no Brasil.* São Paulo: Ática, 2006.

———. *Democracia em pedaços: direitos humanos no Brasil.* São Paulo: Companhia das Letras, 1996.

Dodson, Michael. "Pentecostals, Politics and Public Space." In *Power, Politics, and Pentecostals in Latin America,* edited by Edward L. Cleary and Hannah W. Stewart-Gambino, 25–40. Boulder: Westview, 1997.

Doimo, Ana Maria. *A vez e a voz do popular: movimentos sociais e participação política no Brasil pós-70.* Rio de Janeiro: Relume-Dumará, 1995.

Domingues, José Mauricio. "Cidadania, direitos e modernidade." In *Democracia hoje: novos desafios para a teoria democrática contemporânea.* edited by Jessé de Souza, 213-42. Brasília: Editora UnB, 2001.

Dreher, Martin. "Heutige Situation der Lutherischen Kirche in Lateinamerika und auf der Karibik." In *Lutherische Kirchen,* edited by Michael Plathow, 189–207. Göttingen: Vandenhoeck & Ruprecht, 2007.

———. *História do povo luterano.* São Leopoldo: Sinodal, 2005.

———. *Igreja e Germanidade.* São Leopoldo: Sinodal, 2004.

———. *Kirche und Deutschtum in der Entwicklung der Evangelischen Kirche Lutherischen Bekenntnisses in Brasilien.* Göttingen: Vandenhoeck & Ruprecht, 1978.

———. "Luteranismo e participação política." In *Reflexões em Torno de Lutero,* vol. 2, 121–32. São Leopoldo: Sinodal, 1984.

———. "Reflexões sobre os Sessenta Anos da Escola Superior de Teologia." In *Estações da formação teológica: 60 anos de história da EST,* edited by Lothar Carlos Hoch, et al., 57–70. São Leopoldo: Sinodal, 2008.

Dressel, Heinz F. *Brasilien: von Getúlio bis Itamar.* Berlin: ELA, 1995.

Drogus, Carol Ann. "Review: The Rise and Decline of Liberation Theology: Churches, Faith and Political Change in Latin America." *Comparative Politics* 27/4 (1995) 465–77.

Duchrow, Ulrich. *Christenheit und Weltverantwortung. Traditionsgeschichte und systematische Struktur der Zweireichelehre.* Stuttgart: Klett-Cotta, 1983.

———. *Os dois reinos: uso e abuso de um conceito teológico luterano.* São Leopoldo: Sinodal, 1987.

———, editor. *Lutheran Churches—Salt or Mirror of Society? Case Studies on the Theory and Practice of the Two Kingdoms Doctrine.* Geneva: Lutheran World Federation, 1977.

Dunn, James D. G. *The Theology of Paul the Apostle.* Grand Rapids: Eerdmans, 1998.

Dussel, Enrique. "Theology of Liberation and Marxism." In *Mysterium Liberationis: Fundamental Concepts of Liberation Theology,* edited by Ignácio Ellacuría and Jon Sobrino, 85–102. Maryknoll: Orbis, 1993.

Ellacuría, Ignácio. "The Historicity of Christian Salvation." In *Mysterium Liberationis: Fundamental Concepts of Liberation Theology,* edited by Ignácio Ellacuría and Jon Sobrino, 251–89. Maryknoll: Orbis, 1993.

Ellacuría, Ignácio, and Jon Sobrino, editors, *Mysterium Liberationis: Fundamental Concepts of Liberation Theology.* Maryknoll: Orbis, 1993.

Esperandio, Mary Rute. "Narcisismo e sacrifício: modo de subjetivação e religiosidade contemporânea." PhD diss., São Leopoldo: EST, 2006.

Eugster, Markus. *Der brasilianische Verfassungsgebungsprozess von 1987/88.* Bern: Haupt, 1995.

Faoro, Raymundo. *Os donos do poder: formação do patronato político brasileiro.* São Paulo: Globo, 2001.

Faria, Eduardo Galasso. *Fé e compromisso: Richard Shaull e a teologia no Brasil.* São Paulo: ASTE, 2002.

Farmer, Paul. *Pathologies of Power: Health, Human Rights and the New War on the Poor.* Berkeley: University of California Press, 2005.

Fausto, Boris. *Getúlio Vargas: O poder e o sorriso.* São Paulo: Companhia das Letras, 2006.

———. *História do Brasil.* São Paulo: EDUSP, 1996.

Ferguson, Adam. *An Essay on the History of Civil Society.* Cambridge: Cambridge University Press, 2003.

Fernandes, Rubem César. "Governo das almas. As denominações evangélicas no Grande Rio." In *Nem Anjos nem Demônios: interpretações sociológicas do pentecostalismo,* edited by Alberto Antoniazzi, 163-203. Petrópolis: Vozes, 1994.

———. *Privado porém público: o terceiro setor na América Latina.* Rio de Janeiro: Relume-Dumará, 1994.

———. "Sociedade civil e ecumenismo." *Comunicações do ISER* 12/44 (1993) 55–64.

Fernandes, Rubem César, et al. *Novo nascimento: os evangélicos em casa, na igreja e na política.* Rio de Janeiro: Mauad, 1998.

Fernandes, Sílvia Regina Alves. "Prática religiosa e participação social." *Ceris* (2002) 88–136.

———, editor. *Mudança de religião no Brasil: desvendando sentidos e motivações.* Rio de Janeiro: CERIS, 2006.

Fernandes, Sílvia Regina Alves, and Marcelo Pitta. "Mapeando as rotas do trânsito religioso no Brasil." *Religião e Sociedade* 26/2 (2006), 120–54. Online: http://www.ceris.org.br/download/FERNANDES%20E%20PITTA.mapeando%20as%20rotas_rev.pdf.

Ferreira, Aurélio Buarque de Holanda. *Novo Aurélio século XXI: o dicionário da língua portuguesa,* 3rd revised edition. Rio de Janeiro: Nova Fronteira, 1999.

Ferreira, Marieta de Morais, and César Benjamim. "Goulart, João" In *Dicionário histórico-biográfico brasileiro: 1930–1983,* vol. 2, 1504–1521. Rio de Janeiro: Forense-Universitária, FGV/CPDOC, FINEP, 1984.

Fiegenbaum, Ricardo Zimmermann. "Midiatização do campo religioso e processos de produção de sentido: análise de um conflito anunciado. O caso do Jornal Evangélico da IECLB." Master's thesis, São Leopoldo: Unisinos, 2006.

Fischer, Joachim. "Geschichte der Evangelischen Kirche Lutherischen Bekenntnisses in Brasilien." In *Es begann am Rio dos Sinos: Geschichte und Gegenwart der Ev. Kirche Lutherischen Bekenntnisses in Brasilien,* edited by Joachim Fischer and Christoph Jahn, 83–204. Erlangen: Verlag der Ev.-Luth. Mission, 1970.

———. "Identidade confessional: lições da história" *Estudos Teológicos* 43/1 (2003) 29–42.

———. "Luther in Brasilien." In *Nachfolge Jesu—Wege der Befreiung: Evangelisch-Lutherische Kirche in Brasilien*, edited by Ulrich Schoenborn, 6–22. Mettingen: Brasilienkunde-Verlag, 1989.

Fischer, Joachim, and Christoph Jahn, editors. *Es begann am Rio dos Sinos: Geschichte und Gegenwart der Ev. Kirche Lutherischen Bekenntnisses in Brasilien*. Erlangen: Verlag der Ev.-Luth. Mission, 1970.

Fluck, Marlon Ronald. *Basler Missionare in Brasilien: Auswanderung, Erweckung und Kirchenwerdung im 19. Jahrhundert*. Bern: Lang, 2004.

Follmann, José Ivo. "O Mundo das Religiões e Religiosidades: alguns números e apontamentos para uma reflexão sobre novos desafios." In *Religião, Cultura e Educação*, edited by Cleide C. da Silva Scarlatelli, Danilo R. Streck, and José Ivo Follmann, 11–28. São Leopoldo: Edunisinos, 2006.

Fonseca, Alexandre Brasil. *Evangélicos e mídia no Brasil*, Bragança Paulista: Editora Universitária São Francisco; Curitiba: Faculdade São Boaventura, 2003.

Font, Maurício A. *Transforming Brazil: A Reform Era in Perspective*. Lanham: Rowman and Littlefield, 2003.

Frank, André Gunder. *Capitalism and Underdevelopment in Latin America: Historical Studies of Chile and Brazil*. New York: Monthly Review Press, 1967.

Freire, Paulo. *Pedagogy of the Oppressed*. London, Continuum, 2000.

Freitas, Maria Carmelita de, editor. *Religião e transformação no Brasil*. São Paulo: Paulinas, 2007.

———, editor. *Teologia e sociedade: relevância e funções*, São Paulo: Paulinas, 2006.

Freston, Paul. "Breve História do Pentecostalismo Brasileiro." In *Nem Anjos nem Demônios: interpretações sociológicas do pentecostalismo*, edited by Alberto Antoniazzi, 67–159. Petrópolis: Vozes, 1994.

———, editor. *Evangelical Christianity and Democracy in Latin America*. New York: Oxford University Press, 2008.

———. *Evangelicals and Politics in Asia, Africa and Latin America*. Cambridge: Cambridge University Press, 2001.

———. *Evangélicos na Política Brasileira: História Ambígua e Desafio Ético*. Curitiba: Encontro, 1994.

———. *Religião e Política, sim; Igreja e Estado, não: os evangélicos e a participação política*. Viçosa: Ultimato, 2006.

Freyre, Gilberto. *Casa grande e senzala*. Rio de Janeiro: Record, 2002. [English edition: *The Masters and the Slaves*, New York: Random House, 2000.]

Fridman, Luis Carlos, editor. *Política e cultura: século XXI*. Rio de Janeiro: ALERJ, Relume-Dumará, 2002.

Fukuyama, Francis. *Trust: The Social Virtues and the Creation of Prosperity*. New York: The Free Press, 1995.

Funari, Pedro Paulo. "A cidadania entre os romanos." In *História da Cidadania*, edited by Jaime Pinsky and Carla Bassanezi Pinsky, 49–79. São Paulo: Contexto, 2003.

Gaskyll, Newton J. "Rethinking Protestantism and Democratic Consolidation in Latin America." *Sociology of Religion* 58/1 (1997) 69–91.

Gaspari, Elio. *A ditadura derrotada*.São Paulo: Companhia das Letras, 2003.

Gebara, Ivone. *Teologia ecofeminista*. São Paulo: Olho d'Água, 1997.

Gerstenberger, Erhard. "בטח vertrauen." In *Theologisches Handwörterbuch zum Alten Testament*, vol. 1, edited by Ernst Jenni and Claus Westermann, 300–5. München, Zürich: Chr. Kaiser, Theologischer Verlag, 1984.

Gertz, René E. "Die Lutheraner in der Gesellschaft und Kultur Brasiliens." In *Luther zwischen den Kulturen. Zeitgenossenschaft—Weltwirkung*, edited by Hans Medick and Peer Schmidt, 164–89. Göttingen: Vandenhoeck & Ruprecht, 2004.

Getui, Mary, Luiz Carlos Susin and Betrice W.Churu, editors. *Spirituality for Another Possible World*. Nairobi: Twaweza, 2008.

Gibellini, Rosino. *A teologia no século XX*. São Paulo: Loyola, 1998.

Gilberto, Antonio. *Lições Bíblicas: Mestre. A igreja e sua missão*. Rio de Janeiro: CPAD, 2007.

———. *Lições Bíblicas: A parábola do bom samaritano*. Rio de Janeiro: CPAD, 1990.

———. *Lições Bíblicas: Sal e Luz: as marcas do cristão atual*. Rio de Janeiro: CPAD, 1996.

Gill, Anthony. *Rendering unto Caesar: The Catholic Church and the State in Latin America*. Chicago: University of Chicago Press, 1998.

Giumbelli, Emerson. "O 'chute na santa': blasfêmia e pluralismo religioso no Brasil." In *Religião e espaço público*, edited by Patricia Birman, 169–99. São Paulo: Attar, 2003.

———. *O fim da religião: dilemas da liberdade religiosa no Brasil e na França*. São Paulo: Attar, 2002.

———. "Religião, Estado, modernidade: notas a propósito de fatos provisórios." *Estudos Avançados* 18/52 (2004) 47–62.

Giumbelli, Emerson, and Sandra de Sá Carneiro. "Religião nas escolas públicas: questões nacionais e a situação no Rio de Janeiro." *Revista Contemporânea de Educação* 2 (2006). Online: http://www.educacao.ufrj.br/revista/indice/numero2/artigos/egiumbelli.pdf.

Gohn, Maria da Glória. *O protagonismo da sociedade civil: movimentos sociais, ONGs e redes solidárias*. São Paulo: Cortez, 2005.

Goldmeyer, Marguit, et al., editors. *Luteranismo e Educação: Reflexões*. São Leopoldo: Sinodal, 2006.

Gomes, Flávio dos Santos. "Sonhando com a terra, construindo a cidadania." In *História da Cidadania*, edited by Jaime Pinsky and Carla Bassanezi Pinsky, 447–67. São Paulo: Contexto, 2003.

Gomes, Mércio Pereira. "O caminho brasileiro para a cidadania indígena." In *História da Cidadania,* edited by Jaime Pinsky and Carla Bassanezi Pinsky, 419–45. São Paulo: Contexto, 2003.

Graham, Elaine. "Power, Knowledge and Authority in Public Theology." *International Journal of Public Theology* 1/1 (2007) 42–62.

Gremmelspacher, Georg. "Kirchen als Nicht-regierungsorganisationen und ihr Einsatz für den Menschenrechtsschutz in Transformationsgesellschaften – juristische Aspekte." In *Kirche und Öffentlichkeit in Transformationsgesellschaften,* edited by Christine Lienemann-Perrin, and Wolfgang Lienemann, 177–92. Stuttgart: Kohlhammer, 2006.

Grotefeld, Stefan. *Religiöse Überzeugungen im liberalen Staat: Protestantische Ethik und die Anforderungen öffentlicher Vernunft.* Stuttgart: Kohlhammer, 2006.

Gruchy, John W. de. "From Political to Public Theologies: The Role of Theology in Public Life in South Africa." In *Public Theology for the 21st century, Essays in Honour of Duncan B. Forrester,* edited by William F. Storrar and Andrew R. Morton, 45–62. London: T & T Clark, 2004.

———. "Public Theology as Christian Witness: Exploring the Genre." *International Journal of Public Theology* 1/1 (2007) 26–41.

Guarinello, Norberto Luiz. "Cidades-estado na Antigüidade Clássica." In *História da Cidadania,* edited by Jaime Pinsky and Carla Bassanezi Pinsky, 29–47. São Paulo: Contexto, 2003.

Guider, Margaret Eletta. "Reinventing Life and Hope: Coming to Terms with Truth and Reconciliation Brazilian Style." In *Reconciliation, Nations and Churches in Latin America,* edited by Iain S.Maclean, 111–31. Aldershot: Ashgate, 2006.

Guimarães, Juarez, editor. *Leituras críticas sobre Leonardo Boff.* São Paulo: Editora Fundação Perseu Abramo; Belo Horizonte: Editora UFMG, 2008.

Gutiérrez, Gustavo. "Notes for a Theology of Liberation." In *Liberation Theology at the Crossroads: Democracy or Revolution?* edited by Paul Sigmund, 199–213. New York: Oxford University Press, 1990.

———. "Option for the Poor." In *Mysterium Liberationis: Fundamental Concepts of Liberation Theology,* edited by Ignácio Ellacuría and Jon Sobrino, 235–50. Maryknoll: Orbis, 1993.

———. "Renewing the Option for the Poor." In *Liberation Theologies, Postmodernity, and the Americas,* edited by David Batstone et al., 69–82. London/New York: Routledge, 1997.

———. *A Theology of Liberation: History, Politics, and Salvation.* Maryknoll: Orbis, 2006.

Haacker, Klaus. "Glaube II. Altes und Neues Testament." *Theologische Realenzyklopädie* 13 (1993) 277–304.

Habermas, Jürgen. *Faktizität und Geltung. Beiträge zur Diskurstheorie des Rechts und des demokratischen Rechtsstaats.* Frankfurt a. M.: Suhrkamp, 1998.

———. *Glauben und Wissen.* Frankfurt a. M.: Suhrkamp, 2001.

———. "On the Relations Between the Secular Liberal State and Religion," In *Political Theologies. Public Religions in a Post-Secular World,* edited by Hent de Vries and Lawrence E. Sullivan, 251–60. New York: Fordham, 2006.

———. *Strukturwandel der Öffentlichkeit. Untersuchungen zu einer Kategorie der bürgerlichen Gesellschaft.* Frankfurt a.M.: Suhrkamp, 1990. [English version: *The Structural Transformation of the Public Sphere: an Inquiry into a Category of Bourgeois Society*, Cambridge: MIT, 1989.]

Hagopian, Frances. "Politics in Brazil." In *Comparative Politics Today: A World View,* edited by Gary Almond et al., 520–74. New York: Longman, 2003.

———. *Traditional Politics and Regime Change in Brazil.* Cambridge: Cambridge University Press, 1996.

Hagopian, Frances, and Scott P. Mainwaring, editors. *The Third Wave of Democratization in Latin America: Advances and Setbacks.* New York: Cambridge University Press, 2005.

Hanks, Tomás. "El testimonio evangélico a los pobres y oprimidos." *Vida y Pensamiento* 4/1–2 (1984) 21–42.

Hartmann, M. and Claus Offe, eds. *Vertrauen. Die Grundlage sozialen Zusammenhalts.* Frankfurt, Campus, 2001.

Hasler, Eveline. *Ibicaba: Das Paradies in den Köpfen.* Zürich: Nagel und Kimche, 1985.

Heater, Derek, *A Brief History of Citizenship.* New York: New York University Press, 2004.

Hegel, Georg Wilhelm Friedrich. *Grundlinien der Philosophie des Rechts.* Frankfurt a.M.: Suhrkamp, 1986.

Heidegger, Martin. *Sein und Zeit.* Tübingen: Niemeyer, 1993.

Herberg, Will. *Protestant—Catholic—Jew: An Essay in American Religious Sociology.* Garden City: Doubleday, 1955.

Herbert, David. *Religion and Civil Society: Rethinking Public Religion in the Contemporary World.* Aldershot: Ashgate, 2004.

Herkenhoff, João Baptista. *Direito e Cidadania.* São Paulo: Uniletras, 2004.

———. *Direitos Humanos: a construção social de uma utopia.* Aparecida: Santuário, 2004.

Hess, David J., and Roberto DaMatta, editors. *The Brazilian Puzzle: Culture on the Borderlands of the Western World.* New York: Columbia University Press, 1995.

Hewitt, William E. *Base Christian Communities and Social Change in Brazil.* Lincoln and London: University of Nebraska Press, 1991.

Hick, John. *Religion. Die menschlichen Antworten auf die Frage nach Leben und Tod.* München: Beck, 1996. [Engl. ed.: *An Interpretation of Religion. Human Responses to the Transcendent*, 2nd ed. New Haven: Yale University Press, 2005.]

Hiltbrunner, Otto. *Gastfreundschaft in der Antike und im frühen Christentum.* Darmstadt: Wissenschaftliche Buchgesellschaft, 2005.

Hinkelammert, Franz J. *The Ideological Weapons of Death: a Theological Critique of Capitalism.* Maryknoll: Orbis, 1986.

———. "Liberation Theology in the Economic Social Context of Latin America: Economy and Theology, or the Irrationality of the Rationalized." In *Liberation Theologies, Postmodernity, and the Americas*, edited by Batstone et al., 25–52. New York: Routledge, 1997.

Hoch, Lothar Carlos, editor. "Aconselhamento pastoral e libertação." *Estudos Teológicos* 29 (1989) 17–40.

———. *Formação Teológica em Terra Brasileira. Faculdade de Teologia da IECLB 1946–1986, edição comemorativa.* São Leopoldo: Sinodal, 1986.

———. "Healing as a Task of Pastoral Care among the Poor." *Intercultural Pastoral Care and Counselling* 7 (2001) 32–38.

Hoch, Lothar Carlos, and Susana M. Rocca L., editors. *Sofrimento, resiliência e fé: implicações para as relações de cuidado.* São Leopoldo: Sinodal, EST, 2007.

Hoch, Lothar Carlos, Marga Janete Ströher and Wilhelm Wachholz, editors. *Estações da formação teológica: 60 anos de história da EST.* São Leopoldo: Sinodal, 2008.

Hochstetler, Kathryn. "Democratizing Pressures from Below? Social Movements in the New Brazilian Democracy." In *Democratic Brazil. Actors, Institutions, and Processes,* edited by Peter R. Kingstone and Timothy P. Power, 162–82. Pittsburgh: University of Pittsburgh Press, 2000.

Holanda, Sérgio Buarque de. *As raízes do Brasil* [1936], 26th ed. São Paulo: Companhia das Letras, 1995.

Hollenweger, Walter J. *Charismatisch-pfingstliches Christentum: Herkunft, Situation, Ökumenische Chancen.* Göttingen: Vandenhoeck & Ruprecht, 1997.

Holston, James. *Insurgent Citizenship: Disjunctions of Democracy and Modernity in Brazil.* Princeton: Princeton University Press, 2008.

Holston, James, and Teresa P. R. Caldeira. "Democracy, Law, and Violence: Disjunctions of Brazilian Citizenship." In *Fault Lines of Democracy in Post-Transition Latin America*, edited by Felipe Aguëro and Jeffrey Stark, 263–96. Miami: North-South Center Press, University of Miami, 1998.

Hoornaert, Eduardo. "As comunidades cristãs dos primeiros séculos." In *História da Cidadania*, edited by Jaime Pinsky and Carla Bassanezi Pinsky, 81–95. São Paulo: Contexto, 2003.

Huber, Wolfgang. *Gerechtigkeit und Recht: Grundlinien christlicher Rechtsethik,* 2nd ed. Gütersloh: Chr. Kaiser/Gütersloher Verlagshaus, 1999.

———. *Kirche und Öffentlichkeit.* München: Kaiser, 1973.

———. "Menschenrechte/Menschenwürde." *Theologische Realenzyklopädie* v. 22 (1992) 577–602.

———. "Öffentlichkeit und Kirche." In *Evangelisches Soziallexikon, Neuausgabe*, edited by Martin Honecker et al., 1165–1173. Stuttgart: Kohlhammer, 2001.

———. *Rechtfertigung und Recht: Über die christlichen Wurzeln der europäischen Rechtskultur.* Baden-Baden: Nomos, 2001.

———. *Vertrauen erneuern: Eine Reform um der Menschen willen.* Freiburg: Herder, 2005.

Hünermann, Peter and Juan Carlos Scannone, editors. *Lateinamerika und die Katholische Soziallehre: Ein lateinamerikanisch-deutsches Dialogprogramm.* 3 vols. Mainz: Grünewald, 1993.

Huntington, Samuel P. *Political Order in Changing Societies.* New Haven: Yale University Press, 1968.

______. *The Third Wave: Democratization in the Late Twentieth Century.* Norman: University of Oklahoma Press, 1991.

IBGE [Instituto Brasileiro de Geografia e Estatística]. *Brasil em Números—Brazil in Figures*, vol. 14. Rio de Janeiro: IBGE, 2006.

———. *Censo demográfico 2000.* Online: http://www.ibge.gov.br.

———. *Estatísticas do século XX.* Rio de Janeiro: IBGE, 2003.

IBOPE [Instituto Brasileiro de Opinião Pública e Estatística]. *Confiança nas instituições*, 2005. Online: http://www.ibope.com.br/opp/ pesquisa/opiniaopublica/download/opp098_confianca_portalibope_ago05.pdf.

IECLB [Igreja Evangélica de Confissão Luterana no Brasil]. *Batismo: diálogo com o movimento carismático na IECLB.* Porto Alegre: IECLB, 2006.

———. *Diretrizes teológico-pastorais para atos e diálogos inter-religiosos*, 2009. Online: http://www.luteranos.com.br/articles/11314/1/Diretrizes-teologico-pastorais-para-atos-e-dialogos-inter-religiosos/1.html.

———. *Estatuto do ministério com ordenação.* Porto Alegre; IECLB, 2003.

———. *Manifesto da Chapada dos Guimarães,* 2000. Online: http://www.luteranos.com.br/ articles/8198/1/Manifesto-de-Chapada-dos-Guimaraes---2000/1.html.

———. *Manifesto de Curitiba,* 1970. Online: http://www.luteranos.com.br/articles/8191/1/ Manifesto-de-Curitiba—1970/1 .html.

———. *Motivos de intercessão da IECLB 2003–2006.* Porto Alegre: IECLB, 2006.

———. *Recriar e criar comunidade juntos: Plano de Ação Missionária da IECLB.* Porto Alegre, 2000.

———. *Unidade: Contexto e Identidade da IECLB.* Blumenau: O. Kuhr, 2006.

Iglesias, Francisco. *Trajetória Política do Brasil, 1500–1964*. São Paulo: Companhia das Letras, 1993.
Illich, Ivan. *Tools for Conviviality*. Berkeley: Heyday, 1989.
INP [Instituto Nacional de Pastoral]. *Presença Pública da Igreja no Brasil (1952–2002), Jubileu de Ouro da CNBB*. São Paulo: Paulinas, 2003.
"In God's name: a Special Report on Religion and Public Life." *The Economist*, November 3, 2007. Online: http://www.economist.com/ specialreports.
Ireland, Rowan. *Kingdoms Come: Religion and Politics in Brazil*. Pittsburgh: University of Pittsburgh Press, 1991.
———. "Pentecostalism, Conversions, and Politics in Brazil." In *Power, Politics, and Pentecostals in Latin America*, edited by Edward L. Cleary and Hannah W. Stewart-Gambino, 123–37. Boulder: Westview, 1997.
———. "Popular Religions and the Building of Democracy in Latin America: Saving the Tocquevillian Parallel." *Journal of Interamerican Studies and World Affairs* 41/4 (1999) 111–36.
Jacob, Cesar Romero, et al. *Atlas da filiação religiosa e indicadores sociais no Brasil*. Rio de Janeiro: Editora PUC-Rio; São Paulo: Loyola, 2003.
Jahn, Christoph. "Porto Alegre im Juni 1970: Überforderte lutherische Gemeinden." In *Kirche vor den Herausforderungen der Zukunft. Evian '70. Porto Alegre—Evian-les-Bains 1970. V. Vollversammlung des Lutherischen Weltbundes*, edited by Jürgen Jeziorowski, 24–40. Kreuz: Stuttgart, Berlin, 1970.
Janoski, Thomas. *Citizenship and Civil Society*. New York: Cambridge University Press, 1998.
Jenkins, Philip. *The New Faces of Christianity: Believing the Bible in the Global South*. New York: Oxford University Press, 2006.
———. *The Next Christendom: The Coming of Global Christianity*. Oxford: Oxford University Press, 2007.
Jelin, Elizabeth. "Construir a Cidadania: uma visão desde baixo." *Lua Nova* 33 (1994) 39–57.
Jenni, Ernst, and Claus Westermann, editors. *Theologisches Handwörterbuch zum Alten Testament*, vol. 1. München, Zürich: Chr. Kaiser, Theologischer Verlag, 1984.
Jeziorowski, Jürgen, editor. *Kirche vor den Herausforderungen der Zukunft. Evian '70. Porto Alegre—Evian-les-Bains 1970. V. Vollversammlung des Lutherischen Weltbundes*. Kreuz: Stuttgart, Berlin, 1970.
———. 'Gesandt in die Welt': Der Streit um den Tagungsort." In *Kirche vor den Herausforderungen der Zukunft. Evian '70. Porto Alegre—Evian-les-Bains 1970. V. Vollversammlung des Lutherischen Weltbundes*, edited by Jürgen Jeziorowski, 7–23. Kreuz: Stuttgart, Berlin, 1970.
Joint Declaration on the Doctrine of Justification, Roman Catholic Church and Lutheran World Federation. Grand Rapids: Eerdmans, 2000.
John Paul II. *Veritatis Splendor: The Splendour of the Truth Shines*. Vatican City: Libreria Editrice Vaticana, 1993. Online: http://www.vatican.va/edocs/ENG0222/_INDEX.HTM.
Jüngel, Eberhard. *Das Evangelium von der Rechtfertigung des Gottlosen als Zentrum des christlichen Glaubens*. Tübingen: Mohr Siebeck, 1999.
Juergensmeyer, Mark, editor. *Religion in Global Civil Society*. New York: Oxford University Press, 2005.
Kadt, Emanuel de. *Catholic Radicals in Brazil*. Oxford: Oxford University Press, 1970.
Kant, Immanuel. "Grundlegung zur Metaphysik der Sitten [1785]." In *Werke*, vol. IV, 7–102. Darmstadt: Wissenschaftliche Buchgesellschaft, 1998. [English Edition : *Foundations of the Metaphysics of Morals*, 2nd ed., Prentice Hall, 1989].
———. "Die Metaphysik der Sitten [1797]." In *Werke*, vol. IV, 303–64. Darmstadt: Wissenschaftliche Buchgesellschaft, 1998.
———. "Zum Ewigen Frieden [1795]." In *Werke*, vol. VI, 191–251. (Darmstadt: Wissenschaftliche Buchgesellschaft, 1998. [English edition: *Perpetual Peace and Other Essays on Politics, History, and Morals*. Indianapolis: Hackett. 1983]
Karnal, Leandro. "Estados Unidos, liberdade e cidadania." In *História da Cidadania*, edited by Jaime Pinsky and Carla Bassanezi Pinsky, 135–57. São Paulo: Contexto, 2003.
Keane, John., editor. *Civil Society and the State*. London, New York: Verso, 1988.
———, editor. *Civil Society: Berlin Perspectives*. New York: Berghahn, 2003.
———. *Global Civil Society?* Cambridge: Cambridge University Press, 2003.
Keck, Margaret E. *The Workers' Party and Democratization in Brazil*. New Haven/London: Yale University Press, 1992.
Kern, Bruno. *Theologie im Horizont des Marxismus: Zur Geschichte der Marxismusrezeption in der lateinamerikanischen Theologie der Befreiung*. Mainz: Grünewald, 1992.
Khoury, Raif Georges. "Glaube 4. Nichtchristl. Religionen; exemplarisch: Islam." In *Evangelisches Kirchenlexikon, vol. 2*, 202–5. Göttingen: Vandenhoeck & Ruprecht, 1989.
Kingstone, Peter R., and Timothy P. Power, editors. *Democratic Brazil. Actors, Institutions, and Processes*. Pittsburgh: University of Pittsburgh Press, 2000.
Kinzo, Maria D'Alva G. "Transitions: Brazil." In *Democracy in Latin America. (Re)Constructing Political Society*, edited by Miguel Antonio Garretón M and Edward Newman, 19–44. Tokyo: United Nations University Press. 2001.

Kirche Lateinamerikas, die. *Dokumente der II. und III. Generalversammlung des Lateinamerikanischen Episkopates in Medellin und Puebla.* Bonn: Sekretariat der Deutschen Bischofskonferenz, 1979.

Kirchheim, Huberto. *Novo jeito de ser igreja: textos selecionados.* São Leopoldo: Sinodal, 2002.

Kirst, Nelson. "A reforma do estudo—marca registrada da última década." In *Formação Teológica em Terra Brasileira. Faculdade de Teologia da IECLB 1946–1986, edição comemorativa,* edited by Lothar Carlos Hoch, 51–60. São Leopoldo: Sinodal, 1986.

Klaiber, Jeffrey. *The Church, Dictatorships, and Democracy in Latin America.* Maryknoll: Orbis, 1998.

Kleger, Heinz, and Alois Müller, editors. *Religion des Bürgers: Zivilreligion in Amerika und Europa.* Münster: LIT, 2004.

Klein, Remí, and Sérgio Rogério Azevedo Junqueira. "Aspectos referentes à formação de professores de Ensino Religioso." *Revista Diálogo Educacional* 8/23 (2008) 221–43.

Kliewer, Gerd Uwe. "Uma comunidade evangélica frente aos problemas sociais e à atuação sócio-política da igreja." In *Quem assume esta tarefa? Um documentário de uma igreja em busca de sua identidade,* edited by Germano Burger, 189–211. São Leopoldo: Sinodal, 1977.

———. "O Declínio do Crescimento Natural 1." *Protestantismo em Revista* 3/4 (2004), 82–93. Online: http://www3.est.edu.br/nepp/revista/005/ano03n3_06.pdf

———. "Effervescent Diversity: Religions and Churches in Brazil Today." *The Ecumenical Review* 57/3 (2005) 314–21.

———. "Ex-alunos e ex-alunas da EST." In *Estações da formação teológica: 60 anos de história da EST,* edited by Lothar Carlos Hoch, Marga Janete Ströher and Wilhelm Wachholz, 130–68. São Leopoldo: Sinodal, 2008.

———. *Das neue Volk der Pfingstler. Religion, Unterentwicklung und sozialer Wandel in Lateinamerika.* Frankfurt: Lang, 1975.

Knebelkamp, Ari. "Believing Without Belonging? In Search of New Paradigms of Church and Mission in Secularized and Postmodern Contexts: Brazilian Insights and 'Outsights'." *International Review of Mission* 92/365 (2003) 192–99.

Knirck-Wissmann, Christa-Maria. "Kontextualität und Partikularität der Kirche: zur ekklesiologischen Bedeutung der Auseinandersetzung um die Verlegung der 5. Vollversammlung des Lutherischen Weltbundes von Pôrto Alegre nach Evian." PhD diss., Theologische Fakultät der Universität Heidelberg, 1978.

Knitter, Paul F. "Cosmic Confidence or Preferential Option?" In *The Intercultural Challenge of Raimon Panikkar,* edited by Joseph Prabhu, 177-91. Maryknoll: Orbis, 1996

Kocka, Jürgen. "Civil Society in Historical Perspective." In *Civil Society: Berlin Perspectives,* edited by John Keane, 37–50. New York: Berghahn, 2003.

———. "Zivilgesellschaft als historisches Problem und Versprechen." In *Europäische Zivilgesellschaft in Ost und West, Begriff, Geschichte, Chancen,* edited by Manfred Hildermeier, Jürgen Kocka and Christoph Conrad, 13–39. Frankfurt a.M.: Campus, 2000.

Konder, Leandro. "Idéias que romperam fronteiras." In *História da Cidadania,* edited by Jaime Pinsky and Carla Bassanezi Pinsky, 171–89. São Paulo: Contexto, 2003.

Koopman, Nico. "Some Comments on Public Theology Today." *Journal of Theology for Southern Africa* 177 (2003) 3–19.

Koschorke, Klaus, editor. *Falling Walls: The Year 1989/90 as a Turning Point in the History of World Christianity/ Einstürzende Mauern: Das Jahr 1989/90 als Epochenjahr in der Geschichte des Weltchristentums.* Wiesbaden: Harrassowitz, 2009.

Krischke, Paulo J. "A Gramscian Critique of Della Cava's 'Short-Term Politics and Long-Term Religion.'" In *Debate on Church and Politics in Brazil, 1978,* edited by Ralph Della Cava and Paulo J. Krischke, 39–48. Toronto: Brazilian Studies—Latin American Research Unit,1978.

———. *A Igreja e as crises políticas no Brasil.* Petrópolis: Vozes, 1979.

———. *The Learning of Democracy in Latin America: Social Actors and Cultural Change.* New York: Nova Science, 2001.

Kunert, Augusto E. "Aspectos da relação IECLB e Estado, em uma compreensão histórica e teológica." *Estudos Teológicos* 22/3 (1982) 215–42.

Küng, Hans. *A Global Ethic for Global Politics and Economics.* Oxford: Oxford University Press, 1998.

Kusmierz, Katrin. *Theology in Transition: Public Theologies in Post-Apartheid South Africa.* Münster: LIT, forthcoming.

———. "Vom Umgang mit Schuld: Theologie und Kirche im Kontext der Wahrheits- und Versöhnungskommission in Südafrika." Licentiateship diss., Basel University, Faculty of Theology, 1998.

Kusmierz, Katrin, and James R Cochrane. "Öffentliche Kirche und öffentliche Theologie in Südafrikas politischer Transformation." In *Kirche und Öffentlichkeit in Transformationsgesellschaften,* edited by Christine Lienemann-Perrin and Wolfgang Lienemann, 195–226. Stuttgart: Kohlhammer, 2006.

Kymlicka, Will, and Wayne Norman, editors. *Citizenship in Diverse Societies.* Oxford: Oxford University Press, 2000.

Laclau, Ernesto, and Chantal Mouffe. *Hegemony and Socalist Strategy: Towards a Radical Democratic Politics.* London: Verso, 1985.

Lafer, Celso. *Hannah Arendt: pensamento, persuasão e poder.* São Paulo: Paz e Terra, 2003.

Lagos, Marta. "Between Stability and Crisis in Latin America." *Journal of Democracy* 12/1 (2001) 137–45.

Lalive d'Épinay, Christian. *Haven of the Masses: A Study of the Pentecostal Movement in Chile.* London: Lutterworth, 1969.

Lamounier, Bolívar, editor. *Brasil e África do Sul—uma comparação.* São Paulo: IDESP, 1996.
———. *Depois da transição: Democracia e eleições no governo Collor.* São Paulo: Loyola, 1991.
Lamounier, Bolívar and Rubens Figueredo., eds. *A era FHC—um balance.* São Paulo: Cultura, 2002.
Landim, Leilah, editor. "Associativismo e organizações voluntárias." *IBGE* (2003) 59–87.
———. *Sem fins lucrativos: as organizações não-governamentais no Brasil.* Rio de Janeiro: ISER, 1988.
Latinobarómetro, *Informe Latinobarómetro 2003*. Online: http://www.latinobarometro.org.
Latinobarómetro, *Informe Latinobarómetro 2005*. Online: http://www.latinobarometro.org/uploads/media/2005.pdf.
Latinobarómetro, *Informe Latinobarómetro 2007*. Online: http://www.latinobarometro.org.
Lehmann, David. *Struggle for the Spirit. Religious Transformation and Popular Culture in Brazil and Latin America.* Cambridge: Polity Press, 1996.
Léonard, Emile G. *O protestantismo brasileiro: estudo de eclesiologia e história social.* São Paulo: ASTE, 2002.
Léry, Jean de. *History of a Voyage to the Land of Brazil, otherwise called America.* Berkeley: University of California Press, 1992.
Lessa, Carlos. *O Rio de todos os Brasis: uma reflexão em busca de auto-estima.* Rio de Janeiro: Record, 2005.
Libânio, João Batista. *As lógicas da cidade: o impacto sobre a fé e sob o impacto da fé.* São Paulo: Loyola, 2001.
———. *Olhando para o futuro: prospectivas teológicas e pastorais do cristianismo na América Latina.* São Paulo: Loyola, 2003.
Libânio, João Batista, and Afonso Murad. *Introdução à Teologia: perfil, enfoques, tarefas.* São Paulo: Loyola, 2001.
Liehr, Wilfried. *Katholizismus und Demokratisierung in Brasilien: Stimulierung von sozialen Lernprozessen als kirchliche Reformpolitik.* Saarbrücken: Verlag Breitenbach, 1988.
Lienemann, Béatrice. "Deskriptive und normative Grundlagen der politologischen Transformationsforschung." In *Kirche und Öffentlichkeit in Transformationsgesellschaften,* edited by Christine Lienemann-Perrin and Wolfgang Lienemann, 125–58. Stuttgart: Kohlhammer, 2006.
———. "Vergleichende Betrachtungen zu den Transformationsprozessen." In *Kirche und Öffentlichkeit in Transformationsgesellschaften,* edited by Christine Lienemann-Perrin, and Wolfgang Lienemann, 403–31. Stuttgart: Kohlhammer, 2006.
Lienemann, Wolfgang. "'Eschatologik' als Antipolitik? Politische Ethik zwischen weltlichem Staat und christlichem Friedenszeugnis: Überlegungen im Blick auf Augustins *De civ. Dei XIX*." In *Alles in allem: eschatologische Anstöße – J. Christine Janowski zum 60. Geburstag,* edited by Ruth Hess and Martin Leiner, 409–25. Neukirchen-Vluyn: Neukirchener, 2005.
———. *Gerechtigkeit.* Göttingen: Vandenhoeck & Ruprecht, 1995.
———. "Kirche und Öffentlichkeit in Transformationsgesellschaften. Voraussetzungen, Bezugsrahmen, Leitfragen." In *Kirche und Öffentlichkeit in Transformationsgesellschaften,* edited by Christine Lienemann-Perrin and Wolfgang Lienemann, 21–50. Stuttgart: Kohlhammer, 2006.
———. "Öffentlichkeit und bürgerliche Gesellschaft in der europäischen Tradition." In *Kirche und Öffentlichkeit in Transformationsgesellschaften,* edited by Christine Lienemann-Perrin and Wolfgang Lienemann, 51–86. Stuttgart: Kohlhammer, 2006.
———. "Sklaverei und Menschenrechte. Die exemplarische Funktion des Sklavereiverbots in der europäischen Geschichte für die Bestimmung universaler Menschenrechte." In *Ethik der Menschenrechte: Zum Streit um die Universalität einer Idee, part I,* edited by Hans-Richard Reuter, 135–71. Tübingen: Mohr Siebeck, 1999.
———. "Zwei-Reiche-Lehre." In *Evangelisches Kirchenlexikon, vol. 4,* 1408–1419. Göttingen: Vandenhoeck & Ruprecht, 1996.
Lienemann-Perrin, Christine. "Neue sozialethische Konzeptionen Öffentlicher Theologie in Transformationsprozessen." In *Kirche und Öffentlichkeit in Transformationsgesellschaften,* edited by Christine Lienemann-Perrin and Wolfgang Lienemann, 433–70. Stuttgart: Kohlhammer, 2006.
Lienemann-Perrin, Christine, and Mee-Hyun Chung. "Vom leidenden Volk zur Staatsbürgerschaft. Koreanische Kirchen zwischen *Minjung* und *Shimin*." In *Kirche und Öffentlichkeit in Transformationsgesellschaften,* edited by Christine Lienemann-Perrin and Wolfgang Lienemann, 301–31. Stuttgart: Kohlhammer, 2006.
Lienemann-Perrin, Christine, and Wolfgang Lienemann, editors. *Kirche und Öffentlichkeit in Transformationsgesellschaften.* Stuttgart: Kohlhammer, 2006.
Lima, Delcio Monteiro. *Os demônios descem do norte.* Rio de Janeiro: Francisco Alves, 1987.
Lima, Mirian Assumpção de. *A major da PM que tirou a farda.* Rio de Janeiro: Qualitymark, 2001.
Lindberg, Carter. "Luther on Poverty." In *Harvesting Martin Luther's Reflections on Theology, Ethics, and the Church,* edited by Timothy J. Wengert, 134–51. Grand Rapids: Eerdmans, 2004.
Link, Christian. *Schöpfung: Schöpfungstheologie angesichts der Herausforderungen des 20. Jahrhunderts.* Gütersloh: Gütersloher Verlagshaus, 1991.
Link, Rogério Sávio. *Luteranos em Rondônia: o processo migratório e o acompanhamento da Igreja Evangélica de Confissão Luterana no Brasil (1967–1987).* São Leopoldo: Sinodal, 2004.

Linz, Juan L. "The Future of an Authoritarian Situation or the Institutionalization of an Authoritarian Regime: The Case of Brazil." In *Authoritarian Brazil. Origins, Policies, and Future*, edited by Alfred Stepan, 233–54. New Haven, London: Yale University Press, 1973.

Linz, Juan J., and Alfred Stepan. *Problems of Democratic Transition and Consolidation. Southern Europe, South America, and Post-Communist Europe*. Baltimore/London: Johns Hopkins University Press, 1996.

Lira, Eliezer. *Lições Bíblicas: Mestre. Salvação e justificação: os pilares da fé cristã*. Rio de Janeiro: CPAD, 2006.

Lisbôa, Maria da Graça Cavalcanti. *A idéia de Universidade no Brasil*. Porto Alegre: EST, 1993.

Lissner, Jørgen, and Arne Sovik, editors. *A Lutheran Reader on Human Rights*. Geneva: Lutheran World Federation, LWF Report1/2, n.d.

Locke, John. *Second Treatise of Government* [1690], edited by C. B Macpherson. Indianapolis: Hackett, 1980.

Løgstrup, Knud Ejler. *The Ethical Demand*. Philadelphia: Fortress, 1971.

Lohse, Bernhard. *Luthers Theologie in ihrer historischen Entwicklung und in ihrem systematischen Zusammenhang*. Göttingen: Vandenhoeck & Ruprecht, 1995.

Longuini Neto, Luiz. *O novo rosto da missão: os movimentos ecumênico e evangelical no protestantismo latino-americano*. Belo Horizonte: Ultimato, 2002.

Löwy, Michel. *A guerra dos deuses: religião e política na América Latina*. Translated by Vera Lúcia Mello Joscelyne. Petrópolis: Vozes, 2000. [Engl. original ed.: The War of Gods—Religion and Politics in Latin America, 1996.]

Lugo, Luis E., editor. *Religion, Pluralism, and Public Life: Abraham Kuyper's Legacy for the Twenty-First Century*. Grand Rapids: Eerdmans, 2000.

Lührmann, Dieter. "Glaube 2. Neues Testament." *Evangelisches Kirchenlexikon, vol.* 2, 190–93. Göttingen: Vandenhoeck & Ruprecht, 1993.

Luhmann, Niklas. *Vertrauen: Ein Mechanismus der Reduktion sozialer Komplexität* [1968], 4th ed. Stuttgart: Lucius & Lucius, 2000.

———. "Vertrautheit, Zuversicht, Vertrauen, Probleme und Alternativen." In *Vertrauen. Die Grundlage sozialen Zusammenhalts*, edited by Martin Hartmann and Claus Offe, 143–160. Frankfurt, Campus, 2001.

Luther, Martin. *Luther's Works* [LW], edited by Jaroslav Pelikan (vols. 1–30) and Helmut T. Lehmann (vols. 31–55). Philadelphia: Muhlenberg Press, 1962.

Luther, Martin. *Werke: Kritische Gesamtausgabe* [WA: Weimarer Ausgabe]. Weimar: Hermann Böhlaus Nachfolger, 1883ff.

Luz, Ulrich. *Das Evangelium nach Matthäus, Evangelisch-Katholischer Kommentar I/1*. Zürich etc.: Benziger, 1985.

LWF [Lutheran World Federation]. *Sent Into the World: The Proceedings of the Fifth Assembly of The Lutheran World Federation. Evian, France, July 14–24, 1970*, edited by LaVern K. Grosc. Minneapolis: Augsburg, 1971.

Macedo, Edir. *A libertação da teologia*. Rio de Janeiro: Universal, 1997.

Macedo, Edir, and Carlos Oliveira. *Plano de poder: Deus, os cristãos e a política*. Rio de Janeiro: Thomas Nelson Brasil, 2008.

Machado, Maria das Dores Campos. *Carismáticos e pentecostais: adesão religiosa na esfera familiar*. Campinas: Autores Associados; São Paulo: ANPOCS, 1996.

Machiavelli, Niccolò. *Il Príncipe—Der Fürst* [1532]: *Lateinisch/Deutsch*. Stuttgart: Reclam, 1986.

Maclean, Iain S. *Opting for Democracy? Liberation Theology and the Struggle for Democracy in Brazil*. New York: Peter Lang, 1999.

———, editor. *Reconciliation, Nations and Churches in Latin America*. Aldershot: Ashgate, 2006.

Maddox, Marion. "Religion, Secularism and the Promise of Public Theology." *International Journal of Public Theology* 1/1 (2007) 82–100.

Maduro, Otto. "Once Again Liberating Theology? Towards A Latin American Liberation Theological Self-Criticism." In *Liberation Theology and Sexuality*, edited by Marcella Althaus-Reid, 19–31. Aldershot: Ashgate, 2006.

Mafra, Clara. "Gênero e estilo eclesial entre os evangélicos." In *Novo nascimento: os evangélicos em casa, na igreja e na política*, edited by Rubem César Fernandes, et al., 224–50. Rio de Janeiro: Mauad, 1998.

Mafra, Clara, and Robson de Paula. "O espírito da simplicidade: a cosmologia da Batalha Espiritual e as concepções de corpo e pessoa entre policiais pentecostais cariocas." *Religião e Sociedade* 22/1 (2002) 57–76.

Mainwaring, Scott. *The Catholic Church and Politics in Brazil, 1916–1985*. Stanford: Stanford University Press, 1986.

———. "Grassroots Popular Movements and the Struggle for Democracy: Nova Iguaçu." In *Democratizing Brazil. Problems of Transition and Consolidation*, edited by Alfred Stepan, 168–204. New York: Oxford University Press, 1989.

———. "Multipartism, robust federalism, and presidentialism in Brazil." In *Presidentialism and Democracy in Latin America*, edited by Scott Mainwaring and Matthew Soberg Shugart, 55–109. Cambridge: Cambridge University Press, 1997.

———. *Rethinking Party Systems in the Third Wave of Democratization: The Case of Brazil*. Stanford: Stanford University Press, 1999.

Mainwaring, Scott, and Matthew Soberg Shugart. "Juan Linz, Presidentialism, and Democracy: A Critical Appraisal." In *Politics, Society, and Democracy: Latin America,* edited by Scott Mainwaring and Arturo Valenzuela, 141–69. Boulder: Westview, 1998.

Majewski, Rodrigo Gonçalves. "Assembléia de Deus e teologia pública: o discurso pentecostal no espaço público." Unpublished thesis, Master of Theology. São Leopoldo: EST, 2010. Online: http://tede.est.edu.br/tede/tde_busca/processaPesquisa.php?listaDetalhes[]=227&processar=Processar

———. "Pentecostalismo e reconciliação: uma análise do discurso teológico popular das Assembléias de Deus do Brasil a partir de suas revistas de escola dominical." Unpublished course paper, Master of Theology—Hermeneutics, EST, 2008.

Mantey, Volker. *Zwei Schwerter—Zwei Reiche. Martin Luthers Zwei-Reiche-Lehre vor ihrem spätmittelalterlichen Hintergrund.* Tübingen: Mohr Siebeck, 2005.

Mariano, Ricardo. "Expansão pentecostal no Brasil: o caso da Igreja Universal do Reino de Deus." *Estudos Avançados* 18/52 (2004) 121–38.

———. *Neopentecostais: Sociologia do novo pentecostalismo no Brasil.* São Paulo: Loyola, 1999.

———. "Secularização do Estado, liberdades e pluralismo religioso." 2002. Online: http://www.naya.org.ar/congreso2002/ponencias/ricardo_mariano.htm.

———. "Usos e limites da teoria da escolha racional da religião." *Tempo Social* 20/2 (2008) 41–66.

Mariano, Ricardo, and Antônio Flávio Pierucci. "O envolvimento dos pentecostais na eleição de Collor." *Novos Estudos CEBPRAP* 34 (1992) 92–106.

Mariz, Cecília Loreto. *Coping with Poverty: Pentecostals and Christian Base Communities in Brazil.* Philadelphia: Temple University Press, 1994.

———. "Libertação e ética. Uma análise do discurso de pentecostais que se recuperaram do alcoolismo." In *Nem Anjos nem Demônios: interpretações sociológicas do pentecostalismo,* edited by Alberto Antoniazzi, 204–24. Petrópolis:Vozes, 1994.

———. "Pentecostalism and Confrontation with Poverty in Brazil." In *In the Power of the Spirit. The Pentecostal Challenge to Historic Churches in Latin America,* edited by Benjamin F. Gutiérrez and Dennis A. Smith, 129–46. Mexico City: AIPRAL; Guatemala: CELEP; Louisville: Presbyterian Church (U.S.A.), 1996.

Mariz, Cecília Loreto, and Maria das Dores Campos Machado. "Pentecostalism and Women in Brazil." In *Power, Politics, and Pentecostals in Latin America,* edited by Edward L. Cleary and Hannah W. Stewart-Gambino, 41–54. Boulder: Westview, 1997.

Marshall, Thomas H. *Class, Citizenship, and Social Development.* Garden City: Anchor Books, 1965.

Martin, David. *Pentecostalism: The World Their Parish.* London: Blackwell, 2002.

———. *Tongues of Fire: the Explosion of Protestantism in Latin America.* Oxford: Blackwell, 1990.

Martin, Leonard. "The Call to do Justice: Conflict in the Brazilian Catholic Church, 1968–79." In *Church and Politics in Latin America,* edited by Dermot Keogh, 299–320. New York: St. Martin's Press, 1990.

Martinez, Gaspar. *Confronting the Mystery of God: Political, Liberation, and Public Theologies.* New York: Continuum, 2001.

Martins, José de Souza. "Changes in the Relationship between Society and the State, and the Trend Toward Anomie in Social Movements and in Popular Organizations." In *Brazil: Dilemmas and Challenges,* 73–85. São Paulo: EDUSP, Instituto de Estudos Avançados, 2002.

Marty, Martin E. "Befreiungstheologie I. Kirchengeschichtlich 2. Nordamerika." In *Die Religion in Geschichte und Gegenwart, vol. 1,* 1209f. Tübingen: Mohr Siebeck, 1998.

———. *The Public Church: Mainline—Evangelical—Catholic.* New York: Crossroad, 1981.

———. "Reinhold Niebuhr: Public Theology and the American Experience." *Journal of Religion* 54/4 (1974) 332–359.

———. "Two Kinds of Civil Religion." In *American Civil Religion,* edited by Russell E. Richey and Donald G. Jones, 139–57. New York: Harper & Row, 1974.

Mathewes, Charles. *A Theology of Public Life.* Cambridge: Cambridge University Press, 2006.

Mathwig, Frank, and Wolfgang Lienemann. "Kirchen als zivilgesellschaftliche Akteure in aktuellen politischen Transformationsprozessen: Überlegungen zu einer Typologie." In *Kirche und Öffentlichkeit in Transformationsgesellschaften,* edited by Christine Lienemann-Perrin and Wolfgang Lienemann, 87–123. Stuttgart: Kohlhammer, 2006.

Matos, Henrique Cristiano José. *Nossa história. 500 anos de presença da Igreja Católica no Brasil. Vol. 1: Período Colonial.* São Paulo: Paulinas, 2001.

———. *Nossa história. 500 anos de presença da Igreja Católica no Brasil. Vol. 3: Período Republicano e Atualidade.* São Paulo: Paulinas, 2003.

Mau, Rudolf. "Gesetz V. Reformationszeit. " *Theologische Realenzyklopädie* 13 (1984) 82–90.

McDonough, Peter, Doh C. Shin and José Alvaro Moisés. "Democratization and Participation: Comparing Spain, Brazil, and Korea." *The Journal of Politics* 60/4 (1998) 919–53.

McFague, Sallie. *Life Abundant: Rethinking Theology and Economy for a Planet in Peril.* Minneapolis: Fortress, 2001.

Medeiros, Katia Maria Cabral. "Orientações ético-religiosas." In *Desafios do catolicismo na cidade: pesquisa em regiões metropolitanas brasileiras,* edited by CERIS, 199-251. São Paulo: Paulus, 2002.

Medick, Hans, and Peer Schmidt, editors. *Luther zwischen den Kulturen. Zeitgenossenschaft—Weltwirkung.* Göttingen: Vandenhoeck & Ruprecht, 2004.

Meincke, Sílvio. "Justificação por graça e fé: um novo espaço para a vida." *Estudos Teológicos* 23/3 (1983) 205–30.

Mendes, Gilmar Ferreira, Inocêncio Martires Coelho and Paulo Gustavo Gonet Branco. , *Curso de direito constitucional.* São Paulo: Saraiva, 2007.

Mendonça, Antônio Gouvêa, and Prócoro Velasques Filho. *Introdução ao protestantismo no Brasil.* São Paulo: Loyola; São Bernardo do Campo: IEPG, 2002.

Menezes, Paulo. "Democracia e exigências éticas." *CNBB* (1989), 59–69.

Merkel, Wolfgang, editor. *Systemwechsel 5. Zivilgesellschaft und Transformation.* Opladen: Leske & Budrich, 2000.

———. "Theorien der Transformation." *Politische Vierteljahresschrift* 36 (1994) 30–58.

Michiles, Carlos et al. *Cidadão Constituinte: a saga das emendas populares.* Rio de Janeiro: Paz e Terra, 1989.

Mieth, Dietmar. "Interkulturelle Ethik. Auf der Suche nach einer ethischen Ökumene." In *Wissenschaft und Weltethos,* edited by Hans Küng and Karl-Josef Kuschel, 359–82. München, Piper, 2000.

Miguez Bonino, José. *Doing Theology in a Revolutionary Situation.* Philadelphia: Fortress, 1975.

———. "From Justice to Law and Back: An Argentinian Perspective." In *Public Theology for the 21st century, Essays in Honour of Duncan B. Forrester,* edited by William F. Storrar and Andrew R. Morton, 63–74. London: T & T Clark, 2004.

———. "Latin America." In *An Introduction to Third World Theologies,* edited by John Parratt, 16–43. Cambridge: Cambridge University Press, 2006.

———. "Love and Social Tansformation in Liberation Theology." In *The Future of Liberation Theology: Essays in Honor of Gustavo Gutiérrez,* edited by Marc H. Ellis and Otto Maduro, 121–28. Maryknoll: Orbis, 1989.

Milbank, John. *Theology and Social Theory: Beyond Secular Reason.* Oxford: Blackwell, 2006.

Min, Anselm Kyonsuk. "From the Theology of Minjoong to the Theology of the Citizen: Reflections on Minjoong Theology in 21st Century Korea." *Journal of Asian and Asian American Theology* 5/Spring (2002) 11–35.

———. "Towards a Theology of Citizenship as the Central Challenge in Asia." *East Asian Pastoral Review* 41/2 (2004) 136–59. Online: http://eapi.admin.edu.ph/eapr004/amin.htm.

Moe-Lobeda, Cynthia D. *Public Church: For the Life of the World.* Minneapolis: Augsburg Fortress, 2004.

Moisés, José Álvaro. *Os Brasileiros e a democracia. Bases sócio-políticas da legitimidade democrática.* São Paulo: Ática, 1994.

———. "Cidadania, confiança e instituições democráticas." *Lua Nova* 65(2005) 71–94.

Moltmann, Jürgen. *Erfahrungen theologischen Denkens: Wege und Formen christlicher Theologie.* Gütersloh: Chr. Kaiser/ Gütersloher Verlagshaus, 1999.

———. *God for a Secular Society: The Public Relevance of Theology.* Minneapolis: Augsburg: Fortress, 1999.

———. *Gott im Projekt der modernen Welt: Beiträge zur öffentlichen Relevanz der Theologie.* Gütersloh: Chr. Kaiser/ Gütersloher Verlagshaus, 1997. [English version: *God for a Secular Society. The Public Relevance of Theology* (Minneapolis: Fortress, 1999).]

Mondaini, Marco. "O respeito aos direitos dos indivíduos." In *História da Cidadania,* edited by Jaime Pinsky and Carla Bassanezi Pinsky, 115–33. São Paulo: Contexto, 2003.

Montero, Paula. "Religião, pluralismo e esfera pública no Brasil." *Novos Estudos—CEBRAP* 74 (2006) 47–65.

Montes, Maria Lucia. "As figures do sagrado: entre o público e o privado." In *Historia da vida privada no Brasil, v.4,* edited by Lilia Moritz Schwarcz, 63–171. São Paulo: Companhia das Letras, 1998.

Moraes, Maria Lygia Quartim de. "Cidadania no feminino." In *História da Cidadania,* edited by Jaime Pinsky and Carla Bassanezi Pinsky, 495–515. São Paulo: Contexto, 2003.

Mouffe, Chantal, editor. *Dimensions of Radical Democracy: Pluralism, Citizenship, Community.*London: Verso, 1992.

Mueller, Enio R. "Um balanço da Teologia da Libertação como *intellectus amoris.*" In *Sarça ardente: teologia na América Latina: prospectivas,* edited by Luiz Carlos Susin, 41–77. São Paulo: Paulinas, SOTER, 2000.

———. *Teologia cristã em poucas palavras.* São Paulo: Teológica; São Leopoldo: EST, 2005.

———. "A teologia e seu estatuto teórico: contribuições para uma discussão atual na universidade brasileira." *Estudos Teológicos* 47/2 (2007) 88–103.

Musskopf, André Sidnei. "Até onde estamos disposto(as) a ir? Carta aberta ao Fórum Mundial de Teologia e Libertação." In *Teologia para outro mundo possível,* edited by Luiz Carlos Susin, 471–74. São Paulo: Paulinas, 2006.

———. *Homossexuais e o Ministério na Igreja.* São Leopoldo: Oikos, 2005.

———. "Via(da)gens teológicas: itinerários para uma teologia queer no Brasil." PhD diss., Escola Superior de Teologia, 2008. Online: http://tede.est.edu.br/tede/tde_busca/arquivo.php?codArquivo=96.

———. "'Who is not afraid of Gay Theology'—Comments to Björn Krondorfer." *Theology and Sexuality* 14/1 (2007) 89–94.

Nagle, Robin. *Claiming the Virgin: The Broken Promise of Liberation Theology in Brazil.* New York: Routledge, 1997.

Nalini, José Renato. "Justiça e cidadania." In *Práticas da cidadania,* edited by Jaime Pinsky, 11–19. São Paulo: Contexto, 2004.

Neutzling, Inácio, editor. *A teologia na universidade contemporânea.* São Leopoldo: Unisinos, 2005.

———, editor. "Teologia pública." *Cadernos IHU em formação* 2/8 (2006)

Newbigin, Lesslie. "The Trinity as Public Truth." In *The Trinity in a Pluralistic Age: Theological Essays on Culture and Religion*, edited by Kevin J.Vanhoozer, 1–8. Grand Rapids: Eerdmans, 1997.

Niles, D. Preman. "Justice, Peace and the Integrity of Creation." In *Dictionary of the Ecumenical Movement,* edited by Nicholas Lossky, et al., 631–33. Geneva: WCC, 2002.

Nóbrega, Francisco Adalberto. *Deus e constituição: a tradição brasileira.* Petrópolis: Vozes, 1998.

Norris, Pippa, and Ronald Inglehart. *Sacred and Secular: Religion and Politics Worldwide.* Cambridge: Cambridge University Press, 2004.

Novaes, Regina Reyes. "Crenças religiosas e convicções políticas." In *Política e cultura: século XXI,* edited by Luis Carlos Fridman, 63–98. Rio de Janeiro: ALERJ, Relum-Dumará, 2002.

———. *Os escolhidos de Deus. Pentecostais, trabalhadores & cidadania.* Rio de Janeiro: ISER, Marco Zero, 1985.

Odalia, Nilo. "Revolução francesa: a liberdade como meta coletiva." In *História da Cidadania,* edited by Jaime Pinsky and Carla Bassanezi Pinsky, 159–69. São Paulo: Contexto, 2003.

O´Donnell, Guillermo. "Democracia delegativa?" *Novos Estudos CEBRAP,* 31 (1991) 25–40.

———. "On the State, Democratization and Some Conceptual Problems. A Latin American View with Glances at Some Post-Communist Countries." *World Development* 21 (1993) 1355–1369.

———. "Polyarchies and the (Un)Rule of Law in Latin America: A Partial Conclusion." In *Jenseits von Zentrum und Peripherie: Zur Verfassung der fragmentierten Weltgesellschaft*, edited by Hauke Brunkhorst and Sérgio Costa, 53–79. München/Mering: Rainer Hampp Verlag, 2005.

O´Donnell, Guillermo, and Philippe C. Schmitter. *Transitions from Authoritarian Rule. Tentative Conclusions about Uncertain Democracies.* Baltimore: Johns Hopkins Press, 1986.

O'Donovan, Oliver, and Joan Lockwood O'Donovan, eds. *From Irenaeus to Grotius: A Sourcebook in Christian Political Thought.* Grand Rapids: Eerdmans, 1999.

Offe, Claus. "How can we trust our fellow citizens?" In *Democracy and Trust*, edited by Mark Warren, 42–87. Cambridge: Cambridge University Press, 1999.

———. "Wie können wir unseren Mitbürgern vertrauen?" In *Vertrauen. Die Grundlage sozialen Zusammenhalts,* edited by Martin Hartmann and Claus Offe, 241–94. Frankfurt, Campus, 2001.

Offe, Claus, and Susanne Fuchs. "A Decline of Social Capital: The German Case." In *Democracies in Flux: The Evolution of Social Capital in Contemporary Society*, edited by Robert D. Putnam, 189–243. New York: Oxford University Press, 2002.

Oliveira, Joanyr de. *The Assemblies of God in Brazil. An Illustrated Historical Summary.* Rio de Janeiro: CPAD, 1997.

Oliveira, Marco Davi de. *A religião mais negra do Brasil. Por que mais de oito milhões de negros são pentecostais.* São Paulo: Mundo Cristão, 2004.

Oliveira, Nilton Emmerick. "Jaime Wright (1927–1999)." In *Vidas ecumênicas: testemunhas do ecumenismo no Brasil,* edited by Rudolf von Sinner, Elias Wolff, and Carlos Gilberto Bock, 175–95. São Leopoldo: Sinodal; Porto Alegre: Padre Reus, 2006.

Oliveira, Pedro A. Ribeiro de. "A teoria do *trabalho religioso* em Pierre Bourdieu." In *Sociologia da religião: enfoques teóricos*, edited by Faustino Teixeira, 177–97. Petrópolis: Vozes, 2003.

Oliveira, Raimundo Ferreira de. *Ética cristã: a vida cristã no dia-a-dia.* Campinas: EETAD, 1999.

Oro, Ari Pedro. "Considerações sobre a liberdade religiosa no Brasil." *Ciências e Letras* 37 (2005) 433–47. Online: http://www.fapa.com.br/ cienciaseletras/publicacoes.htm.

Oro, Ari Pedro., et al., editors. *Igreja Universal do Reino de Deus: os novos conquistadores da fé.* São Paulo: Paulinas, 2003.

Paes, José Eduardo Sabo. *Fundações, Associações e Entidades de Interesse Social.* Brasília: Brasília Jurídica, 2006.

Panikkar, Raimon. *The Cosmotheandric Experience. Emerging Religious Consciousness.* Maryknoll: Orbis, 1993.

———. *The Intra-Religious Dialogue.* New York, Paulist, 1978.

———. "The Invisible Harmony: A Universal Theory of Religion or a Cosmic Confidence in Reality?" In *Towards a Universal Theology of Religion*, edited by Leonard Swidler, 118–53. Maryknoll: Orbis, 1985.

———. "The Jordan, the Tiber, and the Ganges. Three Kairological Moments of Christic Self-Consciousness." In *The Myth of Christian Uniqueness,* edited by John Hick and Paul F. Knitter, 89–116. London, SCM, 1988.

———. *La nueva inocéncia.* Estella: Verbo Divino, 1993.

———. "A Self-Critical Dialogue." In *The Intercultural Challenge of Raimon Panikkar,* edited by Joseph Prabhu, 227-91. Maryknoll: Orbis, 1996.

Parlow, Mara Sandra. "Fruto maduro não volta a verde: Promotoras Legais Populares—um estudo de caso." Masters Thesis, São Leopoldo: EST, 2000.

Parratt, John, editor. *An Introduction to Third World Theologies*. Cambridge: Cambridge University Press, 2006.

Pattnayak, Satya, editor. *Organized Religion in the Political Transformation of Latin America*. Lanham: University Press of America, 1995.

Paul VI, Pope. Apostolic Exhortation *Evangelii Nuntiandi*. Online: http://www.vatican.va/holy_father/paul_vi/ apost_exhortations/documents/hf_p-vi_exh_19751208_evangelii-nuntiandi_en.html.

Pauly, Evaldo Luis. *Cidadania e pastoral urbana*. São Leopoldo: Sinodal, 1995.

———. *Ética, educação e cidadania: questões de fundamentação teológica e filosófica da ética da educação*. São Leopoldo: Sinodal, 2002.

———. "Liberdade e laicismo na atual educação brasileira." *Observatório da Laicidade do Estado*, 2008. Online: http:// www.nepp-dh.ufrj.br/ole/posicionamentos6-3.html.

———. "O novo rosto do ensino de teologia no Brasil: Números, normas legais e espiritualidade." *Protestantismo em Revista* 5/2 (2006) 20-35. Online: http://www3.est.edu.br/nepp/ revista/010/10ano05n2 02.pdf.

———. "Sociedade civil e igreja: a justificação pela fé como critério para 'discutir a relação' entre fé e política." In *Congresso Ecumênico 2006: Missão e Ecumenismo na América Latina*, edited by Rudolf von Sinner, 2006. CD-ROM. São Leopoldo: EST, CAPES.

Paviani, Jayme, and José C. Pozenato. *A universidade em debate*. Caxias do Sul: EDUCS, 1979.

PCJP [Pontifical Council for Justice and Peace]. *Compendium of the Social Doctrine of the Church*, Washington/D.C.: United States Conference of Catholic Bishops, 2005.

Pearson, Clive. "The Quest for a Glocal Public Theology." *International Journal of Public Theology* 1/2 (2007) 151–72.

Pereira, Anthony W. "An Ugly Democracy? State Violence and the Rule of Law in Postauthoritarian Brazil." In *Democratic Brazil. Actors, Institutions, and Processes*, edited by Peter R. Kingstone and Timothy P. Power, 217–35. Pittsburgh: University of Pittsburgh Press, 2000.

Peters, Christian. "Werke IV. Kirchengeschichtlich." *Theologische Realenzyklopädie* 35 (2003) 633–41.

Peterson, Erik. "Der Monotheismus als politisches Problem: Ein Beitrag zur Geschichte der politische Theologie im Imperium Romanum." [1935]. In *Theologische Traktate, Ausgewählte Schriften* vol. 1, 23–81. Würzburg: Echter, 1994.

Petrella, Ivan. *Beyond Liberation Theology: A Polemic*. London: SCM, 2008.

———. *The Future of Liberation Theology: An Argument and Manifesto*. London: SCM, 2006.

———, editor. *Latin American Liberation Theology: The Next Generation*. Maryknoll: Orbis, 2005.

Pew Forum on Religion and Public Life, The. *Spirit and Power: A 10-Country Survey of Pentecostals*. Washington: Pew Research Center, 2006. Online: http://pewforum.org/publications/surveys/ pentecostals-06.pdf.

Pfleiderer, Georg. "Politisch-religiöse Semantik. Zur Analytik politischer Religion und ihrer Kontextualität." In *Politische Religion: Geschichte und Gegenwart eines Problemfeldes*, edited by Georg Pfleiderer and Ekkehard W. Stegemann, 19–58. Zürich: TVZ, 2004.

Pfleiderer, Georg, and Ekkehard W. Stegemann, editors. *Politische Religion: Geschichte und Gegenwart eines Problemfeldes*. Zürich: TVZ, 2004.

Pierucci, Antônio Flávio. "'Bye bye, Brasil'—O declínio das religiões tradicionais no Censo 2000." *Estudos Avançados* 18/52 (2004) 17–28.

———. "Liberdade de cultos na sociedade de serviços: em defesa do consumidor religioso." *Novos Estudos CEBRAP* 44 (1996) 3–11.

Pierucci, Antônio Flávio, and Reginaldo Prandi. *A realidade social das religiões no Brasil: religião, sociedade e política*. São Paulo: Hucitec, 1996.

Pinsky, Jaime, editor. *Práticas da cidadania*. São Paulo: Contexto, 2004.

———. "Os profetas sociais e o Deus da cidadania." In *História da Cidadania*, edited by Jaime Pinsky and Carla Bassanezi Pinsky, 15–27. São Paulo: Contexto, 2003.

Pinsky, Jaime, and Carla Bassanezi Pinsky, editors. *História da Cidadania*. São Paulo: Contexto, 2003.

Plou, Daphne S. *Caminhos de unidade: itinerário do diálogo ecumênico na América Latina (1916–2001)*. São Leopoldo: Sinodal, 2002.

Poletto, Ivo. "A CNBB e a luta pela terra no Brasil." *INP* (2003) 333–52.

Power, Timothy J. "Political Institutions in Democratic Brazil: Politics as a Permanent Constitutional Convention." In *Democratic Brazil. Actors, Institutions, and Processes*, edited by Peter R. Kingstone and Timothy P. Power, 17–35. Pittsburgh: University of Pittsburgh Press, 2000.

Prabhu, Joseph, editor. *The Intercultural Challenge of Raimon Panikkar*. Maryknoll, Orbis, 1996.

Prandi, Reginaldo. "Perto da magia, longe da política." In *A realidade social das religiões no Brasil: religião, sociedade e política*, edited by Antonio Flavio Pierucci and Reginaldo Prandi, 93–105. São Paulo: Hucitec, 1996.

———. "Perto da magia, longe da política. Derivações do encantamento no mundo desencantado." *Novos Estudos CEBRAP* 34 (1992) 81-91.

———. *Um sopro do Espírito.* São Paulo: EDUSP, 1997.

Prien, Hans-Jürgen. *Das Christentum in Lateinamerika.* Kirchengeschichte in Einzeldarstellungen IV/6. Leipzig: Evangelische Verlagsanstalt, 2007.

———. *Evangelische Kirchwerdung in Brasilien. Von den deutsch-evangelischen Gemeinden zur Evangelischen Kirche Lutherischen Bekenntnisses in Brasilien.* Gütersloh: Gütersloher Verlagshaus Gerd Mohn, 1989.

———. *Die Geschichte des Christentums in Lateinamerika.* Göttingen: Vandenhoeck & Ruprecht, 1978.

———. "Identity and Problems of Development: The Evangelical Church of Lutheran Confession in Brazil." In *Lutheran Churches—Salt or Mirror of Society? Case Studies on the Theory and Practice of the Two Kingdoms Doctrine,* edited by Ulrich Duchrow, 192–242. Geneva: Lutheran World Federation, 1977.

———. "Lateinamerika (Brasilien/Argentinien)." In *Die Ambivalenz der Zweireichelehre in lutherischen Kirchen des 20. Jahrhunderts,* edited by Ulrich Duchrow and Wolfgang Huber, 195–210. Gütersloh: Gütersloher Verlagshaus Gerd Mohn, 1976.

———. "Präsident General Geisel: Ein distanzierter Protestant." *Lutherische Monatshefte* 13/1 (1974) 4–5.

Puddington, Arch. "Freedom in the World 2007: Freedom Stagnation amid pushback against democracy." Online: http://www.freedomhouse.org.

———. "Freedom in Retreat: Is the Tide Turning? Findings of *Freedom in the World 2008.*" 2008. Online: http://www.freedomhouse.org/uploads/fiwo8launch/ FIWo8Overview.pdf.

Purper, Dornalli L. "Religião e desenvolvimento." In *Quem assume esta tarefa? Um documentário de uma igreja em busca de sua identidade,* edited by Germano Burger, 219–49. São Leopoldo: Sinodal, 1977.

Putnam, Robert D. *Bowling Alone: The Collapse and Revival of American Community.* New York: Simon & Schuster, 2000.

———, editor. *Democracies in Flux: The Evolution of Social Capital in Contemporary Society.* New York: Oxford University Press, 2002.

———, editor. *Gesellschaft und Gemeinsinn: Sozialkapital im internationalen Vergleich.* Gütersloh: Bertelsmann, 2001.

———. *Making Democracy Work: Civic Traditions in Modern Italy.* Princeton: Princeton University Press, 1994.

Quirino, Célia Galvão, and Maria Lúcia Montes. *Constituiçoes brasileiras e cidadania.* São Paulo: Ática, 1987.

Ratzinger, Joseph, and Hans Maier. *Demokratie in der Kirche: Möglichkeiten und Grenzen.* Limburg: Lahn, 2000.

Rau, Johannes. "Vertrauen in Deutschland—eine Ermutigung." Berliner Rede 2004 by President Johannes Rau, delivered on May 12, 2004 at Bellevue Castle in Berlin. Online: http://www.bundespraesident.de.

Rawls, John. *A Theory of Justice.* Oxford: Oxford University Press, 1989.

Reid, William R., and Frank A. Ineson. *Brazil 1980: The Protestant Handbook.* Monrovia: Missions Advanced Research & Communications Center, 1973.

Rega, Lourenço Stélio. "As Diretrizes Curriculares Nacionais para os cursos de Teologia e os conteúdos curriculares", paper presented at the Public Hearing of the (Brazilian) National Council of Education, November 22, 2010.

Reily, Duncan Alexander. *História Documental do Protestantismo no Brasil.* São Paulo: ASTE, 2003.

Renders, Helmut. "A soteriologia social de John Wesley com consideração especial de seus aspectos comunitários, sinergéticos e públicos." PhD diss., Methodist University of São Paulo, 2006.

Renovato, Elinaldo. *Células-tronco: uma visão ética e cristã.* Rio de Janeiro: CPAD, 2005.

———. *Lições Bíblicas: Ética cristã: confrontando as questões morais.* Rio de Janeiro: CPAD, 2002.

———. *Lições Bíblicas: Mestre. Tiago: a prática da vida cristã.* Rio de Janeiro: CPAD, 1999.

Reuter, Hans-Richard, et al., editors. *Freiheit verantworten, Festschrift für Wolfgang Huber zum 60. Geburtstag.* Gütersloh: Chr. Kaiser/ Gütersloher Verlagshaus, 2002.

Ribeiro, Lúcia. *Sexualidade e reprodução: o que os padres dizem e o que deixam de dizer.* Petrópolis: Vozes, 2001.

Ribeiro, Renato Janine. "Religião e política no Brasil contemporâneo." In *Política e cultura: século XXI,* edited by Luis Carlos Fridman, 99–110. Rio de Janeiro: ALERJ, Relum-Dumará, 2002.

Ricœur, Paul. *Le conflit des interpretations,* Paris: Seuil, 1969.

———. *De l'interprétation: essai sur Freud.* Paris: Seuil, 1965.

Rieth, Ricardo Willy. "'*Habsucht' bei Martin Luther: Ökonomisches und theologisches Denken, Tradition und soziale Wirklichkeit im Zeitalter der Reformation.*" Weimar: Böhlau, 1996.

———. "Luther on Greed." In *Harvesting Martin Luther's Reflections on Theology, Ethics, and the Church,* edited by Timothy J. Wengert, 152–68. Grand Rapids: Eerdmans, 2004.

Ritschl, Dietrich. "Der Beitrag des Calvinismus für die Entwicklung des Menschenrechtsgedankens in Europa und Nordamerika [1980]." In *Konzepte: Ökumene, Medizin, Ethik. Gesammelte Aufsätze,* 301-15. München: Chr. Kaiser, 1986.

———. *Theorie und Konkretion in der Ökumenischen Theologie: Kann es eine Hermeneutik des Vertrauens inmitten differierender semiotischer Systeme geben?* Münster: LIT, 2003.

Rodrigues, Alberto Tosi. "Autonomous Participation and Political Institutions in Recent Brazilian Democracy." In *Political Transition and Democratic Consolidation: Studies on Contemporary Brazil,* edited by Adriano Nervo Codato, 103–26. New York: Nova Science, 2006.

Rolim, Francisco Cartaxo. "Pentecostalismo, governos militares e revolução." *Revista Eclesiástica Brasileira* 53/210 (1993) 324–48.

———. *Pentecostalismo: Brasil e América Latina,* Petrópolis: Vozes, 1995.

Roos, Lothar. "Demokratie, Demokratisierung und Menschenrechte in den Dokumenten der Katholischen Soziallehre." In *Lateinamerika und die Katholische Soziallehre: Ein lateinamerikanisch-deutsches Dialogprogramm. 3 vols,* edited by Peter Hünermann and Juan Carlos Scannone, 19–74. Mainz: Grünewald, 1993.

Rorty, Richard. "Religion As Conversation-Stopper." In *Philosophy and Social Hope,* 168–74. London: Penguin, 1999.

Rosa, João Guimarês. *Grande Sertão: Veredas.* Rio de Janeiro: Nova Fronteira, 2008.

Rothstein, Bo. "Schweden." In *Gesellschaft und Gemeinsinn: Sozialkapital im internationalen Vergleich,* edited by Robert D. Putnam, 115–197. Gütersloh: Bertelsmann, 2001.

Rousseau, Jean-Jacques. "Vom Gesellschaftsvertrag oder Prinzipien des Staatsrechtes" [1762], in *Politische Schriften,* Übersetzung und Einführung von Ludwig Schmidts, 2nd ed., 59-208. Paderborn: Schöningh, 1995.

Sader, Emil, and Ken Silverstein. *Without Fear of Being Happy: Lula, the Workers Party and Brazil.* London/New York: Verso, 1991.

Sanchez, Wagner Lopes, editor. *Cristianismo na América Latina e no Caribe: trajetórias, diagnósticos, prospectivas.* São Paulo: Paulinas, 2003.

Sanneh, Lamin. *Whose Religion is Christianity? The Gospel Beyond the West.* Grand Rapids: Eerdmans, 2003.

Santa Ana, Júlio de. *Ecumenismo e libertação,* Petrópolis: Vozes, 1987.

Santos, Joe Marçal Gonçalves, and Luiz Carlos Susin, *Nosso planeta, nossa vida,* São Paulo: Paulinas, 2011.

Sauer, Sérgio. "The Land Issue as a Theological Problem: The Roman Catholic and Lutheran Churches' Social and Political Commitment to the Struggle for Land in Brazil." Master's Thesis, Stavanger School of Mission and Theology, 1996.

Scampini, José. *A liberdade religiosa nas constituições brasileiras: Estudo filosófico-jurídico comparado.* Petrópolis: Vozes, 1978.

Schäfer, Heinrich. *Praxis— Theologie—Religion: Grundlinien einer Theologie- und Religionstheorie im Anschluss an Pierre Bourdieu.* Frankfurt a.M.: Lembeck, 2004.

Scheper-Hughes, Nancy. *Death Withouth Weeping: the Violence of Everyday Life in Brazil.* Berkeley: University of California Press, 1993.

Scherkerkewitz, Iso Chaitz. "O direito de religião no Brasil." 1996. Online: http://www.espirito.org.br/portal/artigos/diversos/religiao/ o-direito-de-religiao.html.

Schindler, Alfred. "Augustin/Augustinismus I." *Theologische Realenzyklopädie* 4 (1979) 646–98.

Schmidt, Manfred G. "Demokratie (J)." In *Evangelisches Staatslexikon, Neuausgabe,* edited by Werner Heun, et al., 325–36. Stuttgart: Kohlhammer, 2006.

———. *Demokratietheorien.* Opladen:Leske + Budrich, 2000.

Schmidt, Martina. "Protestantisme historique et liberation: Exemples d'un renouveau oecuménique dans le Sud e dans le Nord." PhD diss., Lausanne Faculté de Théologie, 2005.

———. "Quand nous joignons notre voix au chant de la libération: Enquête sur la présence luthérienne au Brésil." Unpublished Specialization Thesis, Lausanne Faculté de Théologie, 1999.

Schmitt, Carl. *Politische Theologie: Vier Kapitel von der Souveränität.* Berlin: Duncker & Humblot, 1993.

Schmitt, Flávio. "A cidadania da fé: uma releitura da justiça de Deus em Romanos." PhD dissertation, São Bernardo do Campo, UMESP, 1998.

Schneider, Nélio. *Paulo de Tarso: Apóstolo a serviço do Evangelho de Jesus Cristo e da cidadania.* São Leopoldo: CEBI, 1999.

Schneider, Ronald M. *Order and Progress: a Political History of Brazil.* Boulder: Westview, 1991.

Schoberth, Wolfgang. "Die bessere Gerechtigkeit und die realistischere Politik: Ein Versuch zur politischen Ethik." In *Salz der Erde: Zugänge zur Bergpredigt,* edited by Reinhard Feldmeier, 108–40. Göttingen: Vandenhoeck & Ruprecht, 1998.

Schørring, Jens Holger, et al., editors. *From Federation to Communion: The History of the Lutheran World Federation.* Minneapolis: Fortress, 1997.

Schrage, Wolfgang. *Ethik des Neuen Testaments.* Göttingen: Vandenhoeck & Ruprecht, 1982.

Schreiter, Robert J. *Constructing Local Theologies.* Maryknoll: Orbis, 1985.

Schröder, Friedrich. *Brasilien und Wittenberg: Ursprung und Gestaltung deutschen evangelischen Kirchentums in Brasilien.* Berlin: de Gruyter, 1936.

Schünemann, Rolf. *Do gueto à participação: o surgimento da consciência sócio-política na IECLB entre 1960 e 1975.* São Leopoldo: Sinodal, 1992.

Schuler, Roberto José. *Pfingstbewegungen in Brasilien: Sozio-politische Implikationen der neuen Pluralität.* São Leopoldo: Sinodal, 2004.

Schultz, Adilson. "Deus está presente— o diabo está no meio: o protestantismo e as estruturas teológicas do imaginário religioso brasileiro." PhD diss., São Leopoldo EST, 2005. Online: http://www3.est.edu.br/biblioteca/btd/Textos/Doutor/Schultz_a_td48.pdf..

———. "Misturando os espíritos . . . Algo de simultâneo, escorregadio e ambíguo abala os fundamentos da missão cristã no protestantismo brasileiro." Master's thesis, São Leopoldo EST, 2000

Schultze, Andrea, Rudolf von Sinner, and Wolfram Stierle, editors. *Vom Geheimnis des Unterschieds: Die Wahrnehmung des Fremden in Ökumene—Missions—und Religionswissenschaft.* Münster: LIT, 2002.

Schuurmann, Lambert. "A doutrina dos dois reinos em sua relevância para a situação latino-americana." *Estudos Teológicos* 12/2 (1972) 63–69.

Scott, Peter, and William T. Cavanaugh, editors. *The Blackwell Companion to Political Theology.* Oxford: Blackwell, 2004.

Secco, Lincoln. *Gramsci no Brasil: recepção e difusão de suas idéias.* São Paulo: Cortez, 2002.

Segundo, Juan Luis. *The Liberation of Theology.* Maryknoll: Orbis, 1991.

Serbin, Kenneth. "The Catholic Church, Religious Pluralism, and Democracy in Brazil." In *Democratic Brazil. Actors, Institutions, and Processes*, edited by Peter R. Kingstone and Timothy P. Power, 144–61. Pittsburgh: University of Pittsburgh Press, 2000.

———. *Secret Dialogues: Church-State Relations, Torture, and Social Justice in Authoritarian Brazil.* Pittsburgh: University of Pittsburgh Press, 2000.

Shaull, Richard. *Encounter with Revolution.* New York: Association Press, 1955.

———. "Die revolutionäre Herausforderung an Kirche und Theologie." In *Appell an die Kirchen der Welt: Dokumente der Weltkonferenz für Kirche und Gesellschaft*, edited by Ökumenischer Rat der Kirchen, 91–99. Stuttgart/Berlin: Kreuz, 1967.

———. *Surpreendido pela graça: memórias de um teólogo. Estados Unidos, América Latina, Brasil.* Rio de Janeiro: Rocco, 2003.

Shaull, Richard, and Waldo César. *Pentecostalism and the Future of the Christian Churches. Promises, Limitations, Challenges.* Grand Rapids: Eerdmans, 2000.

Siepierski, Paulo D. "Pós-pentecostalismo e política no Brasil." *Estudos Teológicos* 37/1 (1997) 47–61.

Sigmund, Paul. *Liberation Theology at the Crossroads: Democracy or Revolution?* New York: Oxford University Press, 1990.

Silva, Antônio Carlos Teles da. "As origens do movimento ecumênico na Amazônia paraense." Master's thesis, São Leopoldo: EST, 2005.

Silva, Hélio. *Vargas: uma biografia política.* Porto Alegre: L&PM, 2004.

Silva, Luiz Inácio Lula da. "Discurso do presidente da República, Luiz Inácio Lula da Silva, na cerimônia por ocasião da 9ª Assembléia do Conselho Mundial de Igrejas Porto Alegre—RS, 17 de fevereiro de 2006." Online: http://www.info.planalto.gov.br/download/discursos/PR1047. DOC.

Silva, Vagner Gonçalves da, editor. *Intolerância religiosa: impactos do neopentecostalismo no campo religioso afro-brasileiro.* São Paulo: EDUSP, 2007.

Singer, Paul. "A cidadania para todos." In *História da Cidadania*, edited by Jaime Pinsky and Carla Bassanezi Pinsky, 190–263. São Paulo: Contexto, 2003.

Sinner, Rudolf von. "Der Beitrag der Kirchen zum demokratischen Übergang in Brasilien." In *Kirche und Öffentlichkeit in Transformationsgesellschaften*, edited by Christine Lienemann-Perrin and Wolfgang Lienemann, 267–300. Stuttgart: Kohlhammer, 2006.

———. "Brazil: From Liberation Theology to a Theology of Citizenship as Public Theology." *International Journal of Public Theology* 1/3–4 (2007) 338–63.

———. "The Contribution of the Churches to Citizenship in Brazil." *Journal of International Affairs* 61/1 (2007) 171–84.

———. "Ecumenical Hermeneutics for a Plural Christianity. Reflections on Contextuality and Catholicity." *Bangalore Theological Forum* 34/2 (2002) 89–115. Online: http://www.religion-online.org/showarticle.asp?title=2455.

———. "Healing Relationships in Society: The Struggle for Citizenship in Brazil." *International Review of Mission* 93/369 (2004) 238–54.

———. "Inter-religious Dialogue: From 'Anonymous Christians' to the Theologies of Religion." In *The God of all Grace: Essays in Honour of Origen Vasantha Jathanna.* edited by Joseph George, 186–201. Bangalore: ATC, UTC 2005

———. "Leonardo Boff—a Protestant Catholic." *Cultural Encounters* 3/2 (2007) 7–22.

———. "Menschenrechte in Brasilien. Die Notwendigkeit einer verlässlichen Gesellschaft," Vortrag vor der Forschungsgemeinschaft Mensch im Recht, 6. Juni 2000, Basel. Online: http://www.mensch-im-recht.ch/online/sinner01.html.

———."Ökumene im 21. Jahrhundert: Thesen zur Diskussion." In *Profilierte Ökumene: Bleibend Wichtiges und jetzt Dringliches, FS Dietrich Ritschl zum 80. Geburtstag,* edited by Fernando Enns, Martin Hailer and Ulrike Link-Wieczorek, 76–93. Frankfurt a. M.: Lembeck, 2009.

———.*Reden vom Dreieinigen Gott in Brasilien und Indien: Grundzüge einer ökumenischen Hermeneutik im Dialog mit Leonardo Boff und Raimon Panikkar.* Tübingen: Mohr Siebeck, 2003.

———. "Religion and Power. Towards the Political Sustainability of the World." *Concilium* 40/5 (2004) 96–105.

———. "Religião e transformação no Brasil: Uma perspectiva evangélico-luterana." In *Religião e transformação no Brasil,* edited by Maria Carmelita de Freitas, 159–75. São Paulo: Paulinas, 2007.

———. "Sérgio Costa: Vom Nordatlantik zum 'Black Atlantic'. Postkoloniale Konfigurationen und Paradoxien transnationaler Politik." *Lateinamerika Analysen* 18/3 (2007) 238–40.

———. "Teologia como ciência." *Estudos Teológicos* 47/2 (2007) 57–66.

———. "Trinity, Church and Society in Brazil." In *A World for All? Global Civil Society in Political Theory and Trinitarian Theology,* edited by William Storrar, Peter Casarella and Paul Louis Metzger, 265-281. Grand Rapids: Eerdmans, 2011.

———. "Trust and convivência. Contributions to a Hermeneutics of Trust in Communal Interaction." *The Ecumenical Review* 57/3 (2004) 322–41.

Sinner, Rudolf von, and Rodrigo Gonçalves Majewski. "A contribuição da IECLB para a cidadania no Brasil." *Estudos Teológicos* 45/2 (2005) 32–61.

Skidmore, Thomas E. "Brazil's Slow Road to Democratization." In *Democratizing Brazil. Problems of Transition and Consolidation,* edited by Alfred Stepan, 5–42. New York: Oxford University Press, 1989.

———. "Politics and Economic Policy Making in Authoritarian Brazil, 1937–71." In *Authoritarian Brazil. Origins, Policies, and Future,* edited by Alfred Stepan, 3–46. New Haven, London: Yale University Press, 1973.

———. *Politics in Brazil 1930–1964. An Experiment in Democracy.* New York: Oxford University Press, 1967.

———. *The Politics of Military Rule in Brazil 1964–1985.* New York: Oxford University Press, 1988.

Slenczka, Reinhard. "Glaube VI. Reformation/Neuzeit/Systematisch-theologisch." *Theologische Realenzyklopädie* 13 (1984) 318–65.

Smit, Dirkie. "Notions of the Public and Doing Theology." *International Journal of Public Theology* 1/3–4 (2007) 431–54.

Soares, Esequias. *Lições Bíblicas: Romanos: o evangelho da justiça de Deus.* Rio de Janeiro: CPAD, 1998.

Soares, Luiz Eduardo, et al. *Elite da Tropa.* Rio de Janeiro: Objetiva, 2006.

Soares Filho, Kleber Torres. "Assembléia de Deus na política brasileira: do apoliticismo ao projeto 'Cidadania AD Brasil.' Bachelor's thesis in Social Communication, Universidade de São Paulo, 2006. Online: http://www.mep.org.br/arquivos/assembleiadedeusnapolitica.pdf.

Sobel, Henry. *Um homem: um rabino.* São Paulo: Ediouro, 2008.

Sobottka, Emil A. *Kirchliche Entwicklungsprojekte in Brasilien: Die Zusammenarbeit von Brot für die Welt und EZE mit brasilianischen Partnern als Impuls für gesellschaftliche Transformationsprozesse.* Münster: LIT, 2001.

Sobrino, Jon. "Teología en un mundo sufriente: la Teologia de la Liberación como *intellectus amoris.*" *Revista Latinoamericana de Teologia* 15 (1988) 243-266.

Sodré, Nelson Werneck. *Introdução à Revolução Brasileira.* Rio de Janeiro: Civilização Brasileira, 1963.

Soosten, Joachim von. "Civil Society: Zum Auftakt der neueren demokratietheoretischen Debatte mit einem Seitenblick auf Religion, Kirche und Öffentlichkeit." *Zeitschrift für Evangelische Ethik* 37 (1993) 139–57.

SOTER [Sociedade de Teologia e Ciências da Religião]. *Corporeidade e teologia.* São Paulo: Paulinas, 2005.

———, editor. *Deus e vida: desafios, alternativas e o futuro da Améria Latina e do Caribe.* São Paulo: Paulinas, 2008.

———, editor. *Gênero e teologia: interpelações e perspectivas.* São Paulo: Loyola, Paulinas, 2003.

———, editor. *Sustentabilidade da vida e espiritualidade.* São Paulo: Paulinas, 2008.

Souza, Herbert de. "Os cristãos e a democracia." In *Cristãos: como fazer política,* edited by Clodovis Boff et al., 115–19. Petrópolis: Vozes, 1987.

Souza, Luiz Alberto Gómez de. "Catolicismo em tempos de transição." In *Desafios do catolicismo na cidade: pesquisa em regiões metropolitanas brasileiras,* edited by CERIS, 9–13. São Paulo: Paulus, 2002.

———. "The Origins of Medellín: From Catholic Action to the Base Church Communities and Social Pastoral Strategy (1950–68)." *Concilium* 3 (2002) 31–37.

———. "As várias faces da Igreja Católica." *Estudos Avançados* 18/52 (2004) 77–95.

Souza, Jessé, editor. *Democracia hoje: novos desafios para a teoria democrática contemporânea.* Brasília: Editora UnB, 2001.

———. *A modernização seletiva. Uma reinterpretação do dilema brasileiro.* Brasília: Editora UnB, 2000.

Spliesgart, Roland."*Verbrasilianisierung" und Akkulturation: Deutsche Protestanten im brasilianischen Kaiserreich am Beispiel der Gemeinden in Rio de Janeiro und Minas Gerais (1822–1889).* Wiesbaden: Harrassowitz, 2006.

Stackhouse, Max L. "Civil Religion, Political Theology and Public Theology: What's the Difference?" *Political Theology* 5/3 (2004) 275–93.

———. *Globalization and Grace, God and Globalization vol. 4.* New York: Continuum, 2007.

———. "Public Theology and Ethical Judgment." *Theology Today* 54/2 (1997) 165–79.

———. *Public Theology and Political Economy: Christian Stewardship in Modern Society.* Lanham: University Press, 1991.

———. "Public Theology and political economy in a globalizing era." In *Public Theology for the 21st century, Essays in Honour of Duncan B. Forrester*, edited by William F. Storrar and Andrew R. Morton, 179–94. London: T & T Clark, 2004.

———. "Reflections on How and Why We Go Public." *International Journal of Public Theology* 1/3–4 (2007) 421–30.

———. "Sociedade Civil, Teologia Pública e a Configuração Ética da Organização Política em uma Era Global." In *Teologia publica: lançando o debate,* edited by Ronaldo Cavalcante and Rudolf von Sinner, 37-51. São Leopoldo: Sinodal, 2011.

Staden, Hans. *Brasilien: Historia von den nackten, wilden Menschenfressern.* Lenningen: Erdmann, 2006.

Stålsett, Sturla J. *The crucified and the Crucified. A Study in Liberation Christology of Jon Sobrino.* Bern: Peter Lang, 2003.

———. "Trust in the Market? Social Capital and the Ethics of Vulnerability." 2003. Online: http://www.iadb.org/etica/ingles/index-i.cfm.

Stegemann, Ekkehard W. "'Ich habe öffentlich zur Welt gesprochen.' Jesus und die Öffentlichkeit." In *Glaube und Öffentlichkeit, Jahrbuch für Biblische Theologie* v. 11, 103–21. Neukirchen-Vlyun: Neukirchener, 1996.

Stepan, Alfred, editor. *Authoritarian Brazil. Origins, Policies, and Future.* New Haven, London: Yale University Press, 1973.

———, editor. *Democratizing Brazil. Problems of Transition and Consolidation.* New York: Oxford University Press, 1989.

———. *The Military in Politics: Changing Patterns in Brazil.* Princeton: Princeton University Press, 1971.

Stewart-Gambino, Hannah W., and Everett Wilson. "Latin American Pentecostals: Old Stereotypes and New Challenges." In *Power, Politics, and Pentecostals in Latin America* edited by Edward L. Cleary and Hannah W. Stewart-Gambino, 227–46. Boulder: Westview, 1997.

Stierle, Wolfram. *Chancen einer ökumenischen Wirtschaftsethik: Kirche und Ökonomie vor den Herausforderungen der Globalisierung.* Frankfurt a.M.: Lembeck, 2001.

Stoffel, José Carlos. *Ecumenismo de justiça: reflexão e prática: CECA—uma entidade a serviço do movimento ecumênico.* São Leopoldo: FAAP; CECA; Oikos, 2006.

Stoll, David. *Is Latin America Turning Protestant? The Politics of Evangelical Growth.* Berkeley: University of California Press, 1990.

Storrar, William. "2007: A Kairos Moment for Public Theology." *International Journal of Public Theology* 1/1 (2007) 5–25.

Storrar, William F., and Andrew R. Morton, editors. *Public Theology for the 21st century, Essays in Honour of Duncan B. Forrester.* London: T & T Clark, 2004.

Streck, Danilo R. *Educação para um novo contrato social.* Petrópolis: Vozes, 2003.

Ströher, Marga J., Wanda Deifelt, and André S. Musskopf, eds. *À flor da pele: ensaios sobre gênero e corporeidade.* São Leopoldo: Sinodal, CEBI, EST, 2004.

Stumme, John R. "Algumas teses sobre os dois reinos." *Estudos Teológicos* 23/3 (2004) 249–64.

Stümke, Volker. *Das Friedensverständnis Martin Luthers: Grundlagen und Anwendungsbereiche seiner politischen Ethik.* Stuttgart: Kohlhammer, 2007.

Sundermeier, Theo. "Konvivenz als Grundstruktur ökumenischer Existenz." In *Ökumenische Existenz heute* edited by Wolfgang Huber, et al., 49–100. München: Kaiser, 1986.

Sung, Jung Mo. *Teologia e economia: repensando a teologia da libertação e utopias.* Petrópolis: Vozes, 1994.

Susin, Luiz Carlos, editor. *O mar se abriu: trinta anos de teologia na América Latina.* Porto Alegre: SOTER; São Paulo: Loyola, 2000.

———, editor. *Teologia para outro mundo possível.* São Paulo: Paulinas, 2006.

———, editor. *Terra prometida: movimento social, engajamento cristão e teologia.* Petrópolis: Vozes, 2001.

———, editor. *Sarça ardente: teologia na América Latina: prospectivas.* São Paulo: Paulinas, SOTER, 2000.

Sylvestre, Josué. *Irmão vota em irmão: os evangélicos, a Constituinte e a Bíblia.* Brasília: Editora UnB, 1986.

Sztompka, Piotr. *Trust: A Sociological Theory.* Cambridge: Cambridge University Press, 1999.

Tamez, Elsa. *Bajo un cielo sin Estrellas: lecturas y meditaciones biblicas.* San José, Costa Rica: DEI, 2001.

———. *Contra toda condena: la justificación por la fé desde los excluídos.* San José: DEI, 1991. [English edition: *The Amnesty of Grace. Justification by Faith from a Latin American Perspective.* Nashville: Abingdon, 1993.]

———. "When the Horizons Close Upon Themselves. A Reflection on the Utopian Reason of Qohélet." In *Liberation Theologies, Postmodernity, and the Americas*, edited by David Batstone, et al., 53–68. London/New York: Routledge, 1997.

Tavolaro, Douglas. *O bispo: a história revelada de Edir Macedo.* São Paulo: Larousse, 2007.

Taylor, Charles. "Die Beschwörung der Civil Society." In *Wieviel Gemeinschaft braucht die Demokratie? Aufsätze zur politischen Philosophie,* 64–91. Frankfurt a. M.: Suhrkamp, 2002.

Teixeira, Faustino. *A Gênese das CEBs no Brasil: elementos explicativos.* São Paulo: Paulinas, 1988.

Teixeira, Faustino, et al. *CEBs, cidadania e modernidade: uma análise crítica.* São Paulo: Paulinas, 1993.

Teixeira, Faustino, and Renata Menezes, editors. *As religões no Brasil: continuidades e rupturas.* Petrópolis: Vozes, 2006.

Tepe, Valfredo. "Igreja e democracia: reflexão bíblica." CNBB, *Sociedade, Igreja e Democracia,* 87-95, São Paulo: Loyola, 1989.

Theissen, Gerd. *Die Religion der ersten Christen. Eine Theorie des Urchristentums.* Gütersloh: Gütersloher Verlagshaus Gerd Mohn, 2000. [Engl. ed.: *A Theory of Christian Primitive Religion,* London: SCM Press, 1999.]

———. *The Social Setting of Pauline Christianity: Essays on Corinth.* Philadelphia, Fortress, 1988.

Thiemann, Ronald F. *Constructing a Public Theology: The Church in a Pluralistic Culture,* Louisville: Westminster/John Knox, 1991.

Thigpen, T. Paul. "Catholic Charismatic Renewal." In *The New International Dictionary of Pentecostal and Charismatic Movements,* edited by Stanley M. Burgess and Eduard M. van der Maas, 460–67. Grand Rapids: Zondervan, 2002.

Thomson, Heather. "Stars and Compasses: Hermeneutical Guides for Public Theology." *International Journal of Public Theology* 2/3 (2008) 258–76.

Tillard, Jean-Marie R. "Koinonia." In *Dictionary of the Ecumenical Movement,* edited by Nicholas Lossky, et al., 646–52. Geneva: WCC, 2002.

Tillich, Paul. *The Courage to Be.* New Haven: Yale University Press, 1952.

Tipton, Steven M. "Globalizing Civil Religion and Public Theology." In *Religion in Global Civil Society,* edited by Mark Juergensmeyer, 49–67. New York: Oxford University Press, 2005.

Tocqueville, Alexis de. *Democracy in America.* Chicago: University of Chicago Press, 2002.

Tomita, Luiza E., Marcelo Barros, and José Maria Vigil, editors. *Pluralismo e libertação: por uma teologia latino-americana pluralista da libertação.* São Paulo: ASETT, Loyola, 2005.

Toulouse, Mark G. *God in Public: Four Ways American Christianity and Public Life Relate.* Louisville: Westminster, 2006.

Tracy, David. *The Analogical Imagination: Christian Theology and the Culture of Pluralism.* New York: Crossroad, 1989.

Trevisan, João Silvério. *Devassos no paraíso: a homossexualidade no Brasil, da colônia à atualidade.* Rio de Janeiro: Record, 2004. [English edition: *Perverts in paradise.* Alyson Publications, 1986.]

Turner, Bryan S, editor. *Citizenship and Social Theory.* London: Sage, 1993.

———. "Contemporary Problems in the Theory of Citizenship." In *Citizenship and Social Theory,* edited by Bryan S. Turner, 1–18. London: Sage, 1993.

———. "Outline of a Theory of Citizenship." *Sociology* 24/2 (1990) 189–217.

Tveit, Olav Fykse. "*Mutual Accountability as Ecumenical Attitude. A Study in Ecumenical Ecclesiology Based on Faith and Order Texts 1948–1998.*" Doctoral thesis, Oslo School of Theology, 2001.

UNDP [United Nations Development Programme]. *Human Development Report 2006.* New York: United Nations, 2006.

———. *Human Development Report 2007–2008.* New York: United Nations, 2007.

Unger, Roberto Mangabeira. *Democracy Realized: The Progressive Alternative.* New York: Verso, 1998.

———. *What Should Legal Analysis Become?* New York: Verso, 1996.

Vainfas, Ronaldo. *Trópico dos pecados: moral, sexualidade e inquisição no Brasil.* Rio de Janeiro: Campus, 1989.

Valle, Edénio. "A Renovação Carismática Católica. Algumas observações." *Estudos Avançados* 18/52 (2004) 97–107.

Vanderlinde, Tarcsísio. "CAPA: o jeito luterano de atuar com os pequenos agricultores no Sul do Brasil." *Estudos Teológicos* 46/2 (2006) 143–62.

———. *Entre dois reinos: a inserção entre os pequenos agricultores no sul do Brasil.* Cascavel: Edunioeste, 2006.

Varella, Drauzio. *Estação Carandiru.* São Paulo: Companhia das Letras, 2000.

Vidal, Dominique. "Die Sprache des Respekts. Die brasilianische Erfahrung und die Bedeutung von Staatsbürgerschaft in modernen Demokratien." In *Jenseits von Zentrum und Peripherie: Zur Verfassung der fragmentierten Weltgesellschaft,* edited by Hauke Brunkhorst and Sérgio Costa, 131–45. München/Mering: Rainer Hampp Verlag, 2005.

Vieira, David Gueiros. "Protestantism and the Religious Question in Brazil 1850–1875." PhD diss., Ann Arbor: University Microfilms International, 1973.

Vieira, Liszt. *Os argonautas da cidadania: a sociedade civil na globalização,* Rio de Janeiro: Record, 2001.

Villa-Vicencio, Charles. "From Revolution to Reconstruction: The South Africa Imperative." In *Christianity and Democracy in Global Context,* edited by John Witte, Jr., 249–66. Boulder: Westview, 1993.

———. *A Theology of Reconstruction: Nation-building and Human Rights.* Cambridge: Cambridge University Press, 1992.

Vingren, Ivar, translator. *Despertamento apostólico no Brasil: resumo da missão pentecostal sueca no Brasil.*Rio de Janeiro: CPAD, 1987.

———. *O diário do pioneiro: Gunnar Vingren.* Rio de Janeiro: CPAD, 1982.

———. *Diário do Pioneiro Gunnar Vingren.* Edited by Ivar Vingren. Rio de Janeiro: CPAD, 2005.

Vögele, Wolfgang. *Menschenwürde zwischen Recht und Theologie: Begründungen von Menschenrechten in der Perspektive öffentlicher Theologie.* Gütersloh: Kaiser/Gütersloher Verlagshaus, 2000.

———. *Zivilreligion in der Bundesrepublik Deutschland.* Gütersloh: Kaiser/Gütersloher Verlagshaus, 1994.

Vries, Hent de, and Lawrence E. Sullivan, editors. *Political Theologies. Public Religions in a Post-Secular World.* New York: Fordham, 2006.

Wachholz, Wilhelm. "'IECLB': caminhos de uma confessionalidade (diagnósticos e prognósticos)." *Estudos Teológicos* 43/1 (2003) 14–28.

———. "Luterano? Reformado? Unido? Evangélico! Aspectos históricos e teológicos da União Prussiana." In *Evangelho, Bíblia e Escritos Confessionais,* Anais do II Simpósio sobre Identidade Evangélico-Luterana, edited by Wilhelm Wachholz, 87–109. São Leopoldo: EST, 2004.

Wanderley, Luiz Eduardo W. "Educação, cultura e democracia" CNBB, *Sociedade, Igreja e Democracia,* 71-82, São Paulo: Loyola, 1989.

Walz, Heike. "*Madres* appear on the public *Plaza de Mayo* in Argentina. Towards human rights as a key for a public theology rescuing the liberation heritage." *International Journal of Public Theology* 3/2 (2009) 165–87.

———. *Nicht mehr männlich und nicht mehr weiblich? Ekklesiologie und Geschlecht in ökumenischem Horizont.* Frankfurt a. M.: Lembeck, 2006.

Warren, Mark, editor. *Democracy and Trust.* Cambridge: Cambridge University Press, 1999.

WCC [World Council of Churches]. *Handbook of Member Churches: Profiles of Ecumenical Relationships.* Geneva: WCC, 2006.

Weber, Burkhard. *Ijob in Lateinamerika: Deutung und Bewältigung von Leid in der lateinamerikanischen Befreiungstheologie.* Mainz: Grünewald, 1999.

Weffort, Francisco. "Brasil: condenado a modernização." In *Brasileiro: cidadão?* edited by Roberto DaMatta et al., 185–215. São Paulo: Cultura, 1992.

———. "New Democracies, which Democracies?" In *The Latin American Program Working Paper Series,* nr. 198. Washington: Woodrow Wilson International Center for Scholars, 1992.

———. "Why Democracy?" In *Democratizing Brazil. Problems of Transition and Consolidation.* New York: Oxford University Press, 1989, 327–50.

Weimer, Afonso Adolfo. "Aspectos da inserção da Igreja Evangélica de Confissão Luterana no Brasil na realidade política do Brasil de 1968 até 1980 à luz de seus Concílios e da Folha Dominical/Jornal Evangélico." Bachelor's thesis, São Leopoldo Escola Superior de Teologia, 1991.

Weingärtner, Lindolfo. *A responsabilidade pública dos cristãos, exemplificado no Manifesto de Curitiba.* Blumenau: Otto Kuhr, 2001.

Weithman, Paul J. *Religion and the Obligations of Citizenship.* Cambridge: Cambridge University Press, 2006.

Welker, Michael. *Gottes Geist: Theologie des Heiligen Geistes.* Neukirchen-Vluyn: Neukirchener, 1992 [English edition: *God the Spirit.* Minneapolis: Fortress, 1994.]

Wengert, Timothy J., editor. *Harvesting Martin Luther's Reflections on Theology, Ethics, and the Church.* Grand Rapids: Eerdmans, 2004.

Weschler, Lawrence. *A miracle, a universe: settling accounts with torturers.* New York: Pantheon, 1990.

Westermann, Claus. *Genesis 1–11.* Neukirchen-Vlyun: Neukirchener, 1974.

Westhelle, Vítor. "Befreiungstheologie II. Systematisch." In *Religion in Geschichte und Gegenwart,* 4th ed., vol. 1, 1210–3. Tübingen: Mohr Siebeck, 1998.

———. "O desencontro entre a teologia luterana e a teologia da libertação." *Estudos Teológicos* 26/1 (1986) 37–58.

———. *The Scandalous God: The Use and Abuse of the Cross.* Minneapolis: Fortress, 2006.

———. "O tamanho do paraíso: pressupostos do conceito de pecado na teologia latino-americana." *Estudos Teológicos* 38/3 (1998) 239–51.

———. "The Word and the Mask: Revisiting the Two-Kingdoms Doctrine." In *The Gift of Grace: the Future of Lutheran Theology,* edited by Niels Henrik Gregersen et al., 167–80. Minneapolis: Augsburg Fortress, 2005.

Weyland, Kurt. "The Brazilian State in the New Democracy." In *Democratic Brazil. Actors, Institutions, and Processes,* edited by Peter R. Kingstone and Timothy P. Power, 36–57. Pittsburgh: University of Pittsburgh Press, 2000.

———. "The Growing Sustainability of Brazil's Low-Quality Democracy." In *The Third Wave of Democratization in Latin America: Advances and Setbacks,* edited by Frances Hagopian and Scott P. Mainwaring, 90–120. New York: Cambridge University Press, 2005.

Whitaker, Francisco., et alii, *1989: Cidadão Constituinte—a saga das emendas populares,* São Paulo, 1989.

Wildberger, Hans. "אמן fest, sicher." In *Theologisches Handwörterbuch zum Alten Testament,* vol. 1, edited by Ernst Jenni and Claus Westermann, 177–209. München, Zürich: Chr. Kaiser, Theologischer Verlag, 1984.

Willems, Emilio. *Followers of the New Faith: Culture Change and the Rise of Protestantism in Brazil and Chile.* Nashville: Vanderbilt University Press, 1967.

Wirth, John D., et al., editors. *State and Society in Brazil: Continuity and Change.* Boulder: Westview, 1987.

Witherington III, Ben. *Conflict and Community in Corinth: A Socio-Rhetorical Commentary on 1 and 2 Corinthians.* Grand Rapids: Carlisle, 1995.

Witte, John, Jr. *God's Joust, God's Justice: Law and Religion in the Western Traditon.* Grand Rapids: Eerdmans, 2006.

———. *Law and Protestantism: The Legal Teachings of the Lutheran Reformation.* Cambridge: Cambridge University Press, 2002.

———. *The Reformation of Rights: Law, Religion, and Human Rights in Early Modern Calvinism.* Cambridge: Cambridge University Press, 2007.

Wöhlke, Manfred. "'Land der Zukunft?' Einige kritische Anmerkungen zur Entwicklungsproblematik Brasiliens." In *Brasilien heute: Politik, Wirtschaft, Kultur,* edited by Dietrich Briesemeister et al., 364–75. Frankfurt a. M.: Vervuert, 1994.

Wuthnow, Robert. "The United States: Bridging the Privileged and the Marginalized?" In *Democracies in Flux: The Evolution of Social Capital in Contemporary Society,* edited by Robert D. Putnam, 59–102. New York: Oxford University Press, 2002.

———. "Der Wandel des Sozialkapitals in den USA." In *Gesellschaft und Gemeinsinn: Sozialkapital im internationalen Vergleich,* edited by Robert D.Putnam, 655–749. Gütersloh: Bertelsmann, 2001.

Zabatiero, Júlio P. T. "Do Estatuto Acadêmico da Teologia: pistas para uma solução de um problema complexo." *Estudos Teológicos* 47/2 (2007) 67–87.

———. "Um movimento teológico e sua contribuição para a transformação social. A Fraternidade Teológica Latino-Americana—Brasil." In *Religião e transformação no Brasil,* edited by Maria Carmelita de Freitas, 133–58. São Paulo: Paulinas, 2007.

Zaverucha, Jorge. *FHC, forças armadas e polícia: entre o autoritarismo e a democracia.* Rio de Janeiro: Record, 2005.

Zaugg-Ott, Kurt. *Entwicklung oder Befreiung? Die Entwicklungsdiskussion im Ökumenischen Rat der Kirchen von 1968–1991.* Frankfurt a.M.: Lembeck, 2004.

Zeron, Carlos. "A cidadania em Florença e Salamanca." In *História da Cidadania,* edited by Jaime Pinsky and Carla Bassanezi Pinsky, 97–113. São Paulo: Contexto, 2003.

Ziegler, Béatrice *Schweizer statt Sklaven: schweizerische Auswanderer in den Kaffee-Plantagen von São Paulo (1852–1866).* Stuttgart, Wiesbaden: Steiner, 1985.

Zweig, Stefan. *Brasilien: ein Land der Zukunft.* Frankfurt: Insel, 1997.

Zwetsch, Roberto. *Missão como com-paixão. Por uma teologia da missão em perspectiva latino-americana.* São Leopoldo: Sinodal, Quito: CLAI, 2008.

———. "Nova situação do ensino de Teologia no Brasil: a experiência da Escola Superior de Teologia (EST) da Igreja Evangélica de Confissão Luterana no Brasil." In *Teologia e humanismo social cristão: traçando rotas,* edited by Cecília Osowski, 273–86. São Leopoldo: Editora Unisinos, 2000.

Author Index

Subject Index